Human Development

Karen L. Freiberg, R.N., Ph.D.

Human Development:

A Life-Span Approach

Duxbury Press
North Scituate, Massachusetts

Library of Congress Cataloging in Publication Data

Freiberg, Karen L., 1944–
Human Development, A Life-Span Approach.

Includes bibliographical references and index.
1. Human growth. 2. Human ecology.
3. Human physiology. 4. Human behavior.
I. Title.
QP84.F68 613 78–14741
ISBN 0–87872–177–0

Duxbury Press
A Division of Wadsworth Publishing Company, Inc.

Human Development: A Life-Span Approach was edited and prepared for composition by Eleanor Gilbert.
Interior design was provided by Joanna Prudden Snyder.
The cover was designed by Elizabeth Anne Spear.

L.C. Cat. Card No.:
ISBN 0–87872–177–0
Printed in the United States of America
1 2 3 4 5 6 7 8 9 — 83 82 81 80 79

To Michael,
Kenneth,
and Signe Lise

Contents

Chapter 7 Young Adulthood

Chapter 8 The Thirties

Chapter 9 The Forties

Chapter 10 The Fifties and Early Sixties

Preface

The curricula of many American institutions teaching human development are currently being recast with a focus on human ecology. The limiting and determining effects of the physical and social environment should be studied to clearly understand the individual.

Human Development: A Life-Span Approach presents genetic, health, family, social networks, and other determinants of development on persons of various age groups. This age-organized text will be useful to teachers, students, professionals, and lay readers who desire an integrated account of the interrelatedness of various systems. It draws on research from many fields: biology, genetics, medicine, psychology, sociology, anthropology, and education. An introductory chapter examines determinants of development, research methodologies, and theoretical viewpoints. Five chapters covering the time span from conception to young adulthood carefully emphasize the significance of biology, family, and community on growth and change. Extensive references document the interactive effects of physical, social, and cognitive development. Five additional chapters on adulthood bring together more information and research on the years of maturity than are available in other current life-span textbooks. A unique section in each age-organized chapter details the primary health issues and concerns that characterize that particular span of life. Functional photographs throughout the manuscript enhance the narrative and provide examples of developmental concepts. Chapter summaries and review questions emphasize the relationships of human ecology to human development. The concluding chapter of the text looks at death and bereavement throughout the life span. It ends with a valuable, thought-provoking discussion of perspectives on living that brings the reader to a full-cycle view of development.

Friends who aided in the development of this text are warmly and gratefully acknowledged: Andrew Freiberg and J. Michael Freiberg, M.D.s; Robert Gormley, Edward Murphy, Virginia Lakehomer, Barbara and Leslie Davis, and Diane Wallace, each for his or her own unique contribution. Thanks also to reviewers of the early manuscript: Ann Lyon, Harrisburg Area Community College; Jean A. O'Neil, Boston College; Victor Messier, University of New Hampshire; and Colleen Rand, University of Florida.

Human Development

Contents

Frank Siteman/Stock, Boston

Perspectives on Human Development

All aspects of human development are interrelated and integrated with each other. All the separate aspects of growing, learning, and interacting in family and society affect all other aspects of development from conception through death. The study of the life span gains a valuable sense of wholeness when discussed from several points of view; that is, physical growth, social-emotional and personality development, intellectual development, and health. Reductionist theories (those that try to bring constituent elements into narrow classifications) lose the important considerations of the interactions of many diverse areas of growth with each other. To illustrate the need for an integrated study of human development, consider what the *you* in you would be like if you developed physically and intellectually but not emotionally. Consider ways in which your emotions have an effect on your physique (lack of appetite? overexertion? poor sleep? illness?), on your intellect (lack of attention or persistence? fear? skepticism?), on your family relationships (jealousy? pride? stubbornness?), or on your community relationships (shyness? smugness? ambitions?). It would be similarly astounding to try to consider what you would be like if you developed physically and emotionally but not intellectually.

In the course of human development, a goal of maturation is the ability to achieve a degree of independence (freedom from the influence, control, or determination of another). However, we always exist under some degree of dependence (reliance) on others in the world around us. John Donne said it well 300 years ago. "No man is an island, entire of itself; every man is a piece of the continent, a part of the main."[1] Biological parents are responsible for each one of us. We all interact in the drama of human ecology and in relation to other living plants and animals in the environment. We exist in a state of "interdependency" with family, community, and external environmental factors.

Life-span development

The description of life-span development in this text will be age organized. It will focus on the interactive effects of various systems in specified age groups. It will also consider the changing nature of the human organism in relation to both age and experiences.

Description is a very important aspect of life-span study. Scientists have developed and are continuing to develop measurements of variables that describe growth and development. Descriptions focus both on the commonalities and on the range of differences between and within the variables. Changes that occur in variables, and the nature of the changes are carefully noted.

Once phenomena are described in terms of their range and modulations, scientists attempt to explain their particulars. They look for antecedents to the variables and consequents of them. They look for the underlying processes that may account for any changes that occur. Consider, for example, the phenomenon of "coping style." Where does it come from? Why do different individuals respond to stress in different ways? When and why do humans alter their response patterns? What influence does a "coping style" have on development throughout the life span? This is just one of many kinds of questions for which explanations are sought.

In many research studies related to specific variables, social scientists will take description and explanation one step further. An endeavor will be made to change the course of human development by modifying the expression of the given variable or variables. How and why these alterations are attempted depend on the orientation of the researchers. Nurses may try to modify behavior to improve physical health. Teachers may desire an alteration to enhance learning. Psychiatrists and psychologists may want to optimize life satisfaction on an emotional level. In this text the major emphases will be on describing and explaining phenomena. Research on ways to optimize development will only be presented in the process of narrating and interpreting various phenomena of life-span development.

Determinants of development

Scientists have fractionated the study of human development into so many parts in the past century that a truly integrative account of all the systems known to influence development would require large tomes for a more complete presentation. Consider these influences: genes, nutrition, health, shelter, climate, economy, education, race, sex, religion, fashion, family, nurturance, discipline, social acceptance. In specialized courses students can apply themselves to critical investigation of human development from any number of specialized points of view (e.g., genetics, anatomy, anthropology, sociology, psychology). Even within specialized studies there are further reductions of areas of interest (e.g., within psychology: abnormal psychology, developmental psychology, educational psychology). This is important because the influences of all the different determinants are profound. Different scientists are more concerned with some of the determinants of development than with others.

One system that will receive a great deal of emphasis in this text is the family. Consider how much the family influences your physical growth through genetics, foods provided, and care of injuries, infections, and disease. Consider how much the family setting (past and present) affects your personality and intellect through such things as sex-role conceptions, status, esteem, achievement expectations, intellectual activities, emotional security, eating and health habits, religious practices, traditions, feelings about people of other ethnicities, races, or religions, and feelings about different age groups.

Another system that will receive considerable emphasis as a determinant of development is the social setting of the community. Sections in this book dealing with community influences will both point out the diversity of conditions under which the inhabitants of this country exist and underscore the commonalities of law, organization, and experiences of its citizenry. The community leaves its mark on the development of every individual in a multitude of ways. Consider your physical growth in relation to the availability of health services in your community, the way disease preventions and treatments are delivered, and methods of disease control, the sanitation of your water supply, the quality of foods available to you, the cleanliness of the air you breathe, the dangers of genetic mutations resulting from radiation or pollution in your region, and the accident hazards you encounter. Consider your behavioral development (the ways you have learned to act and react) in relation to your community. Associate your conduct with such societal influences as relative prosperity or proverty, availability of educational or aesthetic resources (the arts), community sports, patriotism, job opportunities, population, and how others in your community feel about all the groups to which you may belong: age, race, sex, ethnicity, religion, social clubs, political party, school, the physically disabled.

First, before looking at how human development occurs at various ages, an overview of some of the methods and problems of research concerned with the study of humans will be presented. Following this will be a discussion of some theoretical viewpoints about the whats and whys of human development.

Research: methods and implications

Research is a controlled, objective, systematic, and patient study of some phenomena in some field that is carried out to learn more about a subject. If the research is undertaken for the primary satisfaction of knowing and understanding the subject, it is called basic or pure research. If it is entered into for reasons of knowing a subject well enough to make changes in the direction of more efficiency or for more benefits to some recipient group, it is called applied research. The findings of basic research often have suggestions for applicability, however, and applied research may make important contributions to basic knowledge of a field.

In the field of human development, questions asked by basic or applied researchers reflect many concerns: the incidence of some phenomena; whether events follow a pattern that could be used as a predictor of the same events in other persons; the explanation for a phenomenon; how a phenomenon gets its start; what are efficient behaviors for achieving objectives; what are the results of specific occurrences; how can problems of human development be solved; what are normal patterns of human growth; and what constitutes "abnormal" in human development.

It is important that you understand some of the basic methods of research. In this text and in many other texts, in journals, newspapers, television reports, or even in word-of-mouth communications, people will report research findings to you. Some of the reports will be quite reliable and worthy of your trust. Others will be contrived, or based on faulty logic. You, as a consumer of research, should be able to question how conclusions were reached. You should also be able to make an intelligent estimate of how reliable the results are, based on the research methodologies used. Very often the same question can be researched in different ways and the resulting answers will be in conflict. Which study should you believe? The following brief introduction to research methodology cannot make you an expert judge of research quality. However, it can make you aware of problems inherent in all research methodologies used to study human development. If you emerge from a careful reading of the following descriptions of research with a feeling of skepticism about the 100 percent accuracy of any human relations research result, this chapter will accomplish its first goal. If you begin to question how research results are obtained in the future, a second important goal will be met.

It is possible to roughly divide research in human development into the categories of experimental research (where some conditions are held constant while others are altered for study purposes) and naturalistic research (where study is conducted under normal, real-life conditions). This chapter will discuss methods falling under each classification separately. It will also discuss the relative benefits and drawbacks of using cross-sectional research (different subjects at the same time) or longitudinal research (the same subjects over a period of time) and of various statistical treatments of research data.

Laboratory-experimental studies

While not all experimental studies are conducted in a laboratory, this is the location of choice for experiments. It is easier to control a whole range of irrelevant stimuli in a carefully prepared laboratory environment. When an experimental study is conducted, a single behavior (or set of behaviors) is allowed to vary. All others are held constant (unchanging). In this way it is possible to know quite precisely what, if any, effect any manipulation introduced by the researcher will have on the subject or subjects. The behavior (or set of behaviors) being manipulated by the experimenter is called the independent or antecedent (coming before) variable. The changes that occur in the subject as a result of the introduction of the independent variable are known as the dependent or consequent variables.

Often, in order to demonstrate that there is an antecedent-consequent relationship between the variables in an experiment, a control group is used. The control group is not subjected to the manipulation of the independent variable under study as are all members of the experimental group. Both groups are observed carefully. If the dependent variables occur only in the experimental group, then it can be assumed that the manipulations of the independent variable were effective in bringing about a consequence that ordinarily would not occur.

The results of laboratory-experimental research can be checked over and over again in replication studies because the experimental conditions are specified so carefully. This lends a special degree of confidence to the research results, especially if replications are carried out by different researchers.

It is always necessary to have a sufficiently large number of subjects in both the experimental and the control groups to ensure that the phenomenon under study is something that characterizes all humans or all people of a special group (e.g., women, sixth graders, Navajo Indians). It is difficult to have confidence in research when an experimenter has selected only a few special persons to be experimental subjects. Instead, subjects should be selected randomly from the total population of the group under investigation. Control subjects should be matched as closely as possible to the experimental subjects in age, sex, environment, and the like to further

Figure 1–1. *Laboratory-experimental research provides greater certainty that subjects do not differ in treatment conditions than does naturalistic research. Naturalistic research, however, gives a better picture of what actually occurs in the real world. Both methods have advantages depending on the nature of the research question.*
Leslie Davis

ensure that it is the independent variable of the experiment that brings about a result, not any chance external factors that make the experimental subjects different from the control subjects.

One criticism frequently voiced about experimental research is that, because it is so highly manipulated and controlled, it does not give a very good picture of what actually occurs in the real world. It is true that there is a degree of artificiality about experimental research, but this does not always negate its value. Consider the following experiment by Jakibchuk and Smeriglio.[2] They were interested in helping preschool children who had a low level of interaction and social responsiveness. They went to several nursery schools and carefully observed all the children, finally selecting a group of twenty-two (eleven boys, eleven girls) who were rated by their teachers as isolates and who seldom interacted with others during observations of free play. They randomly assigned the children to one of four groups: two experimental groups and two control groups. Experimental group one was shown a film of the activities of a model child in which a voice described all the behaviors of the model in first person: "I . . . ." Experimental group two was also shown the film of the model child, but all the model's behaviors were described in the third person: "He . . . ." Control group one was shown a nature film, and control group two was shown no film. Peer social interactions and communications increased in the experimental subjects who had seen a film of a model child interacting with others and describing the actions in the first person. (The dependent variables of social interactions were measured again in free play at the nursery schools on two occasions after the experimental film showing.) This research suggests a way in which preschool isolates can be helped to increase their numbers of interactions with other children. The criticism of artificiality is not important. The artificial situation (showing a filmed model child interacting and speaking) may in itself be useful to help increase social interactions of isolated children. However, while the criticism of artificiality may not mean a great deal in this case, it demonstrates other limitations of experimental research. This study has a very limited range of applicability (to preschool isolates in settings where such a film can be obtained and shown). Similar limitations are true for many experimental studies. This study also cannot be generalized to other populations: to non-nursery school children, to older children, or to children who would not identify with the filmed model child. What is true for one age and cultural group is not necessarily true for others. The study illustrates still another problem. The kinds of stimuli that can be used as independent variables, and the kinds of responses that can be measured as dependent variables in experimental situations are confined within narrow bounds. Only simple behaviors can be manipulated. This kind of research cannot contribute very much to our knowledge of thought processes, emotional feeling tones, or unconscious inhibitors of behavior. It is a precise, replicable, fairly objective way of doing research on a limited number of topics in human development.

Naturalistic studies

Naturalistic studies, as the word suggests, try to investigate behaviors as they occur in the real world. They offer the potential for studying many actions and events that would be impossible to reproduce in the laboratory. In the 1920s and 1930s most studies of human development were naturalistic. With the growth and development of the field of psychology, experimental studies took precedence over naturalistic studies or observations because they were more scientifically precise. Little by little, the pendulum is swinging back toward research in the true-life setting. Electronic recording devices (audiovisual equipment: videotapes, sound movies) make it possible to record behavior as it occurs and then to analyze segments of the behavior carefully and repeatedly at a later date. There are still many problems. As Hutt and Hutt have pointed out, "What is required in observational studies, but is seldom applied, is a degree of rigor in measurement commensurate with that expected of experimental studies."[3] The behaviors to be isolated for analysis from the range of actions and events observed must be very carefully identified and defined. All persons trained to extract these elements must understand the definitions fully. They must reach a high degree of agreement among themselves about what they are seeing. Further, they should not have any preconceived notions about what they ought to be seeing, as this can distort their perception of what they actually see. This state or quality of observing phenomena without bias, in a detached, impersonal way, is called objectivity. Opposed to this is subjectivity: a state or quality of imposing personal prejudices, thoughts, and feelings into one's work. It is hard to overcome subjectivity in the study of human behavior. Experimental studies that deal with counting responses or gathering any measures of quantity avoid subjectivity better than observational studies that rely more heavily on measures of the quality of responses. Condry and Condry provide a good example of how one's subjectivity can contaminate research results.[4] They asked over 200 male and female college students to rate the emotional responses of the same baby to presentations of a teddy bear, a jack-in-the-box, a doll, and a buzzer. (The sequence was filmed on videotape.) One-half of the students were told that the baby was male. The other half were told that the baby was female. There was a significant difference between the ratings of the baby's emotional responses depending on whether the students believed the baby to be a boy or a girl. The data supported the hypothesis that observers may see differences in a child's behavior as a function of the sex-type label alone. Such errors can often happen in research when investigators have personal prejudices about any kind of qualitative responses.

Ethology, the biological study of animal behavior, is the purest form of direct observation. Everything that occurs in relation to the creature under study in a certain time period is recorded in detail, even such external factors as weather conditions. The record is kept as objective as possible, cataloging activities and events, not thoughts and desires. It has long been used by biologists studying animals and has recently gained some popularity as a method of studying humans. The data is so rich and descriptive that new hypotheses can be generated from it, and new theories formulated. It can be analyzed in a great number of ways. It is sometimes difficult, however, to separate out what is meaningful from what is irrelevant for purposes of analyzing and reporting research results.

Field studies, as differentiated from ethological investigations, limit the activities and events that they catalog in any instances of observing naturally occurring behaviors. The research scientist must first have a good idea of the variables he or she is looking for. This imposes a restriction on how much information can be gleaned from the data after it is gathered. It also may prevent looking at a random sample of a population if one or more variables under study are person specific (e.g., male breast cancer). Comparing certain behaviors observed in different groups (e.g., men with breast cancer and men without) may result in invalid conclusions. How can the researcher be sure that the group differences observed were due to the cancer and not some extraneous variable? Although results of field studies are generally more suggestive than conclusive, they contribute a great deal of information to our knowledge of human development that would be impossible to ascertain with either experimental studies or ethological investigations.

The kinds of naturalistic data used in some studies of human development are made by laypersons. Researchers may gain insights and generate hypotheses about factors which affect human lives from the material found in autobiographies, biographies, diaries, letters, record books, baby books, and the like. Records of such quantitative data as height, weight, and measurements at various ages are used to establish norms (the median or average figures for a population) for certain variables.

Interviews are used to collect data about people's behaviors in the past (called retrospective studies) or about their current attitudes and/or behaviors. While a great deal of information can be obtained in this way (and frequently is so obtained by many researchers and pollsters in our nation), there are a number of factors that can make responses somewhat less than accurate. First, there is the obvious fact that most persons like to cast themselves in a favorable light. Second, many persons, in an attempt to please the interviewer, will give the answer they feel is desired. Third, the way that a question is worded or asked can often influence what response will be given. Fourth, people are forgetful. Even if memories are excellent, no one perceives every aspect of every experience. Only certain phenomena that are meaningful are recorded in the mind. Consequently, memories are subjective as well as occasionally unclear about many events. Finally, everyone experiences changes of mind. Truthful answers that are given one day may cease to be true over time.

Questionnaires and tests are liable to many of the weaknesses of interviews. Answers may reflect lack of frankness, forgetting, selective remembering, confusion about or misunderstanding of wording, or vacillating attitudes. Subjects filling in the blanks may be troubled by nervousness, which affects their ability to remember or reason, or by boredom, which can lead to carelessness and to decreased efforts to concentrate on the questions. Nevertheless, when respondents strive to be honest and are motivated to add to a body of research data, these methods can amass a great deal of information that cannot be gathered in other ways.

Clinical investigations usually refer to those done in some facility where people come to receive advice or treatment for problems (medical, social, educational, etc.) and, consequently, usually deal with maladjustments of some nature. Frequently interdisciplinary, clinical investigations may involve in-depth interviews, tests, questionnaires and/or observations by physicians, nurses, social workers, psychologists, educational specialists, nutritionists, or other professional specialists, depending on the nature of the clinic.

The result of the intensive investigation of the symptoms, past history, and current influences on the patient and his or her problem is most apt to be a case study. The focus is on the individual and his or her uniqueness. Research using case studies may try to find commonalities among persons with particular problems or experiences. There are dangers inherent in this kind of research. The investigator may try to force different experiences into the same classification for the sake of doing statistical analyses. Or the researcher may affect the results of the analyses by interpreting the data according to some preconceived notions. Nevertheless, case studies can provide us with a wealth of new information. An alert, receptive member of a clinical team who is involved in studying patients day after day may be able to see patterns developing over time. Such an investigator may be able to draw on stored bits of information in recorded case studies and synthesize them into a unified interpretation of some phenomenon. The collections of data can first be used to evoke hypotheses, then later can be used to test them.

Cross-sectional and longitudinal studies

Cross-sectional studies (which measure different subjects at the same time) are used more frequently than longitudinal studies (which measure the same subjects over a period of time), because they can be completed more quickly. However, they tend to ignore the individual and his or her unique growth and development. This can be especially hazardous if the subjects under study are going through one of the more rapid periods of growth and change that occur in the human life span, such as infancy or adolescence. When infants, for example, ranging in age from birth through three months are grouped together for study, their individual differences, which are vast, are ignored. Another hazard of cross-sectional research is the danger that comparisons of a group of individuals of one age with individuals of another age often may result in findings that are determined by social and generational differences between the age groups as much as by the variable under study. Consider the various impacts on people of environmental situations such as World War II in the 1940s, the relative peace and prosperity of the 1950s, and the discontent, rioting, protesting, and the Vietnam War of the 1960s. These situations could not help but influence the social and emotional development of all those who were aware of them. Would a research finding that belief in violence, war, and aggression as a means of solving problems increases concurrently with age make you skeptical if you knew the persons studied were all aged either 25, 35, or 45? Would you not question whether the positive evaluation of violence was really a factor of what each subject had experienced in his or her youth? When cross-sectional research is used to study groups of individuals who are more similar in age and background, this criticism is less meaningful. Comparisons of associates that are carefully designed to eliminate problems of vast intragroup or social and cultural differences can be fruitful as well as convenient ways of learning a great deal about human behavior.

Longitudinal research is desirable for ascertaining the stability or instability of individual characteristics over time. Many concerns of human development research (e.g., emotional response patterns, physical functions, or intelligence) would be better studied following the same persons over time than by finding comparable persons to group together for a one-time investigation. However, longitudinal research has many problems besides the obvious difficulty of taking so much time. Subjects in longitudinal research get "lost" (i.e., quit, move away, die). The expenses incurred by the investigators over time are enormous. There is also a danger that subjects in a longitudinal study will become investigation-wise (anticipate what the researchers want to see) or else lose their motivation to give their best efforts to the research, or else remember the way they responded in the last session and imitate that response even though it no longer characterizes their behavior or beliefs.

Recently a method of combining cross-sectional and longitudinal research has emerged. Called short-term longitudinal research, it first finds comparable groups of subjects to study in a cross-sectional manner. Then it repeats the cross-sectional studies on the same subjects at spaced intervals of time (e.g., follow-ups at one, two, and three years), usually until the youngest subjects in the first study reach the age of the oldest subjects in the first study. This method combines the desirability of analyzing the unique individual differences of subjects with the relative ease of looking at a greater number of subjects in a shorter time. However, it also runs the risk of contamination through subjects becoming investigation-wise, or unmotivated to continue performing over time.

Statistical analysis of research data

Methods of statistical analysis have been developed, and are continuing to develop, to evaluate data obtained in research. Methods of statistical analysis help to shape the format of research, and, as such, are part and parcel of research methods. Though statistics is a branch of applied mathematics in its own right, with roots in probability theory, its value is stressed here as a tool of human development research. The following brief overview, hopefully, will help you understand some of the statistical terms in research reports.

Descriptive statistics describe and summarize, or help a reader understand the characteristics of data. Observations are translated into quantitative data or numerical measures. "Means," "medians," and "modes" are descriptive statistics used frequently to represent a set of measures as a single number. They give information about the central tendencies or averages of a set of data. The mean is the arithmetic average. The median is the middle number in any ordered series. The mode is the numerical term that occurs most frequently in the data. For instance, if you have scores of 62, 62, 63, 84, and 94, the mean value will be 73, the median 63, and the mode 62. In addition to the average score, it is usually necessary to learn the distribution or spread of a set of scores. Descriptive statistics that assess the spread of a set of data are the range and the standard deviation. The highest and lowest values of the data are indicated by the "range." The degree of spread from the center of the data is described by the "standard deviation." This is based on a normal curve (see Figure 1-2). The standard deviation is calculated for each set of data by determin-

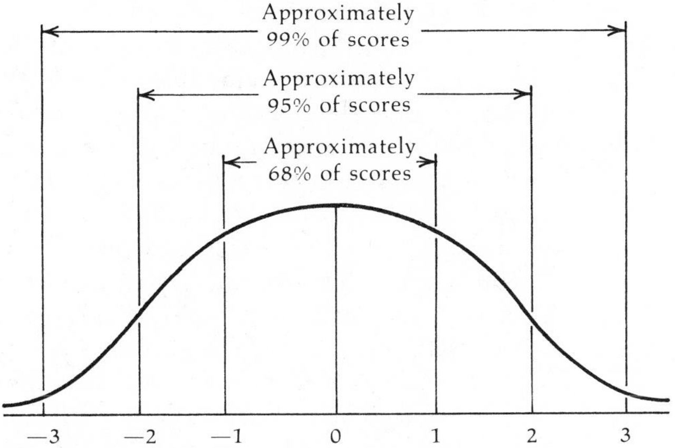

Figure 1–2. *The bell-shaped normal frequency distribution.*

ing the distance of each score from the mean, squaring it, summing the squares, dividing by one less than the total number of scores, and finding the square root of the resulting figure. For large samples, approximately 68 percent of all scores will be expected to fall within one standard deviation above and below the mean. Approximately 95 percent will fall within two standard deviations and 99 percent within three standard deviations above and below the mean.

Another frequently used term in statistics is the "correlation coefficient." It is a numerical value that indicates the degree and direction of the relationship of two variables to one another. When two variables change in the same direction (e.g., height and weight), they are said to be positively correlated. When two variables change in the opposite direction (e.g., high blood pressure and life expectancy), they are said to be negatively correlated. A perfect positive or negative correlation between two variables is indicated by a correlation coefficient of +1.0 and −1.0 respectively. Most correlation coefficients range between +1.0 and −1.0 and are therefore fractions (e.g., +.25, −.55, +.90) that indicate some low, moderate, or high degree of positive or negative association between two variables.

Inferential statistics go beyond description. The characteristics of a population are inferred from the characteristics of a sample of that population. For example, from a knowledge of the birth weights of a sample of infants, one can infer the birth weights of the larger population of infants from which the sample was drawn. Based on sample values, statistical methods can be employed to estimate population values with varying degrees of confidence.

There are many kinds of statistical tests used on different sets of data to answer different types of questions. For example, *T*-tests are often used in evaluating differences in mean outcomes of two treatments. Analyses of variance are used to evaluate differences in mean outcomes among three or more treatments. Chi-square tests are used to evaluate how variables are distributed in a population and to evaluate the independence or dependence among various qualitative features within the elements of a population. Regression analyses are used in testing for significance of relationships among two or more variables. You may learn about these and other statistical tests in a statistics course.

It is important for you to understand what is meant by confidence and significance, whether or not you ever take a statistics course. "Confidence intervals" are mathematical expressions that define a range into which a certain proportion of the values of a variable (or feature of a population) will fall. They are derived from a knowledge of the characteristics of a sample. For instance, we could mathematically define a 95 percent confidence interval that would include the birth weights of 95 percent of infants in a population, based on our knowledge of the mean and standard deviation of the birth weights of a sample of infants drawn from that population. Weights falling outside of this 95 percent confidence interval would be considered distinctly unusual. They could be expected to occur by chance with a probability (expressed as p) of no more than 5 percent (expressed as $p < .05$). The highest and lowest values of the confidence interval are called the "confidence limits." Researchers in a field somewhat arbitrarily decide what the stringency of their confidence limits will be. Influenced by experience, researchers may say that a value of a variable is unusual and "statistically significant" if its chance of occurring is less than 5 percent, or less than 1 percent. Generally, in studies of human development, confidence limits are found in which the probability of a variable having a value greater than the upper limit or less than the lower limit of the confidence interval is less than 5 percent ($p < .05$) or less than 1 percent ($p < .01$).

The determinants of human behavior and various research methods used to study these topics have been explained. Now this chapter will explore some of the theories about human development. These theories try to explain determinants and usually incorporate many research findings.

Theoretical viewpoints

Theories are not fact; they are merely speculations or hypotheses that individuals make for the purpose of explaining and predicting the phenomena of interest to them. Theories include definitions and propositions that specify the interrelationships of variables in a systematic fashion. You have theories of your own. You may not have formalized them or put them in writing, but you have them. Some of your theories are quite firmly entrenched in your thought processes. Others may change each time you discuss a topic, meet someone new, or read a book. Some of your theories are exclusively yours. Others you may have borrowed or adopted from friends, from professors, or from readings. Because of the status of theories as "not well understood" or "not proved," many are frequently altered or exchanged for others. The nature of human development is not at all well charted. It is a complicated and difficult area in which to construct research. The theories to be presented here are respected because of the empirical evidence, derived from valid research, that support their propositions. This is not to say that they are correct or incorrect, but simply that they have received the attention and partial, if not complete, support of some experts and some of the public-at-large. Every time a person sets his or her theories down in print for others to read, that person leaves him- or herself open to controversy and criticism as well as to agreement, praise, and approval. Carefully researched, well-organized, systematic theories with definitions of special terminology are more apt to gain support than poorly constructed or undocumented theories. When and if any of the hunches of a theory are explained by research to the extent that they become fully understood, they leave the realm of theory and become fact. You may feel free to agree or disagree with parts or all of any of the theories to follow.

Psychoanalytic theories

Psychoanalysis or psychoanalytic psychology refers to the study of the unconscious element in psychological behavior. There are many theories that fall under the rubric of psychoanalysis. Each has its own slant, but all share certain similarities.

The father of all the various psychoanalytic theories was Sigmund Freud. Freud's theory will be reviewed first as the prototype of psychoanalytic theories. Second, mention will be made of some of the differences of a few other well-known psychoanalysts.

Freud is generally viewed as one of the most influential of the initiators and contributors to the fields of psychology and psychiatry. His assumptions have become so firmly established in the language of our culture that we usually regard them as facts rather than suppositions (e.g., ego, libido, unconscious).

Sex was considered by Freud as the primary motivator of behavior. (He also acknowledged aggression and hunger as forces that could move people to action.)[5] He described libido as the source of energy for sexual behavior. Sex, he felt, was present in some form in most physical pleasures. He also believed most adulthood neuroses (partial disorganizations of the personality such as anxieties, compulsions, obsessions, tics, phobias) could be traced back to childhood sexual conflicts. His theory has recently been under fire, especially by women, because of his views of sex differences and male supremacy. Many of the sexual conflicts he believed to be developmental were probably once true of children raised in prim Victorian settings such as those that existed in Europe in his lifetime (1856–1939). However, they are not found in all children today, especially not in youngsters raised in cultures or atmospheres where sex is discussed with honesty and candor.

The use of free association of ideas in an intensive interview in a "relaxed" setting was Freud's method of analyzing patients. The image of a psychiatrist sitting back in a chair while the patient reclines on a couch originated in his Vienna office. On occasion, Freud also hypnotized patients to help them review their earlier life experiences.

Freud postulated that personality has three components: the id, the ego, and the superego.[6] Instincts, sexual impulses, the hunger drive, and aggressive urges are all housed in the id. Freud viewed the id as having untamed, animal-like drives that are in need of control. The superego was postulated to be the controlling, moral arm of the personality. According to Freud, it serves as a watchdog to ascertain that our dominant id impulses do not motivate us to engage in socially unacceptable behaviors. The superego represents the conscience. It houses our religious teachings, our moral values, and the ethics and mores of our culture. While it generally is a prohibitive influence on our behavior, it can also motivate us to do good deeds. The superego develops slowly over the course of one's childhood and adolescence. The id, in contrast, is the aspect of the personality that houses and directs psychic energy from birth. Between the id and the superego is the ego. Freud saw the ego as the reality component of the personality. Ego is the self: the problem-solving, realistic, perceiving, remembering, judging, speaking mediator of all the conflicting drives from the id and the superego. Freud believed that personality is a dynamic and changing phenomenon, influenced by the development of each person's id, ego, and superego. Any given individual can at times be more id controlled, and at times be more influenced by the superego. However, Freud felt that these personality components, and the relative way they balance and counterbalance each other, become established by the end of adolescence. At this time, one has a typical response pattern to frustrations, conflicts, and threats. Freud felt that major changes in adult personality can be accomplished only with great difficulty.

Unconscious and subconscious levels of thought are two further important Freudian suppositions. He felt that ideas buried in the unconscious mind can influence us in ways that are beyond our ability to control. The ego represses certain ideas and memories and prevents them from gaining access to the conscious mind, even when they have the power to affect behaviors. At the subconscious level people may be only vaguely aware of the roots of their ideas. For example, you may have brief glimpses or feelings about people, places, or things without being able to get a firm grasp on why they came to mind. Freud felt that all behavior is rooted in mental processes at one of the levels of consciousness. In psychoanalysis some of the unconscious or subconscious thoughts may be revealed to the therapist through verbal associations, dreams, slips of the tongue ("Freudian slips"), flashes of insight (the "aha" experience), through old memories, or through hypnosis.

As Freud sought to understand the early experiences of his patients and to discern ways in which childhood conflicts create adulthood problems, he hypothesized that a sequence of developmental stages exists. He believed they are based on instincts related to body zones that bring sexual pleasure. If a child passes through each stage without trauma (few can, in Freud's opinion), he or she will become a "well-adjusted" adult. Trauma in any given stage will result in some fixation of the personality based on that stage. The first stage, the oral stage, has sexual drives and conflicts related to breast- or bottle-feeding and weaning. Failure to gratify the infant's suckling needs may result in adulthood oral fixations such as habitual nail biting, cigarette smoking, and gum chewing. During the second, anal stage, sexual drives are related to toilet training. Traumatic experiences can leave the future adult with anal fixations such as parsimony, orderliness, punctiliousness, obstinacy, pedantry, and possessiveness. In the third stage, the phallic stage, Freud proposed that sexual conflicts revolve around the fact that the child discovers how genital manipulation can bring both pleasurable feelings and parental anger. The conflict-ridden child eventually falls in love with, and has sexual urges directed at, the opposite-sexed parent. Trauma in this stage can lead to Oedipal or Electra complexes, in which boys become overly attached to their mothers, and girls to their fathers. In the next stage, Freud felt that sexual urges are repressed. He called this phase, occurring in middle childhood from approximately ages six to eleven, the stage of latent (concealed) sexuality. He felt that failure to repress the sex drive can prolong and exaggerate the previously formed Oedipal and Electra complexes. The last period of psychosexual development, Freud believed, occurs in adolescence. Conflicts then arise concerning the sexual urges that develop with puberty. Fixations in this stage can result in failure to develop mature and socially acceptable modes of attaining sexual gratification.

Freud's childhood stages, derived entirely from adult patients rather than from children, are among his most criticized premises. The personality complexes he described may occur for many other reasons. They also may fail to occur even with unfavorable childhood conditions. However, some of the defense mechanisms that Freud proposed as guards against sexual anxieties have received wide acceptance. Many are now a common part of our vocabularies: regression, repression, projection, denial, sublimation, displacement, reaction formation, introjection, asceticism and intellectualization. Regression refers to reactivating behaviors more appropriate to earlier stages of development. Repression means burying something in the unconscious or subconscious level of thought. To project is to attribute a motive to someone else. Denial is a refusal to believe or accept something as it is, but rather to perceive it as one wishes it would be. Sublimation refers to discharging sexual energy in socially approved ways rather than using it to obtain sexual gratification. Displacement refers to a transference of emotion toward an inappropriate person or object rather than toward the person or thing that incurred the strong feelings. A reaction formation is a distortion of a drive to its opposite, as misrepresenting hostility by acts of kindness. Introjection refers to taking into one's own personality the characteristics of another. To be ascetic is to deny oneself gratification of some need(s). Intellectualization refers to separating events and content areas from emotions that impinge on them.

All of these defense mechanisms are characteristic ways in which the ego functions to avoid pain, to modify expression of strong emotions, and to relieve the pressures of excessive anxiety.

Freud based his theory primarily on what he saw and heard from the sick personalities who sought his psychiatric treatment. He did not use any projective personality tests, or experiment, or collect data for quantitative analysis. However, he did check his theory continually against the evidence as he saw it. This resulted in many revisions of his concepts, and eventually in a theory that has endured.

All psychoanalytic theories, Freud's and the neo-Freudians', tend to look for causes of behavior with roots in the past. They pay close attention to what others have done to the individual and tend to ignore what the individual has done to shape his or her own behaviors. They show more concern for helping the individual adjust to society than they do for reforming society. Finally, psychoanalytic theories depend on long-term, deep-delving therapy sessions to discover what went wrong before helping the individual acquire new behaviors.

Carl Jung and Alfred Adler, both students of Freud, developed rival psychoanalytic theories. Jung saw the possibility of lifelong personality development. (His views of adult stages of development will be described in Chapters 9 and 10.) Jung also theorized that a deeper level of consciousness exists than Freud's unconscious. He called it the collective unconscious.[7] He felt we have inherited the wisdom and experience of previous centuries, even from our evolutionary prehuman existence, in this deep consciousness. He felt that religious or mystic experiences, deep trances, or hallucinations might occasionally shed some light on these collective memories.

Alfred Adler saw the drive for superiority and power to be a more potent motivator of behavior than sexual libido. He wrote extensively about inferiority complexes and the mechanisms of compensation and overcompensation that some people use to hide their feelings of inferiority.[8]

The psychoanalytic theory of Freud's daughter, Anna, put more emphasis on ego development in relation to the id and superego. She also placed a far greater stress on the period of puberty and adolescence as a shaper of adult psychosexual behaviors.[9]

Erik Erikson, whose psychoanalytic theory probably has the largest number of supporters today, postulated that humans go through eight stages of psychosexual development, including three stages that occur in adulthood. (All of Erikson's stages will be described in greater detail later in the text.) Erikson felt that an individual must cope with anxieties inflicted on the ego by the self, by the society, and by the individual's reference group in the society, throughout the life span.[10]

Harry Stack Sullivan, whose theory is receiving more attention today, saw the self as a product of an accumulation of meaningful relationships with other people in society.[11] He felt that fear of social disapproval is one of the primary motivators of people's behaviors.

Behaviorist and learning theories

Psychoanalytic theories are based on the premise that the roots of a person's behavior lie in the meanings that earlier experiences have had for that individual. They believe that changing behavior takes a considerable amount of time. It requires an understanding of thought processes acquired over time. In contrast, theories of behaviorism and social learning are minimally concerned with the past and its influence on a person's behavior. They believe that new behaviors can be substituted for old behaviors after a relatively short period of behavior therapy. New behaviors can be taught to, or conditioned in, the individual. Behavior theories and social learning theories are not the same thing, but they have enough similarities to allow for their presentation in a back-to-back fashion.

A Russian physiologist, Ivan Pavlov, is credited with originating behavior theory. In the late 1800s he introduced the idea of changing behavior through a process known as conditioning.[12] He "conditioned" a dog to salivate at the sound of a bell by coupling the bell with every presentation of food over an interval of time. After a while the dog associated the sound of the bell with the arrival of food and, whenever he heard the bell, began salivating (a natural reflex) in anticipation.

John Watson introduced behaviorism to the field of psychology in the 1920s. He wanted more of a separation between psychology and the realms of philosophy and religion. In behaviorism new learning can be observed, measured, and unambiguously stated in technical, scientific language. Behaviorism did not try to speculate about the causes of behavior buried in various mental levels for which no proof could be supplied. Instead, the new breed of psychologists began producing evidence that anxieties and phobias were curable by behavioral means. For example, in 1924 Mary Cover Jones, a student of Watson, published a paper in which she detailed her success in helping a small boy overcome his fear of furry things.[13] She conditioned him to tolerate a rabbit by coupling his lunches with the presentation of the animal. After a while the boy was able to eat calmly with the rabbit on his lap.

B. F. Skinner introduced the concepts of "stimulus-response learning" (S-R learning) and "operant conditioning" (defined below) procedures to behaviorism. His carefully controlled experiments and extensive publications of orderly data, his theoretical explanations of behaviorism, and his arguments for the uses of operant conditioning to modify and/or control human behavior made him a recognized leader of behaviorists from the 1940s through the 1970s. He published two very influential and controversial best-selling books in 1948 and 1971 in which he advocated that operant conditioning be made an integral part of the social order: *Walden Two* and *Beyond Freedom and Dignity*, [14], [15]

Stimulus-response learning refers to the idea that certain stimulus variables can be used to bring about overt, observable responses. If a stimulus brings about an involuntary response (i.e., salivation when food appears), and then a second stimulus is paired with and finally substituted for the original stimulus, the learning that takes place is called classical or Pavlovian conditioning. This is not the most commonly used form of conditioning, because many of the responses desired for modifying behavior are voluntary rather than involuntary.

Operant conditioning was devised by Skinner to increase the number of desirable, voluntary responses an animal or human will make to some stimulus. In operant conditioning a voluntary response is associated with a stimulus by being reinforced (rewarded) when it occurs. Operant conditioning works because animals and humans tend to repeat actions that bring them pleasurable consequences. Skinner only advocated the use of positive reinforcement or rewarding to bring overt responses under the control of stimuli. Some other behaviorists introduced the use of negative reinforcement, which is some form of punishing, to help terminate undesirable voluntary responses.

Skinner designed and built special electronic cages called "Skinner boxes" for use in many of his orderly experiments of conditioned responses in animals. Into his apparatus he would place a rat or a pigeon or a monkey. When the animal pressed a lever (pigeons needed to peck a disk), the specially constructed box would both deliver a small quantity of food to the animal and record its response. At first responses were "shaped" by rewarding every response. Eventually, reinforcers were given on a fixed or variable schedule of reinforcement. Intermittent reinforcement, Skinner discovered, makes a conditioned response stronger and more resistant to fading away than giving a reward for every response. (continuous reinforcement).

Behavioral psychologists who apply Skinnerian principles to bring about operant conditioning in humans, or to teach more complex tasks to animals, may have to spend more time shaping desirable responses. At first, a response that approximates the behavior that the psychologist wants to develop is reinforced. In successive steps the rewards are made contingent on a response that more closely resembles, and finally becomes, the desired bahavior. Consider the following problem and its solution as an example of operant conditioning in action. Procedures of operant conditioning are also known as "behavior modification."

The problem: Johnny won't approach his peers in nursery school, but follows the teacher or her assistants around, demanding their attention.

Step 1. Obtain an operant level. Observe and count the number of approaches Johnny makes to any peer in a certain time interval. Also count the number of advances he makes to the teacher and her assistants.

Step 2. Shape the behavior desired. To begin, each time Johnny plays alone without following a teacher or demanding adult attention, reinforce him with attention. Ignore him when he makes advances toward the teachers. As soon as he can spend short periods of time alone, make reinforcement contingent on a higher level of behavior (e.g., looking at peers playing). When this is achieved, make the reward of attention contingent on a still higher level of behavior (e.g., interacting with peers) until Johnny reaches the desired level of behavior.

Step 3. In the shaping procedures every instance of the desired behavior was reinforced, while undesirable behavior was ignored. Now make the reinforcement schedule variable rather than continuous. Never reward undesirable behavior, but use an intermittent interval reinforcement schedule for the conditioned behavior (in this case interacting with peers). This strengthens the behavior.

In laboratory experiments with operant conditioning, behavioral scientists have been able to demonstrate that their conditioning procedures, not any extraneous factors, are responsible for modifying responses. They can extinguish responses by deconditioning and bring them back by reconditioning. While intermittent reinforcements strengthen responses in the conditioning process, they do not guarantee that the conditioning will be permanent. In order for behaviors to last in the course of everyday living, they must continue to succeed in producing positive rewards for the person performing them.

Programs of behavior modification have been very useful in studying child development in experimental situations (especially nursery schools) in the past few years. Bijou and Baer's theory of child development is based on S-R learning and principles of operant conditioning.[16] Behavior modification programs have also been used successfully to alter adult behaviors: overeating, daydreaming, smoking, alcoholism, poor study habits, aggression. However, the same procedures that are so beneficial in helping humans overcome undesirable habits, or in training animals, can be put to destructive uses, as has happened with brainwashing. In the Korean war, for example, many American soldiers were made to confess to crimes that they never committed or to accept Communist ideology by operant conditioning. They were deconditioned from their own values with negative reinforcers: various forms of physical and mental torture. Then they were reinforced for espousing the desired beliefs: that they had committed crimes, that Americans were evil imperialists. Behavior modification has also been cast in a negative light in futuristic novels such as George Orwell's *1984* and Aldous Huxley's *Brave New World.* Humans are portrayed as becoming so conditioned or standardized that they lose their free will and individuality. While conditioning can conceivably be put to evil uses, it is also a technique with potential for producing many desirable behaviors in man and animals. Skinner advocated its use to eliminate problems such as aggression, wastefulness, and injustice in our society. Opponents of mass behavioral modification programs for societal members fear that its use will go beyond conditioning of beneficial behaviors to the inculcation of undesirable attitudes, values, and beliefs in "captive" persons.

Social learning theories grew out of the problems behaviorists encountered when they tried to teach complex forms of social behavior to animals and humans. Operant conditioning procedures are most effective in teaching one new behavior, or set of behaviors, at a time. Reinforcements must be carefully controlled. No rewards must be given for undesirable acts and the desired behaviors must be attended to continuously at first. This can become tedious and time consuming for teaching behaviors that involve many complicated interrelated parts. In addition, some semblance of a response must occur naturally before it can be shaped into a more desirable response. Social learning theory is broad enough to account for learning that takes place when responses, or some approximation of them, do not occur naturally. It attempts to explain how behaviors are initially acquired before they can be reinforced by conditioning.

In 1941 Neal Miller and John Dollard suggested imitation as an explanation of how novel behaviors are acquired.[17] Their theory was demonstrated and expanded by many psychologists in the following two decades. The writings of Albert Bandura and Richard Walters in 1963[18] and by Bandura in 1969[19] exemplify this belief in learning by imitation. Most of the experiments of Bandura and his colleagues involved observing the behaviors of children after they had watched models demonstrating various actions or feelings. Models were varied from real, to filmed, to cartoon or animal models. They were nurturant, hostile, or neutral at different times and behaved under conditions of positive, neutral, or negative reinforcement. Children were found to imitate the behavior of models more frequently if the models were perceived to be powerful, or if some form of positive reinforcement was given to the models for the behaviors or emotions they demonstrated.

Bandura and Walters discerned three ways in which imitation influences social learning. Many acts are modeled exactly as they are observed: the modeling effect. Other acts are not imitated because they are observed to bring negative consequences in their wake: the inhibitory effect. Still other behaviors that are modeled may remind the viewer of other similar but not identical behaviors, which are then practiced: the eliciting effect.

There are many things that children and adults may perceive as positive reinforcers for given behaviors: material rewards (money, food, gifts); praise; nurturance; inclusion in a group; attention; even criticism if it is seen as a form of attention. Bandura identified two other kinds of reinforcement that may influence social learning: vicarious reinforcement and self-reinforcement. In vicarious reinforcement the person imitating some modeled behavior obtains pleasure from the act, not because he or she is rewarded, but because the model or some other person was rewarded. The reinforcement of the model takes the place of one's own reward. In self-reinforcement the learner actually rewards him- or herself for behaviors or emotions deemed meritorious. Self-administered reinforcers are considered very important in the learning of complex social behaviors.

Robert Sears applied social learning principles to the socialization of children in his theory of child development.[20] Sears felt that parents are the earliest and most frequent models for children's imitations. Consequently their behaviors and their childrearing practices determine the nature of the child's development. The parental admonition "Do as I say, not as I do" is the antithesis of social learning principles. Children do what they see and hear their parents do, not just what their parents tell them to do. Physical punishment of misbehavior is, in Sears's view, much less effective in changing children's behaviors than rewards for appropriate behaviors. In addition to leaving a child in conflict about the misbehavior and the parental retaliation, it serves as a model of parental aggression that will be imitated by the child. Sears used social learning by imitation to explain how identification occurs. The child, dependent on the mother, comes to enjoy her affectionate nurture. The child imitates this powerful and rewarding model. The act of imitation itself then acquires a secondary rewarding value. Imitating her gestures and actions will bring pleasure to the child in her absence.

Social learning theorists are continually modifying their learning theories to account (in stimulus-response terms) for the acquisition of more and more behavioral phenomena. Because they limit their research to very carefully controlled experiments and report their findings completely, they are highly respected. However, social learning theories tend to ignore what they cannot explain in S-R terms or demonstrate in experimental situations. This translates into the existence of a gap in behaviorist learning theories about the role played by past experiences, especially the highly charged emotional experiences that are the concern of the psychoanalytic theorists. Because they are not generally observed in experimental situations, and because any recounting of them is so subjective, they are intentionally left unstudied.

Cognitive-developmental theories

As psychoanalytic theories all have roots in the theory of Sigmund Freud, cognitive-developmental theories stem from the systematic explorations of cognition carried out by Jean Piaget from the 1920s through the 1970s.

Jean Piaget conducted most of his research on cognition (the process of knowing and understanding) in Geneva, Switzerland, using children and adolescents as subjects. He began his career as a biologist, earning a Ph.D. for a study of mollusks. He then found employment in Paris, standardizing intelligence tests for humans. He became fascinated with the way children reason to arrive at answers to questions. The reasoning was frequently confusing. His biological background led him to question how it is that humans come to adapt to their world and to reason with mature, objective, and abstract logic. Thus began his investigations of cognitive development and epistemology (the study of the origin, nature, method, and limits of knowledge). Piaget was more concerned with how we come to know what we know than with our actual range of stored information. How does the infant who "knows" the world through reflex actions (resting, sucking, grasping, looking) come to eventually understand mature hypothetical concepts? Piaget's theory explains the qualitative differences in methods of thinking used by children and adolescents rather than enumerating the quantity of right answers that children can provide at different ages. The theory stresses both biological changes and maturation as determinants of cognitive development and interaction with materials and people in the environment. The theory is concerned primarily with cognition. Consequently, it only peripherally deals with emotional aspects of behavior.

Piaget used his own three children as subjects for many of his early experiments. He was an astute observer of changes in their behavior that indicated a more advanced stage of intellectual development. In addition to observing, he invented many little problems or games for them to test their reasoning abilities. For example, when his daughter Jacqueline was five months and five days old Piaget reports:

> *I then tried the experiment of alternately separating and bringing together my hands as I stood in front of her. She watched me attentively and reproduced the movement three times. She stopped when I stopped and began again when I did, never looking at her hands, but keeping her eyes fixed on mine.*
>
> *At 0;5(6) (five months, six days) and 0;5(7) (five months, seven days) she failed to react, perhaps because I was at the side and not in front of her. At 0;5(8), however, when I resumed my movement in front of her, she imitated me fourteen times in just under two minutes. I myself only did it about forty times. After I stopped, she only did it three times in five minutes. It was thus a clear case of imitation.*[21]

Piaget, like the social learning theorists, found that imitation is one of the important skills that children have to help them learn about and adapt to the adult world. He saw organization and adaptation as two basic functions of all organisms. In their adaptation to the world, humans practice the interrelated processes of assimilation and accommodation. Assimilation refers to an individual's taking in (perceiving) some new pieces of information from the environment and using current structures to deal with the information. Accommodation refers to modifications of current structures that the individual must make due to the impact of some newly assimilated pieces of information. Previous concepts may be radically altered in the process of accommodation. Children are continually revising and refining their thought processes through assimilation and accommodation and becoming cognitively more mature.[22]

Piaget introduced the concepts of equilibrium and disequilibrium to help explain the process of cognitive development. Equilibrium refers to a state of relative balance between assimilation and accommodation of environmental stimuli. In equilibrium one does not have to disturb one's thought processes too much to assimilate the information at hand. However, when a relative state of equilibrium exists, the little inconsistencies in one's knowledge come into clear focus and serve as seeds of destruction for the balanced state.[23] When new information cannot be accounted for by preexisting concepts, and when the mind must work to form new concepts into which the information can fit, a state of disequilibrium is present. The mind continually fluctuates between states of relative equilibrium and disequilibrium as learning takes place. This portion of Piaget's theory parallels the concept of stimulus-response (S-R) learning of behavior theory. The information that upsets a state of equilibrium is comparable to a stimulus, for which a response (new learning accommodation) is necessary to restore the balance.

Piaget postulated that intellectual development occurs by stages. At the end of each of his hypothetical stages, he feels that children attain a feeling of near equilibrium in their assimilation and accommodation of environmental events. The remaining inconsistencies then serve to usher in a new phase of higher learning. The stages he postulated are the sensorimotor period from infancy through about age two, the preoperational period from about ages two to seven, the concrete operational period from about seven to eleven, and the formal operational period during late childhood and adolescence. Each of these stages will be explained in considerable detail in the cognitive development sections of Chapters 3, 4, 5, and 6. Piaget found that progression through these stages is gradual and orderly. In his opinion, the development of intelligence is biologically determined. Every child goes through all of the stages at his or her own pace. Piaget's goal was to study epistemology—how we come to know things—not education. However, he expressed his preference for educational programs that allow children to have free exploration of materials rather than providing them with too many structured learning experiences. Through the manipulation of materials and the experience of experimenting with them, children assimilate and accommodate the aspects of the stimuli that are novel to them, yet familiar enough to be fitted into preexisting schemas. A schema, in Piaget's theory, is a pattern of behaviors (such as an activity or a thought process) that the child or adult is capable of performing. Many concepts that adults try to teach children in formal lessons may either lack novelty and thus be repetitious and boring, or may be too novel to fit into any of the categories of knowledge that the children have so far acquired.

Piaget arrived at many of his conclusions about cognitive development by using a clinical method of asking different questions of each child rather than by uniformly testing a large number of children on the same concepts, or by observing children in natural settings (as he did with his own children in their infancies). The clinical method of questioning can be used to explore a child's reasoning abilities in depth without suggesting that any answers are right or wrong. It is flexible enough so that the questions can be kept at a level that each child understands. Any spontaneous, interesting answers can be pursued. In short, this method allows the examiner to explore each child's own unique reasoning processes with very few constraints. This clinical method has been used to collect data by many of Piaget's students at the research institute in Geneva. It is not used injudiciously, however. Piaget stated that it takes at least a year of daily practice before an examiner can achieve any proficiency at his method of clinical questioning.[24]

Piaget is recognized as one of the most influential and important contributors to the study of human development in the twentieth century. Nevertheless, his theory has been in turn ignored and then roundly criticized for its lack of scientific precision. His descriptions of the development of reasoning abilities during infancy, childhood, and adolescence are rich and voluminous. (He authored over thirty books and more than 400 papers.)[25] However, because he asked no standardized questions and collected no systematic observational data, he did not submit his research to any kind of statistical analysis. His theory also ignores many of the concerns of human development that lie outside the realm of learning. He disregarded Freudian concepts such as the unconscious and psychosexual conflicts. He looked only at children's rational utterances, not at their irrational behaviors. He collected data predominantly on white subjects from the area around Geneva, Switzerland. He did not tell us if he found sex differences, cultural differences, or differences related to factors such as the adequacy of nutrition. These concerns he left to other students of human development. In spite of his scientifically imprecise means of collecting data with clinical questions, replications of his studies have, in general, supported his theory of cognitive development.

Research by Jerome Kagan, Howard Moss, and Irving Sigel expanded Piaget's belief that intellectual processes are qualitatively different during the various stages of cognitive development. They demonstrated the existence of individual differences in cognitive processes among children.[26] The techniques of conceptualizing that a child acquires early in life stays relatively unchanged as that child assimilates and accommodates new information and climbs the ladder of cognitive maturity. While all children go through the stages Piaget postulated, Kagan, Moss, and Sigel believed they may do so with their own unique styles of problem solving.

Laurence Kohlberg extended Piaget's theory of how children learn the moral standards of their social order. Both Piaget and Kohlberg took a cognitive-developmental view of the acquisition of morality. Children are believed to move from a stage of moral egocentricity toward a level of social idealism and social consciousness as they mature. However, while Piaget wrote of two basic moral orientations (that of moral realism where children see rules as sacred and unalterable, and that of moral relativism where rules are seen as modifiable to bring the greatest good to the greatest number), Kohlberg described six stages of moral development. Acquisition of the highest levels, he wrote, depends on cognition, experience, and acquisition of each of the lower levels first. (The levels of morality postulated by Kohlberg will be presented in Chapter 6).

Cognitive-developmental theories deal with different matters than those that are the principle concerns of psychoanalytic and behaviorist learning theories. They stress the cognitive rather than the affective aspects of behavior. In some cases the views of the cognitive-developmental theorists parallel quite closely the views of the other theorists. Psychoanalytical, behaviorist, and social learning theories stress accumulations during development. Cognitive theories stress change. None of the theories is complete. A clearer picture of the course of development through the life cycle is obtained by studying all of these theories.

Humanist theories

The humanist movement is relatively new and untested, especially as compared to psychoanalysis, behavior modification through operant conditioning, and theories of cognitive development. It has been generated more by the observations of nonpsychoanalytic psychiatrists, clinical psychologists, teachers, and parents than by experimental research. There is no one master builder of a humanist theory the way Freud was of psychoanalytic theory, Skinner was of behaviorism, and Piaget was of the study of cognition. It grew in part out of existential philosophies and writings of such people as Soren Kierkegaard, William James, Jean Paul Sartre, and Martin Heidegger. Some of the names frequently associated with the humanist movement include A. S. Neill, Abraham Maslow, Gordon Allport, Carl Rogers, Albert Ellis, Ronald Laing, Rollo May, Thomas Gordon, Sidney Jourard, Clark Moustakas, Donald Snygg and Arthur Combs. We will briefly describe some of the contributions of a few "humanists" in this chapter. First, however, let us explore what is meant by a humanist approach.

Humanists feel that man is too complex to be explained away as a product of psychosexual conflicts of infancy and childhood or as a product of S-R learnings. The humanist viewpoint is that people are born basically good. They strive throughout their life spans to become all they are capable of being. The ways in which persons define their various experiences within their family and their society may either hinder or enhance their potentialities for growth. All humans are different because of their varying experiences and the unique meanings that these experiences have for them. Consequently, humanists believe that theory builders, philosophers, educators, parents, and the like should not try to fit human beings into roles or categories and predict how they should or will behave. The humanist theory stresses individual freedom and responsibility along with a respect for the existence, dignity, and worth of others, whatever their status in life. Qualities such as humor, happiness, hope, creativity, choice, ideals, values, needs, love, and identity are the subjects that concern humanists. The core interests are in the experiencing person, and in the meanings that the individual assigns to feelings, events, and subjective phenomena. By studying healthy personalities, humanists hope to learn more about the potentials that we all have for enhancing our affective lives. In any kind of therapy situation (e.g., encounter groups, sensitivity training sessions, Gestalt therapy, client-centered therapy), the individual is first helped to accept, then like, then love him or herself. A central tenet of humanist theory is that persons cannot love others unless they first love themselves. Childrearing, according to the humanists, should involve less rules, less roles, and less expectations of what constitutes a "good father," a "good mother," or "good children." Each member of the family unit needs freedom to grow and become what he or she can be. Guilt feelings, hostilities, disciplinary actions and the like are counterproductive to the development of healthy personalities. Conversely, when family members feel loved and accepted for what they are, their defenses will disappear and they will feel freer to pursue joy, love, rational behavior, and self-actualization.

The humanist views of A. S. Neill are best described in his book *Summerhill: A Radical Approach to Child Rearing.*[27] Neill started a small private school in England after World War II in which he eliminated assignments, examinations, rules, and punishment. Students were given freedom to choose their own course of study, or to not study. The one overriding concern of Neill was that all teachers and pupils should show respect for everyone else and use their freedom in a responsible way. Neill described the initial problems with the approach but reported that, in time, students became accountable for their own growth, development, and learning in a way seldom seen in traditional school settings. His book presents a strong argument for a more humanist approach to education. His phenomenal success, however, has not been replicated by many other schools or educators.

Abraham Maslow exemplified the positive approach of the humanists in his theory of motivation. It is based on basic needs organized into a hierarchy of relative potency.[28] At the top of the hierarchy is the need for self-actualization. This is a state of being open, autonomous, spontaneous, accepting, loving, creative, democratic, in short, being a happy, fulfilled human being. (We will discuss all the needs more fully in Chapter 7.) Maslow also introduced the idea that persons can have "peak experiences" of extraordinary happiness at special times in their lives.

Gordon Allport argued for a more humanist approach to research in his book *Becoming: Basic Considerations for a Psychology of Personality.*[29] He felt a study of healthy human beings, of law-abiders, and courageous persons should take the place of so much research on neurotic, anxious, hostile, aggressive persons. He is also well known for his trait theory of personality that he evolved in the 1930s. He compiled a list of 17,953 traits from a dictionary (e.g., honest, kind, generous, shy, smug, rude) that he felt motivated behavior in different persons. He felt we all have a few cardinal traits that predominate in our personalities. For example, reverence for life was a cardinal trait of Albert Schweitzer. We also all have many secondary traits that occasionally play a role in our actions.

Another very important contribution to the humanist movement was made by Carl Rogers. He believed that we all help shape our own personalities. In order to change our personalities, we must acknowledge to ourselves what we are. "Self-acceptance is the beginning of change."[30] He practiced and taught a method of client-centered therapy in which the therapist refrained from making value judgments or giving advice. Instead the client was helped to discover for him- or herself what courses of action were desirable to change behavior and what behaviors to change.

The humanist bent of Albert Ellis led him to develop another form of therapy: rational-emotive therapy (RET).[31] Ellis wrote extensively on the concept that neurotic behaviors are often the result of irrational thought processes. Many persons talk nonsense to themselves. They convince themselves that they are afraid, inferior, or unattractive. In RET sessions clients are encouraged to check the validity of their thinking. They consider whether a problem is real, if it is their own problem, and how it can be changed. RET stresses the development of rational thoughts and behaviors that generate satisfaction. "You feel the way you think" is the basis for helping clients to acquire more healthful beliefs about themselves.[32]

Thomas Gordon translated the concepts of Albert Ellis and other humanists into a self-help program for parents called parent-effectiveness training (PET).[33] He outlined ways in which parents can give children both freedom and responsibility. Solutions to conflicts are negotiated in a rational way. Neither parent nor child emerges as winner or loser. According to Gordon, guilt, hostility, and disciplinary actions should become antiquated if PET is practiced daily.

There are many other humanists who have made important contributions to the movement, some whom we have previously named (May, Laing, Jourard, Moustakas, Snygg, Combs), many whom we have not. Humanist theories are very much "in-the-making." The Association for Humanistic Psychology and the *Journal of Humanistic Psychology* are currently encouraging research in the area. Much of the research already assembled is criticized for its scientific imprecision, just as Piaget's research has been. The stress on subjective experiences of individuals has led to a rich collection of case studies but a paucity of statistically analyzable data. Another criticism often voiced about humanist theory and practice is that society is not organized to allow "free" individuals to participate in it comfortably. Even if a family or school classroom can function effectively without rules and role expectations, society still expects conformity. Children raised in humanist ways may become confused when they are denied the right to be themselves in nonhumanist social settings. Adults who have learned to think and behave in rational, free ways may be given negative reinforcement (criticism, ostracism) by nonrational persons in society. "Uptight" individuals may resent the open expression of personal feelings and the unorthodox, self-confident behaviors of "actualized" persons. The humanist movement hopes to move society in the direction of more altruism, less competition, and less aggression.

The person in family and community

Each individual person can be better understood when one learns about the dynamics of his or her life in the family setting and in the community. These two determinants of development have a profound impact through each of the ages of the entire life cycle.

The family can be both held sacred and considered a scourge by an individual. For many it is regarded more often as one than the other. It is difficult to cast the contemporary American family into any one mold. While the functions that families perform are similar, their social and emotional climates can be vastly dissimilar.

A primary function of families in relation to young children is physical care. Human children require years of feeding, clothing, sheltering, and protecting before they can take care of themselves without adult help. A second very important function of families in relation to children is socialization. Social values and appropriate social behaviors need to be taught. The family more than any other institution has the responsibility for instilling religious and moral training and for providing discipline. A third important function of families for all ages is the provision of a sense of belonging. A family connotes ancestors, traditions, intimacy, family rituals, even private passwords or jokes. The tie to one's family is felt and enduring, even if family members feud, or change frequently, or if the home is conflict ridden and crisis prone. A fourth, desirable function of families is the provision of an affection bond. Parents should be a source of love to each other, to their offspring, and to all those who reside in the family household. Provision of a tender, loving, caring, supportive feeling is one of the most important ways in which a family can optimize the development of its members.

The wider world of the community also serves several very important functions related to the growth and development of each individual. Warren has identified five areas in which persons, social systems, and institutions outside of the family are meaningful. These are the areas of socialization, economic welfare, social participation, social control, and mutual support.[34]

While the family may start the work of instilling society's values in their children, the community becomes the testing ground on which all these values and beliefs are tried. All aspects of the socialization process are affected by community interactions. To illustrate this, consider the first two aspects of social development as described by the psychoanalytic theorist, Erik Erikson. He believed that the first, most central social lesson learned by human infants is trust in caregivers. Community members, in the form of babysitters, either enhance an infant's trust in adults as providers or instill feelings of mistrust. The second, central social lesson, which is learned in toddlerhood, is autonomy. The child begins to view him- or herself as a separate person, able to stand alone, with a sense of self-control, pride, and inner goodness. Community members in the form of religious, day care, or nursery school teachers, baby-sitters, parents' friends, and store clerks can either enhance the child's sense of autonomy or foster in the child a sense of shame and doubt. Critical or overprotective others can make a child feel foolish, mistrustful, and dependent again.

Social participation is essential to the well-being of the human organism. Children and adults alike when deprived of social contact for prolonged periods will suffer breakdowns in their emotional health. Law enforcers have long realized that solitary confinement is the most severe form of punishment. Community members supplement or sometimes replace family members as sources of social contact. They provide companionship, reassurance, and emotional security. They cooperate in tasks, share ideas, and provide feedback to each other on patterns of acceptable and unacceptable dress and behavior.

Community members share in the tasks of social control by altering rules, making new ones, adhering to them, and providing law enforcement institutions in their community. They share the task of assuring economic welfare by providing jobs for each other. They give each other mutual support when tasks or problems arise that are too great for any one or two individuals to handle alone (e.g., emergency disaster relief).

Throughout the following chapters you will find references to family influences, community influences, various research methodologies, and various theories. Remember, the existence of every individual person is complex. Consider your own self. Can anyone else ever fully understand you? No research methodology, no theory, and no textbook can ever fully describe all the complexities of human existence.

Summary

In presenting the ecology of human development over the life span, this text focuses on many determinants of development. The process of growth and change is examined in physical, cognitive, social, and health spheres. The impact of the primary ecological setting of the family is stressed, as are the roles of the larger ecological systems in the community. It is important to integrate and interrelate all these various systems with each other in order to understand individual development.

Two major kinds of research—experimental and naturalistic—have been applied to the study of human development. Experimental research is contrived. It provides a control of variables, is fairly objective, and is replicable; however, it has a limited application to the study of areas such as thought processes and feelings. Naturalistic research is a look at "real life." It can contribute a great deal of information about many different subjects; however, it must rely on some subjective judgments and may not be easily replicable.

Research can be cross-sectional (studying many different persons at the same time) or longitudinal (studying the same persons over a period of time). Short-term longitudinal research looks at many different persons at the same time and then does follow-up studies on the same persons over an extended period of time.

The data obtained from any type of research is usually analyzed with statistical methods. Results are expressed numerically in terms of their mean, median, mode, and standard deviation. Relations between variables are expressed in terms of correlation coefficients and in chi-square tests. Inferential statistics extends analysis beyond simple description to predict characteristics of the population from those of a sample.

Theoretical viewpoints are important frameworks in which to look at research data. There are many theories of human development.

Psychoanalytic theories usually focus on the impact and influences of past experiences. Freud described unconscious motivators of behavior, the id, ego and superego, defense mechanisms, and stages of psychosexual development in his classical theory. Neo-Freudians (e.g., Jung, Adler, Sullivan, Erikson) developed alternate psychoanalytic theories.

Unlike psychoanalysts, behaviorists pay less attention to past experiences. They effect behavior changes after relatively short periods of behavior therapy using conditioning. Pavlov originated "classical conditioning." Skinner introduced "operant conditioning" and stimulus-response (S-R) learning. He used positive reinforcement (reward) to change behavior. Some behaviorists also use negative reinforcement (punishment).

Social learning theorists explain how social behaviors are acquired in childhood. Miller and Dollard proposed imitation as a fundamental means. Sears added the concept of identification.

Cognitive-developmental theories are more concerned with cognition than social behaviors. Piaget stressed the need for maturation and experience for cognitive growth. He described the learning processes of assimilation and accommodation and postulated four stages of cognitive development. Kohlberg extended Piaget's theory to explain how children acquire moral behaviors.

Humanists study healthy personalities to see how people constantly strive to be all they can be. Humanist theories stress people's goodness and need for freedom in order to become open, spontaneous, and independent. The ideal, as described by Maslow, is to be "self-actualized."

Questions for review

1. Describe an experiment or naturalistic study you would be interested in doing. Discuss some of the problems you might have in conducting this piece of research.
2. List the pros and cons of using the experimental method in doing research in human development.
3. Why are experiments often considered more scientific than naturalistic forms of research?
4. Some feminists say that very little of the research already done in social science is useful for statements about women since most of it was done by men using male subjects who have had different experiences than women. Do you agree or disagree with this? Why?
5. Some parents feel it is important to limit their child's exposure to the community and its influences as much as possible, especially when the child is quite young. Do you agree or disagree? Why?
6. Imagine you would like to see a therapist for some problem you are having. Would you choose one with a psychoanalytic background, a behaviorist orientation, or a humanist? Explain.
7. Compare Freud's psychoanalytic theory with Piaget's cognitive-developmental theory.
8. Do you agree or disagree with the humanist view that childrearing should involve "less rules and less roles, and less expectations of what constitutes a good father, a good mother, or good children," thus allowing for the self-actualizing of individuals. Discuss.

References

[1]J. Donne, *Complete Poetry and Selected Prose*, C. Coffin, ed. (New York: Random House, 1952).

[2]Z. Jakibchuk and U. Smeriglio, "The Influence of Symbolic Modeling on the Social Behavior of Preschool Children with Low Levels of Social Responsiveness," *Child Development*, 47(3), 1976.

[3]S. Hutt and C. Hutt, *Direct Observation and Measurement of Behavior* (Springfield, Ill.: Charles C. Thomas, 1970).

[4]J. Condry and S. Condry, "Sex Differences: A Study of the Eye of the Beholder," *Child Development*, 47(3), 1976.

[5]S. Freud, *General Introduction to Psychoanalysis*, J. Riviere, trans. (New York: Permabooks, 1953).

[6]C. Hall and G. Lindzey, *Theories of Personality*, 2nd ed. (New York: John Wiley and Sons, Inc., 1970).

[7]C. Jung, *Collected Works, vol. IX, part 1, The Archetypes and the Collective Unconscious* (Princeton, N.J.: Princeton University Press, 1959).

[8]A. Adler, *The Practice and Theory of Individual Psychology* (New York: Humanities Press, 1971).

[9]A. Freud, *The Ego and the Mechanism of Defense*, C. Baines, trans. (New York: International Universities Press, 1948).

[10]E. Erikson, *Childhood and Society*, 2nd ed. (New York: W. W. Norton, 1963).

[11]H. S. Sullivan, *The Interpersonal Theory of Psychiatry*, H. Perry and M. Gawel, eds. (New York: W. W. Norton, 1953).

[12]J. Marquis, "Behavior Modification Theory: B. F. Skinner and Others," *Operational Theories of Personality*, A. Burton, ed. (New York: Brunner/Mazel, 1974).

[13]M. C. Jones, "Elimination of Children's Fears," *Journal of Experimental Psychology*, 7, 1924.

[14]B. F. Skinner, *Walden Two* (New York: Macmillan Co., 1948).

[15]B. F. Skinner, *Beyond Freedom and Dignity* (New York: Alfred A. Knopf, 1971).

[16]S. Bijou and D. Baer, *Child Development. Volume I: A Systematic and Empirical Theory* (New York: Appleton, 1961).

[17]N. E. Miller and J. Dollard, *Social Learning and Imitation* (New Haven: Yale University Press, 1941).

[18]A. Bandura and R. Walters, *Social Learning and Personality Development* (New York: Holt, Rinehart, and Winston, 1963).

[19]A. Bandura, *Principles of Behavior Modification* (New York: Holt, Rinehart, and Winston, 1969).

[20]H. Maier, "The Learning Theory of Robert R. Sears," *Three Theories of Child Development* (New York: Harper and Row, 1965).

[21]J. Piaget, *Play, Dreams and Imitation in Childhood*, C. Gattegno and F. Hodgson, trans. (New York: W. W. Norton Co., 1962).

[22]J. Flavell, *The Developmental Psychology of Jean Piaget* (New York: Van Nostrand Reinhold Co., 1963).

[23]J. Phillips, *The Origins of Intellect: Piaget's Theory* (San Francisco: W. H. Freeman Co., 1969).

[24]H. Ginsburg and S. Opper, *Piaget's Theory of Intellectual Development: An Introduction* (Englewood Cliffs, N.J.: Prentice-Hall, Inc., 1969).

[25]American Psychological Association, "Distinguished Scientific Contribution Awards for 1969: Jean Piaget," *American Psychologist*, 70(1), 1970.

[26]J. Kagan, H. Moss, and I. Sigel, "Psychological Significance of Styles of Conceptualization," *Cognitive Development in Children: Five Monographs of the Society for Research in Child Development* (Chicago: University of Chicago Press, 1970).

[27]A. S. Neill, *Summerhill: A Radical Approach to Child Rearing* (New York: Hart Publishing Co., 1960).

[28]A. Maslow, *Motivation and Personality* (New York: Harper Brothers, 1954).

[29]G. Allport, *Becoming: Basic Considerations for a Psychology of Personality* (New Haven: Yale University Press, 1955).

[30]C. Rogers, *On Becoming a Person* (Boston: Houghton-Mifflin, 1961).

[31]A. Ellis, "Psychotherapy Without Tears," *Twelve Therapists*, A. Burton, ed. (San Francisco: Jossey-Bass, 1972).

[32]A. Ellis, "Rational-Emotive Theory," *Operational Theories of Personality*, A. Burton, ed. (New York: Brunner/Mazel, 1974).

[33]T. Gordon, *Parent Effectiveness Training* (New York: Peter H. Wyden, Inc., 1970).

[34]R. Warren, *The Community in America* (New York: Rand McNally, 1972).

Contents

© Camerique

Prenatal Development

Think back to the birth of a baby who meant something special to you—a sibling, niece or nephew, a friend's child, or your own child. You probably remember the date of the birth as well as such memorable details as sex, weight, facial features, and hair color. You probably celebrate the date of birth every time it appears on the calendar. Birthdays are considered the anniversary of a person's first day of life. Yet for nine and a half months prior to birth, from the moment of conception, life exists as the fertilized egg passes from the stages of zygote to embryo to fetus. The goal in this chapter is to describe the transformations that occur prenatally (before birth), changing the fertilized egg, which is about the size of a tiny dot, into a fully developed neonate (newborn infant). By the time of birth the neonate has already made giant strides toward becoming unique. Except in the case of identical twins, the neonate is a creature different from all others even before he or she takes a first breath of air. We will discuss male and female reproductive anatomy and physiology to trace the course of the ovum (egg) and sperm that unite to make a new human being. We will explore genetics and cell biology to see what it is about genes and chromosomes that make all humans both similar and yet unique in structure and functions. We will also discuss a number of environmental influences, both internal and external to the uterus, that may possibly influence the development of the future person before birth.

Prenatal physiological processes

Can you recall any of your own early naive concepts about the source of a baby in a woman's uterus (womb)? Did you ever wonder if pregnancy resulted from kissing? from overeating? from swallowing a watermelon seed? History suggests that many early people believed that some spirit entered a woman to become her child at that moment when she first felt her baby move.[1] They believed that impregnating spirits came from the wind, the trees, the sun, the moon, food, and water. During the Renaissance (and occasionally still today), people believed that new babies were contained in male sperm.[2] They needed only to be planted in a woman to grow. Babies were often considered the property of men. While a father might have his infant destroyed if the child displeased him, the care of surviving babies was left to women. Even in the seventeenth century Leeuwenhoek, in developing and experimenting with the first microscope, believed he saw miniature human beings in sperm cells. Indeed, our knowledge of the principles of genetic inheritance after the ovum-sperm union is relatively new. A description of the current information on ovum and sperm, the human reproductive cells, follows.

Precursors of a new human being

Human development begins with the fertilization of an ovum by a sperm. The ovum and sperm have to mature before they merge.

The ovum. The ovum originates from one of the two female ovaries located on either side of the uterus. About every thirty days during a woman's fertile years (from puberty to menopause or approximately ages twelve to forty-seven), a mature ovum is set free to be fertilized in the oviduct if sperm are present. Usually only one ovum is discharged, but sometimes two or more are released, presenting the possibility for multiple, fraternal births. The two ovaries alternate months in which they release ova (plural of ovum). The ovaries interrupt their production of one mature ovum every thirty or so days during pregnancy and total lactation (breast-feeding). The maturation and release of ova is brought about by certain hormones that are extremely sensitive and responsive to the physical condition and emotions of the woman. If one ovary becomes diseased or removed, those hormones will stimulate the other ovary to take over the responsibility of releasing one ovum every thirty days on schedule. If another part of the body becomes diseased, or if the woman is under great emotional stress, the hormones may cause the ovaries to delay the process of maturation and release of ova temporarily, as they do during pregnancy and total lactation. The hormones that trigger ovulation (release of an ovum) are under the direct control of the hypothalamus and come from the pituitary gland in the brain.[3] The hypothalamus regulates the pituitary gland's production of these so-called gonadotropic (gonad-stimulating) hormones: follicle-stimulating hormone (FSH) and luteinizing hormone (LH). Each female has approximately 300,000 rudimentary ova in her two ovaries at the time of birth.[4] Each immature ovum is contained in a primordial (primitive) follicle. Every month from puberty through menopause several of the primordial follicles begin to grow under the influence of FSH, but, only one reaches full maturity. During the average woman's life, only about 400 follicles will fully ripen and release their ova (one per month for about thirty-five fertile years, subtracting months of pregnancy, lactation, and/or illnesses affecting ovarian functions). All the follicles that begin to develop each month produce another hormone, estrogen. This ovarian hormone triggers the release of LH by the pituitary gland. The luteinizing hormone then triggers the release of the ovum from the fully ripened follicle (called a Graafian follicle) and from the surface of the ovary, a process called ovulation. After ovulation the several partially developed follicles degenerate. Under the influence of LH the Graafian follicle develops into a structure called the corpus luteum (see Figure 2–1). The corpus luteum secretes some estrogen and another hormone, progesterone. These hormones help the uterus prepare to accept a fertilized

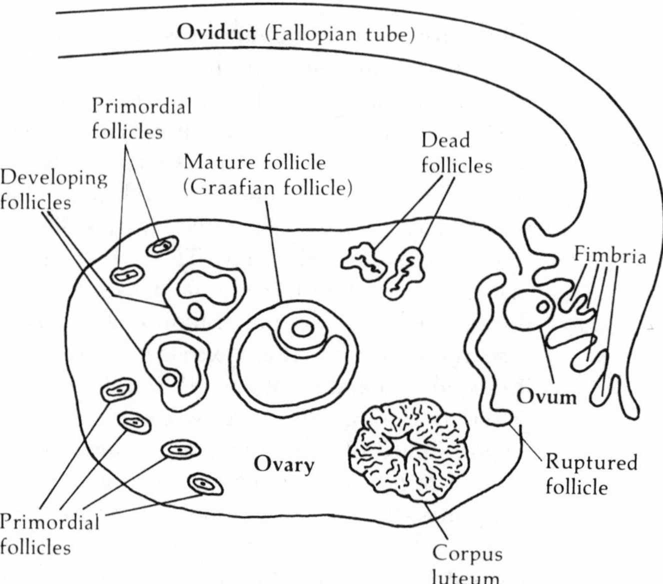

Figure 2–1. Diagrammatic summary of the maturation and discharge of an ovum from the ovary.

ovum. If it is fertilized, the corpus luteum increases its production of estrogen and progesterone during pregnancy. If the ovum is unfertilized, the corpus luteum begins to degenerate at about the same time that the uterus sheds, through menstruation, the lining it had prepared for the possibility of pregnancy.

As the ovum escapes from the Graafian follicle and from the surface of the ovary, it passes briefly into the abdominal cavity before it is picked up by the fimbriated ends of the oviduct (also called Fallopian tube or uterine tube). The ovum moves slowly down the four-inch oviduct and reaches the uterus after two or three days. Unless it is fertilized by a sperm within twelve to twenty-four hours after escaping from the ovary, it dies.[5]

Many women can determine their time of ovulation, and hence their fertile period, by taking daily readings of their body temperature on thermometers that record to fractions of a degree. Body temperature may either rise or fall slightly at ovulation or shortly thereafter. If a woman has very regular menstrual periods, she can also estimate that her ovulation will occur at approximately fourteen days prior to the beginning of each period. However, such things as heightened emotionality and ill health can either accelerate or retard the time of ovulation from month to month.

The sperm. While women are born with all the ova they will ever have, men continually produce sperm at the rate of several hundred million every few days.[6] The sperm are formed in the two testes that lie in the scrotum suspended below the abdomen (see Figure 2–2). This location outside the abdomen is necessary for fertility because spermatogenesis (formation of sperm) requires a temperature lower than that of the body. The scrotum hangs loosely when warm and pulls closer to the body when cool to maintain a relatively stable temperature.

From birth, males have in their testes dormant spermatogonia or primordial germ cells that are the early precursors of sperm. Beginning at puberty these primordial germ cells grow and multiply. In successive steps the activated spermatogonia are transformed into primary spermatocytes, then into secondary spermatocytes, then into spermatids, and finally into spermatozoa, or mature sperm. The differentiation and maturation process from spermatogonia to mature sperm takes between two and three weeks.[7] Most men continually produce sperm from puberty until death. A sperm diminishes in size during this maturation transformation. The cell nucleus condenses and is concentrated into a "head" region. Most of the cell cytoplasm (the colloid, semifluid matter outside the nucleus) is cast off. A long, whiplike tail, called a flagellum, forms. This structure permits the sperm great mobility (see Figure 2–3).

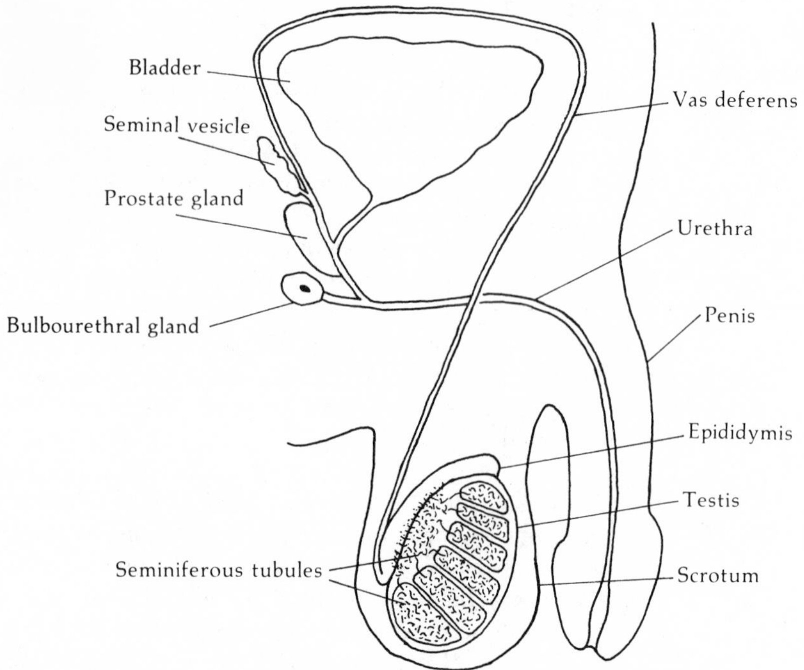

Figure 2–2. *The male sex organs where spermatozoa are produced, stored, lubricated, and released.*

Fully developed sperm move from the seminiferous tubules in the testes to the epididymis (see Figure 2–2) where they may remain for several months. They are lubricated and acquire greater motility while in the epididymis. When ejaculation occurs, a few hundred million sperm travel through the long vas deferens to the seminal vesicles where they are further lubricated by fluids from the seminal vesicles, the prostate gland, and the bulbourethral glands. These fluids both nourish the sperm and provide them with further means of transport. Finally, the sperm are thrust through the urethra and expelled from the penis. During sexual intercourse the sperm are deposited in the vagina near the small opening to the uterus known as the cervix. The cervix is protected by mucous secretions through which the sperm must pass. Then they must cross the uterus, enter the oviducts, and travel to the ends nearest the ovaries in order to fertilize an ovum, if present, while the ovum is still alive. While several million sperm may be deposited near the cervix, only a few hundred may reach the portion of the oviducts near the ovaries.[8] Sperm travel fastest right after ejaculation and slow down considerably after two hours. Some sperm can be expected to reach the ovarian ends of the oviducts after about one hour. Others arrive later. The whiplike movements of the sperm flagellae help them "swim." Travel is also assisted by contractile move-

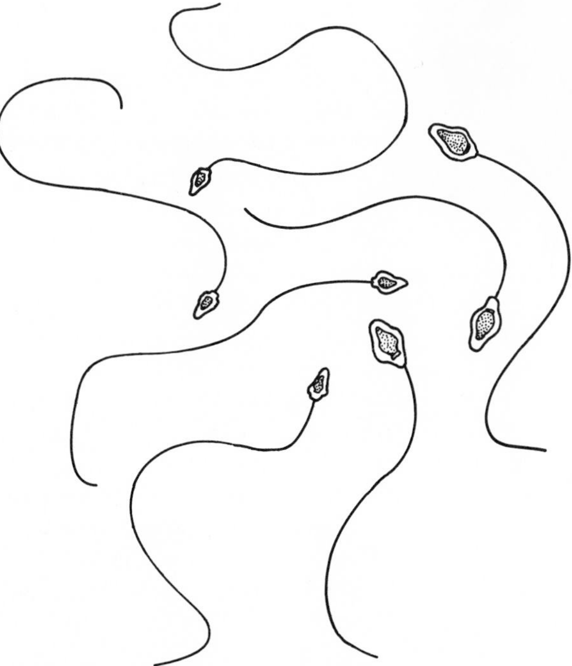

Figure 2–3. *Mature spermatozoa. Those that will produce female offspring have the larger, oval heads and shorter tails.*

ments of the walls of the uterus and oviducts.[9] Sperm can remain alive in the oviducts for from two to four days waiting for an ovum.[10] It has become possible to identify and differentiate sperm that will produce male and female offspring. Sperm that will produce male children (called androsperm) have longer tails and smaller heads and can be expected to reach the far ends of the oviducts most rapidly. However, the sperm that will produce female children (called gynosperm) can survive longer in the oviducts waiting for an ovum due to the extra cytoplasm carried in their "head" region.[11] Sperm undergo still another transformation within the female genital tract. They lose a coating on their heads that allows special enzymes to escape. These enzymes help break down the protective coating on the ovum so a sperm can penetrate it. One and only one sperm fertilizes an ovum. Once the head of a sperm enters the cytoplasm of the ovum, a change occurs on the surface of the ovum that makes it become impenetrable to all other sperm.

Reduction division. In the preceding description of mature ova and sperm, one important difference between these sex cells (called germ cells or gametes) and the other body cells (called somatic cells) was reserved for discussion here. This involves the way they divide and the contents of their nuclei (cell centers) following division. Mature germ cells are different because they have only one-half the normal complement of chromosomes in their nuclei. Chromosomes are structures that contain genes. Genes are important because they contain the "blueprints" for the structure and functioning of our bodies.

All the somatic cells in the human species contain forty-six chromosomes that can be arranged into twenty-three pairs. They are called diploid (double) cells. Mature ova and sperm contain only twenty-three unpaired chromosomes and are called haploid (half) cells. When fertilization occurs, the chromosomes of each of the germ cells merge. They then can be arranged into twenty-three pairs of chromosomes. Thus the fertilized ovum becomes a diploid cell. All the cells of the embryo and later the fetus and finally the mature human body will be formed from divisions of this fertilized ovum and will contain the same chromosomal and genetic materials as this original parent cell.

Somatic cells divide continually. In the prenatal period, cell division is extremely rapid to allow for growth of the fertilized ovum into a neonate. Most of the cells of even mature humans continue to divide in order to replace old, damaged, or discarded cells. Prior to the division of cells, and, in particular, prior to division of the nucleus of each cell, the chromosomes must have exact replicas made of themselves. The process by which the chromosomes in the nuclei divide during cell division is known as mitosis.

Chromosomes are composed of compounds called nucleotides, stranded into long chains known as nucleic acids, and also of associated nucleoproteins. The nucleic acids and nucleoproteins together are also referred to as chromatin material. Each nucleotide in the chromosome is composed of a phosphate group, a sugar group (deoxyribose) and an organic base. Strands of such phosphate–sugar-base units (nucleotides) are called deoxyribonucleic acids (abbreviated DNA). In each chromosome there are two strands of nucleotides that wrap around one another in a double helical pattern (see Figure 2–4). Each base (of a nucleotide) in one strand faces and is bound to a complementary base on the second strand, so that the base sequence of one DNA determines the base sequence of its complementary DNA strand. The four bases in DNA are called adenine, thymine, guanine, and cytosine. While these four bases can be stranded in various arrangements in one strand of DNA, the order of the bases is fixed on the complementary second strand of DNA. This is because adenine always pairs with cytosine. This base pairing is crucial to the exact replication of DNA molecules required for replication of chromosomes seen before any cell division. The phosphate and sugar groups of each nucleotide on one strand are so attached that they contribute to the stability of the helical coils of DNA. The bases are at the center of the

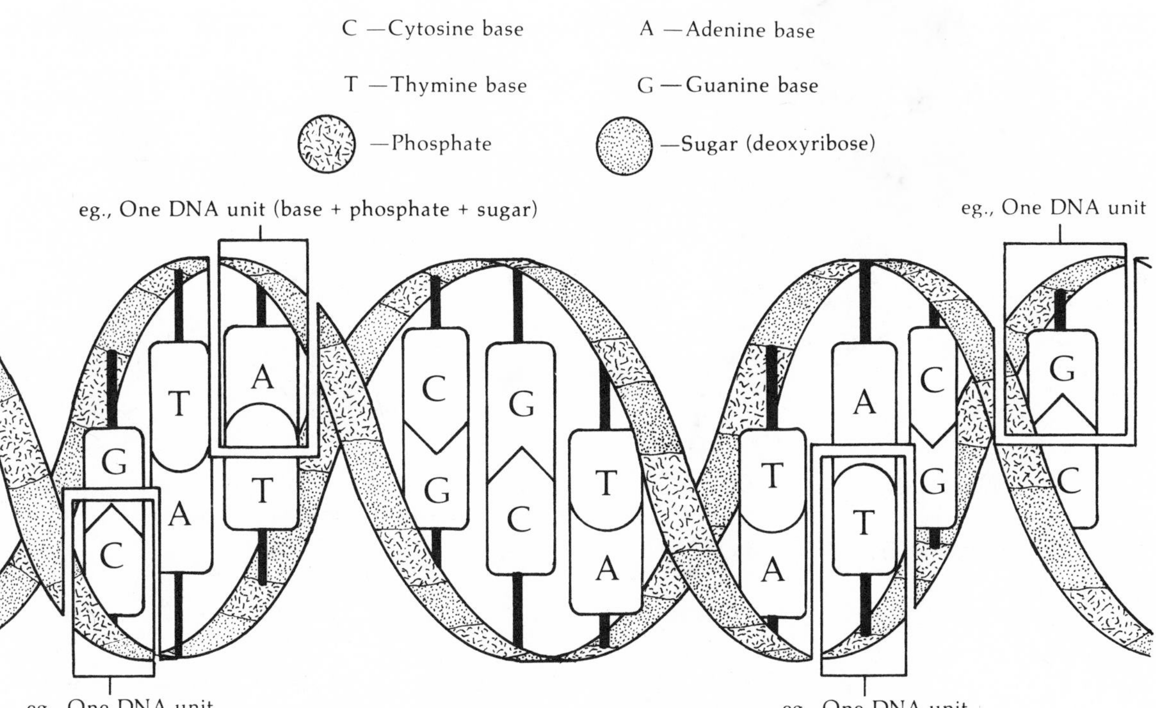

Figure 2–4. *Schematic representation of deoxyribonucleic acids (DNA), of which genes are composed and which appear in chromosomes in a double helix arrangement.*

coils, while the phosphate and sugar groups are on the outside, serving as the "backbone" of the double-entwining helical structure.

In the resting stage of the cell cycle, while the cell is not yet preparing for the division of the chromosomes, the base of the complementary strands of DNA are still attached to each other by certain chemical attractive forces. In the process of replication of each chromosome, the double helical coils of the complementary DNA strands must separate. To each separated strand new nucleotides with complementary bases become attached. (These new nucleotides form from free-floating materials in the cell.) This process results in a replication, nucleotide by nucleotide, of the two strands of complementary DNA. Each DNA strand thus serves as a pattern for its complementary strand. So, by this process, the new set of chromosomes carry exactly the same nucleotides in a double helix arrangement as the original. After the process of DNA replication, the number of chromosomes per cell has doubled. The cell must undergo a division process (mitosis) to return the number of chromosomes back to the original level.

Mitosis occurs in a series of stages termed prophase, meta-

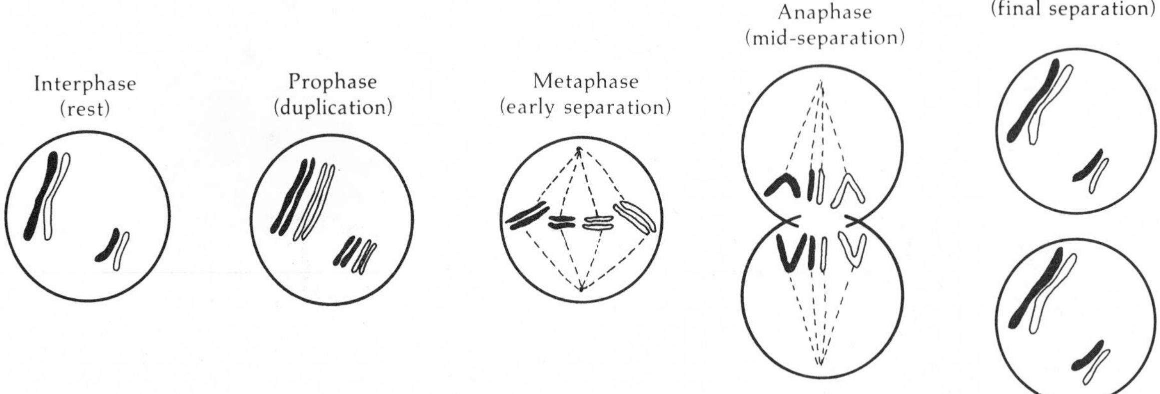

Figure 2–5. *Cell division by mitosis schematically, showing only two pair of chromosomes per cell rather than the full human complement of twenty-three pair.*

phase, anaphase, and telophase (see Figure 2–5). Every chromosome separates from its replica so that a newly formed cell can have genetic material that is perfectly equivalent to that of the original cell.

In preparation for possible later fertilization, germ cells (ova and sperm) have to undergo certain maturation processes that involve their chromosomes. There must be a reduction in the number of chromosomes carried in these germ cells so that after fusion of an ovum and a sperm the resulting product has the normal complement of forty-six chromosomes arranged into twenty-three pairs. The specialized reduction division, resulting in only twenty-three unpaired chromosomes in each mature germ cell, is called meiosis.

Just before the first meiotic division begins, the primitive germ cells replicate their DNA. Thus, at the start of meiosis the ova and sperm contain double the normal amount of DNA. Each of the forty-six chromosomes has a double structure, the original chromosome and its replica, bound at a structure common to both called the centromore (see Figure 2–6). During the first meiotic division, during prophase, there is a pairing of the homologous (alike) chromosome pairs. This pairing is exact, except for the X and Y chromosome pairs, resulting in paired, double-structured chromosomes. During this characteristic lining up of the chromosomes of the germ cells, there occurs an interchange of chromosome segments, a process called crossing-over. This provides an opportunity for exchange of genetic content among homologous chromosomes. During the metaphase of the first meiotic division (see Figure 2–6), there is separation

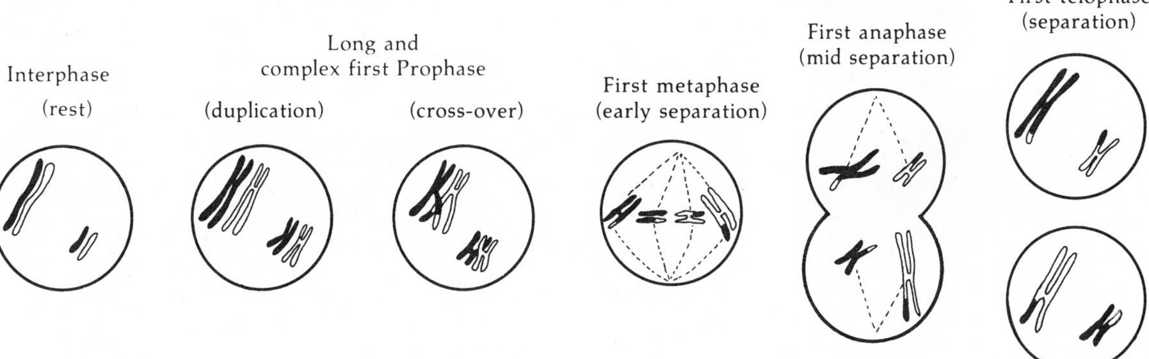

Figure 2–6. *Meiosis: first division. Cross-over may occur between some segments of the intertwined chromosome pairs during the long and complex prophase. (Diagram shows only two chromosome pairs rather than the full complement of twenty-three pairs per cell.)*

of the homologous chromosome pairs. The first meiotic division continues through anaphase and telophase. After the completion of the first division, each offspring cell contains one member of each chromosome pair and has twenty-three double-structured chromosomes. At this point the second meiotic division begins (see Figure 2–7). The twenty-three double-structured chromosomes divide. Each newly formed offspring receives twenty-three single-structured chromosomes. These offspring cells are referred to as haploid (half) cells.

The purposes of the two stages of meiotic or reduction division are to produce germ cells with half the number of chromosomes and half the amount of DNA of somatic cells and to allow for an exchange of small amounts of genetic material between chromosomes of homologous pairs through the cross-over phenomenon.

Only one offspring cell resulting from meiotic division of an immature ovum becomes a mature ovum. The other cells, called polar bodies, degenerate. In the male all four haploid cells become mature sperm.

In Figures 2–6 and 2–7 the process of reduction division was schematically illustrated for only one pair of homologous chromosomes per cell. The same phenomenon occurs with the remaining twenty-two chromosome pairs. Both the cross-over step and the completely random distribution of the twenty-three singlets among the four offspring of the meiotic process in germ cells lead to enormous numbers of different combinations of the genetic material on the twenty-three chromosomes in the mature germ cell. Only identical twins, who develop from one fertilized ovum, can claim to be exactly equal down to the last gene.

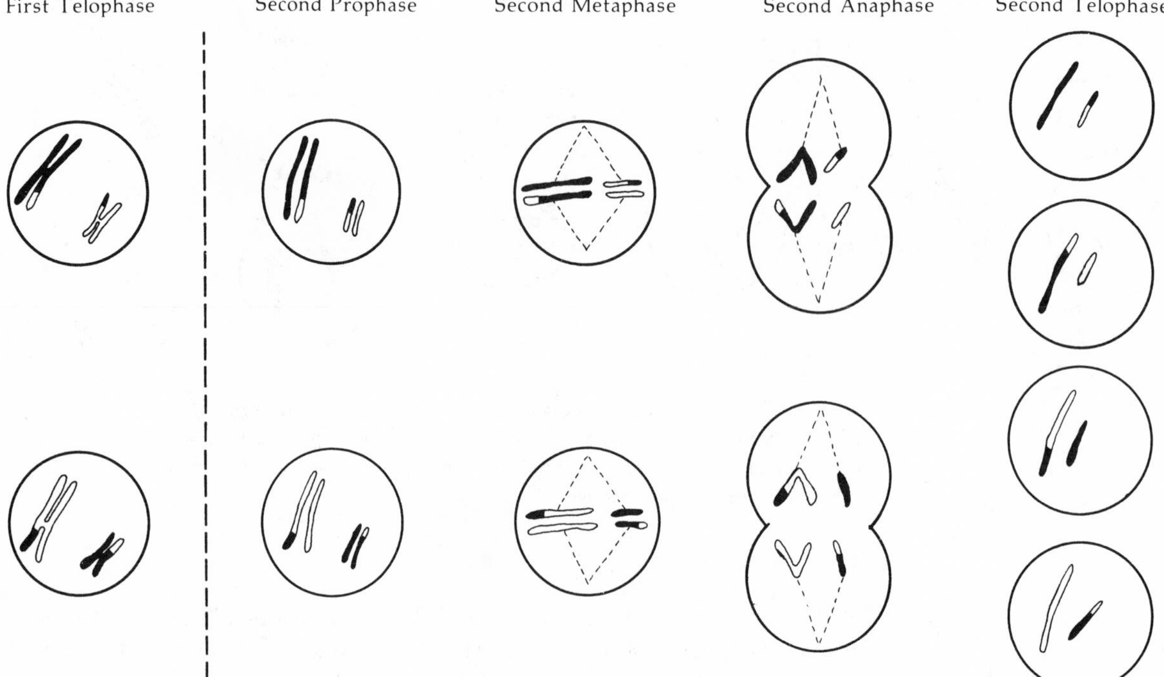

Figure 2–7. *Meiosis: second division with four resultant haploid germ cells. In the female only one germ cell matures after the two-stage meiotic cell division. In the male all four germ cells resulting from meiosis can develop into mature sperm.*

Genetic inheritance

Genes are discrete portions of the chromosomes, or specifically, of the DNA portions of the chromosomes. These portions carry information for building all the proteins of the body. The numbers of genes on chromosomes can only be guessed. It is possible for chromosomes to contain a large number of genes in a condensed space because of the helical coding structure. It is estimated that each chromosome in humans may contain as many as 3000 genes.[12]

Genes code for proteins that determine the many activities of cells. Some genes even code for proteins that control the function of other genes. In this chapter only the role of genes in transmitting "inherited" characteristics will be covered. In humans, in all but the germ cells, there are twenty-two pairs of autosomal chromosomes and either two X sex chromosomes (in females) or one X and one Y sex chromosome (in males). Identical regions of each pair of chromosomes contain genetic information for the same function. These identical regions are called alleles. Humans all inherit genes that make them alike for many traits. For example, all humans have fingers, legs, and toes. For features such as eye color, skin color, hair texture, and blood type, there is obviously different genetic inheritance among individuals. If the genes in the identical regions (allelic portions) in the paired chromosomes contain different information as to how a trait should appear (e.g., one contains information coding for blue eyes, the other for brown eyes), the paired genes are heterozygous (different). If both paired allelic genes code for the same information, they are homozygous (alike) for the trait.

The laws of heredity based on homo- or heterozygosity were initially worked out by an Austrian monk, Gregor Mendel, in the year 1865, long before anyone knew about genes. The principles of homo- and heterozygosity are still referred to as Mendelian law even though knowledge of the essential elements of inheritance has vastly improved since then. Mendel worked out his laws with sweet pea strains that he grew in his monastery garden. This description of Mendelian law will use eye color instead.

A person with brown eyes may be homozygous for brown eyes. If so, that person is both genotypically brown-eyed (genotype refers to one's genetic make-up for a trait) and phenotypically brown-eyed (phenotype refers to the visible expression of inherited traits or what we see when we look at each other).

A person with brown eyes may be heterozygous for brown eyes rather than homozygous. While the phenotype (visible expression) of the genes may be a brown color, one allele on one of the chromosomes may carry a message for blue eye color. Paired heterozygous genes usually work in a dominant-recessive relationship. The dominant gene cancels out the effect of the recessive gene in the phenotype. However, the recessive gene remains in the genotype and can be passed on, unaltered and uncancelled, to offspring. Genetic information determining brown eyes is dominant over such information for blue eyes. Getting back to Mendel's laws, suppose you have brown eyes phenotypically but are heterozygous and carry genes for both brown and blue eye color. Further, suppose you produce children with a person who also carries genes for both brown and blue eyes. Meiotic cell division will result in 50 percent of each of your respective germ cells carrying genes for blue eyes. However, the chances of two phenotypically brown-eyed but genotypically heterozygous persons producing children with blue eyes are only 25 percent. Any combination of a dominant brown gene pairing with a recessive blue gene will produce a brown-eyed child (see Figure 2–8). (For the sake of illustration, we will denote a dominant brown-eye-carrying gene as B and a recessive blue-eye-carrying gene as b.)

Suppose you (hypothetically now a heterozygous brown-eyed individual) produce children with a homozygous brown-eyed person. All of your offspring will have brown eyes like their parents. However, theo-

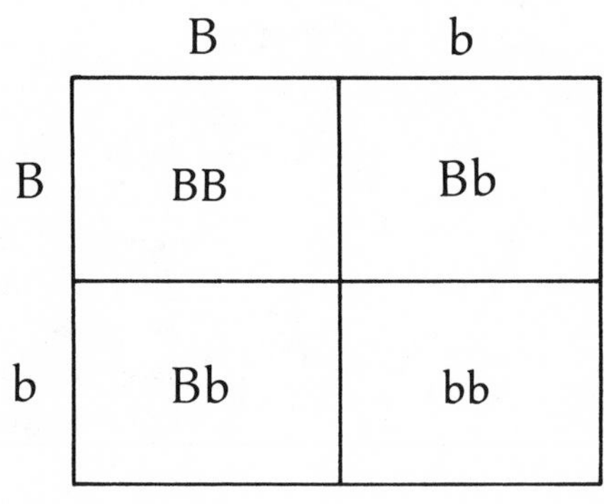

Figure 2–8. *Mendelian square showing the possible genotypes of offspring produced by heterozygous parents carrying genetic information for both brown eye color (B) and blue eye color (b).*

retically 50 percent of them will carry recessive genes for blue eyes that they may pass on to their own offspring (see Figure 2–9).

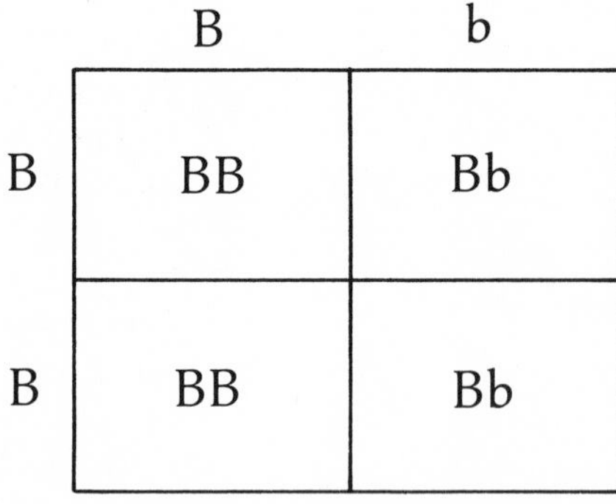

Figure 2–9. *Mendelian square showing the possible genotypes of offspring produced by one parent carrying heterozygous genetic information for both brown eyes and blue eyes (Bb) and one parent carrying homozygous genetic information for brown eyes (BB).*

Suppose you produce children with a partner who is homozygous for blue eyes? What color will the eyes of your offspring be? Theoretically, half of them should have blue eyes and the other half will be phenotypically brown-eyed but genotypically heterozygous for blue eyes as well (see Figure 2–10).

All the offspring of parents who are both homozygous for blue eyes will be blue-eyed. There will be no opportunity for genes to work in a dominant-recessive relationship since the genes on both alleles will transmit the same information determining the color of the pigment in the iris (colored portion) of the eye.

Genetic inheritance is not always determined by simple dominance and recessiveness of genes. Some traits are influenced by multiple genes. Sometimes there are even intermediate effects of genetic information..

The sex of offspring is determined not by genes on alleles but by the sex chromosomes. Every mature ovum contains one large X sex

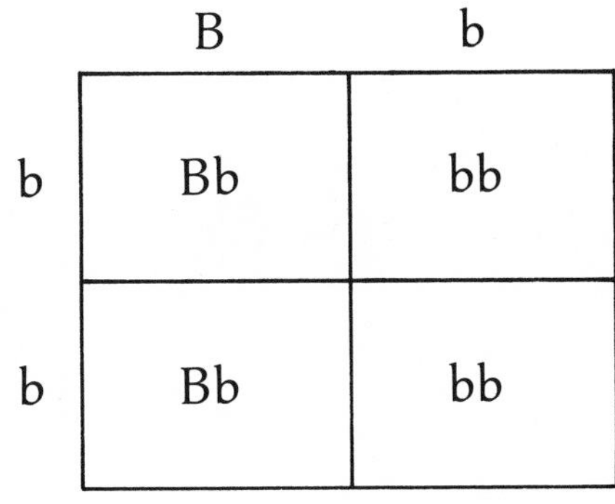

Figure 2–10. *Mendelian square showing the possible genotypes of offspring produced by one parent carrying heterozygous genetic information for both brown eyes and blue eyes (Bb) and one parent carrying homozygous genetic information for blue eyes (bb).*

chromosome along with twenty-two unmatched autosomes. Every mature sperm contains either a large X or a small Y sex chromosome along with twenty-two unmatched autosomes. If a sperm containing an X sex chromosome fertilizes the ovum, the offspring of this conception will be female. Likewise, if a sperm containing a Y sex chromosome fertilizes the ovum, the offspring will be a boy. As mentioned earlier, the male-producing (Y-carrying) sperm are smaller and faster than the X-carrying sperm. More male than female babies are conceived. Some scientists estimate that there are about 40 percent more males conceived than females. But ova impregnated with androsperm are more apt to be spontaneously aborted. There are only an estimated 104 newborn males for every 100 newborn females.[13] The combination of the smaller Y chromosome with the larger X chromosome causes genetic information for male structure and functioning to be related to the cell, while the combination of two X chromosomes relays information for female structure and functioning. Thus, the consequences of fertilization are that the zygote has a full complement (the diploid number) of newly combined chromosome pairs. Further, the sex of the new offspring is determined by the complement of sex chromosomes received from the parent germ cells.

Stages of prenatal development

The growth and development of a single fertilized human ovum into a full-term infant in only approximately 266 days is a truly remarkable phenomenon! From fertilization until birth, every day is marked by notable changes in the baby-to-be. Three stages of prenatal development will be highlighted first: the changes leading up to and surrounding the implantation of the developing ovum into the wall of the uterus; the embryonic stage; and the fetal stage, with an emphasis on anatomy and physiology. A discussion of a multitude of environmental influences (both internal and external to the uterus) that can influence the growing, developing organism will follow in the next section of this chapter.

Implantation. As soon as fertilization and the merging of the twenty-three chromosomes of the ovum and sperm occur, the new cell becomes a somatic cell called the zygote. It will now undergo mitotic cell division. Within thirty hours it will divide into a two-cell structure. By forty hours it will reach a four-cell stage. By seventy-two hours the four cells will have divided twice again to make a sixteen-cell structure called a morula. Each cell will contain the normal somatic cell complement of forty-six chromosomes. This early cell division occurs in the oviduct as the zygote-changed-to-morula structure is slowly transported by peristaltic (rhythmic, wavelike) movements towards the uterus. The ball of cells floats free in the uterus, growing progressively larger, until about the sixth day after fertilization. By this time it will have reached a state called blastocyst and contain over 100 cells. It is now ready to burrow into the well-prepared mucosal lining, called the endometrium, on the wall of the uterus. This endometrium, you will remember, was stimulated to grow by the hormones estrogen and progesterone produced by the corpus luteum after the ovum escaped from its Graafian follicle (refer back to Figure 2–1). The process by which the blastocyst burrows into the endometrium is called implantation. Some women will shed a little blood at this time. The bleeding may be mistaken for a menstrual period since it occurs about six to ten days after ovulation. It usually differs from a normal menstrual flow, however, in both amount and duration of bleeding. The cells of the blastocyst differentiate into embryonic cells and trophoblastic cells as it implants into the uterus. The embryonic cells become the future baby, which is first called an embryo, then a fetus, then a neonate at birth.

In forming the placenta, trophoblastic cells undergo complex changes. Some form villi (minute projections from the surface of the organ) that dig into the engorging blood vessels of the uterus (see Figure 2–11). Others form the placental interior, including the umbilical cord.

The placenta is an organ rich in blood vessels that throughout pregnancy carries oxygen and nutrients from the mother-to-be to the embryo-fetus, and many waste products from the embryo-fetus to the

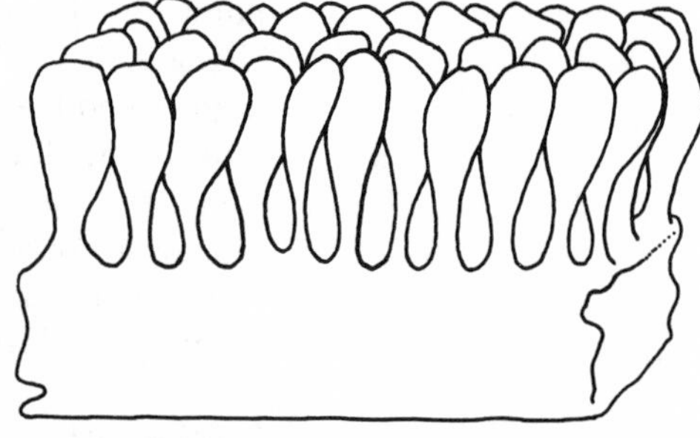

Figure 2–11. Early placental villi are short, stout projections into the uterine mucosa. Later they develop treelike side branches.

mother for excretion. This organ has attachments on the outside to the mother's uterus (villi) and, on the inside, connects with the embryo-fetus by way of the umbilical cord. It will eventually be expelled as the afterbirth following the delivery of the neonate. Figure 2–12 schematically illustrates the changes from fertilized egg to implanted blastocyst in the first two prenatal weeks.

The maternal circulation and the circulation of the developing embryo-fetus are never directly connected. Exchange of oxygen, nutrients, and wastes is accomplished through diffusion through the villi. Other placental cells produce hormones that are essential for the continuous support of pregnancy. These hormones are human chorionic gonadotropin (HCG), human chorionic somatomammotropin (HCS), thyrotropin, es-

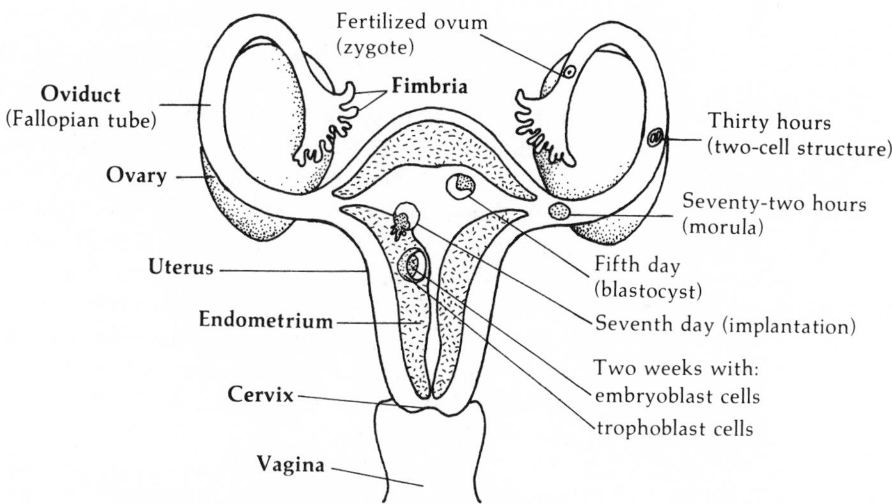

Figure 2–12. Schematic representation of the changes from fertilized ovum to implanted blastocyst in the first two prenatal weeks.

trogen, and progesterone.[14] They cause the "morning sickness" that about 50 percent of women experience in their pregnancies.[15] The trophoblast-placenta cells produce and release HCG as early as two weeks after fertilization. Its appearance and identification in the urine of the mother serves as the basis for the most common pregnancy test.

The fact that the placenta is tolerated in the uterus presents an immunological puzzle that has produced a great deal of investigation, but has not, as yet, been solved. The problem revolves around the fact that the embryo-fetus is not immunologically identical with the mother. It carries transplant antigens (materials that stimulate the body to produce an immune, rejection response) from both the mother and the father. The lack of the rejection reaction until the ninth month is puzzling.

Embryonic period. The placenta expands to form a balloonlike sac, called the amniotic sac, inside of which the embryo grows. It fills with amniotic fluid that serves as a shock absorber for the floating embryo and keeps the walls of the uterus from cramping continued development.

As the embryo grows, the cells of the embryoblast differentiate into the ectodermal, mesodermal, and endodermal layers. These eventually become, in their respective orders, the outer structures (skin, hair, teeth, nails, nerves), the middle structures (muscles, bones, heart, blood vessels), and the inner structures (intestines, endocrine glands, liver, pancreas, lungs, and respiratory tract). The fourth to eighth weeks following fertilization make up the embryonic period. In the fourth week the embryo appears C-shaped. The brain and heart experience the most rapid growth. Thickened areas that will become eyes and ears are visible (see Figure 2–13). In the fifth week the buds that will become arms and legs appear. Growth of the brain exceeds that of all the other body parts. By the sixth week the head is bent over the abdominal bulge. The heart and circulatory system, lungs and respiratory system, liver, pancreas, kidneys, genitals, the nervous system, the mouth, stomach, and intestines are all undergoing very rapid development. A hand with webbed fingers appears. By the seventh week the fingers are all clearly visible and toes appear. The head becomes more rounded and is supported by a neck area. The abdominal bulge and the umbilical cord become smaller. By the eighth week the embryo has a distinctly human appearance. At this point it is called a fetus rather than an embryo.

The period of most rapid growth or development of any structure or function is called its "critical period." The developing human is especially vulnerable to disruptive influences to the organ systems during the critical period of embryonic development. It is remarkable that in spite of the enormous complexity of the organ systems, most babies are born with faultless or nearly faultless, well-integrated, functional systems. One of the reasons for the final perfection rate is the early rejection rate. Many zygotes with genetic or chromosomal imperfections die before they implant, or are not allowed to implant into the uterine lining. Blastocysts that implant incorrectly are likewise rejected. And embryos that are damaged by various extrinsic causes (to be discussed shortly) are frequently aborted. It is estimated that the spontaneous abortion rate in the embryonic period is from 10 percent to 25 percent.[16] Many of these abortions are simply experienced as a normal or slightly delayed menstrual period, the mother having had no prior knowledge of her pregnant state.

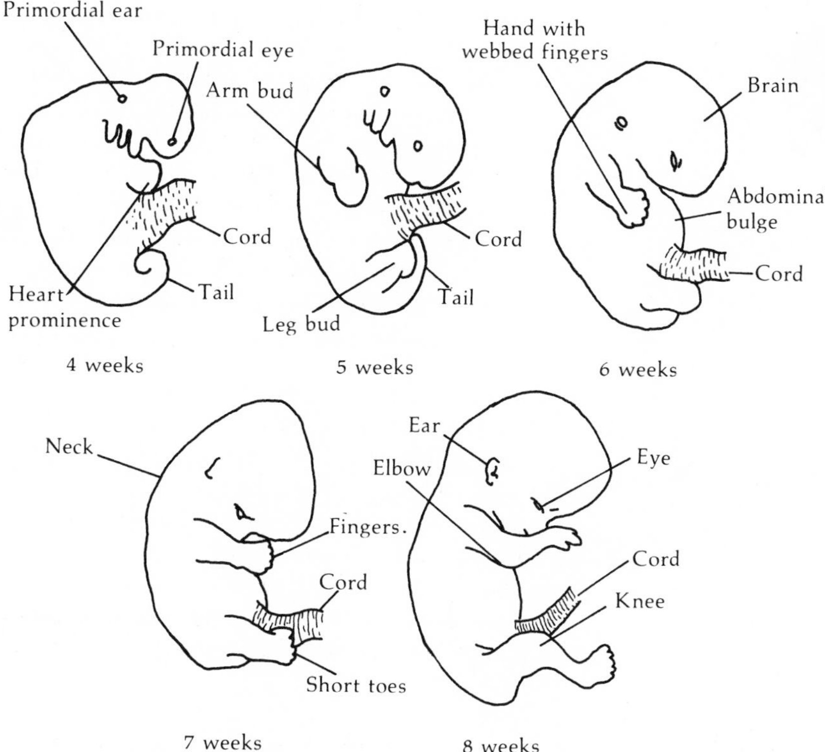

Figure 2–13. Development of the embryo week by week.

Fetal period. The fetus is less susceptible than the embryo to internal and external injuries to its organs, since they are usually past their critical period. The fetal stage is characterized by growth and maturation of all of the structures that were formed in the embryonic stage. Weight gain is extraordinary. By the third month the sex of the fetus is distinguishable externally. By the fourth month the head is erect on the neck, the external ears are formed and stand out from the head, and the legs are well developed. By the fifth month the mother has usually felt movements of the legs or arms (called quickening). At first the movements can be compared to a bubble rising to the surface or a butterfly fluttering, but later they are very noticeably kicks or punches that may cause the mother to wince. By six months the fetus has hair, eyebrows, and fingernails. A fetus born around the twenty-sixth to twenty-ninth week (approximately seven months) can occasionally survive.[17] However, the mortality rate is high because the respiratory system is not yet adequately developed to support life outside the uterus. In the last two months the fetus rapidly accumulates fat deposits to use in the neonatal period. The fatty tissues give the fetus a plump, smooth look. The fetus is usually expelled from the uterus about thirty-eight weeks (or nine months, or 266 days) after conception. The exact mechanisms that trigger hormone changes in the uterus and cause it to contract and push out the fetus are not yet well understood. However, if these trigger mechanisms fail and the fetus is retained in the uterus longer than about forty-two weeks, the delay can be dangerous rather than helpful to the baby-to-be.

Possible prenatal defects

Considering the enormously complicated mechanism of the development of an individual from germ cells to birth, and considering the multitude of factors that can affect the organism in intrauterine life, it is amazing that abnormalities are not more frequent. In this section of the chapter we will describe various reasons for some of the imperfections that do occur. Remember, however, that these are not all risks in every pregnancy. The norm is for full-term, healthy infants to emerge from the nine months of prenatal existence, not defective ones.

Chromosomal abnormalities

When a fertilized ovum contains abnormal chromosomes, extra chromosomal materials, or absent chromosomes, it is usually spontaneously aborted, thus protecting mothers from giving birth to defective infants. However, some disorders due to chromosomal aberrations are more viable than others and occur with enough frequency to merit description here.

At present the chromosome pairs are numbered from one to twenty-two and XY. Down's syndrome, formerly called mongolism, results when one of the chromosomes on the twenty-first pair contains extra chromosomal material. Down's syndrome is also called Twenty-One Trisomy (three bodies) for this reason. The most common cause of the extra material is a failure of the members of the twenty-first chromosome pair to separate during the process of meiosis. This failure to separate is known as nondisjunction. The cell that receives no member of the twenty-first chromosome pair cannot survive but the cell with the extra material, if fertilized, will develop into a person with Down's syndrome. The other cause of extra material is translocation. In this abberation one portion of a chromosome breaks off and attaches to a chromosome of another pair (which is the twenty-first pair if the person is born with Down's syndrome). Nondisjunctions and translocations probably occur in other autosomal chromosomes also, but the recipients of the errors are probably aborted. Infants with trisomies of the eighteenth pair (E syndrome) or of pairs thirteen, fourteen, or fifteen (Trisomy D) have survived for a few weeks after birth but have been severely deformed.[18] An individual with Down's syndrome is mentally retarded, has a dwarfed physical stature, eyes that slant slightly upward, a nose bridge that is small or absent, and a mouth that tends to hang open, allowing the enlarged tongue to protrude.[19] Mortality is high in infancy and childhood. Few Down's individuals survive past their forties.[20] The causes of autosomal chromosomal trisomies are not fully understood, but their frequency is greater in older women than younger. Associations have been demonstrated between autosome errors and aged germ cells, viral infections, maternal irradiation, and chemical agents.[21]

Trisomies of the sex chromosomes are not usually lethal. A male with an extra X chromosome (XXY) is said to have Klinefelter's syndrome. He typically has very small testes with near absence of seminiferous tubules, some breast development, scant body hair, and is sterile.[22]

A male with an extra Y chromosome (XYY) is typically taller and more muscular than the average man. Males with this sex chromosome trisomy were first identified as aggressive members of prison populations.[23] Certainly not all XYY males are aggressive, criminal, or antisocial. The hypothesis that the XYY constitution renders a male more susceptible to emotional stress remains to be proven.[24]

Some males with multiple sex chromosomes (more than trisomies) have also been seen: XXXY, XXXXY. They have small testes, are sterile, and may be mentally retarded.

Super- or metafemales with XXX or XXXX sex chromosomes sometimes have normal ovaries but no menses. They also may be mentally retarded.

Occurrence of only one of a pair of homologous chromosomes is called monosomy. A person with a monosomy can survive if the unpaired chromosome present is an X sex chromosome. An XO recipient is said to have Turner's syndrome. She has abnormal ovarian development, sterility, short stature, and cardiac and skeletal deformities.[25]

Mosaicism is another type of chromosomal abnormality. It results from chromosomal nondisjunction in *some* cells during mitotic cleavage early in embryonic development. The consequence is that certain tissues of the body have abnormal complements of chromosomes, some more and some less than the normal forty-six per cell. The individual with chromosomal mosaicism may appear normal and function normally, since many body cells have normal chromosomes. Abnormal organs alone may have abnormal chromosomal patterns.

Genetic defects

Many diseases existing from the time of birth are caused by deleterious recessive genes rather than whole chromosomal errors. Single gene abnormalities tend to be less lethal than those of whole chromosomes. The recessive disease-producing genes and autosomal chromosomes must be inherited from both mother and father in order to be manifest. However, recessive gene abnormalities may produce disease if they appear only on the X sex chromosome in a male, because in this case there is no allelic dominant gene on the Y chromosome to compensate for, or override, the abnormality. A form of color blindness affecting 8 percent of white males is one example of a "sex-linked" defect caused by a genetic defect on those males' X chromosomes.[26] Hemophilia, a disorder of blood clotting, is another. It affects about 0.01 percent of males.[27] Such disease rarely occurs in females because they would have to receive the recessive, deleterious gene on the X chromosome derived from both their mother and father, a distinctly rare occurrence (see Figure 2–14).

Certain genetic defects have become quite well known, not so much because of their frequency, but because of publicity surrounding them: phenylketonuria (PKU), galactosemia, Gaucher's disease, Tay-Sachs disease, sickle-cell anemia, cystic fibrosis.

With PKU the recessive deleterious inheritance is manifest by lack of the enzyme phenylalanine hydroxylase, needed to convert phenylalanine, one of the essential amino acids found in most protein foods, into tyrosine. Without this conversion, phenylpyruvic acid and other substances are produced through alternate pathways. They build up to toxic levels in the central nervous system causing severe mental retardation, tremors, seizures, weak muscles, and a decrease in hair and skin

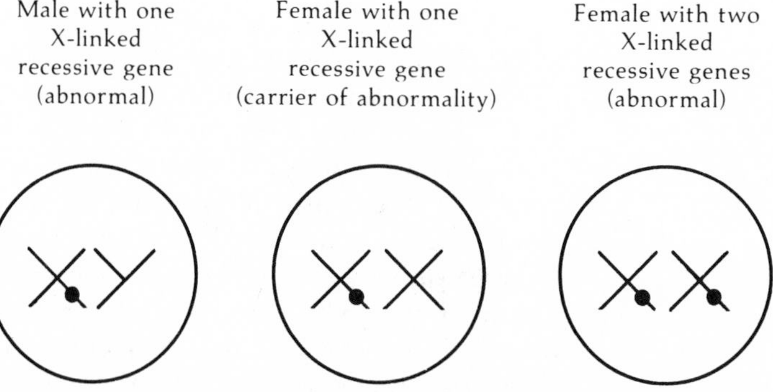

Figure 2–14. *Schematic representation of the sex chromosomes in a cell showing the effects of possession of a recessive X-linked gene on males and females.*

pigmentation.[28] A nationwide screening program is now in effect to test infants born in hospitals for PKU. A few drops of blood from the infant's heel can be used to determine the presence or absence of the disease. If it is present, treatment can be instituted before damage occurs. Special diets containing only a minimal amount of phenylalanine are given to PKU children to prevent build-up of the toxic substances.

Galactosemia is a rare hereditary disorder resulting from the inability to metabolize galactose, a major constituent of the milk sugar lactose. It most commonly results from a genetically determined inability to produce an enzyme involved in converting galactose to glucose. The clinical picture includes failure to thrive, liver disease, cataracts, mental retardation, and bouts of severe hypoglycemia (insufficient sugar in the bloodstream). A screening test is available for early diagnosis. After diagnosis, all sources of galactose must be eliminated from the diet.

In Gaucher's disease an enzyme deficiency results in the accumulation of a lipid found in membranes of all cells of the body. One form of the disease is manifest by severe neurologic disease in infancy. By age three months affected babies have feeding problems, enlarged liver and spleen, and progressive neurologic problems. They seldom survive past age two. In the other form of the disease, symptoms do not appear until adulthood.[29]

Tay-Sachs disease is caused by a deficiency of another enzyme which causes accumulation of certain lipids found in cells throughout the body, causing progressive degeneration of the central nervous system. Symptoms usually appear by about three to six months of age, and affected children seldom survive past age three. The disease generally occurs in Ashkenazic Jewish families. It can be detected in the recessive form by simple blood tests, a valuable aid in genetic counseling.

Sickle-cell anemia differs from the genetically inherited diseases described so far because no enzyme deficiency is involved. Rather, people with the disease have structurally abnormal hemoglobin-S, which tends to crystallize and precipitate in red blood cells that become slightly deoxygenated. This produces the peculiar, elongated sickle-shaped red corpuscles.[30] These sickled red blood cells can clump together and impede flow of blood to any part of the body. They can obstruct vessels causing crises such as loss of blood supply to the bowel, stroke, and death of kidney tissue. There is usually severe anemia, frequent respiratory infections, gallstones, and heart disease. Inheritance of only one recessive gene for sickle-cell disease may cause some sickling to occur during oxygen depletion at high altitudes or after hard exercise. Despite these consequences, the sickle-cell hemoglobin seems to provide some resistance to malaria. This advantage is important to black people (the population most commonly affected by the disease) living in malaria-infested regions of the world. It is not advantageous to blacks in the United States. Sickle-cell tests are available to identify carriers and for diagnosis of disease in children over six months of age.

Cystic fibrosis is an inherited disease of obscure etiology that affects the pancreas, respiratory system, and sweat glands.[31] It usually is manifested in infancy by frequent or chronic respiratory infections, susceptibility to heat prostration, malabsorption from the bowel, and a general failure to thrive. Pancreatic enzymes, needed for digesting fats, proteins, and starches, are insufficient or absent. Thick mucous secretions and frequent mucous plugs develop in the airways and result in severe, recurrent and often fatal respiratory infections. Because of the unusually high content of sodium in the sweat of these patients, they must consume extra salt to compensate for losses in warm weather.

Environmental hazards

The influences of heredity and environment *cannot* be separated. From conception, when the genes on the chromosomes contributed by the ovum and the sperm first provide instructions for the development of structures and functions of the new organism, the environment provided by the mother begins to exert an influence. The genetic make-up of the organism provides a potential for functioning for any given trait in that individual. This potential may or may not then be utilized, depending on certain environmental influences. One tends to think of environment as something experienced after birth; however, there are many areas in which environment before birth can effect changes in the growing, developing embryo-fetus. We will now discuss four of these prenatal influences.

Radiation. All people are exposed to certain amounts of radiation from the sun, diagnostic x-rays, and some types of lamps. The effects of radiation are cumulative over long periods of time. Overexposure to some forms of radiation can cause mutations (changes of form) in genes. It can also cause malformations in the developing embryo and fetus. This was made evident after the 1945 bombings of Hiroshima and Nagasaki, Japan. Surviving pregnant women who were within the fallout range experienced abortions (28 percent), neonatal death of their infants (25 percent), and deformed offspring (25 percent).[32] It is not known how much exposure to radiation can safely be allowed during pregnancy. Dental x-rays are usually considered safe, although many doctors prefer pregnant women to avoid all exposure to radiation. The need for pelvic x-rays to diagnose obstetrical problems sometimes outweighs the possible radiation risks to the unborn child.

Infections. Many infections that the mother contracts during her pregnancy can be dangerous to the embryo-fetus. This is especially true during the first trimester (first three months) of pregnancy, when most organ systems are in their "critical period" of development.

Rubella, or German measles, is caused by a virus that is small enough to diffuse through the villi of the placenta (called the placental barrier). If a mother has had rubella or an immunization against it prior to her pregnancy, her body will contain antibodies that will destroy the virus if she comes in contact with it. However, if she is unprotected and gets the disease, the virus is liable to infect the embryo as well. Common effects of rubella in the first trimester on the infant are heart defects, deafness, cataracts, mental retardation, and growth retardation. Maternal rubella is not as dangerous if it occurs later in pregnancy. By then the organ systems are past their most susceptible "critical period" of development. Also, the immune system of the fetus may be mature enough to produce some of its own antibodies against the virus.[33]

Viruses causing influenza are also small enough to cross the placental barrier and disrupt development during the critical embryonic period. However, the incidence of defects in infants whose mothers had influenza in the first trimester is quite a bit lower than that resulting from rubella infection. Many newborn defects may be the result of minor viral infections of the mother in her first three months of pregnancy—infections so trifling that she hardly noticed them or did not report them.

The spirochete causing syphilis is still another microorganism able to pass through the placental barrier. It can cause death, deafness, mental retardation, hydrocephalus (large brain due to an abnormally large amount of cerebrospinal fluid), microcephalus (small, underdeveloped brain), and osteitis (inflammation of bones) in the embryo or fetus.

Wilson estimates that from 2 to 3 percent of the developmental defects in humans at birth are due to prenatal maternal infections.[34] Bacterial infections that cause illness in the mother but do not traverse the placenta may still be somewhat hazardous to the embryo (or fetus) since the mother who has lost her appetite, become dehydrated, and lost sleep may have difficulty providing optimal amounts of nutrients and oxygen across the placenta.

Maternal metabolic imbalance. Women with certain preexisting health problems who become pregnant may have difficulty providing good uterine environments. Diabetes, thyroid disease, and other metabolic and hormonal disorders, heart defects, high blood pressure, alcoholism, smoking, drug use, and malnutrition are examples of maternal health problems that often adversely affect the developing organism.

Diabetic mothers, even when controlled before pregnancy, may have difficulty readjusting to their increased needs for both nutrients and insulin during pregnancy. Diabetic mothers have a 6 to 10 percent higher incidence of infant mortality and infants born with malformations.[35] At birth their babies are frequently large. Soon after birth they may suffer from hypoglycemia (insufficient sugar in the blood stream). They have a higher than normal incidence of the respiratory distress syndrome of newborns.

Women with heart defects may have difficulty in tolerating the large blood volume changes associated with pregnancy. Normally blood volume increases by 40 percent, and cardiac output increases by 30 percent during pregnancy.[36] If defective hearts cannot adequately handle the extra work load, infants are apt to show growth deficiencies and be born prematurely. Women with high blood pressure are also more apt to deliver prematurely, possibly due to impaired circulation to the uterus and placenta.

Alcoholism and malnutrition are similar in that pregnant mothers suffering from both conditions cannot supply adequate nutrients to their babies prenatally. Consequently, they are prone to miscarriages, stillbirths, higher neonatal mortality, and/or giving birth to babies with growth deficiencies.[37] The malnourished state that is associated with the problems is a chronic rather than an acute one, however. Women who have been generally well fed prior to their pregnancies and then suddenly eat poorly (as may happen with acute nausea and vomiting accompanying morning sickness) usually have adequate reserves to tide the developing embryo over until they can return to better eating habits. This was well illustrated by a follow-up study made of teenagers in the Netherlands whose well-nourished mothers had experienced a wartime famine during their pregnancies. The children had below normal birth weights but were otherwise normal throughout childhood and adolescence. The researchers suspected that the mothers who were not well nourished prior to their pregnancies were not able to draw on reserves and therefore had miscarriages, stillbirths, or lost their babies in infancy.[38] The National Research Council's Committee on Maternal Nutrition urges obstetricians to allow weight gains in pregnancy close to twenty-five pounds.[39] The most essential nutrients for pregnant women are good quality proteins and essential minerals (e.g., calcium, sodium). Recent evidence shows that if a fetus does not get adequate nourishment, especially in the form of proteins, the rate of brain cell division can slow so that a newborn may have significantly fewer brain cells than an adequately nourished fetus.[40] Infants born to poorly nourished mothers not only have fewer brain cells but are smaller in general and are less likely to survive through the critical first twenty-eight days of life.

Preeclampsia (also called toxemia of pregnancy) is a condition in which a woman's blood pressure increases, her body accumulates salt and water, and she develops swelling (edema). Protein can be found in her urine. Eclampsia is a more severe form of the disease in which convulsions may develop. These, in addition to endangering the life of the mother, may result in fetal oxygen deprivation. The causes or origin of preeclampsia and eclampsia are still unknown. They may result from endocrine disturbances or from some impairment to the uterine blood supply. Once they were felt to result from excessive weight gain and/or excessive salt intake, but these are no longer considered causative factors. The problem is generally relieved by the delivery of the baby and the placenta.

Drugs. Some drugs are able to pass from mother to embryo (or fetus) through the placental barrier. Wilson estimates that from 2 to 3 percent of all human birth defects are caused by such drugs.[41] Among the better known offenders are tetracyclines, iodides, progesterone, stilbesterol, thalidomide, and chemically related tranquilizers, narcotics, and nicotine.

Tetracyclines, if taken during the critical period for tooth development (six to ten weeks), are known to stain the enamel irreparably and may cause defective formation. There is evidence that in animals they also inhibit the growth of long bones.

Iodides cause the thyroid gland to enlarge, which in turn can lead to respiratory difficulties postnatally. Many cough suppressants and expectorants that are sold over the counter without prescriptions contain iodides that, while safe normally, can be potentially dangerous during pregnancy.

Synthetic forms of progesterone, a hormone sometimes given to women in their first trimesters to avert threatened abortions, can, in large amounts, cause masculinization of the female genitalia.

A synthetic estrogen diethylstilbestrol (DES), which was formerly given to women to protect them during threatened miscarriages, produces changes in the vagina of female fetuses. Diethylstilbestrol has been linked to a form of vaginal cancer in daughters of women who were given DES during their pregnancy with that daughter.

Thalidomide and its chemically related tranquilizers are banned for use as sedatives in the United States. In the early 1960s they were discovered in Europe to be dangerous if used during pregnancy. Women who used thalidomide in their first trimester gave birth to infants with phocomelia (stunted limbs) and malformations of the heart, digestive, and circulatory systems.[42]

Narcotics (heroin, morphine) addiction or cocaine addiction in pregnant women can be transmitted to the fetus and leads to withdrawal symptoms in the neonate. Such babies suffer from tremendous irritability, seizures, tremors, diarrhea, and vomiting.[43] They usually must be treated with tranquilizers and receive intensive medical and nursing care in order to survive.

Women who smoke a pack of cigarettes or more per day run a greater risk than do nonsmokers of delivering prematurely, having low birth weight babies, or experiencing the death of their infants pre- or postnatally. Scientists are not sure how heavy smoking has adverse effects on the fetus. Smoking may decrease the maternal blood supply to the placenta because the nicotine in smoke causes the arteries to undergo spasms of constriction. The carbon monoxide that is produced by smoking may also diminish the oxygen-carrying capacity of the mother's blood.

Immunological factors. Our immune systems are very sensitive to the presence of foreign substances (e.g., foreign proteins, microorganisms, blood cells with proteins on their surface that are different from those on our blood cells) that enter our bodies. We produce antibodies to attack and help eliminate these foreign substances (called antigens). We continue to manufacture specific antibodies to guarantee us some degree of "immunity" against specific antigens for varying periods of time after our initial exposure to them. There are some fetal products (e.g., red blood cells) that can act as antigens if they cross the placenta to the mother. These "antigens" then stimulate the mother's immune system to produce antibodies that can pass the maternal placental barrier and attack the fetal "antigens." Antibodies directed against fetal cells may produce serious diseases in the fetus or neonate. An outstanding example of this is Rh sensitization.

The Rh factor is a substance found on the surface of red blood cells of approximately 85 percent of the Caucasian population and nearly 100 percent of the black and Oriental population. We say persons have Rh-positive blood if they have this substance on their cells, and Rh-negative blood if they lack it.

If a mother with Rh-negative blood has a child with Rh-positive blood, there is a possibility that some of the red blood cells of the fetus containing the Rh-positive factor may enter the mother's bloodstream at the time of labor or delivery. If so, the mother will build up antibodies against the Rh factor. If second or subsequent children inherit Rh-positive blood, there is a chance that the antibodies in the mother's bloodstream will pass through the placenta and destroy some of the fetus's red blood cells. If this happens the baby may be born with erythroblastosis fetalis (severe jaundice and anemia and on-going destruction of red blood cells) and must have exchange transfusions of fresh Rh-negative blood to survive.

Not all Rh-negative mothers married to Rh-positive men will have problems with Rh incompatibility in their children. If the father is heterozygous for the Rh trait and carries one gene for Rh-negative blood, there is a 50-50 chance that offspring will inherit negative blood. However, if the father is homozygous for the Rh-positive blood trait, all the children will have Rh-positive blood. Rh-positive blood from the fetus does not always enter the mother's bloodstream at the time of delivery, so an Rh-negative mother may bear several normal Rh-positive children without ever developing Rh antibodies. Now, thanks to a new anti-Rh immunoglobulin (Rho GAM), an Rh-negative mother can be protected from developing antibodies with a simple intramuscular injection given within seventy-two hours after delivery or miscarriage. Rho GAM prevents the formation of Rh antibodies by the mother by combining with and destroying any fetal red blood cells that enter the mother's circulation. It must be administered following every delivery or miscarriage to ensure continued protection.

Another example of an immunological problem that may occur prenatally is ABO incompatibility.

Blood cells can be divided into various types according to differences in proteins on their membranes. The most commonly known blood types are A, B, AB, and O; and Rh+ and Rh−. (There are many others: Kidd, Kell, Duffy, Hr, M, N, P, Lewis, etc.) People who have cells with A-type antigens on their membranes spontaneously produce anti-B antibodies, and people with B-type antigens produce anti-A antibodies. Thus crossing blood types A and B can lead to an incompatibility that is manifest by either the clumping or breaking down of cells. If a pregnant woman has a fetus with a different ABO blood type, it is possible for fetal blood entering her bloodstream at the time of labor and delivery to stimulate her immune system to develop antibodies against the incompatible type. Future offspring may be affected by these antibodies. However, A or B isoimmune disease of the newborn is usually milder than Rh incompatibility disease and only rarely requires exchange transfusion.[44]

Birth

Approximately 266 days (thirty-eight weeks, nine months) after conception, the new human being is ready to emerge into the outside world. Most obstetricians give mothers-to-be an expected due date, or EDC (expected day of confinement), figured from the last menstrual period. Only a very small fraction of women actually deliver on their due dates. Most deliver within ten to fifteen days before or after the estimated date.[45]

The uterine contractions that expel the fetus and the placenta are known as labor. Labor differs for every woman and with every succeeding child so that statements about what it is like are, at best, generalizations.

The average length of labor for a first born is thirteen hours—for a subsequent child, eight hours. Few women experience the exact mean. Neither labors lasting twenty-four to thirty-six hours nor precipitous deliveries that occur on the way to the hospital are uncommon.

Mild contractions called Braxton-Hicks contractions occur throughout pregnancy, preparing the uterus for its eventual task of expelling the fetus and placenta. They are painless early in pregnancy but may be felt as "false labor" toward term. These contractions may begin thinning out and enlarging the uterine floor prior to actual labor. False labor may also accompany the dropping of the baby's head into the brim of the pelvis. This is variously known as "lightening," "settling," or "dropping." With first babies it may occur as much as two weeks before labor. "Lightening" usually makes a pregnant woman feel more comfortable and allows a greater range of motion. Since the pressure on her diaphragm is relieved, she can breathe more easily.

As the baby's head presses down on the uterine floor, it begins to efface (thin out) and dilate (enlarge) the opening to the uterus (the cervix). As this happens, a mucous plug, which has been keeping the cervix closed during pregnancy, is expelled. It is frequently streaked with blood and is referred to as the "bloody show." Real labor usually begins after the mucous plug is discharged and when the cervix begins effacing and dilating more rapidly.

Stages of labor

Labor is divided into three stages. In the first stage the cervix effaces and dilates until it is wide enough (usually around four inches, or ten centimeters or five fingers) to allow the baby's head to pass into the vagina. In the second stage the baby emerges from the vagina. In the third stage the placenta (or afterbirth) is expelled.

Presentations

In about 96 percent of pelvic deliveries the top of the skull (vertex) comes out first.[46] If the spine of the fetus is adjacent to the abdomen of the mother, the head descends in an anterior lie (see Figure 2–15). If the spine of the fetus is to the left or right side, the head descends in a transverse lie. With anterior or transverse lies the back part of the skull emerges first, which is the easiest way for it to pass the pubic arch bones. If the spine of the fetus is lined up against the spine of the mother, the head descends in a

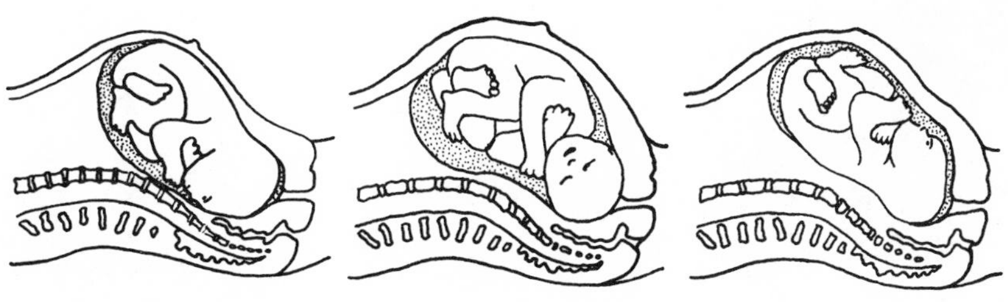

Anterior Transverse Posterior

Figure 2–15. *Possible positions of the fetus in the uterus.*

posterior lie. The posterior position often causes the mother to experience more back pain during labor.

The bones of the fetal skull are not yet completely formed. The membrane covered spaces between the bones, known as fontanels and sutures, allow the bones to overlap each other slightly, making it possible for the head of the fetus to slip past the tightest portion of the maternal pubic arch. This overlap process is known as "molding."

The 4 percent of fetuses who do not emerge with the top of their skulls first may present with their brow, their face, in a transverse or shoulder position, or in a breech (buttocks or feet first) position (see Figure 2–16).

Brow and face presentations are difficult because the diameter of each of these presenting parts is too large to slip through the pelvic arch. If the fetus is very small or the bone structure of the mother is very large, or if the obstetrician can turn the head before it becomes engaged and molded, pelvic delivery may be possible. Frequently, the baby is delivered surgically through an incision made through the abdomen and uterus of the mother (cesarean section).

A fetus cannot be delivered in a transverse lie. When the abnormal position is recognized before or in early labor, the fetus can be turned. If the position cannot be changed, delivery must be by cesarean section.

Breech presentations occur in about 3 percent of all deliveries.[47] There are variations of breech where buttocks alone, buttocks and both feet, single foot, or knee may descend first. Breech babies may be delivered through cesarean section.

As the fetus is forced down through the cervix by uterine labor contractions, the membranes of the amniotic sac rupture and the amniotic fluid gushes out. This is commonly referred to as "the breaking of the bag of water." It occurs during labor for most women but occasionally may precede it.

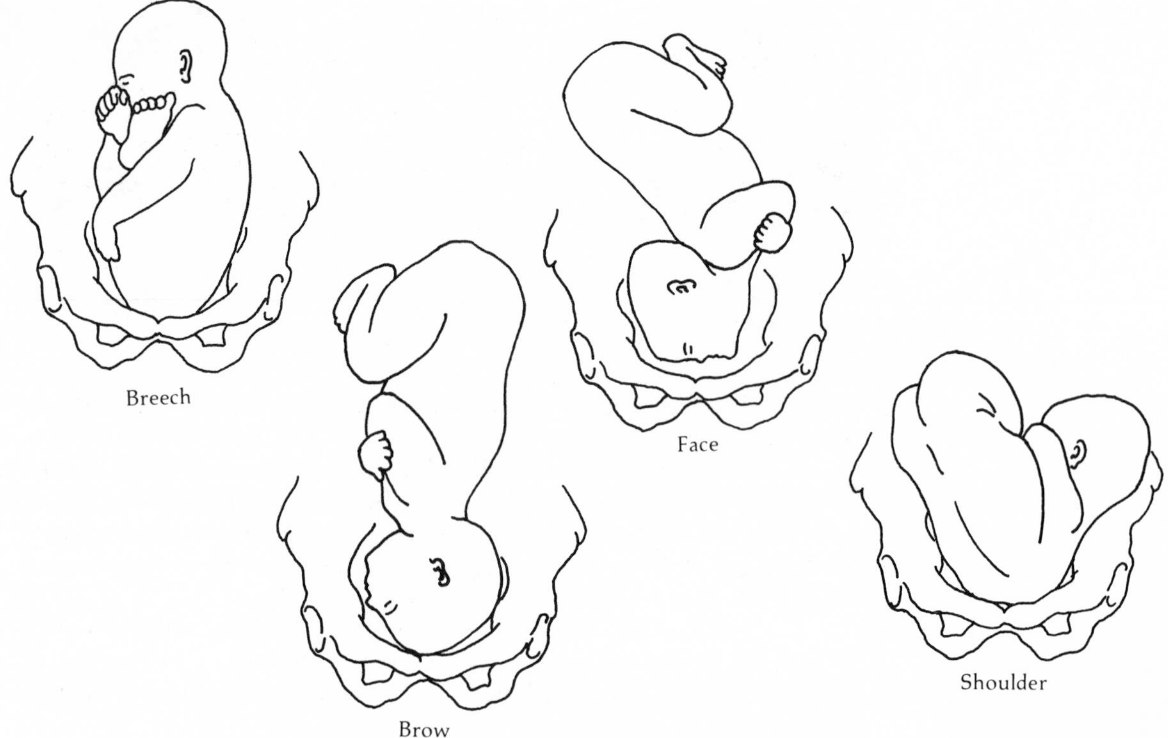

Figure 2–16. *Atypical postures of the fetus.*

Aides to delivery of the fetus

The United States uses the most analgesics and anesthesia for labor and delivery of any of the Western industrialized nations.[48] Analgesics such as tranquilizers, narcotics, and barbiturates help the laboring mother relax and lose her sensitivity to the pain of the contractions. Anesthesia takes away all the sensations either by putting the mother to sleep (general anesthesia) or by deadening the sensations in a portion of her body (regional anesthesia).

All of the anesthetic agents and most of the analgesics have a serious hazard in common. They can be transmitted across the placental barrier to the fetus. This can contribute to a drowsy infant at birth who may have difficulty initiating his or her own respiration.[49] Failure to obtain adequate oxygen soon after birth can lead to brain damage. The baby may also have trouble feeding and lose more weight than normal in the first two to three days after delivery.[50] No form of obstetric anesthesia is 100 percent safe and satisfactory. The obstetrician and anesthesiologist must weigh the dangers of drugs against the need for promoting relaxation or relieving pain for women who do not want to experience it or who have a history of difficulty during labor and delivery.

The use of analgesics and sedatives during labor may also necessitate the use of obstetrical forceps. These are double-bladed tongs that fit over the head of a fetus and grasp it without compressing it. They are used if a mother loses her ability to push the fetus out during the second stage of labor due to the effects of medication or exhaustion. Forceps frequently leave marks showing where they were placed on the infant's head. Such marks disappear in a few days.

Natural childbirth is the delivery of an infant without the use of anesthetics or instrumentation. "Prepared childbirth," often called natural childbirth, refers to the fact that the mother (and usually a partner, such as the father) has been educated beforehand about the physiology of pregnancy, what to expect during labor and delivery, and how to assist in the birth of the fetus. In the United States such preparation usually comes from a series of evening meetings conducted in the Lamaze method or the Grantly Dick Read method. Prepared childbirth encourages parents to experience birth together. It discourages the mother from accepting drugs or

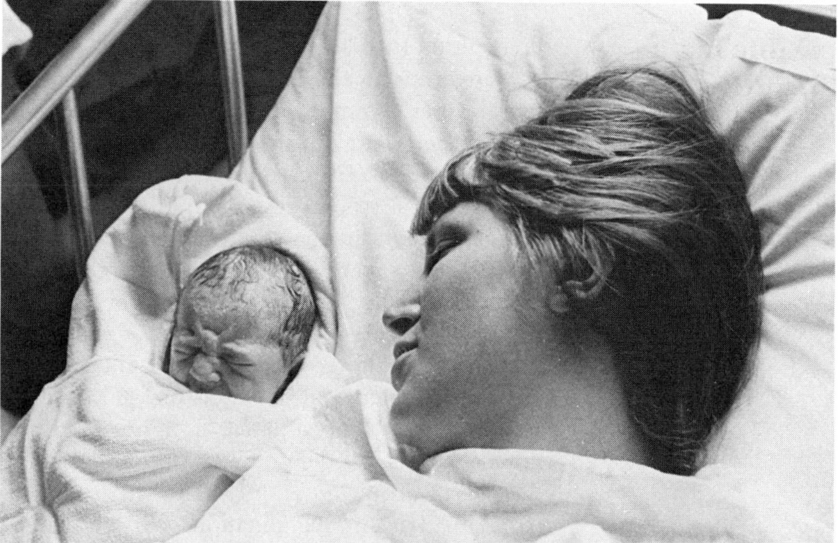

Figure 2–17. *Prepared childbirth allows a mother to experience the incredible moment of her child's birth while fully awake. It minimizes the danger that the infant will be drowsy or have difficulty breathing due to the effects of anesthetics. Anesthesia, however, when carefully administered, is also safe for women who feel the need for it.*
Leslie Davis

tranquilizers that will cause her to sleep through or be hazy during childbirth. Exercises teach her to breathe in a way that minimizes the pain of labor contractions, strengthen her pelvic muscles to aid in childbirth, and prepare her psychologically to face childbirth without fear. This method is becoming increasingly popular. Tanzer and Block estimate that over 50,000 babies are now born to prepared parents every year.[51]

The LeBoyer method of delivery was developed to reduce fetal birth trauma. The delivery room is kept dark and quiet. The newborn is immediately immersed in warm water to simulate amniotic fluid. Handling is kept to a minimum.

Many women have an episiotomy whether or not they use obstetrical medications. This is a straight cut made from the vagina back toward the anus (either straight back or slightly to one side) to enlarge the vaginal opening just before the head delivers. In some hospitals it is done routinely while in others it is performed only if it seems likely that the perineal tissues will tear without an episiotomy. A straight cut is easier to sew up and heals better than a ragged-edged tear. An episiotomy also gives the baby more room to get out.

Possible birth difficulties

Precipitous (sudden or abrupt) deliveries as well as prolonged labors can be dangerous to the fetus. So can both premature and postmature deliveries. Other common problems affecting labor and delivery are prolapsed cord, placenta previa, abruptio placentae, and low birth weight.

Precipitous deliveries are dangerous to the fetus because the skull bones are compressed rapidly rather than molding gradually. This can cause tears in the membranous coverings of the brain or even occasionally the severing of veins in these membranes.[52] Another danger of precipitous labor is that the fetus may be born unattended. Such labors last less than three hours and occur in about 15 percent of all births.[53]

Prolonged labor may result from weak uterine contractions, a large fetus, abnormal positions of fetal head (buttocks or shoulder), from an abnormally shaped pelvic arch, from multiple fetuses, or even for emotional reasons. With prolongation of labor (over 24 hours) the fetus runs the risk of acquiring an infection, suffocating, or sustaining brain damage from insufficient oxygenation. Obstetricians may provide rest for the mother with weak contractions in order to improve them, or may stimulate the contractions with drugs. Obstetricians perform cesarean sections in about 10 percent of such cases.[54]

Premature infants (born before thirty-seven weeks) are now differentiated from low birth weight infants (less than five and a half pounds). A premature infant usually has limited fat deposits, poor temperature control, poor muscle control, poor resistance to infection, poor kidney function (which may lead to electrolyte imbalance), and poor liver function (which may lead to jaundice). Fragile blood vessels may lead to bleeding and bruising. Difficulties are also encountered with breathing, sucking, and swallowing. All of these problems are associated with insufficient time for prenatal growth and development in the uterus. Factors associated with prematurity may be the youthfulness of the mother, infections, poor nutrition, heavy smoking, emotional traumas, and multiple birth.[55] About 15 percent of premature infants get hyaline membrane disease of the lung, which is also called the respiratory distress syndrome of the newborn.[56] Even when recognized early and treated carefully, the infant's survival chances are endangered.

Low birth weight infants may have many of the same problems as premature infants if their intrauterine growth and development was hampered by maternal malnutrition, smoking, by fetal sharing of nutrients with other fetus(es) or by placental malfunctioning. Infants born with low birth weights may also have a genetic inheritance for small size. Whatever the reason for their size, these babies need extra warmth, nutrition, and protection from infections.

A more serious threat to the life of a fetus is prolapsed umbilical cord. The pressure of the descending head of the fetus on a cord that has partially slipped through the cervix ahead of the fetus cuts off the oxygen supply. Unless the doctor can intervene to relieve the pressure on the cord, the fetus will suffocate. If the cervix is fully dilated, the doctor will speed the delivery with forceps. If it is not, the doctor will have to remove the baby by cesarean section.

With placenta previa and abruptio placentae, the placenta separates from the uterus before labor. The fetus can suffocate if enough placenta separates to interfere with oxygen exchange via the uterus. In placenta previa the placenta is implanted abnormally low in the uterus. The dilation and effacement of the uterus that occur with approaching labor cause it to separate. In abruptio placentae the placenta is implanted normally but separates too soon, sometimes because of toxemia or high blood pressure in the mother, or for unknown reasons. In both placenta previa and abruptio placentae, the chances of saving the life of the fetus depend on the amount and speed of the separation and the prompt diagnosis and intervention by trained medical personnel.

Summary

The uterus of the mother is the primary prenatal ecological environment. As protected as the developing infant seems floating in amniotic fluid within an amniotic sac, within a placenta, within a uterus, he or she is dependent on and influenced by other things external to this setting. The greater world of the mother's environment—nutrition, health, rest, shelter, stress—affect the embryo-fetus. The progress of development prenatally also depends on the interactions of the genetic materials inherited from each parent. By the end of nine months, the fetus is ready to emerge into the external world as a truly unique individual.

The ovum and sperm divide by meiosis as they mature and become haploid cells, with only half (twenty-three) the normal (forty-six) cell complement of chromosomes. Conception of a new human being occurs with the union of one ovum with one sperm. This union produces one new cell with forty-six chromosomes, twenty-three inherited from each parent. This new cell proceeds to divide again and again, by mitosis, reproducing other cells, each with forty-six chromosomes, and each carrying the same genetic materials inherited from the parents. It grows and develops in the uterus for nine months. The cells differentiate. Some become the placenta, others become the baby-to-be (skin, muscles, bones, heart, lungs, etc.). For the first three months, the developing organism is called an embryo. At the end of three months, he or she has a distinctly human appearance. For the remainder of the prenatal period, the baby-to-be is called a fetus.

While the norm is for fetuses to survive the nine prenatal months and emerge as healthy full-term infants, some imperfections do occur. Down's, Klinefelter's, and Turner's syndromes are examples of problems caused by chromosomal defects. Tay-Sachs disease, PKU, and sickle-cell anemia are examples of problems caused by genetic defects. The embryo-fetus also can be harmed by factors in the mother's environment such as excessive radiation, some viral infections, poor nutrition, and some drugs.

At the end of nine months the uterus expels the fetus. The contractions that push the baby out are called labor. Most babies are expelled head first. The average length of labor for a first child is thirteen hours and eight hours for subsequent children. If either the fetus or mother has problems that might interfere with a normal vaginal delivery, the baby may be delivered by surgery through the abdomen of the mother (cesarean section).

Considering the enormously complicated process of development from union of ovum and sperm to delivery of a full-term baby, it is amazing that normal infants are the rule, not the exception. Never again in the life span will growth and change be quite as rapid or quite as revolutionary.

Questions for review

1. Describe the process of maturation of ovum and sperm and the fertilization process.
2. If a mother is homozygous for brown eyes, and a father is heterozygous, what is the likelihood of their child having brown eyes? Discuss.
3. Many persons have diets that consist of high amounts of carbohydrates and low amounts of protein. Discuss what effects this kind of diet will have on a developing fetus.
4. The LeBoyer method of childbirth is one in which every effort is made to reduce the trauma of the birth for the infant. Describe some of the pros and cons of using the LeBoyer method.
5. The U.S. is the highest user of anesthesia and analgesics during childbirth. Why do you think this is so?
6. More women today are considering the option of having their children at home, with the assistance of a midwife. List the pros and cons of using this type of delivery.
7. Describe the concept of "critical period" of development.
8. Project over a couple of generations the effect of poor nutrition. Outline a possible program of intervention that might be culturally acceptable and economically feasible.

References

[1]E. S. Hartland, *Primitive Paternity* (Washington, D.C.: American Medical Society, 1909).

[2]J. Needham, *A History of Embryology*, 2nd ed. (Cambridge: Cambridge University Press, 1959).

[3]K. Moore, *The Developing Human: Clinically Oriented Embryology* (Philadelphia: W. B. Saunders Co., 1973).

[4]J. Langman, *Medical Embryology*, 3rd ed. (Baltimore: The Williams & Wilkins Co., 1975).

[5]L. Shettles, "Fertilization and Early Development from the Inner Cell Mass," *Scientific Foundations of Obstetrics and Gynecology*, E. Philipp, J. Barnes, and M. Newton, eds. (London: Wm. Heinemann, Ltd., 1970).

[6]J. Hancock, "The Sperm Cell," *Science Journal* (London, 1970), 6 (31).

[7]K. Moore, *The Developing Human.*

[8]J. Langman, *Medical Embryology.*

[9]C. Austin, "The Egg and Fertilization," *Science Journal* (London, 1970), 6 (37).

[10]D. Jensen, *The Principles of Physiology* (New York: Appleton-Century-Crofts, 1976).

[11]L. Shettles, "Use of the Y Chromosome in Prenatal Sex Determination," *Nature* (London, 1971), 230.

[12]H. Papazian, *Modern Genetics* (New York: W. W. Norton Co., 1967).

[13]P. Swerdloff, *Men and Women* (New York: Time-Life Books, 1975).

[14]K. Moore, *The Developing Human.*

[15]C. McLennan, *Synopsis of Obstetrics,* 8th ed. (St. Louis: The C. V. Mosby Co., 1970).

[16]D. Smith and D. DerYven, "Prenatal Life and the Pregnant Woman," *The Biologic Ages of Man,* D. Smith and E. Bierman, eds. (Philadelphia: W. B. Saunders Co., 1973).

[17]J. Lucey, "Conditions and Diseases of the Newborn," *Principles and Management of Human Reproduction,* D. Reid, K. Ryan, and K. Benirschke, eds. (Philadelphia: W. B. Saunders Co., 1972).

[18]M. Moore, *The Newborn and the Nurse* (Philadelphia: W. B. Saunders Co., 1972).

[19]R. Adams and G. R. DeLong, "Developmental and Other Congenital Abnormalities of the Nervous System," *Harrison's Principles of Internal Medicine,* 7th ed. M. Wintrobe, G. Thorn, R. Adams, E. Braunwald, K. Isselbacher, and R. Petersdorf, eds. (New York: McGraw-Hill, 1974).

[20]Ibid.

[21]J. Wilson, *Environment and Birth Defects* (New York: Academic Press, 1973).

[22]K. Moore, *The Developing Human.*

[23]M. Marinello, R. Berkson, J. Edwards, and R. Bannerman, "A Study of the XYY Syndrome in Tall Men and Juvenile Delinquents," *Journal of the American Medical Association* (1969), 208.

[24]R. Johnston and P. Magrab, *Developmental Disorders: Assessment, Treatment, Education* (Baltimore: University Park Press, 1976).

[25]J. Langman, *Medical Embryology.*

[26]V. McKusick, "Genetics and Human Disease," *Harrison's Principles of Internal Medicine,* 7th ed. M. Wintrobe, G. Thorn, R. Adams, E. Braunwald, K. Isselbacher, R. Petersdorf, eds. (New York: McGraw-Hill, 1974).

[27]O. Ratnoff, "Hereditary Disorders of Hemostasis," *The Metabolic Basis of Inherited Disease,* 3rd ed. J. Stanbury, J. Wyngaarden, D. Fredrickson, eds. (New York: McGraw-Hill, 1972).

[28]W. Knox, "Phenylketonuria," *The Metabolic Basis of Inherited Disease*, 3rd ed. J. Stanbury, J. Wyngaarden, D. Fredrickson, eds. (New York: McGraw-Hill, 1972).

[29]D. Boggs and M. Wintrobe, "Diseases of the Spleen and Reticuloendothelial System," *Harrison's Principles of Internal Medicine*, 7th ed. M. Wintrobe, et al., eds. (New York: McGraw-Hill, 1974).

[30]H. Lehmann, R. Huntsman, and J. Ager, "the Hemoglobinopathies and Thalassemia," *The Metabolic Basis of Inherited Disease*, 3rd ed. J. Stanbury, J. Wyngaarden, D. Fredrickson, eds. (New York: McGraw-Hill, 1972).

[31]P. Snodgrass, "Diseases of the Pancreas," *Harrison's Principles of Internal Medicine*, 7th ed. M. Wintrobe, et al., eds. (New York: McGraw-Hill, 1974).

[32]J. Langman, *Medical Embryology.*

[33]T. Veskari, "Rubella Antibodies in Infants Whose Mothers Had Rubella During the Second and Third Trimesters of Pregnancy," *Scandanavian Journal of Infectious Diseases* (1971), 3.

[34]J. Wilson, *Environment and Birth Defects.*

[35]M. Moore, *The Newborn and the Nurse.*

[36]C. McLennan, *Synopsis of Obstetrics.*

[37]D. Coursin, "Maternal Nutrition and the Offsprings' Development," *Nutrition Today* (1973), 8.

[38]Z. Stein, M. Susser, and G. Saenger, "Nutrition and Mental Performance," *Science* (1972), 178.

[39]R. Shank, "A Chink in our Armour," *Nutrition Today* (1970), 5.

[40]J. Lloyd-Still, *Malnutrition and Intellectual Development* (Acton, Mass.: Publishing Science Group, 1976).

[41]J. Wilson, *Environment and Birth Defects.*

[42]H. Taussig, "The Thalidomide Syndrome," *Scientific American* (August 1962).

[43]D. Marlow, *Textbook of Pediatric Nursing*, 4th ed. (Philadelphia: W. B. Saunders Co., 1973).

[44]Ibid.

[45]K. Moore, *The Developing Human.*

[46]J. Willson, C. Beecham, and E. Carrington, *Obstetrics and Gynecology*, 5th ed. (St. Louis: C. V. Mosby Co., 1975).

[47]M. Moore, *The Newborn and the Nurse.*

[48]H. Chase, "Perinatal and Infant Mortality in the United States and Six Western European Countries," *American Journal of Public Health* (1967), 57.

[49]W. Bowes, Y. Brackbill, E. Conway, and A. Steinschneider, "The Effects of Obstetrical Medication on Fetus and Infant," *Monographs of the Society for Research in Child Development* (1970), 35 (4).

[50]T. Brazelton, "Effect of Prenatal Drugs on the Behavior of the Neonate," *American Journal of Psychiatry* (1970), 126.

[51]D. Tanzer and J. Block, *Why Natural Childbirth?* (New York: Doubleday and Co., 1972).

[52]M. Moore, *The Newborn and the Nurse.*

[53]C. McLennan, *Synopsis of Obstetrics.*

[54]J. Willson, C. Beecham, and E. Carrington, *Obstetrics and Gynecology.*

[55]R. Wennberg, D. Woodrum, and W. Hodson, "The Perinate," *The Biologic Ages of Man*, D. Smith and E. Bierman, eds. (Philadelphia: W. B. Saunders Co., 1973).

[56]Ibid.

Contents

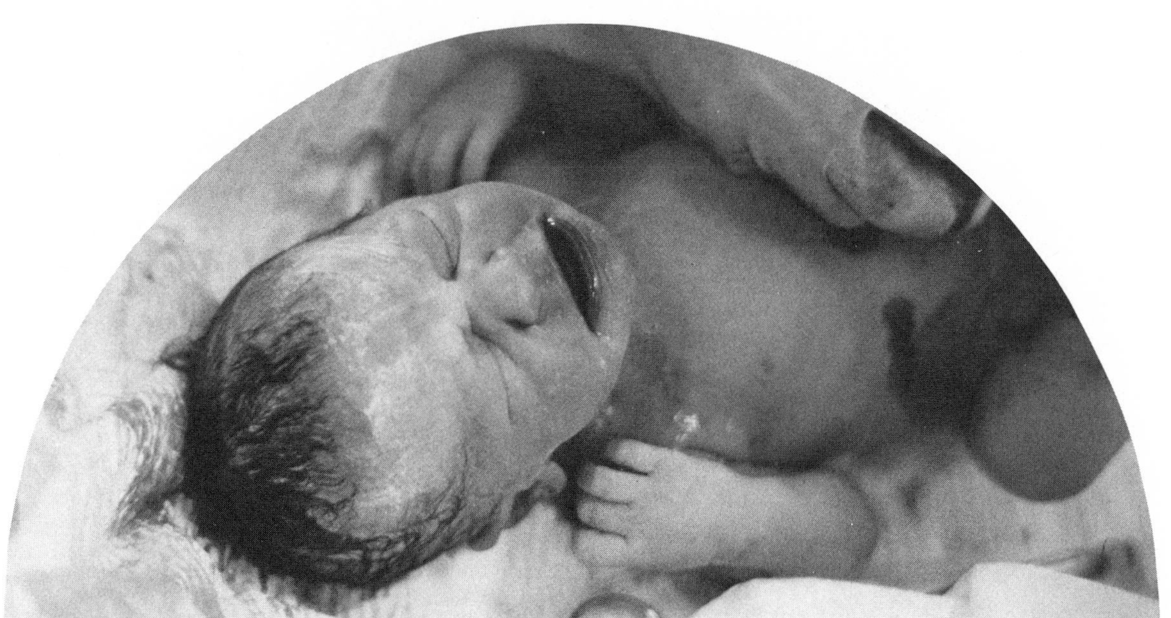

Leslie Davis

Infancy

Specialists in the study of infancy differ in their opinions as to when infancy ends and childhood begins. The word *infant* derives from the Latin *infans,* which literally means "without language." The consensus of many experts is that the advent of meaningful verbal communications marks the end of infancy. However, some babies begin using language before they reach their first birthdays, walk, or perform other childlike activities. Other babies walk, run, are toilet trained, may even reach their third birthdays before they talk. Consequently, this delineation of infancy is often invalid. Other experts use motor milestones such as toddling, toilet training, or self-feeding with a spoon to mark the end of infancy. Such boundaries also have too much variability across infants to make a good case for using them for all babies. Age is a third frequently used demarcation for the end of infancy. Again, controversy exists. Do infants become toddlers at eighteen months? at two years? at three years? This chapter will be eclectic. All three boundaries (language, motor tasks, age) will be encompassed to some extent. Infants will be defined as human beings who have not yet learned to communicate in short sentences, nor toddle around with ease, and who are below the age of two. This admits that some babies will be toddlers before age two, while others will still be babies up through their second birthdays. The term *neonate* is much easier to define. It will be used to describe newborn infants in their first month of life.

Physical development

Physical development in infancy exceeds that of any other time period of the postnatal life span. The neonate is far from a miniature replica of an adult. While the brain stem, heart, and lungs are mature enough to make extrauterine life possible, many other organ systems are still quite immature. They undergo rapid changes during infancy, resulting in a metamorphosis from a totally dependent, reflex-bound neonate to a toddling, talking, thinking child. We will examine the physiological status of the neonate first. This will provide a base from which to discuss the physical growth and development that takes place in the period of infancy.

Physical status of the neonate

At birth the infant must literally conform to a whole new world. The era of floating in a warm amniotic sac filled with fluid, and of having all the necessities of life supplied through the umbilical cord, ends. The transition from intrauterine to extrauterine existence requires many adaptations.

First, survival of newborns requires that the exchange of oxygen and carbon dioxide be immediately transferred from the placenta to

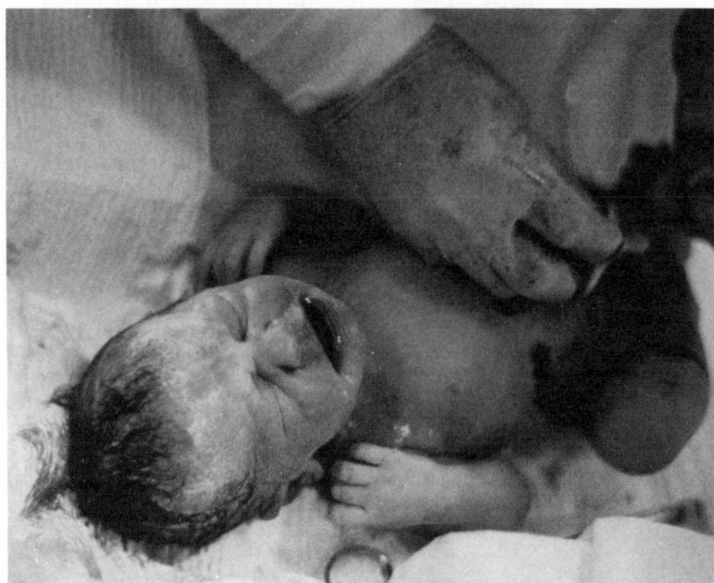

Figure 3–1. *The transition from intrauterine to extrauterine life is a giant step for a neonate. Breathing and blood circulation are transferred to the infant's lungs and heart as the tie to the mother through the placenta and umbilical cord is severed.*
Leslie Davis

the lungs. Respiratory reflexes become activated within seconds after birth. Due to pressure changes infants usually breathe spontaneously and cry, thereby allowing full expansion of their lungs with air. However, if the respiratory passages are still blocked with residual amniotic fluid and mucous from intrauterine life, breathing will be impaired. For this reason babies are held upside down after delivery, allowing such materials to drain out. Some hospitals also routinely suction the respiratory tracts of newborns to hasten free breathing. The belief that the doctor or nurse must slap the baby to start crying is false. Spanking, back slapping, or immersing the baby in cold water can be dangerous. Instead, the newborn's heels are flicked or tapped lightly. If infants do not begin to breathe within sixty seconds of birth, resuscitation measures may be instituted to prevent cell damage or death from lack of oxygen.

Survival of newborns also requires that circulation be transferred from the umbilical cord to the heart and lungs. The blood vessels that pass from the placenta to the baby through the cord must be obliterated. First the cord is "stripped." This means that the doctor or midwife pushes all the extra blood and nutrients from the cord toward the baby's body. Then the cord is clamped shut close to the infant's abdomen. Finally, the cord is cut between the clamp and the placenta (afterbirth). The cord stump remaining on the baby dries up and falls off in one or two weeks. The umbilical site heals to form the navel. Further adjustment of the circulatory system to extrauterine life requires that two openings, present prenatally, now close. The ductus arteriosus, which is a shunt between the aorta and the pulmonary artery, obliterates soon after birth. The foramen ovale, which is the connection between the right and left atrium of the heart, closes more gradually during infancy.[1]

At one minute and again at five minutes after hospital deliveries, babies are given a score for heart rate, respiratory effort, muscle tone, reflex irritability, and color, on a scale developed by Dr. Virginia Apgar (see Table 3–1). Very few infants are oxygenated enough to have pink extremities at one minute. Therefore, the highest score an infant usually first receives is nine. By five minutes healthy infants may receive a score from five to ten. Infants scoring lower than five need some form of prompt diagnosis and treatment.[2]

Survival of the neonate requires that warmth be provided in the period immediately following birth. The temperature control regulating mechanism of the nervous system is not yet sufficiently mature to allow the baby to shiver or sweat to raise or lower his or her own temperature. Also, the intrauterine environment is much warmer than room temperature. The neonate is accustomed to an environment closer to 32° centigrade (90° Fahrenheit).[3] In this so-called neutral thermal environment the baby finds it easier to breathe. Therefore, in hospitals infants are dried and

Table 3–1. *The Apgar scoring method.*

Sign	*0*	*1*	*2*
Heart rate	Absent	Below 100	Over 100
Respiratory effort	Absent	Minimal; weak cry	Good; strong cry
Muscle tone	Limp	Some flexion of extremities	Active motion; extremities well flexed
Reflex irritability (response to stimulation on sole of foot)	No response	Grimace	Cry
Color	Blue or pale	Body pink; extremities blue	Pink

Source: From Virginia Apgar, *Anesthesia and Analgesia,* 32:260, 1953.

placed in warm bassinettes or carriers as soon as respirations are established and the cord is clamped.

The immune system at birth is in an immature stage, requiring that neonates be protected against infections. In hospitals silver nitrate drops or a penicillin ophthalmic solution are instilled in the neonate's eyes immediately after birth as a prophylactic measure against gonorrheal infection. Various hospitals may separate mother and infant for the period of hospitalization (usually two to three days) or may allow modified or complete rooming-in. With separation the infant remains in a nursery and is only taken to the mother for short visiting hours (usually coinciding with feeding for both breast- and bottle-fed infants). With modified rooming-in the baby stays in a crib at the mother's bedside when she so desires and is taken back to the nursery when she wants to rest and/or at night. Complete rooming-in permits the infant to remain with the mother constantly. Each plan has its immunological advantages and disadvantages. When an infant resides in a nursery with other babies, there is a danger of cross-infant spread of infections. When an infant stays in the mother's room, there is a danger of infections being carried in by visitors or the mother. Actually, neonates have some immunity to a few organisms at birth, despite their own very limited ability to produce antibodies. They have received certain antibodies through the placenta prenatally. These will protect them for several months while their own immune system is developing. Neonates who are breast-fed receive additional antibodies, first through colostrum, a sweet, thin fluid that is produced by the breast for two to three days before milk comes in, and then later through the mother's milk. The merits of both breast- and bottle-feeding will be discussed in more detail in the social development section of this chapter.

The neonate is seldom very hungry immediately following delivery. Sleep is the infant's major activity throughout the first few weeks of life. First feedings are either sweetened water or colostrum. Milk is generally not tolerated well for a day or two. Then milk becomes the only necessary source of nutrients for the remainder of the neonatal period.

The central nervous system (brain and spinal cord) is one of the more immature organ systems in the neonate. Because it is so important to survival, the following description of its status in the newborn will be lengthy, including an outline of various structures and functions.

The brain has many divisions and subdivisions that work together to sustain life and to make total functioning possible. The three major divisions are the cerebrum, the cerebellum, and the brain stem. The cerebrum consists of two large lobes called cerebral hemispheres. Each is further subdivided into four smaller lobes. The brain stem consists of three structures: the pons, medulla, and midbrain (see Figure 3–2). At birth the pons, medulla, and midbrain are developed more fully than the rest of the brain.[4] They help regulate respiration, heart beat, blood pressure, coughing, sneezing, swallowing, vomiting, postural reflexes, and some motor coordination. Less well developed in the neonate is the cerebellum, through which motor activities, balance, and joint position sense are coordinated. It develops very rapidly in the early months of life. Also poorly developed and organized at birth are the cerebral hemispheres (cerebrum). They will eventually become so complex as to make humans the most intelligent of all species. They control learning, thought, and memory as well as sensory and motor functions. However, the growth of the cerebrum is slow, spanning infancy, childhood, and adolescence. We will discuss cerebral structure and functions further under sections of intellectual development throughout this text.

All portions of the brain are composed of nervous tissue that consists of three elements: nerve cells, nerve fibers, and the supporting structure of cells and fibers known as the neuroglia, or simply glia.[5] The glial cells (named from the Greek word for glue) account for approximately 90 percent of all brain tissue.[6] Nerve cells, called neurons, in spite of their relatively small number (10 percent of brain cells, or approximately ten billion cells) sustain life, control thought, consciousness, and memory, direct all our involuntary and voluntary muscle movements, and are in charge of all our senses. When we speak of brain cells, we usually

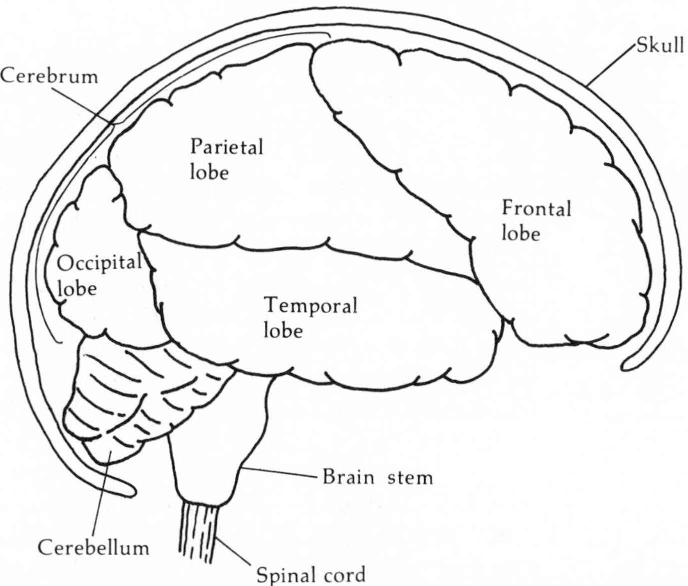

Figure 3–2. *The major structures of the human brain are the cerebrum, cerebellum, and the brain stem. Each cerebral hemisphere is described by a frontal lobe parietal lobe, occipital lobe, and temporal lobe.*

mean neurons, the workers, rather than glia, the supporters. At birth most, if not all, of the neurons that the brain will ever have are present. Glial cells may continue to be added during infancy. The rapid growth and development of the brains of infants consist mainly of additions of glial cells and increases in size of existing neurons rather than proliferation of new cells. The increase in size of neurons is due to increases in materials in the nuclei and cytoplasm of the cell bodies, increases in the length and branchings of the cell processes (an axon and a number of dendrites per cell), and the growth of a layer of fatty, insulating material called myelin around the nerve fibers. Neonates have a paucity of dendritic connections between their various nerve cells. They also have little or no myelin sheathing around the axons and dendrites that do exist (with the exception of some sensory, visual, and auditory fibers).[7]

At birth the brain weighs, on the average, 335 grams (about eleven ounces).[8] Its adult size will eventually be 1300 to 1400 grams (about three pounds).[9] The neurons and glia are massed together in a fashion different from their final organization and relative positions; they await rearrangements, growth and interconnections among fibers, and the development of myelin sheathing.

Damage to brain cells in infancy is just as profound as damage to them at any other point in the life span. Brain cells, unlike other types of human cells, cannot be replaced once they are destroyed.[10] For this reason, the infant brain must be protected very carefully. The bones of the skull ossify (change from cartilage to bone) prenatally and protect the neonate to some extent, although there are still spaces between the bones of the head at birth (fontanelles and sutures). These unossified areas allow the skull bones to overlap each other slightly during labor (molding) to make passage through the pubic bones of the mother easier. The fontanelles are commonly referred to as the "soft spots" in infants. The two largest ones, on the top back and top front of the skull, will not close until about four months and nine to eighteen months respectively.[11] Although they are covered with a tough membrane, care must be taken to prevent injury to the baby's brain and the underlying blood bessels through these fontanelles.

Another grave danger to the infant brain is lack of oxygen, a necessary constituent for cell life. Failure of the respiratory control center to maintain adequate breathing, whereby oxygen is taken into the body, is a leading cause of mortality and brain damage in infants. Likewise, any failure of the cardiovascular system to pump the oxygen-carrying blood to the brain can result in brain injury or death. The demands that the neonate's brain makes for oxygen are huge, taking up as much as 50 percent of the available supply.[12] The blood vessels that supply the brain with oxygen are still quite fragile in the neonate. In addition, the muscular support system for the head is weak. Consequently, the baby's head must be supported carefully and not be allowed to jerk rapidly from side to side. Such careless handling, which can cause blood vessels to break, can lead to brain damage and/or death.

While the skull bones, clavicle, spine, and long bones of the extremities partially ossify before birth, many other bones-to-be in the neonate are still completely cartilage. Ossification continues rapidly in infancy. The abundant supply of the bone-forming substances found in milk is a vital part of the diet. The rate and sequence of bone development has been established by means of x-ray visualization. There is an established correlation between the degree and location of ossification and the age of the infant. This relationship is the basis of the concept of bone age. Factors that interfere with bone maturation, such as severe disease, endocrine disorders producing disturbance in growth, and malnutrition, all influence the development of bones in a way that can be measured by comparing the infant's bone age to chronologic age. At birth, as well as throughout infancy, childhood, and adolescence, girls are more advanced in skeletal development than boys.[13]

The neonate's physical appearance is quite different from that of older infants and much different from adults. The head accounts for about one-fourth of the newborn's length (refer back to Figure 3–1). It may be misshapen for a day or two postnatally due to pressures on it during birth. The trunk is small with rounded shoulders, narrow hips, and protruding abdomen. Skin is generally thin and wrinkled and may be covered with downy hair. The hands remain clutched for several days, and feet and legs remain drawn up in their prenatal posture. Both male and female neonates have enlarged breasts and genitalia due to the prenatal influence of maternal hormones. Jaundice, a yellow coloration of the sclera (white area) of the eyes and of the skin, also appears in from 55 to 70 percent of neonates in the first three days of life.[14] It is caused by the presence of high levels of bilirubin (a bile pigment that is a breakdown product of fetal hemoglobin) in the bloodstream. It usually disappears by one week of age, at which time the infant's liver has developed the ability to metabolize the bilirubin, allowing its excretion. While vision in the neonate is developed enough to allow momentary following of a light or bright object with the eyes, eye muscles are weak. In fact, the eyes may occasionally drift asymmetrically, giving the newborn a cross-eyed appearance. Eye color is initially smokey-blue. The tear ducts do not yet function. The average neonate weighs about 3,000 to 4,000 grams (six and a half to eight and a half pounds). Length is about fifty to fifty-three centimeters (twenty to twenty-one inches).[15] The average here means the ranges where considerable numbers of infants fall. An infant may be above or below average and still be normal. While girls are more advanced in bone maturation at birth, boys tend to be slightly heavier and longer.[16]

Survival of neonates is enhanced by several reflex abilities that exist at birth. When the cheek is stroked or touched, infants will turn their heads toward the contact (rooting reflex) and will begin to make sucking

Figure 3–3. *Neonates reflexively turn their heads to one side or the other when placed in a prone (face downward) position. During the first month they develop the strength to lift their chins for a few seconds. By two months they will lift their chests as well and look around.*

Leslie Davis

movements (sucking reflex) followed by swallowing movements (swallowing reflex). When placed face down on a surface, they will draw their knees up under their abdomens and turn their heads to one side (head-turning reflex). Normal infants are thus protected from smothering unless someone puts a soft pillow or loose cloth under their heads that will block the respiratory tract and/or prevent the lifesaving head turn. When placed on their backs, infants turn their heads to one side and extend their arms and legs on the corresponding sides (tonic neck reflex). Neonates cough, sneeze, and yawn reflexively and frequently. These actions help them clear their respiratory tract and get more oxygen. When they are startled by sudden noises or bumps on their beds, they throw out their arms and legs, then hug them together over their bodies (startle or Moro reflex). This reflex is frequently used to assess the neurological status of the baby.[17] Consistent absence suggests a delay in central nervous system maturation. When supported upright, neonates will appear to take steps (walking or dancing reflex). When well fed and about to drop off to sleep, they will smile (smiling reflex). (This reflexive smile precedes the social smile that occurs in response to interactions with people some weeks later.) When an object or finger is placed in neonates' hands, they will grasp it so tightly that often they can be lifted off the surface on which they are lying (grasping reflex).

Physical changes in the first two years

The physical changes of infancy progress in an orderly, sequential way for all normal babies, although the exact age at which each change occurs varies widely from baby to baby. In the 1930s and 1940s, Arnold Gesell, Frances Ilg, and other colleagues at the Yale University Clinic for Infant and Child Development filmed and studied sequences of infant development. Out of this "cinemanalysis" came the conclusion that growth proceeds in certain developmental directions: from head to foot (called the cephalocaudal direction); from the center outwards (called the proximal-distal direction); and from general to specific movements. Cephalocaudal direction is well illustrated by the fact that the head accounts for about one-fourth of the infant's length at birth. By about one year of age the circumference of the chest finally becomes equal to that of the head. Proximal-distal development can be illustrated by the fact that the first bones to ossify are those close to the central, vital organs (skull, clavicle, spine) that are formed before birth. The bones of the fingers and toes do not begin to ossify until the end of the first year of life. General to specific development can be illustrated by grasping. Infants can crudely hold larger objects with both hands by about four months. They can hold smaller objects in one hand between thumb and forefinger (pincer grasp) by about one year of age. Figure 3–4 illustrates these developmental directions.

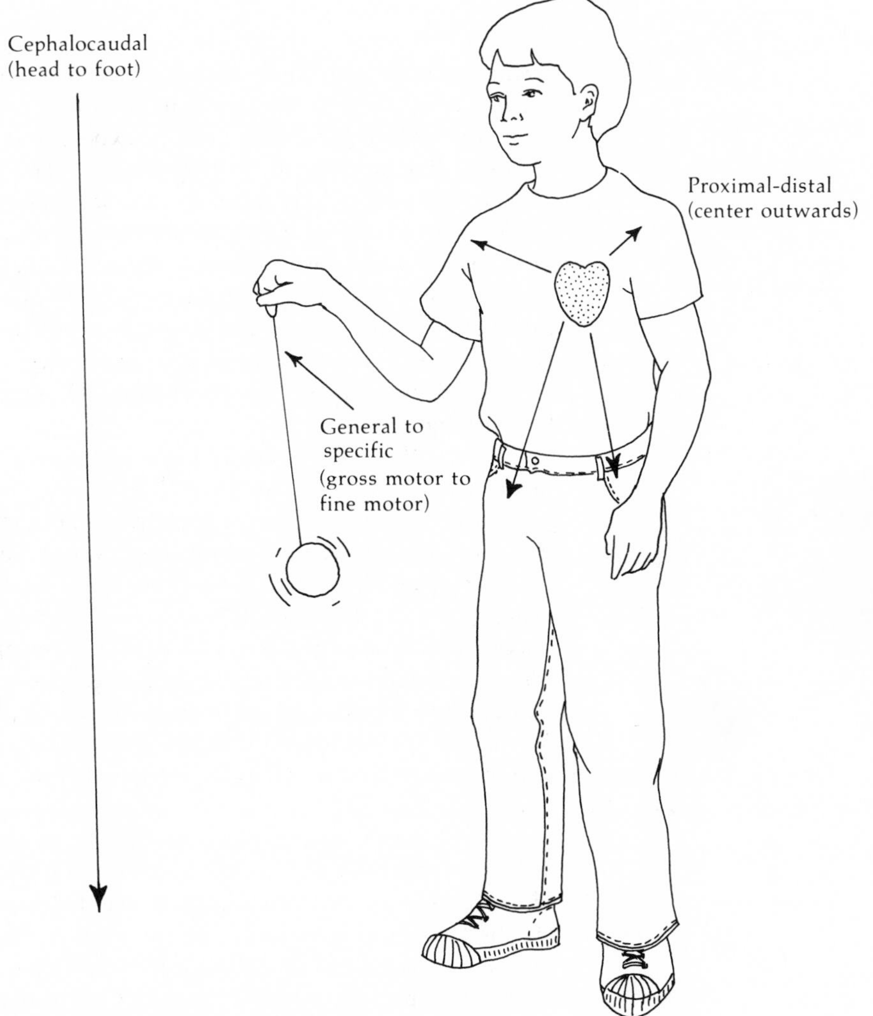

Figure 3–4. *Principles of developmental direction.*

Gesell's studies also indicated that development does not progress in a straight line but rather oscillates back and forth between periods of more rapid and slower maturing. Gesell and his colleagues (notably Frances Ilg and Louise Ames) suggested that infants (also children and adolescents) go through periods of good, pleasant behavior followed by times of troubled, "neurotic" behavior.[18] Knowledge of these normal changes can help parents survive the more troublesome periods of development.

Weight and height both progress at faster rates in infancy than at any other postnatal time of life. Infants tend to gain an average of about twenty grams (two-thirds of an ounce) per day during their first five months and fifteen grams (one-half an ounce) per day for the remainder of their first year of life.[19] They can be expected to double their birth weight by about five months, triple it by one year, and quadruple it by two years of age. Length during infancy can be expected to increase by about twenty-five to thirty centimeters (ten to twelve inches) during the first year and by about twelve more centimeters (five inches) at the end of the second year.[20] The weight of the brain multiplies most rapidly during infancy as cells enlarge, acquire longer, branched processes, and gain myelin sheathing. At the end of the first eighteen months, the brain is 75 percent of its adult weight. By the fourth year, 90 percent of its final weight has been attained.[21]

Nutrition is vitally important to an infant's physical development. Milk is sufficient to meet all of a baby's needs for the first four to six months of life. It does not contain iron, but infants have enough stored iron from birth to last for about the first half year of postnatal life. Solid foods are generally started before four to six months, depending on the advising physician (see Figure 3–5). Cereals or fruit juices are usually introduced first. Some physicians will introduce cereals soon after birth as supplements to milk. Strained fruits and vegetables may be part of the diet by two to three months. Meats may be added by three to four months. All new foods are introduced one at a time. They are continued for a day or two to ensure that no allergic reaction will occur before starting another new food.

Severe malnutrition problems can arise if infants are weaned too early from milk and are not given other foods equally rich in proteins. The effects of malnutrition on brain cell development are profound. During the first eight months of life the proliferation of additional glial cells (supporting cells) can be curtailed by insufficient dietary protein. In addition, lack of protein reduces branchings of the nerve fibers, enlargement of cell bodies, and myelinization of the cell processes.[22] Infancy is a "critical period" for hypertrophic growth of brain tissue. (Critical period refers to the concept of high vulnerability to damage during a period of rapid growth of a structure or function.) This can be illustrated by research on kwashiorkor (a disease caused by protein deficiency) in humans. Infants acquiring the disease in early infancy suffer irreparable brain damage. Infants who are affected by kwashiorkor in later infancy (from fifteen to twenty-nine months) have a milder residual mental retardation. Children who do not get the disease until they are beyond age three can recover normal intelligence once they are cured of their malnourished, diseased state.[23]

Less profound, but also unfortunate, are the effects of overfeeding in infancy. Babies who are fed many more calories than they can utilize from day to day develop additional fat cells to store the unused en-

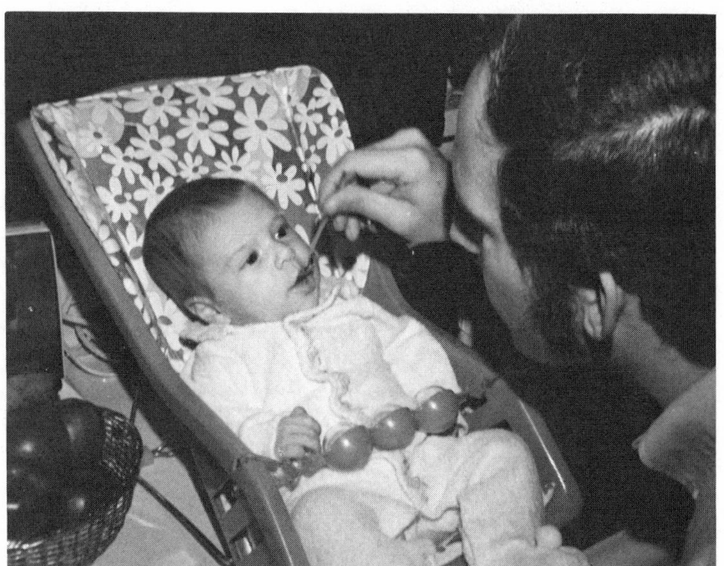

Figure 3–5. *Solid foods may be introduced any time between the third week and the fourth or fifth month, depending on the size and appetite of the infant and the advising physician's preferences. Feedings should be calm, pleasant, uninterrupted times for both baby and caregiver.*
Barbara Davis

ergy sources. Many biologists believe that these fat cells that develop in infancy will continue to replace themselves as children grow. If this theory is correct, adults who were fat as infants will have excess fat cells to fill throughout their lives and will either be obese or have difficulty holding their weight down to their normal range for size. Another theory about the effect of infant overfeeding on adult obesity is that eating patterns become habits that are difficult to change.[24]

Infants generally show a decrease in appetite between about twelve and eighteen months. They are no longer growing as rapidly and, therefore, do not need as many calories.

Sleep needs and patterns oscillate greatly during the first two years of life, both in the life of a single child and between infants. Immediately after birth, infants spend most of their nonfeeding time in sleep. The sleep-wake cycles are short, however, and the neonate can be expected to wake up every two to three hours (even during the night). The age at which the baby sleeps through the night (considered about a six to eight hour stretch) varies greatly from infant to infant. Some babies surprise their parents by doing this shortly after birth while others cannot do so until they are from four to seven months old. Between ages one and two most infants adapt their schedules to a morning and an afternoon nap and a full night (about twelve hours) of sleep.

The ages at which infants reach the milestones of motor development vary considerably. Motor achievements depend on maturation of the central nervous system, genetic factors, nutrition, physical health, environmental space, freedom, and stimulation, and even psychological well-being. One-month-old infants generally can lift their chins up above a surface when lying on their stomachs. By two months they probably can lift their chests up slightly and gaze around. At about three months their locomotor maturation is sufficient to hold their heads steady as they are pulled up. They also begin to reach for objects that attract their attention. At about four months they may grasp and hold objects for which they reach. By age five months infants generally can roll over. They also can hold their heads steady when in an upright position. At six months many infants sit alone. Their grasp is also now practiced enough to allow them to transfer objects from hand to hand. Between seven and nine months, babies may assume a sitting posture on their own, learn to creep or crawl, or stand with support. Between nine and twelve months they begin to take walking steps when their hands are held and to pull themselves up into a standing position alone by holding furniture. They also have practiced their grasp enough to have moved from a whole hand carry to a pincer grasp (opposition of thumb and forefinger). Most babies walk alone by fifteen months. By eighteen months they may be able to run stiffly and even climb stairs.

The ages for eruption of teeth in infancy are far more varied than the ages for accomplishing motor tasks. An occasional infant is born with a tooth. Other infants show no signs of teething until well past their first birthday. Early or late teething patterns appear to have genetic bases and are not related to other aspects of physical and motor development. Generally, Oriental and black infants are ahead of white infants in age of eruption of their first tooth.[25] The average age for acquiring a tooth (usually one or both of the lower central incisors) is six months.

Cognitive and language development

There are many people who believe that infant behaviors (e.g., shaking a rattle, drinking from a cup, walking) are taught by painstaking caregivers or learned in environments carefully supplied with the right kinds of stimuli. There are many other people who feel that infant behaviors will gradually evolve, regardless of caregivers or environmental stimuli, as the baby matures physiologically. Before reading on, consider these two explanations of the acquisition of new behaviors by infants. Which one seems more correct to you? There is an inseparable element of interplay between maturation and experience in infant learning. However, in recent years educators have been forced to accept the idea that many aspects of cognitive behavior are controlled by maturation.[26] Until the central nervous system reaches the necessary degree of maturity for any given skill (e.g., shaking a rattle), no amount of teaching or assisted practice will enable the infant to accomplish the task. Only after the appropriate neuroanatomical development has occurred will experience be of value.

Organization of the infant brain

The structure and functions of various brain parts and nervous tissue (neurons and fibers, glial cells and fibers) were outlined earlier in this chapter. In order for learning to take place in infancy, neurons and glia must become rearranged within the brain. In early infancy cells are denser in the outer layers of the brain. As development proceeds, the cells migrate toward the interior (see Figure 3–6).

Axons and dendrites must grow, branch out, and develop interconnections among each other. In addition, fibers must develop myelin

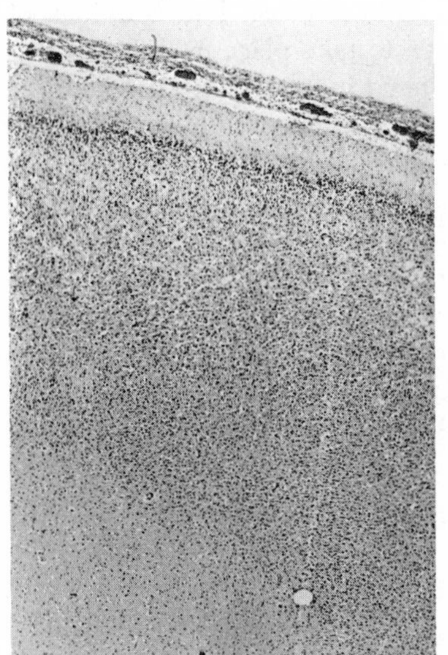

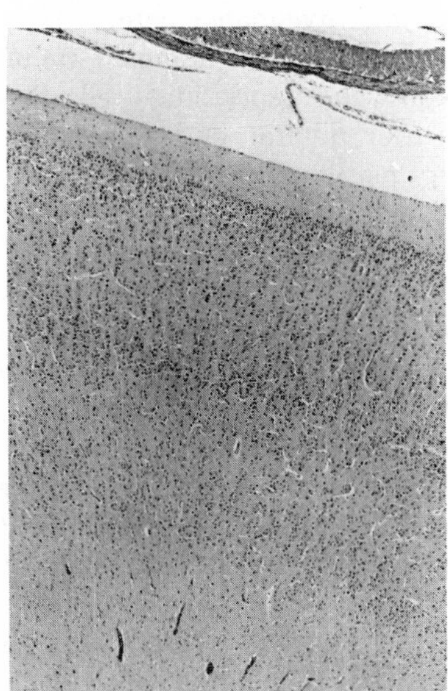

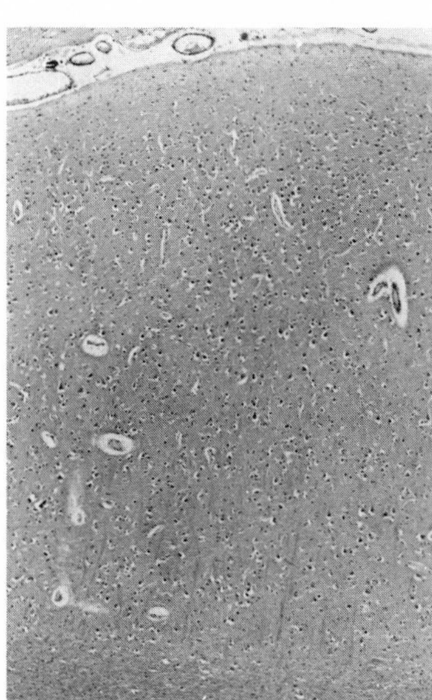

Figure 3–6. *Cells of the cerebral cortex are denser in the outer layers in the immature brain of the neonate, (A). They begin to migrate toward the interior as the infant matures, (B). In the adult cerebral cortex, they exist in well-organized arrangements, (C). (The many nerve fibers [axons and dendrites] connecting cells were not stained for these photos and cannot be seen.)*

Andrew Freiberg

coverings. These processes occur at different times and at different rates in different parts of the brain. Most brain cells probably become functional only after they reach their final locations in the nervous system. After this, their interconnections can become activated as they grow and develop.

Piaget's sensory-motor stage

Piaget's theory of cognitive development stresses four major periods through which humans pass in the course of intellectual maturation: (1) sensory-motor intelligence, (2) preoperational thinking, (3) concrete operational thought, and (4) formal or logical intelligence. Piaget's period of sensory-motor intelligence is easily juxtaposed with knowledge of the organization of the infant brain. As various cells of the cerebral cortex migrate into position, mature, develop interconnections among each other, and acquire myelin sheathing, infants become able to learn increasingly more about the world around them. The cells of the cerebral cortex are of three types: sensory, motor, and associational. Motor cells are concerned with muscle activities. Sensory cells are concerned with input from the senses (vision, smell, hearing, taste, touch). These cells migrate, mature, and become myelinated before the associational cells. The activities of memory, reason, and judgment are believed to take place in the cells that mature last, the associational cells. Piaget stated that in the first eighteen to twenty-four months of life an infant's knowledge of the world comes about primarily through sensory impressions and motor activities. The second stage of learning, the preoperational stage, coincides with increased maturation of the associational cells.

Piaget saw the sensory-motor period of intellectual development as having six distinctive substages, each one of which we will describe separately. Remember, however, that there is no overt end to any substage nor any obvious entrance into the next. Even if infants are watched very carefully for each new substage to emerge, more often than not they are discovered to have acquired new abilities and practiced them enough to be proficient before one quite realizes what has happened. Some infants pass through the succession of stages earlier than others. The rate of intellectual development depends not only on maturation but also on genetic factors, individual differences in patterning of learning experiences, physical and emotional health, nutrition, and the number and kinds of stimuli that the infant receives from the environment. Piaget and his colleagues were hesitant to attach an expected age of emergence on any of the substages of sensory-motor development. Instead they provided a wider approximate range for going through the stages. More important than when the behaviors emerge is the fact that they develop in the sequence that he described.

As infants experience various phenomena through their motions and senses, the complementary processes of assimilation and accommodation are put into play. Assimilation refers to the process of absorbing new information. Any objects or events that elicit exploring behaviors from the infant are being assimilated. Accommodation refers to the process whereby the infant (or child, or adult) alters his or her behaviors to adjust to the requirements of the object or event just assimilated.[27] (For more discussion of assimilation and accommodation, see p. 28.) Assimilation and accommodation allow infants to integrate new learning with old and thus adapt to their ever-expanding environments. As a result of infants' encounters with new stimuli, they acquire increased numbers of schemas. These, according to Piaget, are mentally organized patterns of behaviors.[28] When any structures are assimilated and accommodated into sharply defined schemas, a state of relative equilibrium is said to exist. However, this equilibrium sows seeds for its own destruction.[29] Inconsistencies and gaps previously ignored now become salient. They usher in a new subperiod of exploration of and adaptation to the newly perceived phenomena.

The first stage of sensory-motor intelligence, as described by Piaget, is the reflex stage. Piaget felt that for the first month of life the primary learning that takes place is bound to naturally occurring reflexes: rooting, sucking, swallowing, head-turning, crying, startling, grasping, and smiling. He proposed that assimilation to these reflexes occurs because the infant has a basic tendency to exercise any available behaviors and make them function. In exercising reflexes such as sucking, the infant learns more about the environment. Not only will the infant suck a nipple, but also a finger, a blanket, a piece of clothing, or anything that happens to come in contact with the mouth. During the first stage the infant learns to differentiate between various stimuli and accommodate to them. Thus, before long, when hunger is strong, only a nipple will elicit strong sucking movements. A blanket may elicit a loud howl of protest instead.

The second stage of sensory-motor intelligence commences at about one month and may last two to three months. Piaget called it the stage of primary circular reactions. Piaget's notion of primary circular reactions were described by Ginsburg and Opper:

> *The infant's behavior by chance leads to an advantageous or interesting result; he immediately attempts to reinstate or rediscover the effective behavior; after a process of trial and error, he succeeds in doing so. Thereafter, the behavior and the result may be repeated; they have become "habits."*[30]

Examples of some primary circular reactions (behaviors that become habits) are sucking on a specific object (e.g., thumb, finger, pacifier, toy), turning to look in the direction of a sound, reaching for and grasping an object, smiling at a friendly (later at a familiar) face, and showing anticipatory behaviors before routine procedures (e.g., feeding, diapering, being put to bed).

Infants begin to pay more attention to moderately novel stimuli during this stage. Both events totally assimilated and accommodated and events with no elements of familiarity are given less heed. Infants seem to prefer the challenge of attending to environmental events that almost, but not quite, fit into their preexisting schemas. These events require assimilation and accommodation work.

During the phase of primary circular reactions, infants seem content to focus on objects or events that occur naturally. Soon, however, maturational processes make it possible for them to begin experimenting with novel actions of their own. At first such experimental actions occur by accident. Serendipity! Infants arrive at the fortunate discovery that they can alter stimuli themselves and thus make them slightly novel and more interesting. This development ushers in Piaget's third substage of sensory-motor development.

Piaget called the third substage in infancy the period of secondary circular reactions. "Secondary" refers to the idea that habits developed in the preceding substage can now be embellished with new, more advanced actions. "Circular" refers to the fact that these behaviors are continually repeated by the baby in play. This stage is believed to characterize infants ranging in age from about four months through about eight to ten months. During this phase of development an intentionality in the babies' behaviors becomes apparent. Infants show evidence of finding ways to make interesting events last or be repeated. However, sensory-motor maturation is not yet sufficient to allow infants to mentally invent stimuli. Rather, their efforts to retain on-going events lead to an increased awareness of, and assimilation and accommodation to, various environmental forces.[31] Consider this example: a child was lying on his back in a crib watching a mobile move as he shook his right hand. A string was attached from the mobile to his right wrist. His mother removed the loop from his right wrist and slipped it over his left wrist. He shook his right hand vigorously. He then shook both hands as he became agitated. When the mobile moved, he continued shaking both hands more calmly. Soon he shook only his left hand. On following days he became accustomed to shaking only the hand to which the loop was attached after one or two trials when the mobile-string game was presented. On a subsequent occasion when the mobile was presented without a string, he shook both hands until he fortuitously hit the side of his crib, making the mobile move. In time he discovered that kicking the side of the crib to which the mobile was attached caused greater movement. Thereafter he experimented with the rate and rhythm of his kicks to make this interesting sight last.

During the phase of secondary circular reactions infants will imitate models if the patterns of behavior being demonstrated are familiar. They cannot yet copy novel actions.

Prior to this stage infants behave as if objects out of their sight no longer exist. Now they begin to have a rudimentary object concept. If an object with which they are involved disappears, they will attempt a visual or tactile search for it. However, they will not search for things that have been out of sight for a moderate period of time.

In the next stage infants' behaviors begin to take on an appearance of organization. Piaget called this fourth stage the coordination of secondary schemas. It commences when indications arise that babies have a definite goal in mind for what they are doing, and so is often referred to as the means-ends stage. The approximate age range is from eight to twelve months. By this time infants are more mobile. They can sit alone, reach and grasp, creep, crawl, or perhaps even pull to stand or take a few unassisted steps. "Coordination of schemas" refers to the idea that infants now need and use more than one pattern of behavior to attain the goal they have in mind. They may use one schema as a means for attaining the goal and a second for dealing with the goal.[32] Active experimentation is also evident as infants combine schemas in different ways. New skills and awarenesses emerge as they discover means to ends that were not originally intended.

Infants come to show anticipation of events that do not depend on their own actions. They expect people to act in certain ways, indicating their appreciation of the laws of causality independent of their own behavior. They also acquire the ability to imitate novel behaviors of models. Further, they now show a variety of searching behaviors for vanished objects.

Piaget surmised that during their first year and a half of life infants basically know their worlds through sensory impressions and motor activities. In substage five, which he called tertiary circular reactions, he first acknowledged the roots of some rudimentary associational cell functioning. (He did not call it associational cell functioning.) New schemas are still incorporated into old ones. Piaget believed that by this time, approximately twelve to eighteen months, babies can incorporate both the actions of combining schemas and the results of their experiments into their mental storehouse of knowledge. Piaget located the beginnings of rational judgment and intellectual reasoning in this cyclic behavior.[33] When confronted with obstacles, infants can now invent new means for handling them. They do not have to rely solely on schemas that were successful before.[34] They now also recognize causes and effects quite clearly. For example, a fourteen-month-old baby accidentally drops a toy on the floor of the car. She cannot retrieve it herself because she is buckled into a car seat. After only a moment's hesitation, she reaches for her mother's hand (cause) and pushes it down toward the object, indicating her desire to have the toy returned (effect). Object concept is so well established that even if something is hidden in a succession of places, the infant will search for it in the place where it was last seen.

The last of the sensory-motor phases postulated by Piaget is the invention of new means through mental combinations. By this time, approximately eighteen months to two years, infants can understand and use some language. Language is used to form mental symbols for patterns of behavior. Infants now try to think about problems and develop solutions on a mental rather than a physical level. Simple new forms of behavior are initiated and carried through without the past trial-and-error steps. For example, a twenty-month-old baby pushing himself around on a kiddy car catches a wheel on the edge of the carpet. He stands up and peers under the vehicle to see what is obstructing his movement. He then lifts the wheel up over the carpet immediately and proceeds on his self-propelled ride. Infants are now proficient at imitating behavior that occurred some time earlier. They have formed some mental representations of the behaviors that they can copy rather than requiring a physically present model. This last substage heralds the beginning of a whole new period of symbolic thought: that of preoperational intelligence.

Some people feel that infants may be able to generate mental hypotheses about their experiences sooner than Piaget surmised. We know from studies of older children and adults that when humans actively think about something (e.g., memorization) or work at something (e.g., calculations) their heart rates increase. Kagan studied a group of infants ranging in age from five and a half to eleven and a half months as they listened to discrepant speech phrases. They all showed increases in heart rates. The older infants' heart rates rose the most, suggesting that they were working harder mentally to understand the speech.[35] Zelazo found a similar increase in heart rates when eleven-month-old infants watched an unusual event.[36] Many other research studies using different methodologies have also demonstrated the advent of mental processes in infants at earlier ages than postulated by Piaget. Infants may be smarter than Piaget's stages would indicate. However, the sequence in which he described development has been well replicated. In addition, we are convinced that maturation of the central nervous system must precede the acquisition of increasingly intelligent behaviors.

Language beginnings

Language appears at the end of infancy, as suggested by the word *infans*, meaning "without language." In their early development, even though infants are not yet speaking, they are actively learning about the words that they hear spoken. As their neurological development progresses, they become increasingly able to organize and comprehend language. As their cognitive development progresses, they find increasing numbers of things for which some representational symbol would be helpful (i.e., the objects that are out of sight, but not out of mind; the people or things that cause pleasant or interesting stimuli to occur).

The ability to understand the spoken word is called passive or receptive language. It is, in fact, the primary or fundamental aspect of language. The ability to produce meaningful utterances (called expressive language) is always secondary to understanding what others are saying.

From birth the auditory nerve tracts are myelinated enough to allow infants to hear. They show signs of actively listening and trying to tune in sounds which caregivers make to them in feeding, diapering, and soothing situations. They also attend to sounds of distress and respond in like fashion. (Any newborn nursery nurse can verify the fact that when one baby starts crying, others will soon do the same.) A discrimination of different intonations is soon followed by the ability to differentiate between various vowel and consonant sounds. Using heart rate increases as a sign of mental work (as described in Kagan's study on p. 102), two separate researchers found that young infants (ranging from four to twenty-eight weeks) could already discriminate between different sounds. In each study infants heard one sound until they were accustomed to it. Then a new cue was introduced. Increases in heart rate indicated that they could perceive the change.[37] Using the sucking reflex as a sign of interest (infants suck more vigorously when they are alerted), another research study found that four-week-old infants could distinguish between sounds as subtly different as "pa" and "ba."[38] Understanding of language becomes increasingly proficient as babies get older. Whether they are responding to intonation, to actual words, or both, it is possible to either soothe or upset a baby of three to four months with comforting or frightening statements. By nine to eleven months receptive language is organized to the point that infants will obey spoken commands (e.g., give me the ball, play pat-a-cake, finish your juice).

There are many precursors of expressive language also present at birth. The sensory nerve fibers that control speech are myelinated enough to allow infants to utter sounds, although neither the associational cells nor the motor cells are mature enough to allow the production of meaningful words. It is interesting that the speech center in the brain, which is located in the sensory cortex on the left side of the cerebrum (the right side in left-handed persons), borders on the areas of the motor cortex, which control both mouth-tongue movements and hand movements. This proximity of the speech center to the hand control area of the motor cortex is important. We all express ourselves with our hands as well as with our mouths. Infants especially use many gestures in association with simple words as they acquire language.

The earliest sounds made in infancy are cries. As any infant caregiver can confirm, it is possible to tell from the rhythm, tone, and pitch of a cry very soon after birth whether a baby is hungry or uncomfortable, angry, or in pain. Even a colicky pain can be discerned from other pain sounds. By about three weeks of age infants add new sounds to their repertoire. Noncry sounds such as coos or gurgles usually are produced just minutes before fussing begins.[39] However, these sounds soon are practiced whenever the babies are alert and contented. It seems, as Piaget stated it, that infants have a basic tendency to exercise any available behaviors and make them function.[40] During the first two to six months of life, infants in all cultures produce all the possible sounds of every known language.[41] They try out whistles, snorts, chuckles, squeals, gutteral sounds, nasal sounds, trills, glides, even "Bronx cheers." However, by about six months they begin to have what linguists call "phonetic drift." They concentrate on producing only the sounds (phonemes) that they hear spoken. We have forty-five phonemes in English. Some languages have as many as seventy-one. Phonemes are fundamental sounds. Some of our alphabetical letters represent several different phonemes (e.g., *ō*, *ô*, *o͞o*, *oo*, *oi*, *ou* are all represented by *o*). The infants' drift towards reproducing only the phonemes that they hear spoken indicates the beginnings of organization of language in the brain. As early as age three months infants show a tendency to babble more when they are alone. When a caregiver approaches, they quiet to attend to the caregiver's utterances. They may try to repeat sounds that adults make, if the sounds are ones they have already produced and practiced. At about six months it is common to hear infants string syllables together (e.g., gumgumgumgum, duhduhduhduh). By about ten months they make efforts to imitate novel sounds, ones that they have not practiced previously. Finally, at about one year, many babies make their first meaningful words. Very frequently they are labels for caregivers (e.g., mama, dada, nana, papa).

In all cultures the first meaningful words of babies are nouns.[42] Next to emerge are verbs, the action words. The early utterances usually refer to subjects or objects on which the baby acts, not familiar things to which caregivers attend (e.g., diapers). Between ages one and two infants generally acquire the ability to produce holophrases. These are one-word sentences that convey a complete message (e.g., Up). Next, infants learn to expand their holophrases by attaching them back-to-back to other nouns or verbs. They thus form two-word sentences (e.g., Mommy milk, Daddy come). The one- and two-word sentences used by babies are generally accompanied by many gestures that, together with the context, make them comprehensible. For example, the single word *chair* might mean, I want to get up in the chair; I want the chair moved; I want you to get out of the chair; or simply be a label, This is a chair; or a question, Is this a chair? The words produced by infants are usually the most salient portions of any message. Early speech is often referred to as telegraphic speech because, as in telegram messages, the articles, pronouns, prepositions, conjunctions, and auxiliary verbs are omitted. In organizing and coding receptive language, infants acquire an understanding of the most meaningful units of speech. No one teaches them to use nouns and verbs first. They learn this sequence on their own.

Noam Chomsky proposed that humans (as opposed to other species) have an innate capacity to learn language, which he labeled the language acquisition device (LAD).[43] During infancy, as neurological maturation proceeds, the unique ability of the brain to sort out basic sounds and to extract from sentences the most meaningful elements becomes apparent. During early childhood the brain's language acquisition ability becomes even more sophisticated. Children will implicitly use underlying rules for constructing sentences in their native tongue. They will invent new sentences that they have never heard adults utter. They will also make rule-based mistakes (e.g., adding *-er* and *-s* incorrectly to irregular verbs and nouns). These aspects of language development will be discussed further in Chapter 5.

Role of the family in fostering learning

Parents and other caregivers can have an enormous influence on their infants' intellectual development, within the limits set by heredity. Language can be stimulated in many verbal ways. Cognition can be enhanced by providing exciting stimuli to be assimilated and accommodated, as well as through various behaviors of the caregivers.

The more infants are talked to directly the better. From birth on, caregivers should talk to their babies when they are awake and alert, as during feedings and diaper changes. This early practice helps form habits of talking to infants that are invaluable later. This early talking also helps soothe babies and allows them to become familiar with and form attachments to their caregivers. Many parents are not sure what they should say to their babies. It is not important what is said, only that speaking occurs. Infants can be told the plans for the day. They can be sung to or told nursery rhymes. There is an old Norwegian saying that a much nicknamed baby is a much loved baby. Infants can be called all kinds of affectionate things and can be complimented over and over without any damage.

At about three or four weeks, when infants begin cooing,

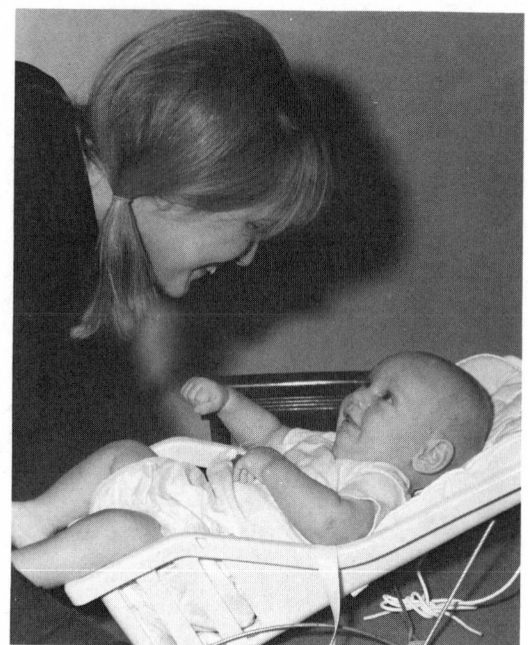

Figure 3–7. Language development is enhanced by face-to-face vocal interactions between infant and adult. The infant enjoys both hearing the adult's words and hearing his own sounds imitated back to him.
Leslie Davis

caregivers can increase the rate at which babies play with sounds by imitating some of them. These vocal games should continue right up to and beyond the time when infants produce their first words. After about six months babies will begin to imitate some of the caregivers' sounds as well as vice versa. From two or three months on, when infants begin working to understand words with their receptive language capabilities, caregivers should begin labeling things clearly (e.g., bottle, dog, blanket). They should show enthusiasm and encourage infants to label things as well, even if the baby's word for an object is incomprehensible. With infants' increasing ages, explanations can be given for all the activities of infant care. Questions may be asked, and after a few moments, answered. All of these verbal activities will stimulate language development in infants.

Once babies begin making holophrases (one-word sentences) and gestures in attempts to communicate, every attempt should be made to understand these messages. If caregivers cannot comprehend, they can ask the baby, "Show me." Sometimes, if another child is present, the child will understand what the baby is saying. When caregivers grasp what infant vocalizations mean, they should expand the holophrases or gestures into longer sentences, both encouraging the baby's word and modeling additional language (e.g., "Up."—"Up? Very good! Billy wants to go up. Up Billy goes. Up into the chair").

The same kinds of verbal stimulation that are useful in fostering language also encourage cognitive growth. Caregivers should be responsive to infants' calls for information, for encouragement, for a change of play materials, or for a change of scenery.

In earliest infancy babies spend most of their time either in their cribs or with a caregiver—being fed, changed, bathed, or comforted. While in their cribs, infants can be placed on their stomachs a portion of the time. Their head-turning reflex will prevent smothering. They will try to lift their heads and eventually develop enough strength to lift their chests also. The view from this position can be stimulating. While on their backs, infants should not have to stare at a blank ceiling. A mobile, toys strung on elastic, or a friendly face is infinitely more interesting. Caregivers can foster intellectual growth during feedings, baths, and diaper changes by talking, singing, showing toys, and even just by holding babies so they can view the caregivers' faces. Facial features are very potent stimuli to infants and hold their attention longer than any other configurations.[44] Other games are also stimulating (e.g., touching baby's nose, bouncing baby on a knee, blowing on baby's stomach).[45]

By about three months infants begin to reach for things and should be given opportunities to do so. Mobiles or toys strung on elastic and placed over the crib or across infant recliner seats are good. When infants can grasp the toys, it is important to keep safety in mind. While expensive toys are not necessary, babies should not be given objects small enough to swallow, wooden toys with slivered, rough surfaces, or peeling or paint-chipped toys. Even some new toys can be dangerous (e.g., hard, thin plastic objects that break into sharp pieces, breakable rattles filled with bee-bee pellets, stuffed animals with button or prong eyes that pull off easily). Babies explore everything with their mouths as well as with their hands.

The right learning toy for a baby at any age is one that produces pleasure and excitement and is safe. Hunt called finding such toys "the problem of the match."[46] If the toy is too familiar, the baby will be bored. If it is too novel, the baby will ignore it. The best learning toys are ones with both elements of familiarity and challenge (i.e., something new to be assimilated and accommodated). Toys with different colors or sounds or textures or shapes should be provided. Several safe, manipulatory objects can be kept in one place to present to babies at playtimes. This allows them to select their own "match."

When babies acquire the motor coordination to hold their own heads steady, they can be propped or carried in upright positions more of their waking hours. This opens up whole new horizons of interesting sights for them. Caregivers who provide many social stimulations for their infants go a long way in fostering intellectual development. Babies learn a great deal from walks, visits to stores or other people's houses, and from being with adults and other children in their own homes. While playpens have their uses, it is good to give babies freedom to explore more than just a small square space from day to day. Back, front, or shoulder carriers are available that allow caregivers to take infants wherever they go with minimal difficulty.

During the latter half of the first year of life, babies become quite mobile. They will roll over, sit up alone, scoot, creep, crawl, pull themselves up to stand, and eventually walk. They will explore anything they can touch, which necessitates putting unsafe things out of reach. This is a time of active learning. Caregivers should respond to babies' bids for help, movement, encouragement, and the like. Play objects that no longer attract attention should be removed and new ones provided. It is also good to organize days so that changes of play objects or scenery occur frequently enough to prevent boredom.

One very important way in which families can foster intellectual development in infants is to provide diets with enough protein (e.g., milk and milk products, meat, poultry, fish, beans) for maximum neurological development. Diets also need to be balanced out with other essential foods (fruits and vegetables; cereals and grains). They should not be so calorie laden, however, that infants become too fat to move about freely.

Social development

In the preceding sections we learned that social-emotional well-being has an important influence on the development of motor skills and the acquisition of cognitive skills and language. Many of the things families do to foster learning also foster social development. The most important person in any infant's life is the primary caregiver, usually the mother or mother-substitute. However, fathers and other family members also are very important persons to infants.

As babies grow, their waking social periods lengthen. Let us look at "social" human beings as they develop during infancy. By about two months babies will smile spontaneously at any human face. If the recipient responds, babies will usually make happy noises. Between two and five months babies begin reaching for and grasping objects, including human noses, glasses, hair, and clothing. Whatever they successfully grasp, they bring to their mouths. By five or six months (or whenever the first teeth emerge), babies will also bite any objects brought to their mouths. At about the half-year mark babies begin trying to feed themselves. They also hold on to objects that they have grasped tightly and resist the efforts of caregivers to take them away. If objects are put out of reach, they will try hard to get them. By seven to nine months social games such as peek-a-boo and drop and fetch are fun. Babies may insist on continuing such sport to the annoyance of caregivers. At about this time babies also become shy or anxious around strangers. They may cling, cry, and vigorously protest any separation from the primary caregiver(s). When caregivers are present, babies may explore everything. As mobility increases, their curiosity leads them to every nook and cranny and through every door possible. Safety precautions become vital.

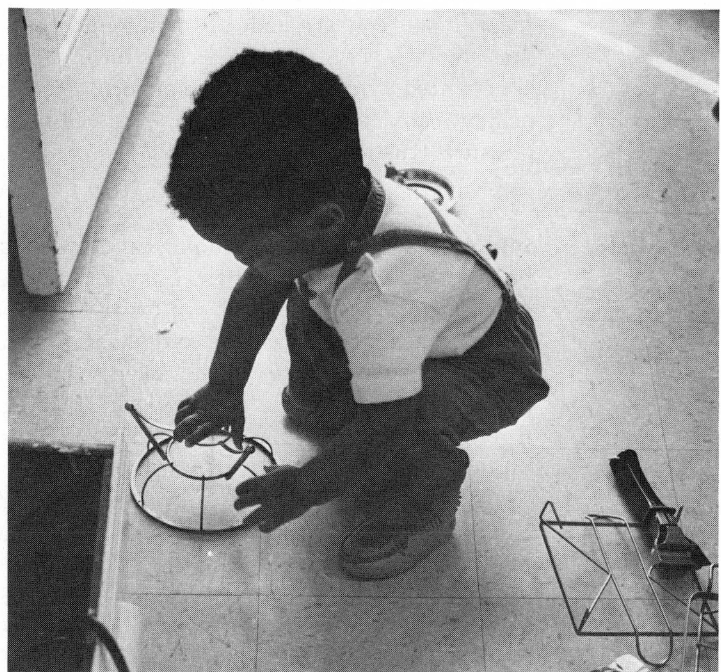

Figure 3–8. *When babies sit alone or walk, their hands become free for exploration. They attempt to pick up everything in reach. They examine what they grasp with hands, mouth, and teeth.*
Burk Uzzle/Magnum Photos, Inc.

By about one year of age babies begin indicating what they want with gestures or holophrases. If babies do not receive gratification when they seek it, or if they are thwarted or frustrated in obtaining some goal, they may have anger outbursts (temper tantrums). Mealtimes may be chosen as prime time for demonstrations of self-help skills: drinking from a cup, using a spoon. They also may be chosen as opportunities to test the word *no.* Food likes and dislikes may be exaggerated in the process. By age eighteen months most babies are walking and finding additional ways to satisfy their curiosity. They imitate many of the behaviors of their caregivers, in social-emotional behaviors as well as physical actions. They will also attempt to undress and dress themselves—the first rather well, the second with many frustrations. They may not have as much stranger anxiety by this time, but they still desire a very close personal relationship with their primary caregiver(s). Jealousies become evident—of other adults, other children, even of pets or time-consuming activities such as housework or phone conversations. The word *no* enters into what appears to be virtually all requests made of them by parents and others ("negativism" or "resistance").[47] As you can see, by the end of infancy babies have already experienced a fairly wide range of social-emotional reactions (e.g., distress, delight, anxiety with strangers, attachment to caregivers, curiosity, pleasure, frustration, anger, jealousy, and negativism).

Significance of the family in social development

Infants are born new psychological as well as new physiological human beings. We all know that babies cannot survive without physical care. But physical care is not enough. In order to support the developmental tendency of neonates to become competent, healthy infants and infants to become competent, healthy children, psychological care is also essential. It must begin at birth and be provided by caregivers in abundant measure throughout the psychologically as well as physically dependent periods of infancy. Psychological care refers to the tender, holding, warmth-providing, loving behaviors sometimes believed to gush forth instinctively from mothers. While some mothers are easily able to provide high quality psychological care, other mothers find this kind of caregiving quite foreign. Likewise, while some fathers are naturally affectionate with their babies, others must learn the tender touch. Research can tell us quite a bit about the necessity for psychological care in infancy.

Contact hunger. Back in the 1940s and 1950s a few studies were made of infants raised in overcrowded orphanages. In general, the foundlings received only physical care. They were kept in cribs with covered sides, possibly to prevent the spread of infections, and were only picked up on alternate days for baths. Bottles were propped in the cribs. Visual contact with the caregivers and other babies was minimal due to the covered crib sides. Verbal stimulation was limited, and no toys were provided. Rene Spitz, in one study, found that after two years of such care 37 percent of the infants had died, and the survivors seemed "emotionally starved."[48] In another study, Wayne Dennis found that over 60 percent of such deprived infants could not sit up alone at age two, and 80 percent could not walk by age four.[49] Dennis "enriched" one institution by adding one woman caregiver for every three infants. The women held the infants,

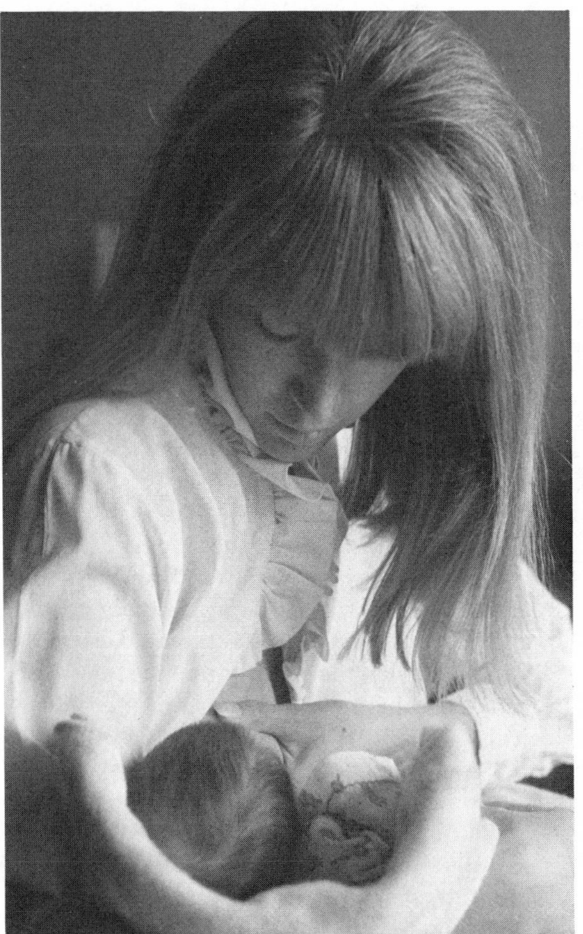
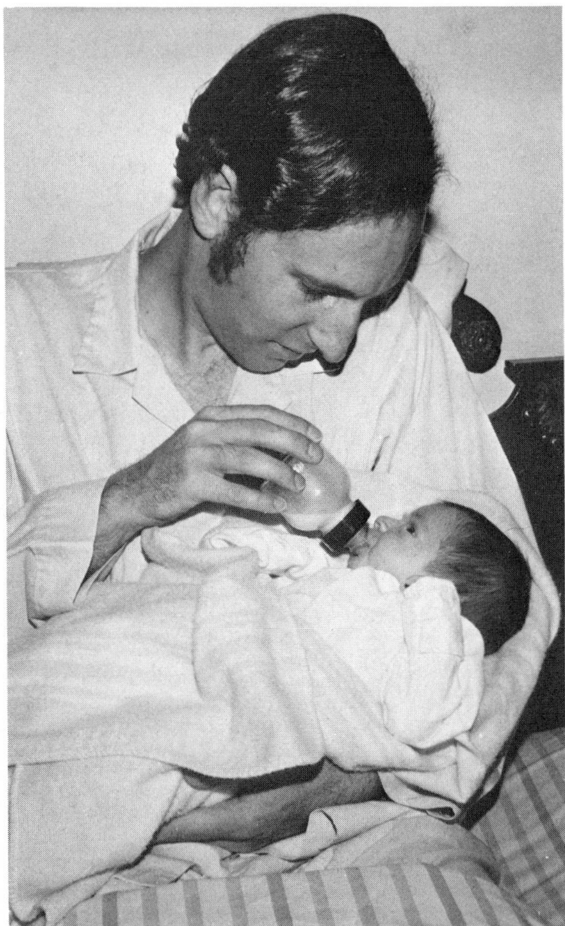

Figure 3–9. *Both breast- and bottle-feeding can satisfy an infant's need for contact comfort when adults cuddle the baby close and provide face-to-face attention.*
Leslie Davis

talked and played with them, and, in general, provided tender loving care. These orphans sat and stood at the normal ages.[50]

Harry and Margaret Harlow demonstrated the importance of cuddling (contact comfort) for emotional well-being when they raised newborn rhesus monkeys with either cold, chicken wire-covered or warm, terry cloth-covered "surrogate" mothers.[51] Infant monkeys spent much more time with the warm, cloth-covered "mothers" even when they were fed from bottles placed in the wire "mothers." When a frightening object like a moving toy was placed in their cages, they ran to the cloth-covered "mother" for comfort, even though, in some cases, the Harlows had fashioned these "mothers" with fright-producing faces. If the warm, cloth-covered "mothers" were absent, the baby monkeys became extremely agitated. They did not seem to be comforted by the presence of the cold, wire "mothers," even with milk and/or kindly faces. The Harlows attributed this to "contact hunger." Human infants also have a psychological need for close contact with a warm, soft mother or mother-substitute.

The fact that infants are born with enough neurological maturation to cry bodes well for them. Crying is, in fact, an excellent way to begin obtaining contact comfort. It is an aversive sound to adults. As such, it elicits behaviors directed toward soothing the baby to make the crying stop. Very often crying babies will not be comforted until they are held.

The feeding situation is another way in which babies should have their contact hunger satisfied (see Figure 3–9). There is no way to breast-feed an infant without holding him or her nestled close. This is an advantage of nursing, as important as many of the other advantages (convenience, digestibility, low cost). Bottle-feeding, too, can satisfy contact hunger as well as physiological hunger. Not only can the mother cuddle the baby close during feedings, but so can the father, grandparent, nurse, or other loving person. In many cases mothers are very tired after having their babies and find it difficult to stay awake, much less provide tender loving care (TLC) during every feeding (including night feedings). Bottled milk allows mothers more freedom to rest and gives other significant family members a chance to get acquainted with the infant. Feeding babies by bottles is often, in fact, recommended if mothers are malnourished, ill, or overtired, or if babies suckle with difficulty due to prematurity or a cleft lip defect. The most important lesson to be learned when bottle-feeding an infant (beyond providing clean, warm, properly prepared formula) is to hold the baby close. Holding a bottle for a baby left lying in a crib, or propping a bottle for the baby and then leaving, deprives the infant of the contact comfort for which he or she has such an overwhelming need.

An advantage of partial or complete rooming-in for newborns in hospitals is the speed with which mothers and fathers learn to hold, cuddle, and caress their baby. The sooner they get over their fears of handling the tiny neonate, and the sooner they feel comfortable caring for their own offspring, the sooner the baby will begin to receive the psychologically important warm, tender touch.

Attachment. In ethological research (the study of the behavior of animals through direct observation), biologists have labeled the characteristic following and imitation of the mother animal by the young as "imprinting." In the human species motor coordination is not sufficiently developed at birth to allow for much following or imitating, although psychologists believe a form of imprinting called "attachment" does occur. Various attachment behaviors of the very young infant toward the caregiver that have been identified include grasping, crying, visual following, clinging, reaching, and smiling. One can be quite sure attachment has occurred when certain behaviors are observed, such as separation anxiety, fear of strangers, repeated visual or tactile contacts with the caregiver while exploring unfamiliar territory, and the kinds of following and imitative behaviors that characterize imprinting in other species.

Crying, grasping, and some visual following occur at birth. As mentioned earlier, the human face is an especially potent stimulus for infants. By about two months infants begin smiling at any human face. If the human smiles back, infants will usually make happy gurgling noises and reach toward the person. Between three and six months babies show signs of differentiating between the primary caregiver(s) and others.[52] The primary caregiver(s) get the biggest smiles and the most babbling and cooing responses. Attachment becomes more obvious between six and fifteen months when separation reactions and stranger anxiety emerge. Separation reactions (distress and/or crying at the caregiver's departure) cannot appear until after a focused relationship between the infant and mother-figure has developed.[53] Crying upon separation seems to vary widely from child to child, as does fear of strangers. Some infants show marked reactions of this sort, while others show little or none. Ricciuti suggested that these behaviors might be less marked in infants who have experienced rather wide contact with a variety of strangers, under circumstances that attenuate the initially fearful reactions that are likely to occur.[54] While separation protest and stranger anxiety may be taken as a clear indication that an attachment has been formed, the absence of such protest in everyday, nonstressful situations does not necessarily suggest that an attachment is either absent or weak.[55]

Erikson's concept of trust versus mistrust. Erik Erikson, a neo-Freudian psychoanalytic theorist, postulated that humans go through eight stages of social-emotional development in the life span. At each stage there exists a nuclear conflict that is a critical period for the development of certain attitudes and the resolution of certain conflicts. While nuclear conflicts are never completely resolved during the stage in which they emerge, a satisfactory resolution of most of the conflict leaves a person with the judgment and ability to handle repeated upsurgings of the basic conflict throughout life. A person who has passed through a stage successfully achieves a feeling of well-being related to the "sense" just developed.

Erikson proposed that in infancy, the most crucial sense to be formed is a sense of trust, a feeling of confidence and reliance in the caregivers. Erikson's sense of trust does not explicitly deal with attachment; however, it is implicit in the theory that an attachment does form between the infant and the caregiver as trust develops. Erikson suggested that when a primary caregiver meets the infant's needs consistently, with sameness and continuity, the infant learns to rely not only on the external provider but also on him- or herself.[56] Trust is learned very early through situations such as feedings and diaperings. If infants are fed when hunger first appears rather than being allowed to develop strong hunger pangs, they are more comfortable in their surroundings. Likewise, if they are diapered when they first wet rather than being left cold and dirty, a feeling that the world is a good place is more apt to develop. Mistrust, the other alternative to this nuclear conflict, develops when infants are allowed to experience frequent bouts of overwhelming hunger, or are left dirty, uncomfortable, irritated, and irritable. Effective caregiving for the development of a sense of trust involves far more than just taking care of an infant's bodily needs. It prospers with warm, tender touching, verbal soothing, verbal stimulation, smiles, and sensory arousal with toys and changes of scenery. It flounders with careless holding, dropping, and an absence of things to see and do while awake. Table 3–2 presents some of Erikson's descriptions of the sense of trust versus the sense of mistrust and some adult behaviors that foster each attitude.

Individual differences. Few people believe today, as John Locke postulated in the seventeenth century, that the infant is born a "tabula rosa" (clean slate) or a moldable piece of clay. The kind of adults that infants become is most certainly influenced by caregivers and care received, but behaviors of caregivers do not create the whole physique, intelligence, and personality of adults. Infants come into the world equipped with their own unique characteristics for physical stature, for learning, for behaving. In the area of the "psychological human being" normal babies differ remarkably. Some infants, when held, cling. Others need considerable support and behave more like rag dolls. Some infants sleep a great deal more than others. Individual differences in babies have been noted in their activity, rhythmicity, adaptability, approach, threshold, intensity, moods, distractability, and persistence.[57] Babies also differ in the amount of their crying, soothability, and capability for self-comforting behavior as well as in their capacity to assimilate and accommodate sensory stimuli.[58] In a longitudinal study (one that follows subjects over an extended time) of more than 200 infants in New York City, Chess, Thomas, and Birch identified three particular types of infants that they called "easy babies," "slow-to-warm-up babies," and "difficult babies."[59] The easy babies ate and slept well and had positive, sunny dispositions. The slow-to-warm-up babies seemed cautious and hesitant about new foods, new people, new places, and new things. The difficult babies had intense negative reactions

Table 3–2. *Erickson's first nuclear conflict: trust versus mistrust.*

Sense	*Eriksonian descriptions*	*Fostering adult behaviors*
Trust	– ease of feeding, depth of sleep, relaxation of bowels	– caregiving techniques with consistency, continuity, and sameness
	– feeling of inner goodness	– sensitive attention to the baby's individual needs
	– reliance on outer providers	– firm sense of personal trustworthiness; conviction that there is meaning to what one is doing
	– trust in the capacity of one's own organs to cope with urges	
vs.		
Mistrust	– sense of having been deprived, divided, abandoned	– inconsistent, neglectful caregiving
	– anxiety, rage, lack of control of urges	– withdrawal from situations where baby tests the relationship and demands attention to his or her needs

Source: Based on material from "Eight Ages of Man" from *Childhood and Society*, 2nd Edition, Revised, by Erik H. Erikson, with the permission of W. W. Norton & Company, Inc. Copyright 1950, © 1963 by W. W. Norton & Company, Inc.

to just about everything. Difficult babies were different from colicky babies (to be described in the health section of this chapter), who seemed to have difficulty only with feeding situations.

The behaviors of infants have very definite effects on the behaviors of their caregivers. Moss demonstrated that the crying of an infant in the first three months of life elicited soothing procedures from the mother. Later, the infants who responded to the mother's soothing in the early months of life got more soothing. The more intractable infants were left to cry.[60] In another study, Ainsworth and Bell showed that a mother's prompt response to crying in the first four months produced infants who cried less at one year of age.[61] Social development in infancy is multifaceted, with both infants and adults affecting the outcomes.

Many studies have shown sex differences in infants. Boy babies have been shown to fuss and cry more and to soothe less easily, which may eventually lead to fewer attempts to soothe them by caregivers.[62] Girl babies have been shown to babble to faces and voices more and in turn to receive more face-to-face vocal exchanges.[63] As infants move into their second year of life, boys have been observed to show more aggression, independence, and active playing, while girls have been observed spending more time close to adults, vocalizing.[64] Arguments as to whether observed sex differences are genetically or environmentally induced, or both, are unresolved.

Discipline. Discipline in infancy may seem out of context to you after the preceding discussions of tender loving care, contact comfort, attachment, and trust. It is not. Discipline refers to limit setting, to training that develops self-control. It is a very important part of helping babies feel safe and secure. It helps them gain the ability, as Erikson stated it, to "trust oneself and the capacity of one's own organs to cope with urges; . . . to consider oneself trustworthy enough so that the providers will not need to be on guard lest they be nipped."[65] This feeling of emerging inner goodness and self-control is best brought about through consistent, predictable caregiving routines within the family setting.

At birth infants' wake-sleep-hunger cycles are irregular. Initially, it is a good idea to offer food each time babies awaken from sleep, although before long babies will develop their own feeding schedules, based on their intestinal absorption patterns and the amount of milk they can tolerate at each feeding. In general, periods of hunger vary from two and a half to four hours apart. Soon caregivers will recognize hunger cycles and will discover the approximate rhythm of their own infants. At this point they can begin to modify their infants' demands to fit a pattern. Knowing the approximate length of time between hunger cycles will help establish another rhythm, the day-night sleep pattern. Most neonates will automatically have one longer nap (ranging from four to eight hours) per day and several shorter ones (ranging from one to three hours). The longer nap does not necessarily occur at night, but a knowledge of the approximate time between hunger pangs during the short nap periods will enable caregivers to "move" the longer nap to night. They simply can wake the baby for feedings every two and a half (or three, or four) hours during the day and provide a warm, quiet atmosphere conducive to sleep at night. The "longer" night nap may only be four hours initially, but it gradually lengthens until babies "sleep through the night." The age at which an "eight-hour-plus night" occurs varies widely from infant to infant. A few will do this from birth. Others may not oblige until five to seven months of age. Other ways that caregivers can demonstrate consistency and continuity and help establish disciplined, patterned days for their infants are by bathing the baby at approximately the same time each day and by making feedings routine (i.e., feeding, burping, feeding, burping, diapering, talking).

As babies get older, naps get shorter, although most infants still require a morning as well as an afternoon nap and an uninterrupted sleep through the night. Babies who are consistently put to nap at certain times are less likely to resist being put to bed than babies who are put down irregularly.

Food likes and dislikes are common in infancy. To avoid confrontations over foods, caregivers should try a new food when the baby is neither tired nor painfully hungry. If babies resist, caregivers should stay calm. They can try the food again later. Food jags are also normal. Infants may resist all but one food (e.g., cereal) for a few days, but these jags seldom last long. It is more important to have regular, pleasant meals than to insist on eating exactly what is on a plate at every sitting. If meals are kept pleasant, and patterns of interpersonal relationships include mutual affection and trust, the "imitative" older infants will soon want to eat the same foods that the caregivers eat. When self-help urges surface, finger foods can be supplied (e.g., fruit slices, raw or cooked and cooled vegetables, cheeses, meat cubes, cereals, bread cubes).

Biting usually follows teething. Infants learn what not to bite (caregivers, siblings, furniture) and what is acceptable (teething toys, dry toast, biscuits) through the caregiver's prompt substitution of appropriate teething materials for inappropriate ones.

Mobility requires a certain amount of household engineering and an acceptance of the word *no* as voiced by caregivers. Household engineering consists of such things as moving dangerous items out of reach or locking them away, using gates as necessary on stairwells or off-limits areas, putting safety plugs in electrical outlets, and keeping pins, nails, or other sharp or poisonous items off the floors. Infants also learn to respect and obey the word *no* if it is used only when needed and reinforced by removing the infant from the temptation (or vice-versa). However, if it is voiced often and indiscriminately with no follow-up, it will eventually be ignored.

Temper tantrums are often avoidable if caregivers are alert to signs of hunger, exhaustion, boredom and/or frustration in their babies. Angry outbursts are much more likely to occur when babies are hungry and tired than when they are fed and rested. Likewise, they occur more frequently when toys, scenery, or social contacts thwart or frustrate some goal than when babies are able to observe or explore phenomena that interest them. If an infant desires something forbidden and must be thwarted with a *no*, it is a wise caregiver who can quickly find an acceptable substitute goal for the baby or in some way distract attention to another interesting stimulus.

Significance of the community in social development

Most babies spend more time within the context of the family than away from it. While many babies have frequent social outings, these are usually taken with a caregiver and thus are still "family" activities. Increasingly, mothers are returning to work after they have their babies, so that provisions must be made for the infant's care while the mother and father are both away from home. Some parents choose to use a baby-sitter (grandparent, relative, other adult) who either comes into the family home or takes the baby into his or her own home, thus maintaining a family atmosphere. Other parents choose to use a professional day care center for their child's care. Infants can adapt to and do well with more than one primary caregiver. The important consideration is choosing child care that provides consistent, long-term, nurturing care.

It is not possible to discuss the effects of all the possible permutations of infant care in this chapter. (Indeed, the effects are not well known.) However, the following section will include a brief review of the significance of infant day care centers on infant socialization.

Infant day care. In infant day care situations, a few adults provide care for several infants. This poses certain limitations on the establishment of close, one-to-one relationships between infants and caregivers. Most infant day care centers are aware of the importance of consistency and sameness in an infant's life and will make efforts to have one or two adults care for the same babies every day to provide a measure of continuity. However, there are problems. Infants are brought to day care centers early in the morning before the hour that the parent must be at his or her own job. They are picked up to be taken home late in the afternoon or early evening, after the parent has finished work and perhaps run a few errands. An infant's time at the day care center averages eight and a half to ten hours a day. Employees of day care centers usually work eight hour days, and, in addition, may leave for holidays, vacations, lunch or coffee breaks, and sick days. In spite of efforts to have just one or two adults provide most of the care for any given infant, that infant, in fact, will experience an array of caregivers over time. Infants will also experience the need to share their favorite caregiver (the one to whom they become most attached) with other infants. They will have experiences of waiting and watching while other infants are being held, cuddled, fed, changed, and entertained by their adult. If they become sick, their caregiving is either taken over by a relatively unfamiliar nurse in the day care center, or they must remain at home, often with an equally unfamiliar babysitter. However, in spite of some of these roadblocks to establishing caregiving characterized by consistency, continuity, and sameness, many day care centers do a good job of providing sensitive attention to each infant's individual needs.

The research we have on the effects of day care centers on an infant's social-emotional development shows very little harm occurring from such caregiving. Caldwell, Honig, Wright, and Tannenbaum studied mother-infant attachment behaviors in infants who spent full days with their mothers and infants who spent eight or more hours a day in a center for five days of every week.[66] They found the day care center babies as attached to their mothers as the home-reared infants. The group care experience had not interfered with a close interpersonal bond forming between infants and their natural mothers. Some day care centers have found that the effects of quality care in a center can have a carry-over effect in the homes. This has been especially demonstrated by research programs where parents have been involved in the center's activities and where staff from the center have made visits to the various infants' homes.[67,68] Keister assessed day care and matched home-reared infants on many variables of development, cognitive as well as social, and found that there were few substantial differences on any measures.[69] Long-term effects of day care have been assessed in countries like Israel where infants once raised in group settings on kibbutzim are now adults. Rabin suggested that prior to age ten some kibbutz-reared children show shallowness in their interpersonal relations, but this disappears.[70] By adulthood they are considered to be among the most responsible and stable citizens of the country.[71]

These researches have all been conducted on infants given very high quality group care. While they demonstrate that group care need not be detrimental, they do not suggest that it is better than care by a single caregiver or a single family unit.

Hospitalization. Research reports on the effects of infant-caregiver separation for hospitalization are in contrast to the findings of little or no emotional trauma engendered by day care separations. The situations, however, differ in many respects. A healthy baby goes to a cheerful, familiar day care center everyday. A sick baby goes to a busy, unfamiliar hospital for the first time in his or her memory. It is far easier to adjust to a new environment where substitute caregivers behave like primary caregivers (e.g., holding, talking, entertaining with toys) than to accept a setting where a multitude of strange adults poke, pry, and administer painful or distasteful treatments and medicines.

Research on the effects of hospitalization show a steady change in a baby's behavior over time, related to the length of the hospital stay. Robertson classified these changes into three progressive stages: protest, despair, and denial.[72] They are illustrated in the following vignette.

An eighteen-month-old baby enters the hospital in his mother's arms, sick and frightened. A stranger in white takes him from his mother and carries him to a strange room, past other staring or crying or busy people. She places him in an unfamiliar, cagelike crib and undresses him. His mother is requested to leave the room. His clothes disappear. Other strangers approach, stick cold things in him, hold him down, tell him to stop crying. When they finally go away, they pull bars up around him. Mother eventually reappears and is crying. She says she must leave, and does. He feels sick, hurt, rejected, frightened. He shakes the crib bars and screams (protest). For a day or two the protesting is vigorous. He calls for his mother when she is gone and cries when she is present. He is not only uncomfortable from the illness (or other reason for hospitalization) but also angry at everyone who approaches. He is grief-stricken each time his mother or other family members depart. Gradually his behavior becomes subdued, passive, more obedient. He is "settled-in." He starts to keep his emotions bottled inside rather than exhausting himself with futile protests. He may regress in feeding and/or toileting practices (despair). For the next few days he becomes increasingly more pleasant toward the hospital staff and more and more hostile toward his family. If he is hospitalized for an extended period, he withdraws attachment behaviors from all adults. He appears self-sufficient, even happy. He hardly notices when adults, especially his primary caregiver(s) come and go (denial). If a baby is separated long enough to begin denying his attachments to loved adults, his normal social-emotional development may be in jeopardy. It may take an extended period of time for him to learn to trust his caregiver(s) again. When the baby is discharged from the hospital, another series of behaviors are typical. At first he is withdrawn. He warms up to auxiliary family members first. For hours, or days, he demonstrates hostility toward his primary caregiver. He demands things and is jealous of his siblings. Then for several days he clings to his primary caregiver. He also is defiant, destructive, disobedient, and negativistic. He must relearn feeding, dressing, and any bowel or bladder control. For weeks he remains babyish, anxious, fearful, has sleep difficulties and nightmares, is easily angered, and has temper tantrums. If his parents treat him with sympathy and love, in a few months he will probably recover from his trauma.

These behaviors, as reported by Robertson and many other researchers, can be alleviated to a great extent by unrestricted visiting privileges or rooming-in for the primary caregiver during the baby's hospitalization. However, factors such as the nature of the child's illness, the necessities of caring for other children at home, or the primary caregiver's emotionality may make frequent visiting imprudent. The worst age period for hospital-based separation from the primary caregiver(s) is from about seven months to three years.[73] Prior to seven months, attachments may not be fully developed. After age three, a child begins to understand reasons for the separation and hospitalization.

Health considerations

The first month of life is a high-risk period in terms of health of an infant. During this time the neonate's respiratory and digestive systems are becoming acclimated to extrauterine existence. The majority of full-term, normal birth weight infants are able to make the transition successfully. The remainder of the first and second years of life still have health hazards, but as infants mature, their defenses against disease become better. First, we will describe caregivers' behaviors that help sustain and enhance life and health in infancy. Following this we will review some of the more common health problems of babies, both during the neonatal period and through the first two years of life.

Health maintenance

Although we discussed physical and emotional development separately in this chapter, they are, in fact, inseparable in the human being. Health maintenance, as suggested previously, demands more than just providing for physiological needs. It also requires careful attention to emotional needs. Trust and attachment are important elements in the feeling of well-being that contributes to actual health.

One of the most important ways in which caregivers first provide for both physiological and emotional health is by supplying appropriate nutrients in a loving manner. Neonates' initial requirements are for colostrum (the thin, sweet, fluid first produced by the breasts before milk comes in) or sweetened water. By the third or fourth postnatal day, they will require breast milk or formula. Caregivers have the responsibility to ensure that the nutrients provided are appropriate, germ free, available when requested in sufficient supply, and offered concurrently with tender touching to assuage the "contact hunger" of infants. As infants mature, it is necessary to add to the diet to ensure that babies have sufficient protein, iron, calcium, and vitamins for the most active growth period of their life. Contact hunger and the need for cognitive stimulation also grow, not diminish, during the early months of life.

A second important aspect of infant health maintenance is protection from infection. While some degree of immunity from pathogens to which the mother is immune is passed on prenatally, the infant is still highly susceptible to disease. Persons with known active infections (e.g., colds, influenza, "strep" or "staph" infections) should not kiss and cuddle or even be in contact with infants. If the primary caregiver becomes ill, another person should help meet the baby's needs until the caregiver can recover.

Because infant skin is so sensitive, it must be protected, especially from sun and from diaper rash. Diaper rashes are common, even in the cleanest homes, because of the ammonia that forms from urine in wet diapers. It burns and irritates the skin, causing redness and/or blisters. Protective powders or creams may be necessary to supplement prompt changing of wet diapers if rashes are common. If blisters become infected, further diagnosis and treatment are required.

Many infections that contributed in the past to high infant mortality and morbidity in later life can now be prevented through a series of immunizations: diphtheria, whooping cough (pertussis), tetanus, poliomyelitis, measles, mumps, and rubella (also typhoid fever and tuberculosis—depending on locale). All babies should be taken to a private physician or well-baby clinic for immunizations, assessment of infant development, and guidance in diet progression. The usual schedule is for three immunizations for DPT-OPV (diphtheria, whooping cough, tetanus, and oral polio vaccine) and one for measles, mumps, and rubella at approximately monthly intervals as decided by the physician. Injections are not given at the scheduled visit if an infant has an active upper respiratory infection or other illness. The exact timing of immunizations is not nearly as important as the fact that the infant receive all of the injections eventually.[74]

Regularly scheduled visits to a doctor's office or clinic during infancy are important for health maintenance above and beyond immunizations (see Figure 3–10). Trained personnel are able to weigh, measure, and examine the baby and determine the presence of any possible disorders or developmental delays that may require attention. They can provide counseling for questions and problems. Establishing contact with medical supervisors also aids the supervisors' capacity to respond appropriately to patients in emergencies.

An additional important aspect of health maintenance for infants is accident prevention. In the social development section of this chapter, we stressed household engineering to prevent mishaps, especially when babies become mobile. It is worth repeating. Infants must be protected from falls: out of cribs or playpens, down open stairwells, off furniture. They must be kept away from open fires, matches, hot stoves, hot radiators, and out of the paths of motor vehicles. Poisons, pins and nails, and any small objects that could be swallowed must be kept out of reach.

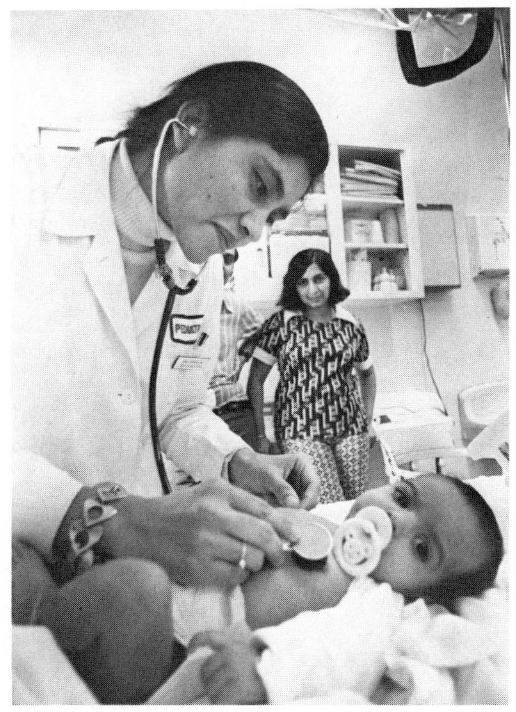

Figure 3–10. *Regular well-baby examinations by a pediatrician, family practitioner, or nurse practitioner prevent many health problems and identify others before they become serious.*
Forsyth/Monkmeyer Press Photo Service

Any large containers of water (bathtubs, swimming pools) are also hazardous. Finally, infants must be taught to respect and obey the command "no" for their own safety's sake.

Common health problems in infancy

Infections of the digestive system and the respiratory tract are the leading health problems of infants from birth to one year of age in the United States. From one to two years of age, accidents and respiratory infections cause the most difficulty.[75]

Colic is a very common problem in infants between about one week and three months. It is characterized by excessive crying, drawn-up arms and legs, reddened face, and hardened abdomen following feedings. Both suspected causes and methods for treating colic are numerous. A colicky baby may suffer from an immature nervous system, an intestinal disorder, a food allergy, excessive air swallowing, too rapid feeding, overfeeding, or may be responding to his mother's nervousness with tenseness of his own digestive system. Reasons for colic may differ from infant to infant. The problem usually disappears on its own at about three months. Until it does, doctors may advise caregivers to try changing formulas, feeding smaller amounts more frequently, giving cold formula, burping the baby more frequently, applying hot water bottles to the abdomen, rocking or walking the baby, or sedating him or her with drugs.

Diarrhea and vomiting are also frequent problems in young infants and are usually related to irritation of the digestive system by new foods, contaminated foods, or ingestion of nonfood substances. Because infants become dehydrated very quickly when they lose fluids due to the smaller total fluid volume of their bodies, diarrhea and vomiting must be treated promptly.

Respiratory illnesses common in infancy include croup, influenza, colds, bronchitis, pneumonia, and ear infections. Research points to the fact that infants living in homes where two or more people smoke run twice as much risk of having frequent respiratory illnesses, including attacks of pneumonia or bronchitis, as infants in homes where nobody smokes.[76]

Croup is a mild form of laryngitis common in infancy and is rarely serious unless complicated with other infections. Croup produces a loud spasmodic cough that can be very frightening. It may sound like the infant is strangling. Humidifiers generally liquefy the secretions blocking the larynx and thus relieve the coughing spasms.

Influenza and colds are more common between age six months (when immunities from birth wear off) and age two. Fevers are seldom present. However, the nasal passages may become filled with thick, bubbling mucus. Decongestants are usually prescribed promptly to prevent the infecting agent from obstructing breathing or entering the eustachian tube. Ear infections are common sequelae to colds because the eustachian tube is short and wide in infants. Ear infections must be treated promptly to prevent rupture of the eardrum and possible hearing loss from tissue destruction.

The heartbreaking syndrome of crib death, known as sudden infant death syndrome (SIDS), in which apparently normal, well-developed infants suddenly stop breathing, is being studied intensively in many centers. Though the fundamental cause of SIDS is unknown, efforts are made to identify infants who have frequent apnea (inability to get a breath) episodes in the hospital. These infants are watched closely. At discharge from the hospital their caregivers may be instructed to monitor breathing with the help of a machine that signals apnea occurrences. Usually just moving the baby is enough to restore breathing. Someone from the baby's family must always be close enough to hear the monitor in case it should give its warning ring. As the infant matures, the apnea episodes become less frequent and are eventually outgrown. The monitor can then be returned to the hospital for use with another potential SIDS baby.

Approximately one-fifth of all children experience at least one significant accident per year.[77] In infancy the most common accidents are from falls, aspiration of foreign bodies in attempts to swallow them, from burns, poisonings, and from motor vehicle mishaps. Should a serious accident occur, the baby should be rushed to the nearest doctor's office or hospital with someone telephoning ahead. If the problem is aspiration, and the infant chokes and turns blue, a caregiver should first try to dislodge the object blocking the airway with the Heimlich Method. Make a fist and press it just under the rib cage with a sudden thrust. (The other hand may be used to push the fist in and upward.) This may be repeated several times if necessary. In many cases this sudden pressure between the navel and rib cage will cause the obstructing object to be dispelled from the trachea much as a cork pops from a bottle. If the infant has swallowed poison, water should be given to dilute it and then, with certain exceptions, the baby should be made to vomit. This can be accomplished by tickling the back of the throat with a blunt object, or by giving one tablespoon (15 cc, 1/2 ounce) of syrup of ipecac in a cup (240 cc, 8 ounces) of water. Do not induce vomiting if the infant has swallowed strong acid, lye, or petroleum products (gasoline, kerosene, paint thinner).

Iron deficiency anemia is the most common infant and adult nutritional disorder in the United States. Many babies do not get enough iron from their diets of milk, cereals, fruits, and mixed dinners (usually containing more vegetables than meats). An iron deficient infant appears pale and tires easily. Unless iron is supplemented, or iron rich foods are added to the diet, both physical and mental growth can be stunted. Severe malnutrition problems such as kwashiorkor (lack of protein), rickets (lack of vitamin D), and scurvy (lack of vitamin C) are also occasionally seen in the United States in areas where families live on marginal incomes and find it difficult to buy meats, fruits, and vitamin-fortified products. Ignorance and negligence may also produce the same effect.

Eczema is an allergic reaction to one or more things and is characterized by inflammation of the skin and intense itching. It may be a wet form with running sores or a dry form with bright red patches of scales. The tendency to become allergic is inherited, but an infant's eczema may be a reaction to a food or substance quite different from the food or substance to which the parents are allergic. Doctors frequently have difficult times determining the source(s) of the infant's problem. Until they do, medication is usually prescribed to help relieve the itching.

An increasing amount of heart surgery is being done to repair congenital anomalies in early life for compelling reasons. Some of the other frequent reasons for surgery in infancy are repair of cleft lip or palate, repair of intussusceptions (a telescoping of one portion of the intestine into another), hernias (outpouching of a portion of the intestine), and hydroceles (accumulation of fluid around the testes). Any surgery that can wait until a baby is three years or older is usually delayed because of the traumatic effects of hospitalization and separation from caregivers during infancy.

Child abuse

Physical abuse of infants and children (called the "battered child syndrome") is distressingly common in our society. Each year in the United States over 700 children are killed and thousands more given serious physical and mental injuries by adults—primarily their caregivers.[78] Child abuse is defined as the intentional, nonaccidental use of physical force, or intentional nonaccidental acts of omission, on the part of a parent or other caregiver interacting with a child in his or her care, aimed at hurting, injuring, or destroying that child.[79] It is not a new phenomenon. However, research studies and media reporting have only recently brought it out from behind closed doors and into national awareness. In the early 1970s many states passed new laws making it easier for doctors, nurses, social workers, and law enforcement officers to report cases of child neglect or abuse.

Research indicates that abusive adults can be found in all socioeconomic levels in our society and in all ethnic groups. Many factors, singly or in combination, contribute to high risk situations in which child abuse is more likely to occur.

While adults with particular problems of neurosis, sadism, or sociopathic personality may be abusive, a battered child is not evidence of such pathology. More often, very normal adults become abusive due to situations of environmental stress of such magnitude that they lose their self-control.[80] If adults have no sources of support when they are under stress, they may become excessively aggressive or violent out of frustration.

Research also suggests a strong connection between the behavior of abusive adults and their own experiences of being punished in childhood.[81] An attitude of permissiveness, even approval, of childrearing tactics involving excessive aggression and use of physical force may be passed on from generation to generation. Family patterns of childrearing involving minimal demonstrations of affection and a lack of emotional warmth in parent-child interactions may also be learned behaviors.

Our relatively recent awareness of the prevalence of battered children in our society has led to new programs to help abusive parents and to intervene on behalf of injured children. Effective programs for adults should be multidisciplinary to provide aid in the many areas in which they suffer their seemingly insurmountable stresses and to educate them in areas of self-control and childrearing techniques. Programs for parents should also not be incriminating. Self-help groups and parents anonymous programs are especially effectual.[82] Programs for children, such as specialized day care centers, should emphasize the affectionate, trustworthy side of adults. They should also help the abused children overcome their feelings of unworthiness and develop more positive self-concepts. With increased understanding of the factors involved in the battered child syndrome, with increased efforts to provide intervention and treatment facilities in our communities, and with concern for psychological as well as physical health maintenance practices in our homes, it is hoped that child abuse (as well as other forms of violence in our society) will soon begin a downward spiral.

Summary

The primary ecological setting of infancy is the home and family. However, as babies mature they are increasingly affected by higher order ecological systems in the neighborhood and community.

The neonatal period (birth to one month) is a high-risk period in the life of the new human being. Neonates are dependent on others to meet their needs for food, warmth, tender loving care, and protection from infectious agents.

Growth and change are rapid in the first two years of life. Babies double their birth weight by about five months, triple it by one year, and quadruple it by two years. They add about twenty-four centimeters to their length in the first year and about twelve more centimeters in the second year.

Piaget described a sensory-motor stage to explain the cognitive changes that occur during infancy. In six progressively more complex phases, babies move from predominant exercise of preexisting reflexes to actions that require remembering and planning.

Learning to talk has its roots in receptive language. The baby listens to communications of others and begins to sort out meanings of words. Expressive language (talking) usually begins with nouns (e.g., mama, dada, nana, papa). Verbs are usually added next. Holophrases, which are one-word sentences, may consist of nouns or verbs (e.g., "Up"; "Bottle"). Eventually the baby begins to string nouns and verbs together (e.g., "Daddy come"). Early speech is described as telegraphic because, as in telegrams, only the most salient words are reproduced.

Tender loving care is a crucial ingredient in the make-up of emotionally healthy infants. Babies show contact hunger as well as nutrient hunger. They become attached to their primary caregivers and show joy at reunion and anxiety at separation. Erikson described the most crucial social learning in infancy as trust, a sense of confidence and reliance in the caregivers. Trust develops when caregivers are consistent with schedules and discipline as well as sensitive to the baby's needs.

Babies show individual differences early: in motor abilities, physical stature, sleep-wake cycles, activity levels, disposition, and adaptability. Babies shape their caregivers' behaviors as well as respond to them. While the mother or father is usually the primary caregiver, babies are exposed to varying amounts of contact with other adults and children through such things as visits, walks, shopping, baby-sitters or attendance at day care centers.

Health maintenance requires providing psychological care (the tender touch) and stimulation as well as physical care. Nutrition, rest, and shelter are important aspects of physical care. Infections should be treated promptly. Many infections can be prevented through a series of immunizations. Safety precautions to prevent accidents become important as the infant learns to roll over, sit, crawl, then walk.

Questions for review

1. What might be the developmental consequences for an infant who receives little or no stimulation?
2. The number of women in the labor force has been increasing over the past twenty years. Many of these women are placing their infants in day care centers. Discuss the pros and cons for families. In your discussion, consider the needs of all family members—mother, father, and child.
3. Infants require a great deal of attention to both their physical and psychological needs. Describe some of their psychological needs.
4. Describe the process that occurs immediately after birth, when the baby adapts from intrauterine to extrauterine life.
5. Discuss how families can foster cognitive development in infancy.
6. The rate of teenage pregnancy has been a concern for a number of years. The rate of infant abuse and infant neglect among very young mothers is often high. Describe why this might be so. Consider the various demands of a developing infant in your discussion.
7. A common way of dealing with child abuse and child neglect is removal of the child from his or her home. Discuss the pros and cons of such a program of intervention.
8. Children may reside in foster homes for a number of years, often being moved from one home to another. Consider the future implications of this lifestyle on such children. Speculate as to the resolution of Erikson's trust-mistrust conflict in these situations. Also, discuss the consequences regarding the formation of the attachment bond.

References

[1]J. Basmajian, *Grant's Method of Anatomy*, 9th ed. (Baltimore: The Williams and Wilkins Co., 1975).

[2]V. Broadribb, *Foundations of Pediatric Nursing* (Philadelphia: J. B. Lippincott Co., 1967).

[3]R. Wennberg, D. Woodrum, and W. Hodson, "The Perinate," *The Biological Ages of Man*, D. Smith and E. Bierman, eds. (Philadelphia: W. B. Saunders Co., 1973).

[4]B. King and M. Showers, *Human Anatomy and Physiology*, 5th ed. (Philadelphia: W. B. Saunders Co., 1963).

[5]E. Bickerstaff, *Neurology for Nurses* (London: English Universities Press, Ltd., 1971).

[6]King and Showers, *Human Anatomy and Physiology.*

[7]A. Dekaban, *Neurology of Early Childhood* (Baltimore: The Williams and Wilkins Co., 1970).

[8]Ibid.

[9]J. Crough, *Human Anatomy and Physiology*, 2nd ed. (New York: Wiley, 1976).

[10]S. Robbins, *Pathologic Basis of Disease* (Philadelphia: W. B. Saunders Co., 1974).

[11]W. Nelson, V. Vaughn, and R. McKay, *Textbook of Pediatrics*, 10th ed. (Philadelphia: W. B. Saunders Co., 1975).

[12]R. Bailey, *The Role of the Brain* (New York: Time, Inc., 1975).

[13]W. Nelson, V. Vaughn, and R. McKay, *Textbook of Pediatrics.*

[14]D. Marlow, *Textbook of Pediatric Nursing* (Philadelphia: W. B. Saunders Co., 1973).

[15]M. Moore, *The Newborn and the Nurse* (Philadelphia: W. B. Saunders Co., 1972).

[16]W. Nelson, V. Vaughn, and R. McKay, *Textbook of Pediatrics.*

[17]M. Moore, *The Newborn and the Nurse.*

[18]F. Ilg and L. Ames. *The Gesell Institute's Child Behavior* (New York: Harper and Brothers, 1955).

[19]W. Nelson, V. Vaughn, and R. McKay, *Textbook of Pediatrics.*

[20]Ibid.

[21]K. Holt, *Developmental Pediatrics* (Reading, Mass.: Butterworths Inc., 1977).

[22]M. Winick, "Nutritional Disorders During Brain Development," *The Nervous System, vol. II: The Clinical Neurosciences*, D. Tower and T. Chase, eds. (New York: Raven Press, 1975).

[23]S. Fomon, *Infant Nutrition* (Philadelphia: W. B. Saunders Co., 1967).

[24]S. Fomon and E. Ziegler, "Food and the Child," *Childhood* (Chicago: Blue Cross Association, 1976).

[25]M. Steggerda and J. Hill, "Eruption Time of Teeth Among Whites, Negroes, and Indians," *American Journal of Orthodontics and Oral Surgery*, 26 (1942).

[26]J. Kagan, "Do Infants Think?," *Scientific American*, 226 (3) (March 1972).

[27]T. Bower, *Development in Infancy* (San Francisco: W. H. Freeman and Co., 1974).

[28]H. Ginsburg and S. Opper, *Piaget's Theory of Intellectual Development* (Englewood Cliffs, N.J.: Prentice-Hall, Inc., 1969).

[29]J. Phillips, *The Origins of Intellect: Piaget's Theory* (San Francisco: W. H. Freeman and Co., 1969).

[30]H. Ginsburg and S. Opper, *Piaget's Theory of Intellectual Development.*

[31]H. Maier, *Three Theories of Child Development* (New York: Harper and Row, 1969).

[32]H. Ginsburg and S. Opper, *Piaget's Theory of Intellectual Development.*

[33]H. Maier, *Three Theories of Child Development.*

[34]H. Ginsburg and S. Opper, *Piaget's Theory of Intellectual Development.*

[35]J. Kagan, "Do Infants Think?"

[36]Ibid.

[37]B. Friedlander, "Receptive Language Development in Infancy," *The Competent Infant*, L. Stone, H. Smith, and L. Murphy, eds. (New York: Basic Books, 1973).

[38]P. Eimas, E. Şiqueland, P. Jusczyk, and J. Vigorito, "Speech Perception in Infants," *The Competent Infant*, L. Stone, H. Smith, and L. Murphy, eds. (New York: Basic Books, 1973).

[39]P. Wolff, "The Natural History of Crying and Other Vocalizations in Early Infancy," *Determinants of Infant Behavior*, vol. IV, B. Foss, ed. (London: Methuen & Co., Ltd., 1969).

[40]J. Piaget, *The Origins of Intelligence in Children*, M. Cook, Trans. (New York: International Universities Press, 1952).

[41]J. Deese, *Psycholinguistics* (Boston: Allyn and Bacon, Inc., 1970).

[42]D. Slobin, "They Learn the Same Way All Around the World," *Psychology Today*, 6 (1972).

[43]N. Chomsky, *Language and Mind* (New York: Harcourt, Brace, Jovanovich, Inc., 1972).

[44]R. Haaf and R. Bell, "A Social Dimension in Visual Discrimination by Human Infants," *Child Development*, 38 (1967).

[45]J. Watson, "Smiling, Cooing and the Game," *Merrill-Palmer Quarterly*, 18 (1973).

[46]J. Hunt, "How Children Develop Intellectually," *Children*, 11 (3) (1964).

[47]H. Ricciuti, "Emotional Development in the First Two Years," Unpublished manuscript prepared for adaptation in *Developmental Psychology: An Introduction* (New York: CRM Books / Random House, 1970).

[48]R. Spitz, "Hospitalism: An Inquiry into the Genesis of Psychiatric Conditions in Early Childhood," *Psychoanalytic Study of the Child*, 1 (1945).

[49]W. Dennis and P. Najarian, "Infant Development Under Environmental Handicap," *Psychological Monographs*, 71 (Whole No. 436) (1957).

[50]W. Dennis, "Causes of Retardation Among Institutional Children: Iran." *Journal of Genetic Psychology*, 96 (1960).

[51]H. Harlow and M. Harlow, "The Affectional Systems," *Behavior of Nonhuman Primates, vol. II*, A. Schrier, H. Harlow, and F. Stollnitz, eds. (New York: Academic Press, 1965).

[52]R. Wahler, "Infant Social Attachments: A Reinforcement Theory Interpretation and Investigation," *Child Development*, 38 (1967).

[53]L. Yarrow, "Separation from Parents During Early Childhood," *Review of Child Development Research: vol. I*, M. Hoffman and L. Hoffman, eds. (New York: Russell Sage Foundation, 1964).

[54]H. Ricciuti, "Emotional Development in the First Two Years."

[55]M. Ainsworth, S. Bell, and D. Stayton, "Individual Differences in Strange-Situation Behavior of One-Year-Olds," *The Origins of Human Social Relations*, H. Schaffer, ed. (London: Academic Press, 1972).

[56]E. Erikson, *Childhood and Society*, 2nd ed. (New York: W. W. Norton & Co., 1963).

[57]A. Thomas, S. Chess, H. Birch, M. Hertzig, and S. Korn, *Behavioral Individuality in Early Childhood* (New York: New York University Press, 1963).

[58]A. Korner, "Individual Differences at Birth: Implications for Early Experience and Later Development," *American Journal of Orthopsychiatry* (1971).

[59]S. Chess, A. Thomas, and H. Birch, *Your Child Is A Person* (New York: Viking Press, 1972).

[60]H. Moss, "Sex, Age, and State as Determinants of Mother-Infant Interaction," *Merrill-Palmer Quarterly*, 13 (1) (1967).

[61]S. Bell and M. Ainsworth, "Infant Crying and Maternal Responsiveness," *Child Development and Behavior*, F. Rebelsky and L. Dorman, eds. (New York: Alfred A. Knopf, 1973).

[62]H. Moss, "Sex, Age, and State as Determinants of Mother-Infant Interaction."

[63]J. Kagan, "Continuity in Cognitive Development During the First Year," *Merrill-Palmer Quarterly*, 15 (1969).

[64]S. Goldberg and M. Lewis, "Play Behavior in the Year-Old Infant: Early Sex Differences," *Child Development*, 40 (1969).

[65]E. Erikson, *Childhood and Society.*

[66]B. Caldwell, C. Wright, A. Honig, and J. Tannenbaum, "Infant Day Care and Attachment," *American Journal of Orthopsychiatry*, 40 (3) (1970).

[67]D. Weikart and D. Lambie, "Preschool Intervention Through a Home Teaching Program," *Disadvantaged Child, vol. II*, J. Hellmuth, ed. (New York: Brunner/Mazel, 1968).

[68]I. Gordon, "Early Stimulation Through Parent Education," *Final Report: Institute for Development of Human Resources* (Gainsville, Fla.: submitted to U.S.D.H.E.W., Children's Bureau, June 1969).

[69]M. Keister, *The Good Life for Infants and Toddlers: Report on a Demonstration Project* (Washington, D.C.: National Association for the Education of Young Children, 1970).

[70]A. Rabin, "Infants and Children Under Conditions of Intermittent Mothering in the Kibbutz," *American Journal of Orthopsychiatry*, 28 (1958).

[71]M. Kaffman, "Comparative Psychopathology of Kibbutz and Urban Children," *Children in Collectives*, P. Neubauer, ed. (Springfield, Ill.: Charles C. Thomas, 1965).

[72]J. Robertson, *Hospitals and Children: A Parent's Eye View* (New York: International Universities Press, Inc., 1962).

[73]M. Petrillo and S. Sanger, *Emotional Care of Hospitalized Children* (Philadelphia: J. B. Lippincott Co., 1972).

[74]W. Nelson, V. Vaughn, and R. McKay, *Textbook of Pediatrics.*

[75]W. Wenner and B. Veer, "Infancy: The First Two Years," *The Biological Ages of Man*, D. Smith and E. Bierman, eds. (Philadelphia: W. B. Saunders Co., 1973).

[76]J. Colley, W. Holland, and R. Corkhill, "Influence of Passive Smoking and Parental Phlegm on Pneumonia and Bronchitis in Early Childhood," *The Lancet* (November 2, 1974).

[77]W. Wenner and B. Veer, "Infancy: The First Two Years."

[78]D. Gil, *Violence Against Children: Physical Abuse in the United States* (Cambridge, Mass.: Harvard University Press, 1970).

[79]Ibid.

[80]J. Garbarino, "A Preliminary Study of Some Ecological Correlates of Child Abuse: The Impact of Socioeconomic Stress on Mothers," *Child Development*, 47 (1) (1976).

[81]B. Steele, "Intra-familial Violence and Child Abuse," Paper presented at the An-

nual Meeting of the National Council on Family Relations, Chicago, Oct. 7–10, 1970.

[82]N. Ebeling and D. Hill, *Child Abuse: Intervention and Treatment* (Acton, Mass.: Publishing Sciences Group, 1975).

Contents

Joanna Prudden Snyder

Early Childhood

Somewhere between eighteen and thirty months of age infants develop motor coordination and speech skills to such an extent that their parents and other adults view them as toddlers rather than as babies. They walk, they have increased success with talking, and they strive for a measure of self-reliance and independence. This chapter will describe the various aspects of physical development, cognitive and language development, social development, and health separately as in other chapters. However, these boundaries serve only to help the reader visualize the developments in each area more clearly. Remember that young children develop in all ways each day. Keep in mind that physical growth influences cognition, language, social development, and health. Likewise, cognition, language, and social development have an interactive effect on each other and can also affect physical growth and health. Try, if you can, to visualize children you know (or have known) who are approximately ages two, three, four, and five. Keep each whole child in mind as you read about development in the separate areas. The two-year-old is quite different from the five-year-old. In each section the contrasts between younger and older children will be stated. Early childhood in this text will include the period of time between infancy and elementary school. (Elementary does not include nursery school or day care.) Late childhood (to be described in the next chapter) will encompass the years from beginning elementary school to adolescence. Within early childhood two other age parameters will occasionally be used: toddlers and preschoolers. Toddlers are younger children, ages two and three. Preschoolers are children ages four and five.

Physical development

The rate of growth in the early childhood years is slower than in infancy but follows the same general principles. Development proceeds from head to foot (cephalocaudal direction), from the center outwards (proximal-distal direction), and from general to specific movements (see Figure 3-4, page 93). Consider these examples. To illustrate cephalocaudal development, let us look at head and leg circumferences of five-year-olds. Mean head circumference is approximately fifty centimeters, or about 90 percent of its adult size.[1] In contrast, leg circumference is only about twenty-two and a half centimeters, less than 45 percent of its adult size.[2] As an example of proximal-distal development, the young child will develop the ability to use the muscles of the upper arms (pushing) and upper legs (jumping) long before the ability to use the finger muscles (molding clay) or toe muscles (picking up marbles) develops. To illustrate the principle of development from general to specific, consider finger muscles again. First, the young child will have the gross motor ability to push a lump of clay from round to flat then to round again. Later, the fine muscles will acquire the necessary coordination to push the clay into a shape roughly resembling what the child desires.

Physical changes occur at a relatively slow, even, and continuous pace. Only occasionally will starts and stops be noticeable. Sometimes a child will concentrate so intently on one aspect of development (e.g., tricycle riding) that other emerging abilities will seem to falter or even regress (e.g., sphincter muscle control). Most children will also show some seasonal variations in the speed of their growth. Data from European and American sources show that increases in height occur more rapidly in the spring, while increases in weight occur more rapidly in the fall.[3] Illnesses and periods of malnutrition can temporarily slow children's rates of growth, but when diseases are cured or missing nutrients supplied, a catch-up phenomenon usually occurs. Exceptions depend on the length and severity of the disease or malnourished state and on the organs affected. The brain is more susceptible to permanent injury because its cells are not replaced once they are destroyed.[4] (To some extent, other brain cells may take over the functions of missing cells.)

For you to appreciate some of the physical changes that occur in early childhood, motor norms (the average motor achievements by age for a large number of children) will be presented. Then some of the physical differences between children of ages two, three, four, and five will be discussed. Finally, the factors involved in the development of increased neuromuscular skills in early childhood will be considered.

Arnold Gesell (introduced in Chapter 3, page 92) and his colleagues at the Yale Clinic of Child Development (later at the Gesell Institute of Child Development) accumulated an impressive amount of information about children's age-related behaviors from the 1930s through

Table 4–1. *DDST gross and fine motor accomplishments of early childhood.*

Gross motor accomplishments	*Age range in years*	*Fine motor accomplishments*	*Age range in years*
Throws ball overhand	2–2½	Imitates vertical line	2–3
Balances on one foot 1 second	2–3¼	Dumps raisin from bottle	2–3
Jumps in place	2–3	Builds tower of 8 cubes	2–3¼
Pedals tricycle	2–3	Copies circle	2¼–3¼
Broad jumps	2–3¼	Imitates bridge with 3 cubes	2¼–3½
Balances on one foot 5 seconds	2½–4¼	Picks longer line, 3 of 3	2½–4¼
Balances on one foot 10 seconds	3–6	Copies plus sign	2¾–4½
Hops on one foot	3–5	Draws man, 3 parts	3¼–5
Heel to toe walk	3¼–5	Imitates square (demonstrated)	3½–5½
Catches bounced ball	3½–5½	Copies square	4½–6
Backward heel to toe walk	3¾–6	Draws man, 6 parts	4½–6

Source: Adapted from Frankenburg and Dodds, Denver Developmental Screening Test (DDST) University of Colorado Medical Center, 1967.

the 1950s.[5, 6, 7] Their developmental rating scales, the *Gesell Developmental Schedules*, give milestones that typical children accomplish at each of several ages between four weeks and six years. These scales, which are widely used, separate behaviors into categories of (1) motor accomplishments, (2) adaptive behaviors, (3) language skills, and (4) personal-social skills.

Many other normative schedules have been developed that allow an examiner to ascertain how much a child has matured in various areas. Table 4–1 and Figure 4–1 illustrate portions of a scale with greater age flexibility, the *Denver Developmental Screening Test* (DDST). Table 4–1 presents the gross and fine motor accomplishments expected in early childhood. Gross motor accomplishments are those that involve use of the large muscles (e.g., arms, legs). Fine motor tasks are those which require use and coordination of smaller muscles (e.g., fingers).

Figure 4-1 depicts the actual DDST rating sheet used by examiners. It has bars that represent the age span between which 25 percent and 90 percent of children perform each item. It alerts professionals to the possibility of developmental delays so that appropriate diagnostic studies may be pursued. It is *not* designed to give a score of a child's developmental or mental age or a developmental or intelligence quotient (IQ).[8]

The average American two-year-old stands about eighty-one to eighty-four centimeters high (thirty-two to thirty-three inches) and weighs about eleven to thirteen kilograms (twenty-six to twenty-eight pounds).[9] By age five the average American five-year-old stands about 109 to 111 centimeters high (forty-three to forty-four inches) and weights about eighteen to nineteen kilograms (thirty-nine to forty-one pounds). Remember that "average" refers to the sum of many quantities divided by the number of quantities that were added together. No one child should be expected to be average in every respect. Weight gain in early childhood averages about two kilograms (four pounds) per year, and height increases range from six to eight centimeters (two-and-one-half to three-and-one-half inches) per year.[10]

Studies of well-nourished European and American children over the past 100 years have revealed a trend toward increased height each decade.[11] This ever-increasing height phenomenon is still seen in Europe but appears to have leveled off in some affluent sections of the United States. When you next visit a museum with artifacts from bygone eras, notice how much smaller the people must have been to wear or use the items on display.

While the average two-year-old may be about eighty-two centimeters tall and weigh twelve kilograms, there is a wide range of normal heights and weights for children of every age. These can be found by referring to a table of standard measurement percentiles for age (see Figure 4–2). Individual variations in height and weight are influenced by such factors as inheritance, ethnicity, sex, hormones, nutrition, health, and living conditions. Each child's growth in height and weight tends to follow a trajectory (curved path) that maintains its place in relation to other children's height and weight trajectories over time. Thus, a two-year-old child whose length is in the ninetieth percentile can be expected to continue to be tall for his or her age, following the ninetieth percentile trajectory throughout childhood into adulthood. Studies have revealed a correlation of +.76 between height at age three and final adult height.[12] (Weight is more susceptible to dietary factors and cannot be predicted as successfully.) Improvements in nutrition and living conditions can increase height only within certain limits imposed by genetic inheritance and

DENVER DEVELOPMENTAL SCREENING TEST

STO.=STOMACH
SIT=SITTING

PERCENT OF CHILDREN PASSING

Date
Name
Birthdate
Hosp. No.

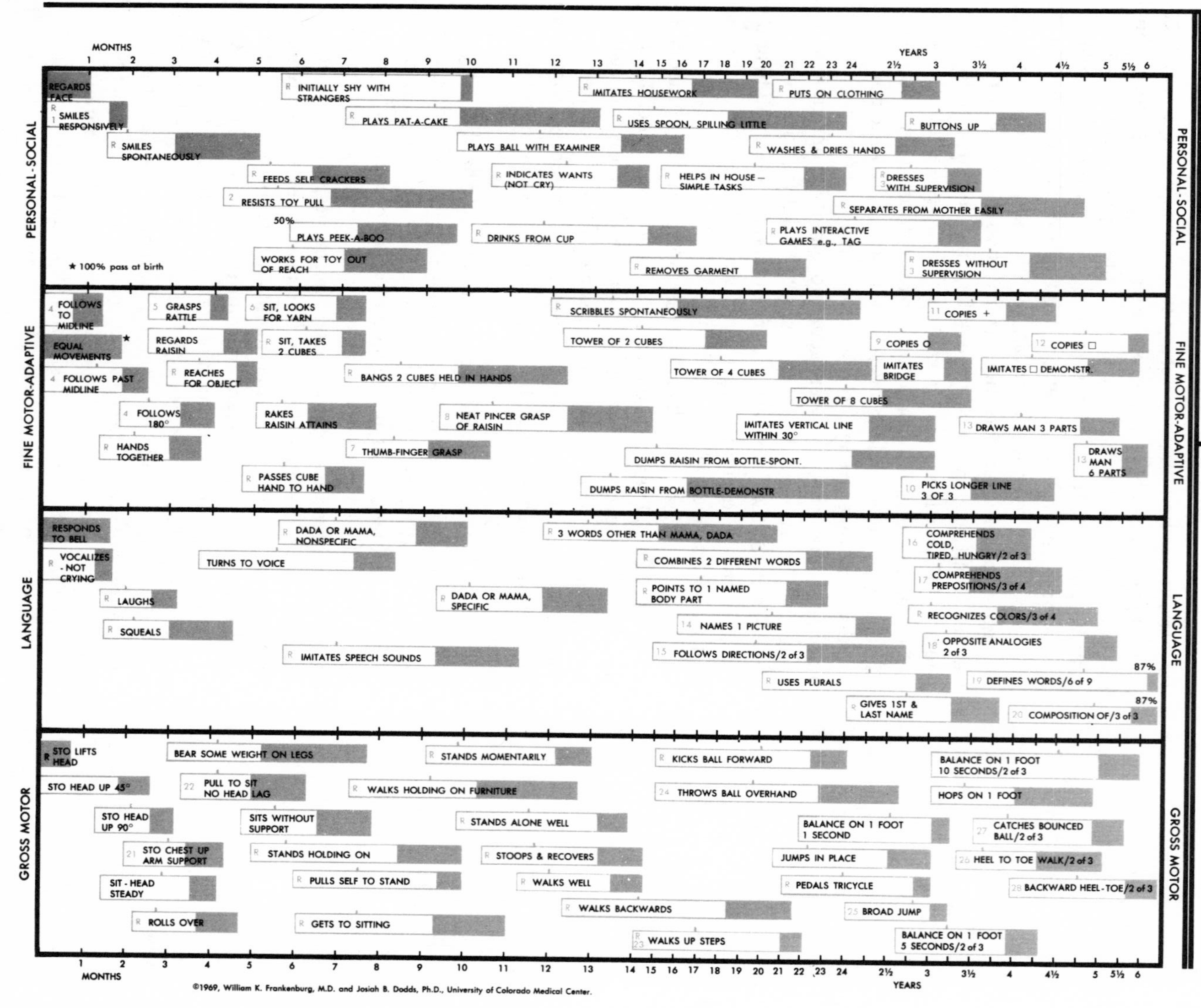

secretions of growth-promoting hormones. Likewise, very deprived conditions are thought to contribute to only about a 5 percent reduction in final mature height.[13]

Arms and legs grow fastest during early childhood, trailed by trunk growth. Head growth follows at a much slower pace, mainly because head circumference has already reached approximately 68 percent of its adult size by age two. It reaches about 70 percent of its adult size by age five.[14] The top-heavy, short-legged appearance of babyhood changes to proportions more nearly resembling those of adults between ages two and five. When two-year-olds bend over, they can usually touch their heads to the floor without bending their knees. By age five they can simply place their hands flat on the floor without bending their knees. When two-year-olds wave good-bye, their arms go straight up without any elbow bending, yet their hands reach only slightly above their heads. Five-year-olds' hands reach considerably higher up into the air. Potbellies are typical of toddlers, due to the forward placement of the bladder in their relatively short trunks and to the lordosis (curvature) of their, as yet, unelongated spines. By age five to six potbellies and the lordosis disappear.

Consider the following comparisons of neuromuscular skills of toddlers and preschoolers. At age two children walk upstairs holding onto a hand, rail, or wall. They place both feet on each step before proceeding to the next. By age three they begin to alternate their feet, one to a step. By age four they have usually ceased to hold on to anything and alternate steps going both down and up. By age five they may well run up the stairs. For many two-year-olds holding a glass of liquid and drinking without spilling is a feat. By age three children can drink well and feed themselves complete meals with very little assistance. At age three children undress (quite successfully) and attempt to dress (less successfully). By age five, children dress without assistance, including washing faces, hands, and brushing teeth. Five-year-olds may even be able to tie the laces of their shoes in neat bows. Three-year-olds learn to jump over or off objects and maintain their balance. Five-year-olds learn to jump rope in rhythm. Two-year-olds may or may not be toilet trained for daytime. If they are, there are still generally some accidents. Three-year-olds may or may not be night trained. Five-year-olds generally take care of their own toilet needs, unannounced and unassisted.

Neuromuscular skills emerge, become practiced, and are refined as children grow older due to several factors. Muscles grow larger and increase in strength. Children learn, or are taught, how to control and

Figure 4–1. *Denver Developmental Screening Text (DDST).*
Adapted from Frankenburg and Dodds, Denver Developmental Screening Test (DDST), University of Colorado Medical Center, 1967.

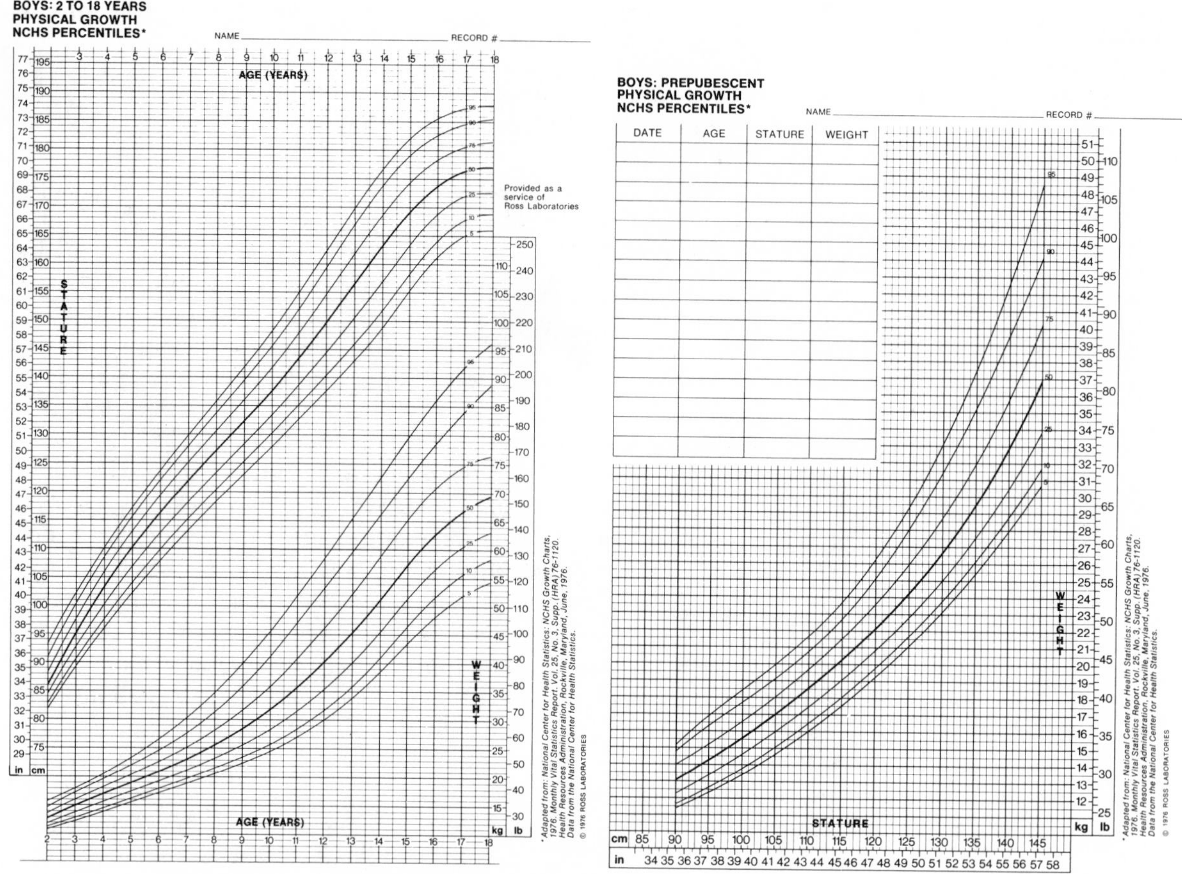

Figure 4–2. *Standard measurement percentiles for height and weight of children.*
Data from the National Center for Health Statistics © 1976 Ross Laboratories.

use various muscles. They store this information in their memories. Such memory patterns then aid them in repeating motor acts. As they improve their performance through practice, they continue to store information about more efficient ways to use their muscles. However, the growth and development of the entire nervous system influences the ways in which muscles are used. Memory is just one of many aspects of nervous system functioning. The term motor, which has been used many times already, refers to muscle activities initiated by the nervous system. Many of our muscle movements are voluntary (under our conscious control). Voluntary actions receive their directions from the motor cortex in the frontal lobe of the brain. This area is made up of rather large nerve cells, called pyramidal cells due to their triangular shape.[15] The motor cortex command center sends out messages across motor nerve fibers grouped together in tracts called pyramidal tracts. These tracts are not fully developed at birth. Dur-

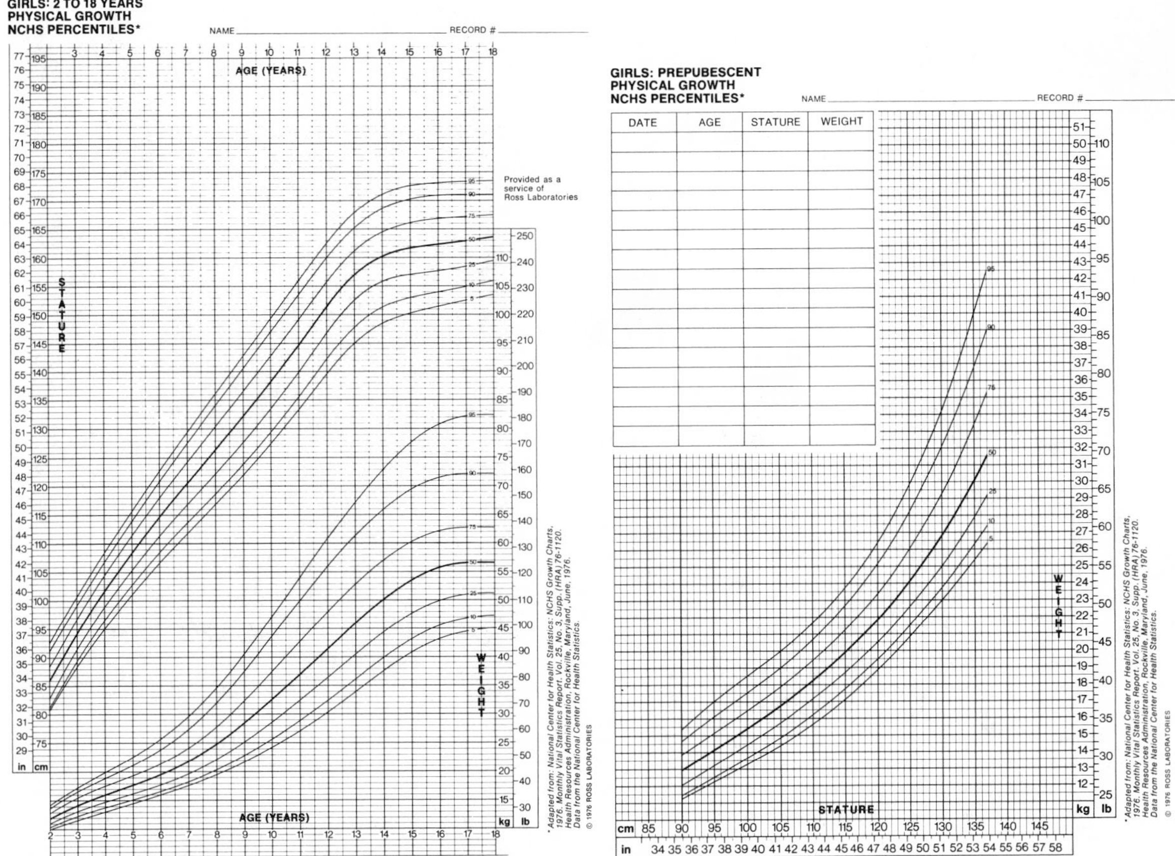

ing early childhood the nerve fibers in the tracts become much more intricate and efficient. They send out branches that connect them to other nerve cells. They also acquire a sheathing of insulating, fatty material called myelin that enables them to transmit signals more rapidly. Motor development in children proceeds as the pyramidal tracts gradually expand and become able to serve all of the 600-plus human muscles more effectively. This, however, is not the whole story. Other parts of the brain also exert influences on muscle movements.[16] Various sensory centers receive and transmit information from muscles, tendons, joints, and other skeletal structures about their positions in space, rate of movement, and so on, all of which serve to modify and smoothen voluntary movements.[17] In the parieto-occipital area of the brain are centers that provide information about the body's orientation (position and balance) in space. The premotor cortex seems to be responsible for the sequential ordering of separate units

Figure 4–3. *Two-year-olds' arms are so short that only their hands extend above their heads when they raise their arms. Five-year-olds' arms reach the top of the head at midpoint on the forearm. Adult arms are long enough so that the elbow usually extends above the top of the head.*
Leslie Davis

of behavior.[18] It helps stop one movement and makes a transition to the next. Those movements are involuntary (not under our conscious control). Between all of the above-mentioned brain areas run tracts of nerves that work in conjunction with the pyramidal (motor cortex) tracts. They are derived from the cerebellum and the extrapyramidal systems, whose nerve cell bodies lie in the centers of the brain called basal ganglia, which are apart from the pyramidal cells. The tracts from the cerebellum and extrapyramidal system help to regulate and coordinate movements so that muscles contract smoothly, with the proper amount of force, and the correct opposing muscles relax.[19] Well-coordinated muscle movements emerge only gradually during early childhood as all these various brain cells enlarge and develop more connections among each other.

Cognitive and language development

It is far easier to explain how motor activities emerge and become refined during early childhood than it is to give reasons for human acquisition of knowledge and understanding. We do not yet completely comprehend how or where the brain stores memories. Karl Lashley, a respected neuropsychologist who spent thirty years searching for memory's locale, stated that it is so elusive it is nearly impossible to accept the fact that we learn.[20]

This section will discuss these elusive neuroanatomical roots of learning. Piaget's view of the preoperational stage of intellectual development will be discussed, and the further acquisition of language by toddlers and preschoolers will be presented. This will be followed by a consideration of the role that caregivers play in fostering cognitive and language development. Finally, the meaning of early schooling in young children's lives will be reviewed.

Neuroanatomy of learning

Elusive though memory is, a few hypotheses about it have persisted. The most frequent view is that it has two stages: immediate, short-term memory (often called "telephone-number" or "scratch-pad" memory) and distant, long-term memory. Some evidence also suggests that there may be an intermediate third stage, or even several intervening stages. Still other research suggests an asymmetry of cerebral hemisphere functions that accounts for the stagelike character of memory.[21]

The first phase of an answer to the question "How is memory stored?" is given a suggestive answer by the short-term–long-term hypothesis. Short-term memories are believed to consist only of electrical impulses. The electrical activity that is generated by the millions of bits of incoming material recorded by the brain every minute may be so brief and shallow as to be dissipated rather quickly, before there is a chance to imprint anything in a long-term memory storage system. On the other hand, some bits of incoming information may excite a great deal of electrical activity, enough to overflow the boundaries of the short-term registration system and to generate some longer term retention of knowledge with potential for retrieval.

Research suggests that a pair of small structures in the brain play a vital role in pushing some information into a retention process rather than allowing it to dissipate and be forgotten. These are the hippocampi, small seahorse-shaped structures located within both temporal lobes. The hippocampi are a part of the limbic system, a major function of which appears to be the regulation of emotions. Bits of information registered in the brain that excite some emotional reactions are more apt to be converted into long-term memories through the hippocampi than are such things as telephone numbers. The role of the hippocampi has been made clear through brain surgery. Neurosurgeons discovered that if the hippocampus in only one side of the brain is accidentally or unavoidably destroyed, memory functions are only temporarily disrupted. However, if both the hippocampi are destroyed, memory functions cease entirely.[22] Images stored before the loss of the hippocampi will still be intact, but the formation of new memory is impossible.

The role of the hippocampi in discriminating between trivial information and relevant material to commit to memory is very important to intellectual functioning. A Russian psychologist, A. R. Luria, reported a case study of a man whose brain sent too many things into his long-term memory bank.[23] Although he could reproduce lengthy series of numbers or words or describe minute details of any given scene, he appeared to be dull-witted. He remembered whole situations rather than singling out key points. Consequently, his understanding of the meaning of any given subject matter was poor. He also could not forget images he no longer needed. New impressions collided with old in a chaotic manner.

Some children also have the ability to remember minute details of a situation. We call this "eidetic," or photographic, memory. It is usually lost in the maturation process, since intelligence requires the ability to blot out irrelevant stimuli and to focus on only the important elements of a situation.

A second phase of an answer to the question "How is memory stored?" concerns the mechanisms by which the brain changes short-term impressions into long-term memories. Here neuroscientists are puzzled. For years memories were believed to be laid down in electrical circuit patterns called engrams. For the most part, searches for the location of engrams were frustrating. Karl Lashley taught rats to run mazes, then systematically cut away portions of their cortices to see where the information had been stored. Yet, even with 90 percent of their cortices removed, the rats still staggered through the mazes. Memory seemed to be everywhere rather than localized.[24] Some visual memories have been demonstrated to be stored in the temporal lobes of monkeys.[25] However, the search for stores of various images in humans continues. One rather recent hypothesis is that human memories may be stored as holograms.[26] Holograms are three-dimensional pictures that are made on photographic film without the use of a camera. They consist of interference patterns caused by splitting a laser light into two parts: one is bounced off an object or scene, and the other interacts with this reflection. Several interference patterns can be superimposed on a single holographic plate so efficiently that millions of bits of material can be stored and retrieved with ease. If even a small part of a hologram is illuminated with an appropriate stimulus, a whole object or scene will be reproduced in detail. It may be years before we understand if brain cells store information as holograms, or if some other sophisticated mechanisms are responsible for our memories.

Research studies have given us reason to believe that chemical changes and the synthesis of new protein materials by the brain cells are involved in the transfer of bits of incoming information from short- to long-term memory. For example, in Sweden Holger Hyden trained rats in certain tasks and then killed them to study their brains. He found that the neurons' output of ribonucleic acid (RNA), a substance necessary to the manufacture of protein, was increased.[27] In the United States David Kresh, Mark Rosensweig and others have found increases in glial cells, in cholinesterase (an enzyme present in glial cells), and in acetylcholinesterase (an enzyme involved in synaptic transmission of neural impulses) in rats after they had been taught new tasks. Furthermore, rats raised in stimulating environments or trained in various skills were found to have heavier brains than unstimulated rats raised in barren cages. Likewise, rats fed high protein diets learned more efficiently than malnourished rats.[28] More support for the idea of chemical changes and protein synthesis to accommodate new learning has emerged from research on the effects of drugs on memory. Bernard Agranoff demonstrated that puromycin, a drug that interferes with protein synthesis, would prevent a goldfish from remembering a task if it was injected either prior to, or immediately after, learning of a new skill. If the injection was delayed an hour, the memory of the skill was fixed, and the fish remembered.[29] Other researchers have also found certain drugs that improve the brain's ability to fix memories. However, these drugs have side effects: some are poisonous; some cause convulsions; some are addictive.[30] It may be possible that in the future safer drugs will be manufactured that will help push more bits of information into a retention system and help synthesize the necessary chemicals to store them permanently. In the meantime, we are left with the knowledge that sufficient dietary intake of protein is essential to the neurophysiology of remembering. We can also be comforted by the knowledge that too much remembering is chaotic, and our ability to focus on some things and forget others is essential to intelligent behavior.

Piaget's preoperational stage

Preoperational thought, which characterizes children from about ages two to seven, is advanced over sensory-motor intelligence in many ways. Basically, children have the emerging ability to think mentally rather than to assimilate and accommodate new phenomena primarily through exploration and manipulation using their sensory and motor apparatus. This is not to say that exploration and manipulation are forfeited in early childhood. Quite the contrary! Such play is still a very important activity of young children. It is a major means of coming to know and understand the world around them. However, by acquiring the ability to think mentally, children can play at new levels. They are no longer limited to here-and-now explorations and imitations. They can transcend time and space and remember and think about things in the past as well as about things that are out of sight. Their play becomes more symbolic, filled with fantasy figures and elements of "let's pretend."

Piaget explains the new ability to think about situations, rather than just behaving in them, in terms of symbolic functions, or the formation of mental images. While the acquisition of expressive language marks the beginning of the preoperational stage of intellectual development, mental images are not always words. A word is one limited kind of mental sign. It refers to an object or situation, the meaning of which the child shares with all others in the environment (e.g., up, milk, Daddy). Other mental images are very personal (e.g., the feeling of cold and fright that accompanies being put on an adult toilet seat rather than on a child's seat or potty chair). While mental symbols may have words associated with them, they are also partly nonverbal. You can appreciate this if you consider your own thought. When you think in words, your mental progress is considerably slower than when you allow whole images to flash by at a time.

Piaget gave specific names to both the mental images that a child forms to represent an object or situation, and the objects or situations themselves. The mental images (words, nonverbal symbols) are called signifiers. The objects or events to which they refer are called the significates.[31] In the dual processes of assimilation (taking in and consolidating information) and accommodation (changing concepts to fit with the newly assimilated information), young children apply signifiers to more and more diverse phenomena (significates).

The ability to use mental images, while a major achievement in cognitive development, does not become refined for a number of years. For example, young children sometimes have difficulties differentiating between the real and the unreal, or between actual events and their fantasies. They also have a limited appreciation of the point of view of anyone but themselves. They try to find explanations for things based on their own personal needs and experiences. Their receptive and expressive language abilities, while expanding daily, also leave them puzzled about many things they see, hear, or experience. They are unable to phrase adequate questions to clarify all of their confused thoughts. In many cases, they do not feel confused but simply "understand" events in illogical ways that make sense to them. (We will discuss more of the idiosyncrasies of young children's thought shortly.) Piaget referred to this early phase of mental reasoning as preoperational. Young children's logic does not function according to "operations," which are systematic, orderly ways of mentally turning an action over to its starting point again and again and integrating it with other reversible actions.[32] This reversible, thoughtful kind of logic does not begin to emerge until the next stage, the concrete operations period, at about age seven.

Piaget subdivided the preoperational period into two phases: preconceptual and intuitive. Preconceptual refers to the young child's tendency to group together facts as they are acquired, not separating the real from the fantasized, and not classifying or defining objects and events in a systematic manner. Intuitive refers to the emerging ability of young children to separate disparate objects and events into some rudimentary classification. However, the classifications are still faulty by standards of adult logic. Preconceptual reasoning characterizes children from about two to four. Intuitive logic begins to be evidenced in children from about four to seven.

Piaget saw imitation as a bridge between sensory-motor intelligence and preoperational thought. In infancy imitations are first manifest as repetitions of ongoing behaviors—if such behaviors are encouraged and copied by caregivers. Eventually, infants become able to repeat novel behaviors demonstrated by caregivers. In the final stage of sensory-motor development, infants begin to imitate absent models. In the preoperational period, the character of imitations is advanced further. Long periods of time may elapse between observations and imitations. When imitations occur, they may be very abbreviated forms of the original actions. The child is no longer bound to physical repetitions of behaviors. The imitations can be performed mentally. In other words, imitations are internalized.

Young children use play as a means of assimilating and accommodating themselves to numerous bits of information newly acquired through sensory-motor skills and through mental images. Symbolic functions lead to a new kind of play: symbolic (also called dramatic) play. This is one of the chief synthesizers of ego, emotions, cognition, and socialization in early childhood. Internalized imitations can be repeated, not verbatim, but with the stress where the child desires (e.g., on words or behaviors that were not well understood, on words or behaviors that brought pleasure, or with words or behaviors that caused pain or frustration eliminated or altered). Piaget saw symbolic play as a very important aspect of a child's emotional life as well as his or her cognitive development. Children use symbolic play to adjust to reality and to get reality to conform to their own personal needs and desires. They can act out conflicts. They can acquire power. They can project their shortcomings or limitations onto others. They can make their wishes come true. Play serves a multitude of functions. When you observe children in play, you will learn a great deal about what they are trying to comprehend. For example, Signe, age two and one-half, was left with a babysitter while her parents attended a concert. The following day she announced that she would attend a concert. She went to the closet for the shoes her mother had worn. She then went to stand next to her crib, the last place she had seen her mother stand prior to the concert. Her father, observing this, asked her if she knew what a concert is. He then explained that it is a musical performance. She immediately began singing, "Mary had a little lamb. . ." Signe was not only trying to understand about a concert, she was also

Figure 4–4. *Play is a child's richest learning medium. It contributes to physical, cognitive, language, and social-emotional development.*
Leslie Davis

reenacting a situation that had frustrated her. She had been quite unhappy about her parents' departure the previous evening.

Piaget described the thoughts of young children as egocentric. They view everything in relation to themselves. It is very difficult for them to see fully any other point of view. When they take the role of another person in symbolic play, they make some strides towards such an understanding. The ability to think more systematically about the needs and experiences of others helps mark the transition into a higher level of cognitive functioning, the concrete operations stage.

The egocentricity of young children often leads them to believe that their thoughts and actions are shared by others, especially by the primary caregivers. It therefore seems unreasonable to them for an adult to say "I don't understand." They are unable to reconstruct their thought processes to show how they arrived at their conclusions and help others understand. Because they think that saying or thinking something makes it so, they frequently feel no need to justify their conclusions anyway.

Communication difficulties arise, not only because young children are just learning to label things, phrase requests, ask questions, and make statements, but also because they presume that much is understood without its being voiced. A small portion of young children's speech is also not aimed at communicating. It is practice speech and resembles a monologue. While it may be directed toward another person, the child will make little or no effort to be sure the listener hears or understands. Like adults, children may frequently hear only what it seems they want to hear. However, there may be a difference between the selective listening of a child and an adult. A young child may lack the competence to understand a message that is adequately imparted. Adults may simply lack the will to understand.

Egocentricity leads to another problem in reasoning that Piaget called centration or centering. Young children focus on one point of view, their own. They center on one need, or desire, or aspect of a problem and find it very difficult to shift their attention elsewhere. This cognitive limitation can make them appear very persistent, very single-minded, and sometimes very stubborn.

Preoperational children deal with things exactly as they appear to them in their here-and-now egocentric perception. Piaget called this perception realism. Psychological events such as thoughts, dreams, and names are things of substance to the child. For example, names are believed to inhere in a thing. When Piaget asked a young child how people know that the sun was called the sun, he got this answer: "They saw it was called the sun because they could see it was round and hot."[33] For another example of realism, Piaget discussed preschoolers' views of dreams. They are believed to come from outside, sometimes from God, can be made of wind, and sometimes can punish their viewer for misdeeds of the day.[34]

Facts acquired by young children can be described as animistic, artificialistic and syncretistic. Animism refers to the child's endowment of life, consciousness, and will to physical objects and events (e.g., pincushions feel the prick of a pin, clouds feel rain, and grass feels hurt when it is pulled). However, animistic notions may be fleeting, (e.g., the pincushion may not be sentient until stabbed; grass may not feel the child playing on it, but only another person's pulling on it). Artificialism refers to the child's tendency to believe that all objects and events in the world were made by humans for humans (e.g., clouds exist to give us shade; rain comes to make splashy mud puddles; and lakes were put on earth for swimming or boating. Night comes so we can sleep). Syncretistic thought refers to the child's tendency to fuse a multitude of diverse phenomena together. If you were to ask a young child a question (e.g., "Why does the water flow downstream?"), the answer is apt to be based on some cooccurring phenomenon (e.g., "The rocks push it down").

Reasoning in the preoperational period is most apt to be from particular to particular. Piaget called this transductive reasoning. It is midway between the two forms of reason which adults use—inductive and deductive. When we induce something, we use a few particulars to arrive at generalizations. For example, after meeting several persons from Denmark, all of whom have blonde hair, we might generalize that all Danes are blonde. When we deduce something, we reason from general to particular. For example, after observing many college students wearing blue jeans, we might word an invitation to a coed, "Wear your blue jeans," assuming that she must own a pair. The results of young children's transductive reasoning may or may not be logical by adult standards. (They are always logical to the child.) They are usually fascinating. Piaget provided these examples:

> J. at 2 years, 9 months: "She hasn't got a name." (a little girl a year old).—Why?—"Because she can't talk."
>
> J. at 2 years, 10 months: (showing a postcard) "It's a dog."—I think it's a cat.—"No, it's a dog."—Is it? Why?—Why do you say it's a dog?—Why do you think it's a dog?—"It's grey."[35]

The ability to separate objects or events into classes in an ordered, systematic way is absent in the preoperational stage, although some children begin to see relationships among diverse phenomena from about ages four through seven. Piaget felt that they may be unaware of why they do what they do. Therefore, he called this phase intuitive. When young children are asked to classify a set of materials, they either make small, partial alignments (an array of materials with some groupings but no overall guiding plan) or complex objects (arrangement of the materials into an interesting form or picture).[36]

Time and number concepts are hazy in early childhood since a genuine understanding of them requires the operation of classification. Toddlers can learn to wait a minute and to recognize times for bodily activities like eating and sleeping. The concepts of yesterday and tomorrow gradually become meaningful, but, even though preschoolers may voice the words next month or next year, they have little appreciation for the length of time involved. Thus they may wait impatiently for Christmas in September, regardless of their knowledge of the three-month wait. They may count numbers fluently yet be unable to correctly select which of an array of candies is greater if one is piled and the other is spread out. Even after counting the candies, they are apt to want the array that looks bigger to them, even if it actually has fewer candies.

Piaget referred to preoperational thought as bad thought or thought akin to daydreams, because it lacks the sophistication of adult logic. However, it is advanced over sensory-motor intelligence and improves continually as the child experiences more and increasingly adapts to his or her environment.

Language acquisition

In Chapter 3 we presented Noam Chomsky's proposition that humans have an innate ability to acquire language. While imitation is also considered an important factor in language acquisition, most linguists are now paying more attention to the relationship between cognition and language. Children are known to dissect rules and structural principles (syntax) from whatever language they hear. The special information-processing abilities in their brains make it possible for them to invent their own sentences as they begin speaking.[37] While not always grammatically correct, such sentences adequately convey their intended messages (e.g., "All gone nap"; "Mommy up teddy"). Children can interpret from the massive input of language they hear what is relevant. They learn first to impart back to others only what is necessary to be understood. Later they learn to embellish their sentences with the auxiliary parts of speech. While language is first acquired spontaneously, and while rules of construction operate automatically, language acquisition continues to span both early and late childhood. Many adults, in fact, are still attempting to make their word usage more polished, precise, and correct.

The first words used by children are holophrases (entire ideas expressed by one word). The words used are generally nouns or verbs. It requires mental planning by children to move to the next stage of speech, selecting out appropriate nouns and verbs from their repertoire to make an understandable two-word sentence. Piaget, for this reason, used acquisition of language as the end point of sensory-motor intelligence and the beginning of preoperational thought, which requires the use of mental processes.

Toddlers embellish their two-word, telegramlike utterances with additional meanings through gestures and intonations. "More milk," for example, may be a meager, bashful request made with head lowered and hands clutching a glass close to the body. It may be a loud demand voiced in an insistent tone with the glass thrust out in both hands. It may also be a question, evidenced by a rise in pitch at the end of the utterance.

Many of the first words of toddlers become overextended in their meanings. For example, a child may call several four-legged real and stuffed animals "kitty" because they resemble a cat which is so named.

Three-word sentences generally emerge around the middle of the second year. They usually take the form of subject-verb-object (e.g., Billy feed kitty. Daddy go car). Some of the common constructions involve requests for actions, requests for repetitions, labeling of phenomena, claims of possession, signs of disagreement or negation, descriptions of location, descriptions of absent objects, and questions.[38] In addition to forming three-word sentences, children begin voicing nearly incessant "whys." They seem more interested in keeping adults talking than in receiving answers. For example, an adult begins: "I'm going to make lunch." The child responds, "Why?" "Because I'm hungry." "Why?" "Because I haven't had anything to eat since breakfast." "Why?" "Because I've been busy." "Why?" . . . And so it goes.

A short while after children master two- and three-word sentences, they begin constructing longer messages. At first they often put two short ideas together end to end. For example, a child may say, "Candy is gone, on the table." It will be a while before they can embed one idea within another (e.g., "The candy on the table is gone").

During the early phases of language acquisition, pronounciation of words may be understood only by regular caregivers. It is not uncommon for a child to impart a message to an unfamiliar person and have it received as gibberish. However, if the recipient of the message calls on the caregiver, he or she can usually decipher it quite easily.

Between ages two and a half and three, children begin to use pronouns, especially *I, me, you,* and *it.* They often confuse *I* and *me.* The possessives my and mine emerge soon after the noun-verb stage, as do the articles *a, an,* and *the.* Children also begin to add inflections to their nouns and verbs about this time, especially to plurals and past tenses. Idiomatic nouns are pluralized by the same rule as regular nouns (e.g., sheeps, foots, gooses, tooths, mices, oxes, fishes, deers). Idiomatic verbs are given the same past tense as regular verbs (e.g., seed [saw], goed [went], braked [broke], singed [sang], gived [gave], and doed [did]). A few contractions are also attempted, some correctly (e.g., isn't, didn't), some incorrectly (e.g., amn't, ain't, willn't).

Word usage multiplies rapidly once a child begins speaking. The average number of words used may sprout from fifty at age two to 1000+ by age three.[39] While average refers to a number representing the mean of a wide range of observed children, it does not necessarily suggest what a normal child should accomplish. In the area of language development, where individual differences are vast, average is not synonymous with normal. Some children learn to speak earlier than the ages indicated in the preceding descriptions. Other normal children acquire language much later. Many persons who became quite famous in their adult lives are known to have been slow to speak in childhood (e.g., Albert Einstein, Winston Churchill, Virginia Woolf).[40] Females generally acquire language at slightly earlier ages than males.[41] They continue to excel in verbal skills throughout childhood.

The speech control center is located in the dominant cerebral hemisphere.[42] For most persons this is the left side. (It is the right side for left-handed persons.) Girls show advanced development of their left cerebral hemispheres during infancy and early childhood, which possibly accounts for some of their accelerated verbal fluency.[43] However, the right hemisphere can take over control of speech if the speech area of the left hemisphere is injured in childhood. Lenneberg reported that left-sided injuries that occur before speech is learned have little or no effect on language acquisition.[44] The right hemisphere simply develops a speech center, and learning progresses on schedule. If a speech center injury occurs after language acquisition, but prior to adolescence, the child temporarily loses language. When it is relearned, it is acquired in much the same way as it first developed (by holophrases and telegraphic sentences, etc.), but at a more rapid rate. The critical period for speech center development in the nondominant hemisphere, however, seems to end at puberty. After this, speech center injuries leave people with a very limited or nonexistent ability to reacquire language.

Role of the family in fostering learning

Experiences—rich and varied opportunities to personally observe, hear, taste, smell, or touch a multitude of objects and circumstances—are the *sine qua non* for fostering intellectual growth. Without experiencing phenomena children cannot assimilate and accommodate them into their mental structures. In addition, the emotional climate in which a child learns about his or her world is important. An insecure, frightened, unhappy child seldom evidences much curiosity or interest in the events taking place around him or her other than those things that relate directly to their emotional problems. Nutrition is also important to learning. A hungry child is often lethargic and seldom very curious. Severe malnutrition can limit a child's ability to form new memories as well as interfere with interest and attention.

There exists a controversy over the possibility or impossibility of increasing children's cognitive abilities or intelligence quotients (IQs). Some persons feel that IQ is innate. They believe children inherit an ability to learn that is well demarcated from birth. Smart babies will acquire skills and information rapidly, while dull babies will be delayed, not only as infants, but throughout their lives. Other persons feel that IQ is flexible. They believe that while children inherit a tendency to learn quickly or slowly, they can learn more information when placed in stimulating environments with caregivers who provide incentives. Boring environments with cognitively uncaring or unaware adults will not foster rapid intellectual growth. It is nearly impossible to determine if IQ can be increased in early childhood by special teaching techniques and materials because of the nature of IQ testing of preoperational children. Language difficulties are only part of the problem. Young children are also very situation prone. They may test quite low one day and quite high the next, depending on their interest, their rapport with the examiner, their emotional needs, their physical needs (e.g., for food, water, toileting, sleep), and their health. It is not until after age five that correlations between childhood IQ and final adult IQ, or between successive IQ tests begin to show a degree of stability and predictability. (IQ testing will be discussed in more detail in Chapter 5.)

Persons who adhere to the notion that IQ is innate usually allow for a degree of flexibility or stretchability to intelligence. Arthur Jensen, after examining several studies supporting the genetic basis of intelligence, arrived at the ratio of 80/20 for fixed versus flexible learning abilities.[45] Even given 20 percent of intelligence as stretchable (it may be much more than this), there are specific things that caregivers can do to foster learning.

While a stimulating environment is essential for fostering intellectual development, caregivers must be certain that the child for whom they are making provisions is able to concentrate on stimuli. Is the child adequately nourished and relatively free of negative emotions? Does he or she get enough sleep? Are any chronic health problems interfering with energy and interest levels?

The right learning environment is one that produces pleasure and excitement in children. In such a setting parents and others involved in the child's care will not have to push. The children's interests will propel them to explore and discover more and more. The stimuli in the environment must satisfy what Hunt has called "the problem of the match."[46] They must not be too familiar, or they will bore children. If they are too novel, they will be ignored. Outings, trips, toys, games, and household articles that have elements of both familiarity and novelty will capture and hold children's interests (see Figure 4–5).

Verbal stimulation is also very important to children's intellectual development. Parents should spend time every day talking and listening to their children in face-to-face communication. It is not the amount of speech heard by children that fosters language, but the way in which communications occur. A child may be bombarded with human vocalizations throughout the day (e.g., from television, other children, other adults), but unless words are spoken to the child directly, they will have little meaning. The most meaningful communications are those that come from the adults to whom the child has the greatest attachments. Parents and other significant adults can foster language by encouraging children's efforts to communicate. Holophrases and short sentences can be repeated approvingly and then expanded into longer sentences with the addition of the auxiliary parts of speech. Adults can explain objects or events to a child as they interact together and help the child move towards a greater comprehension of the world and its properties. It is also important that adults attend to children's questions. Although a steady stream of "whys" can be exasperating, children who ask them want either information, attention, or both. The best time to provide both is when children are open and recep-

Figure 4–5. *Parents can do much to enrich their children's environments and stimulate their cognitive development through outings, books, games, plenty of one-to-one interaction, and attention to needs for nutritious food, rest, safety, and love.*
Leslie Davis

tive. Caregivers who repeatedly say "Not now" or "Wait," and then fail to find a few minutes to spend with the child, will discourage further attempts by the child to obtain explanations or information from them.

Television as a source of intellectual stimulation has been both over- and underrated. Some programs developed especially for children are excellent. They capture and hold a child's interest, while presenting very good information about concepts and relationships within the child's comprehension range. However, too much of a good thing ceases to be good. Television viewing can become habitual, an unstimulating, passive, escapist activity. Children may remain in front of televisions in spite of their boredom, because the alternatives to watching it are even less stimulating.

Reading aloud to children will entertain and stimulate them at a level that television programming can never achieve. Children cannot ask for and get instant replays of a television scene, nor can they ask questions and get answers from electronic gadgetry. In addition to the pluses of being able to turn pages back, ask questions, and discuss interesting aspects of the pictures in books, reading provides a warm emotional climate between child(ren) and caregiver.

Research studies looking at caregiver styles of interacting with and stimulating children have found that some adults have a decided impact on cognitive achievements. Hess and Shipman found that effective caregivers more often give specific, well-organized instructions, encourage children to ask questions or talk about activities, engage children in interactions, and praise progress.[47] Burton White found that caregivers of competent children provided safe environments with a variety of toys and interesting household objects where children had a great deal of freedom for exploration. He also found that these caregivers set very definite limits to dangerous behaviors and were available as consultants to answer questions, give directions, or provide encouragement when children needed it.[48]

Early schooling

Preschool programs have been available to American parents for over 100 years. Susan Blow began the first kindergarten in the United States in St. Louis, Missouri, in 1873. It was modeled after the teaching styles of Friedrich Froebel, a German educator who provided the name *kindergarten* (meaning child's garden) to his preschools in Europe. It stressed sitting down and learning. Within a few years other preschools opened that stressed play and group interactions rather than rigid lessons for very young children.

John Dewey, an American educator, espoused the need for young children to receive individual experiences in meaningful activities geared to teach societal adjustment (e.g., handicrafts, gardens, nature studies).[49] The activities were guided by the teacher, but not forced. His theories had a profound influence on American progressive education during his long (ninety-three years) lifetime.

Dr. Maria Montessori, an Italian physician-turned-educator, developed preschools in Europe (first in Rome, later in Holland) that stressed individual experiences in meaingful activities of a cognitive nature (e.g., sandpaper letters, graduated cylinders to teach size concepts, numbers' games).[50] Like Dewey's activities they were guided by the teacher, but not forced. Her schools emphasized quiet, good manners, respect for others, and a regard for the upkeep of all the educational materials. Montessori schools spread to the United States in the early 1900s. In the 1920s they were eclipsed by schools following Dewey's philosophies. However, in recent years modified Montessori programs have again become very popular in the United States. While her rigid schedules and strict insistence on quiet have been somewhat relaxed, many of her teaching materials are used just as she developed them at the turn of the twentieth century.

Day care centers grew up out of the work programs established by Roosevelt to help the United States out of the depression of the 1930s. They expanded during the 1940s to provide care for children whose mothers went to work during World War II. They practically became extinct during the 1950s and early 1960s. The women's liberation movement, however, has catapulted day care centers into an increasingly popular position in American society in the 1970s.

Nursery schools emphasizing socialization, group play, and creativity (and marked by permissive discipline) became popular after World War II. They were frequently attached to colleges or universities to provide a setting for training student teachers and for doing child development research, as well as for early schooling of young children whose parents could afford the tuition. The postwar era also saw the development of free half-day kindergartens for five-year-olds that were attached to elementary schools. In some areas of the country, attendance at kindergarten before entering first grade even became mandatory.

Emphasis on socialization became partially displaced by an emphasis on cognitive development in the 1960s. The nation became especially concerned about its underprivileged children. Compensatory (to make up for deprived conditions) programs were developed such as project Head Start in 1965 and project Follow Through in 1968. They taught academic and language skills to children from low income families. In addition, they provided for some of the children's physical, nutritional, and dental needs, stressed behaviors such as curiosity, creativity, self-discipline, and self-confidence, and tried to foster better child-family and family-school ties. Critics of Head Start, Follow Through, and many of the other compensatory education programs claimed that they failed because the IQ gains demonstrated between starting and finishing preschool could not be sustained in the public schools. However, it is unfair to judge the success of preschool programs solely on IQ tests, which are known to be unreliable predictors of academic success for young children. There were no tests made of the happiness, security, social skills, and improved self-concepts of children given the opportunity to attend the compensatory programs.

Today caregivers may be able to choose (depending on their locale) from a vast array of specialized preschool programs that can provide a positive atmosphere for the acquisition of both cognitive and social skills. How these programs will enhance a child's intellectual and social-emotional development depends on many factors. The child's unique personality must be considered. Some programs serve the needs of shy children better than others. Likewise, some programs and teachers are more effective with active children. Some stress only the acquisition of cognitive or language skills. Others stress social adjustment. Many are eclectic. Some children enjoy a program more if it is not too long or too frequent (e.g., half-days two or three times a week). Others enjoy full-day programs five days per week. The reasons why caregivers send children to early childhood education programs can also influence the children's enjoyment and progress in the centers. If parents believe in the programs and cooperate with the teachers, their children are more apt to find the atmosphere pleasant than are children whose parents resent the intrusions of the school or feel guilty for leaving their children a part of the day.

Social development

The process of socialization is no longer viewed as a one-way street with family and community members acting on the child to bring about socialization. For example, cognitive-developmental theorists and humanists believe that children's unique characteristics and ways of interacting with the world influence the ways in which others react to them. Socialization is thus seen as a reciprocal process where children influence adult behaviors as certainly as adults influence children's behaviors. In the preceding two chapters facts that suggested personality differences are present at birth were presented. In discussing social development in early childhood, keep in mind that there will be children whose patterns of behavior range from shy to bold, passive to active, cuddly to distant, lethargic to alert, serious to carefree, and so on. The same adult behaviors aimed at socialization of each child can have different effects.

Significance of the family in social development

Healthy young children emerge from infancy with strong attachment bonds to family members, especially the primary caregiver(s). The nature of the attachment is based both on the infant's innate patterns of behavior and the family members' personalities and styles of interacting. Babies must depend almost completely on their caregivers to meet their needs. During the early childhood years they move, with the family's help, toward independence.

This section will emphasize the family's role in social development. We will look at familial behaviors as they influence the nuclear conflicts of autonomy versus shame and doubt and initiative versus guilt as described by Erik Erikson, the important sense of feeling loved and wanted as described by Rudolf Dreikurs, and the need for a strong identification as stressed by social learning theorists. We will also describe the intrafamilial dynamics involved in discipline, moral development, sibling relationships, sex typing, and sex education.

Erikson's nuclear conflicts of early childhood. Given a sense of trust in the caregivers to whom they are attached, children move into what Erik Erikson described as the second nuclear conflict of life, that of achieving autonomy versus shame and doubt. Erikson, as a psychoanalytic

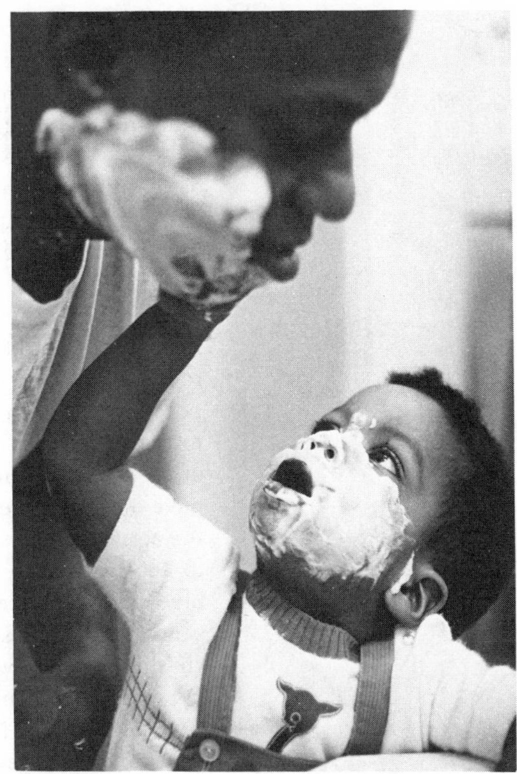

Figure 4–6. *Children are born with some of their own innate personality characteristics. They influence the ways in which their caregivers interact with them as surely as adult behaviors help shape their emerging personalities.*
Burk Uzzle/Magnum Photos, Inc.

theorist, followed Freud's lead in viewing toilet training and anal functioning as a foremost concern of the child at about age two. As young children develop the sphincter control necessary for holding on and letting go, caregivers begin to ask them not to wet or mess their pants. Children have the power to obey or disobey, which, for them, can be a heady feeling. If accidents are cleaned up without much fuss, if children are encouraged to hold on long enough to get to a toilet, and if praise is given for toileting successes, children will gain a sense of self-control, of inner goodness, and of pride. These feelings are basic to autonomy as Erikson described it. However, if children are punished and made to feel foolish for their accidents, a sense of shame will be encouraged. If they are kept in diapers and given no opportunities to control their uges, a sense of doubt will be fostered. Feelings of shame and doubt are not healthy personality attributes. As Erikson stated: "Too much shaming does not lead to genuine propriety but to a secret determination to try to get away with things, unseen—if, indeed, it does not result in defiant shamelessness."[51] Doubt is the brother of shame. It is a sense of inner badness and secondary mistrust with a need to look back or behind. Erikson believed that many adult persecution complexes may have their origins in the compulsive doubting that begins in early childhood.[52]

While toilet training methods play a role in the nuclear conflict of learning autonomy versus learning shame and doubt, they are by no means the only caregiving techniques involved. During the second and third years of life, toddlers are very actively trying to stand on their own two feet, literally as well as figuratively. Increased neuromuscular development gives them the capabilities for walking, running, climbing, pushing, pulling, holding on tight, and exploring their worlds in ways heretofore impossible. Likewise, cognitive and language development make it possible for them to think about their actions and make their wills known to their caregivers. "No!" and "Me!" (meaning "Let me do it myself") are often-repeated holophrases of two- and three-year-olds. Caregivers do not have an easy time of helping children develop a sense of autonomy in all the activities of daily living. Toddlers need many experiences of being able to choose among alternatives (e.g., to play inside or outside, to wear the blue pants or the brown pants, to have a peanut butter or a bologna sandwich). However, caregivers should carefully phrase questions for children to allow situations in which either choice will be acceptable. When a particular behavior is necessary (e.g., going to bed, holding hands to cross a street, letting go of another child's hair), caregivers should not give a choice. Rather, they must exercise firm control over the toddler's wish to be in command. Young children do not have the wisdom or the sense of discrimination to know what behaviors are acceptable or unacceptable, healthy or unhealthy. If caregivers give in too often to children's stubborn streaks and insistent demands, children may develop long-lasting personality conflicts. They may become fearful of their own powers. If their willfulness leads them into too many unfortunate accidents, they may develop what Erikson describes as a sense of shame and self-doubt. Autonomous behaviors are best nourished in a climate where both experiences of free choice and firm control of anarchy are continuously available (see Table 4–2).

Remember that although Erikson's theory describes a primary time for resolving each of the ego's eight conflicts during a lifetime, he stresses that personality development is a continuous process. All of the conflicts of the ego can be present even at times when they are not of central importance. Children who develop a strong sense of trust in infancy will still experience feelings of suspicion and fear in later life. However, they will be able to resolve these conflicts of trust versus mistrust more easily if their infant experiences were predominantly trust promoting. Likewise, children who develop a strong sense of autonomy as toddlers should be able to emerge from conflicts of autonomy versus shame and doubt without undue difficulty throughout life.

Table 4–2. Erikson's second nuclear conflict: autonomy versus shame and doubt.

Sense	*Eriksonian descriptions*	*Fostering adult behaviors*
Autonomy	– sense of inner goodness	– encourage child to stand on own feet
	– sense of self-control	– firm control of child's anarchy due to lack of sense of discrimination
	– sense of good will and pride	– gradual and well-guided experiences of free choice
vs.		
Shame	– sense of premature or foolish exposure	– shaming as punishment technique
	– sense of being too visible	– suppression of self-expression
	– desire to sink out of sight	– overcontrol of actions
		– little free choice
Doubt	– sense of inner badness	– critical of self-help efforts
	– secondary mistrust with a need to look back or behind	– overprotective

Source: Based on material from "Eight Ages of Man" from *Childhood and Society,* 2nd Edition, Revised, by Erik H. Erikson, with the permission of W. W. Norton & Company, Inc. Copyright 1950, © 1963 by W. W. Norton & Company, Inc.

In the preschool period (about ages four to five) children begin the work of resolving Erikson's third nuclear conflict, that of acquiring a sense of initiative versus guilt. Having discovered that they can do for themselves, they become curious about how much they can do, and when, and where. They also wonder about who else they can be. They explore answers to these questions by pretending to be other people and by scrutinizing more and more diverse phenomena. Acquiring a sense of initiative involves thrusting out into a wider world of childhood and assuming new interests and activities. Energy levels are high, curiosity is profound, and explorations are vigorous.

Erikson, following Freud, saw elements of genital interest and sexual conflicts accompanying the nuclear conflict of acquiring initiative versus assuming guilt. Curiosity and cognitive maturity lead young children to take note of the differences between males and females. Their role-playing imitations of other people include pretending to be husband and pretending to be wife. Children most frequently assume the roles of the adults in their lives whom they recognize as sharing sexual sameness. According to psychoanalytic theory, Oedipal and Electra complexes are common at this time. Oedipus was a legendary Greek king who killed his father and married his mother. A boy with an Oedipus complex presumably wants to replace his father as his mother's husband. Many boys become very attached to the females in their lives during the preschool period. Electra was a legendary Greek woman who harbored an intense love for her murdered father and bitterly hated her mother, whom she blamed for the father's death. A girl with an Electra complex supposedly wishes to replace her mother as her father's wife. Many preschool girls become very attached to the men in their lives.

Erikson wrote that jealousy and rivalry directed at the same-sexed parent is part of the conflict of initiative versus guilt. As he stated it, "Initiative brings with it anticipatory rivalry with those who have been there first and may, therefore, occupy with their superior equipment the field towards which one's initiative is directed."[53] The jealousy and rivalry that accompanies the nuclear conflict of initiative versus guilt can also be directed at other children (siblings, friends) and at other adults.

The development of a sense of initiative involves a great deal more than sex-role jealousies and rivalries. Erikson describes initiative as a quality of undertaking, planning, and attacking a task. It involves creativity and assertiveness. Children need to be given opportunities to plan for and carry out their own activities during the preschool years. They need to begin to develop a feeling that they are, to some extent, masters of their own fates.

During this period of childhood a rudimentary sense of conscience, or the superego as the psychoanalysts call it, becomes apparent. Preschoolers begin to show signs of anxiety about their misbehaviors, even while they find it difficult to control their impulsive, assertive, and/or aggressive actions. Erikson calls this feeling of concern about misdeeds a sense of guilt. Preschoolers try to take control of their own behaviors as well as to manipulate the behaviors of other objects or persons. Sometimes they are harsher critics of their own behaviors than are their caregivers. Erikson warns that children who are frequently criticized, derided, and inhibited from initiating behaviors may learn to overcontrol and overconstrict themselves to the point of self-obliteration. They may develop deep regressions. They may also form lasting resentments of caregivers who do not live up to the high standards they exact for themselves. No

Table 4–3. Erikson's third nuclear conflict: initiative versus guilt.

Sense	*Eriksonian descriptions*	*Fostering adult behaviors*
Initiative	– quality of undertaking, planning and "attacking" a task	– provide opportunities for child to plan and carry out own activities
vs.		
Guilt	– anxiety about own behavior being bad	– inhibit child from starting own activities
	– fear of wrongdoing leading to overcontrol and overconstriction of own activities	– deride child's efforts at doing for self

Source: Based on material from "Eight Ages of Man" from *Childhood and Society*, 2nd Edition, Revised, by Erik H. Erikson, with the permission of W. W. Norton & Company, Inc. Copyright 1950, © 1963 by W. W. Norton & Company, Inc.

child emerges from early childhood without some feelings of guilt for initiating behaviors beyond the realms of what the caregivers or the larger social order find permissible. Learning the rules, regulations, and limits of behavior involves exploration of confines and occasional overstepping of bounds. Adults need to help children establish a sense of right and wrong without laying on their shoulders an unduly heavy burden of guilt for all the mistakes that naturally accompany active, curious, exploration of people (through role playing), places, and things (see Table 4–3).

Dreikurs's stress on family interactions. Rudolf Dreikurs, another neo-Freudian social psychologist who followed Adler more closely than Freud, stressed the role of the whole family unit (parents, siblings, all live-in persons) on children's social development. Dreikurs wrote that unless children feel worthwhile and protected by their family unit, they may go through one or more of four progressive stages aimed at capturing attention and a sense of being wanted. The stages involve behaviors that are usually unpleasant for the adult(s) involved in parenting: (1) seeking attention directly through loud talking, interrupting, annoying, being cute; (2) seeking power through stubbornness, assertiveness, rebelliousness; (3) seeking revenge through aggressive acts aimed to injure or inflict pain; and, finally, (4) giving up altogether and retreating into a silent, passive stance.[54] Most children have times when they feel the need to overcome feelings of inferiority by seeking attention or power or revenge (see Figure 4–7). Parents who reassure their children that they are loved and wanted can reduce these attention-seeking behaviors. But Dreikurs fears that if children cannot get a feeling that they are worthwhile and protected by their families, they may give up altogether any efforts to interact in a social way with others.

Identification with caregivers. Heinz Werner described human development as a movement from global, undifferentiated activity to organized, integrated, and differentiated activity. He saw identification as an early way in which children begin to differentiate self from others.[55] With increased cognitive maturity, children's imitations of others become more and more complex. They choose whom they will imitate, how much, and how often. Through these role-playing imitations they begin to appreciate their own unique sense of self. Identification is a term derived from psychoanalysis that refers to the process whereby a child willingly assumes some of the characteristics of others into his or her own unique selfness. While introduced by Freud, the importance of identification to young children's social development has been stressed more by social learning theorists. It goes far beyond simple imitations. It includes a degree of permanency and generalization of acquired behaviors. When a child identifies with an adult, he or she imitates many of the characteristics of that adult (e.g., walking, eating, talking, relaxing) much of the time.

Chapter 1 introduced identification as a major element in Robert Sears's social learning theory of child development (see p. 26). Sears believed identification with caregivers follows attachment bonding.[56] Children learn to enjoy and look forward to contact with the caregivers who are their primary sources of nurture and affection. This affective attachment bond motivates children to imitate or model the behavior of the loved adult(s) frequently. Such imitations bring pleasurable consequences when observed by the nurturant, powerful, and rewarding adults. The rewards increase the rates at which the imitations occur. Imitations are performed not only in the caregivers' presence, but also in their absence. Sears pointed out that imitating absent caregivers has a secondary reinforcing value. It makes the caregivers seem closer. Children's incorporations of adult behaviors into their own acts can give them a sense of security, a sense of greater strength, and can aid them in controlling their own emotions and behaviors.

Young children identify to some extent with many persons in their environments (e.g., caregivers, siblings, friends, even television characters). The strength of the identity bond is related to factors such as af-

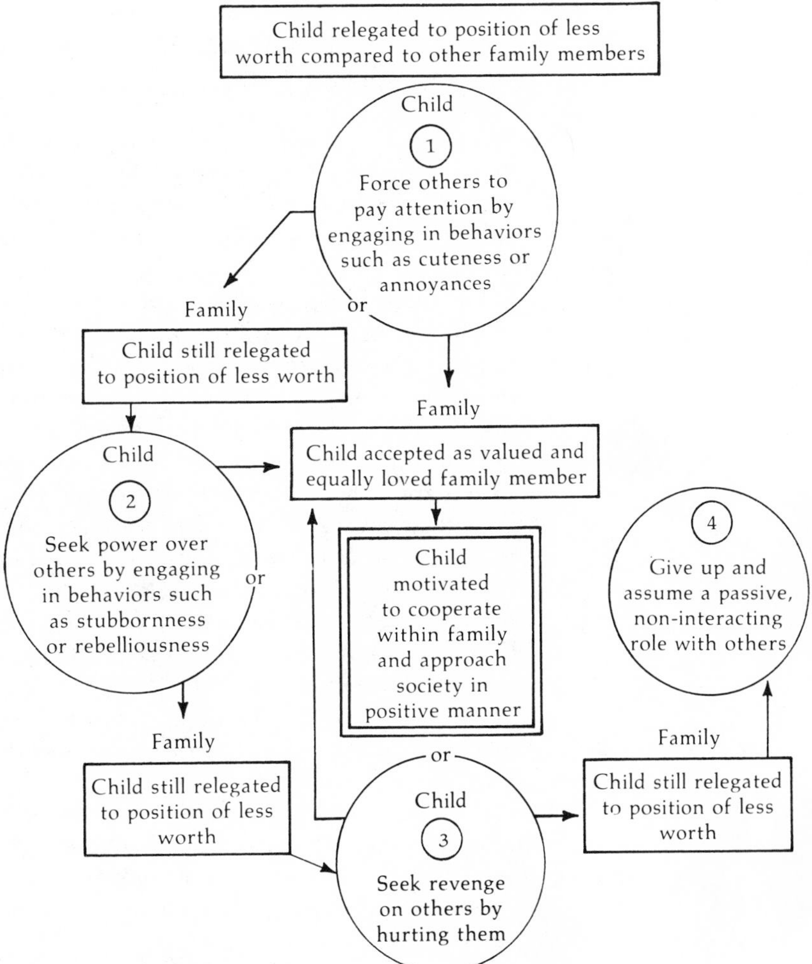

Figure 4–7. *Dreikurs's theory of interfamilial social interaction patterns.*
Based on material from R. Dreikurs and V. Soltz, *Children: The Challenge.* New York: Hawthorn Books, Inc., 1964.

fection bonds, responsiveness of others to imitations, recognition of similarities between self and others, and to perceptions of power. Albert Bandura and his associates found that adults who are recognized as wielding power and controlling status are more salient as identification models than are those adults or children who are simply rewarding.[57] Knowledge of this perception-of-power component in strong identification bonds may bring comfort to some parents who fear the effects of peer models, television models, or super-rewarding (spoiling) adult models on their children.

While children practice many different roles in their play, they are most apt to take on the characteristics of the most loved, nurturing, and powerful persons in their lives.

Sex-role learning. Sex typing refers to the process whereby children establish stronger identification bonds with nurturant, powerful adults of their own gender than with opposite-sexed adults. It does not occur all at once but continues gradually throughout the course of development. It is not an all-or-none phenomenon at any time. While boys gradually imitate and acquire more and more of the behavior patterns typical of the meaningful men in their lives, they also still identify with and imitate the characteristics of meaningful women. Likewise, girls continue to imitate some of the attributes of significant men in their lives while acquiring stronger identity bonds with significant women. Many factors are related to the strength of sexual identity. Cognitive maturity leads children to recognize the differences between males and females and to acknowledge their own greater similarities to persons of the same sex. Concurrently, social learning is taking place. Boys are usually attended to and rewarded more for behaviors that society deems masculine. Girls are usually given more attention and praise for feminine-typed behaviors. Comments from other people add to the sexual identity effect (e.g., "That boy is just like his father," or "That girl is just like her mother").

Freud felt that the cross-sex identifications (boys with their mothers and girls with their fathers) that occur during early childhood are the cause of tremendous personality conflicts. He not only posited Oedipal and Electra complexes but also believed that castration fears and penis envy take place in boys and girls respectively. Freud believed that it is not until about age six that emotionally healthy boys and girls repress and/or renounce their desires for their opposite-sexed parent and identify with the same-sexed parent.

Social learning theorists have proposed that sex typing occurs much earlier. Soon after attachment bonds are formed, boys and girls begin to imitate the behaviors of adults they perceive as nurturant, powerful, and/or bearing strong resemblance to themselves. Sexual identity grows stronger with the passing of time. Boys are rewarded and praised for masculine behaviors, while girls are rewarded and praised for feminine actions. Both may be punished or ignored for inappropriate sex behaviors. Thus, according to social learning theory, boys and girls learn appropriate sex behaviors both because they imitate the behaviors of all the adults whom they find nurturant and powerful and because of the rewards and attention that these appropriate behaviors bring. Single parents can promote and support both male and female sex typing by providing differential rewards and attention for children's behaviors depending on gender.

Cognitive theorists reject much of Freud's psychosexual theory of sex-role acquisition and emphasize the cognitive aspects over the reinforcement aspects of the social learning theory. They view role taking more as a developmental phenomenon. While agreeing that reinforcement of sex-appropriate behaviors occurs, cognitive theorists feel that children model the like-sexed parent because first, they perceive their resemblance to that parent, and second, they want to imitate the person whom they most closely resemble. This gender identity is not completed until children acquire the cognitive ability to differentiate classes and conserve notions of class constancy.

There are some analogies in each of these theories of sex-role learning, even though they may appear at first to contradict each other. The psychoanalytic theory recognizes the role of social learning. Boys and girls eventually repress or renounce their desires to be like the opposite-sexed parent and identify instead with the same-sexed parent, presumably because their sex-inappropriate behaviors have been ignored or punished. Both psychoanalytic and social learning theories recognize the role of cognitive maturity in sex-role acquisition. The differences in the theories are more of what is primarily emphasized (e.g., sexual libido and unconscious motives, systems of rewards and punishments, cognitive maturity) than in what actually occurs. The Oedipal, Electra, castration and penis envy conflicts proposed by Freud are not seen as frequently as they once were, probably because the Victorian practice of hiding sexuality and punishing any interest in it has been replaced with more openness and honesty about sexuality.

The definitions of male-appropriate and female-appropriate behaviors are becoming less clear in our contemporary culture than they were when Freud, the social learning theorists, and the cognitive-developmental theorists put their ideas on paper. Toddlers and preschoolers now usually all sport pants and shirts, regardless of sex. Many caregivers make a conscious effort to teach their sons to avoid fights, to express emotions, to nurture dolls, or animals, or other children, and to help with cooking and housework. Daughters are rewarded for doing the same things but are also taught to assert themselves, to run, climb, and roughhouse, and to help with garbage collection and mechanical fix-it tasks (see Figure 4–8).

Often the first exposure that toddlers have to sexual differences between males and females occurs when toilet training is begun, usually between eighteen months to two and a half years of age. At this time, if not before, children may be allowed to accompany opposite-sexed adults or other children into the bathroom for training purposes.

The concept of sex differences acquired in toddlerhood through toileting and other situations becomes of greater concern to pre-

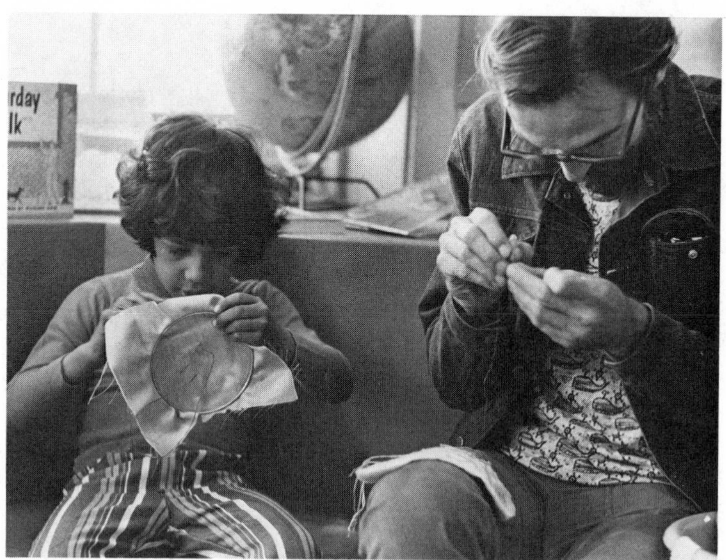

Figure 4–8. *Children today are becoming less conscious of sex-role stereotypes such as blue, baseball, and roughhousing for boys, and pink, perfume, and keeping house for girls.*

schoolers as they mature cognitively. They begin to discern sex similarities and differences in their friends, siblings, and acquaintances as well as in their caregivers. Curiosity leads to questions: Is that man the same as my father? Where do babies come from? Why is it forbidden to touch genitals in public? Even extreme efforts to shelter children from a knowledge of sex differences usually end in failure. The differences are too obvious to remain unnoticed. Some children learn that it is taboo to ask their caregivers questions about sex. So they ask their siblings or friends or invent their own answers. Often they acquire a great deal of emotionally upsetting misinformation in this manner. Caregivers who try to be open and honest about sexual matters and who answer all questions directly when and where they occur report surprise at how easily children accept the answers and go back about their play. Most psychologists believe that sex education is best accomplished by such direct information. However, it is not easy for all families to give on-the-spot, simple answers to questions, especially if they have had a lifetime's practice in keeping sexual matters hidden. Their embarrassment may be acute. Children can sense their parents' timidity and may quit asking questions. Many books for preschoolers are available to help families explain sex roles (see, for example, those by Gordon,[58] Evans,[59] and Gruenberg[60]). Writers of such books present answers to the questions that they know preschoolers ask in order to help caregivers provide the information in a less embarrassing way.

Sibling relationships. The presence of one or more brothers or sisters in a family adds new dimensions to social development beyond the caregiver-child behaviors discussed so far. Children may form affectionate bonds to each other in spite of the fact that the outward demonstrations of their relationship seem to consist mainly of fights. Younger children imitate their older siblings as well as their caregivers. They may play with them, learn from them, and receive some measure of help and nurturance from them. Young children may also experience the conflicting and painful emotions of fear, jealousy, anger, or hatred directed toward another sibling, especially a new arrival or one who consistently receives favored treatment from the caregivers. Sibling rivalry varies from family to family. Several interacting variables can affect its relative intensity, strength, and endurance. One factor that plays an important role in the formation of jealousies is the quality and quantity of time and attention that caregivers bestow on each individual child. The greater the differential treatment and favoritism shown, the more intense are the rivalries that develop. While it is not always possible for caregivers to treat children equally, explanations should be given to children about the reasons for any preferential treatment that is protested as unfair. As much as possible, caregivers should try to be fair with the time, attention, and favors they give each child. Two other factors that, along with parental treatment, have an interactive effect on sibling rivalry are sex and age spacing. Koch found that the stresses of sibling rivalry are greater between opposite-sexed than between same-sexed children.[61] Children who are spaced closer together have more rivalry than children who are born further apart. Koch found that the most stressful spacing is between two to four years apart. If a toddler is less than two when a new baby is brought into the home, the jealousy is not as intense. The two- to four-year age range is the period of time when toddlers are beginning to establish a sense of self. They have strong attachment and dependency bonds with their primary caregiver(s). They struggle for a sense of autonomy and yet are very vulnerable to feelings of shame and doubt. Their cognitive immaturity prevents their understanding why the caregiver must spend time with the baby. They resent the intruder who has usurped their favored status. After age four preschoolers are better able to understand reasons for sharing the caregivers' time with a new sibling. They also are more independent of adults and can initiate and carry through more of their own activities without assistance. Parents can help prepare a toddler for the arrival of a new sibling by explaining what life will be like with an eating, sleeping, crying baby in the house. When the infant arrives, parents should expect some jealousy and anger from the toddler, or perhaps some regression toward more infantile behaviors. The child should be helped to understand that such feelings are normal, but cannot be expressed in acts of physical aggression toward baby, mother, or

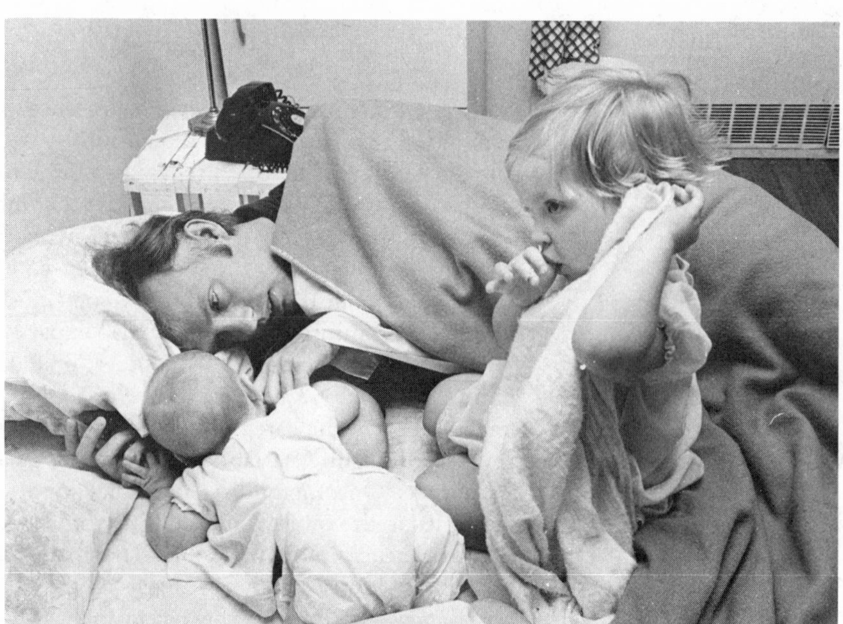

Figure 4–9. *Sibling rivalry is universal. It is generally more intense when babies are born close together than when they are spaced a few years apart. While rivalry is unavoidable, it can be minimized. Each child should be given individual attention, allowed to follow his or her own interests, and praised and encouraged for helping siblings rather than competing with them.*
Abigail Heyman/Magnum Photos, Inc.

self. Parents should spend as much time as possible with the toddler when the baby is asleep and reassure him or her of their love. Sibling rivalry can be further reduced by allowing the older child to help the adult nurture and protect the baby (e.g., holding, feeding, diapering, entertaining).

Studies of large groups of first-born, middle-born, and youngest children have revealed certain personality traits that are apt to characterize people of different birth orders. One must be cautious in interpreting these studies too literally. While a significant number of persons of a particular birth order may share similarities, any one person can be quite different from the group and still be normal. First-born children have been shown to begin talking sooner than later borns. They model and identify more with their parents. They have more motivation to perform well in school. And more than a fair share of them achieve high status employment for their adult years (e.g., doctors, lawyers, professors, engineers, architects, business executives). Parents tend to spend more time with first-born children. Although every developmental task accomplished is new and unique, parents pressure first borns to perform more. Research by Schacter shed a negative light on first-born children in this regard. The pressures on them to be the star performers can interfere with the give-and-take of establishing and keeping lasting friendships. According to Schacter, first-born children do not know how to get along with others as well as children raised with older siblings. They more often exploit friends and lose them. They are also more apt to have unsuccessful marriages.[62] Second- and middle-born children have been described as more easygoing and cheerful, or, occasionally, as neglected. Youngest children have been variously described as more immature and self-conscious or as more popular and outgoing.[63] When families are very large, children usually have fewer pressures on them in the cognitive and social realms. Bossard and Boll reported that families with six or more children usually insist on a handful of very firm rules but thereafter give the children a lot of freedom to do their own things.[64]

Discipline. It would be much easier to be a parent if experts in child development could produce an easy formula for stopping all children's bad behaviors and quickly inculcating high moral standards and pleasing behaviors. They cannot. There is an abundance of advice available on how to discipline children, but it is not simple or straight-forward. It is full of ifs, ands, and buts. This is because children are not all alike. And their behaviors change from day to day, even from minute to minute. In addition, parents are not all alike, and parental behaviors are subject to mood swings just as are children's actions. The long-range goal of discipline is to help children develop a conscience that will guide their behavior toward the positive and away from the negative. This conscience (or superego) formation involves gaining an understanding of the moral codes of the social order (i.e., learning right from wrong). It also involves gaining mastery over one's own behavior (i.e., learning self-control). The short-term goal of discipline is to stop behaviors that are dangerous, destructive, pain producing, or annoying. Some forms of discipline are more effective in bringing about the long-range goal of helping children guide their own behaviors according to society's moral standards. Other forms of discipline better serve the short-term goal of stopping an ongoing set of bad behaviors.

The various forms of discipline used by caregivers have been grouped into three patterns: power assertion, love withdrawal, and induction.[65] Power assertion includes deprivation of material objects or privileges, physical punishment (slapping, spanking, pulling, pushing, kicking, and all those ways by which adults punish with bodily hurt), or the threat of any of these. Love withdrawal includes scolding, ignoring, refusing to speak or listen to the child, isolating, giving dirty looks, explicitly stating a dislike, or any of the behaviors that adults use to temporarily withhold affection and approval from the child. Inductive discipline is an attempt to control the child's actions by explaining reasons for requiring a change of behavior or by explaining the consequences of the undesirable deed in terms of its bad effect on others. Most parents use all three kinds of discipline at different times depending on what has transpired and how tired they are. Often two or even all three methods are used simultaneously. Occasionally families get in the habit of using one method more than the others. Let us look at the developmental consequences of using each form of discipline.

Power assertion usually has the most immediately successful effect of halting misbehavior. It may be necessary when a child's actions are endangering another child, an adult, an animal, a valuable property, or the child's own person. It is relatively easy to use and is apt to occur more frequently when adults are rushed, tired, or irritable. However, predominant use of power assertion has harmful side effects. It leaves children feeling resentful. This resentment can be ameliorated to some extent if the punitive adult takes the time later to explain to the child the reasons why the behavior was halted, or why the adult felt it was necessary to dole out such an unpleasant punishment. If resentment is always ignored, it can seriously weaken the parent-child affection bond. In addition, exclusive use of power assertion does not further the long-term goal of discipline, the development of a conscience. Predominant use of physical force in childhood has been correlated with a low level of moral development in adulthood, based on fear of punishment.[66] Persons reared with a great deal of physical punishment will obey the letter of the law if they think they are being watched, but they often transgress quite freely if they think no one will catch them. This is because physical punishment has the ability to free one from feelings of guilt. Once a child (or adult) has paid for a misbehavior by being physically hurt, they may consider the score even. It is no longer necessary to consider the ill effects of the misbehavior on others. Physical punishment also serves as a model of aggression for the punished to imitate at a later time.

Love withdrawal is effective when a bond of love and an enjoyment of interacting exists between parent and child. The parent's anger then leaves the child anxious about endangering this pleasant relationship. In order to assure continuation of the parent's love, children will make amends. They will take whatever steps are necessary to get back in the parent's good graces: confessing, explaining, apologizing, making reparation, or promising not to repeat the action. Their guilt usually continues until the parent(s) again demonstrate love, affection, and forgiveness. Predominant use of love withdrawal has the initial effect of intensifying a child's efforts to obey and imitate the parents in order to assure continuation of their love, but it becomes less effective with increased use. Children can become resentful of adults who continually deride them or behave in a cold, aloof manner. This resentment can erode the bond of love and trust between them. Eventually the bond may be so damaged that parents have little love left to withdraw to sustain good behavior. Another possible effect of the overuse of love withdrawal in some children is repression. Children who appear too good may in actuality be quite inhibited. Fears of wrongdoing and loss of love may lead some children to overcontrol and overconstrict their activities to the point of not being able to acquire or sustain the Eriksonian "sense of initiative" that is so important in the preschool years. The predominant use of love withdrawal as a disciplinary technique in childhood is apt to lead to an adult morality level based primarily on the desire to maintain the good relations and approval of others. Kohlberg describes this as an intermediate level of moral development.[67] More mature moral orientations allow adults to respect authority, accept democratically contracted laws, and behave according to their own principles of conscience, regardless of the reactions of others.

Induction, as opposed to power assertion or love withdrawal, has much less potential for leaving children resentful. This is especially true if adults can speak with a calm voice rather than with harsh or angry tones when trying to induce changes of behavior. Inductive discipline has the most potential for directing conscience formation. It also increases the possibility that as they mature children will be able to channel their behavior into avenues that include consideration for the rights and needs of others. Children who are continually given other-oriented reasons for right and wrong learn to evaluate their own behavior in terms of its effects on others. They cannot depend on parents to relieve their guilt by physically punishing them or withholding possessions, privileges, or love when they hurt another person. They must bear the guilt alone. Predominant use of inductive disciplinary techniques in childhood leads to a high level of morality in adulthood, one in which persons are guided by their own individual principles of conscience rather than by the reactions of others. However, in order for induction to work with very young children, explanations must be kept at a very simple level. It is sometimes impossible for toddlers and preschoolers to comprehend or respond to an exclusive use of induction.

The consequences of the three major patterns of discipline just described are related to a nearly exclusive use of each one. Effects of discipline are less clear-cut when parents use a mixture of all three patterns of behavior as their children mature.

Many conflicts between adults and children are avoidable. Adults should be cognizant of normal behaviors of growing children at different ages and should not insist on rules and regulations that completely interfere with the acquisition of autonomy and initiative. Nor should parents insist on rules and regulations that are beyond the child's ability to understand or obey.

Discipline is not easy, but it is necessary. Children want and need help in controlling their impulsive actions in early childhood. Parents who are prepared to give this help in a thoughtful manner, without resorting to an overuse of power assertion or love withdrawal, can be successful disciplinarians.

Significance of the community in social development

Communities exert influence on the socialization of children in many ways—through traditions, customs, and the social norms of ethnic, religious, and racial groups and through direct contact with community members. For example, Quakers and Mennonites socialize children to abhor physical violence. Poussaint and Comer's book, *Black Child Care*, details specific advice to black parents on how to raise black children.[68] Navajo and Zuni Indian mothers carefully teach their children to respect and use nature wisely. They also discourage them from competing with each other for material possessions.

Children come into direct contact with a wide variety of individuals who exert influence on them: playmates, preschool teachers, babysitters, sales clerks, neighbors, other adults they see from time to time, and older children. In addition, they are influenced by television and books.

Although young children are encouraged to play with other children, it takes several years to learn to play cooperatively. At all ages, most children are keenly interested in the activities of other children. Two-year-olds usually engage in solitary play (alone), onlooker play (watching others), or parallel play (alone but with another child close at hand). Confrontations over desired toys are common. With increasing age, the children move to more associative play in which some shared activity and communication occurs. Finally, around school age, they move to more cooperative play in which there are rules and goals to their activities.

Children learn both good and bad things from each other: sharing, helping, encouraging, fighting, taunting, teasing, even cursing. However, in the early childhood years youngsters predominantly model the adults who do the nurturing and control the power. As children enter school, the influences of community members on social practices become much greater. Peers become more influential in later childhood and adolescence.

In group experiences such as neighborhood play groups, preschool programs, or day care centers, young children can gain additional independence and self-confidence and learn to relate to children and adults outside the family. Children without these experiences enter kindergarten somewhat cautiously. It is their first time away from home. Within a short time, however, they learn to adapt socially, assert themselves, share, and communicate with others.

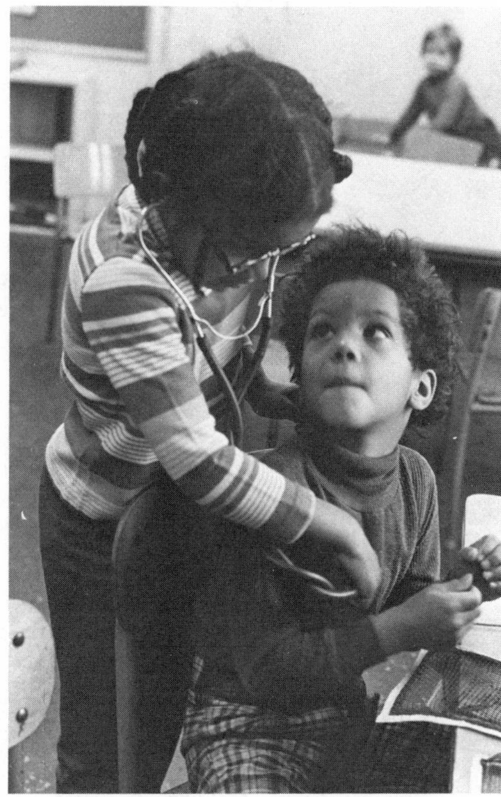

Figure 4–10. *Dramatic play allows children to assimilate and accommodate new bits of information into their existing mental structures. It lets them transform experiences into novel situations more to their liking. It also contributes to the child's growing sense of mastery of the world.*
Suzanne Szasz/Photo Researchers, Inc.

Television is considered an influential, extrafamilial agent of socialization in American culture today. Its role is similar to that of radio and movies in past generations. Programs such as Sesame Street and the Electric Company bring a great deal of enrichment to young children's lives. It is not uncommon to see preschoolers incorporate parts of these programs or characters from them into their fantasy play. (They also imitate situations or characters from any of the less enriching programs they watch.) Viewing time varies from child to child, day to day, and home to home, but may average about three or four hours a day and more on cartoon day (Saturday). In the early 1970s Gerbner took the time to count violent episodes in children's cartoons and got an average rate of 25.1 per hour.[69] Some recent research has found that children model the violence they see on television. Television networks, on the other hand, cite sources that refute this claim. Networks often claim violence in children is a result of general violence in society rather than the effect of television violence. Children also experience violence in their physical punishment, in the fighting between children and between adults, and in children's books.

Health considerations

When your parents were children, safeguarding health loomed very large as a concern of early childhood. Caregivers relied on daily rituals to promote good health (e.g., one hour of fresh air, one spoonful of cod liver oil) and used many palliative medicines (e.g., castor oil, jalap, calomel, mustard plasters) or patent medicines (those containing secret ingredients) to ward off illnesses. Mortality rates were high from infectious, contagious diseases (e.g., scarlet fever, typhoid fever, poliomyelitis) and complications of colds or influenza (e.g., pneumonia and encephalitis). Physicians did not yet have penicillin or other antibiotics.

Many of the diseases you had (or your parents feared you would contract) in early childhood are now less commonly seen. There are immunizations against measles, mumps, poliomyelitis, and rubella. In addition, medical technology and current pharmaceutics allow physicians to diagnose and effectively treat common infections before they lead to complications such as pneumonia, rheumatic fever, or acute glomerulonephritis (a kidney infection).

Today, improved diagnostic measures, new medicines, more immunizations, better sanitation, and a higher standard of living have relieved many parents of an overriding concern about their children's health. However, a high resistance to infection and freedom from dangerous illnesses cannot be taken for granted. Caregivers still have a responsibility for helping young children maintain a state of physical well-being.

Health maintenance

Adequate nutrition, sufficient sleep, exercise, freedom from emotional stress, avoidance of close contact with persons with contagious diseases, and protection from accident hazards in the environment are important ways to safeguard health in early childhood. In addition, young children should have regular medical examinations by a physician on an annual basis and be immunized against the preventable childhood diseases.

Adequate nutrition consists of a diet balanced with proteins, carbohydrates, and fats plus sufficient vitamins and minerals. It can be achieved by giving children two or more servings every day from each of the four basic food groups: (1) milk, (2) vegetables and fruits, (3) meat (or protein), and (4) breads and cereals. However, a well-balanced diet may be more difficult to attain during early childhood than it was during infancy. Appetites decrease and fluctuate from day to day. Children use mealtimes to test their independence with food refusals, food jags, or dawdling. They discover "junk" foods (e.g., candy, soda) and demand them. Between-meal snacks are common. They are also sometimes necessary because active young children burn up their intake of mealtime calories rapidly, although snacks may interfere with intake of more nutritious foods at mealtimes.

Caregivers can help assure adequate nutrition in early childhood by providing snacks with substantive nutritive value (e.g., milk, cheese, nuts, whole grain cereals or bread, fruit, vegetables). If young children have not been allowed to spoil their appetites with junk foods, and if their food refusals do not receive a great deal of attention, they will eat most of the foods served at meals in imitation of their caregivers. Food dislikes are generally related to highly seasoned or strong flavors or the foods that the caregivers also dislike. Vitamin supplements are rarely necessary if young children have balanced diets. Some physicians recommend vitamins with iron if the child shows signs of iron deficiency anemia. Others may recommend fluoride pills to help prevent tooth decay.

Sufficient sleep varies from child to child. In general, two-year-olds will probably require ten to twelve hours of sleep at night in addition to a midday nap. By age five preschoolers may cease napping during the day and only require about ten hours of sleep at night. On days when the child has been very active or emotionally keyed-up, sleep requirements may be greater than on days when excitement is minimal. Young children feel more secure with regular schedules and are more apt to get sufficient sleep if bedtime is the same time each night than when it varies according to the caregivers' moods. Extra sleep, when necessary, can be caught in the mornings or in afternoon naps.

Routine medical examinations on an annual basis during early childhood serve a multitude of purposes. Booster shots for immunizations received in infancy are necessary. Physicians are also able to detect problems that may be hidden from caregivers. Regular check-ups may reveal developmental delays, visual or hearing defects, heart murmurs, iron deficiency anemia, unsuspected urinary tract infections, perceptual problems, cerebral dysfunctions, or many other conditions that may otherwise remain undetected until the child enters school. The sooner they are discovered, the better the chances are of correcting them before they become severe or permanent problems. In addition, physicians can be excellent sources of information about childrearing concerns (e.g., toileting, feeding, sleep problems, discipline). If they cannot answer questions themselves, they may make referrals to agencies or professionals who are better equipped to help.

The leading causes of death in early childhood are (1) accidents, (2) neoplasms (cancers), (3) congenital malformations of the heart, circulatory, central nervous, and urinary systems, (4) influenza and pneumonia, and (5) gastrointestinal problems.[70] The most frequent nonfatal health problems for which physicians treat young children are accidents and infections. The following section will discuss accidents, infections, physical disabilities, neoplasms, and congenital malformations.

Accidents

Young children are especially vulnerable to hazardous conditions in their environments because of their cognitive immaturity and their strivings for autonomy and initiative. They cannot be trusted to remember and obey safety rules. Explanations of rules may be poorly understood. Young children also often act impulsively to gratify their immediate, egocentric needs or desires, rather than considering their knowledge of rules and regulations.

Motor vehicle mishaps account for about 40 percent of the fatal accidents of early childhood.[71] Caregivers have a dual teaching responsibility in relation to automotive safety: precautions while riding in a motor vehicle and precautions while playing near areas where motor vehicles travel.

Many in-car fatalities can be avoided if children are taught from infancy to stay in seat belts or restraining devices. If a driver does not have one of the specially designed car safety seats for children, a regular seat belt can be used with the child sitting up on a cushion. In addition, children must be taught to keep their hands and feet away from all the instruments used by the driver. The back seat is, in general, a safer place for children than the front, and the center seat is safer than the window seats. A child riding on an adult's lap is not safe.

Young children should not be allowed to play in streets or busy driveways at any time and should be supervised while playing in areas accessible to roadways. In addition, toddlers and preschoolers should cross streets only with adult supervision. Young children should be taught the correct, cautious, "stop, look, and listen" procedures whenever they are near traffic.

Another leading cause of fatal accidents and serious injury to young children is ingestion of poisonous substances. The three household areas from which toddlers and preschoolers most often take and taste poisonous materials are under the kitchen sink, the medicine cabinet, and the garage (or storage area for shop, automotive, and garden supplies). Mothers frequently fail to realize that detergents and other cleaning aides can seriously injure or kill children when eaten or drunk in relatively small quantities. All household cleaning products should be stored on a high shelf out of children's sight and reach. Likewise, paints, paint removers, petroleum products, fertilizers, insecticides, and the like should be high and hidden from view. Medicine cabinets should be kept locked, and medicines should never be stored with foods. If cough syrups or liquid antibiotics must be refrigerated, they should be kept separate from foods in covered containers. Safety caps should be replaced securely (see Figure 4–11).

All potentially poisonous materials should be kept in the original, labeled containers in which they are purchased. If a supply must

Figure 4–11. *Small children can be expert at climbing to reach the attractive items they see their parents use. All household poisons and medicines should be kept out of sight and out of all possible reach.*
Leslie Davis

be transferred to another box, can, or jar, caregivers should never choose one which has been associated with food (e.g., soda bottle, soup can). The new container should also be clearly labeled as to contents and precautions. Young children should be taught not to play with any supplies belonging to adults. Even hair spray or perfume can cause fatalities. Children should especially be taught not to taste or eat anything unless it has been given to them by a parent or known caregiver. When medicines are necessary, caregivers should caution the child that the substance is a medicine, not a candy, and should only be taken when given by a known adult.

Other accidents that are seen frequently in early childhood include burns and scalds, animal bites, drowning, and electrocution. Caregivers must assume the responsibility for protecting toddlers and preschoolers from sources of flame or heat, from strange animals, from open water, and from sources of electrical current. Active, curious young children cannot be expected to remember all rules and dangers and protect themselves from environmental hazards.

Infections

As reported earlier, many of the fatal diseases of the early childhood years are now rare because of immunizations against them or because of improved medical care. However, there are still many infectious diseases for which we have no immunizations, such as many viral common colds, chicken pox, meningococcal meningitis, staphylococcal infections (boils, impetigo), streptococcal infections (strep throat, scarlet fever, impetigo), simple gastroenteritis, and tuberculosis.

Children will build up some natural immunity to many of the disease-producing organisms after they are exposed to them, although in early childhood the immune system is not fully mature and youngsters are very susceptible to infections.

Often bouts of sickness follow the beginning of preschool or kindergarten when the child is suddenly exposed to many other children and many new microorganisms. Continued good nutrition, adequate sleep, emotional security, and prompt medical attention all improve children's chances of recovering from infections without serious complications. But infections are hard to avoid altogether, and the child who is sheltered from all microorganisms does not have an adequate chance to develop immunities to them. The average child will have three or more upper respiratory or gastrointestinal infections each year.[72]

Caregivers should not hesitate to call a physician for symptoms of upper respiratory infections such as sore throat, fever, earache, coughing, wheezing, difficult breathing, or swollen glands. A physician is the best judge of whether or not the child should be seen after hearing the symptoms described on the telephone. What appears minor to the parent may be considered more serious by the doctor, especially if he or she has knowledge of some epidemic in the community. The opposite may also be true; the physician may reassure the parent that the symptoms that seem so serious are, in fact, transient and do not endanger the child's life.

Symptoms of gastrointestinal infections such as vomiting, cramps, or diarrhea should also be reported to a physician. It is not safe to assume that the child has "flu," a stomach upset, or an intestinal virus. The problem may be one of a magnitude requiring surgery, such as appendicitis or intussusception (an obstruction of the bowel caused by a telescoping of one portion of the intestine into another). Even if the gastrointestinal upset is due to a virus, young children can become seriously dehydrated quite quickly. They may also go into shock from loss of fluids and salts after a prolonged episode of vomiting and diarrhea.

Physical disabilities

Some young children are born with or develop physical disabilities that are not life threatening but that remain with them for a lifetime. These include sensory defects (visual and hearing problems) and motor defects (cerebral palsy or congenital-orthopedic impairments).

Visual defects frequently remain undetected until toddlerhood. Parents may begin to suspect that vision is faulty if they see their child hold an object very far from or very close to the face while examining it. Friends or neighbors may point out problems such as squinting or crossed-eyes that parents have grown so accustomed to viewing that they ignore them.

Most young children are normally hyperopic (farsighted).[73] When the globe of the eye expands to rounder, fuller, more adultlike proportions at about age six, this farsighted condition will correct itself. However, some children with a higher grade of hyperopia in early childhood may experience headaches and eyestrain from this refractive error. If so, they should be fitted for glasses to relieve such symptoms and to improve their near vision. Glasses will not interfere with the progressive development of the eye and the accompanying decrease of hyperopia. Two other refractive errors of the eyes that young children may experience are myopia (nearsightedness) and astigmatism. In astigmatism one or more of the refractive surfaces of the eye have unequal curvature, which interferes with clear focusing. Glasses will correct the errors of both myopia and astigmatism and should be prescribed for and worn by young children as soon as the defects are discovered.

Strabismus (crossed-eyes, walleyes) is estimated to affect about 10 percent of the world population.[74] It is difficult to diagnose in infants because their eye muscles normally allow the eyes to drift occasionally. However, by age six months eyes should move in parallel (conjugate eye movement). Many parents ignore strabismus, believing it will correct itself in time. While some cases of strabismus lessen with the passage of time, the more usual course of events is for the child to get used to using only one eye. This may eventually allow the turning eye to lose its visual function. Uncorrected strabismus is one of the leading causes of monocular (one-eyed) blindness. It is preventable with early diagnosis and treatment. In general, vision can be saved if the deviating eye is brought back into binocular (two-eyed) functioning before about age six. Children should be taken to an ophthalmologist for correction of strabismus whenever it persists beyond infancy. Not only will treatment prevent monocular blindness, but it will protect the child from the psychologically damaging effects of being cosmetically different (cross-eyed, walleyed) from others.

Mild or moderate hearing defects are frequently unrecognized during early childhood. Caregivers or physicians may become suspicious of a hearing defect in early childhood if children do not attempt to speak by age two, if they fail to respond to out-of-sight noises, or if they tilt their heads or assume straining-forward postures while listening to communications. While some hearing defects are congenital, others may be acquired in early life as a result of severe ear infections or accidental ear injuries. As soon as hearing defects are suspected, they should be given medical attention for confirmation, diagnosis, and treatment, as hearing is very important to the development of language, cognition, and social skills in young children. If a hearing defect cannot be corrected with a hearing device, a child may be started in lip reading and sign language instructions as early as two to three years of age, the period when language development occurs in hearing children. Caregivers should also learn to communicate in sign for the benefit of the child.

Motor defects, such as spasticity (increased muscle tone with sudden, burstlike movements), other forms of involuntary movements, difficulty walking, and lack of coordinated muscle movements may not become obvious until early childhood. Motor defects in young children are most frequently the result of cerebral palsy, spina bifida, or some congenital orthopedic problem.

Cerebral palsy (CP) is a condition characterized by nonprogressive disturbances of control of motor power and coordination. It is related to developmental defects, intrauterine degeneration of some parts of the brain, anoxia, or brain trauma at the time of birth. In addition, it can sometimes result from postnatal factors (e.g., accidents, meningitis, encephalitis). There are many types of CP: spastic hemiplegia (one-sided body involvement, arms more involved than legs), spastic diplegia (all four limbs involved), spastic double hemiplegia (four limbs involved, arms more than legs), athetosis (involuntary writhing movements, usually of the hands and fingers), ataxia (uncoordinated movements), flaccidity (lack of tone in muscle movements), or mixed types.[75] With early diagnosis and physiotherapeutic treatment, speech training, or corrective orthopedic devices children with CP can be helped to gain some degree of control of their muscle movements.

Spina bifida refers to a congenitally defective development of the spinal column in which there is an absence of a portion of the vertebrae. Through this resultant space, there is a protrusion of the spinal cord membranes with or without spinal cord tissue. In the mild occulta form the defect may be unnoticeable or present simply as a slight protrusion over the spine that is covered with a growth of hair. In the more serious cystic form a sac protrudes from the spine, usually in the lumbosacral region.

Spina bifida occulta rarely creates any symptoms.[76] If the spinal cord is injured, symptoms associated with occulta defects may be muscle weakness, gait disturbances, or difficulty in controlling the bowel and bladder sphincter muscles.

Spina bifida cystica may take one of several forms. More common forms of spina bifida cystica are meningocele and meningomyelocele. In the former the cyst is composed of spinal meninges (membranes surrounding the cord) with the cord and nerve roots usually normal. In the latter the cyst contains neural tissue of the damaged cord. A meningocele is usually removed by elective surgery. It seldom causes neurologic symptoms since the cord is usually normal. The infant or young child with a meningocele must be kept from laying on or injuring the sac until surgery is performed. A meningomyelocele, depending on location on the spinal column, may cause flaccid paralysis, absence of sensations, inability to control bowel and bladder sphincters, leg and foot deformities, or spasticity in the lower extremities. The most serious abnormality associated with the meningomyelocele is hydrocephalus (excessive accumulation of cerebrospinal fluid in the brain). The biggest danger of the meningomyelocele is that the exposed neural tissue will become infected and lead to bacterial meningitis and death. It is, therefore, usually repaired as soon after birth as possible. If hydrocephalus is present, the accumulated cerebrospinal fluid, often under great pressure, may be removed by a shunt into the large veins leading to the heart. Children surviving surgery for cystic forms of spina bifida and hydrocephalus have varying degrees of motor impairment, mental retardation, and varying needs for rehabilitation training, depending on the extent of involvement of the cord, nerve roots, and the brain itself. Many of these children will be confined to wheelchairs for life.

Terminal illnesses

The second leading cause of death in early childhood is from neoplasms (cancers). The third leading cause of death is from complications of severe congenital anomalies of the central nervous system (such as meningomyelocele and hydrocephalus) or defects in the heart and circulatory systems, respiratory system, genitourinary system, or musculoskeletal system.[77]

Parents usually expect the possibility that a cancer or congenital anomaly will make their child's life expectancy short. Most still hope that surgery, improved medical techniques, protection from accidents and infections, or a miracle will give their child additional years of life. Toddlers and preschoolers themselves have only a vague concept of what it will mean to die. Death may be viewed simply as a transient phenomenon, similar to sleep. (In Chapter 12 we will present an in-depth discussion on children's concepts of death, related to their levels of cognitive maturity.) While death itself may not be overly fear-provoking, young children do experience stress, anxiety, and fears related to the symptoms of their illness. They also sense and react to the fears and anxieties observed in their caregivers. As difficult as it may be, caregivers should treat terminally ill children much the same as they treat normal children. Overindulgence can be more upsetting than helpful. Children feel more secure knowing that there are limits to the things they may request and the actions they may perform.

Cancers, unfortunately, claim the lives of many preschoolers each year. The predominant form of cancer of early childhood is leukemia. Brain tumors are also among the most common malignant tumors seen in young children. Leukemias of early childhood nearly always have acute onset (98 percent) with anemia, bruises, limb pain, spleen and liver enlargement, and fever.[78] Without treatment acute leukemia may be fatal within four months, although with expert management life expectancy may be prolonged, on the average, about four years. A small number of children may survive for many years.

Summary

Toddlers' and preschoolers' ecological environments gradually widen to include social networks outside the home. These, along with the primary family caregivers, help shape abilities and behaviors.

Physically, children stretch out in early childhood. Arms and legs grow fastest, helping to alter the top-heavy, short-legged appearance of babyhood. Motor skills emerge and improve (e.g., running, stair climbing, tricycle riding, ball throwing).

Piaget described the cognitive developmental stage of early childhood as preoperational. Children explore, manipulate, and think. The new dimension of improved mental functioning and use of mental images makes possible rapid acquisition of language and stimulates symbolic (dramatic) play. Play is a major synthesizer of ego, emotions, cognition, and socialization used to assimilate and accommodate more and more information. However, children in play and in other situations do not yet classify and systematically define their thoughts. They have difficulty separating fantasy from reality. They view their worlds from an egocentric perspective. Quite often they are very persistent and self-centered about felt needs or desires. By the end of the preoperational period, children begin to use rudimentary classifications. They also recognize some rights and needs of others and become less egocentric.

Language development reflects the egocentricity of early childhood. *I*, *me*, and *mine* are often heard. *Why?* is also common. Word usage multiplies rapidly, going from the few holophrases of beginning speech to more than a thousand words in a year. The age of beginning speech varies greatly from child to child, some starting shortly after their first birthdays, others waiting until after their third. One-to-one verbal stimulation fosters language usage.

Many young children attend preschools oriented toward cognitive and language development, toward socialization, or both. Day care centers usually combine a range of preschool-type activities with caregiving: meals, naps, nurturing. Neighborhood play groups help children relate to children and adults outside the family as well. The community influences development through cultural, religious, and ethnic customs and norms as well as through direct personal contact with the child.

Erikson described the nuclear conflicts of early childhood as first achieving a sense of autonomy versus shame and doubt and then thrusting out into the wider world with initiative rather than guilt. Learning self-help skills (feeding, dressing, toileting) and having freedom to explore and communicate are basic to autonomy. Shame and doubt, and then guilt, may arise if children's independence strivings bring continued negative feedback.

Discipline is essential in early childhood. Three kinds may be used alone or in combination: power assertion, love withdrawal, and induction. Induction has the greatest potential for directing conscience formation.

Health maintenance requires adequate nutrition, sleep, exercise, protection from accidents, and affection. Regular check-ups and immunizations can prevent or control many serious diseases and childhood disabilities.

Questions for review

1. Parents have generally been socialized to believe that having only one child will be harmful to that child. Do you agree or disagree with this? If you feel it would be harmful, how old do you think the first child should be before parents have another child? Discuss.
2. How does the preoperational stage described by Piaget differ from the sensory-motor stage that occurs in infancy?
3. Why do you think the age of two is commonly called the "terrible twos"?
4. What gifts (toys, games, etc.) do you think would be good for a child in early childhood? In your answer consider the developmental needs of a child at this time in the life span.
5. Children as young as the age of five—possibly younger—have been diagnosed as being emotionally disturbed. Do you agree or disagree that it's possible for a child at this age to be severely emotionally disturbed? In your answer, consider the theories presented by Erikson and Dreikurs.
6. Imagine you are the physician or nurse practitioner working with a family who has a child with a severe physical handicap. What would you advise the family in terms of coping with this handicap? Consider the coping needs of the child and the parents in such a situation.

7. Do you agree or disagree that the violence seen on television and in other parts of society is producing more violence in children? Discuss.

8. Jamie is an only child who is very active, bright (but not precocious), healthy, and extremely inquisitive. His parents are looking for a preschool setting for him to attend mornings. Describe a nursery setting that would be most appropriate for Jamie. Consider the various emphases in these settings (e.g., emphasis on socialization, emphasis on cognitive development). Also consider whether a Montessori school or a Dewey-type school might be more appropriate for this child. What qualities should the parents look for in the teachers? in the physical environment?

References

[1]D. Smith and E. Bierman, *The Biologic Ages of Man* (Philadelphia: W. B. Saunders Co., 1973).

[2]W. Nelson, V. Vaughn, and R. McKay, *Textbooks of Pediatrics*, 10th ed. (Philadelphia: W. B. Saunders Co., 1975).

[3]J. Tanner, "Physical Growth," *Carmichael's Manual of Child Psychology: volume I*, 3rd ed., P. Mussen, ed. (New York: J. Wiley and Sons, 1970).

[4]S. Robbins, *Pathologic Basis of Disease* (Philadelphia: W. B. Saunders Co., 1974).

[5]A. Gesell, *The First Five Years of Life* (New York: Harper and Brothers, 1940).

[6]A. Gesell, L. Ames, and G. Bullis, *The Child From Five to Ten* (New York: Harper and Brothers, 1946).

[7]A. Gesell, F. Ilg, and L. Ames, *The Years From Ten to Sixteen* (New York: Harper and Brothers, 1956).

[8]W. Frankenburg and J. Dodds, *Manual: Denver Developmental Screening Test* (Denver: University of Colorado Medical Center, 1967).

[9]White House Conference on Children, *Profiles of Children* (Washington, D.C.: U.S. Government Printing Office, 1971).

[10]W. Nelson, V. Vaughn, and R. McKay, *Textbook of Pediatrics.*

[11]J. Tanner, "Physical Growth."

[12]B. Bloom, *Stability and Change in Human Characteristics* (New York: J. Wiley and Sons, 1964).

[13]Ibid.

[14]D. Smith and E. Bierman, *The Biologic Ages of Man.*

[15]R. Truex and M. Carpenter, *Human Neuroanatomy*, 7th ed. (Baltimore: The Williams and Wilkins Co., 1976).

[16]Ibid.

[17]R. Bailey, *The Role of the Brain* (New York: Time, Inc., 1975).

[18]A. Luria, "The Functional Organization of the Brain," *Scientific American*, 222(3) (March, 1970).

[19]E. Bickerstaff, *Neurology for Nurses*, 2nd ed. (London: The English Universities Press, Ltd., 1971).

[20]K. Lashley, *The Neuropsychology of Lashley: Selected Papers*, F. Beach, ed. (New York: McGraw-Hill Book Co., 1960).

[21]R. Joynt, "Human Memory," *The Nervous System: vol. II, The Clinical Neurosciences*, D. Tower and T. Chase, eds. (New York: Raven Press, 1975).

[22]M. Pines, *The Brain Changers* (New York: Harcourt, Brace, Jovanovich, Inc., 1973).

[23]A. Luria, *The Mind of a Mnemonist*, L. Solotaroff, trans. (New York: Basic Books, 1968).

[24]K. Lashley, *The Neuropsychology of Lashley.*

[25]C. Gross, C. Rocha-Miranda, and D. Bender, "Visual Properties of Neurons in Inferotemporal Cortex of the Macaque," *Journal of Neurophysiology*, 35(1) (1972).

[26]K. Pribram, "The Neurophysiology of Remembering," *Scientific American* (January, 1969).

[27]M. Pines, *The Brain Changers.*

[28]M. Rosensweig, E. Bennett, and M. Diamond, "Brain Changes in Response to Experience," *Scientific American* (February, 1972).

[29]B. Agranoff, "Memory and Protein Synthesis," *Scientific American* (June, 1967).

[30]M. Pines, *The Brain Changers.*

[31]J. Phillips, *The Origins of Intellect: Piaget's Theory* (San Francisco: W. H. Freeman & Co., 1969).

[32]J. Piaget and B. Inhelder, *The Child's Conception of Space*, F. Langdon and J. Lunzer, trans. (London: Routledge & Kegan Paul, Ltd., 1956).

[33]J. Piaget, "Children's Philosophies," *A Handbook of Child Psychology*, C. Murchinson, ed. (Worcester, Mass.: Clark University Press, 1933).

[34]J. Flavell, *The Developmental Psychology of Jean Piaget* (New York: Van Nostrand Reinhold Co., 1963).

[35]J. Piaget, *Play, Dreams and Imitation in Childhood*, C. Gattegno and F. Hodgson, trans. (New York: W. W. Norton and Co., Inc., 1962).

[36]H. Ginsburg and S. Opper, *Piaget's Theory of Intellectual Development* (Englewood Cliffs, N.J.: Prentice-Hall, 1969).

[37]N. Chomsky, *Language and Mind* (New York: Harcourt, Brace, Jovanovich, Inc., 1972).

[38]R. Brown, *A First Language: The Early Stages* (Cambridge, Mass.: The Harvard University Press, 1973).

[39]E. Lenneberg, I. Nichols, and E. Rosenberger, "Primitive Stages of Language Development in Mongolism," *Disorders of Communication*, D. Rioch and E. Weinstein, eds. (Baltimore: Williams & Wilkins, 1964).

[40]D. Thomson, *Language* (New York: Time, Inc., 1975).

[41]B. Hamburg, "The Psychobiology of Sex Differences: An Evolutionary Perspective," *Sex Differences in Behavior*, R. Friedman, R. Richart, and R. VandeWiele, eds. (New York: John Wiley and Sons, 1974).

[42]N. Geschwind, "Language and Cerebral Dominance," *The Nervous System Volume II: The Clinical Neurosciences*, D. Tower and T. Chase, eds. (New York: Raven Press, 1975).

[43]B. Hamburg, 'The Psychobiology of Sex Differences."

[44]E. Lenneberg, *Biological Foundations of Language* (New York: John Wiley and Sons, 1967).

[45]A. Jensen, "How Much Can We Boost I.Q. and Scholastic Achievement," *Harvard Educational Review*, 39 (1969).

[46]J. Hunt, "How Children Develop Intellectually," *Children*, 11(3) (1964).

[47]R. Hess and V. Shipman, *Parents as Teachers: How Lower Class and Middle Class Mothers Teach* (Urbana, Ill.: ERIC Clearinghouse on Early Childhood Education, 1967).

[48]B. White, *Experience and Psychological Development* (Englewood Cliffs, N.J.: Prentice-Hall, 1971).

[49]J. Dewey, *Democracy and Education* (New York: The Macmillan Co., 1916).

[50]M. Montessori, *The Montessori Method* (New York: Frederick A. Stokes Co., 1912).

[51]E. Erikson, *Childhood and Society*, 2nd ed. (New York: W. W. Norton & Co., 1963).

[52]Ibid.

[53]Ibid.

[54]R. Dreikurs and V. Soltz, *Children: The Challenge* (New York: Hawthorn Books, Inc., 1964).

[55]H. Werner, *Comparative Psychology of Mental Development* (New York: International Universities Press, 1957).

[56]H. Maier, "The Learning Theory of Robert R. Sears," *Three Theories of Child Development* (New York: Harper and Row, 1965).

[57]A. Bandura, D. Ross, and S. Ross, "A Comparative Test of Status Envy, Social Power, and Secondary Reinforcement Theories of Identificatory Learning," *Journal of Abnormal and Social Psychology*, 67 (1963).

[58]S. Gordon, *Girls are Girls and Boys are Boys: So What's the Difference* (New York: The John Day Co., 1974).

[59]E. Evans, *The Beginning of Life: How Babies are Born* (New York: Crowell, Collier, and MacMillan, Inc., 1969).

[60]S. Gruenberg, *The Wonderful Story of How You Were Born* (Garden City, N.Y.: Doubleday and Co., 1970).

[61]H. Koch, "Some Emotional Attitudes of the Young Child in Relation to Characteristics of His Siblings," *Child Development*, 27 (1956).

[62]S. Schacter, "Birth Order and Sociometric Choice," *Journal of Abnormal and Social Psychology*, 68 (1964).

[63]B. Sutton-Smith and B. Rosenberg, *The Sibling* (New York: Holt, Rinehart and Winston, 1970).

[64]J. Bossard and E. Boll, *The Large Family System* (Philadelphia: University of Pennsylvania Press, 1956).

[65]M. Hoffman, "Moral Development," *Carmichael's Manual of Child Psychology*, vol. 2, 3rd ed., P. Mussen, ed. (New York: John Wiley and Sons, Inc., 1970).

[66]Ibid.

[67]L. Kohlberg, "The Cognitive-Developmental Approach to Socialization," *Handbook of Socialization*, D. Goslin, ed. (Chicago: Rand McNally, 1969).

[68]A. Poussaint and J. Comer, *Black Child Care* (New York: Simon and Schuster, 1975).

[69]G. Gerbner, "Violence in Television Drama: Trends and Symbolic Functions," *Television and Social Behavior Volume I: Media Content and Control* (Washington, D.C.: U.S. Government Printing Office, 1972).

[70]American Public Health Association, *Vital and Health Statistics Monographs: Mortality and Morbidity in the United States*, C. Erhardt and J. Berlin, eds. (Cambridge, Mass.: Harvard University Press, 1974).

[71]V. Holm and N. Wiltz, "Childhood," *The Biologic Ages of Man* (Philadelphia: W. B. Saunders Co., 1973).

[72]Ibid.

[73]L. Apt and G. Breinin, "The Eyes," *Pediatrics*, 15th ed. H. Barnett and A. Einhorn, eds. (New York: Appleton-Century-Crofts, 1972).

[74]Ibid.

[75]H. Jolly, *Diseases of Children*, 3rd ed. (Oxford, England: Blackwell Scientific Publications, 1976).

[76]W. DeMyer, "Prenatal and Developmental Defects," *Pediatrics*, 15th ed. H. Barnett and A. Einhorn, eds. (New York: Appleton-Century-Crofts, 1972).

[77]American Public Health Association, *Vital and Health Statistics Monographs*.

[78]H. Jolly, *Diseases of Children*.

Contents

Owen Franken/Stock, Boston

Late Childhood

The years from six to twelve are sometimes called middle childhood as well as late childhood. The latter rubric will be used here as an inclusive term. Middle childhood suggests that the early adolescent age range comprises late childhood. Most adolescents would consider late childhood a misnomer. The term middle childhood will be used occasionally to describe children of ages six, seven, and eight.

The most vivid memories of childhood are usually those from the late childhood period covered in this chapter: best friends (the "at-home" ones like neighbors and siblings, and the "at-school" ones who probably changed frequently); school; lunch hours at school; teachers and classes; after-school activities; homework; chores; sports; clubs; summer vacations; secrets; places to hide when one wanted to be alone.

During late childhood peers become extremely important. For this reason some writers call it the "gang age." It is also called the "dirty age" for reasons of both language and laundry. It is a time of considerable development physically, socially, emotionally, cognitively, and linguistically. The old adage that a child's personality is set by age seven has not been supported by research. Personality is a dynamic phenomenon, influenced throughout life by all kinds of environmental pressures. One should not become locked into the notion that the late childhood years are simply a latent passage of time in which a child grows bigger but otherwise emerges unchanged. Early childhood experiences do have a profound impact on the continuous development of children in the physical, cognitive, and social-emotional realms as they grow older. For example, the manner in which the Eriksonian conflicts of trust, autonomy, and initiative are resolved in the early years influences the way children react during their school years. However, new conflicts arise, new solutions are generated (interpreted by the accumulation of past experiences), and children change as they grow.

Physical development

Between the ages of six and twelve, children's proportions become more adultlike. Arms and legs get longer, the abdomen flattens, and the shoulders and trunk broaden. While the size of the head changes very little, facial proportions are altered considerably. The forehead broadens, the nose grows larger, the lips get fuller, and the jaw juts out from the chin. All of this takes place at a very gradual but steady pace. Growth is slower than it was in early childhood and slower than it will be in adolescence. Height increases by about five to seven centimeters (two to three inches) a year, and weight gains vary from one and a half to two and a half kilograms (three to six pounds) a year. Pediatricians may examine children carefully if they do not grow taller in a year's time, but they do not get as concerned about failure to gain weight. This is because weight is influenced by exercise and environment as well as by diet. A well-fed, well-nourished child may get taller but not add kilograms (pounds) over a one-year time span and still be well within a normal range. Fat deposits are burned off, and many muscles grow stronger during the elementary school years. Normal, healthy children engage in plenty of acrobatics—jumping, climbing, and group sports—and often learn to throw and catch, skate and swim, ride horses, bicycles, and skate boards. They may also be required by their families to engage in other less pleasant muscle-building activities like daily chores. They may take up stamp collecting, weaving, clay modeling, painting, model car or airplane building, cooking, sewing, photography, or any number of other activities that help develop their fine motor skills.

Late childhood may begin with a seemingly toothless grin caused by the shedding of deciduous teeth in preparation for the permanent ones. Throughout late childhood deciduous teeth are lost, and permanent teeth are gained, until by age twelve most youngsters have twenty-eight out of the eventual number of thirty-two permanent teeth. (Lacking are the wisdom teeth that may or may not manage to arrive during adolescence.) Teeth often grow in crooked. Numbers of children learn to cope (and sometimes even feel part of the gang) with their orthodontist visits and braces. Straightening of teeth not only gives a more pleasing appearance but also allows for a more satisfactory development of the lower part of the face and for a better bite.

Roughly 25 percent of school-age children need to wear glasses.[1] Most children are normally hyperopic (farsighted) until after about age six when their eyes begin to reach more adultlike proportions. Some children, however, are myopic (nearsighted), a problem that is not outgrown. Others have problems with astigmatism (a situation in which images are improperly focused on the retina due to faulty curvature of the cornea or lens). Glasses can correct hyperopia, myopia, and astigmatism and should be worn to prevent eyestrain and/or progressive loss of visual function. (see Figure 5–1).

Less than 5 percent of school-age children have some degree of temporary or permanent hearing loss.[2] However, even a mild, fluctuating hearing impairment such as that resulting from serous otitis media (condition in which the middle ear, the portion just behind the ear drum, is filled with fluid) can interfere with learning and should not be ignored. Children with chronic infectious otitis media or serous otitis media may eventually sustain a permanent conductive hearing loss from damage to the hearing structures. Other causes of hearing losses include accidental ear injuries and congenital defects. Hearing tests should be conducted annually on school-age children. Significant hearing loss is often an overlooked cause of learning difficulties. If schools do not do routine hearing screening, parents should ask their physician to include this in the child's annual physical check-up.

Figure 5–1. *Children with visual defects such as myopia and astigmatism should wear glasses. Failure to correct vision can result in blurred or distorted images that confuse children and interfere with learning.*
Freda Leinwand

Cognitive and language development

Piaget's descriptions of cognition in late childhood will be examined first in this section, followed by the various processes involved in learning, the testing of intelligence, the debate over how much of intelligence is inherited, factors involved in creativity, and, finally, language development in late childhood. Cognitive and language development move from the realm of predominant parental concerns to the sphere of school interests during the years from six to twelve. An assortment of teachers help children learn increasingly complex cognitive skills and try to stimulate their drives for mastery and achievement. School becomes the center of children's extrafamilial lives, occupying about one-half of their waking hours Monday through Friday nine months of each year. As we shall see in the social development section of this chapter, the school plays an important role in instilling many attitudes not related to academics. Some critics of schools in America feel that, in fact, schools may contribute to academic frustration and failure rather than to intellectual curiosity and achievement.[3]

Piaget's concrete operations stage

Piaget postulated that the period of concrete operations begins somewhere between ages six and eight, depending on each particular child and his or her maturation, physical experiences, and social interactions. Some children may begin some concrete operations as early as age five.[4]

As we discussed in Chapter 4, the preoperational child (approximately aged two to seven) gradually acquires the ability to see a few relationships between things and to handle some simple classifications. Piaget felt such successes, however, were more intuitive than reasoned. The period of concrete operations is differentiated from preoperations by the fact that children now learn to reason about what they see and do. In fact, psychologists and educators sometimes call the years between six and eight the age of reason because children do acquire the ability to think things through.

During concrete operations children develop the ability to apply rules to the new things they see and hear. Such rules help them understand and classify new phenomena. The rules constantly undergo revisions and expansions. For example, a child in the concrete operations stage who sees a baby alone in a room will reason that a mother must be near because babies cannot take care of themselves. When a group of adults enter a room, the child will search out the most probable mother. If the mother is not present, and a father attends the baby instead, the child will have to revise the rule to include the fact that adults other than mothers also take care of babies.

Children who perform concrete operations can reverse their thoughts and mentally imagine things as they were before any actions were taken. In the previous example the child who had expected to see a mother can think back to the moment the baby was discovered alone and realize that, although a mother was expected, what he or she actually knew was that some adult must be near.

The ability to use and reverse mental operations makes possible an important concrete skill described by Piaget, that of conservation. Conservation involves the ability to understand that a quantity does not change simply because the form it takes varies. For example, an amount of water does not change when it is poured from a tall thin glass to a short fat glass. Likewise, an amount of playdough does not change when it is rolled from a ball shape into a snake shape. In order to conserve, children must be able to look over the whole field of a problem. They must pay attention to more than one characteristic at a time. For instance, they must be able to perceive changes in width as well as changes in height. They also need to be able to reverse the operation mentally and visualize what the properties were like before the change in form occurred. Preoperational children find conservation difficult because they center on only a limited aspect of the

Figure 5–2. *Children in Piaget's stage of "concrete operations" find games like chess challenging. They utilize their abilities to apply rules, comprehend ordering and classifications, reverse their mental calculations, and conserve equivalency.*
Leslie Davis

task and do not reverse their thoughts. Conservation of mass or quantity develops first.[5] Conservation of weight, where children need to have a relative knowledge of the weights of different materials as well as attend to size, develops more slowly. It may be acquired between ages nine and twelve depending on cognitive ability and experiences. Conservation of volume develops last. In his experiments Piaget seldom found children able to conserve volume before age twelve.[6]

Another demarcation separating preoperational from concrete operational children is the ability to comprehend numbering. Piaget explained that children become more adept at handling number correspondence and ordering problems during the concrete operations period because they use rules, reverse their mental calculations, and conserve. When preschoolers are shown a bouquet of flowers bunched together and an equal-sized bouquet spread out, they will choose the separated bouquet as larger because it looks larger. Even when they count the flowers and determine that the two bouquets have an equal number of blossoms, they will again be deceived about size when one bouquet is spread out. In contrast, concrete operational children handle problems of judging more, less, and the same by using a numerical count whenever possible. They will then conserve equivalency or nonequivalency no matter what form the rearrangement takes.

Piaget viewed numbering as a synthesis of two other operations: ordering and classifying.[7] If preoperational children are asked to place in order a group of articles that come in a range of sizes, they will order them haphazardly, often letting them represent some figure such as a house or train. Concrete operational children develop the ability to order them from largest to smallest, or vice-versa. If new gradients are introduced, the concrete operational children will insert them correctly into their series. In the concrete operations period children will also ascertain what objects belong to the same class, what objects differ, and how. They do this concurrently with ordering and, ultimately, with numbering. When presented with a box containing ten chocolates, five jelly beans, and five marbles and asked, "Which is most—chocolates, candies, or toys?", a preoperational child will most probably say that there are more chocolates than candies. They will not see that the chocolates are also in the class of candies. Concrete operational children would not have this difficulty. They can handle many classifications and subclassifications while ordering a series of objects.

Time conceptions (i.e., days, months, years) become increasingly well differentiated during this stage, but ideas of historical time and far future may remain vague until ages ten to twelve, depending on maturation, physical experiences, and social interactions. Many an adult has been horrified to learn that a school-age child may equate the days of the adult's youth with the days of the Civil War, for example, or fail to understand that some of the projections of science fiction might be possible by his or her own adult years. Space perceptions also develop gradually in the concrete operations period. Perception of self in space develops early. However, an understanding of geographical distances, such as those between states and countries, or of celestial distances, such as those between the earth, sun, moon, and stars, develops considerably more slowly.

Another notable achievement during the concrete operations period as described by Piaget is an understanding of the differences between physical and psychological causality. Young children with their animistic and artificialistic ideas (see p. 151) listen for or invent psychological causes for events. For example, many preschoolers who ask about the flame in a cigarette lighter would not be satisfied with an explanation of flints and lighter fluid. They would feel better answered if it were explained that the flame shot up so you could light your cigarette. As children grow older, they want to understand physical causes, although an interest in and knowledge of physical causality may not entirely replace ideas of psychological causality. Older children (even adults) may understand and be able to explain the physical cause for an occurrence (e.g., a higher flame on a cigarette lighter resulting from more oxygen intake) yet speak of a psychological cause for the same occurrence as well (e.g., "Aha, the flame is shooting up to get you!").

The concrete operational abilities do not all appear at once. They develop gradually as children have more and more experience manipulating objects and discovering rules about sizes, shapes, weights, classes, volume, time, space, and causality. All the operations become more refined and sophisticated with age and experience until children finally bridge the gap between concrete operations and the formal operations that characterize the reasoning of most literate adolescents and adults.

The learning process

Children use various processes to assimilate and accommodate their experiences and newly acquired information into their range of knowledge. An appreciation of how information is processed is central to a comprehension of cognitive development.

In the neuroanatomy of learning (see pp. 145–147), we discovered that some facts are stored only briefly (short-term memory), while others are retained over a longer period of time (long-term memory). The hippocampi, structures that are part of the limbic system of the brain, seem to play a vital role in pushing some information into a retention process rather than allowing it to dissipate.[8] The major function of the limbic system is the regulation of emotions. It does not seem merely coincidental that new information that arouses some personal emotional reaction is more apt to be remembered longer than information that is emotionally neutral.

Emotional and aesthetic (a sense of the beautiful) perceptions also guide cognition of objects or events. Psychologists differ in their opinions as to how judgment conceptualization develops in children. Gestalt psychologists feel that young children perceive whole objects first and have only vague awareness of the separate parts composing the whole.[9] They emphasize that as children gradually become conscious of parts, they continually redefine their idea of the whole to include each newly discerned part. Heinz Werner emphasizes the importance of the development of sensual awareness in all modes of this whole-to-part perceptual awareness.[10] Maturing children learn about the structures and functions of objects and events through such things as play, body movement, music, dance, stories, and language. Other psychologists believe that children first observe one or more of the distinct features of an object or event before they acquire the ability to pay attention to the whole.[11] A child may be so engrossed in a new noise that he or she may be oblivious to the rest of the toy, other toys, and all other surrounding objects or activities. Regardless of which awareness comes first, between the ages of six and seven part-to-whole perception reaches a level where children become adept at seeing both. Then, to succeed in school they must learn to pay attention to only a selected area of perceptual cues pertaining to a task and ignore other extraneous cues. Central nervous system development together with learned behaviors usually allows them to do this. The attention span for working at any given task also increases with age and experience.

Children learn to use perceptual features (e.g., round, happy, large, blue, middle, least) to help them label the new information they comprehend. They then try to fit the new information into some classification (e.g., food, game, chore, friend, animal, vehicle, word). By a process of using selective attention and encoding procedures, they are using reason as well as sensory perception for learning.

During late childhood boys and girls begin to develop an awareness of their own memory skills. This knowledge and awareness of the memory is called metamemory.[12] Young children are unlikely to think about trying to remember things for future retrieval. They have what Flavell has called a "production deficiency."[13] However, with increasing age, children develop strategies for remembering subject matter that they deem important. They learn to categorize incoming information in various ways: encoding stimuli with a word or series of words, encoding with pictorial images, or encoding with concepts. Some children develop more effective strategies for remembering than others. Some adults continue to develop their memories by attending classes such as the Dale Carnegie self-improvement course or reading books that teach them new learning skills. The more experience children have in finding ways to remember subjects, the more adept they become at fixing memories. However, the amount a given person can memorize at any one time is limited by the development and functioning of the brain cells. An average six-year-old can usually remember and repeat five digits presented verbally. By age ten it is usually possible to remember six digits.[14] Superior adults may have immediate recall of up to eight or nine digits. A six-year-old may remember and repeat two unrelated words presented verbally. A ten-year-old may remember three or four unrelated words. An adult may be able to handle up to six.[15] Short-term memory of adults is generally longer lived than short-term memory of children.[16] The ability to recall and retrieve various objects and events from the memory is greatly enhanced by the comprehension and use of a large vocabulary. For example, an adult would be hard pressed to remember more than two or three words presented verbally in a foreign language. Or, for example, if children were asked to draw ϕ ψ Ω from memory, they would have difficulty unless they had previously learned the Greek alphabet. If children know the Greek alphabet, they can use the names *phi, psi, omega* to mediate the image of the Greek symbols they see. Mediation refers to a middle step between perceiving and remembering that aids with the latter. Verbal mediators, in the case of the Greek letters, would help children remember and respond with a correct drawing. This is much simpler than trying to remember the descriptions: circle with a vertical line through it, vertical line with a half circle open on top attached at midpoint, and so on. Mediation involves using skills already acquired to help develop new skills or acquire greater dexterity at old skills. Mediators are frequently verbal (i.e., words we tell ourselves between taking in new information and responding to it). Sometimes nonverbal mediators like pictures are used. The abilities of deaf children to respond to new information quickly and accurately illustrates the use of some nonverbal mediators.

School-age children learn new information best when they have some definite verbal or physical example with which to encode and mediate their responses. Abstractions are still difficult for the child in Piaget's stage of concrete operations. Invisible, intangible concepts such as the grace of God, infinity, and algebraic equations cannot be readily grasped during late childhood.

Testing of intelligence

Piaget became interested in cognition and epistemology (the study of the origin, nature, method, and limits of knowledge) when he went to work at the laboratory of Alfred Binet in Paris in 1920. Binet and his colleague, Theophile Simon, were then standardizing the first widely accepted intelli-

Figure 5–3. *Reading contributes to competency in all cognitive and learning skills such as assimilating and accommodating new concepts, attending, encoding, mediating, remembering, and increasing the total range of knowledge. Children prefer books with plenty of action, sustained suspense, humor, and new information.* Jeanne Hamilton/Editorial Photocolor Archives

gence test. A version of Binet's original examination, revised at Stanford University and now called the Stanford–Binet Intelligence Test, is still used today. Piaget was not so much interested in the development of tests to measure a person's intelligence quotient (IQ) as in the nature of the intellect. Therefore, he soon left the lab of Simon and Binet. However, Simon and Binet continued their work because others wanted tests. Today there are hundreds of IQ tests: individual tests, group tests, long forms, short forms, culture-fair tests, even tests based on Piaget's studies in epistemology. As the number, complexity, and uses of IQ tests have grown, so have the criticisms of them.

The advocates of IQ testing support their use on multiple grounds. Most importantly, IQ examinations can gauge how well or poorly a person has learned academic materials in comparison with others of the same age group. In addition, IQ tests can also predict, to some degree, how well or poorly a person will continue to learn academic subjects in the future.

Critics of IQ testing argue against their use on many other grounds. Primarily, they point out that for a test to fairly gauge and predict the relative learning abilities of a group of people, the members of the group should all have had equal exposure to the kinds of information required on the test. One seldom finds so homogeneous a group. Also, to be fair, test takers should all be relaxed during an examination so they can think clearly. They should be motivated to answer the questions correctly to the best of their ability. Test anxiety or lack of motivation to perform can severely mask real abilities. Language problems further complicate test giving and test taking. Even when both tester and subject speak the same language, directions can be misunderstood. When the subject's first language differs from that of the tester, the difficulties multiply. Some nonlanguage IQ tests exist, but like culture-fair tests, they are limited in the skills and abilities they can test. They cannot gauge what a child has learned from his environment as well as culture-bound and language-bound tests.

Children may have tremendous fluctuations in their IQ scores from test to test, as much as from twenty to thirty points, depending on the circumstances surrounding the test administration. For example, one child's tested IQ dropped fifty points after the death of his mother, and another's IQ score increased thirty points after psychotherapy relieved some anxieties. When such variations due to environmental conditions are possible, the accuracy of any one measurement is necessarily open to question.

The one thing on which test advocates and critics agree is that a child's success in learning school subjects is predicted better by the IQ test than by any other instrument. It is important, however, that parents, educators, and other lay people remember that an IQ score remains, at best, an inexact estimate of academic learning ability.

The heritability of intelligence

Arguments wax and wane about whether children inherit their ability to learn from their parents (grandparents, distant relatives) or whether parents and teachers inspire and motivate them to learn well (the nature versus nurture controversy). Most people believe that both heredity and environment influence intellectual ability. The argument became heated in 1969 when Berkeley psychologist Arthur Jensen published a review of several studies of intelligence.[17] He concluded that about 80 percent of intelligence is inherited. He testified before a U.S. Senate Committee on Education that with only about 20 percent of intellect influenced by environment, the vast sums of money spent on compensatory education, in his opinion, were wasteful. (Compensatory education programs, such as Head Start, were trying to provide intellectually stimulating environments to preschool children from deprived backgrounds before they began formal schooling.) Tempers flared, especially among educators trying to provide better educational opportunities for poor children. Jensen was accused of being a racist since lower IQ scores were associated with nonwhite Americans, and many poor nonwhites were in the compensatory education programs. Richard Herrnstein wrote in support of Jensen and added fuel to the fire of controversy.[18] He suggested that since different people inherit different intellectual abilities, we should educate people for jobs according to their merit, or practice a system of meritocracy. A Nobel Prize-winning physicist, William Shockley, further suggested that persons with inherited low IQs might be monetarily rewarded for being sterilized to halt the production of more low IQ children.[19]

Counter-arguments were abundant. Supporters of Head Start and other compensatory education programs emphasized that children given enriched environmental stimulation through early schooling could enhance the extent to which their genetic potential was realized.[20] Others questioned whether the impoverished and suppressive environments of these children were not more responsible for failing to evoke and nurture their IQs than realized by Jensen, Herrnstein, Shockley, and others. Additional benefits of early schooling such as social and emotional development were also stressed as reasons for supporting Head Start. Many educators refused to argue whether nature or nurture was more important but asked instead, as Anastasi asked in 1958, how the genotype and the environment could interact to produce the phenotypic characteristic recognized as intelligence.[21]

No matter where one stands on the nature versus nurture question, IQ tests cannot measure inherited abilities. They simply estimate how well or poorly a person can answer the kinds of questions on a test compared to other people of the same age, assuming equivalency of experience, motiviation, nervous tension, physical health, and emotional health.

Creativity

Creativity is variously defined as the ability to think flexibly, divergently, imaginatively, inventively, or productively. Is it good to be creative? A paradox exists in contemporary American schools about creativity. While its merits are extolled, its development is frequently inhibited. Examinations, for example, usually have only one right answer. Any novel, unconventional ideas, even though practical and correct in their own way, are penalized. Children who have been fond of freestyle drawing, sculpturing, and building in their preschool years may be encouraged to make school products look like the models in workbooks or those that their teachers have made. Creative children can become embarrassed or ashamed of work that differs from the norm. They learn to inhibit their originality and their urges to strike out on their own. A child's attendance at school five days a week learning conventional school subjects also reduces the amount of time he or she has for creative enterprises. A young Mozart would be hard pressed to write two operas and a large number of arias, serenades, symphonies, masses, and divertimenti during late childhood today.

School-age children display varying degrees of creativity that are not at all synonymous with academic ability. Creative development is fostered by adults who are tolerant of unconventional products or responses, who encourage free use of materials and free flow of conversation, who accept children's own best efforts, and who allow children to

Figure 5–4. *Creative children are able to express their experiences or dreams and fantasies in original, unique ways. They use materials freely rather than repeating tried and true procedures. Adults can foster creativity by encouraging and praising new productions and refraining from giving specific "how-to-do-it" directions.*

Bill Anderson/Monkmeyer Press Photo Service

proceed on tasks without a lot of specific directions.[22] Special rooms are needed where messy projects are permitted and time is unlimited. Such places are not conducive to maintaining clean, quiet, well-ordered households or to teaching large classrooms of children certain required subjects in short school terms. Teachers who are firmly committed to developing creativity in their students might also find their efforts inhibited by administrators or parents who value conventional academic performance more highly than originality and imagination.

Language

Growth in vocabulary and use of language continue throughout adulthood. The average six-year-old may have about 2,000 words at his or her disposal.[23] Adults can pick and choose from about 50,000 words. Children not only gain larger vocabularies during their late childhood years, they also correct grammatical and pronunciation errors and learn subtle meanings of old words. Puns and figures of speech finally become meaningful. Inflections allow children to alter the meaning of what they say. Language becomes fun! School-age children usually enjoy the play of words and invent or adopt word games that allow them to show off and improve their speech proficiency. Jokes based on double word meanings, slang, colloquialisms, curse words, feigned accents, secret languages, and ciphered messages abound between ages six and twelve.

School-age children acquire new sophistication in their sentence constructions. Sentences may be compound or complex and may contain compound subjects, compound verbs, and relative clauses. Children's understanding of certain syntactical forms (arrangements of words) in sentences also improves. Noam Chomsky, who postulated the language acquisition device (LAD) in humans (see pp. 105 and 153), believes there are two levels of language: surface and deep structures.[24] For example, the sentences "Helen is easy to please" and "Helen is eager to please" have the same surface structure, but their deep structure, their underlying meanings, are very different. School-age children come to understand that Helen is the object of the first sentence (others try to please her), whereas she is the subject of the second and will try to please others. Younger children may have difficulty with the first sentence. They may be confused about what Helen is to do.

During late childhood children still use vocabulary words that they do not fully understand (e.g., radar, communist) or understand expressions incorrectly, according to what they believe the words should mean. Krauss and Glucksberg found that certain general concepts were misunderstood and used incorrectly by several persons in the same school class until the eighth grade.[25]

Social development

During the years from ages six to twelve, the school and the peer group join the family as major influences on the socialization of the growing, developing child. How potent the school and the peer group can become depends in part on how strict or relaxed the family members are in exerting their own forces on shaping behaviors. A second factor that plays an important role in determining the relative strength of family versus school versus peers in socialization is the stoutness of the family's affectionate bond. Children from ages six to twelve still identify with and model their behavior after the people they perceive as most nurturant and powerful. Strong family ties relegate peers and school to a position of lesser importance, while weak family ties escalate the influence of significant others in the community.

Significance of the family in social development

The American family has changed profoundly in the last few years, moving from existence in a predominantly rural society to a suburban and urban one. Many people have divorced themselves from dependence on members of the extended family and learned to value the privacy and self-sufficiency of the nuclear unit (father, mother, children) or simply to rely on themselves alone. With this emphasis on self-sufficiency has come a hesitancy to ask too much of relatives, friends, or neighbors. Today many American families do not know, or even care to know, the names of the families living next door to them. This closed-door tendency is partially due to the high mobility rate of Americans. Neighbors are apt to move away and be replaced by strangers rather frequently.

Twenty-five years ago most mothers stayed home to raise their children. Now approximately half of the mothers in the United States go to work at jobs outside the home each day.[26] Childrearing responsibilities are being shared by baby-sitters, by day care centers, by family day care homes, and, increasingly, by fathers who arrange work schedules flexible enough to allow them to stay home part-time with their children.

In this section on social development in late childhood, we will examine both the theories of what families should provide for optimal socialization and some of our common practices today.

Erikson's industry versus inferiority stage. Erik Erikson's fourth stage in his concept of "The Eight Ages of Man" is the nuclear conflict between developing a sense of industry versus developing feelings of inferiority. True to his Freudian background, Erikson saw the middle to late childhood period as one characterized by a latent interest in sex. Oral, anal, and genital concerns are supposedly sublimated. As the child becomes master of many of the concerns of early childhood (e.g., autonomy, walking, running, talking, toilet training, initiative, sex role identification), he or she moves beyond the womb of the family. "The inner stage," as Erikson put it, "seems all set for 'entrance into life,' except that life must first be school life, whether school is field or jungle or classroom."[27] The nuclear conflict between developing a sense of industry and acquiring an uncomfortable sense of inferiority remains paramount throughout the elementary school years.

School, with its objectives, methods of instruction, discipline, and system of rewards and punishments, is an influential force in shaping or negating a sense of industry. In school, children concentrate on the important but impersonal tools of the adult world: reading, writing, arithmetic, science, and social studies. They must apply themselves to tasks and persist in the work involved until some satisfactory completion point is reached. This ability to persevere is fostered by increasing cognitive maturity, by social reinforcements, and by children's own drives for industry. The ability to bring a productive situation to completion carries with it a sense of pleasure and pride in accomplishment. The more experiences children have winning recognition from others and feeling inner pride, the more anxious they become to finish projects and produce or accomplish things. The mere exploration of or experimentation with materials as practiced in early childhood becomes less rewarding. Schools foster industry by requiring that tasks be finished (e.g., completing a reader; writing sentences, paragraphs, compositions; learning to spell; learning arithmetic computations). They often teach children to work together toward some stated goal (the division of labor principle). Two or three children may be assigned a joint project, or the whole class may work together on some undertaking that will then be displayed to other classes or to parents. In some foreign countries children actually begin working together during their elementary school years to produce articles for sale to the outside community. The recognition that comes to a whole group for their production serves to bolster the sense of industry of each participant. While the school has the potentiality for fostering a sense of industry in each pupil, this possibility is not always realized. Standards used by various schools or teachers to measure adequacy, such as tests, praise for classroom performance, and report cards, can leave some children well recognized and others frequently reproached for mediocrity or inadequacy. When children fail to win recognition for their efforts to accomplish things or for the products they effect, they are in danger of developing a sense of being inferior.

Erikson wrote that too many experiences of being made to feel inadequate and inferior in the early years of elementary school may cause a child to revert back to the more isolated, less industry-conscious stage of the Oedipal and Electra attachments.[28] He warned that families have a responsibility for preparing children for the realities of school life with its competitiveness and its emphasis on accomplishments. Likewise, the school has a responsibility to sustain the promises of worth and respectability made by families to children. Each child should be helped to feel industrious and adequate no matter how his or her skills compare with others. Children who are continually made to feel inferior during their elementary school years may be doomed to feeling mediocre or inadequate throughout their lives. Just as babies who fail to develop a sense of trust in infancy will have lifelong difficulties in trusting others, children who fail to develop a sense of industry in the elementary school years will have lifelong underlying weaknesses when it comes to taking their productive places in the world.

The family is a very important source of feedback for children to assure (and reassure) them that their industry is both recognized and approved. Children who have learned the pleasure of work completion in school will try to win approval at home through the demonstration of various achievements and productions. It is important that parents give children this needed approval. It is also important that children be given projects or work to do at home to help foster their growing sense of industry. While boys and girls may bemoan the addition of chores to their daily activities, such household tasks provide a sense of contributing to the work of the family unit (see Figure 5–5). They also give children a sense of pride in accomplishment when their completion is recognized, approved, or rewarded with praise or some other tokens of appreciation. Favoritism is one way in which families detract from the child's sense of industry and contribute to his or her sense of inferiority. Sensitive parents will be careful not to continuously praise or reward one sibling over another. They will avoid the use of comparisons to motivate behaviors. Instead, they will help all their children feel adequate with their own special skills and accomplishments.

There are many activities in which elementary school-age children can participate outside of the home and school that serve to enhance their sense of industry. Many organized clubs offer individual recognition in such forms as uniforms, badges, pins, award ribbons, trophies, or even monetary prizes. Depending on age, children can join the Cub Scouts or Brownies, Boys and Girls Clubs, 4H, Boy or Girl Scouts, Demolay or Rainbow, religious groups, and many other organizations where they can work together with others learning new skills of the adult world. Erikson pointed out that it is by no means always in schools with special teachers that children receive systematic instruction.[29] Many adults teach their specialized skills to children simply by dint of gift and inclination. Often the most effective teachers are older siblings, neighbors, and friends, both within and outside of organized groups.

Figure 5–5. *Daily chores can help children develop a sense of industry as described by Erikson, if family members approve their efforts. Chores can also help children feel that they are contributing to the work of the family unit.* Charles Harbutt © Magnum Photos, Inc.

Sports activities and games provide still another avenue for developing a sense of industry in childhood. In group sports children work together for a common goal, and all members of a team can share the glories of a victory. In individual competitions a child often has the prerogative of choosing a rival of equal or similar abilities so winning happens in a balanced ratio with losing.

In discussing inferiority Erikson warned of the danger that threatens individuals and society when the schoolchild is made to feel that his or her worth is related to skin color, parental background, or fashionable clothes.[30] Parents, teachers, neighbors, or club leaders can be guilty of conscious or unconscious prejudicial judgments about some children's accomplishments. Such adult prejudices often make children feel inferior. And, unfortunately, at this time in children's lives self-concept is usually not well defined. During the elementary school years children are apt to believe adult evaluations rather than recognize prejudice for what it is. It is important for parents and friends to reassure children of their worth if and when the children report the prejudicial comments of others. While some experiences of feeling inadequate are bound to occur during late childhood, a sense of industry can be fostered by sensitive adults who counterbalance their criticisms with constructive suggestions, recognition of completed work, and praise (see Table 5–1).

Table 5–1. Erikson's fourth nuclear conflict: industry versus inferiority.

Sense	*Eriksonian descriptions*	*Fostering adult behaviors*
Industry	– application of self to given skills and tasks	– give systematic instruction in skills and tasks
	– effort to bring productive situation to completion	– give recognition of things produced
	– attention and perseverence at work with pleasure obtained from effort	– specialized adults and older children outside family also instruct and recognize progress
	– work beside and with others brings sense of need to divide labor	
vs.		
Inferiority	– disappointment in own tool use and skills	– family failed to prepare child for life in school and with other adults and unrelated children
	– sense of inadequacy among tool partners	
	– lost hope of association in industrial society	– school failed to sustain promises of earlier stages
	– sense of being mediocre	– adult makes child feel that external factors determine worth rather than wish and will to learn

Source: Based on material from "Eight Ages of Man" from *Childhood and Society*, 2nd Edition, Revised, by Erik H. Erikson, with the permission of W. W. Norton & Company, Inc. Copyright 1950, © 1963 by W. W. Norton & Company, Inc.

Moral development. The acquisition of society's moral standards is influenced by identification, modeling, cognitive growth, and the predominant kind of discipline used to correct a child's unacceptable behaviors (power assertion, love withdrawal, induction; see pp. 173–176).

The goal of morality training is to produce a person whose conscience will direct his or her behaviors toward the good and away from the bad without continual external reminders.

Freud believed that children learn early moral standards through two kinds of identification with their caregivers: by anaclitic identification (based on a fear of losing love) and by aggressive identification (based on a fear of punishment by the aggressor or authority figures).[31] Anaclitic identification is used more by girls in identifying with their mothers, while aggressive identification is used more by boys in identifying with their fathers. Identifications of girls with their fathers and boys with their mothers can be either anaclitic or aggressive. Freud saw these identifications as a basis for children's knowledge of right and wrong. The fears of losing love and/or the fears of punishment are the forces that help children avoid unacceptable behaviors.

Social learning theorists emphasize the fact that children model the behavior of adults with whom they most strongly identify.[32] Children's modeling takes the form of striving to incorporate everything about the loved or powerful adults into their own lives, including moral standards and values. Learning theorists claim that children receive a sense of security and approval when they emulate caregivers' behavior. This modeling of behavior then becomes a need because of the emotional rewards it brings to the child.

Although identification with and modeling of the loved caregivers within the family is felt to be the *sine qua non* for beginning moral development, children also learn moral rules by modeling the behavior of friends, neighbors, teachers, and other associates, especially during late childhood.

Research has amply demonstrated that principles of stimulus-response learning apply to the development of moral behaviors. When a response to a given behavior is attention, approval, praise, or some material reward, that behavior will be repeated. When the response is negligence or punishment, the behavior is less apt to be repeated. However, ignoring bad behavior can sometimes be misconstrued by a child to mean approval. Siegal and Kohn found that children misbehaved more frequently in the presence of a permissive adult than they did when they thought no adults were around.[33] They suggested that this misbehavior probably occurred because the children felt that the permissive adult, by not correcting the bad behaviors, was giving tacit approval for its continuance.

Piaget distinguished two moral levels in children. The earliest is a morality of constraint that puts wrongdoing in terms of damage done and emphasizes submission to authority. The second moral level is a morality of cooperation that judges wrongdoing by the intent of the doer and establishes rules by mutual agreement.

In the period of morality of constraint, according to Piaget, children feel an obligation to comply with rules because they see them as sacred and unalterable. They measure the degree of wrongness of an act by the amount of damage done, without consideration of motivation. Here are two sample stories that Piaget used to question children to help him determine their level of morality.

A. Alfred meets a little friend of his who is very poor. This friend tells him that he has had no dinner that day because there was nothing to eat in his home. Then Alfred goes into a baker's shop, and as he has no money he waits until the baker's back is turned and steals a roll. Then he runs out and gives the roll to his friend.

B. Henriette goes into a shop. She sees a pretty piece of ribbon on a table and thinks to herself that it would look nice on her dress. So while the shop lady's back is turned she steals the ribbon and runs away at once.[34]

A child in Piaget's stage of morality of constraint would judge the first offense as more serious because the roll was bigger and more expensive than the ribbon. In effect, the child would ignore the intent of the transgressor. The sin would simply be judged by its magnitude. In this case the worse crime would be stealing the larger, more expensive item. At this stage children also believe that punishment wipes away the sin. The more severe the punishment is, the fairer it is. During this stage they see punishment as inherent in the external world, a view that Piaget called a belief in immanent justice. The following question asked by Piaget illustrates a belief in immanent justice:[35]

Piaget: In a class of very little children the teacher had forbidden them to sharpen their pencils themselves. Once, when the teacher had her back turned, a little boy took the knife and was going to sharpen his pencil. But he cut his finger. If the teacher had allowed him to sharpen his pencil, would he have cut himself just the same?

6-year-old: He cut himself because it was forbidden to touch the knife.

Piaget: And if he had not been forbidden, would he also have cut himself?

6-year-old: No, because the mistress would have allowed it.

Children in this level of morality believe that all misdeeds are ultimately punished. If adults fail to punish, nature somehow intercedes. It is common for children to believe that accidents, bad dreams, or illnesses are the just punishments for their sins of the day.

During late childhood Piaget believed a morality of cooperation replaces the morality of constraint. As children begin to help make the rules for their games, they see them as less absolute and immutable. Children begin to see others' points of view and realize how different motivations underlie different actions. Justice comes to be viewed in a social context and in terms of equity and equality.

Kohlberg expanded Piaget's ideas of moral development, postulating six stages rather than two. Brief summaries of his stages are as follows:[36]

Stage 1: Punishment and obedience orientation.

Stage 2: Acts that are satisfying to self and occasionally satisfying to others defined as right.

Stage 3: Morality of maintaining good relations and approval of others.

Stage 4: Orientation to showing respect for authority and maintaining social order for social order's sake.

Stage 5: Morality of accepting democratically contracted laws.

Stage 6: Morality of individual principles of conscience. Do what seems right regardless of reactions of others.

Kohlberg asserted that Piaget placed too much emphasis on the child's respect for rules and authority in the morality of constraint. He said young children's obedience was instead a recognition that the parents are more powerful. He emphasized both cognitive growth and social experience as requirements for moving to advanced moral stages. Kohlberg stated that children advance in sequence from one stage to another, rather than by leapfrogging any of them. However, some older children may be morally behind due to lack of experience and/or cognition, while younger children may advance to higher levels than might be expected for their ages. Research by Turiel supported Kohlberg's theory. Turiel gave his subjects stories like the one below and asked them to choose an ending and explain the reasons for their choices.

> In Europe, a woman was near death from a special kind of cancer. There was one drug that the doctors thought might save her. It was a form of radium that a druggist in the same town had recently discovered. The drug was expensive to make, but the druggist was charging ten times what the drug cost him to make. He paid $200 for the radium and charged $2000 for a small dose of the drug. The sick woman's husband, Heinz, went to everyone he knew to borrow money, but he could only get together about $1000, which is half of what it cost. He told the druggist that his wife was dying and asked him to sell cheaper or let him pay later. But the druggist said, "No, I discovered the drug and I'm going to make money from it." So Heinz got desperate and broke into the man's store to steal the drug for his wife. Should the husband have done that?[37]

Answers such as "You really shouldn't steal the drug" or "The druggist should get some profit from his business" are conventional role-conforming answers, stages 3 and 4. A stage-6 answer would reflect the acceptability of changing a conventional rule when unusual circumstances make it desirable.

In Piaget's and Kohlberg's views, moral development can be influenced by identification and modeling, but it is mainly tied to cognitive development. To reach higher moral levels children need many experiences with choosing right and wrong and opportunities to reason out the whys and wherefores of the choices.

How then do parents, teachers, and other adults help provide for optimal moral development? In order to develop a mature moral orientation and the ability to guide one's own behavior toward the positive and away from the negative, children need (1) to know right from wrong, (2) the ability to control their own urges to do wrong, and (3) thoughtfulness to consider the rights and needs of others before acting. By middle to late childhood children can be expected to understand most of the things that family and society define as unacceptable, but they cannot always be expected to have control over their urges toward selfish or aggressive acts. Nor can they or anyone be expected always to consider the rights and needs of others. Adults can help children learn both self-control and consideration of others.

In helping school-age children learn to control their own behaviors, adults should be mindful of the child's own needs for industry, approval, and respect. An involved, happy child is more apt to be in control of his or her behaviors than a frustrated, unhappy, or bored child. Adults can help school-age children find challenging work and play activities that are neither too simple nor too difficult. They can remain close by to supervise children's activities and be ready to suggest alternatives if it seems frustration or boredom is imminent. When fighting occurs, adults can let children share in the process of deciding right from wrong and the way to correct the situation. Adults should not impose all rules and regulations on school-age children. Rather, children should have many opportunities to discuss rules in a democratic fashion and to help decide on the final regulations. As children mature, they can be given more and more adultlike responsibilities, both in their work and play and in their decision-making activities. When they achieve, they can be given ample respect, approval, and praise.

In helping school-age children learn to respect the rights and needs of others, adults can tell children as often as possible how misbehaviors make them feel, and how they suppose the wrongful actions make others feel. During middle and late childhood it becomes possible for children to see others' points of view and to consider others' motivations, although they often need to be reminded. The more practice children have considering how others feel, what motivates other people's actions, and what other people need, the more apt they are to consider these factors before acting in the future.

Discipline. Adults responsible for the care of older children are still obliged to provide some form of control over misbehavior, although the discipline may take many different forms from that used with younger children. Inductive techniques of discipline are often effective. These are attempts to control the child's actions by explaining reasons for a change of behavior or explaining the consequences of the undesirable deed in terms of its effects on others. Many psychologists also recommend programs of behavior modification to help parents alter their children's unacceptable behaviors. Interestingly, parents must usually change their behavior first before they can modify their child's behavior. Parents need to realize that they may be subtly rewarding a child for some behaviors that they find unpleasant, since these behaviors persist along with the good behaviors they knowingly reward. Parents must learn to reinforce alternative behaviors that they choose as more desirable.

An example will help make a behavior modification program more understandable. A set of parents who came to a Child Development Clinic complained that their six-year-old son continually pestered them. An interaction between the parents and their son was videotaped for about fifteen minutes and then played back for the parents. They were able to see that while their son entertained himself with toys, they read their magazines or newspapers and ignored him. However, when he threw a toy at them or grabbed at their reading materials, they quit reading and tried to discipline him. The parents saw that they paid attention to their son only when he pestered them. In effect, they were positively reinforcing the attention-seeking behaviors they hated. To eliminate pestering the parents first agreed to set aside time to talk to, play with, or read children's books to their son. They then decided what to use as a negative or neutral stimulus when the undesirable behavior occurred. (A negative stimulus is a punishment such as social isolation. Neutral is nothing, an ignoring of the behavior.) They also agreed on a positive reinforcer for a desired behavior to replace the aversive act. (Positive reinforcers may be material rewards such as money, candy, or toys; privileges such as watching television or going to favorite places; or social reinforcers such as attention, affection, praise, or reassurance.) At first the child was rewarded for behaviors that approximated the desired actions. Later the child had to complete a longer segment of good behavior to get a reward. Still later the child had to complete several instances of desirable behavior to get the reward. Material possessions were used as reinforcers at first, and social reinforcers were later substituted for the material rewards. Finally the child's behavior maintained itself without continual rewards. The parents were consistent, firm, and calm during the program. When they gave positive reinforcers, they told the child what the behavior was that they were rewarding to assure that their son knew what they wanted and liked.

Often when behavior modification fails, the parents' motivation is at fault. They may not really want their child to change. Lack of consistency is also a problem. When a child is rewarded for a bad behavior, he or she is apt to try the bad behavior again and again to get another reward.

Critics of behavior modification feel that such engineering of human behavior is disrespectful of free will and somehow lowers children to the level of trained animals. Proponents, especially B. F. Skinner in his book *Beyond Freedom and Dignity,* argue that conditioning of human behavior occurs all the time anyway.[38] In Skinner's opinion, it is better to carefully think through desirable behaviors for children than to let behaviors contributing to the hostile, aggressive side of human nature be taught and/or learned without any attempts to modify or control them.

Rudolf Dreikurs (see pp. 165–166) feels that discipline will succeed most if parents avoid any kind of power play with their children.[39] He proposes that children be left to discover the negative consequences of bad behavior for themselves. If they fail to put clothing in the hamper, they will soon find themselves with no clean clothes to wear. If they annoy the cook, their dinner will be delayed. If they leave toys where they do not belong, the toys will disappear. This is actually a form of inductive discipline. The inducement to behave is more felt than heard. (Parents can give reasons for the child's suffered consequences based on the child's own actions whenever they are not immediately apparent.) Dreikurs advocates a family democracy where all family members feel loved, wanted, worthwhile, and of equal importance. He fears that when parents set themselves up as the exclusive lawmakers and law enforcement agents, they assume a position of being more equal than the children.

Baumrind's research on parental discipline looked at the overall social climate that parents establish in the home. She identified three major patterns of parental behavior: authoritarian, authoritative, and permissive.[40] The authoritarian parent assumed complete control over rules and regulations and stayed somewhat detached and cool toward the children. The authoritative parent was in control but allowed feedback from the children about rules and regulations and was receptive and warm toward them. The permissive parent seldom asserted control, made few demands about rules and regulations, and was warm to the children. For the most part Baumrind found social responsibility greatest in the children with authoritative parents. Too much authority held back the socialization of independence and responsibility-taking, and lax control sometimes led to socially disruptive behaviors.

Baumrind also found a few parents (whom she called harmonious) who seemed to practice more what Dreikurs advocated. They let "honesty, harmony, justice, and rationality in human relations" take precedence over "power, achievement, control, and order."[41] Baumrind found that such parents had control but did not need to exercise it. She saw too few cases of harmonious parents to study the effectiveness of this type of behavior on children, but her impression was that it was highly effective.

Sex typing. Chapter 4 presented different theories about how and why children learn to adopt behaviors appropriate to their own sex. Freud believed that by about age six boys renounce their Oedipal complexes and identify with their fathers and girls renounce their Electra complexes and identify with their mothers, primarily through repression. Social learning theorists state that boys identify with their fathers and girls with their mothers by age six because of the rewards and attention such sex-appropriate behaviors bring. Cognitive theorists claim that children model the like-sexed parent because they perceive their resemblance to that parent and want to imitate the person whom they most closely resemble. Kohlberg, a cognitive theorist, feels that sex identity is already firmly developed by age five.[42]

Freud called late childhood the latency period. By this he meant that children's interest in sex is repressed and remains dormant, or at a low ebb. Freud said sexual interest would not reemerge enough to affect behavior until adolescence. Now psychologists debate whether sexual interest has any decline at all during late childhood. There is a great deal of same-sex play during this age (clubs, gangs, etc.). However, most people that work with school-age children see evidence of an ongoing interest in sex, which may or may not be subdued.

When children are old enough to join clubs, stay overnight with friends, and spend at least half of their waking hours outside the home, they develop other sex-role models besides their parents. The sex-appropriate behaviors they learned at home are tested against a wider sam-

Figure 5–6. *Sex-role stereotypes are less clear-cut in today's society. Both boys and girls can now feel more comfortable demonstrating needs for dependency and independency, pursuing both instrumental and expressive tasks, dressing in similar fashion, playing the same games, and, eventually, choosing the same careers. This photo shows two girls and one boy.*
Leslie Davis

ple of men and women, boys and girls. When confusion develops, children are most apt to model the adults who are nurturant, powerful, and who dole out the rewards for appropriate sex modeling, which may mean learning a double standard. For example, a girl may learn that her liberated Mom wants her to fight her own battles at home, but that her more traditional schoolteacher believes girls should never fight. Or a boy may be told at home that it is inappropriate to cry and then learn from a teacher a message such as "It's all right to cry."

In the past and in some families today girls are expected to develop an expressive orientation to life. They are supposed to be nurturant, sympathetic, dependent, and emotional. Boys are expected to develop an instrumental orientation to life. They are supposed to be task-oriented, brave, independent, and unemotional. The women's liberation movement is doing much to have these sex-role stereotypes eliminated. Why should a girl be taught that she is weak and needs to depend upon a man? Why should a boy be taught that he must be strong and never depend on anyone? Would it not be better, many argue, to allow girls and boys to develop according to their own capabilities? Their own individual strengths and weaknesses should be recognized. All children can be helped to develop healthy forms of dependence, independence, and interdependence and emote more naturally.

Several researchers have looked at the way father absence affects a boy's masculine sex-role identity. If an uncle, grandfather, older brother, neighbor, or other male figure interacts with the boy, the sex-role acquisition usually proceeds normally. With a missing male model, however, the course of the boy's sexual identity is more determined by the mother's behaviors.

A good mother can encourage independence and task mastery, praise her son's strengths and capabilities, present maleness in a positive light, and allow the boy to interact with other boys and men in the course of everyday living.

Some mothers may overprotect their sons and reward their dependence. This may be due to these mothers' own needs for love and attention. Such mothers may encourage physical contact, discourage any signs of aggression or self-assertion, interfere with the boys' attempts at task mastery by helping them with their work, and reward their compliance with maternal wishes. Such boys usually become underachievers, timid and retiring, and have a low sense of worth in terms of their maleness.[43]

Some mothers who engage in overprotective behaviors also add a barrage of negative comments about men to their childrearing tactics. This is more apt to happen after an unhappy affair or marriage, especially if the son resembles his father. The mother's comments about the inadequacy, incompetence, or worthlessness of men further decreases the boy's sense of masculine worth and may contribute to his feminization.

In some cases of father absence the mother is strapped with worries about finances, work, and her own needs to the point of withdrawing from or neglecting her children. This may be especially true of sons who she expects can take care of themselves and maybe even her. Boys so treated may dramatize their masculinity, toughness, and independence from their families, yet they may still have an underlying low sense of worth as males.

Research on mother absence is not as prevalent as research on father absence. Helen Bee has predicted that girls without mothers or mother-substitutes will adopt more instrumental orientations to life and become somewhat stereotypically masculinized.[44] She has also predicted that boys will see their fathers fulfilling the stereotypically feminine family roles and will become somewhat feminized. This may lead to more equality in sex roles. The same process may take place when mothers work outside the home and fathers assume some of the responsibility for housework and child care. More research is needed on the effects of mother absence on male and female children.

Today single men may adopt children. Widowers more frequently raise their children alone, rather than hiring a housekeeper, or asking "Grandma" to move in. Also, fathers are asking for and getting custody of their children after divorce. A 1977 survey revealed that approximately 1 percent of all children under eighteen in the United States are being raised by the father only.[45]

Significance of the community in social development

During late childhood children meet and interact with a whole new world of outsiders. Some of these nonfamily people can have appreciable influences on a child's social development. This section will explore a number of the possible influences of schoolteachers, peers, and members of one's own ethnic group.

Schoolteachers. A well-liked schoolteacher, especially one who resembles a child in some way (sex, race, religion, ethnicity) may be taken on as a role model by a child. Sometimes a teacher will be aware of the child's modeling, often he or she will not. Consider these examples of teachers' impacts. James Conant, a scientist who helped develop the atom bomb, attributed his early interest in chemistry to a teacher. In his autobiography he wrote, "I doubt if any schoolteacher has ever had a greater influence on the intellectual development of a youth than Newton Henry Black had on mine."[46] Helen Keller paid an even greater tribute to her teacher. She wrote, "All the best of me belongs to her—there is not a talent, or an aspiration or a joy in me that has not been awakened by her loving touch."[47]

A classic study by Lewin, Lippitt, and White helped make educators aware of the ways in which a teacher can influence the social behavior of the members of a group.[48] They compared autocratic (dictatorial), democratic, and laissez-faire (let people make or do what they choose) teaching styles. They discovered that while the autocratic teachers ostensibly had good classes, the democratic teachers actually had the better ones. When the autocratic teachers left their groups, fighting broke out immediately. The laissez-faire teachers had fighting occur even in their presence. In the democratic atmosphere policies were established by the group, and the children felt some responsibility for the rules they helped make. They showed little aggression in either the teacher's presence or absence. They also liked the democratic leaders and worked harder for them.

Yando and Kagan studied styles of teaching impulsive children (those who raise their hands or blurt out answers quickly) and reflective children (those who think through problems carefully and do not volunteer answers unless they are sure they are correct).[49] In the first grade reflective habits facilitate learning to read. If impulsive children can be placed with reflective teachers (those who prefer children who take time to get answers right and who practice thinking before speaking themselves), impulsive children can learn to delay their response time. This is much more difficult for them if they are placed with impulsive teachers (those who prefer speedy answers and who react quickly themselves). Therefore, a teacher's personality not only contributes to the child's socialization but also to his or her academic progress.

The effect of a teacher on in-classroom social behavior is better known than the carry-over effect of socialization practices from class to home life. Much carry-over modeling depends on the child's perception of the importance of the teacher's nurturance and power. Much also depends on how well caregivers understand, agree with, and are willing to adopt different school socialization practices in their homes.

Carry-over of socialization practices from school to home has been demonstrated more clearly in the Soviet Union than here. Character education is considered one of the most important functions of Soviet schools. Parents and community members are duty bound to uphold the socialization procedures begun in the schools. Children are taught to help each other and work together for the good of the class, the school, and, finally, for the good of the community and their country. They learn to praise and criticize their own and others' shortcomings rather than hide them. The group then decides on rewards or punishments for behaviors. Selfishness is one of the most serious offenses. A book by A. S. Makarenko is the Soviet equivalent to our Dr. Spock.[50] But, while Spock deals predominantly with physical health, Makarenko's book deals with character education and informs parents how to raise socially upright citizens.

Peers. Just as a schoolteacher may have an impact on social development, so too can friends. But peers' influence on a child's behavior depends on several factors: (1) the amount of time spent with peers, (2) the stoutness of the parent-child affectionate bond, (3) the amount of time spent in family activities, (4) the family's acceptance of various peer group members, (5) various peer group values and activities, (6) the child's own self-esteem, and (7) the child's position in the group. Children use their friends as sounding boards and testing grounds for the values and attitudes they have learned at home. In many cases the peer group can be more democratic than the home. Instead of rules being laid down by authority figures, they are debated, with some or all of the group having a say in what they should be. Home values and attitudes may be upgraded or watered down, depending on the participants in the group.

Gamer demonstrated how children learn prosocial considerations for the sake of being accepted by the peer group.[51] At ages six and seven the children she studied rated shared interest in activities as the primary consideration of friendship. However, by ages nine and ten they viewed friendship as including support, help, availability, reciprocity, and unselfishness as well. One of the major functions of peer group social interaction is the loss of one's egocentric perspective. Children learn to give up their selfish demands and consider the feelings and perspectives of other children in the group in order to retain popularity.

During late childhood friendships become more stable. Friends are usually of the same sex and often of the same race, religion, culture, or socioeconomic standing in the community. Organized activities such as scouting, sports, and religious group projects tend to strengthen friendships and add a cohesive element to a group. When children work together, they learn new respect for each other. Occasionally after a group failure or defeat members will turn against each other, but, in general, teamwork strengthens friendships.

Children in groups will often do things they would never do on their own. This can take the form of increased altruism (e.g., visiting nursing homes) or increased delinquency (e.g., destroying property). Many a quiet, well-behaved child has joined fights or used vulgar language along with a supporting group. A classic study by Berenda demonstrates the susceptibility of children's judgments to peer influence.[52] He asked children to judge lengths of lines on a card after hearing other children (who were confederates with Berenda) repeatedly misjudge lines. Peer group pressure was so strong that subject children almost invariably judged the lines wrong. Conforming to peer judgments was greatest between the ages of seven and ten years. While increased ego strength decreases the influence of peer pressures, not all children develop the needed self-esteem to resist conforming to the group by age ten. In fact, many adults still would rather follow the crowd than risk the social disapproval that comes with being different or taking an unpopular stand.

Minority group membership. Being a member of a minority group within a larger community frequently presents special problems for school-age children. If the minority group is large enough so a child can find a cohesive group of like-sexed friends, the going is easier. Without the benefit of other minority group members to have as friends, it is often difficult for a child to feel worthwhile or acceptable in the mainstream culture. By the elementary school years children have learned many of the prejudices of their parents. Prejudice is an insidious thing. Even members of minority groups may adopt the mainstream culture's prejudice against themselves. For example, in a 1971 study black and white children were asked to sort a stack of photographs according to most and least preferred faces. The children used skin color as a criterion for preference, with light faces being more preferred than darker faces. This was true of black children as well as white children.[53]

Prejudice can be leveled at religious, language, cultural, and economic groups as well as different racial groups. Fat children, handicapped children, even homely children may find themselves the objects of their peers' ridicule. Communities and neighborhoods differ in what they find acceptable and unacceptable. Most communities have a "wrong side of town" whose inhabitants are held in low regard. Children may be ostracized if they come to school with ragged clothes or speak with accents or in a different dialect. Lack of spending money for movies, candy, or other things purchased by the majority may further interfere with social acceptability.

Unacceptability by childhood peer groups can severely affect a child's self-concept and self-esteem. Low self-esteem may be associated with learning as well as social-emotional developmental problems.

Schoolteachers frequently engage in social labeling and treat minority group children according to preconceived notions about performance. Rosenthal and Jacobson demonstrated how influential expectation can be on actual performance in their widely known study, *Pygmalion in the Classroom.*[54] After giving intelligence tests to all the children in a class, the teachers were misled for research purposes. They were told that certain children with just average test scores were going to bloom and show unusual academic growth during the school year. At the end of the year they retested the children. Those who were singled out as bloomers actually had improved and showed higher retest scores. The teachers' belief that they were going to bloom was held to be responsible for their higher scores.

Non-English-speaking minority group children can have an especially devastating course of social and intellectual development during the elementary school years. Unless steps are taken to teach the English language before other academic subjects are introduced, children fall further and further behind and may be classified as retarded in spite of very adequate intelligence.

In 1970 the Massachusetts Task Force on Children Out of School estimated that as many as 10,700 children were excluded from the Boston Public Schools, many of them Spanish-speaking.[55] More than half had never registered, while the rest had rarely attended or dropped out. In 1974 the Children's Defense Fund, a Washington research project, found children out of school in all areas of the country. While both white and minority children were excluded, the highest nonenrollment rates were among non-English-speaking children: Mexican-American 11.4 percent, Portuguese 8.3 percent, and Puerto Rican 7.8 percent.[56] In 1969 Congress passed the Bilingual Education Act, which funds school projects to teach the English language to children before attempting to teach them other academic subjects. The schools themselves must set up programs and find teachers to conduct English-language classes in the children's native languages. With this kind of support and assistance, non-English-speaking American children may be enrolled in schools with greater frequency. Once they learn English, they may attend school longer and find it more beneficial to them in their day-to-day living.

Health considerations

When school-age children are ill during the months from September through June, they suffer academic loss and deprivation of peer group and social interactions. Many children will hide symptoms of illness in order to go to school to be with friends. Others will feign all kinds of symptoms to avoid attending school. Illnesses, in general, are less prevalent in late than in early childhood.

Health maintenance

The maintenance of good health in the school-age years is greatly affected by the maintenance of good nutrition, good family relationships, satisfying peer relations, adequate sleep, attention to health problems, and the practice of safety precautions.

Good nutrition in middle and late childhood does not necessarily mean eating the same foods as adults. For example, adult breakfasts are often toast and coffee, or just coffee. What should a growing child have for breakfast? Many television advertisements would have them eat a sugary, vitamin-fortified, degermed, bleached, artificially flavored and colored, packaged cereal. If one watches carefully, these television commercials and cereal boxes also mention, parenthetically, that children should include milk, orange juice, and toast for a complete breakfast. However, in the rush to get off to school, few children want to eat large breakfasts. Some protein food should certainly be part of breakfast (e.g., a glass of milk, an egg, nuts, cheese, meat, soybeans, or some high-protein cereal). If the protein foods chosen for breakfast are low in carbohydrates (e.g., egg, nuts, meat), some other higher carbohydrate food should also be provided (e.g., milk, orange juice, toast, rice, or cereal). Fat, such as provided by butter or margarine, is also necessary for the normal functioning of the body. However, it is usually found in protein foods in sufficient quantity to make it unnecessary to add separately. Sugar is not necessary to good nutrition and may even be harmful. Because overweight is generally a bigger problem than underweight in American homes, and because super-sweetened foods contribute to such problems as tooth decay, most children should decrease their intake of sugars. In a normal day a growing child should have three servings of milk or milk products (skim milk, yogurt, cheese), two servings of protein foods (fish, poultry, meat, peanut butter, nuts, dried beans and peas, lentils, eggs), three or four slices of bread or its equivalent (rice, pasta, cereal), one fruit or fruit juice, and two vegetables.[57]

Adequate sleep for school-age children decreases with age. A six-year-old probably should get from ten to twelve hours of sleep. A twelve-year-old probably should get from eight to ten hours of sleep. Adequate sleep varies from child to child. If children go to sleep easily, sleep soundly, and wake refreshed, they are getting enough rest. Sleep disturbances such as restlessness, periods of wakefulness, and nightmares may be symptoms of emotional upsets rather than excess sleep. School-age children may find sleep difficult for reasons such as unhappy relationships with schoolteachers or friends, poor academic progress, quarreling between parents or siblings, fears, feelings of low worth, or guilt. Parents can help alleviate sleep disturbances by having a set bedtime hour that is followed firmly with few exceptions, by avoiding severe bedtime punishments, by providing an atmosphere conducive to discussing problems that have occurred in the course of the day, by reassuring the child that he or she is a valued and loved family member, and by soothing away fears.

A school-age child's health should be safeguarded with an annual routine physical examination. Some school systems provide this service free of charge to parents. If they do not, the family should make arrangements to have each child visit a physician yearly. Although it may seem unnecessary for apparently healthy children, there are conditions that may go unrecognized by parents (e.g., heart murmurs, high blood pressure, anemia, low-grade infections, developmental delays, glandular disorders). In addition, parents should call or take children to a medical facility for treatment whenever they have prolonged problems with colds, fever, abdominal pains, earaches, vomiting, weight loss, infections, or when they sustain serious injuries.

School learning problems

Two commonly diagnosed school learning problems are dyslexia and hyperactivity. Many professionals consider these "junk terms." They are often blanket names thrown over a host of problems that may require very different solutions.

The rubric dyslexia is used to describe many reading problems that involve recognition difficulties such as those between words (*tone* and *note*, *chain* and *cain*), or between letters (*d* and *b*, *p* and *g*, *c* and *o*), or reversals of letters (ꓘЯAM, ИHOꓩ), directional confusion (left-right, up-down), illegible writing, imperfect speech, or word rotations (YDNA). In the United States boys have more learning disabilities than girls.[58] In addition to recognition difficulties dyslexia may also be used to describe a condition children have with spelling disabilities and problems with arithmetic. Some learning disabilities may result from mixed or cross-dominant body-brain patterns. Most of us have unilateral body-brain dominance.[59] If we are right-handed, we are also right-eyed and right-footed, and the left hemisphere of our cerebrum is dominant. A mixed dominant person is ambidexterous, without a consistent preference for left- or right-sidedness. A cross-dominant person may be left-handed and right-footed or vice versa.

Hyperactivity simply refers to the fact that a child moves around a lot. However, the term has also become associated with a syndrome of minimal brain dysfunction (MBD), also called minimal brain injury (MBI) or minimal cerebral dysfunction (MCD). Children suspected to have minimal brain dysfunctions may be restless, unpredictable, impulsive, explosive, aggressive, irritable, emotionally unstable, and have short attention spans, difficulty concentrating, and may perseverate (repeat an action over and over). They also often have perceptual and reading difficulties.[60]

The causes of MBDs may lie in prenatal factors (e.g., maternal disease, especially in the first trimester, maternal drug intake, radiation), postnatal factors (e.g., premature birth, birth trauma, anoxia at birth), factors related to an early childhood accident (e.g., a blow to the head, ingested poison), or factors related to an early childhood disease (e.g., encephalitis, meningitis). Hyperactive behaviors can also be caused by some emotional disturbances and have no relation to MBDs. The relationships between MBD children and their parents may also become emotionally taut due to the MBD problem. The afflicted child is difficult to handle. Parents, especially if they do not know the diagnosis, may feel frustrated and guilty about the supposed inadequacies of their childrearing procedures.

School learning problems, whether called dyslexia, perceptual handicap, MBD, or hyperactivity, may occur in as many as one out of every ten to fifteen children in varying degrees.[61] Schoolteachers may be the first to notice a problem and advise parents to seek medical help.

The diagnosis of MBD is difficult. Electroencephalograms (recordings of electrical rhythms of the brain) and neurological exams are administered, but their findings are often inconclusive. However, drugs are available that help control the hyperactivity and make it possible for children to attend regular school classes. Drug use, though common, is questioned today by many professionals. In some communities physicians have overlabeled and overdrugged active, difficult children who were actually free of MBD symptoms. This dangerous practice and its exposure by the mass media with resultant lawsuits has recently made many health professionals wary of any quick diagnoses and prescriptions for hyperactivity.

Handicaps

Children with handicapping conditions may have to miss school or have special school arrangements made for them. When possible, it is preferable to keep the child within a normal school setting for the accompanying benefits to social and emotional development. Some of the more common chronic handicapping conditions of childhood are partial or complete blindness, cerebral palsy, partial or complete deafness, diabetes, epilepsy, mental retardation, emotional disturbance, and speech disorders.[62]

Diabetes mellitus, sometimes referred to as sugar diabetes, may begin in childhood. In the juvenile form of diabetes, there is an impaired ability to utilize carbohydrates due to a lack of insulin production by the pancreas. Acute symptoms of insulin deficiency include increased hunger and thirst, loss of weight, frequent urination (sugar can be found in the urine), weakness, collapse, and finally a comatose condition if treatment is not initiated. Treatment consists of giving the child insulin (by injection) and regulating the diet and the activity of the child. A child may go into a hypoglycemic state (state of low blood sugar level, also referred to as insulin shock) when he or she fails to consume enough carbohydrates, exercises too much (exercise facilitates uptake of sugar by the body's muscles so not as much insulin needs to be administered to maintain the same blood sugar level), or if he or she takes too much insulin. A hypoglycemic state may first be noted by behavior changes such as inattention, confusion, daydreaming and sleepiness, or irritability and aggressiveness. Headaches, sweating, trembling, and visual disturbances may follow. If the child does not ingest some form of sugar, loss of consciousness or convulsion may occur. For this reason diabetic children usually carry candy with them or ask for sweet food or drink whenever they experience any of the symptoms of hypoglycemia.

Having diabetes mellitus may make children feel angry and frustrated. They have difficulty achieving autonomy due to the dependence on others caused by the disease. They must always remember their medicine, watch their diet and their exercise, and be concerned about infections or suffer consequences that hardly, if ever, affect their nondiabetic friends. Diabetic children also must learn how to safely give themselves insulin injections.

Epilepsy is the condition in which a person has recurring seizures or loss of consciousness accompanied by convulsive muscle movements. There are several forms of epilepsy: grand mal, petit mal, psychomotor, focal-motor, myoclonic, and akinetic seizures. About 0.5 percent of the childhood population has some form of epilepsy.[63] Once the condition has been diagnosed, the child can usually be kept symptom-free with daily medication.

In grand mal epilepsy the attack most often begins with a warning called in aura. The aura may take a variety of forms, from the hallucination of a smell, taste, vision, or sound to an abnormal feeling in some part of the body.[64] Immediately after that, consciousness is lost. The child falls to the ground and may suffer injuries in so doing. There then appears rigidity of the muscles, followed by sharp, short, interrupted jerking movements. When the convulsions stop, the child may remain unconscious for only a few seconds or for a long period of time. He or she is generally sleepy and may have headaches for a few hours following each seizure.

In petit mal seizures children suddenly lapse into blank stares. They are unaware of their surroundings and may blink or smack their lips. The spell may only last ten to fifteen seconds. Children do not fall, have convulsive movements, or feel sleepy during or after petit mal seizures.

Convulsive movements that are associated with loss of consciousness may be due to a recognized cause such as electric shock, high temperatures, brain infections or tumors, low blood sugar, or inflammatory disease of blood vessels in the brain. Such seizures are called symptomatic seizures. The underlying disorder in the brain causing grand mal or petit mal epilepsy is not known.

A discussion of all the various emotional disturbances that can handicap school-age children is beyond the scope of this text. However, it seems appropriate to mention two common emotionally based illnesses of late childhood—school phobia and psychosomatic disease.

School phobia is a condition where a child actually develops physical symptoms of illness when left at school (e.g., headache, vomiting, cramps, diarrhea, hysteria, crying). It is most common when a child first starts school but may also occur after a trauma such as the death of a parent. The root of the child's anxiety is usually not the school or the teacher, but a fear of being separated from the parent(s). Symptoms decrease if a parent stays in the classroom. To help children overcome school phobia, parents need to be made aware of the ways in which they consciously or unconsciously convey the impression to their child that all will not be well during the absence.[65] School phobic children may sense that the parent will be lonely without them or that the parent does not believe the school environment is as safe, healthy, and loving as the home environment. Parents differ in their readiness to accept their own roles in their child's problem. Many need help in adjusting to their child's being in school all day.

Psychosomatic disease refers to any health problem that is suspected to result from emotional stress too great for a person to handle in the course of everyday living. Developing a physical illness gives the person "time off." Most psychosomatic illnesses are not recognized as such. Allergies, rashes, headaches, stomachaches, cramps, indigestion, and backaches are often psychosomatic or emotionally based, although these conditions can also be caused by physical problems or a combination of factors. As many as one-fifth of the children taken to pediatricians or family practitioners may be suffering from purely psychosomatic disorders.[66] When parent-child (or, more rarely, peer-child) relationships are improved, the disease fades. Drug treatment is at best superficial and usually wasteful. Unless the emotional disturbance can be alleviated, the disease will persist or one illness will be substituted for another.

Infections

As reported in Chapter 4, immunizations have made many of the dread infectious diseases rare today. However, school children still stay home with respiratory infections (colds, flu, laryngitis, tonsillitis, bronchitis, pneumonia); viral skin diseases such as measles and chicken pox; streptococcal infections such as strep throats and impetigo; staphylococcal infections such as boils, and conjunctivitis; meningitis; and even tuberculosis in some sections of the country. In fact, infections account for approximately 70 percent of school absences.[67] Many children continue school when sick and spread their disease to other children. Infections are less threatening than a generation ago because of the availability of antibiotics and immunizations, but untreated infections still may lead to serious complications (e.g., strep infection leading to rheumatic heart disease and glomerulonephritis) that occasionally result in the death of a child.

Accidents

Accidents manage to take the lives of approximately 15,000 American children yearly. Approximately 19,000,000 others sustain injuries.[68] School-age children most commonly get hurt in motor vehicle accidents. They also swallow or come in contact with poisons, burn themselves, have serious falls from bicycles, trees, or buildings, have water-related accidents, and play in high-risk areas. Although adults cannot always watch

Figure 5–7. *Normal, healthy school-age children delight in attempting daring deeds that demonstrate their gross and fine motor coordination and muscular agility. Adult supervisors should remind children to play in safe areas and obey safety precautions. Most of the 19 million annual accidental injuries to school-age children are preventable.*
Peter Karas

school-age children, they can repeatedly warn them against accident hazards and help them find safe play areas.

Allergies

Some form of allergy occasionally affects about 15 percent of all children.[69] Common allergens (substances that evoke allergic responses) are feathers, fur, plants, smoke, chemicals, and foods. Common manifestations of allergies include hay fever, hives, and asthma. If an allergy is caused by one or two known specifics, treatment may consist simply of avoiding them. Allergy desensitization programs alleviate the allergic reactions of many children. Several classes of drugs are available (e.g., antihistamines, bronchodilators, steroids) to alleviate allergy symptoms.

A common allergic complaint of school-aged children is bronchial asthma. This disease sometimes appears in several members of a family. It is associated with exposure to allergens in the environment (e.g., plants, animals, medicines) but can also be aggravated by emotional factors. An attack involves wheezing that may become so serious that one wonders if the child will be able to catch his or her next breath. Persons witnessing such attacks are often frightened. The child's own fear, together with onlookers' fears, only serves to make the attack worse. It is more helpful if persons attending an asthmatic attack remain calm and keep onlookers away. It is difficult not to overprotect and be anxious about asthmatic children. Asthma treatment has many facets: drugs, control of suspected or known environmental allergens, allergen desensitization programs, relaxation exercises, parental counseling, and child counseling. Parents can help their children most by understanding the underlying causes of attacks, reassuring the child of his or her continued worth and loved position in the family, setting definite limits on the child's behavior rather than "spoiling" him or her after attacks, and by remaining calm and reassuring during and after the attacks.

Nutritional problems

Obesity, malnutrition, anemia, and even tooth decay may be real health problems in school-age children with poor eating habits.

Compulsive eating is sometimes considered a psychosomatic disorder and may reflect a disturbed parent-child relationship (e.g., the child uses food to compensate for lack of attention, or the parent forces food on a child to alleviate his or her guilt or insecurities about parenting). Obesity may also result from learned family behaviors (e.g., all family members overeat) or from some body malfunction (e.g., underactive thyroid). Obesity handicaps a child physically and socially. Peers are often extremely cruel in their ridicule of an overweight child.

Undereating, or improper eating, is less easily spotted but is also very hazardous to good health. A malnourished child may have growth retardation, weakness, fatigue, anemia, tooth decay, poor posture, and a lowered resistance to infection. In some cases food deprivation may be a form of child neglect. More commonly, the malnourished child is fed, but for reasons of economics, ignorance, or overuse of convenience foods, the child is given insufficient protein, vitamins, and iron. Some properly fed children are also malnourished because they refuse to eat the foods placed before them. Lack of appetite may be due to filling up on empty-calorie snacks (soda, candy, cookies), poor health, lack of exercise, emotional tensions, or a desire to be thin.

The maintenance of good health in the school-age years is affected by many variables, including those in the social-emotional as well as the physical realms. Families can promote good health through attention to health problems, the practice of safety precautions, provision of safe places to play, attention to sibling and peer group activities, reassurances to all the children of a family that they are valued and loved, provisions for nutritious meals and snacks, firm expectations for children to follow routines for school work, chores, and bedtime hours, and by allowing children to pursue industrious activities and develop their own skills, talents, and self-esteem. Community members can also make significant contributions to the health of school-age children. They can help safeguard food and water supplies, protect the environment from accident and pollution hazards, provide for health facilities in the area, and ensure that school systems are as free as possible from bigotry and as excellent as possible in serving children's needs for academic stimulation and healthy social interactions.

Summary

Middle and late childhood is a time when the community begins to play a much greater part in children's lives. Peers, neighbors, and schoolteachers often spend as much or more time with children as children spend with their families.

Physical growth is slower than it was in early childhood and slower than it will be in adolescence.

Cognitive growth proceeds in what Piaget called the concrete operations stage. With experience children develop abilities to apply rules, reverse mental operations, conserve, order, classify, conceive of distances in time and space, and understand physical and psychological causation. Learning processes that children may use to assimilate and accommodate new information include perception, mediation, encoding, and memorization.

Testing of intelligence (IQ) is advocated by some, criticized by others. IQ tests give an inexact estimate of children's abilities to learn school subjects but do not accurately predict abilities to learn other life-situation skills. While both heredity and environment affect intelligence and IQ scores, the relative strength of each influence is unknown. Creativity can adversely affect test scores when only one answer is acceptable. While creativity is extolled, its development may be inhibited in many structured situations.

Language is fun in late childhood. Children practice accents, secret languages, foreign words, slang, and words with double meanings. Sentences acquire sophistication as understanding of complex syntactical forms develops.

Erikson described the nuclear conflict of this age group as that of developing a sense of industry versus developing feelings of inferiority. Family members, the school, peers, and other community members all have power to enhance or defeat a child's sense of industry. Children need many experiences of applying themselves to tasks and persisting through their completion. They also need positive feedback that their efforts are worthwhile.

Moral development is enhanced by identification with and modeling of adults with high ethical standards. It is also tied to cognitive development. To reach higher moral levels, children need many opportunities to deal with choices of right and wrong and to reason out the whys and wherefores of the choices. Warm, receptive adults who allow feedback about rules and regulations but maintain control seem to have the greatest potential for directing social responsibility in these late childhood years.

The influence of the peer group on children is related to their self-concepts, parent-child affectionate bonds, and the amount of time spent with peers. Children in groups will often do things they would not do on their own.

During this age, as in previous ages, good health is maintained through good nutrition, adequate sleep, and satisfying family, school, peer, and community relationships. Children continue to get many respiratory infections. Accidents, while not as numerous as for younger children, also occur frequently.

Questions for review

1. What side would you take on the inheritance of intelligence question? Do you believe that most of intelligence is factually determined by inheritance and that only a minimal amount of intelligence can be affected by environmental stimulation, *or* do you agree that intelligence is almost equally affected by inheritance and environment? Discuss. If possible, use some real-life examples to support your answer.

2. In evaluating intelligence (using an IQ test), what variables do you think should be accounted for when compiling the results of the test?

3. Learning involves an ability to select out or discard certain amounts of irrelevant material. How do you think the following affect the learning process: depression, unhappy home atmosphere, poor health, feelings of inferiority. Be specific in your answer. Consider what has been discussed in previous chapters on cognitive development and emotional development.

4. Proponents of progressive education or "classrooms without walls" argue that this kind of educational setting encourages children's creativity, motivation, and ability to learn. Opponents of this type of setting argue that it is unstructured, undisciplined, and too scattered for children to be able to learn. What are your views? Discuss.

5. There is often a tug-of-war between the values children are exposed to in the home and those of their peers. How can parents be consistent and adhere to their values without creating greater conflict within the child by putting down the child's friends?

6. Discuss particular ways in which the family can foster the positive resolution of what Erikson described as the industry versus inferiority conflict during middle-late childhood. Also describe the ways the family can negatively influence this resolution.

7. Some individuals argue that male children and female children are "born different," and that most behavior is only minimally influenced by environment. Others argue that "male" and "female" behavior is generally socialized into children and is not innate. Which viewpoint do you subscribe to? Discuss.

8. Children who belong to a minority group are constantly faced with feeling different from or feeling inferior to those in the mainstream of society. Project what these feelings might do to the ambition and motivation of these children and their ability to meet challenges in the future.

9. Develop an informational program that would make parents and teachers more aware of school learning problems and alert them to resources to deal with these problems.

References

[1]V. Holm and N. Wiltz, "Childhood," *The Biologic Ages of Man*, D. Smith and E. Bierman, eds. (Philadelphia: W. B. Saunders Co., 1973).

[2]Ibid.

[3]J. Kozol, *Death at an Early Age* (Boston: Houghton Mifflin, 1967).

[4]B. Gholson, J. O'Connor, and I. Stern, "Hypothesis Sampling Systems Among Preoperational and Concrete Operational Kindergarten Children," *Journal of Experimental Child Psychology*, 21 (1976).

[5]H. Ginsburg and S. Opper, *Piaget's Theory of Intellectual Development* (Englewood Cliffs, N.J.: Prentice-Hall, 1969).

[6]J. Flavell, *The Developmental Psychology of Jean Piaget* (New York: Van Nostrand Reinhold, 1963).

[7]J. Phillips, *The Origins of Intellect: Piaget's Theory* (San Francisco: W. H. Freeman & Co., 1969).

[8]M. Pines, *The Brain Changers* (New York: Harcourt, Brace, Jovanovich, Inc., 1973).

[9]H. Pick and A. Pick, "Sensory and Perceptual Development," *Carmichael's Manual of Child Psychology*, vol. I, 3rd ed., P. Mussen, ed. (New York: John Wiley and Sons, Inc., 1970).

[10]H. Werner, *Comparative Psychology of Mental Development*, 2nd ed. (New York: International University Press, 1957).

[11]E. Gibson, *Principles of Perceptual Learning and Development* (New York: Appleton-Century-Crofts, 1969).

[12]J. Flavell, A. Friedrichs, and J. Hoyt, "Developmental Changes in Memorization Processes," *Cognitive Psychology*, 1 (1970).

[13]J. Flavell, "Developmental Studies of Mediated Memory," *Advances in Child Development and Behavior*, vol. 5, H. Reese and L. Lipsitt, eds. (New York: Academic Press, 1970).

[14]F. Lumley and S. Calhoun, "Memory Span for Words Presented Auditorally," *Journal of Applied Psychology*, 17 (1934).

[15]Ibid.

[16]F. Morrison, K. Eisenberg, M. Haith, and P. Mindes, "Short-Term Memory for Visual Information in Children and Adults," Paper presented at the Eastern Psychological Association Meeting, Washington, D.C., April 1968.

[17]A. Jensen, "How Much Can We Boost I.Q. and Scholastic Achievement?," *Harvard Educational Review* (Winter 1969).

[18]R. Herrnstein, "I.Q.," *Atlantic Monthly* (October 1971).

[19]W. Shockley, "Dysgenics, Geneticity, Raceology: A Challenge to the Intellectual Responsibility of Educators," *Phi Delta Kappan*, 53 (1972).

[20]S. Scarr-Salapatek, "Race, Social Class and I.Q.," *Science*, 174 (1971).

[21]A. Anastasi, "Heredity, Environment, and the Question 'How?'," *Psychological Review*, 65 (1958).

[22]E. Torrance, *Guiding Creative Talent* (Englewood Cliffs, N.J.: Prentice-Hall, 1962).

[23]F. Bryan, "How Large Are Children's Vocabularies," *Elementary School Journal*, 54 (1963).

[24]N. Chomsky, *Language and Mind* (New York: Harcourt, Brace, Jovanovich, Inc., 1972).

[25]R. Krauss and S. Glucksberg, "The Development of Communication: Competence as a Function of Age," *Child Development*, 40 (1969).

[26]P. Swerdloff, *Men and Women* (New York: Time-Life Books, 1975).

[27]E. Erikson, *Childhood and Society*, 2nd ed. (New York: W. W. Norton & Co., 1963).

[28]Ibid.

[29]Ibid.

[30]Ibid.

[31]S. Freud. *A General Introduction to Psychoanalysis*, J. Riviere, trans. (New York: Permabooks, 1953).

[32]A. Bandura and R. Walters, *Social Learning and Personality Development* (New York: Holt, Rinehart and Winston, 1963).

[33]A. Siegal and L. Kohn, "Permissiveness, Permission, and Aggression: The Effect of Adult Presence or Absence on Aggression in Children's Play," *Child Development*, 30 (1959).

[34]J. Piaget, *The Moral Judgment of the Child* (London: Routledge and Kegan Paul, 1932).

[35]Ibid.

[36]L. Kohlberg, "The Cognitive-Developmental Approach to Socialization," *Handbook of Socialization*, D. Goslin, ed. (Chicago: Rand McNally, 1969).

[37]E. Turiel, "An Experimental Test of the Sequentiality of the Developmental Stages in the Child's Moral Judgments," *Journal of Personality and Social Psychology*, 3 (1966).

[38]B. Skinner, *Beyond Freedom and Dignity* (New York: Alfred Knopf, 1971).

[39]R. Dreikurs and V. Soltz, *Children: The Challenge* (New York: Hawthorn Books, Inc., 1964).

[40]D. Baumrind, "Current Patterns of Parental Authority," *Developmental Psychology*, 4 (1971).

[41]Ibid.

[42]L. Kohlberg, "A Cognitive-Developmental Analysis of Children's Sex-Role Concepts and Attitudes," *The Development of Sex Differences*, E. Maccoby, ed. (Stanford, Calif.: Stanford University Press, 1966).

[43]R. Stoller, *Sex and Gender* (New York: Science House, 1968).

[44]H. Bee, "On the Importance of Fathers," *Social Issues in Developmental Psychology*, H. Bee, ed. (New York: Harper and Row, 1974).

[45]J. Nordheimer "The Family in Transition: A Challenge from Within," *New York Times*, November 27, 1977.

[46]J. Conant, *My Several Lives* (New York: Harper and Row, 1970).

[47]H. Keller, *The Story of My Life* (New York: Doubleday & Co., Inc., 1954).

[48]K. Lewin, R. Lippitt, and R. White, "Patterns of Aggression in Experimentally Created Social Climates," *Journal of Social Psychology*, 10 (1939).

[49]R. Yando and J. Kagan, "The Effect of Teacher Tempo on the Child," *Child Development*, 39 (1968).

[50]U. Bronfenbrenner, *Two Worlds of Childhood: U.S.–U.S.S.R.* (New York: Russell Sage Foundation, 1970).

[51]E. Gamer, "The Long View: Looking at the Life Span," *APA Monitor*, 8(7) (July 1977).

[52]R. Berenda, *The Influence of the Group on the Judgment of Children* (New York: King's Crown Press, 1950).

[53]S. Richardson and A. Green, "When Is Black Beautiful? Colored and White Children's Reactions to Skin Color," *British Journal of Educational Psychology*, 41 (1971).

[54]R. Rosenthal and L. Jacobson, *Pygmalion in the Classroom: Teacher Expectation and Pupils' Intellectual Development* (New York: Holt, Rinehart and Winston, Inc., 1968).

[55]Task Force on Children Out of School, *The Way We Go To School* (Boston: Beacon Press, 1970).

[56]Children's Defense Fund, *Children Out of School in America* (Cambridge, Mass.: Washington Research Project, Inc., 1974).

[57]S. Fomon and E. Ziegler, "Food and the Child," *Childhood*, E. Miller, ed. (Chicago: Blue Cross Association, 1976).

[58]R. Wagner, *Dyslexia and Your Child: A Guide for Parents and Teachers* (New York: Harper and Row, 1971).

[59]D. Kimura, "The Asymmetry of the Human Brain," *Scientific American* (March 1973).

[60]H. Haywood and J. Gordon, "Neuropsychology and Learning Disorders," *Pediatric Clinics of North America*, 17 (May 1970).

[61]H. Bakwin and R. Bakwin, *Behavior Disorders in Children*, 4th ed. (Philadelphia: W. B. Saunders, Co., 1972).

[62]J. Apley, *Pediatrics* (Baltimore: Williams and Wilkins, Co., 1973).

[63]V. Holm and N. Wiltz, "Childhood," *The Biologic Ages of Man*, D. Smith and E. Bierman, eds. (Philadelphia: W. B. Saunders Co., 1973).

[64]R. Bannister, *Brain's Clinical Neurology*, 4th ed. (London: Oxford University Press, 1973).

[65]L. Vettkamp, "School Phobia," *Journal of Family Counseling*, 3(2)(Fall 1975).

[66]J. Apley, *Pediatrics.*

[67]V. Holm and N. Wiltz, "Childhood."

[68]White House Conference on Children, *Profiles of Children* (Washington: U.S. Government Printing Office, 1970).

[69]V. Holm and N. Wiltz, "Childhood."

Contents

George Bellerose/Stock, Boston

Adolescence

A boy grew six inches in the summer between his sixth (elementary school) and seventh (junior high school) grades. He truly felt himself to be a different person (taller, new school) as he entered his thirteenth year. Most people cannot recall so clearly a particular time when they entered adolescence and left childhood behind. In our society the adolescent period often seems to be a holding pattern between childhood and adulthood. In early adolescence it is easy to slip back into the role of a child to suit a particular purpose. In early adulthood many persons choose to slip back into adolescent roles. Adolescence is often defined by both physical and social hallmarks. It is a period of time marked by the biological changes of puberty, and it is a transitional time socially. The adolescent becomes identified as a person increasingly able to make his or her own decisions about school, leisure, employment, and friends. It ends with an independence from the family of origin, brought about by marriage or a full-time job. For some people adolescence may begin at age eleven or twelve and go on through the mid- to late twenties. For others it may start at age fourteen or fifteen and end within a year. Physical, cognitive, and social factors all help determine the length of the adolescent period.

Physical development

The physical changes of adolescence lead to new problems for the growing, developing human being. It is not easy to adjust to all the bodily changes that occur. When an adolescent looks in the mirror, he or she is apt to constantly see changes in appearance, real or imagined. In addition to changes in height and weight, budding sex organs, body hair, facial blemishes, oversized hands or feet, or in the male, an enlarging Adam's ap-

Figure 6–1. *The self-concepts of adolescents often undergo rapid changes—from child to adult, from dependent to self-sufficient, from unity to opposition with families. Old and new tasks are combined in the ever-changing challenge of moving from childhood to adulthood.*
Julie O'Neil/Stock, Boston

ple are just some of the changes that may confront the adolescent. The lack of these things, if friends have them, may also worry the teenager.

Puberty encompasses the one to two years of very rapid growth and development before a girl or boy becomes capable of reproducing children. Sexual maturity for a girl is often defined as the time of the first menstrual period, but this is slightly inaccurate. Most girls are not immediately fertile after beginning to menstruate. They may have anovulatory cycles (not productive of mature ova) for one or two years before they can actually bear children.

It is harder to mark a point in time when boys reach sexual maturity or have the ability to produce and ejaculate sperm. One sign sometimes used to mark sexual maturity is the experience of wet dreams. However, wet dreams are environmentally influenced and may occur long after sexual maturity. A more scientific way to determine male fertility is to microscopically examine urine for evidence of sperm.

In both girls and boys a spurt of growth accompanies puberty. If one feels the need to pinpoint sexual maturity, one can keep regular measurements of changes in height, weight, and body proportions during adolescence. The period of most rapid growth is a good indication of the time when sexual maturity is being achieved.

The physical hallmarks of pubescence (changes accompanying arrival of sexual maturity) vary from individual to individual. Pubic hair may be the first indication a child has of approaching adolescence. Then, the breasts of girls and the testes of boys begin to enlarge. Girls begin menstruating. Their hips also grow wider as the pelvic structures expand to make childbirth possible. One of the later pubescent changes is growth of hair on the face, chest, and armpits. Girls may also have facial and chest hair, but it does not grow as coarse and thick as it does on males. Both boys and girls also experience voice changes. Girls' voices become fuller and richer. Boys' become lower and louder. The deeper male voice results from enlargement of the larynx (the Adam's apple) and the lengthening of the vocal cords. In the process of acquiring a mature male voice, a boy may occasionally experience embarrassing voice breaks or squeaks in the middle of sentences. While parents may be proud of this sign that their son is maturing, siblings and friends usually giggle. Pubescent changes all take time. There may be from two to five years between the first notice of pubic hair and the final development of full sexual maturity.

The age at which sexual maturity is reached in American girls varies from ten to seventeen years, with an average age of first menstruation now standing at slightly less than thirteen years.[1] The range for sexual maturity in American boys is estimated to be from twelve to eighteen. Girls, on the average, reach sexual maturity about two years ahead of boys. As noted in Chapter 4, there is a trend toward each generation growing larger than the last. A similar trend has been at work in pushing the age of puberty down with each successive generation. In 1840 the average girl's first menstrual period occurred in her seventeenth year.[2] Health and nutritional factors may be responsible for this change, as they are suspected to be for the trend toward increased height; however, hereditary factors and hormones also influence the age of puberty.

The physical changes of adolescence encompass much more than sexual changes, although the sex hormones (estrogen and testosterone) do spur on many of the other physical developments.

The heart approximately doubles its weight during adolescence, growing slightly larger in boys than in girls.[3] Blood pressure also rises appreciably, with males eventually having higher systolic pressure than females. Girls may reach their adult body proportions somewhere between ages sixteen and eighteen, but boys may not stop growing until they are twenty, usually growing taller than girls. They also, on the average, grow stronger. Before adolescence girls and boys are similar in muscle strength. However, during pubescence boys develop more muscle mass and more force per gram of muscle.[4] Boys develop proportionately longer limbs, while girls have proportionately larger trunks and wider pelvic girdles. The femurs of females are attached to the pelvis at more oblique angles than those of males. Many of these physical differences between the sexes give the average male an advantage over the average female in our traditional sports, although there are always exceptions.

The physical fitness norms of American teenagers today are behind the norms of adolescents a century ago and behind the norms of youth in other countries. Many factors contribute to this decline in muscle use (e.g., greater availability of cars, sedentary watching of television and movies, listening to longplaying records, experiencing stiffer competition to make sports teams, having fewer intramural sports, and having fewer chores). Social factors further discourage muscle development in girls, while only minimally encouraging the same in boys.

The extreme awkwardness that some youth experience during pubescence is a result of rapid and uneven development. Arms and legs or hands and feet may reach adult proportions before the rest of the body. Teenagers may discover that their big feet and longer legs are only two strides away from the snack table rather than three as they knock it over, or misjudge the distance they have to reach for the milk with the same results. Girls as well as boys may experience some of these judgment problems. Such problems probably result from failure to adapt quickly enough to changed body proportions. Some teenagers never go through an awkward stage. Others seem to learn to be clumsy and continue having difficulties long after any physical adjustment problems can be blamed.

In addition to all the other physical changes of adolescence, the sweat glands become active, or overactive. They begin secreting fatty substances that contribute to body odor, blackheads, and acne (see p. 270). The problems of very early or very late maturation will also be discussed in a later section.

Cognitive development

The new levels of intellectual functioning that usually emerge in adolescence, along with the physical changes of puberty, profoundly influence the social development of teenagers. For this reason we will discuss changes in intelligence before describing the social problems and advances of adolescence.

Piaget saw formal operations as the last phase of cognitive development, the highest level of intellectual functioning. Although his descriptions of earlier intellectual stages have been well accepted and supported by research, the formal operations stage is frequently criticized, both for going too far and for not going far enough.

Those who criticize Piaget for going too far cite research studies that show a lack of formal operational thought in many adults, both in this country and abroad. Ausubel and Ausubel contend that the attainment of formal operations is determined by experience.[5] Children who have opportunities to manipulate relationships with concrete props, who learn vocabularies with abstract words, and who are encouraged to develop ordering concepts, usually shift from concrete to formal operational thinking somewhere around adolescence. Greenfield and Bruner suggest that it is the form of education a person receives that accounts for the shift to formal operational thinking.[6] In areas where children begin school early and are instructed with extensive written language, formal operations emerge slightly before the teenage years. Written language (symbolic thought) helps children deal with ideas that go beyond concrete here-and-now perceptions of the world. Children who read are helped to think in terms of abstract possibilities as well as in terms of actuality. Nonreaders, poor readers, and people in cultures that do not ordinarily use written language may not reach formal operations in the Piagetian sense.

Other arguments criticize Piaget's formal operations stage for not going far enough. Some contend that the intellectual abilities of people like Marie Curie, Albert Einstein, or Jean Piaget go far beyond the abilities of adolescents. They claim another stage should be added that better describes the creative genius of certain persons. Other criticisms focus on the fact that Piaget took little account of the identity confusion or increased sexual libido of adolescents in his analysis of their cognitive reasoning abilities.

Piaget's formal operations

In the period of concrete operations children become proficient at what Piaget called first-order operations—abilities such as classification, serialization, and one-to-one correspondence. In the formal operations stage, youth acquire second-order operations—abilities to see new kinds of logical relationships between classes or between and among several different properties. The reasoning behind first-order operations is called intrapropositional thinking, since it deals within the context of just one property (e.g., weight). The more advanced reasoning of second-order operations is called interpropositional thinking, since it involves handling relationships among several different properties (e.g., density, size, and weight). The term propositional thinking simply refers to an ability to take objects that have been ordered into classes or correspondence in one way and then to see relations among the classes in some new, logical ways.

In formal operations a person also becomes proficient at what Piaget calls combinational analysis, which involves seeing all the possible variations of a problem, or separating out all the possible variables, and then testing them systematically. Imagine all the possible sums of money one can make from a quarter, a dime, a nickel, and a penny. Formal operators will systematically set about the task of combining the coins in some set order such as:

Penny (P) + nickel (N)	=	6¢
P + dime (D)	=	11¢
P + quarter (Q)	=	26¢
N + D	=	15¢
N + Q	=	30¢
D + Q	=	35¢
P + N + D	=	16¢
P + N + Q	=	31¢
P + D + Q	=	36¢
N + D + Q	=	40¢
P + N + D + Q	=	41¢
P alone	=	1¢
N alone	=	5¢
D alone	=	10¢
Q alone	=	25¢
no coins	=	0¢

People still functioning with concrete operations will combine coins to make various sums but will not do so systematically. They will forget what combinations they may already have used. Piaget tested youths' level of operations by asking them to do such things as discover the right combination of chemical liquids to produce a yellow-colored liquid, or to discover how rods of different composition, length, thickness, and form varied in their ability to bend when weights were attached. When people have the ability to think logically and work systematically, they often enjoy trying to solve such problems. They may even resent the chance of hitting the correct solution on an early manipulation, thereby losing out on the fun of trying all the other possibilities.

When one sets out on a task with the idea of testing each possible variation to discover the correct solution (s), one is practicing what Piaget called hypothetical-deductive reasoning. Such reasoning involves solutions that are real (what can be seen, or felt, or experienced) and also encompasses abstract "what-if" solutions to the problem—in short, all the possible variations. A set of hypotheses is derived, and then tested to deduce the correct answer(s). Piaget described formal operations as the combination of interpropositional thinking, combinatorial analysis, and hypothetical-deductive reasoning. The total process, as he described it, is characterized by painstaking accommodation to detail and careful, thoughtful analyses and observations.[7]

The new ability to see all the possible variations of a problem or situation that emerges in the formal operations stage has repercussions on personality and social development (see pp. 255–267).

Creativity

The abstract reasoning abilities of the formal operations period usher in both new creative skills and renewed creative urges in many teenagers. No longer limited to concrete perceptions of the world, they may express their new visions of possibilities in art forms such as painting, sculpturing, music, dance, poetry, short stories, diaries, religious tracts, science projects, or inventions. Many creative products of the teenage years show a certain raw-edged sensitivity and originality that is often missing from more mature works. As many creative preschoolers seem to give up original productions when they enter school, many creative teenagers also become inhibited about, or embarrassed by, their creative expressions when they enter the world of adults. Artists who continue to produce as they pass from adolescence to adulthood usually tone down and refine their works so they are more socially acceptable and salable, sometimes at the expense of the freshness of the product.

Sex differences in mental abilities

By adolescence most girls show a preference for subjects involving human relationships and/or verbal skills (literature, composition, foreign languages, history), while boys show a preference for subjects with numerical and spatial relationships (math, science). Many people argue that these academic preferences are learned; others contend that they have genetic links.

On the environmental learning side, most girls are consciously or unconsciously encouraged to like subjects that will make them better wives and mothers. If they voice a desire for a career, they are encouraged to choose one in which they can help others (e.g., secretary, nurse, teacher). Boys, on the other hand, are encouraged to show off their own individual abilities, to excel as individuals. Working at self-improvement, it is assumed, is as important for a boy as working to help others is for a girl. Boys are encouraged to pursue occupations where they can be competitive, assertive, and logical (e.g., business, law, electronics, mechanics). These are broad generalizations but nevertheless hold true for a great proportion of our society. Many people contend that the differential treatment of the sexes begins at birth. The pink and blue colors attached to babies cue in adults as to what to expect from and do for the infants. In childhood girls are "nearness trained" and kept close to home, while boys are "independence trained" and encouraged to behave more like Tom Sawyer. Girls are praised for making good conversation (verbal skills), and boys are attired in reinforced play clothes and expected to wander far afield (spatial skills). Grown-ups tend to worry more about boys who do not go exploring and irreparably stain or tear their clothing than about those who do.

On the nature-inheritance side, despite myths about societies of "Amazon women," all cultures have sex-role stereotypes somewhat similar to our own. Men are generally physically stronger and predominate in aggressive, protector, provider roles. Cross-cultural tests of mental abilities usually replicate the sex differences found in our society. Women do better at tasks involving fluency, grammar, spelling, and other aspects of language, while men excel at tasks requiring spatial abilities (e.g., copying geometric figures, assembling block designs, discerning embedded figures, finding paths through mazes). Our own IQ tests are carefully balanced with tests of verbal skills and spatial abilities to assure that neither men or women will have a scoring advantage over the other. Biologists suggest that the sex differences in mental abilities are better explained by organizational differences in the brain than by environmental dissimilarities. In females the dominant cerebral hemisphere of the brain develops earlier than it does in males. The speech center is located in the dominant hemisphere (the left side of the brain for right-handed people). This may account for the earlier use of language by girls. Spatial ability is localized on the nondominant hemisphere. The minor hemisphere appears to become more highly developed in males over time. As mentioned in Chapter 5, children with mixed or cross-dominant hemispheric functioning usually have problems handling spatial abilities.

Biologists often contend that hormonal factors may also contribute to differences in mental abilities.[8] In nonhuman species injections of androgens (male hormones) into females cause increased independence and aggressiveness. Girls' and boys' cognitive styles become more obviously at variance in adolescence when the levels of their sex hormones increase. Klaiber, Broverman, and Kobayashi showed that increased levels of testosterone and androgen in human males increased their ability to do simple repetitive tasks.[9] More research on the effects of the sex hormones on mental abilities is hard to justify because of the ethical concerns about injecting or manipulating hormones in humans.

Present evidence does not support either the conclusion that sex differences in mental abilities are learned or biologically determined. Girls' language abilities may be reinforced more simply because they occur earlier. Likewise, boys' spatial skills may be rewarded more because they occur with greater frequency. Remember, with mental skills as well as with physical prowess there are vast individual differences among girls and boys. A normal boy may excel in areas of verbal fluency, and a normal girl may be especially talented in math, science, or a field requiring well-developed spatial abilities.

Figure 6–2. *Adolescence is often a period of social-emotional upheaval in our society. Teens are apt to argue every rule laid down by adults, even when they approve the rules. Familial and societal values that were accepted during childhood are now reexamined, debated, and sometimes revised.*
Ellis Herwig/Stock, Boston

Social development

Adolescence in our society is often a period of storm and stress. Even if a youth experiences a gradual, rather uneventful physical transition from childhood to adulthood, he or she is apt to experience many social and emotional traumas. The social problems of teenagers today are different from the problems of yesterday's youth. However, a turbulent adolescent period has been a fact of life in the Western world at least since the industrial revolution and earlier in some other cultures. Only in societies where the transition from childhood to adulthood is rapid (as over a day or two of an initiating puberty rite) and where adulthood has very well-defined functions (e.g., marriage, hunting, cooking, defending the settlement) is the adolescent storm-and-stress period less tumultuous or nonexistent.

Significance of the family

Families differ in the ways they help youth move from childhood to adulthood. While some families expect adult behaviors from teenagers, others try to keep their offspring as dependent, childlike creatures longer. As young people change physically, experience new sexual urges, begin using hypothetical-deductive reasoning, and approach the end of the schooling required by law, they question, "Who am I? Where have I been? Where am I going? Where should I go?" In spite of family pressures to be this, that, or the other, youth in our society are frequently encouraged to take hold of their own lives and steer themselves towards a destiny of their own making and choosing. This leads to what Erik Erikson has called the identity crisis of youth.

Identity. Erikson, like Freud, recognized the forces that growing sexual impulses exert on behavior during adolescence. However, he felt that the quest for identity is an even more powerful motivating force than sex. He revised and expanded the Freudian concept of adolescence to include the study of identity.

Sigmund Freud emphasized the psychosexual stages of childhood and played down youth. What Freud did write about the adolescent period was almost purely sexual. He called pubescence the genital stage and saw in it a second Oedipal conflict. Youth, he felt, must expand their circle of friends to include opposite-sexed persons, or else their growing sexual libido may be inverted toward homosexuality. He felt they also need to free themselves once again from love for their opposite-sexed parent. He commented that in so doing adolescents frequently choose parent-substitutes as their first outside love objects: girls have crushes on older men, and boys have crushes on older women. Normal adolescents, Freud said, finally move away from self-love, same-sexed friend attachments, and parental dependency and place their libidinal interest in opposite-sexed, extrafamilial friends. In Freud's opinion, a healthy self-concept and emotional health are achieved along with the change from infantile sexual impulses to mature heterosexuality. The fact that several years may pass between a youth's desire for and achievement of an extrafamilial heterosexual relationship was largely ignored by Freud.

Erikson felt that youths' changed physique and sexual impulses also contribute to an identity confusion. Finding a heterosexual love partner does not confer on one a sense of identity. Youths must still assess their assets and liabilities and decide what they want to do with their lives. They use their same- and opposite-sexed friends and their family members as sounding boards on which to test their different identities. Erikson felt that young love is usually more conversational than sexual because youth need to project their developing self-images confidentially to a second person. They then have it reflected back to them. In love relationships youths feel more secure that their secrets can be confided without the danger of ridicule, abuse, or broadcasting. But many youths prefer to use their family members as sounding boards for the same reasons. Erikson wrote that the failure of so many teenage marriages may be linked to the fact that one cannot give oneself to another until one knows one's own identity. Erikson has been criticized for being sexist in his discussion of the identity strivings of women and men. He wrote that "something in the young woman's identity must keep itself open for the peculiarities of the man to be joined and of the children to be brought up."[10] He did not discuss the converse, that something in the young man's identity must keep itself open for the peculiarities of the woman to be joined and of the children to be brought up. Unless youths work at affirming and strengthening their identity in adolescence, Erikson feels they will suffer from role diffusion. They may imitate others but feel confused about their own sense of self. It is especially difficult for youths to discover their own uniqueness if parents and peers pressure them to conform and acquiesce to the will of others (see Table 6-1).

Independence. Adolescents typically fluctuate from wanting privileges in keeping with near-adult status (e.g., use of car, no curfews) to wanting the support and protection afforded them in childhood (e.g., no upkeep of room and clothes, meals prepared). Just as it is difficult for youths to achieve a sense of identity during adolescence, so too is it difficult for families to react to youths who are aesthetics one day and slobs the next or adults one day and children the next. Parents who allow teenagers a great deal of freedom deprive them of some of the direction and support they both need and crave. Likewise, teenagers who have no freedom feel thwarted in their efforts to be adult.

Kandel and Lesser compared parental behaviors vis à vis teen-

Table 6–1. *Erikson's fifth nuclear conflict: identity versus role confusion.*

Sense	*Eriksonian descriptions*	*Fostering behaviors*
Identity	– sense of sameness between self-concept and how one appears in the eyes of others	– others reflect back belief that youth has qualities that match self-image
	– felt continuity between identities prepared in the past, the meaning of one's identity for others, and the promise of career	– opportunity to pursue choice of activities in keeping with aptitudes and endowment
vs.		
Role confusion	– doubt about sexual identity	– lack of interaction with opposite-sex peers
	– inability to find occupational identity	– overidentification with heroes of cliques or crowds
	– personality confusion as evidenced by delinquent, withdrawing, or suicidal behaviors	– lack of attention or feedback as somebody worthwhile

Source: Based on material from "Eight Ages of Man" from *Childhood and Society*, 2nd Edition, Revised, by Erik H. Erikson, with the permission of W. W. Norton & Company, Inc. Copyright 1950, © 1963 by W. W. Norton & Company, Inc.

agers in the United States and Denmark. They found that American youths were kept childlike longer than Danish youths.[11] Americans were given more money to spend but were not otherwise expected to engage in adult behaviors. American parents more often set out arbitrary rules and regulations without discussing the reasons for them. They also expected their offspring to remain in school and be dependent longer on them for room, board, and sustenance.

Independence training is hampered by both authoritarian discipline (parents make the rules) and permissive discipline (teenagers choose their own rules). Youths raised under either persuasion tend to have more storm and stress with their parents. They tend to seek sanctuary with and guidance from their peers rather than from their primary caregivers.[12] The democratic parent-child relationship more successfully allows youths to work through their identity crises and gain a more secure independence. Goethals and Klos have described the ideally adequate parent as (1) one who recognizes the adolescent as an independent, competent person who is gratifying rather than threatening; (2) one who shows genuine care and concern for the adolescent and offers help and involvement without imposing it; (3) one who is open to changes in the ongoing relationship rather than insisting on old and inadequate ways of interacting.[13] In the past males have been encouraged to assume more independent roles in adolescence than females.[14] Women have been expected to transfer their dependency from their parents to a husband and to find their identity in his lifestyle. Increasingly, however, women are striving for more independent roles. Many now feel a need to define themselves as competent, self-respecting individuals before marriage. When and if they marry, they

Figure 6–3. *The conflict of identity versus role confusion is becoming increasingly problematic for females who may be torn between their desires to pursue careers and their concerns about wifehood and motherhood.*

Burt Glinn/Magnum Photos, Inc.

want to have a mutually interdependent relationship rather than one in which one partner becomes subject to the control of the other.

As youths perform more and more tasks successfully, they gain confidence in their ability to move out into the adult world. They learn about economic independence (a subject influenced by chance and skills as well as knowledge) as they begin to earn, budget, and spend their own money. Older and younger siblings often exert a profound influence on independence achievement. The oldest child may be treated like a child longer, while the younger children may strive to have the privileges of the older siblings at an earlier age.

Storm and stress. Families are often stunned when their gregarious, kindly, obedient older children become egocentric, unruly, argumentative teenagers. They may also feel guilty or ashamed. All their very best efforts to raise morally upright children seem to have been for naught. Where, they wonder, did we go wrong? Actually, although some families do err in the direction of too much, not enough, or inconsistent discipline of adolescents, the new cognitive abilities of the formal operations period also have an effect on social behaviors. The ability to see all the possible variations of any problem or situation contributes to a growing argumentativeness and egocentrism.

As youths see many alternatives to their parents' directives, they become unwilling to accept commands without questioning them. However, they see so many alternatives that they become confused. Frequently teenagers egg their parents into debate just for the sake of discussing alterations of decisions. This may occur even when they approve of the decision. They also turn to their peers to discuss modifications of nearly everything. Using, in Piaget's terms, interpropositional thinking, combinatorial analysis, and hypothetical-deductive reasoning, youths may construct an ideal society, an ideal religion, an ideal school, or an ideal family. They compare their ideals with reality and find the adult ways of constructing society lacking. This may contribute to a strong feeling of a generation gap. Youths, however, seldom make any great efforts to bring about their own best of all possible worlds. As Elkind put it, "The very same adolescent who professes his concern for the poor spends his money on clothes and records, not on charity."[15] While moral idealism may be high in adolescence, the behavior of teenagers is unpredictable and generally quite self-centered.

Piaget suggested that there are three periods of great egocentrism in the process of development: infancy, early childhood, and adolescence.[16] He linked adolescent egocentrism to cognitive development. In this new form of egocentricity, where all the realms of possibility are viewed, adolescents fail to distinguish between their own conceptualizations and those of the rest of society. They believe everyone should come to terms with their own idealistic schemes. They fail to take into account the fact that others may not like or want what they want. This egocentricity also takes the form of believing that everyone is extremely concerned with adolescents' appearance and behavior. When they walk into a crowd, they feel that all eyes are on them, a perception that accounts for the many hours teenagers spend grooming and preening before a mirror. They believe everyone will admire what they admire, which helps explain their failure to understand why adults criticize their faddish clothes, their music, and/or their friends (see Figure 6–4).

Youthful egocentrism is also frequently turned into self-criticism. When young people find themselves lacking in some way, they believe the whole world will see the same deficiency. They may plunge

Figure 6–4. *Piaget wrote that adolescents' egocentrism is a symptom of their ability to conceptualize not only their own thoughts but the thoughts of other people as well. They often believe that others are as preoccupied with their appearance and behavior as they are. This causes them to be both vain and self-conscious at the same time.*

into self-improvement exercises or write diaries full of resolutions to change. They may also shroud their efforts to better themselves in secrecy. This desire for privacy in adolescence often leads to lying. In the elementary school years children tell lies that are generally tall tales. They may even come to believe their own stories. In adolescence young people hide behind deceitful screens they erect to confuse others. However, they know the truth full well in their own minds.

Piaget felt that the egocentricity of adolescence is modified with age as a consequence of hypothetical-deductive reasoning. Feelings of omnipotence, near-genius insightfulness, and absolute uniqueness are, in fact, hypotheses to be tested. As a consequence of the testing process, youths come to realize that the whole world is not focused on their thoughts or appearance but that others have their own preoccupations. Youthful idealism is modified as teenagers gain independence and begin functioning in a world full of the everyday problems of existence. They begin to see themselves in relation to other people, nations, races, and in relation to living and nonliving things. Gradually they become able to appraise their own situations more objectively.

Morality. Many of the problems of American youths (e.g., drug and alcohol abuse, violence, vagrancy, larceny, sexual promiscuity) are blamed on a lack of hope for the future in a society thought to be decadent, corrupt, and nearly bankrupt. While this may be a factor in youths' "tuning out," experts are increasingly pointing the finger of blame back at the home and family situations. They see a striking lack of parental involvement with many young people. The decline in parent-child interaction has led to an upsurge of peer-peer dependency. Research by Condry and Simon indicated that the most peer-influenced adolescents described their parents as unaffectionate and lax in discipline.[17] The same teenagers also had poor self-concepts and negative views of the friends with whom they spent so much time. Mealtimes are not family affairs in many homes, due to convenience foods, variously scheduled activities, avoidance of togetherness, or affluence that allows family members to eat out. Television viewing may be the major family activity. However, it is scarcely an interactive pastime. Viewers seldom talk except during commercials. The prevalence of two or more televisions per household further reduces the chance that family members will communicate between programs.

Discipline is difficult during adolescence. Youths often feel that they are too old to be punished. They may rebel against the injustice of physical and love-withdrawal techniques. They argue about almost every decision made that affects them. Therefore, some parents find it easier to allow teenagers to be responsible for their own behavior. They may hope that their past teaching plus example will be sufficient to keep their teenagers out of trouble. Other parents may become dictatorial and insist that certain behavioral standards be met in exchange for allowance, clothes, privileges, meals, or shelter. Both permissive and authoritarian parents are usually guilty of maintaining a low level of actual parental involvement. They communicate less, show less affection, and offer less companionship than democratic families. During adolescence inductive techniques of discipline (reasoning and explanation) are most acceptable to youth and also correlate with higher levels of moral development. However, these methods should be initiated long before adolescence to be most effective. In Chapter 5 we presented Kohlberg's cognitive-developmental approach to morality. In his view moral thinking invariably develops according to the following sequence:[18]

Stage One:	Obedience and punishment orientation
Stage Two:	Instrumental relativist orientation
Stage Three:	Interpersonal concordance orientation
Stage Four:	Orientation toward authority, law, and duty
Stage Five:	Social contract orientation
Stage Six:	Universal ethical principles orientation

Kohlberg calls stages one and two the premoral levels, stages three and four conventional morality, and stages five and six the levels of principled moral reasoning. Inductive techniques of discipline are related to a principled level of morality. Formal operational thought, as described by Piaget, is also believed by Kohlberg to be a prerequisite for principled reasoning. Nevertheless, in a 1971 study of Americans aged sixteen and above, only about 10 percent of them were found to be using moral principles at the highest level.[19] The majority of the people studied were using conventional morality.

As stated earlier, some teenagers are apt to espouse very idealistic concepts, while behaving in contradictory fashion. At the same time they see the inconsistencies in adults' behaviors and may admonish their elders to practice what they preach.

Some teenagers are in trouble with the law before they are old enough to be arraigned in adult court. In 1975 the American juvenile justice system processed more than one million children, the same number as graduated from college that year.[20] A large percentage of juvenile crimes are serious: motor vehicle theft, burglary, grand larceny, drug pushing, aggravated assault, rape, and murder. Many others are "status offenses": school truancy, ungovernability, running away from home.[21] Juvenile delinquents are frequently out of school and unemployed. Many are alcoholics, drug abusers, or have serious emotional problems. Children from one-parent families are arraigned more frequently than those from two-parent families.[22] Many have no parents or have a history of being neglected or abused as children. The juvenile justice system is frequently lenient with youthful offenders. Rarely are they fingerprinted or phototgraphed before age sixteen or eighteen (depending on the state). Frequently their cases are dismissed rather than tried. When tried, punishments are often merciful: stern lectures, paroles, short stays in juvenile rehabilitation camps or correctional facilities. Many social scientists see rehabilitation as multifaceted: increasing family responsibilities for wayward youths, increasing youths' feelings of responsibility for their own actions, and helping them see the enormity of their offenses and the effects on others. The availability of respected adult role models can be enormously beneficial to these youths.

Sexuality. The one aspect of moral training that caregivers usually postpone until adolescence is the area of sexuality. Sex education in schools, popular music with sexual themes, sex on television, sex in the cinema, street language, pornography and the like are blamed for teenagers' sexual problems. Social scientists often point the finger of blame back at the parents. Many teenagers do not get information at home about sex. They are hesitant to ask questions of their embarrassed parents. Consequently, they seek information wherever they can get it. Hit-or-miss sex education from movies, books, the dictionary, and friends can be confusing and misleading. Gordon found that most adolescents have misconceptions about sex.[23] He asked many groups of teenagers to write their questions about sexual myths without fear of being identified. He found that nearly 100 percent had questions that revealed a surprising ignorance and a belief in a host of "old wives'" and "old husbands'" tales. Common questions concerned pregnancy, sexual fantasies, masturbation, perversions, penis size, homosexual thoughts, pornography, venereal disease, birth control, abortion, and the morality of premarital sex. Ignorance is not necessarily bliss. Sexual experience is often inversely related to knowledge about sex.[24] Those with the least understanding about birth control may be the most sexually active. An estimated 200,000 babies are born to unwed mothers each year.[25] Many teenage girls have abortions (legal, illegal, or self-inflicted). Pregnancy is the most prevalent reason why females drop out of school before graduation.

Sex education should begin in early childhood. Parents who answer early questions with simple, straightforward facts will find it easier to give more detailed biological, psychological, and moral facts as the child grows. Children will be more willing to ask, caregivers will be less embarrassed about answering, and the persons involved will have a foundation of knowledge on which to build. Ideal as this sounds, it is not frequently practiced. Sorenson found that 72 percent of boys and 70 percent of girls could not or would not discuss sexual problems with their parents.[26] When the home fails, religious or educational institutions may assume some responsibility for sex education. Accurate sexual facts, along with moral values, are more desirable than ignorance or erroneous "street" facts.

Significance of the community

The role community members play in the socialization of teenagers when families are only minimally interactive can be tremendous. The peer group is often very significant to teenagers, even when their families are close

Figure 6–5. *After puberty one's basic maleness or femaleness leads to sexual urges. Coming to terms with emotional attitudes toward sex may be difficult for teenagers. Families have the major responsibility for sex education and can best serve the needs of their youth by demonstrating love, justice, and healthy approaches to sexuality in the home and by willingly supplying factual sexual information throughout childhood and adolescence.*
Leslie Davis

and supportive. In addition to the peer group, youths may be profoundly influenced by other adult role models, organized school teams and groups, and by community religious and cultural organizations.

Peers. The importance of the peer group for testing new and different roles during adolescence was discussed in Erikson's theory of the identity crisis. Then, discussion of Piaget's theory of formal operations (i.e., combinatorial analysis, hypothetical-deductive reasoning) mentioned how important the peer group is for debating possible variations of decisions and situations. Looking back through history, one finds that teenagers have been profoundly influenced by the convictions of peer groups. There are many reasons for believing that youths today, and yet tomorrow, will be affected by the behaviors and beliefs of their peers.

In the 1960s it was in vogue to talk about the alienated youth, the youth culture, or the counterculture, usually with some reference to problems created by urban rioting or the war in Vietnam. Prevailing social problems help shape the ideology of youth movements. In the 1920s people discussed the decadence of youth during prohibition; in the 1940s they compared the hardworking youth of the depression years to the reckless youth of World War II. In the 1950s (cold war, Sputnik) youth groups often reflected the patriotic zeal for national ascendency. However, prevailing social situations do not always affect all adolescents in the same way. There are always many variations, subcultures, and even countermovements to the prevailing cultural norms.

Peer groups can evolve around shared interests such as athletics or the arts; they may grow between persons with common experiences such as doing well scholastically or becoming popular on the dating circuit. They may reflect neighborhood proximity or be organized around political or religious interests. Or they may reflect a fondness for certain modes of behavior like drinking or "turning on" with drugs. Any one teenager may belong to two or more peer groups simultaneously. Some groups identify themselves with a certain fashion of dress, grooming, or behavior. More often several groups prefer a certain form of dress that follows the fads and fashions of the day. The kinds and numbers of peer groups any one individual can join and the degree and type of influence the group exerts on the individual (or vice versa) depend on the individual. Personality factors like introversion, extroversion, self-esteem, motivation and situational factors like spending money, free time, sex, family rules, and school obligations all determine the strength of peer influence. Every teenager, whether leader or follower, active or passive, accepted or rejected, pays a great deal of attention to the behaviors and opinions of other young people with whom he or she comes in contact. "Doing one's own thing" is not typical until early adulthood when a sense of identity and a degree of independence are established (see Figure 6–6).

Figure 6–6. *The adolescent peer group provides the individual teenager with a sense of security and acceptance and fosters a sense of group loyalty.*
Patricia Hollander Gross/Stock, Boston

School groups. Organized school teams or groups provide ready-made (usually adult-supervised) peer groups for teenagers to join, if they can meet certain requirements. Sports teams, band, orchestra, drama club, school paper, debate, future farmers, future nurses, and other groups give adolescents a chance to interact with young people who have interests similar to their own. If the organized unit works together for a common goal, its members usually develop a certain amount of cohesiveness and group loyalty. Such special interest groups, organized within a school system, help break down the racial, ethnic, and social class barriers that often characterize outside peer groups. Consequently, school groups can serve two very useful functions: (1) they allow not-so-popular teenagers a chance to experience a sense of belonging and acceptance; and (2) they allow youths from different backgrounds to learn more about each other as they work or play together.

Community groups. Community groups more often consist of youths from the same neighborhood, social class, ethnic group, or religion. This kind of exclusive organization helps give teenagers a feeling of identity within their own subculture. While not furthering the American melting-pot ideal, such group feeling can provide a sense of security and pride to many teenagers who are confused about their own sense of self.

Community groups also allow not-so-popular youths to belong to a clique, especially if membership is determined by religion, social class, parents' group membership (e.g., Masons-Demolay), or ethnicity. Within organized community groups with a heterosexual membership, teenagers can also find opposite-sex friends with whom they share common backgrounds or interests and of whom families may approve.

Health considerations

During periods of more rapid growth when the body experiences greater demands on it for physiological functioning, susceptibility to disease increases. Rest periods and adequate nutrition are essential for maintaining good health. However, the adolescent period is typically one where teenagers prefer hectic activity, late nights, and diets composed predominantly of snack foods and soda. While some teenagers come close to running or starving themselves to death, others pay so much attention to their bodies that they could model for health-spa advertisements. We will discuss some of the more common health concerns of adolescence in the following sections.

Infectious mononucleosis

Depending on the attitudes of one's family and peer group, infectious mononucleosis (usually referred to simply as mono) may either be a status disease or a blight. It is often referred to as "the college kissing disease," because the organisms causing it have a low communicability. They must be spread by direct contact such as kissing or eating or drinking from the same utensils. A quality of exclusivity may link together the "have-had-mono" sufferers from the "have-nots." However, the disease has its dangers. The most characteristic symptom of mononucleosis is extreme tiredness. Sufferers discover themselves lacking their usual get-up-and-go. They also may have fever, sore throats, develop an enlarged spleen, develop faint skin rashes, or have enlarged lymph glands (especially in the neck, axillae, and groin.) Nearly 80 percent of mononucleosis sufferers develop some temporary abnormal liver functioning.[27] Some of them may also develop hepatitis, an inflammation of the liver. The treatment of infectious mononucleosis varies according to the symptoms that are manifested. It always includes rest. Usually the diet has increased protein, vitamins, and iron. The period of convalescence from infectious mononucleosis may be quite prolonged depending on complications and the previous health of the patient. The most serious complication is rupture of the enlarged, fragile spleen with massive blood loss and shock. This requires surgery and removal of the spleen.

Nutritional problems

Teenagers need to eat more during pubescence to provide their bodies with the nutrients necessary for rapidly accelerating growth. Appetites normally correspond with the need for more food. However, many teenagers get into trouble nutritionally. They eat the wrong kinds of foods, they overeat, or they refuse to eat to keep fashionably slim.

Nutrient deficiencies. Calcium and iron have been identified as the most common deficiencies in adolescent diets.[28] Protein deficiency also frequently accompanies iron deficiency. The substitution of sodas for milk and snack foods for meals helps to account for these deficits.

Calcium deficiency can lead to osteomalacia, better known as rickets, although this disorder is generally due to a deficiency of vitamin D that prevents the efficient absorption of calcium from the intestine. Most milk is fortified with vitamin D, but if teenagers do not get adequate amounts of milk or other dairy products and avoid exposure to the ultraviolet light of the sun, which initiates production of vitamin D from precursors found in the skin, they may get symptoms of osteomalacia. These include softening and bowing of the long bones and subsequent problems such as backache, kyphosis (humpback), and loss of height.

Iron deficiency results in a reduced amount of blood hemoglobin, the substance that carries oxygen from the lungs to the tissues, and anemia (a reduced amount of red blood cells). The anemia may be manifested by lack of energy, quick fatigue on exertion, shortness of breath, and a pale appearance. While both sexes may have iron deficiency anemia, it is much more common in teenage girls. They lose iron each month in their menstrual flow and may not eat enough of the iron-rich foods to replace it.

A lack of protein can lead to a malnourished state. Malnourished people can appear of normal weight due to their intake of carbohydrates, but they are more susceptible to infections, are mentally sluggish, have low attention spans, tend to be irritable, and have the same problems of fatigue that the anemic person has.

Obesity. One out of every ten American teenagers is more than 20 percent above his or her ideal body weight.[29] Many of these overweight individuals can also be malnourished because they support their eating habits with carbohydrates and fats rather than proteins. Obese youths are prone to both health problems and personality problems.

Obese youths usually see themselves as unattractive in appearance and socially less acceptable than their thinner peers. They may spend a great deal of time and money on diets, exercises, and slimming plans. Lacking signs of immediate improvement, they become discouraged and often eat more as a way to assuage their feelings of failure. This vicious circle may repeat itself over and over. Meanwhile the obese youth's self-image remains low.

Diets should begin with a complete medical examination. Because adolescents frequently rebel against having someone else supervise their eating, they should be given a great deal of nutritional information. If they can understand what they should eat and why, the diet has a greater chance for success. Drugs that suppress the appetite should be used only under the direction of a physician, since the effects of drugs decrease with continued use and are usually gone after a few weeks. Self-control must be learned. In order to be effective, any adolescent diet program should also include a generous amount of counseling in which underlying reasons for eating, such as negative self-concepts and fears about one's developing sexuality, are handled. Unless youths develop more positive self-images and learn to cope with or eliminate their fears, they may regain any weight lost. Finally, an adolescent diet should allow the youth to take part in peer group activities as much as possible.

Anorexia nervosa. When a person experiences a severe weight loss without the presence of a disease associated with weight loss (e.g., diseases of the bowel, tumors, or severe infections), anorexia nervosa may be suspected. This is a self-inflected diet gone out of control. It is a good example of a psychosomatic disease. Most sufferers of anorexia nervosa (called anorexics) are teenage girls. Unlike a dieter who takes pleasure in pounds shed, the anorexic feels dissatisfied. A dieter usually loses energy with decreased food intake. The anorexic becomes hyperactive. Girls with anorexia nervosa often diet until they lose hair, muscle tone, skin tone, and their menstrual periods. Encouraging them to eat only generates hostility. Not until sufferers are of skeletal proportions will they feel somewhat satisfied. The nutritional problems that accrue can be fatal. Some anorexics commit suicide before they can literally starve themselves to death.

Anorexia nervosa is becoming increasingly common in our country. A typical anorexic is intelligent and ambitious. Their families are usually striving middle to upper income people, anxious to do well. Anorexics may perceive that they are not meeting their family's high standards or that peer group popularity is not what it should be.

Psychologists differ in their opinions as to whether anorexics starve themselves to get attention, to retreat to a more childlike state, to avoid developing sexually, or to exert control over something (the body in this case).

Successful treatment must ascertain the underlying problems that led to the diet. These problems must be resolved, and the anorexic must be helped to develop self-respect and self-esteem at a normal weight.

Family therapy is often recommended to help the caregivers and siblings understand the pressures and conflicts that led the patient to quit eating.

Acne

Acne infrequently occurs outside the adolescent period. It is characterized by blemishes, pimples, blackheads, whiteheads (pustules), and cysts of the skin. These most often appear on the face, shoulders, back, and buttocks. Some of the pustules and cysts may become infected and result in permanent scarring of the skin below.

Acne is caused by an increase in the activity and secretions of the sebaceous glands of the skin. Their overgrowth and oversecretion are felt to be related to increased production of the sex hormones during adolescence. The thick substance secreted by the glands, called sebum, blocks hair follicles, causing all the blemishes.

Some teenagers seen to be able to avoid acne simply by normal cleansing of the skin. For others, frequent washing is essential. Occasionally, infected acne is treated with antibiotic therapy or ultraviolet light.[30] Most acne sufferers are warned to avoid eating chocolates, nuts, and fried foods. They are also cautioned not to squeeze or rub their pimples or to cover them with greasy cosmetics. A few special acne preparations are available that help hide the blemishes without further blocking the pores. The favored therapy is frequent cleansing of the skin and shampoos at least twice a week.

Accidents

Adolescents often behave very recklessly in their bids for identity and independence. Accidents are the leading cause of death among teenagers. (Other frequent causes of mortality are homicides, suicides, drownings, accidents involving firearms, and poisonings.)[31] Many accidents are believed to have an emotional basis. Youths who feel depressed about such things as school failure, popularity problems, obesity, or family fights may be especially accident prone. Alcohol and drug abuse may also make adolescents more accident prone. The rate of suicide attempts jumps up markedly after age fourteen.[32] Attempts are more common in females but are more successful in males.

Venereal diseases

Venereal diseases are now occurring in epidemic proportions in our country. In 1972 500,000 of the reported cases occurred in persons under age twenty-one.[33] It is difficult to guess how many unreported cases exist.

Gonorrhea. Contrary to popular notions, gonorrhea and syphilis are not picked up from toilet seats or door knobs. The germs causing the diseases die quickly unless they are in warm, moist areas such as those within the penis, vagina, anus, and mouth. Gonorrhea may cause painful urination in men and women and a slight vaginal discharge or pelvic area pain in women. Women more frequently notice no symptoms of disease.[34] To date there is no blood test to determine the presence or absence of the disease. Cure can be achieved with penicillin or antibiotic therapy, but the disease may be contracted again and again. Physicians usually prefer to treat people who even suspect they may have been infected rather than wait for dubious symptoms. They also try to locate and treat the persons with whom the patient has had sexual contact. Untreated gonorrhea can lead to sterility and, on occasion, infection of the valves of the heart or joints (gonococcal arthritis).

Syphilis. The first symptom of syphilis is usually a painless sore called a chancre. It heals fairly quickly and disappears. A man may notice such lesions on his penis, but women cannot detect chancres occurring within their vaginas. However, blood tests are available to detect syphilis infection. Long after the chancre has disappeared, new symptoms develop: a rash on the palms or soles, a complete body rash, and hair loss. If syphilis remains untreated, it goes into a latent tertiary stage. During this time it may be slowly and insidiously destroying parts of the body by its peculiar living habits in the blood vessel walls. Untreated tertiary syphilis can lead to disease of the aorta and many forms of neurologic disease such as blindness, paralysis, or insanity. Treatment is penicillin or other antibiotic therapy. Physicians must trace sexual contacts and attempt to get them in for treatment when the disease is diagnosed. This is done confidentially, often with the help of specially trained personnel of local health departments.

Late maturation

When teenagers fail to develop signs of sexual maturity at the time when their friends are changing, their self-concept and self-esteem can sometimes be adversely affected. They may feel different, unacceptable, alone.

Girls usually are less affected by late maturation than boys because a small or flat-chested female is not without sex appeal in our society. A late-maturing girl may also find that her lithe, slender body makes it easier for her to excel in sports. However, late-maturing girls may gravitate toward a younger peer group to find acceptance, or they may be excessively modest among their own age-mates. Many late-maturing girls are taken to physicians to ascertain if they have some endocrine disturbance contributing to the delays.

Late-maturing boys have been shown to feel inferior and less secure, be more emotionally expressive (eager, animated, energetic, talkative) and unstable, and have more body concerns than their normally maturing peers.[35] Occasionally they may withdraw from social activities, possibly due to embarrassment about their small size, smooth faces, and high-pitched voices. Often they seek out attention in uninhibited, bossy, talkative, or smart-alecky ways. Late-maturing boys tend to be more passive in boy-girl relationships. They usually do not date as early as their age-mates.[36]

Early-maturing youths have a much easier time than late-maturing youths. Girls may temporarily seek out older girls for friends and usually begin dating earlier than their age-mates. Early-maturing boys are usually looked up to by their peers and rank high in dominance hierarchies. More early-maturing youths are independent, self-assured, and capable of playing an adult role in interpersonal relationships.[37]

Summary

The ecology of adolescence includes vast numbers of interacting changes. Consider, for example, the impact of sexual maturation, more logical reasoning abilities, and greater independence on a teenager's social functioning. The developing personality is particularly vulnerable to pressures from family members, peers, school, and community groups.

Puberty, the period of rapid growth preceding sexual maturity, may occur anywhere from ages eight to eighteen and may last from a few months to a couple of years. While both early and late maturers have special problems, late maturation can be especially traumatic because of its impact on self-concept and peer acceptance.

Piaget postulated a stage of formal operations to explain the cognitive changes of adolescence. It is characterized by interpropositional thinking, combinatorial analysis, and hypothetical-deductive reasoning. Persons using formal operations pay close attention to details and thoughtfully analyze new problems and situations.

Adolescent males frequently excel in cognitive tasks requiring spatial abilities. Females often show superior verbal skills. These sex differences in intellectual functioning may be genetically based, environmentally conditioned, or both. They often influence career choices.

Turbulence frequently mars the relationships between adults and adolescents in Western industrialized societies. New cognitive abilities contribute to a rise in youthful egocentrism, idealism, and argumentativeness.

The quest for identity, as described by Erikson, is marked by a search for a sense of continuity and sameness between one's own and others' view of the self. Concerns about sexuality, popularity, future occupation, and independence are especially troublesome and time-consuming.

Family members and other significant adults may contribute to adolescents' role confusion by rejecting their own self-directing.

The focal points for health maintenance in adolescence are safety and nutrition. Accidents are the leading cause of deaths and disabilities. Independence strivings and peer pressures make many teenagers particularly reckless. A plethora of health problems relate to nutrition: obesity, dangerous fad dieting, anorexia nervosa, anemia, drug and/or alcohol abuse, and acne.

The teenage years bring changes from child to adult body proportions and from reliance on adults to independence from the family of origin. They are years marked by heightened sexual awareness, excitements and fears, and by great ambivalence about one's own sense of self.

Questions for review

1. Adolescents often feel ugly, ungainly, and not as physically attractive as their peers. Flattery by parents usually doesn't help. How can parents help their teenagers deal with these feelings without sounding superficial?
2. Compare the abilities children have in the concrete operations stage with the abilities adolescents have in the formal operations stage.
3. John, age 15, arrived home at the usual time after a school day. He had not been to school that day. His mother knew it. She asked if he had been at school and he answered yes. How should his mother handle this situation?
4. It might seem that the ability that is developed in adolescence to see all variations of a problem would enable an individual to feel more confident and secure. Is this what happens when adolescents develop this ability? Discuss.
5. Adolescents can be difficult to be around—argumentative at one moment, flattering at another, affectionate at another, and rejecting and angry at another—often all in the course of one day. Imagine you are an adolescent's parents. What sorts of things would you keep in mind to help *you* in dealing with all these mood changes and the feelings they stir up in you?
6. There is an increasing trend among pregnant teenagers to keep their babies, even if they decide not to marry. What are the implications of this decision for the girl, her family, the baby, and society?
7. You are a parent who has spent time discussing sex with your children. You have answered all their questions as openly and hon-

estly as possible. Your daughter, age 16, comes to you, telling you she has decided to begin using birth control and wants your help in going to the doctor and choosing a method. She has no steady boyfriend. What would you say to her?

8. Young adolescents are sometimes removed from their homes because of neglect or child abuse and placed in foster homes. Often they run away from these homes, skip school, and often return to their parents' homes. They sometimes are then taken to court on a status offense, removed from the foster home, and placed in an institution. Describe a better method of intervention in these situations.

References

[1]R. E. Muuss, "Adolescent Development and the Secular Trend," *Adolescence*, 5 (1970).

[2]Ibid.

[3]M. Marsh, "Growth of the Heart Related to Bodily Growth During Childhood and Adolescence," *Journal of Pediatrics*, 2 (1953).

[4]J. M. Tanner, *Growth at Adolescence*, 2nd ed. (Oxford: Blackwell Scientific Publications, 1962).

[5]D. Ausubel and P. Ausubel, "Cognitive Development in Adolescence," *Review of Educational Research*, 36 (1966).

[6]P. Greenfield and J. Bruner, "Culture and Cognitive Growth," *International Journal of Psychology*, 1 (1966).

[7]J. Piaget and B. Inhelder, *The Psychology of the Child*, H. Weaver, trans. (New York: Basic Books, 1969).

[8]A. Buffery and J. Gray, *Gender Differences: Their Ontogeny and Significance*, C. Ounsted and D. Taylor, eds. (Baltimore: Williams and Wilkins, 1972).

[9]E. Klaiber, D. Broverman, and Y. Kobayashi, "The Automatization Cognitive Style, Androgens, and Monoamine Oxidase," *Psychopharmacologia*, 11 (1967).

[10]E. Erikson, *Identity: Youth and Crisis* (New York: W. W. Norton, 1968).

[11]D. Kandel and G. Lesser, "Parent-Adolescent Relationships and Adolescent Independence in the United States and Denmark," *Journal of Marriage and the Family*, 31 (1969).

[12]E. Devereux, "The Role of Peer Group Experience in Moral Development," *Minnesota Symposia on Child Psychology*, J. P. Hill, ed. (Minneapolis: University of Minnesota Press, 1970).

[13]G. Goethals and D. Klos, *Experiencing Youth: First Person Accounts* (Boston: Little, Brown, 1970).

[14]W. Mischel, "Sex Typing and Socialization," *Carmichael's Manual of Child Psychology*, vol. II, 3rd. ed., P. Mussen, ed. (New York: John Wiley and Sons, 1970).

[15]D. Elkind, *Children and Adolescents: Interpretive Essays on Jean Piaget* (New York: Oxford University Press, 1970).

[16]J. Flavell, *The Developmental Psychology of Jean Piaget* (New York: Van Nostrand Reinhold Co., 1963).

[17]J. Condry and M. Simon, "An Experimental Study of Adult versus Peer Orientation," Unpublished manuscript (Cornell University, 1968).

[18]L. Kohlberg, "The Cognitive-Developmental Approach to Socialization," *Handbook of Socialization*, D. Goslin, ed. (Chicago: Rand McNally, 1969).

[19]L. Kohlberg and C. Gilligan, "The Adolescent as a Philosopher: The Discovery of the Self in a Postconventional World," *Daedalus*, 100 (1971).

[20]H. London, *Family Court Decisions: A Study of the Relationship Between Family Structure and Dispositions of Persons in Need of Supervision Cases in Onondaga County, 1970–1972*, unpublished Ph.D. dissertation (Maxwell School, Syracuse University, 1976).

[21]J. Downey, "Why Children Are in Jail," *Children*, 17(21)(1970).

[22]H. London, *Family Court Decisions.*

[23]S. Gordon, *The Sexual Adolescent* (North Scituate, Mass.: Duxbury Press, 1973).

[24]Ibid.

[25]Ibid.

[26]R. Sorenson, *Adolescent Sexuality in Contemporary America: Personal Values and Sexual Behavior, Ages Thirteen to Nineteen* (New York: World Press, 1973).

[27]S. Hammar and J. Owens, "Adolescence," *The Biologic Ages of Man*, D. Smith and E. Bierman, eds. (Philadelphia: W. B. Saunders Co., 1973).

[28]E. Wilson, K. Fisher, and M. Fugua, *Principles of Nutrition*, 3rd ed. (New York: John Wiley and Sons, Inc., 1975).

[29]S. Hammar and J. Owens, "Adolescence."

[30]J. Apley, *Pediatrics* (Baltimore: The Williams and Wilkins Co., 1973).

[31]S. Hammar and J. Owens, "Adolescence."

[32]Ibid.

[33]S. Gordon, *The Sexual Adolescent.*

[34]S. Hammar and J. Owens, "Adolescence."

[35]M. Jones and N. Bayley, "Physical Maturing Among Boys as Related to Behavior," *Journal of Educational Psychology,* 41 (1950).

[36]J. Monet, "Components of Eroticism in Man, I. The Hormones in Relation to Sexual Morphology and Sexual Desire," *Journal of Nervous and Mental Diseases,* 132(1961).

[37]P. Mussen and M. Jones, "Self-conceptions, Motivations and Interpersonal Attitudes of Late and Early Maturing Boys," *Child Development,* 28 (1957).

Contents

Frank Siteman/Stock, Boston

Young Adulthood

In our society people in their twenties usually branch out from their families of origin and establish themselves in somewhat independent lifestyles. The activities and patterns of living pursued by different young people may be worlds apart. Consider, for example, the differences between struggling or unemployed ghetto youth and affluent young persons who can move into their families' businesses. Consider the gulf between persons secluded in convents or seminaries and those following rock bands. The examples can go on and on. The lives of young people who get married are vastly different from the lives of those who remain single. Those who pursue advanced education differ from those who never finish high school. Those who earn their own living differ from those whose parents support them. Children and adolescents, because of required school attendance, share similar experiences. People in their twenties often do not. This chapter will describe some of the concerns of young adults, no matter what path they choose. The choice is profound. As Robert Frost put it:

> *Two roads diverged in a wood, and I—*
> *I took the one less traveled by,*
> *And that has made all the difference.*[1]

Physical development

Given proper diet, exercise, rest, and freedom from preexisting handicaps or disease, a person between ages twenty and thirty should enjoy a body performing in peak condition. The archetypical young adult can expect to have muscles and bones that are strong and resilient, freedom from serious infectious or degenerative disease, normally functioning endocrine glands, and a digestive system that functions smoothly. Physical stamina should be sufficient to keep up with all the social, economic, and emotional tasks of this period.

Body shape and proportions finally reach their finished state, with the exception of weight and muscle mass. Fat accumulation and muscle mass are under more environmental influence (e.g., diet and exercise) and may fluctuate throughout a person's life. Skeletal development is slowly completed as the long bones of the upper legs and arms finish their ossification process (change from cartilage to bone with a concurrent increase in length). During childhood the head was larger than the trunk and the trunk more developed than the limbs. With the limbs, development proceeded from foot to calf to thigh and from hand to forearm to upper

Figure 7–1. *The twenties are years usually characterized by peak physical performances with strong muscles and plenty of stamina for vigorous activity. Retention of these capacities is dependent on the continued use of appropriate exercises and diet and avoidance of health and safety hazards and stressful lifestyles.*

Ira Kirschenbaum/Stock, Boston

arm. For some adolescents this meant outsized feet or hands, which caused a degree of clumsiness until the near ends of their limbs caught up with peripheral growth. As bones ossify, the shaft of the bone develops first. In some bones ossification also takes place in scattered outlying areas called epiphyses. Between the ossified shaft and the epiphysis there is a non-ossified area, the epiphyseal line, from which the bone continues to grow in length. In the twenties these epiphyses fuse with the main shafts of the bones. Once epiphyseal lines are calsified (or closed), the lengthwise growth of bones ceases. Attainment of final adult height coincides with this fusion. A simple radiograph can be used to analyze bone development and determine if final adult skeletal growth has been achieved. A few millimeters may be added to the width of some bones later by surface deposition. Head length and breadth, facial diameters, and the width of bones in the legs and hands may increase slightly by this process throughout life.

Muscles continue to gain strength throughout the twenties and reach peak strength at about age thirty, depending on exercise and genetic endowment.[2] Men have larger muscles that can produce more force than the muscle tissue of women. They also have a greater capacity for carrying oxygen in the blood to the muscles and a greater capacity for neutralizing the chemical products of exercising muscle.

Dental maturity is finally achieved in the twenties with the emergence of the last four molars, called wisdom teeth. For some young adults these last teeth are the cause of severe toothaches, as they sometimes become impacted (wedged between the jawbone [mandible] and the next most forward molars) and need to be removed. The molars, which grind food, are not well utilized by persons who partake of soft, modern diets. The absence of one or more of the wisdom teeth causes no hardship.

The reproductive systems of both men and women are fully mature by the twenties. Kinsey reported that male libido peaks between ages fifteen and twenty.[3] For women Kinsey reported a peak in the sex drive between ages twenty-six and forty.[4] However, sex drive remains relatively high in most people for several decades, often into the sixties and seventies. Regardless of libido, the best years for reproducing children for both men and women are in the twenties. Evidence suggests that the likelihood of finding mutant genes in sperm cells increases tenfold between ages thirty and sixty.[5] For women the likelihood of finding mutant genes or chromosomal aberrations in ova also increases greatly with advanced age. As stated in Chapter 2, the incidence of Down's syndrome (a chromosomal defect) is much greater in women over age thirty-five. Older mothers also have more miscarriages, premature babies, stillborn babies, and babies born with various kinds of neonatal problems.

Evidence suggests that both men and women experience involuntary cyclic alterations in their sex hormone production. Exley and Corker found variations in testosterone production in men occurring in cycles of about eight to ten days.[6] Estrogen/progesterone cycles in women are more complex and are about twenty-eight to thirty days in duration. High estrogen/progesterone levels have been associated with feelings of increased well-being and mood elevation in women. This phenomenon has been especially noted during pregnancy, when estrogen and progesterone levels are much increased, and during the postovulatory phase of the menstrual cycle. Low levels of estrogen and progesterone have been associated with feelings of depression, anxiety, or irritability in women.[7] Research has not as clearly labeled comparable mood swings in men related to high and low testosterone levels. Moods, it must be remembered, are affected by environmental conditions and personality as well as by hormones and can usually be controlled by conscious effort. Most women show little if any outward signs of mood change related to their estrogen/progesterone cycles in the course of everyday living.

The effects of the sex hormones on the secretion of oils (sebum) from the sebaceous glands of the skin become less pronounced in the twenties. Acne usually disappears, and young adults generally find they do not have to shampoo daily to keep their hair clean.

Brain cell development also reaches its peak in the twenties. Actually, the final number of brain cells (about 10 billion) that each individual possesses is determined by the end of the first postnatal year of life, but the cells themselves continue to grow and become more complex during childhood and adolescence. The cell fibers (axon and dendrites) and the myelin sheathing surrounding the fibers increase in size, number, and intricacy. Memory is thought to peak at the time when brain weight peaks. After this the brain cells slowly begin to degenerate. Myelin sheathing decreases as do the size and number of cells. This gradual shrinking of the brain cells after about age thirty is not a cause for great concern. We hardly begin to use all of the brain cells we have at any point in our lives. The mental processes of many people in their sixties and seventies are still keen enough to control empires or make important contributions to the world of arts and science.

Just as a trend has been noticed toward increased height and earlier maturation in successive generations of well-nourished peoples over the past hundred years (see pp. 139 and 249), there also has been a trend toward increased head circumference and brain weight. Simultaneously, a distinct rise in IQ scores has occurred.[8] Perhaps this trend will level off just as height and maturation age seem to be leveling off in areas where affluence allows for adequate nutrition and maintenance of good health and living conditions.

Cognitive development

In Piaget's description of cognitive development it was noted that the highest level of intellectual functioning, formal operations, is acquired unevenly during adolescence. Acquisition of formal operational thought is related to innate intelligence, education, and life experiences. Some people never attain this higher level of functioning. Some acquire it in midlife, given further opportunities that enhance its development. Others attain the ability to use interpropositional thinking, combinatorial analysis, and hypothetical-deductive reasoning and then lose their grasp of these skills in old age.

In the twenties young people make considerable use of their "grey cells," as brain cells are called, at whatever level of functioning is available to them (usually formal operations). Many American young people go to work (whether outside or inside the home) when they leave high school and must learn all the new skills, both technical and interpersonal, that relate to their jobs. They also have many roles to learn while achieving social and economic independence. Other American young people continue to pursue formal education in their twenties. They enroll in trade schools, colleges, and graduate schools and may temporarily postpone some of the other kinds of experiential learning.

Psychologists and educators call the need to learn well and do well need-achievement or achievement motivation. It is quite different from innate abilities and cognitive development but enhances the latter. Cognitive ability plus need-achievement contribute to successful learning far more than either attribute alone. Although caregivers can and do stimulate cognitive development in their children, they have a more potent role to play in stimulating need-achievement. In a classic study by Rosen and D'Andrade, the characteristics common to parents of boys with high need-achievement were reported.[9] Fathers were more competitive, took pleasure in problem-solving tasks, showed more father-son involvement, gave their sons more things to manipulate, and displayed more affection and emotion. Mother were more dominant, stressed success and achievement over independence, and held high aspirations for their sons.

The need-achievement of women, especially by the time they reach their twenties, is frequently far below that of men. It is also below what could be expected of them considering their scores on IQ tests and their past performances in grade school and high school. A popular notion of women's intellect based on their achievement is that they start out ahead of boys, level off, and then retrogress with increasing age. There is no evidence to support this. Women and men can both reach the same levels of cognitive functioning, and women can maintain their high level functioning as well as men. Evidence does point to a falling off of most women's need-achievement.[10] Horner found that college women taking achievement tests could do well, but when asked to compete with men, they dissolved into bundles of nerves. She suggested that women fear too much achievement and success.[11] Academic and professional accomplishments may jeopardize their chances of finding husbands or of maintaining good relationships with their husbands after marriage. Men may feel threatened by women who are high achievers. Hoffman suggested that women's affiliative needs are higher than achievement needs due partly to their socialization, and they prefer rapport with others to a position of being the brightest and the best.[12]

Social development

In Chapter 6 we defined adolescence as that period of time between the biological changes of puberty and independence from the family of origin. Using this definition, we find that some teenagers become young adults before reaching age twenty. Likewise, some people in their twenties remain adolescent. (Kenneth Keniston refers to some individuals in their twenties as youth rather than adolescents or young adults. His theory will be described shortly.) While age is not as good a criterion for life stage as are the pursuits of an individual at a given time, nevertheless, certain pursuits tend to coincide with certain ages.

Figure 7–2. *Youth has, unlike adolescence, a stable sense of self, but is searching for vocational and social roles.*
Owen Franken/Stock, Boston

Young adulthood suggests maturity. Opinions differ widely as to what constitutes maturity.

Freud wrote that maturity is the ability to discipline oneself in work and in heterosexual relationships.[13] Neither the id (pleasure-seeking impulses) nor the superego (self-restricting impulses) dominate the balanced ego. He felt maturity arrives in the postadolescent period for most people.

Carl Jung, on the other hand, believed maturity should not be claimed by most people until middle adulthood.[14] First, individuals must go through the trials of many life experiences.

Erik Erikson wrote that maturity develops gradually as adults work their way through the last three nuclear conflicts of their lives: intimacy versus isolation, generativity versus stagnation, and ego integrity versus despair.[15]

Lawrence Kohlberg, a cognitive-developmental theorist, described maturity as a cumulative process without a well-defined beginning or end point.[16] He saw the highest level of moral development as more mature than the conventional level, yet conceded that few people reach the higher stage. He warned that settling too quickly into a static lifestyle can inhibit the development of moral maturity.

Abraham Maslow, a humanist whose theory is dealt with in detail later in this chapter, also saw maturity as a cumulative process. Individuals progressively meet their physiological needs, safety needs, love and belonging needs, self-esteem needs, and need for self-actualization.[17] Maslow stated that while all people have the innate potential for becoming self-actualized, societal conditions are such that many people only advance as far as trying to meet their love and belonging or self-esteem needs.

The remainder of this social development section will examine the influence of the family of origin, the commitment of oneself to a career, and the procreation of a family. The information about twenty- to thirty-year-olds in these sections are generalizations, more applicable to describing the masses of young people in this age range than to describing any one particular person.

Decreasing influence of the family of origin

A great many young people continue to let their primary caregivers provide for part or all of their economic needs during their twenties. Fewer still look to their families to meet their social and emotional needs. It is becoming common practice for postadolescent young people to lay claim on a few years of an adulthood moratorium (a period of time in which a person is permitted to delay meeting an obligation). Such moratoriums lengthen the time until the young adult must assume responsibility for a full-time job and/or marriage. The time may be filled with college, graduate school, exploratory travels, temporary jobs, and, in some cases, military service. The young person enjoying an adulthood moratorium usually still considers home base to be the family of origin. However, even without making a declaration of independence, these young adults tend to function with more self-sufficiency. Friends and various adult mentors (faithful counselors) can become important as role models and sources of social and emotional gratification.

Conventional young adults. The majority of American young people are considered conventional in their behavior. While they may feel a tension between self and society, they work at becoming a part of the adult culture. Although they may deliberate the need for reform in such things as employment, taxation, welfare, political parties, the penal system, the military, and big business, they spend their time pursuing money or education or enjoying leisure activities. Some may experiment with the practices of less conventionl youth, but they generally spend more time adhering to the customs of their mainstream culture.

Keniston's youth stage. Kenneth Keniston gave the classification "youth" to the millions of young people in the Western industrialized world who are between adolescence and adulthood.[18] To come under this rubric a young person must have acquired a stable sense of self (as opposed to being an adolescent seeking an identity). "Youth," however, are still searching—for a vocation, a social role they can comfortably play, the road to take, a place in the existing society. They feel tension and ambivalence about traditional practices vis-á-vis the developed sense of individuality. Some young people never experience this stage, some pass through it quickly, and others remain in it for prolonged periods.

Activist youth. Not all youth are activists, just as not all youth are students. Young people, especially college students, are all to frequently viewed as a group of activist, dissident malcontents by the more staid constituents of our society. In fact, very few youth make up the activist groups who periodically receive so much bad press. They are seldom found at religious, technical, or teachers colleges, and at the large universities they are in fringe groups that rarely constitute more than 3 to 4 percent of the student population.[19] Activists are generally above-average students. Like all youth as described by Keniston, they feel a tension between maintaining personal integrity and becoming effective and acceptable in society. However, activists either feel more estranged or are more willing to do something about the estrangement they feel. They stage strikes, sit-ins and marches, print and pass out statements, and organize campaigns for reform. If they find their jobs or education irrelevant, depersonalized,

Figure 7–3. *Young adults are as varied as their backgrounds and experiences. Some may prefer a stance of non-involvement while others may be activists.*
Jim Jowers from Nancy Palmer Photo Agency, Inc.

or absurd, they say so. They roundly refuse to compromise their high ideals for status and success in a society that to them seems morally offensive. They embrace social or political causes where they perceive they can benefit greater numbers of harassed peoples. Activist campaigns are seldom undertaken simply for self-glorification. In a study of the morality levels of activist students (using Kohlberg's levels), Brewster Smith found that many displayed a highly principled level of morality.[20] Keniston has commented that, given concomitant characteristics of love, compassion, and empathy, they may help make our society a happier place in which to live. However, he has also warned of the truth of the old adage: Compassion without morality is sentimental and effusive, while morality without compassion is cold and inhumane.[21]

Alienated youth. Very different from activist students are those whose feelings of estrangement from society are manifested by a turning inward of frustrations. Rather than participate in organized groups, alienated youth try to escape from society through such means as drugs, alcohol, or adherence to socially unacceptable lifestyles and actions. They are likely to have had preexisting personality problems before young adulthood descended with its tensions and ambiguities.

Family relationships. During the adolescent identity-seeking period the relationships between young persons and their families and friends tend to be somewhat shallow and one-sided. The young use other people as sounding boards for developing their own self-concepts. Once young people have established a stable and satisfying sense of self, they generally prefer to keep and develop more meaningful relationships with a few others. They usually choose friends who complement and enhance their own uniqueness. They become interested in who others are and where others are going. While family contacts become less frequent as the young person moves out of the home, friendships with parents may go either way: dissolve or be strengthened. For some young people who become alienated from their primary caregivers, a reunion may be delayed until middle or late adulthood, or may never occur. But for other young people the twenties may be the first time in their lives that they have really explored the interests, feelings, values, problems, and welfare of the adults who raised them. They begin to give support and direction as well as take it. This turning of the tables ("You have cared for me, now I will care for you") indicates a real feeling of independence on the part of the young adult.

Committing oneself to a career

A major element of Erikson's description of the nuclear conflict surrounding identity versus role confusion concerned career choice (see Table 6–1, page 257). During adolescence there may be a host of people to give advice about various careers: guidance counselors, primary caregivers, mentors, peers, siblings, and other relatives. Teenagers can feel very tense about making such weighty decisions for their lives. Many steal time by simply saying they are college bound for a liberal arts education that will help them decide, or they declare themselves without choice, saying they must get a job wherever they can. Thus, in the twenties the crisis of career choice remains a foremost issue.

Advice on career choice usually abates in the twenties. Would-be advisors believe that young people have already made up their minds about a career. Young people often give lip service to the vocational choice they are pursuing or are hoping to pursue. They hesitate to admit their uncertainty. They often seek less advice because they feel they should decide for themselves.

When looking for a career, young people consider what interests them and what they might be able to do with their given aptitudes.

They also consider prospective salaries, the amount of education or preparation required, the prestige that goes with the job and today, often, the possibility of finding employment in their chosen field after spending considerable time preparing for it.

The young person who chooses to start a career after high school may try out several different jobs before deciding on a preferred form of employment. Young persons who choose a career that entails advanced preparation at a trade school, college, or graduate school invest more of themselves (time, money, dreams) in a future job. They also may quit the job later, but at a greater expense. Hopefully, their enthusiasm for their chosen career will grow as they progress through the educational process. Some will have had summer work or part-time jobs in related areas or will have seen and heard about the work from relatives and friends. They will feel more secure in the commitment they are making. Some will have practicum courses built into their education. These experiences will help them decide whether or not they have made the right vocational choice. If they do not like the work, they may be able to drop out of the particular career program and choose another. In some schools and for some curricula, practicum experience is missing. Some young persons may spend years preparing for a job without any feel for what it will be like.

One may look back wistfully to the days of apprenticeship learning. Children once worked alongside their parents and neighbors or at least had more access to places of employment. Children knew a great deal about the world of work and different occupations. When they decided what job they wanted to pursue as adults, they could, by an agreement between their caregivers and a skilled craftsman, go to learn the line of trade by working daily with the master craftsman. While some aspects of the apprenticeship system can be admired, contemporary culture offers so many possible kinds of work that deciding on any one direction to take is now appreciably more difficult. Specialization within jobs also makes apprenticeship learning more complicated. Increases in business size and rapid technological change also make it less practicable. Finally, education and child-labor laws keep children out of much of the work world until they reach the age of sixteen.

Most employment today involves on-the-job training no matter how little or how much education the employee has had ahead of time. A worker often does not perform well in a job until he or she has had a few months to learn the techniques of the work to be done. The settling-in process involves the establishment of interpersonal working relationships with the employer and other employees as well as learning the details of the job.

Most young people need from a few months to a few years to

enter a field of employment: job changes, job training, and further education prolong the process. They then need a few years to stabilize in the job or career to which they finally make a commitment.

Disillusionment is not uncommon in the months or years spent entering a field of employment. Young persons may choose a job because of the stereotype it has, without a realistic understanding of the work entailed. Medicine, for example, is a high-prestige career with an aura of glamour. However, doctors and nurses must deal with death and disease, maintain patient rapport, and handle many other less enchanting problems in their day-to-day lives. Modeling may look glamourous but requires hours of posing for takes and retakes under hot lights and a rigorous regime of diet and exercise in off-duty hours. Stereotypes differ outside and inside places of employment also. The physician and the model may be envied their salaries and their limelight by the outside world but suffer from many forms of unpleasantness within their work-a-day worlds.

Disillusionment may also take the form of boredom. Employment that seems exciting for a month or a year or two may eventually become routine and unstimulating. Some employers try to provide changes and challenges in assignments to keep their employees interested and motivated at their jobs, but this is not always possible. There are many highly technical jobs that must be done one way and one way only by well-trained, practiced hands. In some large businesses boredom is accompanied by a strong feeling of depersonalization. The worker feels simply like another cog in the machinery and cannot capture a sense of importance, uniqueness, or even self-direction at work.

Young persons in search of careers frequently change jobs. These shifts are more easily accomplished when people are young, do not require large salaries, and can travel. However, tight job markets, family pressures, too little or too much education, even fear of discrimination may make young people hesitate to look for better jobs. In spite of equal opportunity employment laws, factors such as age, race, sex, marital status, health problems, and handicaps can jeopardize one's ability to find work.

Too many job changes can leave young people as dissatisfied with the world of work as can any one routine. Most human beings have a need for some sense of permanence, of belonging. There is often a certain comfort (as well as possible boredom) in having work which is well defined and predictable. Even in large, depersonalized organizations employees can meet in informal groups for coffee breaks or lunch and give each other personal attention and a sense of uniqueness. Some jobs are made more permanent by the promise of salary increments and pension benefits that accrue over time. Alvin Toffler, in his book *Future Shock*, warned of the dangers of too many job changes, including those brought about by upward mobility, promotions within an organization, or promotions to other branches of the same company in far-away locations.[22] There is always a great deal of tension, sometimes more than a person can handle, accompanying a change of job. The work is unfamiliar. One must learn quickly and do well to assure job continuance. One's old friends are gone. Even a promotion within the same organization may put one's old friends at a distance because of sudden social inequality. If the job change involves a move to a new location, there are many extracareer tensions: finding housing, moving the family, starting children in new schools, locating new employment for a spouse.

For women in our contemporary culture, a commitment to a career has concerns beyond those already described. In spite of the women's liberation movement, many people feel that women (especially women with young children) belong in the home. Employers hesitate to hire women of childbearing age for long-term jobs for fear that they will become pregnant and leave. Other employers still hold on to old prejudices against women, believing that they are intellectually inferior or that they are incapacitated by their menstrual periods.

While being discriminated against at the time of job seeking is a threat, the more frequent concerns of women contemplating careers are role-related. Do I want to be married? Can I combine marriage with a career? Do I want to have children? Can I combine childrearing with a career? Will day care centers or baby-sitters be available so that I can work while I have children? Are day care centers or baby-sitters good for children? Are they reasonably priced? Will I be able to take a break from my career to raise children and then return to work?

Some women pursue career education beyond high school without really wanting a career for themselves. There are psychological risks inherent in this plan of action. A subtle indoctrination occurs as a woman studies for and interacts with other people studying for a particular career. She sees herself in the role. She develops self-confidence performing the role. It is then hard for her to give it up and become a full-time wife and mother. A woman who has had a career may miss her contacts with her working friends. She may long for the feelings of competence, self-esteem, respect, and importance she found in her job. Unfortunately, being exclusively a wife and mother is not given due respect by many people in our culture. In her book, *The Feminine Mystique* (1963), Betty Friedan described the loneliness and lack of self-esteem of some housewives as "the problem that has no name."[23] Although it is by no means a universal problem, it is not uncommon. Friedan's book was a great impetus to the renewal of the women's liberation movement in the 1960s.

In summary, career commitment is a problem sufficiently large to consume a considerable amount of the time and energy of people in their twenties. There are many decisions to be made both by women and men about choice of work, preparation for work, or whether to enter a career, leave it, or stabilize oneself in it for a long time.

Establishment of an independent life

Once young adults gain a feeling of independence from the family of origin, they begin to consider how they will build up their own lives. Should they marry? Should they have children? If so, when? Erik Erikson's theory of the eight ages of man considers the marriage question paramount to the early adulthood stage of life.

Erikson's intimacy stage. Erikson described the sixth nuclear conflict of life as that of finding intimacy versus feeling isolated (see Table 7–1). Once young adults have acquired a sense of who they are and where they are going (identity), they begin to feel a need to reach out to others. Having severed their former close ties to caregivers, siblings, and schoolmates, they seek new friends with whom to share life's joys and sorrows. The persons with whom one relates do not necessarily have to be prospective marriage partners. A sense of intimacy (defined as closeness) can develop between people who work together, face various kinds of battles or stresses together, share leisure activities, or who are roommates. While intimacy usually develops between marriage partners, Erikson cautions that some marriages really amount to an *isolation à deux,* two people living in solitude together.[24]

Erikson saw the development of the kind of mature intimacy described by Freud as being necessarily postponed until after youths have defined themselves in terms of their social, sexual, and career identities. They cannot fully relate to others until they have dealt with the problem of self. Remember from Chapter 6 that Erikson felt young love is usually more conversational than sexual. Young people use their friends as mirrors from which to reflect their developing self-images. Sexual relationships that are self-centered or exploitive or engaged in for erotic pleasure only are immature. Mature love includes self-giving, other-centeredness, or a fusion of one's self with another directed toward mutuality of pleasure. The utopia of intimacy as described by Erikson should include:

1. mutuality of orgasm
2. with a loved partner
3. of the other sex

4. with whom one is able and willing to share a mutual trust
5. and with whom one is able and willing to regulate the cycles of
   a) work
   b) procreation
   c) recreation
6. so as to secure to the offspring, too, all the stages of a satisfactory development.[25]

Table 7–1. *Erikson's sixth nuclear conflict: intimacy versus isolation.*

Sense	*Eriksonian descriptions*	*Fostering behaviors*
Intimacy	– a fusion of identity with that of others(s)	– others confirm sense that mutuality of efforts is beneficial
	– commitment to concrete affiliation(s) and partnership(s)	– others prove faithful to cooperative and intimate sharings and interactions
	– strength to abide by commitment to other(s)	– experiences of making sacrifices and compromises to maintain relationships
vs.		
Isolation	– avoidance of contacts that commit to intimacy	– experiences of being victimized, abused or exploited by others
	– distantiation: readiness to isolate forces and people whose essence encroaches on one's own territory	– shaky sense of identity that causes a repudiation of things foreign to self
	– deep sense of self-absorption	– experiences showing need to compete, not cooperate

Source: Based on material from "Eight Ages of Man" from *Childhood and Society,* 2nd Edition, Revised, by Erik H. Erikson, with the permission of W. W. Norton & Company, Inc. Copyright 1950, © 1963 by W. W. Norton & Company, Inc.

However, even while he defined the utopian, Erikson warned that in our complex society factors of tradition, opportunity, health, and temperament interfere with satisfactory mutuality. He also stated that while persons should be potentially able to accomplish mutuality, they should also be able to bear frustrations without undue regression.

Isolation as the alternative to intimacy is fairly common in our culture. Many young peple have had little or no experience with making sacrifices, or compromises, or practicing altruistic behaviors prior to leaving their families of origin. Intimacy cannot develop without a sharing and giving of the self to other(s). Many young people also have had bad experiences trying to show regard for others. They have been exploited, abused, and victimized. They have learned that competition serves them better than cooperation. They fear any further openness with others.

Many of our contemporary psychotherapies seek to help people find intimacy in contrast to isolation. Psychoanalysis typically goes back to an exploration of the parent-child relationship to help a person work through reasons for fearing intimacy. Behavior therapies seek to change the environments that stimulate or maintain isolation. Desensitization programs, assertiveness training, modeling, even biofeedback programs (where an individual becomes aware of his bodily processes by the use of monitoring instruments) can help people alter the external or internal environments that contribute to their isolation. Humanistic therapies help people assess themselves and improve their self-concepts, allowing them to move toward honest, open interactions with others. Sensitivity groups, T-groups (training to recognize and respond to needs of self and others), encounter groups, sensory-awareness training, and nondirective counseling sessions can help people understand and appreciate themselves so they can relate more fully to others.

Maslow's needs hierarchy. The humanist theories of development that stress the central role of "self" have been given a great deal of attention in recent years. Abraham Maslow, Carl Rogers, Gordon Allport, Clark Moustakas, and Ronald Laing, to name only a few of the theorists, have made us aware of how a person's perceptions of him- or herself influence his or her choice of activities. Such terms as *perceptual, third force,* and *phenomenological* are also used to describe humanist psychologists. Humanists see humans as unique, dignified, rational, thinking, planning beings. They believe that individuals actively shape their own environments and influence their own growth rather than just passively wait for others to pressure them into responses.

One of the more prominent humanists, the late Abraham Maslow, defined his concepts as epi-Freudian and epibehaviorist (epi meaning upon) as well as humanist.[26] He stressed positive growth, normality, and excellence rather than abnormality, depression, and antisocial behaviors. He postulated a hierarchy of needs that are common to all humans. The highest needs, those for self-actualization, self-understanding, and the understanding of others, can only emerge when our lower needs are satisfied. The hierarchy of needs, from lowest to highest includes the following:[27]

Physical needs — food, drink, sleep, activity; relief from pain and discomfort.

Safety needs — freedom from threats to supplies or life; secure, orderly, predictable environment.

Belonging and love needs — acceptance; affectionate relations with others.

Esteem needs — competence, confidence, task mastery, recognition, prestige; respect and approval from others.

Self-actualization — realized potential; feeling that one is what one is capable of being.

According to Maslow, gratification of a need makes a person feel good while deprivation breeds illness (mental or physical).[28] A deprived person will prefer gratification of the missing need over everything else under conditions of free choice.

The emergence of self-actualization rests on prior satisfaction of the other four needs. It is a goal toward which healthy persons continually strive. Along with self-actualization, human beings have a high-level need to know and understand. Healthy people are attracted to the mysterious in life. They have impulses to satisfy their curiosity and find explanations for diverse phenomena. The characteristics Maslow attributed to self-actualizing persons include adequate perceptions of reality, comfortable relations with reality, a high degree of acceptance of themselves and others, a feeling of belonging to all humankind, close relationships with a few friends or loved ones, a need for privacy, an unhostile sense of humor, resistance to socialization pressures, autonomy, problem-centeredness, creativeness, spontaneity, a freshness of appreciation, a strong ethical sense, and frequent mystic experiences.[29]

The mystic or peak experiences that Maslow described are feelings of great joy and intense happiness. One may feel that one's boundaries have evaporated, and one has become a part of all humankind and even of all nature. These experiences may occur when one has finished a long-term project, after a particularly good sexual experience, after one has done something special for someone else, even when one becomes aware that he or she is loved.[30] The ever-present pursuit of the needs for belonging and love or for self-esteem prevents the emergence of self-actualizing experiences in many people.

Singlehood. To marry or not to marry is an important decision facing people in their twenties. There are a great many pressures, both internal and external, for marriage.

Internal pressures include those described by Erikson—the seeking of an intimate companion to share life's joys and sorrows and a desire for a true intimacy and mutuality in sex, and those described by Maslow—desire to gratify the needs for belonging, love, self-esteem, and self-actualization. As the twenties pass, many young people feel the exigency to grab hold of life, master it, and establish themselves as self-reliant persons. For some, marriage appears to be one avenue toward accomplishing these goals.

External pressures for marriage may include family prodding,

Figure 7–4. *Marriage is one way in which young adults meet their needs for belonging and love, for esteem, respect, and approval from others. The average age for marrying is increasing with growing numbers of young adults desiring singlehood for at least a portion of their twenties.*
Robert Bianchi

watching one's friends get married, peer group prodding, dwindling social life as friends marry, religious convictions, external urgings to marry to improve financial or social status, even the pressure from an employer for marriage in order to enhance career opportunities.

The median age for marrying in our country is about twenty years for women and twenty-three years for men.[31] Nevertheless, there are approximately thirteen million single young adults in America between the ages of twenty and thirty-four.[32]

A certain portion of young adults resist the pressures for marriage in their twenties for various reasons. Some are busy concentrating on their careers. Some may have the responsibilities of caring for older parents or younger siblings. Some may not meet a woman or man they want to marry, or one who wants to marry them. Others may form intimate alliances with opposite-sexed partners, possibly including cohabitation, but avoid the legal bonds of matrimony. Numerous young people seem to be disillusioned about marriage. They cite troubles they have witnessed between their parents or their friends as reasons for not marrying.

While singlehood has advantages (i.e., freedom to come and go at any hour, freedom to spend time and money as one chooses, autonomy concerning meals and housework), it also carries with it the ever-present threat of loneliness. Single persons may spend considerable amounts of time seeking companions and nurturing relationships. Then, if they lose friends or end attachments themselves, they must start all over again seeking new companions. There are many aids to finding associates for single adults today (singles' clubs, singles' parties, singles' bars, computer-arranged dates, dating services). However, mate seeking is uppermost in the minds of most of the people who use these services. If one is seeking amiable companionship without marriage, one has more difficulty. In our marriage-minded society it is not easy both to remain single and have a fulfilling social life.

Marriage. The joining of two persons into a legal partnership called marriage is easily accomplished by a justice of the peace or an authorized representative of a religious institution. The molding of the lifestyles of the two people into a workable team where joint interests are served involves a great deal of additional effort. Even couples who have lived together prior to marriage agree that the status of legality and the concomitant expectations of permanence of the union place new constraints on them. They must renew their attempts to live together harmoniously. Marriage means compromise and sacrifice. It means acceptance of each other's variations in moods, in needs, and in personality. It means emotional intimacy as well as sexual intimacy. A certain degree of romanticism accompanies mate selection. Wherever courtship takes place, the individuals involved put their best selves forward and try to hide their flaws. In marriage one sees the other's weaknesses as well as strengths. Our society offers very few courses in marriage preparation. To obtain a license one must simply prove legal age (or have consent of a guardian) and freedom from syphilis as shown by a blood test. The best preparation most young adults have are a few premarital counseling sessions or a few lectures. Consequently, many people enter marriage with a very unrealistic idea of what is to follow.

The honeymoon period of a marriage seldom lasts very long. Arguments soon break through the enchantment. Major sources of marital disagreements include money, use of leisure time, in-laws, chores, responsibilities, sex roles, and power. Quarrels, though viewed by many as destructive, can be constructive. They serve to clear the air and relieve tension. People tend to say what they really mean when they are angry. They boast. They gripe. They admit fears and uncertainties. Several other forms of communication, however, serve these ends as well as arguing. A willingness to engage in open, honest communication without game playing is one of the keys to a workable marriage. Another is to develop a relationship where partners are neither completely dependent on each other nor completely independent from each other, but rather have a certain amount of interdependency.

Kieren, Henton, and Marotz described and defined marital morale as a more accurate indicator of the state of a relationship than happiness or stability.[33] It is a measure of contentment with a marriage based on the number of personal and interpersonal goals that are being achieved. Happiness and stability may be marriage goals for some couples, but they are not necessarily goals in every marriage. You can probably think of some people who maintain their unions in spite of what may appear to you to be overwhelming incompatibilities. Other couples are obviously still very much in love when they divorce. If the expectations of both partners in a marriage are being met, the marriage is likely to persist. If expectations fail, separation usually ensues.

Divorces (also annulments and separations) are frequent in our society. The commonly quoted statistic that one in four marriages ends in divorce, however, is not altogether accurate. It is a ratio of total divorces per year over total marriages per year, rather than one of total marriages existing in the population under study. A 1967 survey of a large number of adults under age seventy showed that approximately 17 percent of women and 15 percent of men had been divorced.[34] Young people seem to be more ready to divorce than older people. Divorce rates are highest for those marrying young (one-half of teenage marriages involving a pregnant bride end in divorce) and for those with low incomes, poor education, or uncertain employment. While grounds for divorce are now quite broad in some states (adultery, cruelty, desertion, nonsupport, alcohol or drug addiction, felony conviction, impotence, fraudulent contract), the legal costs and the emotional trauma involved still make most people think twice before seeing a lawyer.

Parenthood. Shortly after marriage most couples begin to feel pressure from parents, in-laws, peers, and friends to have children. The desire to oblige these people and conform to expectations is frequently given as a reason for procreation. Other reasons may include love of children, continuance of the family name, failure of birth control, proof of sexuality, improvement of the marriage, religious reasons, loneliness, security, status, tax exemption, and ability to afford them. Children can bring a great deal of love, warmth, and laughter into a home. They also bring extra work and added financial responsibilities.

During a woman's pregnancy both fathers and mothers usually begin to anticipate and prepare for the changes that children will bring into their lives. Husbands may feel a surge in their masculinity as they watch their wives' abdomens expand and feel unborn children move. They may begin helping and sheltering their wives more. In fact, pregnancy may usher in the first concept in the man that he is the guardian and defender of his wife and family. Women may feel either more or less feminine as they carry children. Some women decry the loss of their figures and the inconveniences of their pregnant stage. Others take great pride in their protruding figures and enjoy the legitimized reduction in their self-help activities.

Birth is usually a joyous occasion. For a short while parent(s) enjoy receiving congratulations and hearing their very own infant's cry. But, sooner or later, the sound of the baby crying reminds parent(s) just how exhausting parenthood can be. LeMasters, after interviews with a wide spectrum of modern American parents, reported that 83 percent of them experienced extensive or severe marital crises after the birth of a baby.[35] Suddenly the family relationships must all change to include the new member. There will be mother-father, mother-child, father-child, and if there are other children, all the new child-child combinations. Schisms and jealousies ensue. The problems that existed in maintaining marital morale before the child's arrival now become aggravated. Sex is temporarily restricted while the mother heals. Freedom to come and go as one is accustomed to doing is inhibited by the need to provide baby care. The extra money from pay checks that once served as a basis for leisure activities is now diverted into baby necessities. In many families the infant's arrival marks a diminution or end to the mother's wage-earning activities. Exhaustion from night feedings, extra housework, and tensions related to the baby are common. Feelings of inadequacy are also frequent. Children seldom, if ever, really improve a marriage by themselves. What may happen is that couples on an upswing work even harder to communicate their problems and needs to each other and/or seek outside help for any difficulties they encounter. Couples on a downswing find their marital adjustment problems magnified. They also may finally turn to outside help to try to resolve their troubles. Once children are involved, divorce becomes more complicated. Adults can sever their relationships with each other but usually not with their offspring. Someone must provide for the well-being of a child for a full sixteen or more years after the child's birth.

Maternal instinct is a myth. Not all women discover an overwhelming love and protective feeling welling up inside them on behalf of their own child(ren). Some women resent and dislike their offspring very much. Yarrow, Scott, deLeeuw, and Heinig found that women who have good self-concepts and enjoy their roles in life are more apt to be good mothers than those who are dissatisfied with what they are doing.[36] Paternal instinct in the human species has never been given as much attention as maternal instinct. Until recently, the mainstream American father-figure was expected to earn a living for his family and leave childrearing to the woman. A father who interacted with his brood over the weekend was considered a "super Dad." Some men love children. Others resent and dislike them very much. Unfortunately, many young people do not know whether they will like or dislike children until they have them.

There are reasons to be optimistic about parenthood as an influence on the development of young adults. Children can be immeasurably enriching and rewarding to adults who want them and are ready to love and care for them. Erik Erikson's seventh nuclear conflict, that of generativity versus stagnation, will be discussed in this regard in the next chapter. Other effects of children on adult development will also be covered.

For some people in their twenties, parenthood is a foreign concept. For others, it is one of the most important influences on their own growth and development. Increasing numbers of young people are delaying having children until they have had a few years on their own to maximize their own development and/or to adjust to their marriages. Some couples are deciding that they do not like children and, therefore, are not having them. There are other indicators that some people approach parenthood with an earnest regard for the seriousness of the task. Courses in childrearing are popular. Books on childrearing are in demand in libraries and bookstores. There is also evidence of a growing feeling among men that it is both admirable and desirable to help care for children.

Figure 7–5. *Parenthood is a challenging task—one of the most important roles of adulthood! Fathers and mothers shoulder the responsibility for helping their offspring grow into trusting, autonomous, initiating, industrious, self-knowledgable, and loving human beings in about eighteen short years.*

Freda Leinwand

Health considerations

As mentioned earlier in this chapter, the twenties are generally years of excellent health and peak physical abilities. Most of the allergies of childhood disappear after the adolescent growth spurt (exceptions are hay fever and asthma). By the twenties young people have developed immunities to many of the infectious agents that troubled them in the past.

Because of well-developed immune defense mechanisms, infections that are contracted are usually not life threatening.

The threats to health that loom largest are those related to poor control of emotional stress (accidents, alcohol and drug abuse, and stress-related illnesses). Preexisting diseases (diseases of the heart, congenital malformations, endocrine disorders) continue to trouble some people in their twenties. Fertility problems may also be discovered in some otherwise healthy young adults.

Accidents

Accidents account for approximately 44 percent of the total deaths of young people between the ages of fifteen and twenty-four.[37] A large percentage of these fatal accidents (61 percent) involve motor vehicles.[38] Statistics do seem to indicate that during the twenties drivers become increasingly more careful. In a California survey, about 65 percent of drivers under twenty who were involved in motor vehicle accidents were held to be at fault. By ages twenty-five to twenty-nine, only about 50 percent of drivers were held at fault.[39] Whites have more fatal motor vehicle accidents than nonwhites, and men have more fatalities than women.

During the twenties a large percentage of mortality is due to self-inflicted or other-inflicted injuries. Suicide as the cause of death in young adults ranks third for white males, fifth for white females, and fifth for nonwhite males.[40] Homicide (killing of one human being by another) ranks second as the cause of deaths in nonwhite males, third in nonwhite females, and fourth in white males.[41]

Drug abuse

Drug abuse is not a phenomenon seen primarily among young people. It is practiced by all kinds of people in every age bracket. Many accidents and illnesses are directly related to what may be considered a harmless use or misuse of pharmaceutical preparations. People use drugs for almost every possible effect today. They use them to go to sleep, to wake up, to get hungry, to lose their appetites, to stimulate activity, to relax, to deaden pain, to make sensations more acute; the list can go on and on. Drug abuse is not limited to illegally obtained substances. People abuse laxatives, vitamins, antacids, coffee and tea, aspirin, cigarettes, glue and other volatile (quickly evaporating) materials, and especially alcohol. Any drug is potentially harmful when misused. Some people have conscious or unconscious accidental or suicidal intents when they abuse drugs. Many others do not realize what they are doing. They save prescription medicines to use the next time they are sick or to give to other sick people as an economy move. They take over-the-counter preparations for their symptoms and delay seeking medical attention until they are seriously ill. Some drugs that work for one person cause allergic reactions or poisoning in others. The drug abuses of young adults often relate to desires for a "high," a feeling of good cheer, or for a "down," a feeling of relaxation.

Alcohol. The favorite mood-altering drug in the United States is alcohol. The amount of alcohol misused in our country far exceeds the amount of abuse of all other drugs. Not only is it the most important drug abused because of the quantity consumed but also because of the social consequences of its misuse. Alcohol is closely related to the number-one cause of death in this age group: accidents. The seventh leading cause of death in adults in the United States is cirrhosis of the liver (a destruction of liver cells and function caused by alcohol and its products). In some metropolitan areas (including New York City), it is the third most frequent cause of death in adults.[42] In addition to the problems of alcohol-related accidents and alcohol-related cirrhosis, the United States has approximately nine million known alcohol addicts (alcoholics).[43]

In our culture social drinking of alcoholic beverages is not only

Figure 7–6. *Social drinking is part and parcel of the American lifestyle. Prohibition, tried in the 1920s, was a failure. However, our thirst for beer, wine, and spirits is not without occasional adverse side effects, physically, socially, and emotionally.*

acceptable, but also sometimes expedient or even a requisite of the peer group in certain situations. Although the general effects of alcohol ingestion are the same for all people, the individual effects of a glass of beer, wine, or spirits on each person are unique and change with time. Alcohol taken on a full stomach will not reach the bloodstream and cause intoxication as quickly as alcohol taken on an empty stomach. Some people can break down (metabolize) alcohol better than others and consequently can drink more without becoming intoxicated. The brains of people who drink a great deal develop a tolerance to the effects of alcohol in their bloodstream, and these people must increase their intake to achieve the feelings that accompany intoxication.

An intoxicated (drunk) person is often considered amusing, "the life of the party." There are many social rewards for drinking but few penalties, unless people drive while drunk. Intoxication brings in its wake a feeling of excitement and elation. While some people may become aggressive and boisterous in an alcohol-influenced state, more often drunken people just become noisy and silly. They lose muscular control and show signs of incoordination. They also have slowed reaction time and a loss of judgment.

Addiction to alcohol may occur after various degrees of drinking, depending on the unique physiological functioning of the drinker. Many people in their twenties have already become alcoholics.

Once people become alcoholics, they must either have a continual source of alcohol to prevent withdrawal symptoms or never drink for fear of needing to continue drinking to prevent withdrawal symptoms. Withdrawal makes people agitated, apprehensive, and weak. They sweat profusely, have tremors, have an elevated blood pressure, and experience nausea, vomiting, and insomnia. Some alcoholics go into convulsions.

Marijuana. Large portions of the United States population have experimented with or occasionally use marijuana (also called maryjane, grass, Indian hay, pot, hashish, stuff, the weed, reefers, or joints). Individual states vary in their laws concerning its use. In some it is now legal to use it and to possess it in small quantities. In others it is criminal to have even traces of it found on one's person or belongings. A great deal of emotionalism surrounds the decriminalization of marijuana. Many myths also exist about its effects.

Marijuana comes from the hemp plant (*Cannabis sativa*), a weed that grows freely in most parts of the world. Preparations are usually smoked but may also be consumed in drink or food. Unlike alcohol, it is not an addictive drug.[44] Users neither need to increase the dosage needed for a high over time, nor do they experience withdrawal symptoms when they do not use it. A high from marijuana produces a euphoric release from inhibitions, tensions, and anxieties. Users also report feelings of bodily lightness, increased perceptual awareness, and heightened sensitivity to external stimuli. In very large doses it may cause vomiting, diarrhea, and loss of muscle coordination.

One argument used to support the laws against marijuana in our country is that its use leads to the use of the more dangerous narcotics. Supporters of tough laws point out that the pushers who handle marijuana also handle other illegal drugs and encourage buyers to try them as well. Opponents of laws making marijuana illegal argue that it is just as likely that alcohol, tobacco, or other drugs that help people relax will lead to narcotics use.

Marijuana has not been shown to incite people to violent or aggressive behavior. It causes less impairment of driving than alcohol. It does not unduly stimulate sexual desires, though some users report more enjoyment of sex, as well as more enjoyment of other sense-related stimuli (art, music) when high. There is no proof that marijuana produces any physical or mental deterioration or contributes to any organic diseases.

The hallucinogens. Much more dangerous than marijuana are the various hallucinogenic drugs: peyote, mescaline, phencyclidine (PCP), psilocybin, psilocin, LSD, STP, DMT, DET. Their use may produce subjective perceptions of things that do not exist. Hallucinations may give the impression of things larger or smaller or more vividly colored than life and may simultaneously involve two or more senses. They may even give a person a sense of being outside the self, depersonalized. In addition to disturbing the thought processes, the hallucinogens can cause severe nausea, vomiting, loss of appetite, flushing, changes in blood pressure, headaches, palpitations, tremors, even seizures. They may alter a person's sense of time, space, and of objects and people in their environment. Some people prefer to use the term *psychedelic* for the hallucinogenic drugs because the perceptual changes that come to mind may be enticing, pleasure-giving insights into reality rather than hallucinations. In some cases perceptions also mimic psychosis, which has led to the labeling of the drugs as psychotomimetic.[45]

Lysergic acid diethylamide (LSD), the best known of the hallucinogens, is man-made. It has been used with some success in controlled amounts to produce schizophrenialike states in studying model psychosis. The LSD produced and sold for "trips" can vary greatly in strength and purity. Some of the preparations are potentially very dangerous. A poorly understood effect of LSD is its ability to cause flashbacks. A person may suddenly fall into another "trip" with hallucinations and disrupted perceptions months after taking the drug.

The natural hallucinogens—peyote and mescaline, derived

from a cactus, and psilocybin and psilocin, derived from mushrooms—are sometimes used for religious services, mainly by Indian peoples in western Canada, the United States, and Mexico. The side effects of nausea and vomiting are considered purifying. The feeling of depersonalization is an aid to meditation and self-understanding. The altered perceptions that occur may be viewed as communion with supernatural powers.

In several states members of the Native American Church are allowed to use small amounts of peyote legally for their worship services. All other hallucinogens are considered controlled substances, available to investigators with state or federally funded research grants, but illegal for possession by lay people.

Barbiturates and amphetamines. About one-half of the barbiturates and amphetamines used by Americans are obtained through prescriptions; the rest are procured illegally. These drugs are abused by more people than are narcotics, as a tolerance to both will develop with prolonged use. Users must have more and more of the drugs to produce the desired effect. Eventually, physical dependency results. Withdrawal from barbiturate use causes severe headaches, tremors, restlessness, insomnia, irritability, palpitations, and convulsions. Withdrawal from amphetamine use causes depression.

Barbiturates (downs, goof balls, red devils) are sedatives. They tranquilize people, allay irritability, and relieve pain. In larger doses they have a hypnotic effect, producing a sleeplike condition in which the user is responsive to the suggestions of others. In overdoses they produce unconsciousness and respiratory depression that can result in death.

Amphetamines (ups, bennies, speed, pep pills) are stimulants. They decrease fatigue, reduce the appetite, generate excitement, and give an exaggerated sense of well-being. They may impair reflex activity and intellectual performance. In larger doses they can cause aggressive behavior, delusions of self-importance, hallucinations, or paranoia. In overdoses they cause tremors, rapid breathing, elevated blood pressure, confusion or panic, nausea, vomiting and diarrhea, convulsions, coma and/or death.

Narcotics. The strongly addicting properties of narcotics like opium, morphine, heroin (smack, horse, H), cocaine (snow, coke), codeine, and Demerol make them especially dangerous drugs. They relieve pain, and like the barbiturates they confer tranquility. When first taken, they produce a feeling of exultation. This is followed by a euphoria, a buoyancy, and a feeling of well-being. The effects of narcotics depend on dose, method of administration, and tolerance of the user. They can be inhaled (snorted), mixed with other substances and smoked, or injected under the skin (popped) or into blood vessels (mainlined). Repeated use leads to the need for larger and larger doses and eventually to addiction. Once a person is addicted, he or she must have a continual supply of the drug to avoid withdrawal symptoms. Early signs of withdrawal include dilated pupils, perspiration, watering eyes and nose, restlessness, and insomnia. Later symptoms include nausea, vomiting, diarrhea, and violent abdominal cramps.

An overdose of narcotics produces unconsciousness and respiratory depression leading to death. The total number of narcotic addicts in our nation has passed the one-half million mark.[46] The drug problem was once predominantly seen in urban ghettos. It is now also found increasingly in middle-class neighborhoods, especially among the youth.

Stress-related illnesses

People differ considerably in their abilities to handle stress. It has been suggested that such simple behaviors as exercising, shouting, or crying can give vent to restrained emotions. Crying especially is credited with helping to restore mental and physical equilibrium during periods of tension and strain.

People who do not have ways to cope with their tensions, or who are placed in situations where the stress is too great to handle, are often afflicted with stress-related illnesses. In Chapter 5 we described psychosomatic illnesses as those that relate to the influence of the mind (emotions, fears, desires, frustrations, anxieties) on the malfunctioning of the body. Psychosomatic diseases are very real, not imagined. However, successful treatment depends on the removal or alleviation of the sources of stress as well as on pharmaceutical and physical measures. Stress that is restrained and hidden from the outside world can affect individuals in any number of ways. Skin lesions may erupt, e.g., neurodermatitis (scales, itchy areas produced by nervous itching of the skin), herpes (shingles), or urticaria (hives). Disorders of the gastrointestinal tract may appear, e.g., heartburn, chronic diarrhea, constipation, ulcers, compulsive overeating, or loss of appetite. The respiratory system may show its susceptibility to psychic stimuli, e.g., hyperventilation or aggravation of asthma. The cardiovascular system may be affected by palpitations, fainting spells, or large fluctuations in blood pressure as may the central nervous system, e.g., migraine headaches, tics, stuttering, tremors, or nervous breakdown. Many other diseases may have psychosomatic bases. It is always difficult to separate the physical from the psychological causes of illness. However, we do recognize that stress predisposes a person to disease.

Many people turn to alcohol and drugs to alleviate stress. As discussed earlier, these remedies may lead to bigger problems. There are a number of other current ways in which people try to come to grips with their anxieties, especially young people. Some turn to professional counselors or talk over problems in sensitivity, encounter, or T-groups. There is a growing interest in the use of special diets and megadoses of vitamins to help individuals tolerate stress better. Also popular are transpersonal therapies, especially transcendental meditation (TM), Arica training, and psychosynthesis. These are techniques that help people relax, achieve harmony within themselves, and release creative energies that will benefit others as well.

Infertility

Couples who try and fail to conceive a child are beset with a variety of concerns and fears. Is one partner sterile? Are they doing something wrong? Will an infertility study be embarrassing? expensive? helpful? Many functional difficulties can be corrected with medicines or surgery. Approximately 60 percent to 90 percent of infertility problems have psychogenic rather than physiological causes.[47] Ignorance about reproduction is frequently a contributing factor. Couples may have misconceptions about the fertile period. They may use home remedies to assure fertility that actually interfere with conception. Drugs or alcohol taken to stimulate sex may actually decrease libido. Too frequent intercourse may make the sperm count fall below the level needed for impregnation. Prolonged continence may depress sperm motility. A state of mind (fear, anger, hostility, worry) can interfere with fertility. In women, tensions can lead to pain during intercourse, spasms in the vagina that prevent coitus, uterotubal spasms preventing fertilization, uterine hypercontractility preventing implantation, or disturbances in ovulation. In men, tensions can lead to loss of libido, premature ejaculation, functional impotence, or a decreased sperm count.

Physical examinations for both wife and husband are needed to ascertain the possible reason(s) for infertility. When no physiological cause can be found, supportive counseling can often do more to further conception than sending the couple home to try harder. Trying too hard may be one of the contributing factors to the infertility problem. Counseling that explores knowledge of the reproductive process, encourages expression of attitudes and concerns about the marriage and/or about children, and helps the couple relax usually works better than scheduling sex by the calendar.

Summary

Young adults can be found in many settings: e.g., jobs, institutes of higher education, their families of origin, new families, singles' residences.

Given proper diet, exercise, rest, and freedom from preexisting handicaps or diseases, persons in their twenties should be in peak physical condition. For both men and women the twenties are the best years for reproducing offspring. However, childbearing is often postponed for social, economic, educational, career, or other considerations.

Entering a suitable field of employment often takes time. Young adults may change jobs frequently before making a commitment to one field. Some persons spend many years in educational centers preparing for a career before they take their first job. Women may choose to be wife/mother/homemaker, to pursue a career, to do one then the other, or to do both simultaneously. Men are increasingly taking more of a role as husband/father/homemaker when the wife also has a career.

The nuclear conflict of young adulthood proposed by Erikson is that of finding intimacy versus feeling isolated. Intimacy involves reaching out to others and is usually seen in the context of marriage. However, it can also be achieved outside of marriage.

Maslow proposed a needs hierarchy common to all humans. Physical needs, safety needs, belonging and love needs, esteem needs, and the need for self-actualization are progressively and cumulatively sought. While some young adults may be struggling with physical and safety needs, many others are trying to meet their needs for belonging and love and then for esteem. Self-actualization cannot occur unless the first four needs are being successfully met.

While many young adults enjoy singlehood, others choose marriage. Marriages have the greatest potential for lasting when partners' expectations are being met and when interdependency rather than a dependent or independent relationship exists.

Parenthood may bring persons in their twenties both joy, warmth, and laughter, and added work, stress, and financial burdens.

The threat to health that looms largest in young adulthood is stress. Accidents, alcohol and drug abuse, and many psychosomatic illnesses have their origin in persons' inabilities to cope successfully with the stresses of adult living.

Questions for review

1. Consider the various definitions of maturity presented in Chapter 7. How would you define maturity? Do you agree that young adulthood suggests maturity? Discuss.
2. Horner found that women fear achievement and success. Some feminists suggest that women learn this fear from the time they are young. Do you agree or disagree? Discuss.
3. Some parents have difficulty accepting their young adults' indepen-

dence, maturity, and sexuality. Imagine you are a counselor working with a couple who is having difficulty accepting their twenty-year-old's independence. How would you counsel this couple?

4. Newspapers often have headlines about a young adult committing some violent act. Many of these individuals are characterized as being loners. Why do you think a loner would be more likely to commit a violent act than someone else?
5. Young adulthood is a time of establishing a feeling of self and independence, of choosing a career. Do you think men or women experience more stress and conflict in making these decisions and taking these steps? Or do you think both experience the same amount of stress? Explain your answer.
6. Our society has traditionally expected people in their twenties to find a mate, marry, and have children. Much has been written about freedom now to do otherwise. Do you believe individuals are truly any freer to be single, live together, or remain childless? Or do you believe these variations in lifestyle remain stigmatized by the majority of society? Why?
7. Why do you think individuals in their twenties, at a peak time of physical and mental ability, have a high incidence of suicide, drug abuse, and stress-related illnesses?
8. Describe how the resolution of the sixth nuclear conflict, intimacy versus isolation, is affected by the resolution of earlier nuclear conflicts described by Erikson.

References

[1]R. Frost, "The Road Not Taken," *Complete Poems of Robert Frost* (New York: Holt, Rinehart, and Winston, 1949).

[2]J. M. Tanner, "Physical Growth," *Carmichael's Manual of Child Psychology*, vol. 1, 3rd ed., P. Mussen, ed. (New York: John Wiley & Sons, 1970).

[3]A. Kinsey, *Sexual Behavior in the Human Male* (New York: W. B. Saunders Co., 1948).

[4]A. Kinsey, *Sexual Behavior in the Human Female* (New York: W. B. Saunders Co., 1953).

[5]D. Smith, "Preparation for New Life," *The Biologic Ages of Man*, D. Smith and E. Bierman, eds. (Philadelphia: W. B. Saunders Co., 1973).

[6]D. Exley and C. Corker, "The Human Male Cycle of Urinary Oestrone and 17-Oxosteroids," *Journal of Endocrinology*, 35(1) (1966).

[7]M. Ivey and J. Bardwick, "Patterns of Affective Fluctuation in the Menstrual Cycle," *Psychosomatic Medicine*, 30(3) (1968).

[8]D. Smith, "Growth," *The Biologic Ages of Man*, D. Smith and E. Bierman, eds. (Philadelphia: W. B. Saunders Co., 1973).

[9]B. Rosen and R. D'Andrade, "The Psycho-Social Origins of Achievement Motivation," *Sociometry*, 22 (1959).

[10]V. Gornick, "Why Women Fear Success," *New York Magazine*, December 1971.

[11]M. Horner, "Toward an Understanding of Achievement-Related Conflicts in Women," *Journal of Social Issues*, 28(2) (1972).

[12]L. Hoffman, "Early Childhood Experiences and Women's Achievement Motives," *Journal of Social Issues*, 28(2) (1972).

[13]S. Freud, *An Outline of Psychoanalysis*, J. Strachey, trans. (New York: W. W. Norton, 1949).

[14]J. Hillman, "Archetypal Theory: C. G. Jung," *Operational Theories of Personality*, A. Burton, ed. (New York: Brunner/Mazel, 1974).

[15]E. Erikson, *Childhood and Society*, 2nd ed. (New York: W. W. Norton, 1963).

[16]L. Kohlberg, *Stages in the Development of Moral Thought and Action* (New York: Holt, Rinehart and Winston, 1970).

[17]A. Maslow, *Motivation and Personality*, 2nd ed. (New York: Harper & Row, 1970).

[18]K. Keniston, "Youth: A 'New' Stage of Life," *American Scholar*, 39(4) (Autumn 1970).

[19]K. Keniston, "The Sources of Student Dissent," *The Journal of Social Issues*, 23(3) (1967).

[20]K. Keniston, "Moral Development, Activism and Society," *Youth and Culture*, H. Kraemer, ed. (Monterey, Calif.: Brooks/Cole, 1974).

[21]Ibid.

[22]A. Toffler, *Future Shock* (New York: Random House, 1970).

[23]B. Friedan, *The Feminine Mystique* (New York: W. W. Norton & Co., 1963).

[24]E. Erikson, *Childhood and Society.*

[25]Ibid.

[26]A. Maslow, "Toward a Humanistic Biology," *Youth and Culture*, H. Kraemer, ed. (Monterey, Calif.: Brooks/Cole, 1974).

[27]A. Maslow, *Motivation and Personality.*

[28]Ibid.

[29]A. Maslow, *Toward a Psychology of Being*, 2nd ed. (New York: Van Nostrand Reinhold, 1968).

[30]Ibid.

[31]U.S. Bureau of the Census, "Social and Economic Variations in Marriage, Divorce and Remarriage: 1967,"*Current Population Reports* P-20, (223) (Washington, D.C.: U.S. Government Printing Office, 1971).

[32]U.S. Bureau of the Census, *1970 Census of Population, Subject Reports: Marital Status* (Washington, D.C.: U.S. Government Printing Office, 1972).

[33]D. Kieren, J. Henton, and R. Marotz, *Hers and His: A Problem-Solving Approach to Marriage* (Hinsdale, Illinois: The Dryden Press, 1975).

[34]Ibid.

[35]E. LeMasters, *Parents in Modern America* (Homewood, Illinois: The Dorsey Press, 1970).

[36]M. Yarrow, P. Scott, L. deLeeuw, and C. Heinig, "Child-Rearing in Families of Working and Nonworking Mothers," *Sociometry*, 25 (1962).

[37]American Public Health Association, *Vital and Health Statistics Monographs: Mortality and Morbidity in the United States*, C. Erhardt and J. Berlin, eds. (Cambridge, Mass.: Harvard University Press, 1974).

[38]Ibid.

[39]R. McFarland, G. Tune, A. Welford, "On the Driving of Automobiles by Older People," *Journal of Gerontology*, 19 (1964).

[40]American Public Health Association, *Vital and Health Statistics Monographs.*

[41]Ibid.

[42]C. Lieber, "The Metabolism of Alcohol," *Scientific American*, 234(3) (March 1976).

[43]A. Goldstein, L. Aronow, and S. Kalman, *Principles of Drug Action*, 2nd ed. (New York: John Wiley & Sons, 1974).

[44]L. Grinspoon, "Marijuana," *Scientific American*, (12) (December 1969).

[45]F. Barron, M. Jarvik, and S. Bunnell, "The Hallucinogenic Drugs," *Scientific American*, (4) (April 1964).

[46]A. Goldstein et al., *Principles of Drug Action.*

[47]M. Taymor, *The Management of Infertility* (Springfield, Illinois: Charles C. Thomas, 1969).

Contents

Jim Harrison/Stock, Boston

The Thirties

Have you heard it said, "Never trust a person over thirty"? This generalization frequently made about people in their thirties suggests that they surrender to the establishment. They give up youthful idealism and replace it with a more realistic perception of what they must do to survive in their particular social network. They relinquish the freedom of words and actions of their twenties and behave according to the constraints of the social order. They even develop a concern for their reputations. In effect, according to the popular notion, they become more conventional.

It is always dangerous to generalize about members of any given group. There are apt to be as many differences between individuals within the group as between members and nonmembers. In fact, not all people in their thirties become conventional, just as not all individuals in their twenties wave banners proclaiming idealistic views. This chapter will describe some of the hallmarks of the thirties. The reader should note that the characterizations that emerge will not be a perfect fit for any individual person.

Physical development

Physically, adults begin to gradually slow down in their thirties. This slowdown, however, need not show in physical performance. How the body functions in the thirties is very much dependent on diet, exercise, rest, stress, genetic constitution, and freedom from disease or disabilities.

Muscle size, strength, and reflex speed can be maintained with regular exercise. Without it muscles begin a progressive decline. Some muscle tissue is capable of regeneration. Size and strength that is lost from disuse can be regained in the thirties through rigorous exercise.

Skin begins to lose its resilience and elasticity. It can no longer stretch as tightly across the muscles and bones. Both women and men usually begin to notice wrinkles in their thirties. Wrinkle creams and other patent or home remedies may temporarily shrink the skin, but they cannot effect a permanent cessation of these early signs of aging. Men usually worry less about wrinkles than women since society considers a lined masculine face to be more handsome or to have more character. The same lines in women are thought to signal a loss of beauty.[1] Advertisers have long applauded the beauty of a tan color on white skin to help sell sunlamps or tanning lotions and creams. In fact, excessive exposure to ultraviolet light accelerates these skin changes: dryness, thinner skin, less rapidly growing skin, and skin that is more susceptible to skin cancer.

Hair may grow more slowly, be lost, or occasionally lose its pigmentation (evidenced by grey hair) during the thirties. Genetic predisposition toward baldness or early greying, nutritional factors, disease, drugs, or hormones may cause these changes. Androgens (male sex hormones) often affect hair growth. Masculine balding or receding hair line after puberty is a well-known and frequent occurrence.

The discussion of the physical changes of the thirties should not cause too much apprehension. Individual differences abound throughout life. Some people may be grey before forty, others not until their sixties or seventies. Some people may grow flaccid and flabby, while others remain lithe and limber. Diet, exercise, sleep, absence of stress, a cloudier climate, avoidance of sunlight, and artificial measures such as hair dyes, make-up, and corrective surgery can retard or hide the signs of aging. Or one may be proud of a physical appearance that shows signs of experience (and character) rather than looking young, naive, and "still wet behind the ears."

Intelligence and creativity

Intellectually, the thirties are very good years. Brain cell maturation and brain weight peaked in the late twenties, and a very gradual but progressive shrinking is now in progress. However, mental acumen is still high. Cattell proposed a model of the intellect that makes a distinction between two dimensions of mental abilities: fluid and crystallized intelligence.[2] Fluid intelligence refers to capabilities such as associative memory, inductive reasoning, and dealing with figural relationships. Crystallized intelligence refers to skills such as verbal comprehension and the handling of word relationships. The former are closely aligned to innate intellect, while the latter are more dependent on learning and experience. Horn presented data suggesting that while fluid intelligence may diminish very slightly following adolescence, crystallized intelligence increases with advancing years.[3] This increase in crystallized intelligence may account for an interesting finding related to adult IQ test scores. Kangas and Bradway reported that between ages thirty and forty-four some superior adults actually increase their IQ scores.[4] Other researchers have found little if any change in IQ test scores of adults until they reach age fifty and begin to show lowered performance.

Many women and some men return to school in their thirties. Women find they have more time to study once their children enter the elementary grades. They may feel a need for more intellectual stimulation. Perhaps they did not finish high school or attend college earlier because of marriage. Occasionally women and men return to school not so much for intellectual stimulation as to enable themselves to obtain more interesting jobs. Whatever their reasons or combinations of reasons for returning to school, people in their thirties often perform at a higher level than younger students, due to their greater achievement motivation.

Creativity peaks in the thirties. Lehman, in an historical study of the lives of thousands of creative men and women, reported that the peak years for most creative ventures have been young.[5] The mean peak years for symphony writing have been thirty to thirty-four. Great contributions to chemistry have been made most frequently between ages

Figure 8–1. *During the decade of the thirties, many young adults have a high quality output of fresh, creative ideas. Their productivity can enhance their careers and family lives, and provide useful contributions to the community.*

Chester Higgins, Jr. from Rapho/Photo Researchers, Inc.

twenty-six and thirty. Mathematical revelations have come between ages thirty and thirty-four, and medical discoveries have been made by men and women most often between the ages of thirty-five and thirty-nine. Creativity and intelligence, as mentioned in Chapter 6, are not synonymous. Some highly creative individuals may have an average intellect. Dennis found that creative persons usually continue to produce important works throughout their adult lives, even though they accomplish their more unique and original contributions early.[6] In areas where creative endeavors require a larger amount of accumulated and systematized knowledge (e.g., medicine), the outstanding productions occur at slightly older ages.

Social development

Havighurst proposed that the primary social concerns of early adulthood are rearing children, managing a home, taking on civic responsibility, and finding a congenial social group.[7] Of course, not all people in their thirties will choose to take on the responsibilities of home and family. Nor will all want to become involved in civic and/or social activities. Nevertheless, this chapter will discuss the social concerns involving family and community relationships, since these concerns are the most common for this age group. It must be noted, however, that while people may appear to be much the same in a given age range (or sex, or ethnic, or social group), they are in many ways quite different. Each individual has her or his own preoccupations, goals, hopes, dreams, problems, and ways of living.

Family relationships

The establishment of a family of procreation (marriage and children) is the conventional behavior that society assumes young adults will follow. The Puritans once punished young people who failed to marry and procreate.[8] Although society is no longer so condemning, it does exert pressures on people to fit the conventional molds. Society rewards adults who marry and procreate with celebrations, gifts, income tax breaks, and ease in obtaining bank loans and credit. People worry about the unmarrieds and persistently try to find eligible mates for them. They pressure the married but childless adults to hurry up and have children before they pass their years of fertility or youthful energy for childrearing.

Generativity. Erik Erikson saw the nuclear conflict of the adult years as that of achieving a sense of generativity versus that of stagnation (see Table 8–1). In Erikson's view, generativity involves more than just producing offspring. Mature adults who have achieved a sense of identity and intimacy begin to take a global view of their own lives. They ask, "What is

Table 8–1. *Erikson's seventh nuclear conflict: generativity versus stagnation.*

Sense	*Eriksonian descriptions*	*Fostering behaviors*
Generativity	– concern for establishing and guiding the next generation	– encouragement and devotion from progeny
	– concern for others including "belief in the species"	– others demonstrate their dependence on and need for the adult's guidance.
	– concern for productivity and creativity as well as for progeny	– others reflect back the value of one's productions
vs.		
Stagnation	– self-concern, self-indulgence	– early childhood impressions leading to excessive self-love
	– early physical or psychological invalidism, personal impoverishment	– feedback from others that own resources for generativity are doubtful
	– regression to obsessive need for pseudointimacy as opposed to real intimacy	

Source: Based on material from "Eight Ages of Man" from *Childhood and Society,* 2nd Edition, Revised, by Erik H. Erikson, with the permission of W. W. Norton & Company, Inc. Copyright 1950, © 1963 by W. W. Norton & Company, Inc.

life all about?" Generativity involves answers that reflect some benefit to others. Adults can make a contribution to future generations through nurturing, teaching, and serving children or other adults. Producing offspring and guiding them through their nuclear conflicts of developing trust, autonomy, initiative, industry, and identity is an important aspect of generativity. However, Erikson wrote that one need not have one's own children. One can achieve generativity nurturing nieces, nephews, neighbor children, or school children. One can also accomplish a genuine sense of generativity through involvement with the welfare of future generations. Creative skills can be applied to improving the quality of life.

Contributions can be made to societal causes. Productivity can be viewed as one way to give back to the world as much, or more, than one has taken from it.[9]

Stagnation, in Erikson's view, involves a lack of productivity. Instead of leaving one's mark on the world in some contribution (i.e, children, work), one behaves parasitically. One takes without repaying. Stagnation is often associated with those persons of low self-esteem who believe any contribution they might make would be worthless anyway. Such persons are seen to vegetate with the exception of grinding through the minimal necessities of daily living. However, stagnation may also be applied to active, pompous, selfish individuals who work only to accumulate wealth and possessions for their own self-glorification. Such people exploit others and manage to shut out any thoughts of how they might provide for or give to others in return.[10]

Rearing children. Many of the concerns adults have about children were presented in Chapters 3 through 6 on child development. In this childrearing section we will briefly review the needs and concerns of parents with various aged children.

Chapter 7 mentioned that children can bring a great deal of warmth, love, and laughter into a home. They continually demonstrate their dependency and make adults feel needed. They provide adults with both verbal and physical affection. They also can be very amusing. Children can help fulfill adults' belonging and love needs, as expressed by Maslow, in many ways.[11]

Chapter 7 also mentioned the extra work and added financial burdens that children bring. The day-to-day provision of food, clothing, shelter, and discipline can be very trying. Some parents find that they appreciate their children most when they are absent from them or when the children are asleep. Roger Gould, in his description of adult time zones, described the early thirties as much more difficult than the twenties.[12] Parents feel weary. They want to accept their children for what they are becoming and not impose roles on them. At the same time they want to be accepted for what they are as adults, not for what they are supposed to be.[13]

Parenthood is one of the most important roles people can take upon themselves in life. Yet it is a role for which society offers little formal preparation. People assume it comes naturally. There is a plethora of books, articles, and columns on childrearing; they offer a gamut of advice ranging from punishing to ignoring and from providing profuse affection to maintaining a restrained distance.[14] Few printed resources, however, can answer the specific questions of individual parents who have unique children, special problems, and different extenuating circumstances.

Figure 8–2. *Parenting, while abounding with challenge and frustrations, can be an enormously satisfying experience. Laughter, a hug, and "I love you" can wipe away unhappy memories or disappointments. Even small successes by children can generate a triumphant warmth in family relationships.*
Leslie Davis

Parents often think the pediatrician, who might be a good resource, is too busy handling life-or-death illnesses to answer questions. Psychologists are thought to be too expensive. Free or inexpensive clinics where staff can answer questions about childrearing generally receive little publicity. So parents call their own parents, their friends, or their neighbors for advice. Maybe the advice is good, and maybe it is not, but parents may take it because it's all they have. Then, almost invariably, parents hear or read somewhere that what they did was wrong or questionable. Some parents can maintain their self-esteem and confidence that they are doing their best, given their own particular circumstances. Others may find that their years of childrearing are fraught with feelings of guilt, anger, and self-doubt. Supportive counseling would help some parents deal with their feelings and be more comfortable in their roles as parents.

As babies grow into toddlers, they begin to test limits. Their pushes for autonomy frequently occur at the worst possible times of day. Their developmental milestones may be too early or too late according to the time that experts report they should occur. Young children interrupt or postpone all kinds of adult behaviors, from sexual intercourse to quarreling. One child seems to double the problems of organizing time and money. A second child seems to magnify the problems at least three- or fourfold. With one child the intrafamilial problems and jealousies revolve around mother-father, mother-child, and father-child. With a second child relationships double to child one-child two, child one-mother, child one-father, child two-mother, child two-father, and mother-father. Each subsequent child further multiplies and complicates the interrelationships.

As children enter school, they begin to make demands on parents for spending money, unsupervised excursions with friends, and parental participation in school activities. They want trips to all the places their friends have been; they request fad clothes, bad foods, and all the things that they see so enticingly advertised on television. They also bring home to their parents new worries about grades, adequacy of the school system, disputes with teachers, behavioral problems that involve parents with neighbors, other parents, school personnel, community workers, or possibly even the law. Discipline—how much and what kind—becomes a primary concern. As with other childrearing concerns, one can find abundant advice on discipline. Parents may try, at various times, reasoning, behavior modification, deprivation of privileges, hollering, or spanking. The disciplinary techniques that become habitual depend on what the parents have read or heard, how they were disciplined as children, what they perceive as working best, and what their spouse, relations, neighbors, and friends reward them for using. In order for the more effective inductive techniques of discipline to predominate over love withdrawal or physical punishment, the parents must have positive feedback from the significant people in their environment. They also must be concerned about their children's internalization of moral rules and must be convinced that reasoning is the best way to help children develop conscience.

Mothering, when it means the exclusive care of young children without the help of the father, grandparents, or a baby-sitter, is hard work. Our culture predominantly stresses the mother's responsibility for all child care. Consider the job: night feedings, diapers, meals, snacks, shopping, laundry, mending, cleaning, straightening, entertaining, comforting, and protecting from danger. The entertainments preferred by young children are seldom really stimulating or amusing to "Mom." She may miss the hours she once had for sleep, beauty routines, other work, social activities with companionable adults, and exclusive attention from her husband. The "happy homemaker" image of a wife and mother, so glorified by advertising in the mass media, imposes an unrealistic ideal. Mothers who remember that the actresses or models in the media are being paid to play a role can accept themselves better than mothers who measure themselves against the yardstick of the glorified Haus-frau. Likewise, mothers whose husbands, families, and friends value their efforts and achievements are usually happier than mothers whose associates criticize and devaluate their daily efforts and exertions.

For years, our society has placed greater emphasis and value on paid labor. Generally, this means that men's value has been greater than women's, since men are the ones who traditionally earn the money.[15] Women have begun to express their dissatisfaction with this inequity. Research by Tavris indicates that the more children a woman has, the less satisfied she becomes with her homemaking role.[16] Bernard reports that neurosis is very high among housewives and that they are nine times as likely to commit suicide as women who are not housewives.[17] In recent years the women's movement has highlighted and publicized the fact that women's work has not, at least economically, been valued similarly to men's work. Some individuals interpret this to mean that feminists are encouraging all women to go to work outside the home. Others argue that feminists are pointing out that women need to have other options—to be able to go to work or stay at home with equal valuing and satisfaction. The same should hold true for men. In order to effect this kind of freedom for individuals, society must grapple with how it determines the value and labors of an individual—by the amount of money he or she earns or by other criteria.

Fathers are increasingly being recognized as important persons in the day-to-day socialization of children. The social changes emphasizing equality of all peoples, regardless of sex, race, age, religion, or country of origin, and the women's liberation movement have helped to break down some of our old masculine/feminine stereotypes about work. As mothers are increasingly working outside the home (about 43 percent now do),[18] some fathers are taking on more cooking, cleaning, and child care. They can even admit doing so, in some social settings, without damage to their masculine egos. In fact, some men now dub themselves "househusbands" with a great deal of pride.

In the late fifties Bernstein and Cyr reported that fathers' interest in and involvement with their children dropped off after babies reached about two months of age.[19] Perhaps this reflected mothering practices. Babies will respond to almost anybody in the neonatal period. After about two months, when they begin to smile, they reserve their biggest smiles and coos for the people they see most often. If mothers protect their baby from the father, and vice-versa, except for ceremonial hellos, the baby will not be apt to greet "Daddy" with big smiles. A cry is just as likely. Fathers may feel rejected and consequently become less interested and involved with the baby.

In interviews with Chicago mothers in the mid-sixties, Lopata found that very few of them expected many fathering duties from their husbands.[20] The predominant expectations from fathers were that they should be breadwinners. Secondarily they were expected to be fathers. Only tertiarily were they expected to be husbands. In the same interviews Lopata discovered that the women saw themselves primarily as mothers, and only secondarily as wives.

While househusband is not a label all men welcome, and while to be "macho" (masculine, male, vigorous, with connotations of not doing women's work) is still very important to some men, times are changing. Chapter 2 cited the increasing numbers of American parents who attend prepared childbirth classes before their babies are born. These classes strongly recommend the father's participation in the birth event. This is a

Figure 8–3. *Society has seen several rises and falls in paternal interest in parenting. Some fathers are now making themselves increasingly available to their children. We need to support and encourage such participation. Research evidence indicates many benefits from paternal nurturance, few from father absence.*

Leslie Davis

good start for a father-child relationship. Rooming-in and relaxed hospital visiting arrangements for fathers further allow them to become familiar with their infants. The more a man interacts with his offspring, the more comfortable he feels providing food, clothing, and contact comfort. Mothers learn in the same way, through observation and experience. If the father participates frequently in infant caregiving activities, the baby will form a strong attachment bond to him. The infant will smile and coo at him and later show signs of missing him (normal separation anxiety) when he departs.

Most studies of parenting are really studies of mothering. Studies of fathers tend to deal with fathering in lower animals, fathering in the past, fathering in other cultures, theories about father roles, father-mother relationships, and absent fathers (see Chapter 5, pp. 223–224), rather than with contemporary father-child interactions and interaction effects. Research needs to take a longer, harder look at fathers. More good quality research in this area is necessary, especially since fathers are increasingly asking, "What should I do to help rear my children besides earn money and mete out discipline?"

Household organization. The task of organizing a home, defined by Havighurst as one of the major concerns of early adulthood, is closely aligned to parenting but is not synonymous with it. There are probably as many ways of managing a household as there are people trying to do so.

A home may be kept by a single person, by related or unrelated roommates, by spouses with or without children. In spite of the rhetoric on shared roles and equality, most individuals occasionally fall into patterns of boss and bossed. Only an individual living alone escapes this, and then only if her or his associates, parent(s), and friend(s) resist the temptation to give directions.

In the traditional nuclear family setting, the husband is usually perceived as having the managerial role. In fact, the wife, because of her more continuous proximity to the home, directs as many if not more of the tasks. Occasionally, children are allowed to have input about what is to be done and who is to do it. The husband usually makes financial decisions in this type of household. However, the wife, children, and sometimes even interested outsiders like grandparents may help decide how to spend available monies.

In nontraditional families and in nonfamily settings, the management of the household has more chance of being egalitarian than in families trying to conform to conventional social customs. However, it is still possible for one person to assume an administrative role and for others to be dominated. Frequently, as in traditional families, one person will dictate some tasks while other(s) dictate the remaining ones.

Household organization is perceived by some to be simpler today due to modern appliances and convenience foods. Tasks are different from 100 years ago, but not necessarily simpler. Society is more complicated. Moves are frequent. Support systems in the larger community are disappearing. Managing a household, even a simple efficiency apartment, calls for paying bills; organizing time for work, meals, and leisure; socializing and entertaining; struggling with machines; repairing or replacing gadgets that seem engineered to break down; and dealing with meter readers, solicitors, repair people, telephone service, landlords, bill collectors, social service workers, neighbors, garbage collection, and pick-up or delivery of mail, newspapers, laundry, and groceries. People with children must organize and plan time for transportation to school and after-school events as well as cope with children's accidents, truancy, and disobedience. For some people household organization is undesirable or untenable. Home means a crowded, chaotic, noisy place where tranquility only reigns when inhabitants are asleep or absent. Smooth, efficient running of a household is a major organizational task.

In-law relations. Married adults not only have to adjust to each other's idiosyncrasies, organize a household, and possibly rear children, but they also have to either design workable in-law relations or become estranged from their original families. In-law relations require a certain amount of diplomacy, compromise, and sacrifice, even with the best of all possible parents-in-law. The best parents-in-law shoulder many of the necessary sacrifices and compromises themselves for the sake of maintaining ties with their married children.

When people marry, they should not expect complete freedom from their families of origin. What young marrieds can expect is that parents and in-laws will give them some freedom, tone down or hide some of their concerns, and refrain from too much advice giving.

Mothers-in-law come in for more accusations of interference than fathers-in-law, due partly to the fact that mothers usually have more to give up in the way of parenting responsibilities. However, all relationships with in-laws are potentially problematic.

The wife's mother may feel that she has to help her daughter learn more about cooking, cleaning, and child care to the extent that the daughter has difficulty gaining a sense of self-esteem as a mature, capable wife/mother in her own right. She may resent her mother (even while being thankful for the help), and her husband may resent that his wife looks to her mother rather than to him.

The husband's mother frequently has difficulty seeing another woman take her place in her son's life. She may genuinely like her daughter-in-law, yet find it hard not to mention all those things that her son liked when she was mothering him. These suggestions may be taken as veiled criticism or advice giving by a sensitive wife rather than as helpful suggestions. Some wives and mothers-in-law actually vie with each other for the attention, affection, and approval of the husband/son. The wife's father may be problematic in the same way as the husband's mother. Fathers tend to persist in their beliefs that their daughters are naive, unaware, and immature. A father-in-law may be jealous of the husband who has taken his place in his daughter's life and may resent the husband for taking away the daughter's innocence. Daughters may aggravate the problem by comparing their husbands to "Daddy."

The husband's own father may give his son advice about finances, his role in marriage, fathering, or any number of other things to the point where the son has difficulty feeling self-confident about his role as husband/father. The wife may resent her husband's leaning on his father rather than managing his home and marriage alone.

In-law problems are more common among adults who marry young.[21] Adams reported that problems are also more frequent when families give financial aid to their married children.[22] Aid may have certain spoken or unspoken strings attached. It also prolongs the young couples' feelings of dependence on their parents. While financial aid may contribute to in-law friction, it is also very much needed and appreciated by some married persons. Living with in-laws may be easier than living close to them. When adults exist under the same roof, they often work out their misunderstandings and agree upon acceptable roles and responsibilities.[23]

Designing workable in-law relations can be very rewarding. Some married couples really look forward to weekends and holidays with in-laws. They accept their parents' desire to spoil them, cook, clean, and give gifts and compliments. They welcome their role as grandparents. They shower their parents with gifts, compliments, love, and affection in turn. They may both give and accept help with finances, children, illness, and crises. Couples may be able to look on in-laws as role models and learn from them.

Changing American family. Many individuals are worried about the status of the family as a basic societal institution. Some, like Cooper in *Death of the Family*, call for its demise.[24] They feel that the family has outlived its usefulness and has become a malignant force in shaping human development. Why the pessimism? Parents are struggling to make sense of their own lives in our rapidly changing world. Many are living under so much stress that they scarcely have time to interact with their children. For many the future is so uncertain that a bewilderment exists about what kind of preparation to offer their children. Parents no longer use memories of their own childhood as guides, since the present is so different from the past. A few years ago children were raised predominantly in smaller towns or in cities where neighborhoods and extended families provided a sense of belonging to the larger community. Children felt a degree of continuity and sameness in their lives. Moves were infrequent and were occasions for neighborhood get-togethers and sorrowful farewells. Families were predominantly traditional: instrumental father, expressive mother, three or more children, close links to grandparents, aunts, uncles, cousins, community, and religion. Divorce, adultery, and illegitimacy, while occurring, were kept as quiet as possible.

Today, divorce, adultery, and illegitimacy are more common and openly discussed. Meanwhile, family units primarily exist as isolated groups of kin. A 1975 census report revealed that nearly half of U.S. households are inhabited by only one or two persons.[25] The report indicated that this dramatic change in the composition of households is due to a rise in divorce and separation, a lowering of the birthrate, an increased number of single parent families, an increased number of single persons living alone, and separation of older people from their children. More peo-

Figure 8–4. *The increased frequency with which young adults move places a great deal of stress on family relationships, since moving necessitates many psychological readjustments: to new jobs, new living quarters, new neighbors, new schools, and new social affiliations.*
Leslie Davis

ple now live in burgeoning metropolitan and suburban areas. They often remain isolated from their neighbors. They may have to face the threats of unemployment, rising costs, uncertain economy, shrinking energy reserves, pollution, poverty, crime, and the like. Bronfenbrenner suggested that the impact of all the societal changes on families is leading to a breakdown in the process of making human beings human.[26] The support systems once available to the family institution need to be rebuilt to allow parents and other caregivers to function effectively in their child-rearing roles and to have more self-esteem and satisfaction in their lives.

Divorce and remarriage. The societal changes that have weakened the traditional family form (e.g., increased mobility, loss of sense of community, relaxation of social mores) have also weakened the marriage bond. Divorces are now quite common. Fidelity and monogamy, while still valued, are not considered the be-all and end-all for a relationship. Counselors may help persons clarify their feelings about their physical and social-emotional needs and/or health and enable them to make a decision to leave a marriage if these needs are unmet.

Throughout history humans have sought and found some alternatives to the conventional lifestyle. Today, there are several variations of the traditional marriage: part-time marriage with partners living separately due to careers or the like; open marriage with sexual freedom for both partners; modified open marriage with sex-role equality but reins on sexual liaisons; cohabitation without marriage; "swinging" (mutually agreed-upon exchange of partners with other couples); amicable separations; three-person marriages; group marriages; even large-scale communal marriages. These alternatives may still be more popular in newspapers, magazines, books, television, and the theater than in the population at large. Some people experiment with alternatives for brief periods of time. They may feel it is more comfortable to conform to the expectations of relatives, friends, and society than to confront others' negative reactions to their lifestyles. Divorce and remarriage are still more accepted than the newer commitments. However, just as changes are occurring in the American family, changes are occurring in American marriage/divorce norms.

Divorce, as reported in Chapter 7, has affected the lives of about 20 percent of Americans under age seventy.[27] The ratio of divorces to marriages each year now ranges between 20 percent and 60 percent, depending on the area of the country under study.[28] Current estimates are that about one out of every four new marriages will fail.

The popular old story about marriages reaching their crisis point after seven years ("the seven-year itch") has been discredited by recent research. Reports by Carter and Glick and Monahan indicate that separations are most likely to occur in the first year of marriage and divorces within the first three years.[29,30] More than half of all divorces occur within the first five years of marriage.[31]

Divorce is emotionally upsetting to all persons involved: partners dissolving the bond, the "other woman" or "other man" if implicated, relatives and friends, and children. Even in the most amicable divorces, the marriage partners often go through identity searches.[32] They must resolve their inevitable feelings of failure. They ask the question "Why?" over and over to themselves and to others. Even if they can avoid self-accusation, there are sometimes overt or covert accusations made by family and friends. Social ties with family and friends must be redesigned to accommodate the absent spouse. New financial arrangements are frequently necessary. Loneliness may be a threat. Decisions about new directions are essential.

If children are involved, the problems of divorce are often compounded. Children ask for and need to receive reasons for the change in their family. It is important that the reasons given for the divorce do not portray either parent in a bad light. It is also essential to reassure children that they are not at fault. Their needs to feel important and loved and wanted are frequently magnified when separation and divorce occur. If decisions about custody or financial responsibilities are problematic, the arguments should be kept out of children's earshot. Once custody and visiting privileges have been settled, the absent parent should keep promises to visit as faithfully as possible. The custodian parent should help the child(ren) understand if visits are postponed and not use such occasions to turn the child(ren) against the absent parent.

Dating is also problematic for divorced parents with children. While some children have a strong desire for a stepparent, they may also fear having one. They may fear losing their parent's love to the stepparent. Or they may feel jealous of the new person in their family. Older children may make a parent feel embarrassed or guilty as they compare and pass judgments on the person who is replacing their absent parent.[33]

Remarriage can bring the same kinds of comments, jealousies, and competition between parent, stepparent, and children as dating. A majority of divorced people do remarry, however.[34] In their own way each new couple resolves the question of who is to discipline, how, and for what. Children may refuse to obey the stepparent. Bids for attention are frequent. With or without children, remarriage involves the same kinds of issues as first marriages—designing relations with in-laws, organizing the household around belongings, and making decisions about housework, leisure time, and sex.

Community relationships

Earlier in this chapter we listed Havighurst's social concerns of early adulthood: rearing children, managing a home, taking on civic responsibility, and finding a congenial social group. All people in their thirties are not equally concerned with civic or social activities, but most have some regard for these matters. Civic responsibilities can be viewed as all the ordinary affairs of social living: obeying laws, paying taxes, working and maintaining a courteous demeanor toward other people. They also may include more specific roles such as voting, supporting causes for the common good, joining civic-minded groups, and running for public office. Social activities may range from infrequent family get-togethers to party hopping on the social circuit nearly every night.

Havighurst's concerns focus on all people. Recent studies done predominantly on white middle-class American males show other concerns of the thirties. Levinson found American men struggling to make sense of life in their thirties. One terminates one's relationship with the mentor acquired in the twenties and becomes one's own man.[35] Levinson found that men often have incompatible goals—for upward mobility, for stability and order, for freedom from restraint.

Vaillant, in his interviews with American men, found the following comments to be typical for better adjusted subjects: "At twenty to thirty I think I learned how to get along with my wife. From thirty to forty I learned how to be a success at my job."[36]

Career. Most men and about one-half of adult women pursue careers outside their homes in their thirties. Their jobs are part of their identity. They spend half of their waking hours at work and more time preparing for and getting to and from the places of employment. Careers certainly play a central role in social development of young adults. They help determine mobility patterns, social status, lifestyles, and the quality of satisfaction with one's life.

Not all people have the same attitude toward their jobs. Johnson, in 1831, noted that business was almost the only pleasure for the English, while pleasure was almost the only business for the French.[37] While such a generalization was certainly unfair to many industrious Frenchmen and many happy-go-lucky Britishers, there is truth to the theme that work means different things to different people. Most people can pick and choose a few goals for their jobs. The hierarchy of order for their goals is apt to differ, however, even if people have the same goals. Here are some of many goals of employment:

income
security
stability
pension benefits
insurance benefits
convenient hours

social affiliations
prestige
societal recognition
enjoyable work
serving others through work
challenging work
competitive work
accomplishment at work
responsibility at work
self-direction at work
independence
creative outlet

Terkel, in the book *Working: People Talk About What They Do All Day and How They Feel About What They Do,* pointed out that there are vast differences between humans in the ways they view their jobs.[38] Job satisfaction is a feeling of contentment based on the number of personal and interpersonal goals that are being met by one's position and work.[39] A quick cost accounting of job satisfaction can be done by jotting down goals and rating how well they are being met. Quinn, Staines, and McCullough found that over 90 percent of individuals in their thirties and

Figure 8–5. *While men and women seek suitable occupations during their twenties, the thirties are customarily the years when they become stabilized in their jobs. They attempt to keep their places or grasp the right opportunities to advance.*

James Foote from Photo Researchers, Inc.

beyond reported job satisfaction in the ten-year span between 1964 and 1974.[40] They foresaw no trend toward unrest. However, other experts predict future insurgency. Kay reported that not only are blue-collar workers dissatisfied with the monotony of their work, but middle managers are also expressing discontent.[41] Some refuse promotions that they feel would disrupt their personal lives. Others change jobs in search of more opportunity for growth and development. Job changes, though, may be a hazard of "future shock," a potential threat to mental health, according to Toffler.[42]

Satisfaction at work is influenced by expectations from others as well as by personal needs. One usually has a certain timetable in one's mind for work progression (i.e., "I will probably be advanced to ________ level by the time I am ________"). One's spouse, parents, or friends may have radically different expectations. Associates may press for salary increments or work promotions when the individual would be quite content to stay put. Significant others may make it difficult for a person in the thirties to feel job satisfaction without some visible signs of upward mobility. People in many fields may devote considerable time in their thirties to pursuing career advancement through night classes, journal reading, studying, experimenting, practicing, working overtime, or attending meetings. Professionals and nonprofessionals alike may concentrate on gamesmanship skills in hope of speeding up promotions: socializing, being seen at the right places, learning when to compete and when to cooperate, ascertaining when to comply with directives and when to ignore them, studying how to "win friends and influence people," and practicing authority roles. By and large the twenties are considered years for work preparation, job exploration, and settling in. The thirties are considered years for work advancement.[43]

It is possible for career upward mobility to have a negative as well as (or instead of) a positive effect on social and emotional well-being. The hazard of losing one's friends when promotions put a gap between social status standings was mentioned earlier. One may also lose one's sense of worth and achievement with a promotion. Peter and Hull in *The Peter Principle* stated the premise: "In a hierarchy every employee tends to rise to his level of incompetence," and a corollary, "In time, every post tends to be occupied by an employee who is incompetent to carry out his duties."[44] Peter and Hull suggested that people who do a job well should stay at the job, not be rewarded upward to something they cannot handle. While many management experts admit the occasional operation of the "Peter principle," they deny its pervading influence and destructive effect.[45]

Big businesses may strip individuals of a sense of personal accomplishment and self-worth. Persons often become numbers or simply insignificant cogs in a computerized machine. Good management strives to give employees self-esteem, pleasure, and a sense of achievement at work while also generating a feeling of loyalty to the company. Such things as shares of stock, rewards for completion of units of work, and individual praise in newsletters help bolster employee morale. Some labor management relations seem to be moving in the direction of praticing humanistic values. Negotiation with and consensus of workers are utilized in developing directives rather than having them dictated by the power structure.

Changing roles of women and men. Community relationships are altering to accommodate the changing roles of women and men just as family dynamics are undergoing modifications.

Many thirtyish women are happy homemakers. Others are more accurately described as neurotic housewives. Some of the latter may assuage their discontent with alcohol or drugs. Some have psychosomatic diseases or nervous breakdowns. Some turn to affairs or get out of their marriages. All of these solutions may affect society adversely.

Many women find positive solutions to assuage their dissatisfaction with housewifery. Some leave their homes part-time to become volunteers in community affairs. They work in church groups, P.T.A., charitable organizations, political parties, hospital auxiliaries, garden clubs, sewing circles, craft classes, and children's groups such as scouts or 4H. Women are also increasingly becoming politicians and community leaders.

Many women seek gainful employment rather than staying home or doing voluntary work. Seligman has reported that about 20 percent of women who seek outside jobs can only find openings in clerical work.[46] Many of these jobs involve tedious, low-paying work. Some women then find the work world no more fulfilling than being at home. However, the majority of women who go to work fare better and achieve a sense of personal fulfillment through their jobs.[47]

The upgrading of women from housewives to independent, active participants in the society has had a negative effect on the functioning of some men. Husbands may no longer find their wives subservient. Wives may refuse to entertain or move at their husband's say-so. Men may suffer loss of promotion because of their wives' independence. Men may lose their jobs to women or find that their new boss is a woman. Men who believe in masculinity as superiority can suffer confusion as to the meaning of being male. Their ego identities may be further shattered when wives strip them of the role of breadwinner by bringing home fatter paychecks or strip them of their role as authoritarian leader by practicing democratic family decision-making processes.

New support systems for both men and women are needed to

help them deal with these societal changes and to enable them to feel good about themselves while maximizing their own unique potentialities in less sex-stereotyped ways.

Friends. Babchuck and Bates found that young adults socialize most with family friends and other couples with job or social ties.[48] However, the preferred friends of each individual may be some same-sexed persons with whom one can be more honest. Family friends are usually of similar social status.[49] Preferred friends may be selected more on the basis of shared concerns (i.e., children, religion, sports, proximity in the neighborhoods).

Friends can have a strong impact on each other's emotional ad-

Figure 8–6. Friends and social gatherings can be very important to persons in their thirties.

Minoru Aoki from Rapho/Photo Researchers, Inc.

justment. They do a great deal of data processing for one another. A person tells a friend of joys and sorrows, problems, and worries. A friend may respond in a way that is rewarding and has a favorable influence on a personality or in a way that is upsetting. The same friend may be helpful one day and unresponsive the next. Friends tend to react to each other not only on information imparted and received but also with aspects of their own needs, desires, and motivations coming into play.

Harry Stack Sullivan based his theory of personality primarily on interpersonal relationships.[50] He felt social approval is as great an influence on one's behavior as physical needs. One's self-concept is formed by the nature of one's relations with others. Rewarding interactions contribute to mental health, while upsetting relations lead to a disturbed personality. Sullivan postulated six stages in the development of personality. In infancy the baby develops a sense of self versus other and experiences the personal attributes of the primary caregivers. In childhood the self is further integrated through experiences with playmates, dramatic play, anxiety-producing events, language, and sex-role training. In the juvenile stage the self learns to accept subordination to authority figures outside the family. In the preadolescent stage genuine relationships with others are formed. In the early adolescent stage heterosexual contacts enter into interpersonal relationships. In the late adolescent stage the self assumes the responsibilities and satisfactions associated with mature social living. Social living necessitates contacts with many different people. A mature person with a stable self-concept can use communication skills to protect the self from conflict with others. An insecure person with a less well-consolidated self may not be able to escape so readily from the hostility of others.

Sullivan's theory provided the basis for much of the transactional analysis of social relationships currently practiced by psychotherapists. This is a method of examining transactions between individuals to determine how they perceive themselves and others. Many young adults are insecure and face their friends with the attitude "You are O.K., but I'm not O.K." They continually seek advice and help from their associates. Therapists try to help them develop an "I'm O.K., you're O.K." attitude instead. Two other unhealthy perceptions underlying the behavior of some young adults toward their friends are "I'm not O.K., you're not O.K." or "I'm O.K., you're not O.K." Psychiatrist Thomas Harris identifies the former as a give-up position and the latter as an antisocial, criminal-type position.[51] Psychiatrist Albert Ellis states that rational living necessitates a consideration of interpersonal relationships to determine if altercations are due to one's own behavior or to another person's problems.[52] If a person's own behavior is immature, she or he should try to change. However, if the source of a conflict is the jealousy, vindictiveness, or greed of another, the mature rational adult should accept it as such and maintain his or her own feelings of adequacy and self-esteem.

Friends certainly play a central role in the social development of young adults. They help determine self-concept, self-esteem, perception of and trust in others, and, to some extent, overall social demeanor in the community.

Health considerations

In general, adults in their thirties enjoy good health. Their immunity is usually adequate to prevent serious infections. As is true of the health of young adults in their twenties, physical well-being is threatened more by noninfectious agents (i.e., alcohol, drugs, smoking, pollution, accidents, the stresses of everyday living) than by pathogens or degenerative processes.

Except for presenting information on the prevalence of self-inflicted health hazards in the thirties, this section will not repeat the topics of Chapter 7: accidents, drug abuse, stress-related illnesses, and infertility. However, these continue to be important health considerations of people in their thirties.

Accidents as the cause of death drop from about 44 percent among fifteen- to twenty-four-year-olds to about 16 percent among twenty-five- to forty-four-year-olds.[53] Alcohol abuse, causing death through liver cirrhosis and gastrointestinal bleeding, steadily climbs in the thirties. It accounts annually for 0.3 deaths per 100,000 Americans between the ages of fourteen and twenty-four years and for 4.7 deaths per 100,000 Americans between the ages of twenty-five and thirty-four years. Between the ages of thirty-five and forty-four years, 20.4 per 100,000 Americans die each year from alcohol abuse.[54] Alcohol-induced liver cirrhosis continues to climb as a leading cause of death with advancing age.

Many chronic diseases (e.g., chronic bronchitis and emphysema, hypertension) have their onset in the thirties but do not become serious health threats until later in life. Other diseases (e.g., cancer, diseases of the heart and cardiovascular system) not only have their onset but also prove fatal to people in their thirties. Because of their increased prevalence in later years, a discussion of these problems will be postponed until the next chapter.

Health maintenance

The care people take to avoid exposure to infectious agents, physical dangers, known irritants, and conditions that lower one's resistance to infectious organisms (i.e., poor nutrition, physical exhaustion) affects good health. In addition, the promptness of treating illness and injury and the adequacy of the treatments administered are influential. People in their thirties are usually responsible for their own health maintenance.

The existence of accidents, alcoholism, drug addiction, obesity, chain smoking, violence, and suicide among thirty-year-old adults demonstrates some of the ways people damage their health. The existence of

Figure 8–7. *Diet and exercise often become greater concerns of adults as they pass through their third decade. Exercise, especially of the leg muscles, improves cardiovascular functioning and advances physical fitness and overall health.*

Charles Harbutt/Magnum Photos, Inc.

health spas, diet groups, and exercise programs demonstrates some of the ways people invest time and energy toward improving or maintaining their health. Health maintenance in the thirties often requires more than just avoiding or treating infectious diseases. Exercise and diet become very important health considerations in these years.

The maximum benefits of exercise are derived from daily exercising, since physical stamina and fitness deteriorate with a lack of training. Many people in their thirties are aware of the role exercise plays in their health. They schedule regular aerobic exercises (e.g., jogging, swimming, cycling) or isometrics (e.g., weight lifting) into their daily lives.

Dietary needs vary according to the amount of energy expended in the course of everyday living. Many Americans slow down in their thirties, but they continue to eat the same amounts of food as they did in their twenties. Consequently, they begin to develop excess fat, the "middle-age spread." The kinds of foods consumed by many Americans also contribute to the development of excess fat. Rather than balanced diets with leaner protein foods (poultry, fish) and plenty of vegetables, Americans generally eat foods rich in cholesterol and triglycerides (pork, beef, butter, cream) and plenty of carbohydrates (beer, soft drinks, bread, desserts). Excess weight is often accompanied by elevated blood levels of cholesterol and triglycerides. These lipids are involved in producing the lesions of atherosclerosis, which leads to the most prevalent fatal disease process of adults, coronary heart disease. Also, the incidence of gallstones is higher in overweight individuals. Obesity helps to bring out the adult form of diabetes mellitus, which is associated with elevated insulin levels and tissue resistance to insulin. Obesity is also known to aggravate other chronic conditions (e.g., degenerative arthritis of the hips and knees and varicose veins). Finally, overweight persons are more accident prone, have lowered resistance to infection, and are poorer risks for surgery. Overweight individuals have a much shorter life expectancy than people of average weight. This fact is illustrated by the higher life insurance rates of overweight people of every age. At the other extreme, malnourished persons may have lowered resistance to infection, tend to lack energy, and may develop anemia due to lack of key nutrients required for normal blood cell formation.

Acute conditions

Even the most cautious thirty-year-olds who exercise regularly, eat and sleep well, and avoid excesses of alcohol, tobacco, and drugs may become ill from bacterial invasions. The following sections discuss some respiratory infections, digestive disturbances, and urinary tract infections. Their severity depends on the number and virulence of the pathogenic organisms to which one is exposed and on the body's state of immune responsiveness and freedom from anatomical or physiological abnormalities.

Respiratory illnesses. Upper respiratory infections (URIs) are a common cause of lost time from work in this age span. Infections of the upper respiratory tract include sinusitis, otitis media, nasopharyngitis, pharyngitis, tonsillitis, and laryngitis. While the common cold is caused by a large number of infectious viruses, infections of the middle ear, sinusitis, pharyngitis, and tonsillitis very often are caused by bacteria (e.g., streptococcus and pneumococcus). Upper respiratory infections can range from mild and short-lived to severe and life-threatening illnesses, depending on the organisms and the general health and immune responsiveness of the affected person. Infections caused by bacteria can be treated with antibiotics. Viral infections cannot be treated with antibiotics because the viruses themselves are not sensitive to these medications. Untreated streptococcal infections of the respiratory tract (or of the skin as in impetigo) can be followed in a few weeks by such complications as rheumatic fever and glomerulonephritis. For this reason, "strep" infections are routinely treated for at least ten days with penicillin or other suitable antibiotics.

A true influenza (as opposed to a stomach upset called intestinal flu) is caused by an influenza virus of one of several subgroups. New viral strains are continually emerging. Influenza initially makes a person feverish, weak, and gives muscle pain and headaches. Then, upper respiratory tract symptoms such as running nose and sore throat and lower respiratory tract symptoms such as coughing and shortness of breath may appear. The illness may be relatively brief (three to seven days). However, it often predisposes the victims to secondary bacterial infections of the lungs (pneumonia) that may be very serious, and occasionally fatal, even in young people.

Bronchitis (infection of the large air passages in the lungs) and pneumonia (infection of the air sacs in the lungs) can occur in anyone but are more common among smokers, persons with asthma, and persons continually exposed to irritating vapors or dust. Bronchitis and pneumonia may result from either viral or bacterial infections. Their symptoms include difficulty in breathing, sputum production (mucus from air passages in the lungs), cough, chest pain, and fever. As with upper respiratory infections, responsiveness to antibiotics will depend on the causes.

Chronic bronchitis is quite different from acute bronchitis. It is more common among habitual smokers and inhabitants of smog-laden areas. The cough of a person with chronic bronchitis is persistent over a period of months and is usually associated with sputum production. Chronic bronchial irritations may predispose an individual to frequent secondary bacterial or viral bronchial infections. Chronic bronchitis is a forerunner of emphysema and often of lung cancer as well.

Adult asthma is characterized by wheezing, coughing, labored breathing, and mucus production. Asthmatics may have disabling attacks of wheezing and difficult breathing that last from hours to several days. Asthma may also lead to emphysema.

Diseases of the digestive system. All the organs of the gastrointestinal (GI) tract (the esophagus, stomach, duodenum, jejunum, ileum, colon) and the organs that are intimately related to the GI tract (liver, biliary tract and gall bladder, pancreas) are subject to infection from pathogens, insult from irritants (e.g., toxins in foods and drinks), and to inherited diseases. During their thirties individuals generally do not have too many difficulties with their digestive systems. A few of the more common problems that occur are peptic ulcer disease, gastritis, gastroenteritis, appendicitis, gallstones, hernias, and ulcerative colitis.

Ulcers are eroded or scooped-out lesions on any mucous membrane or skin surface with superficial loss of tissue and inflammation. Peptic ulcer disease (ulcers of the stomach and duodenum) are among the most commonly reported illnesses in the United States, affecting from 10 to 15 percent of all people at some time in their lives.[55] Though gastric and duodenal ulcers may look alike, they are very different diseases. Duodenal ulcers comprise 80 percent of all peptic ulcers.[56] They are most common between the ages of twenty and fifty years. They occur more often in men, with the ratio of males to females about seven to one.[57] Gastric ulcers are also more common in men, with the ratio being about 3.5 males to one female. They tend to occur at later ages than duodenal ulcers. Duodenal ulcer disease is associated with high levels of gastric acid production, whereas gastric ulcers are found with generally low acid production, often with the use of aspirins and steroids. Peptic ulcers usually occur singly, although multiple ulcers of the duodenum or stomach, or both, are sometimes encountered. Emotional crises, high tension conditions, smoking, alcohol, excesses of spicy foods, aspirin, and certain other medications are among the agents suspected to cause or aggravate peptic ulcers.

The symptoms of an ulcer are feelings of an ache, gnawing, or burning in the upper abdomen. Often nausea also occurs. Antacids or eating may relieve the pain, but it will usually recur. Bleeding from ulcers may be manifested by skin pallor, general weakness, lightheadedness, tarry, black stools, or bloody vomitus.

The courses of duodenal and gastric ulcers differ. Duodenal ulcer disease is usually a chronic problem. While some persons may have a single bout of duodenal ulcer, the tendency is for periods of worsening to occur after periods of complete clearing (remission). About 7 percent of gastric ulcers lead to cancer of the stomach, so physicians carefully follow the healing of gastric ulcers.[58] Failure to heal a gastric ulcer indicates a need for exploratory surgery.

Ulcer patients must practice dietary regulation and moderation in their daily activities. Symptoms are most apt to recur in times of stress or after indiscretions in intake of foods, alcohol, or drugs that increase gastric acidity or cause gastric irritation. As many as 10,000 lives are lost yearly in the United States as a result of the hemorrhaging or perforation of ulcers.[59] Both intractable bleeding from penetration of an ulcer into an artery or perforation of the wall of the gut into the peritoneal cavity require emergency surgical procedures.

Gastritis refers to an inflammation of the stomach caused by an excessive intake of alcohol, aspirin, highly spiced food, or by ingestion of foods containing certain bacterial toxins or poisons. Its symptoms include nausea, vomiting, upper abdominal pain, sometimes vomiting of blood, and weakness. Treatment is generally supportive, including antacids, medications to control nausea and vomiting, analgesics, and sometimes intravenous fluids if the symptoms persist.

Gastroenteritis is an acute inflammation of the lining of the stomach and intestine. The causes may be the same as for gastritis. Onset is generally rapid with symptoms such as weakness, loss of appetite, nausea, vomiting, abdominal cramping, and diarrhea. The treatment includes restraint from eating or drinking during the acute episode and medications for control of nausea, vomiting, intestinal spasms, and pain.

Appendicitis is the most common acute abdominal condition that usually requires surgery. It may occur at any age but tends to occur more commonly in young adults. The vermiform appendix, a small, nonfunctional structure attached to the first part of the colon, may become inflamed and distended. Symptoms of appendicitis include abdominal pain, loss of appetite, nausea, and vomiting. Once a diagnosis of acute appendicitis is made, the appendix is surgically removed. The consequences of delayed treatment of appendicitis are peritonitis (inflammation of the membrane lining the abdominal cavity and its contents) and death from sepsis (overwhelming bacterial infection).

Diseases of the gallbladder and bile ducts also account for a large proportion of the abdominal surgery in this age group. The gallbladder stores bile, a digestive fluid produced in the liver and used in the gut for the digestion of fats. The biliary ducts transfer bile from the liver to the gallbladder, and from the gallbladder to the duodenum. Inflammation of the gallbladder is called cholecystitis. An acute bacterial infection in the gallbladder produces an acute cholecystitis. Symptoms may include nausea, vomiting, chills, fever, and upper abdominal pain. Treatment includes antibiotics, medication for pain, nasogastric suctioning, and intravenous fluids. Several weeks after the acute inflammation subsides, a cholecystectomy (surgical removal of the gallbladder) is done. About 10 to 20 percent of the adult population harbors gallstones.[60] Prevalence among women is about four times greater than among men. Obesity and pregnancy predispose a person to gallstone formation. Gallstones are composed of some of the constituents of bile—cholesterol, calcium carbonate, or calcium bilirubinate. Gallstones usually form in the gallbladder but can also form in the bile ducts. Gallstones are very often present without producing symptoms. Attention may be called to their existence when a person has an attack of acute cholecystitis, or when a small gallstone passes into the biliary duct and abruptly produces severe upper abdominal pain (biliary colic), nausea, and vomiting. This is treated very much like acute cholecystitis. It may require surgical removal of the gallbladder and sometimes of the stone obliterating the flow of bile through the biliary ducts.

Another common reason for abdominal surgery in adults in their thirties is the presence of a hernia. A hernia is a protrusion of a part of an organ through a channel in a wall that normally contains it. Hiatal hernias are protrusions of a part of the stomach up through the esophageal opening in the diaphragm. Inguinal hernias, femoral hernias, and umbilical hernias are protrusions of loops of the intestine through the inguinal, femoral, and umbilical channels respectively. Frequently, herniated portions of the intestine retract (reduce) themselves spontaneously or can be returned to their normal location with pressure applied by skilled hands. Some people wear binders over areas prone to herniation to prevent the protrusion from recurring. A hernia usually causes some pain and tenderness at the site of protrusion. A herniated structure is in danger of becoming confined or imprisoned in its opening ("incarcerated"). As its veins become compressed, blood drainage is impaired. It swells up so that reducing it becomes even more difficult. Eventually its blood (arterial) supply may be cut off, leading to tissue death. In cases of incarceration, emergency surgery must be performed to reduce the hernia, prevent tissue death and gangrene, and to narrow the opening of the channel so that herniation will not occur again.

Ulcerative colitis is an inflammatory and ulcerative disease of the colon (large intestine). The disease usually has its onset in the early adult years. The cause is unknown. The disease may occur gradually with increased urgency for bowel movements, abdominal cramps, and bloody mucus, or very abruptly with lower abdominal pain, marked weakness, rapid weight loss, and stool containing pus, blood, and mucus. Complications include abscesses of the tissues surrounding the rectum, massive hemorrhaging, and/or colon perforation with peritonitis and septicemia. Uncontrolled hemorrhaging or perforations are frequently indications for an emergency colectomy (removal of a segment or all of the colon surgically). Colon cancer develops in 5 to 10 percent of patients who have had ulcerative colitis for more than ten years.

Diseases of the urinary system. Urinary tract infections are more common in females than in males due to their shorter urethras that facilitate the retrograde entry of bacteria into the lower urinary tract. Bacteria may normally be present in the outermost part of the urethra. However, when they reach the urinary bladder, they may cause an infection known as cystitis. Symptoms of cystitis include lower abdominal pain, often radiating into the sacral region of the back, frequent, painful urination, bloody urine, fever, and chills. The urine normally flushes out bacteria from the urethra during voiding, thus preventing cystitis from occurring. Women are more prone to cystitis during pregnancy, after childbirth, and after frequent coitus (thus the frequent occurrence of "honeymoon cystitis"). Treatment generally includes the use of antibiotics and liberal intake of fluids.

Pyelonephritis, an acute bacterial infection of the kidneys, may be a sequel to cystitis. Once the kidneys become infected, they may continually seed the bladder with infecting organisms and cause a prolonged bout of cystitis. Symptoms of pyelonephritis include flank pains, fever, chills, urgent, frequent, and burning urination, and frequently nausea and vomiting. All kidney infections have the potentiality of damaging the kidney tissue, becoming chronic infections, and ultimately causing renal failure. They must be treated rigorously with appropriate antibiotics. Care must also be taken to ascertain that no other obstruction or anomaly exists in the urinary tract that might predispose it to infection.

Glomerulonephritis is the general term for several inflammatory (not infectious) disorders of the kidney, primarily involving the glomeruli or filtering structures of the kidneys. It affects males about twice as often as females.[61] About 85 percent of cases follow a B-hemolytic streptococcal infection of the upper respiratory tract. An immunologic mechanism is known to play an important role in the cause of glomerulonephritis. Symptoms include edema, hypertension, blood in the urine, decreased urine excretion, back pain, fever, and nausea. Although most patients recover completely, glomerulonephritis sometimes becomes chronic causing hypertension, edema, anemia, even uremia (the complex of symptoms of chronic renal failure), or congestive heart failure.

Crippling conditions

Some of the acute conditions just discussed may become chronic conditions that serve to limit a person's daily activities for life. For example, kidney infections may recur and result in progressive loss of renal function; chronic bouts of asthma or bronchitis may lead to emphysema. A duodenal ulcer may flare up whenever stress is present or a dietary regimen is forgotten. Other crippling conditions affecting adults in their thirties include certain forms of arthritis, multiple sclerosis, and paraplegia.

Arthritis. Arthritis is the general term for inflammation of the structures of joints. Rheumatism refers to afflictions of the joints. The conditions are not synonymous with old age. Rheumatoid arthritis, which accounts for about one-third of all arthritic conditions, has an early onset, usually between ages twenty and fifty.[62] Gouty arthritis (gout), which is an inherited metabolic disease, may be diagnosed in early childhood. Osteoarthritis (or degenerative arthritis or degenerative joint disease) usually occurs later in life in the weight-bearing joints, but may be diagnosed in younger people, especially following trauma or injury to a joint area. (A further discussion of osteoarthritis will be made in Chapter 11.)

Rheumatoid arthritis (RA) is a chronic inflammatory disease with involvement of joints and other structures. The cause is unknown. It may be precipitated by such things as emotional or physical stress. The initial symptoms include low-grade fever, muscle weakness, and pain on movement in the multiple joints of the hands. It slowly progresses and causes disabling stiffness, pain, swellings, and tenderness in other joints as well. The symptoms are frequently more pronounced in the morning and after other periods of physical inactivity. The therapy for rheumatoid arthritis is not a cure. There are frequent spontaneous remissions. Drug therapy may involve use of aspirin, motrin, gold compounds, and sometimes steroids. The use of medication allows relief of pain so function can be restored. In addition to medicines, treatment may include physiotherapy, exercises, and even surgery to prevent contracture of muscles and to restore muscle strength and mass. Most patients with rheumatoid arthritis have some degree of disability all their lives.

Gout is a disease due to a disorder in the metabolism of uric acid. The consequences of this disorder are gouty arthritis, which causes recurrent attacks of painful joint swelling, painful uric acid stones in the urinary tract, and chronic kidney failure. The attacks of gouty arthritis most often affect the joints of the large toes, ankles, feet, knees, fingers, wrists, and elbows. They appear without warning and may be precipitated by minor trauma, infections, or surgery. Gout is a genetically inherited disease whose cause cannot be corrected but whose manifestations can be controlled by medications. During acute attacks of painful joints, treatment consists of medication. Since gout is usually the result of increased production of uric acid, current drug treatment aims at decreasing this production. The advent of new drugs has changed the course and outcome of gout very favorably for many people.

Multiple sclerosis. Multiple sclerosis (MS) is frequently referred to as the great crippler of young adults. It is a chronic and slowly progressive disease of the central nervous system characterized by spotty and diffuse areas of loss of the myelin sheathing around axons of nerves in the brain and spinal cord and by a multitude of other symptoms. The age of onset for multiple sclerosis is typically between twenty and forty. The cause is unknown, though scientists suspect it may be related to some viral infection or autoimmune process. The patient gets attacks of neurological disability followed by periods of remission of the disease, but with subsequent recurrences and progressive worsening. As each successive attack occurs, more nerve tissue is damaged. Eventually some victims reach a stage of helplessness. Some common manifestations of multiple sclerosis include muscular weakness or paralysis, paresthesia, double vision, transient blindness, taxia, and speech disorders. A great deal of research time and money is being spent to try to find the cause, some effective treatment, and a way to arrest the occurrence of multiple sclerosis. At present there are approximately 500,000 persons afflicted with MS in the United States.[63]

Paraplegia and quadriplegia. Paraplegia refers to paralysis confined to the lower extremities and, generally, the lower trunk. Quadriplegia refers to paralysis of all four extremities and of the trunk. The causes of paraplegia and quadriplegia include accidents affecting the spinal cord, fractures of the vertebral column causing pressure or severing of the spinal cord, or some disease affecting the cord such as poliomyelitis, a tumor causing compression of the cord, or Pott's disease (tuberculosis of the spine). Quadriplegics and paraplegics not only lose their ability to move their lower trunk and extremities below the level of the spinal cord injury, but also lose control of their bladder and bowel functions. They often develop urinary tract infections from retention of urine or from catheterization of the bladder. Chronic urinary infections and renal failure may shorten their life spans. They also may develop bed sores at pressure points such as the buttocks. Some handicapped persons using wheelchairs to locomote can lead moderately active lives. Their intelligence and manual dexterity are unaffected by the lower paralysis. Quadriplegics are, of course, much more limited. Campaigns such as "Hire the handicapped," public relations programs, supportive and self-help organizations, and simple architectural considerations such as the addition of ramps in buildings are helping to make it less difficult for people with these crippling conditions to adjust emotionally, socially, and economically.

Summary

The ecological settings of the thirties encompass the home, place(s) of outside employment, and places for leisure pursuits and social activities. During the thirties people struggle for their own place in the social order.

Physically, signs of aging appear. However, with exercise, a nutritious and judicious diet, rest, and the ability to recognize, attack, and overcome stressors, the thirties can be years of peak physical prowess.

Intellectually, the thirties are very good years. Many people return to school or continue studying. The output of unique, original materials by creative persons peaks in the decade between thirty and forty.

Social concerns may include rearing children, managing a home, taking on civic responsibility, and finding a congenial social group.

Erikson saw the nuclear conflict of the adult years as that of achieving a sense of generativity versus that of stagnation. Generativity involves nurturing, teaching, and serving children and/or other adults. One can achieve generativity without having one's own children through creative skills, productivity, and contributions to the quality of life of others and of future generations. Stagnation involves a lack of productivity or concern for others.

Parenthood can bring extra work, financial burdens, and feelings of guilt, anger, and self-doubt to adults. Many parents need the support and reassurances of persons around them that they are competent in childrearing. Children can also add warmth, love, and laughter to adults' lives.

Household organization can be very complicated, especially with frequent moves, limited space, overextended budgets, and with all adult members of the household holding part- or full-time jobs.

Support systems in the larger community, which once were very important in the lives of adults, are now disappearing in many of today's transient neighborhoods.

Marriages are not as stable today as in past years. Divorce now follows about one in four new marriages, usually occurring within one to five years of the union. Divorce is made more complicated by the presence of children. A majority of divorced persons do remarry.

Careers are usually very important to persons in their thirties. While the twenties were years for choosing a vocation, the thirties represent the decade for learning to be a success at one's job.

Friends are often chosen on the basis of aspirations for upward mobility, status, and job advancement. They also are apt to be people with similar concerns (religion, neighborhood, children). Closest friends are usually those with whom one dares to be more honest. Friends can create situations of conflict and stress or give support and reassurance to each other.

Health maintenance requires attention to diet, excercise, rest, safety precautions, and prompt treatment of infections. Acute respiratory, digestive, or urinary disturbances can turn into chronic problems (e.g., chronic bronchitis, emphysema, ulcers, colitis, loss of renal function). Other chronic conditions affecting adults in their thirties include certain forms of arthritis, multiple sclerosis, and paraplegia.

Questions for review

1. A number of people believe that men's aging is viewed differently from women's aging in our society. Illustrations of this, they say, exist in the mass media. Give examples that support this view and examples that refute it from either magazines, television, or newspapers.
2. For a number of years the emphasis in American society has been on the maintenance of youth and the needs of the young. What sorts of implications do you think this has for people in their thirties who are beginning to see signs of their own aging?
3. Erikson stated that stagnation is often associated with persons of low self-esteem. Why do you think this is so? Relate this to the resolution of nuclear conflicts described in earlier chapters.
4. Imagine you have been married for ten years, are thirty-five-years-old and are going through a divorce. Would you turn to your friends or family for emotional support? Why?
5. As a health professional, how would you counsel a couple where the man, a father of two young children, has recently become a paraplegic as a result of a car accident? What do you view as the most important issues for a couple dealing with this crisis?
6. Increasing numbers of married women are entering the labor force. What sorts of issues does this raise for men in terms of their role within a family? Include suggestions on how men may deal with these issues.
7. Your relationships with your in-laws has always been a problem. Yet you value the special relationship they have with your children. How do you keep your problems separate from your children's relationship with their grandparents?
8. Some social scientists express concern about women's changing roles, saying that, as mothers enter the work force, there is no one providing tender, loving care for the children. How would you respond to these social scientists? In your answer consider solutions to the care of children other than having women remain home full-time.

9. All around us the message is to be a couple. What sorts of implications does this have for single and divorced persons and widows and widowers?

References

[1]I. Bell, "The Double Standard," *Trans-Action*, 8(12)(1970).

[2]J. Horn, "Organization of Data on Life-Span Development of Human Abilities," *Life-Span Developmental Psychology*, L. Goulet and P. Baltes, eds. (New York: Academic Press, 1970).

[3]Ibid.

[4]J. Kangas and K. Bradway, "Intelligence at Middle-Age: A 38-Year Follow Up," *Developmental Psychology*, 5 (1971).

[5]H. Lehman, *Age and Achievement*, vol. 33, Memoirs Series (Princeton: Princeton University Press, 1953).

[6]W. Dennis, "Creative Productivity Between the Ages of Twenty and Eighty Years," *Journal of Gerontology*, 21(1)(1966).

[7]R. Havighurst, *Developmental Tasks and Education*, 3rd ed. (New York: McKay, 1972).

[8]J. Demos, *A Little Commonwealth: Family Life in Plymouth Colony* (London: Oxford Univeristy Press, 1970).

[9]E. Erikson, *Childhood and Society*, 2nd ed. (New York: W. W. Norton and Co., Inc., 1963).

[10]Ibid.

[11]A. Maslow, *Motivation and Personality*, 2nd ed. (New York: Harper and Row, 1970).

[12]R. Gould, "The Phases of Adult Life: A Study in Developmental Psychology," *American Journal of Psychiatry* (November 1972).

[13]Ibid.

[14]A. Clarke-Stewart, "Popular Primers for Parents," *American Psychologist*, 33(4)(1978).

[15]P. Swerdloff, *Men and Women* (New York: Time Inc., 1975).

[16]C. Tavris, "Woman and Man," *Psychology Today*, 5(10)(1972).

[17]J. Bernard, *The Future of Marriage* (New York: World Publishing, 1972).

[18]U. Bronfenbrenner, "The Roots of Alienation," *Influences on Human Development*, U. Bronfenbrenner, ed. (Hinsdale, Ill.: The Dryden Press, 1972).

[19]R. Bernstein and F. Cyr, "A Study of Interviews with Husbands in a Prenatal and Child Health Program," *Social Casework*, 38 (1957).

[20]H. Lopata, "The Secondary Feature of a Primary Relationship," *Human Organization*, 24 (1965).

[21]E. Duvall and R. Hill, *Being Married* (Boston: Heath, 1960).

[22]B. Adams, "Isolation, Function and Beyond: American Kinship in the 1960's," *Journal of Marriage and the Family*, 32 (November 1970).

[23]J. Udry, *The Social Context of Marriage*, 2nd ed. (Philadelphia: J. B. Lippincott Co., 1971).

[24]D. Cooper, *Death of the Family* (New York: Pantheon, 1970).

[25]U.S. Bureau of the Census, "Household and Family Characteristics: March 1975," *Current Population Reports*, P–20 (291) (Washington, D.C.: U.S. Government Printing Office, 1976).

[26]U. Bronfenbrenner, "The Roots of Alienation."

[27]D. Kieren, J. Henton, and R. Marotz, *Hers and His: A Problem-Solving Approach to Marriage* (Hinsdale, Ill.: The Dryden Press, 1975).

[28]U.S. Bureau of the Census, *1970 Census of the Population. Subject Reports: Marital Status* (Washington, D.C.: U.S. Government Printing Office, 1972).

[29]H. Carter and P. Glick, *Marriage and Divorce: A Social and Economic Study* (Cambridge, Mass.: Harvard University Press, 1970).

[30]T. Monahan, "When Married Couples Part: Statistical Trends and Relationships in the Divorced," *American Sociological Review*, 27 (1962).

[31]R. Ravich and B. Wyden, *Predictable Pairing* (New York: Peter H. Wyden, 1974).

[32]D. Kieren, J. Henton, and R. Marotz, *Hers and His: A Problem-Solving Approach to Marriage.*

[33]R. Gardner, *The Parents Book about Divorce* (New York: Doubleday, 1977).

[34]H. Carter and P. Glick, *Marriage and Divorce.*

[35]D. Levinson, "The Psychosocial Development of Men in Early Childhood and the Mid-Life Transition," *Life History Research in Psychopathology: III*, D. Ricks, A. Thomas, and M. Roff, eds. (Minneapolis: University of Minnesota Press, 1974).

[36]G. Vaillant and C. McArthur, "Natural History of Male Psychologic Health: I. The Adult Life Cycle from 18–50," *Seminars in Psychiatry*, 4(4)(1972).

[37]O. Tanner, *Stress* (New York: Time Inc., 1976).

[38]S. Terkel, *Working: People Talk About What They Do All Day and How They Feel About What They Do* (New York: Pantheon Books, 1974).

[39]R. Quinn, G. Staines, and M. McCullough, *Job Satisfaction: Is There a Trend?* U.S. Dept. of Labor, Manpower Research Monograph No. 30 (Washington: U.S. Government Printing Office, 1974).

[40]Ibid.

[41]E. Kay, "The World of Work—Its Promises, Conflicts and Reality," *Quality of Life: The Middle Years*, Congress of the American Medical Association (Acton, Mass.: Publishing Sciences Group, Inc., 1974).

[42]A. Toffler, *Future Shock* (New York: Random House, 1970).

[43]G. Sheehy, *Passages: Predictable Crises of Adult Life* (New York: E. P. Dutton & Co., Inc., 1976).

[44]L. Peter and R. Hull, *The Peter Principle* (New York: William Morrow & Co., Inc., 1969).

[45]R. Steinberg, *Man and the Organization* (New York: Time Inc., 1975).

[46]N. Seligman, "Working Mobility for Women," *Quality of Life: The Middle Years*, Congress of the American Medical Association (Acton, Mass.: Publishing Sciences Group, Inc., 1974).

[47]Ibid.

[48]N. Babchuck and A. Bates, "The Primary Relations of Middle-Class Couples: A Study in Male Dominance," *American Sociological Review*, 28 (1963).

[49]Ibid.

[50]H. Sullivan, *The Interpersonal Theory of Psychiatry* (New York: Norton, 1963).

[51]T. Harris, *I'm OK–You're OK* (New York: Harper and Row, 1967).

[52]A. Ellis and R. Harper, *A Guide to Rational Living* (Hollywood, Calif.: Wilshire Book Company, 1966).

[53]American Public Health Association, *Vital and Health Statistics Monographs: Mortality and Morbidity in the United States*, C. Erhardt and J. Berlin, eds. (Cambridge, Mass.: Harvard University Press, 1974).

[54]Ibid.

[55]S. Robbins, *Pathologic Basis of Disease* (Philadelphia: W. B. Saunders Co., 1974).

[56]Ibid.

[57]Ibid.

[58]Ibid.

[59]W. Silen, "Peptic Ulcer," *Harrison's Principles of Internal Medicine*, 7th ed. (New York: McGraw-Hill, 1974).

[60]S. Robbins, *Pathologic Basis of Disease.*

[61]Ibid.

[62]H. Aunet, *Physician Service Patterns and Illness Rates* (New York: Group Health Insurance, Inc., 1967).

[63]C. Anderson, *Community Health* (St. Louis: The C. V. Mosby Co., 1973).

Contents

Jeff Albertson/Stock, Boston

The Forties

Physical development

At some time between forty and forty-nine, most people confront the fact that they have left youth behind them. The physical signs of aging become more and more obvious. The forties are frequently years of many life changes (children leaving home; possible death of associates, relatives, or parents; career upsets). Social crises take their toll on a person's physical stamina. The reverse is also true. Declining physical stamina takes its toll on a person's social life. In general, the forty-plus-year-olds who seem the most youthful are those who have experienced the fewest of or been least affected by the stresses of everyday living and the insults to the body caused by disease or hard labor. Most people begin to feel some symptoms of aging during their forties (e.g., muscle or joint stiffness, decreased energy). Some welcome aging as a sign of maturity with its concomitant prestige and worldly wisdom. Others spend a good deal of time, effort, and money trying to hide the physical changes that indicate their age (e.g., grey hair, wrinkles).

Physical changes

There are vast individual differences between people in their forties in terms of physical changes. Some fortyish people are just marrying. Others are already grandparents. Some may have smooth skin and healthy, plentiful hair. Others may have wrinkled skin, grey hair, or bald spots. Some are in peak condition. Others have a number of health problems. In general, there is a gradual slowing down in the forties of all physiological functions and a decrease in the capacity of tissue regeneration.

Bone elongation ceased in the late teens. By the forties the bones have already lost some of their mass and density. As the cartilage between the vertebrae start to degenerate from normal wear, the vertebrae

Figure 9–1. *Persons in their forties vary greatly in appearances and behavior. Some look and act much younger, some much older. However, most confront the fact that their youth is behind them. They pause to consider their accomplishments and their aspirations, and many renew the directions of their lives.*

© Elizabeth Crews/Jeroboam, Inc.

become compressed and the spinal column gradually begins to shorten. As adults age, they actually lose some of their height due to this compression of the spinal column. With increasing age the cartilage in all joints has a more limited ability to regenerate itself. The bumps and jolts of everyday living and the pressures on the joints from carrying weight often lead to some degree of degenerative joint disease by the mid- to late forties.[1] By the forties muscle mass has declined in bulk and strength compared to what it was at its peak in late adolescence and the early twenties. Muscle strength of most men continues to be greater than most women's throughout the life span.

In addition to skeletal and muscular changes, there are age-related changes in the endocrine glands, the hormone-producing structures that control growth, metabolism, homeostatis, and reactions to stress. The secretion by the adrenal glands of cortisol, which is essential for life, appears least affected by age. The blood levels and amounts excreted allow older individuals adequate steroid secretion in response to stress. While the blood level of the thyroid hormone thyroxine (T_4) does not vary with age, the active form of the thyroid hormone triiodothyronine (T_3), which is formed by the tissues from T_4, does decline. Accompanying the decrease in T_3 is a decline in basal metabolic rate. The reactivity of target tissues to hormones also varies with age. For example, the receptors on cell surface membranes for noradrenalin and adrenalin decreases, possibly in relation to the decreased production of T_3. This loss of responsiveness to the adrenal hormones is manifest by a slower heartrate, less constriction of arteries, and a smaller cardiac output. The reactivity of target tissues to insulin also decreases. This results in a decreased effectiveness of insulin in reducing blood glucose after glucose is administered and, no doubt, is related to the increased prevalence of diabetes with age.

The respiratory system, heart, and circulatory system have parallel changes occurring with age. The lungs and bronchi become increasingly less elastic, causing a progressive decrease in maximum breathing capacity. It takes individuals longer to catch their breaths after exercise in their forties than when they were younger. The ability of the heart muscle to contract decreases, leading to a lower cardiac index (the cardiac output per minute per square meter of body surface). Arteries, too, become less elastic; blood pressure increases with every decade.

Weight increases are common in middle age due to a decreased energy expenditure without a concomitant decrease in caloric intake. The unneeded calories are stored as fat deposits, commonly in the wall of the abdomen ("spare tire") or the hips, thighs, and chest wall (the "middle-age spread"). The entire digestive system may slow its process of digesting, absorbing, and eliminating foods. Constipation becomes an increasingly common complaint with age.

The skin continues to lose its elasticity and produces less sebum in the forties. The wrinkles that probably first showed in the thirties become more pronounced. Meanwhile, new creases are added. Exposure to the sun and blustery winds aggravates the problem of thinning, dry, wrinkled skin. Hair begins to thin out, dry out, and may become grey.

The senses of hearing and vision may begin to show age changes in the forties. A hearing loss limited first to high pitches may cause persons to stand or sit closer to the source of sound than previously. They may strain to hear or may talk in compensatory louder tones. A visual problem primarily affecting near vision (presbyopia) may necessitate reading glasses or bifocals for close work. The lens of the eyes gradually becomes less elastic with age, causing the eyes to lose their ability to bring near-point visual images into clear focus. Presbyopics usually can read far-off signs long before younger passengers in a car but have difficulty reading the numerals on the odometer or the car radio without glasses.

While most of these changes begin to occur in the forties, it is important to keep in mind that these changes occur gradually. Many people in their forties are active and quite youthful, exhibiting few of these signs of aging.

Reproductive changes

The reproductive organs of both men and women begin to atrophy with advancing age, eventually rendering them sterile. While records indicate that some men into their ninth decade father children, and some women in their sixties bear children, the norm is for humans to cease bearing children in their thirties or forties.[2] The end of the female reproductive cycle is relatively clearly marked by the menopause. The male climacteric is gradual and less obviously concluded. Neither menopause nor the male climacteric need appreciably affect the sex drive. It may remain powerful throughout the life span.

Menopause. The term *menopause* comes from two Greek words meaning month and cessation and refers broadly to all of the physiological changes that occur when a woman experiences a discontinuation of her monthly menstrual function. As mentioned earlier, many hormone levels in the blood decline gradually with advancing age. At the menopause the levels of the pituitary gland hormones—luteinizing hormone (LH) and follicle-stimulating hormone (FSH)—are high. However, the ovary, which has been gradually shrinking since the late twenties, responds less to the pituitary hormones and produces less estrogen and progesterone of its own. There are fewer ova left to be released and fewer ripen. Menopause, then, is a consequence of ovarian "failure." As estrogen and progesterone production tapers off, the endometrial bleeding known as menstrual flow is triggered less often. For most women, therefore, menopause is experienced as an increased irregularity in time of menstrual flow. Some women simply experience a gradual slowing down of flow with no irregular timing. Others experience changes in both timing and amount of flow or else an abrupt stop to their menses.[3]

The average age at which American women experience

menopause is forty-seven years, with a range from age forty to age fifty-five.[4] In some cases women may cease menstruating as early as thirty-five or as late as sixty. An early menopause may occur as the result of an oophorectomy (removal of the ovaries), a hysterectomy (removal of the uterus), from prolonged nursing, poor health, from living in an extremely cold climate, or from excessive exposure to radiation. The age of onset of menopause also has a link to genetic inheritance.

The decreasing levels of estrogen cause some vasomotor and other physical changes in some, but not all, women. One of the more common vasomotor symptoms of menopause is the hot flush. The body becomes warm and flushed, usually from the breasts up. Perspiration is followed by chills. The flush may last from a few seconds through several minutes and may recur several times a day. Hot flushes are more common during the months of missed periods. Some women may also experience nausea and vomiting, constipation or diarrhea, gas, frequent or painful urination, low backache, an appetite change, headaches, dizziness, heart palpitations, numbness in the fingers or toes, breast tenderness, and insomnia during the menopause.[5] The vagina becomes less elastic, shorter, and has less acidic secretions with decreased estrogen. It may become ulcerated or infected in some cases. The hair of both scalp and genitalia thins out, and lip hair may appear.

Estrogen replacement therapy can alleviate or eliminate the symptoms of menopause in most women. Medical opinion differs as to the desirability of giving estrogen, however. Some doctors do not want to interfere with nature. Some give estrogen only for major problems with vasomotor changes. Others give estrogen replacement daily as soon as unpleasant menopausal symptoms begin. Some continue it for the woman's lifetime. Women continue to produce some estrogen from the adrenal glands or by conversion of adrenal androgen in the liver even after menopause. Replacement therapy supplements the naturally produced hormone, bringing it up to a level that provides relief from symptoms related to insufficient hormones. Estrogen retards many of the aging changes in women such as shrinking of vagina and breasts, development of facial hair, thinning and loss of skin tone, and increased porosity and brittleness of bones. Research pointing to a greater frequency of endometrial cancer among women taking estrogen is not conclusive. However, the threat of such an occurrence keeps many physicians from prescribing estrogen.

The psychological changes of menopause are often grossly exaggerated. The stereotypic menopausal woman is portrayed as depressed, tearful, unpredictable, forgetful, unattentive, frigid, and haggard. In fact, in a study by Neugarten, Wood, Kraines, and Loomis, about 75 percent of women felt that menopause did not change them in any important way.[6]

Only about 50 percent of them found the menopause unpleasant. The remaining 50 percent were not troubled by it. Young women were more concerned about it than women experiencing it, perhaps due to fear of the unknown.[7] Many women find an end to their menses a happy relief. Their sex life remains good or even improves after menopause. For other women menopause may suggest an end to their sex appeal and an end to their usefulness. It often coincides with children leaving home and marks an end to their major mothering and homemaking roles. The severe depression that a few women experience after menopause (involutional depression) will be discussed in the health section (see pp. 385–386).

Male climacteric. The term *climacteric* comes from the Greek term for a critical time. There is a great deal of confusion and debate about whether there really is a male climacteric and, if so, when it occurs. Social scientists feel quite sure that most men go through a transitional period in their forties.[8] They reexamine their lives and may make radical changes in the way they do things. The transition period may erupt in a crisis (i.e., leaving wife, leaving job, turning to drugs or alcohol) for some men. These emotional repercussions will be discussed in more detail in the social development section (see pp. 364–368). The question of whether these changes are brought about or influenced by the normal male reproductive changes that accompany aging is moot.

Androgen levels decline slowly with age. As the production of these hormones tapers off, men may experience a delayed erection time, a reduced ejaculatory volume, pressure, and demand, and a gradual loss of facial and body hair. Some men also experience a gradual rising of their voice pitch. These changes occur so slowly that they may go unnoticed or may only be detected in the seventh or eighth decades. A few men may have an abrupt onset of symptoms, suddenly becoming impotent. The latter occurrence is felt to be a reaction to aging triggered more by financial, social, familial, or marital problems than by hormones. Such impotence may last for a few weeks, a few years, or forever, depending on emotional health, physical health, and therapy.

The physical changes that occur due to decreasing androgen levels are accompanied by other normal physical changes of the forties (i.e., decreased muscle strength, wrinkles, greying hairs, possible digestive disturbances, or fat accumulation). Potentially traumatic psychological events may occur (i.e., seeing a son or daughter become sexually mature, having new financial burdens appear). The events of the forties (or fifties or sixties) for some men may cause depression, unpredictability, forgetfulness, loss of attention, irritability, headaches, insomnia, fatigue, loss of sex drive, appetite changes, flushes, or, in short, any of the symptoms associated with female menopause.[9] The male climacteric, when and if it occurs, may have physical and psychological causes compounding the hormonal effects just as the female menopause does.

Cognitive changes

The weight of the brain gradually decreases with age due to a loss in the number and size of brain cells and the loss of myelin sheathing. As people age, impulses travel slightly more slowly across neurons and axons, causing a decrease in reaction time. In spite of these degenerative changes throughout the nervous system, most human beings retain the full use of their intellectual abilities through their forties and, often, much later.

As mentioned in Chapter 8, fluid intelligence (skills with more innate bases such as inductive reasoning and figural relationships) may very gradually diminish during middle to late adulthood while crystallized intelligence (skills based on learning and experience such as verbal comprehension and handling word relationships) may increase. Birren demonstrated an improvement in the abilities of middle-aged persons to organize and process incoming information and to handle larger vocabularies.[10]

A report by Kangas and Bradway suggested that while men may show a slight increase in their IQ scores during the adult years, women may show a slight decline.[11] Many social scientists feel that this drop in women's IQ scores may be a result of the different life experiences of adult men and women. Men usually go out daily to pursue an income for their families and consequently make constant use of various mental abilities. In contrast, many women stay home and are primarily engaged in child care, housework, or socializing. Sontag, Baker, and Nelson found that adult women with declining IQ scores were stereotypically dependent on men and oriented toward social activities.[12] If intelligence develops through experience, however, women at home should be gaining increased insight into the nature of solving problems related to interpersonal interactions and household management, while men at jobs gain insight into solving problems related to their work. Many intelligence tests only give credit for certain skills that would be apt to increase in out-of-the-home jobs.

Horner suggested that social-emotional factors may contribute to women's declining IQ scores in adulthood.[13] As cited in Chapter 7, Horner found that college women taking achievement tests could do well, unless asked to compete with men, at which point they cease to do their best. Their need to achieve drops far below that of men. Women, in fact, may fear too much success. They often prefer the tasks of maintaining good relationships with their husbands, children, and others, and watching over the socioemotive aspects of living, because these are more socially approved tasks for women.

Biologists feel that hormonal changes or the variation in the

Figure 9–2. *Research has indicated the possibility of both intellectual increments and declines in the adult years. Many persons take on tasks requiring greater use of their intellectual functions in midlife, while others use their abilities less and less.*
Freda Leinwand

growth and development of the two cerebral hemispheres in the brains of men and women may account for the sex differences in adult intelligence. We mentioned in Chapter 7 that the dominant cerebral hemisphere develops later in males than in females. The earlier development of the speech center, located in the dominant hemisphere, gives girls a head start in many verbal skills. Girls are more apt to enjoy studies related to the use of verbal skills (human relationships, literature, composition, foreign languages), while boys often prefer subjects that call for skills involving the handling of numerical or spatial relationships (mechanics, science, math). Hormones that may cause cyclic changes in moods of women at varying times of the month may also affect women's achievement versus affiliation needs at varying times of the month, biologists say. Low levels of estrogen and progesterone, known to contribute to feelings of depression, anxiety, and irritability in some women, may interfere with their concentration and the use of their other mental abilities. This might be especially true as women experience lower levels of the hormones during menopause.

In concluding this discussion of intellectual changes in the forties, it is important to remember that research evidence only suggests that some women show slightly decreased IQ scores during this decade. A great deal more research is needed that uses other measures of women's abilities in addition to standardized IQ tests and that includes more working women in the same population. More research is also needed on the factors that may contribute to this possible sex difference in intellectual functioning.

Social development

Psychologist Robert Havighurst suggested that there are seven developmental tasks that most adults pursue during middle age:

> Achieving adult civic and social responsibility.
>
> Establishing and maintaining an economic standard of living.
>
> Assisting teenagers to become responsible adults.
>
> Developing leisure-time activities.
>
> Relating to one's spouse as a person.
>
> Accepting the physiological changes of middle age.
>
> Adjusting to aging parents.[14]

Both psychologist Daniel Levinson and psychiatrist Roger Gould in their respective adult development studies found that the early forties are characterized by unrest. Toward fifty, adults settle down and pay more attention to their families.[15,16]

In this chapter the family relationships of people in their forties will be examined first, followed by a look at their community relationships. These descriptions are generalizations and will not fit every individual in his or her forties equally.

Family relationships

Family social and emotional relationships are generally not easy for persons in their forties. Middle-aged adults go through a period of midlife transition, sometimes termed the midlife crisis. Both sexes face a turning point in their lives. They need to cope simultaneously with age changes, reproductive changes, their spouse's confusion, their own uncertainty, and children leaving home.

The midlife transition. Most students of the middle adult years agree that a transition occurs around the forties, give or take a few years depending on the individual. At some point the adult realizes that she or he is no longer young. This realization sets in motion a process of exploring the past, the present, and the future, and making an attempt to fuse them together in some logical way. The transition is often called the midlife crisis, suggesting the pain, the stress, the crucial decisions, and the changes that accompany the transition. It is not easy to dispose of dreams that will never come to pass or to face the reality of what is now and what may be left of one's life.

Men and women share the problems of a midlife transition. However, the bulk of research on the stresses that occur emphasize the male's confusion. A woman's midlife transition is often explained away as menopause, and any confusion she feels about the direction of her life is attributed to her reproductive change of life. Some attempt has been made to call the male transition the male climacteric, as discussed before. However, the male midlife crisis usually occurs well before the female menopause. It also has obvious roots in social and emotional factors that suggest its consideration as a developmental stage quite apart from a hormonal-based change of life.

Freud's student, Jung, was one of the earlier psychiatrists to

Figure 9–3. *Jungian theory proposes that it is not until the forties that men and women come to terms with the outer world and begin to experience inner growth. This maturing brings a unification of ideas and greater self-realization, which Jung referred to as "individuation."*
Leslie Davis

describe a midlife transition. He believed that it is a crucial period of development. Here decisions for a lifetime must be made to assure a well-adjusted psyche. Jungian theory proposes that maturity does not evolve until the forties, after the trials of a number of life experiences. Before this, adults work at divesting themselves of their childish ways. They face outer reality and come to terms with it. Then, after their forties (transition), they begin to discover their inner selves. They try to unify their former fantasies, hopes, and dreams with the actuality of their lives. Jung describes the period of life after the transition as the period of individuation. It is only during these years, in his opinion, that adults finally move towards self-realization.[17]

Erik Erikson wrote that the nuclear conflict of trying to achieve generativity (bringing up the next generation—fathering or mothering children or younger adults) versus the opposite extreme, stagnation (lacking growth or personal contribution) is still the dominant life theme of most people in their forties. While Erikson does not spell out the details of a midlife transition, he implies that such a change occurs before and during the final nuclear conflict of life, "integrity versus despair." In this last stage the adult goes through a thorough soul-searching of "one's one and only life cycle."[18] (See further exposition of this stage on pp. 410–412.)

Bernice Neugarten, in her many studies of middle-aged adults, found that the transition may begin with a painful awareness of being viewed as old by youth. For example, in her investigations one respondent said, "When I see a pretty girl on the stage or in the movies . . . and when I realize, 'My God, she's about the age of my son,' it's a real shock. It makes me realize that I'm middle-aged."[19] Another said, "Mentally I still feel young, but suddenly one day my son beat me at tennis. . . ."[20] Neugarten found that the midlife transition is clocked more by life contexts—body, career, family—than by chronological age. For example, the family cycle runs its course differently in various social classes. In one study Neugarten calculated that the wife of an average unskilled worker finishes school by fifteen, marries by eighteen, and has her last child by twenty-three. An average professional worker's wife finishes school by twenty, marries by twenty-three, and has her last child by thirty.[21] For unskilled workers middle age has arrived by forty and old age by sixty. For the professional worker the age of forty is considered prime time. Middle age arrives about fifty and old age not until seventy.[22]

Daniel Levinson's studies of adult men have led him to describe the early forties as "A Time of Assessment." This follows the stages of "Getting Into the Adult World" in the twenties, "Settling Down" in the early thirties, and "Becoming One's Own Man" in the late thirties.[23] The fortyish men Levinson studied were trying to appraise their past life experiences for the purpose of redirecting their future. They often asked, "Does life begin or end at midlife?" Levinson found men in this transition anxious and fearful. They became irritated with others whom they perceived as trying to lead them, or push them, or hold them back. Their assessment was personal—something they had to do alone. Many suffered from depression during their transitions. Some tried to bury their troubles in various ways: overeating, alcohol, psychosomatic disease. Some made radical changes in their lifestyles: leaving a job, leaving the family, having extramarital affairs. In fact, Levinson suggested that most transitional men tend to have fantasies about young, erotic girls and also about older nurturing women. He believed that this may still be related to an attempt to cut free from mother. No matter how the assessment process is manifest in a man's life, Levinson stated that it is normal. From his viewpoint, a man cannot go through this stage of life unchanged. Life will have a different meaning to him, and he will be on a new personality level.[24]

In Roger Gould's studies of adult patients (both sexes), the same inevitable transitional rumblings were heard in the early forties (age range thirty-five to forty-three): "Have I done the right thing?" "Is there time to change?"[25] The adults seemed to experience a feeling of desperation as they became aware of the squeeze of time. They turned on their parents for creating some of their problems. They found fault with their teenage children for causing some of their problems. They blamed their spouses for a lack of sympathy and affection. Gould found a new motif emerging in the late forties (age range forty-three to fifty). The "die is cast" feeling was present and was seen as a relief from the internal tearing apart of the immediately preceding years, even though it was a bitter pill to swallow.[26]

Neugarten found that the restless, discontented feelings accompanying the midlife transition could become a powerful incentive to accomplish further deeds in one's lifetime. One respondent told her, "I know what will work in most situations, and what will not. I am well beyond the trial-and-error stage of youth. I now have a set of guidelines. . . . And I am practised. . . ." Another said, "When I think back over the errors I made when I was twenty-eight or thirty or thirty-five I am amazed at the young men today who think they can take over their companies at twenty-eight. They can't possibly have the maturity required. . . . True maturity doesn't come until around forty-five."[27]

The stress of the midlife transition leads some individuals to real crises or decisions to make changes in their lives before it is too late. Some midlife alterations are well known, such as Gauguin's moving to the South Seas Islands to paint, or England's Edward VIII giving up his throne to marry a commoner. Executives may give up positions of power to start their own small corporations; priests and nuns may leave their orders to marry; and the affluent may leave their riches and become involved in work for charitable causes. Change is not an uncommon phenomenon in the forties.

Woodruff and Birren found that behavior in midlife is often closely aligned to behavior in the earlier years. They followed a group of adults longitudinally for twenty-five years and found that people who were more neurotic in midlife tended to be neurotic in college also. Those who were well adjusted in college had better mental health in midlife.[28] Kelly also studied a group of adults longitudinally and found that very little change occurred in basic personalities over the years other than a diminished energy level and a narrowing of interests.[29] The cross-sectional studies that reveal the phases of the adult life span should always be considered with an appreciation of the uniqueness and mental health of every individual approaching or going through the phase.

Spouse relationships. Two decades ago sex researcher Alfred Kinsey reported that infidelity reaches a peak in the early forties.[30] Contemporary researchers still find marital relationships are troublesome in the forties. Levinson stated that, while less than one-third of the fortyish men he studied were actually involved in affairs, most of them had fantasies of affairs and wondered about their commitments to their wives.[31] Rollins and Feldman reported that the years when children begin to leave home (usually the decade of the forties) are the years in which most married couples are least satisfied with each other.[32]

Consider the factors that may contribute to rough going in marriage between a person's fortieth and fiftieth year: signs of loss of youth, reproductive changes, the midlife psychological transition, coping with spouse's uncertainties, and coping with teenagers' identity confusions. Bernard suggested that such increased marital stress leads to a decreased self-esteem that in turn leads to more marital stress.[33] There is a sharp rise in divorce during this period of family life.[34]

Husbands in their midlife confusion often use their wives as scapegoats for their lack of satisfaction with personal accomplishments. A husband might, for example, blame his wife for a vocational rut: "She held me back." "She pushed me too much." "She didn't keep pace with me intellectually." "She refused to be cooperative or gracious to my associates." He may somehow feel it is his wife's fault that he is losing his youthful appearance: "She feeds me all the wrong foods." "She interferes with my exercise program." "She causes my grey hairs." Or he might blame his wife for his children's shortcomings: "She was too permissive." "She was too busy with her own concerns to be a good mother." "She did not teach them to value money or property." Or a husband might criticize his wife for spending too much time with the children and not enough time with him. He may suspect her of having affairs. There are many ways in which husbands blame their wives for their own problems.

Meanwhile, wives, confused about their own life goals and accomplishments, may find their husbands at fault for their shortcomings, too: "He ignored me for his job." "He held me back, and wouldn't let me develop my potentials." "He never gave me enough money." "He never helped me with the children or the house." They may suspect their husbands of having affairs. They may feel that their husbands are totally unsympathetic to their problems of household organization, childrearing, loneliness, or menopausal symptoms. This is an especially rough period for women who have defined their role predominantly in terms of mothering. As children prepare to leave the home, some of these women are left facing a gap in their lives, a feeling of uselessness.

For those who survive the stresses of marriage during the midlife transition—and many do—marital satisfaction frequently climbs to a new high. Once the children are gone, husbands and wives may redefine their relationship in terms of lovers and/or companions rather than as parents. They may have fewer financial responsibilities, more free time, more geographic mobility, and more ability to plan activities without direction from the children. Deutscher found that a typical female comment about marriage after the departure of the children was, "I don't have as many meals to prepare anymore, and my health is better now."[35] A typical male comment was, "It took a load off me . . . I didn't have to support 'em anymore."[36]

Communicating with teenagers. In attempts to get their own way, adolescents frequently criticize their parents with comments like, "You are so old-fashioned," or "You're really out of it." The teenager may soon forget his or her grievances, while the parent(s) continue to feel confused and perplexed about how to govern their offspring.

Duvall compares parenting of teenagers with the exercise of walking a tightrope.[37] Parents must give directions, advice, or assistance on such things as planning for the future (job, college, marriage), dating and sexuality, drug or alcohol use, independence strivings, and school problems. They may remember things from their own adolescence that they promised they would never inflict on their own children. Yet, due to the changing times, such promises now seem difficult to fulfill. The lifestyle of today's fortyish parents twenty years ago was quite different. Life was simpler, slower, and more predictable. The mass media were less pervasive. Fewer families had television, such as it was—small-screened, black and white, often obstructed with static and "snow." Public transportation was slower and less readily available. Cultural norms, mores and folkways, standards of conduct, etiquette, and moral codes—all were more clear-cut and widely accepted. Norms today are in a state of flux and are often ambiguous. Parents can see or hear a full range of values and disciplinary techniques exhibited by their associates, the media, their religious leaders, and their friends.

Parents often see their teenage children as marks of their own success. They may have nurtured dreams about their offspring's futures such as "my son, the doctor," or "my daughter, Miss America," for many years. It is not easy for them to realize that their hopes and dreams may not come to fruition. If they must settle for less, or something else, they try to assure themselves that the something else will still reflect well on them. Many parents cannot help seeing their children as end products of their own parenting and reflections of their own adult worth. The pressures that such attitudes place on both parents and children are sometimes unbearable. Bart found that depression in middle-aged women was frequently related to their overinvolvement and overidentification with their children.[38] They are bewildered by their sons' and daughters' behavior: refusing to obey, refusing to study, exhibiting temper tantrums, running away, having scuffles with the law, using drugs.

Some parents in our society have a different problem with their teenage children: they see them as standing in the way of their own success. Family for them is simply an aggregate of persons living under the same roof. Parents may not want to be bothered with the social, emotional, or financial problems of their offspring when they are struggling so hard to make sense of their own lives. Mothers and fathers may resent their children receiving the complimentary glances that were once thrown their way. They may feel angered and threatened by teenage idealism that criticizes their own lifestyle. They also may intensely dislike having their authority questioned.

Parents who are overinvolved, parents with a degree of both overidentification and resentment, and parents who reject their demanding teenage children all find it difficult to assist children when they are in trouble. Communicating with teenagers is best achieved by parents who have kept an interchange of thoughts and opinions alive since early childhood. Adolescents (as discussed in Chapter 6) need freedom to exercise their own judgment within limits. They also need dependable persons to turn to as sounding boards when they fail. Whatever the difficulties of parenting teenage children and assisting them to assume their own independent lifestyles, it is sometimes comforting to realize that, in time, most children do appreciate the problems the parents had in raising them.

Assisting aging parents. One of Neugarten's findings about the reassessment process of midlife was that some adults in transition come to sympathize with their own parents and other aging people in a new way.

One person interviewed told her, "My parents, even though they are much older, can understand what we are going through; just as I now understand what they went through. . . ."[39] This change in the way some fortyish persons view their parents may lead to more confiding in them and more advice seeking from them. The middle-aged adults can appreciate that the older people understand their problems.

At the same time that the fortyish adults may acquire a new sympathy for their parents, their parents may turn to them for aid—financial, emotional, physical, or the like. This may present new problems for the midlife generation. It is difficult to criticize one's own parents, realizing that time is running out for them. Yet Gould found that, on occasion, the adults he studied were quite vocal in their criticism of their parents. They blamed the older generation for many of their own life problems.[40] Levinson found that having to assist one's own aging parents caused a great deal of emotional turmoil. The men he studied had to let go of their dependency on their own parents at this point. They had to redefine their relationships with their parents in terms of changed roles. The father, for example, could no longer be viewed as the man whom the interviewee had known as a child.[41]

Figure 9–4. *Individuals in their fourth decade often find themselves giving advice and assistance to growing children and aging parents as well as seeking advice from the latter.*
Leslie Davis

A call to assist one's aging parents is a test of maturity that may arrive for some adults very early in life, for others very late in life, and for others not at all. How a person responds to the request for assistance depends not only on the person's maturity and moral values but also on the extent of the request, the previous relationship with one's parents, other responsibilities, and resources for the aging parents.

Community relationships

As suggested in the discussion of the midlife transition (see p. 364), people in their forties define themselves not only in terms of their family successes or failures, but also in terms of their position in the community. Common yardsticks against which individuals measure themselves are associates at work, neighbors, brothers, sisters, same-aged cousins, former schoolmates, and friends. While "keeping up with the Joneses" is a common theme of one's community relations in midlife, it is not the only concern. Many adults are kept so busy with projects for the good of their community or society that they have no time to worry about their status vis-à-vis others.

Civic responsibilties. Between the ages of twenty and forty, young adults generally tend to focus on career and family development. Their civic responsibilities may include obeying laws, paying taxes, being courteous to others, voting, supporting causes that directly affect their lives, and joining some civic-minded groups. In the decade of their forties, many adults become increasingly conscious of what contributions they can make to their community. Their career development may look limited. Their family responsibilities are slackening. Rather than stagnate in their quest for usefulness and achievement, they look for ways to make contributions to their society.

In spite of our culture's emphasis on youth, we tend to confer positions of leadership to persons of both advanced age and experience. By the time individuals reach their forties, they may receive credit for their past accomplishments by election or appointment to status or authority positions. Many people in their forties are elected or appointed to such responsibilities as school board member, church board member, officer of an organization, member of a board of directors of a professional or service organization, or political leadership. Many others accrue notable records of accomplishments in community activities of their choice without any desire for external recognition.

Neugarten and Moore found that persons in middle age become more strongly identified with their political party.[42] They are also more apt to run for and get elected to political office. In general, the more responsibility the office carries, the older the person is who gets elected to

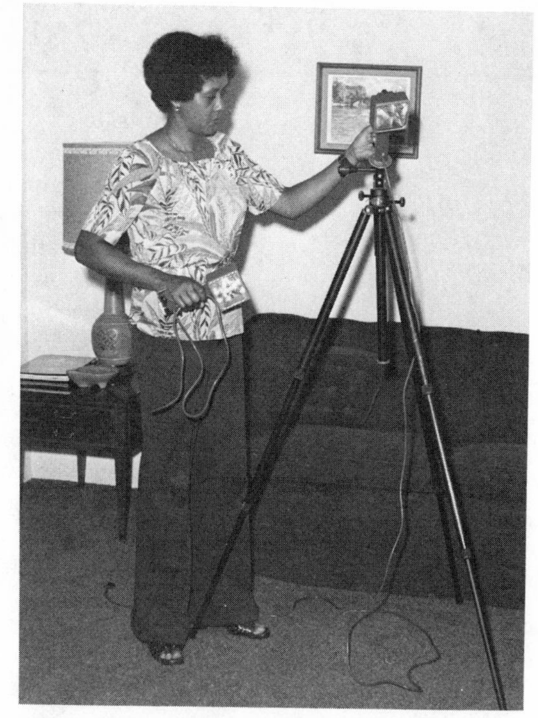

Figure 9–5. As adults become more efficient at home- and job-related duties, they often seek new challenges or opportunities for service. Many assume civic responsibilities or become involved in politics, education, the arts, religion, or other organizations that affect their lives.
Leslie Davis

fill it. At the state levels, Neugarten and Moore found that representatives were younger than senators who in turn were younger than governors.[43]

Women's roles in the community have changed a great deal in the past few years. While boards of directors and party politics were once men's domain, women are now sitting in responsible chairs sharing in decision-making processes. In the 1950s women generally sought volunteer roles in the community after their children were grown.[44] Now they seek careers, elected offices, or paid part-time positions.

The decline of volunteerism among women may in part be due to the societal feeling that only paid work is valuable work. Women, like men, want to feel that their efforts are valuable. Much volunteer work is busy work—address typing, envelope stuffing, or similarly routine, monotonous tasks. When a task is not fulfilling in terms of meeting the needs to feel wanted, needed, goal-oriented, intellectually stimulated, or financially rewarded, a person is not as inclined to persist with the task. Many government and social agencies that once depended heavily on volunteers now have hired employees to do the work to avoid the confusion, tensions, mix-ups, carelessness, and absenteeism that were hallmarks of the volunteers.[45] The volunteer work that survives is the work that allows the performer to meet his or her needs for affiliation and usefulness in well-appreciated, serious jobs.

Close to one-half of all American women now hold paid positions outside of their homes. When asked why they work, about 85 percent of American women cite reasons of necessity such as to help support the family, to help with household expenses, or to help pay for the children's college educations.[46] They also offer reasons touching on their needs for affiliation and achievement. They want to escape the drudgery of housework, escape the loneliness and boredom of the home, meet people, be intellectually stimulated, and feel independent. The kinds of employment available to women are frequently lower status, lower salaried jobs: sales clerks, office workers, maids, teacher aides, nurses aides. Working women often find it difficult to get the job benefits offered men, or raises, or promotions, or tenure, or credit, or bank loans, or many of the other fringe benefits of having a career. Swerdloff reported that, on the average, a working woman in the mid-1970s earns only about 60 percent of the salary paid to a comparable working man.[47] Some women protest the inequalities. Many do not. The reason that so many women remain in

Figure 9–6. *Many women in their forties return to full-time careers after their children enter school. Females now comprise about one-third of the American work force. They work outside the home for a variety of personal, social, and economic reasons. Gradually they are moving toward equitable pay and just respect for their labors.*

Mahon/Monkmeyer Press Photo Service

lower status, lower salaried jobs may lie in the fact that they need the money and realize they will not find better paying work.

Some American women relate to their community through service and social organizations as well as, or instead of, volunteer work or paid employment. Women's groups allied to a religous body, a political cause, their husbands' profession, or to their husbands' social organizations can be found in every community. Most of these groups exist to complete projects of service to some segment of society as well as for social reasons.

Social activities. Gould found that an interest in an active social life climbs in adults between the ages of forty and fifty.[48] Both men and women show a greater interest in church and church-related activities. They join more clubs and participate in more family gatherings. They also tend to socialize more in career-related functions. This may be due to a desire to hang on to or improve a job, to bid for a promotion, or simply because they now have more free time, more money, and more status to enable them to mingle socially with their business associates.

Many of the social, leisure-time pursuits of people in their forties show a decrease in energy expenditure over their activities of earlier years. They prefer less rigorous sports—golfing, bowling, hunting, fishing. They play more cards or tabletop games. While some people seek new concerns and hobbies to get them "out of a rut," their interests and attitudes usually reflect their preferred undertakings in the past.

Health considerations

The prevalence of both chronic disease and fatal illness increases with advancing age. The decade of the forties may be a period of excellent health or a time of increased disability due to illness. The state of one's health is strongly related to one's genetic predispositon to diseases, to lifestyle (especially stress factors, smoking history, diet and exercise), to the body's immune responses, and to the availability and utilization of medical, surgical, and pharmacological therapeutic aides in the event of disease. As has been the case in other chapters, not all the diseases that strike individuals in their forties will be covered. Rather, some of the more common problems of people in this decade of life that have not been discussed previously will be highlighted.

The five leading causes of death between the years of forty-five and sixty-four are diseases of the heart, cancers, diseases of blood vessels other than of the heart, accidents, and cirrhosis, a liver disease related to alcohol.[49] Heart diseases account for about 38 percent of all deaths. Cancers cause about 20 percent of middle-age mortality.[50] Heart disease, some cancers, and mental illness will be discussed in this chapter. Accidents and cirrhosis were discussed in Chapter 7 (see pp. 303–305).

As people get older, they are much more prone to chronic disease conditions that limit their activities to varying degrees. The national health statistics for the middle years indicate that men are more apt to have their activity curtailed by disorders involving their bones or joints and by digestive conditions. Women are generally disabled by disorders of their joints, high blood pressure, and digestive disturbances.[51] Digestive disturbances and disorders of the joints were discussed in Chapter 8 (see pp. 342–346). High blood pressure (hypertension) will be discussed in this chapter. Mental illness, unlike heart diseases and cancer, is not a major cause of death. However, it is one of our most serious national health problems. Approximately 5 to 10 percent of our population, and the population of every country in the world, has experienced serious mental illness, despite the gratifying progress made in the treatment of such disorders.[52]

Vascular diseases

The blood vessels of the body include the arteries, arterioles, veins, venules, and capillaries. These vessels become less elastic, more fibrous, and more beset by pathology with advancing age. Vascular diseases refer to disorders of these blood vessels.

The most frequent vascular disorder is arteriosclerosis, a thickening and hardening of the walls of the arteries.[53] Atherosclerosis, which is one form of arteriosclerosis, involves mainly the intima (the innermost lining) of the arteries. Arteriosclerosis involves the media (muscle portion) of the arteries as well. With aging there is a progressive increase in the thickening of the media and intima of arteries. Subsequently, there is a progressive rigidity (loss of elasticity) of these vessels. Other changes of arteries include dilation (widening), elongation, tortuosity (winding course instead of a straight course), calcification of the media, and aneurysm formation (ballooning out of vessels).[54]

Although the exact mechanism of formation of arteriosclerosis is unknown, studies suggest that obesity, physical inactivity, diabetes mellitus, hyperlipidemia, hypertension, and cigarette smoking are associated with a premature or accelerated course of the disease. The lesions seen are patchy areas of fatty substances (cholesterol and other lipid materials) or slightly raised areas of intimal hardening called fibrous plaques or atheromas. The aorta and the large arteries of the neck show fatty streaks in infancy. These reach a peak between twenty and thirty years. The coronary arteries and arteries of the brain begin to contain fatty streaks during puberty. While a few fibrous plaques may be asymptomatic and produce no disease, the presence of too many of them may impede blood flow through the arteries and eventually cause symptomatic arteriosclerosis (i.e., diseases such as heart attacks and strokes).

Varicose veins are dilated, tortuous, superficial veins found most commonly on the calves and thighs. They affect from 10 to 20 percent of Americans.[55] Overweight individuals, women who have been pregnant, and people with a family history of varicosities are most often affected. Normal veins have one-way valves that prevent a backward flow of blood. This is especially important in humans, who are upright animals and consequently have high venous pressure in their legs. When these valves become incompetent and allow a backflow of blood, varicosities result. In mild cases they may produce little problem aside from cosmetic discoloration. However, they may also cause pain, a feeling of heaviness, fatigue, and swelling of the legs. Sometimes they require surgical removal. People with varicosities often wear support stockings to support the vessels and prevent swelling.

Other vascular diseases of the veins are thrombophlebitis and phlebothrombosis. In the former, veins become inflamed and become the site of blood clots. In the latter, there is an absence of inflammation associated with the presence of a clot (thrombus). Venous thrombosis (blood clot in the vein) has been associated with such things as varicose veins, injury to the legs, use of birth control pills, prolonged bed rest as after surgery or in the postpartum period, congestive heart failure, and certain malignancies. The features of thrombophlebitis include pain, tenderness, redness, and swelling of part of the leg. However, there may be no symptoms with phlebothrombosis, and a person may first know that a venous thrombosis is occurring when a clot dislodges and travels to the lung, producing symptoms of pulmonary embolism (obstruction of lung vessel by a clot). Venous thrombosis may also lead to destruction of venous valves, resulting in more varicose veins. Walking or leg muscle exercises are strongly recommended for pregnant women, obese persons, people with sedentary lifestyles, and postoperative and cardiac patients in an attempt to prevent venous thrombosis and its possible embolic consequences.

Heart disease

Heart disease among middle-aged Americans is of epidemic proportions. Mortality related to the heart is increasingly affecting younger adults, especially men. Many of the problems stem from lifestyle. Stamler identified the factors that predispose a person to heart disease and separated them into factors relating to their degree of control.[56] Those factors that a person can control are a diet high in calories, refined sugars, saturated fats, and cholesterol; cigarette smoking; and sedentary living habits. Factors that a person can control with the help of modern medicine are hypertension, hypercholesterolemia (too much cholesterol in the blood), hyperlipidemia, hyperglycemia, hyperuricemia, hypothyroidism, and detected and diagnosed irregular heart rhythms. Factors that a person cannot control are sex and age. Ischemic (referring to a diminished blood flow) heart disease is the most prevalent form of heart disease.[57]

Ischemic heart disease. Ischemic heart disease is the newer term for coronary artery disease. It is almost invariably due to advanced atherosclerosis, which affects the blood vessels of the heart.[58] There are several patterns of ischemic heart disease (IHD): (1) myocardial infarction (MI, heart attack), (2) congestive heart failure, (3) sudden death from an abnormal rhythm generated within an ischemic area, (4) chronic abnormal rhythm of the heart, (5) angina pectoris, and (6) totally asymptomatic atherosclerosis of the coronary arteries.

A myocardial infarction (MI, heart attack) results from a sudden arrest or insufficiency of blood flow to a part of the heart because of a sudden obstruction or narrowing of the coronary artery supplying it. When it occurs, myocardial (heart muscle) cells become damaged, leading to their death (necrosis). The most common complaint of an MI is severe, crushing chest pain. There is some radiation of pain into the upper arms, jaw, and neck. There may also be shortness of breath, sweating, weakness, and fainting. A few MIs may be painless. If the area of necrosis is extensive enough, the heart muscle may not be able to pump vigorously enough to maintain blood pressure. If the blood pressure becomes so low that organs of the body cannot have their demands met for oxygen, nutrients, and waste removal, a state of shock results. Victims of MIs should be kept warm, quiet, and horizontal and should be taken to a medical facility as rapidly as possible.

The inability of the heart to pump effectively can lead to a back-up of blood into various organs, a condition known as congestive heart failure. Congestive heart failure can occur even unrelated to the sudden necrosis associated with an MI. The more gradual loss of muscle effectiveness is most commonly due to multiple small areas of necrosis. The features of congestive heart failure are presence of edema, shortness of breath, fatigue with exertion, an enlarged heart, a rapid and sometimes irregular pulse, and signs of congestion in various organs due to a back-up of blood.

Angina pectoris is a condition characterized by a feeling of heaviness or pressure in the chest that falls short of an MI. Angina pectoris is almost always associated with severe atherosclerosis of the coronary arteries and results from transient relative inadequacy of blood to a portion of the heart, but it is not severe enough to cause necrosis of the myocardium. The pain and pressure of the recurrent spasms can be controlled by medication that angina sufferers usually carry at all times.

The various patterns of ischemic heart disease are not mutually exclusive. Congestive heart failure and/or angina pectoris and/or abnormal heart rhythms may precede MIs. Persons who recover from MIs may still have congestive heart failure, abnormal rhythms, attacks of angina, or subsequent MIs.

Sudden death, which is mainly a result of ischemic heart disease, affects more than 400,000 Americans yearly.[59] Though most of the deaths are unexpected, about one-half of the victims have previously known heart disease, and an additional one-fourth have known hypertension and/or diabetes.

Hypertension. High blood pressure, also known as hypertension or hypertensive vascular disease, has many definitions. There is no one set line between normal and abnormal blood pressure. Rather, abnormal is the point at which any individual shows evidence of deleterious effects of his or her own high blood pressure. The values 160/95 are often used as the upper limits of normal for resting adults. Using these values, from 15 to 20 percent of the adult population of the United States has abnormal or high blood pressure. The upper value (systolic) refers to the peak pressure and the lower value (diastolic) refers to the bottommost pressure in the arteries during each cycle of heart contraction and ejection of blood and of the blood's distribution.

In general, high blood pressure appears to be caused by an excess of normal substances that either cause retention of salt by the body or cause the arteries and arterioles to contract. If hypertension is caused by recognized factors such as renal disease, adrenal disease, or use of oral contraceptives, it is called secondary hypertension. If its cause cannot be determined, it is called primary or essential hypertension. As the years pass, the causes of hypertension are being increasingly recognized. The complex role of the central nervous system in the maintenance and regulation of blood pressure needs to be better understood. It is widely accepted that as much as 50 to 60 percent of hypertension is neurogenic, that is, due to a disorder in blood pressure regulation by the central nervous system and in the "tuning" by the autonomic nervous system.[60]

The consequences of high blood pressure are higher incidences of symptomatic ischemic heart disease, stroke, renal failure, and thoracic aorta aneurysm. Prognosis for untreated hypertension has been shown to be worse for men than for women and for blacks than for whites.[61]

Accelerated hypertension (also called malignant hypertension) is not a separate disease but is a phase in the course of severe, untreated hypertension. It is manifested by any or all of the following: (1) rapidly worsening kidney failure, (2) heart failure, (3) retinal hemorrhages, and (4) dysfunction of thought processes and decreased level of consciousness. Failure to treat hypertension when it is at this stage will result in death.

The availability of a large number of antihypertensive medications facilitates the treatment of high blood pressure. If the underlying cause of hypertension can be determined, its removal is preferred (e.g., surgically in the case of certain adrenal tumors or discontinuing the use of oral contraceptives). However, more than 90 percent of hypertensives will require drug treatment and such measures as weight loss and reduced salt in the diet.

Cancers

Cancers are growths of abnormal cells that behave differently from the normal cells of the body part in which they develop. Cancers are one form of tumor (masses of abnormal tissue). It should be noted that some tumors are benign (have a limited growth, do not spread, and are not generally life-threatening). Only those tumors that are malignant are called cancers. If a malignant tumor can be removed completely and no new growth appears within several years, a person is often considered cured of that cancer.

Most malignant tumors have a more rapid rate of growth than the normal tissue from which they are derived. They may invade surrounding tissues or the blood vessels and lymphatics and may spread via those vessels to distant parts of the body. The spread of malignant tumors from one part of the body to another is called metastasis. Cures are more unlikely when metastases have occurred, although in certain forms of cancer such cures may still occur.

The pathways through which cancers develop are still unknown. However, there are many recognized carcinogenic agents (cancer-producing substances), the avoidance of which can reduce one's chances of developing certain types of cancer. For example, lung cancer is more apt to occur if a person frequently inhales the smoke of cigarettes. Skin cancers are more apt to occur if a person comes in contact with a class of organic chemicals called polycyclic aromatic hydrocarbons or has frequent exposure to ultraviolet rays from the sun. Many scientists feel that cancer is not a single entity, but rather a multitude of different disorders that have in common the development of abnormal cells. Some families seem to have a genetic predisposition toward growth of various cancers. Cancers that develop in one body organ are not necessarily like cancers that develop elsewhere in terms of growth rate and behavior.

The search for a viral cause of cancer is one of the leading areas of cancer research. It is also one where hopes of isolating a specific virus have been repeatedly shattered. The proof of viral causation of cancer is still limited to animal research. The only documented viral-induced growth in man is the common skin wart.[62]

Some scientists feel that cancer may have two stages of development. In the initiation stages some carcinogen (be it a virus, chemical, or source of radiation) causes a group of normal cells to undergo abnormal changes. In the second stage, the promotion stage, something triggers replication of the abnormal cells rather than their death. It is felt that people have an immune response of sorts to the various carcinogenic agents with which they come in contact. This response of the immune system may prevent abnormal changes from occurring in one's cells, or, in persons who do not develop cancer, it may inhibit the proliferation of abnormally developed cells. A further possibility is that immune persons may go through the promotion stage so slowly that the abnormal cells formed in the initiation stage develop into benign tumors rather than malignant ones. It may be that there are many factors in our environment that serve to enhance malignant cell proliferation (e.g., stresses, hormones, tissue irritations, tissue wounds, infections) just as there are many agents in our environment that serve to initiate malignant cell development (e.g., carcinogens). A clearer understanding of the mechanisms behind the development and spread of malignant cells would allow for more prevention of cancers and for speedier, more effective treatment.

The American Cancer Society has produced a list of seven warning signals to alert persons to possible cancer: (1) any sore or lesion that does not heal within two weeks, (2) a lump or mass in the breast or anywhere else in the body, (3) any unusual bleeding or discharge, (4) any change in the size, color, or appearance of a wart or a mole, (5) persistent indigestion or difficulty in swallowing, (6) persistent hoarseness or cough that does not clear up within two weeks, (7) any change in normal bowel habits.

The most common sites of cancer in women are the breast, uterus, and large intestine. Men most frequently have malignancies of the lungs, gastrointestinal tract, and prostate gland.[63] Breast, uterine, and skin cancers will be discussed in this chapter. A discussion of the other cancers will be postponed until Chapter 10.

Breast and uterine cancers. Breast cancer and uterine cancer occur more frequently in the middle-aged population. Breast cancer accounts for about 26 percent of all cancers in women, followed by uterine cancer, which accounts for about 14 percent of female malignancies.[64]

Cancer of the cervix (opening portion of the uterus) has shown a marked decline in occurrence in the last twenty years. The reason for this decline has been attributed mostly to the microscopic examination of the cells of the surface of the cervix by Pap smears. This examination detects abnormalities that, when not treated, can lead to cancerous growths. Pap smears allow for the possibility of detecting and treating lesions of the cervix in the precancerous stages and thus prevent progression to cancer. Pap smears also allow early cancerous lesions to be treated in the preinvasive stage, at which time the cure rate is still almost 100 percent. If the patient had to depend on symptoms to warn of the presence of cervical cancer, the disease would already have progressed too far to be curable. All adult women should have regular pelvic examinations, including a Pap smear.

Cervical cancer is more common in women who have chronic vaginal infections, whose sex partners are uncircumcised, who have borne many children, who have early, frequent, or numerous sexual partners, and who have genital area herpes (a viral infection).

Breast cancer frequently metastasizes to the nearby lymph nodes. Metastasis may already be present by the time a woman first feels a breast tumor. Women are encouraged to examine their own breasts for lumps at regular monthly intervals. Doctors may examine suspicious nodules further by means of mamography and xeroradiography (breast x-ray) or biopsy (removing a suspicious piece of tissue for microscopic examination). The earlier a breast tumor is removed after detection, the better the woman's chance of being cured. However, the longer the tumor remains in the breast, the greater the chance of metastasis and the lower the cure rate. Breast cancer is more common in certain groups of women than others. Zippin and Petrakis have identified seven high-risk groups: (1) Jews, (2) those of higher socioeconomic status, (3) those with a family history of breast cancer, (4) those with previous breast disease, (5) single women, (6) nonparous (nonchildbearing) women, and (7) those with early menarche (before age twelve).[65] Women who breast-feed their infants have a lower incidence of breast cancer, as do Japanese women.

Skin cancer. Skin cancers account for approximately 1 percent of cancers in men and women.[66] They affect white men more often than white women (2:1 ratio) and rarely occur on people with dark skin. Carcinomas (cancers) of the skin are most common on people who spend a great deal of time outdoors exposed to direct sunlight and wind (e.g., sailors, farmers, year-round outdoor sports enthusiasts). They also are frequently found on persons who have prolonged, unprotected exposure to radioactive materials or irritating chemicals. Skin tumors generally grow quite slowly in a compact mass and, consequently, can be removed quite easily with irradiation or local surgery. The cure rate for treated basal cell carcinomas (those growing on hair-bearing surfaces, especially the face and scalp) is excellent (98 percent).[67] Unattended skin cancers generally metastasize first to the lymph nodes, then to other parts of the body.

The two most common forms of skin cancer are basal cell carcinomas and squamous cell carcinomas (those growing on scalelike surfaces).[68] They generally grow quite slowly in a compact mass and can be removed quite easily with local surgery or irradiation. Squamous cell carcinomas have a greater tendency to metastasize to lymph nodes than do basal cell carcinomas.

Another important form of skin cancer is the melanoma.[69] This is a cancer originating from pigment-containing cells of the skin. Melanomas are the carcinomas referred to in the fourth warning sign of cancer (see page 381); the symptom is any change in size, color, or appearance of a wart or a mole. These tumors, which may occur at any age, are highly malignant and require an early recognition and radical surgery for possible cure.

Mental illness

Psychopathology is one of our nation's most important health problems, costing several billion dollars each year. Persons in their late thirties and early forties seek the most psychiatric care and also are the age group most frequently admitted to mental hospitals.[70]

There is no single criterion for diagnosing mental illness. Persons showing great personal distress, who disturb others, who become incapable of performing their usual jobs, or who have marked personality changes may be manifesting psychopathology. In the following pages some of the more common mental disorders afflicting persons in their forties will be discussed.

Alcoholism is frequently categorized among the personality disorders. It is a major problem of many midlife individuals. Over one third of psychiatric inpatient admissions are related to misuse of alcohol.[71] Alcoholism is a condition said to occur when a person habitually drinks enough to interfere with personal and social functioning and/or when the drinking damages health.

Excessive alcohol consumption may be associated with neurological, muscular, and gastrointestinal complications such as alcohol withdrawal syndrome (delirium tremens, DTs); head injury from falls; polyneuropathy (weakness of muscles, numbness and tingling of the extremities); cerebellar degeneration, producing disorders of gait or speech disorders; Wernicke's syndrome (paralysis or weakness of eye movements, double vision, nystagmus [involuntary movement of the eyeballs], unstable gait—all related to a deficiency of thiamine); Korsakoff's syndrome (disorders of retentive memory with inability to sort out events in their proper sequence and the making up of stories); cirrhosis (degeneration of the liver); gastritis (inflammation of the stomach); and pancreatitis (inflammation of the pancreas). In addition to strictly medical problems, alcoholism leads to severe disruption of family and community relationships and may lead to death by accident or suicide.[72]

Organic brain syndromes refer to variously caused conditions with clinical features such as impaired memory, inability to think with the usual clarity, decreased comprehension, loss of insight, irritability, loss of initiative, and changes in social behavior (e.g., untidiness, rudeness). Some organic brain syndromes result from acute and partially or completely reversible conditions (e.g., subdural hematoma, hypothyroidism). In other cases they result from chronic, irreversible conditions (e.g., degeneration of cerebral lobes from contusion, Korsakoff's syndrome). Other causes of organic brain syndrome include nutritional deficiency, bromide poisoning, neurosyphilis, brain tumor, and brain trauma.

Schizophrenia is another common type of mental disorder that may be of varying severity and have varying symptomatology. Its cause is unknown. Common features include misinterpretation or idiosyncratic distortions of reality, delusions, hallucinations, inappropriate moods, and odd to bizarre behavior and appearance.[73] In the quiescent phases of the illness, the person may be apathetic and joyless. The mood is often described as flat. These quiescent phases are typically interrupted with periods when the disease intensifies and the person manifests signs of profound anxiety and one or more of the above psychotic features.

There have been many attempts to describe different kinds of schizophrenia (or different diseases falling under the umbrella term of schizophrenia) according to various predominating symptoms or various suspected causes. However, it is difficult to find clinical or physiologic rationales for these categories and subcategories that can be generalized to the one out of every 100 persons in the world who become ''schizophrenic'' at some time in their lives.

The risk of becoming schizophrenic at some time in the life span is greater if there are family members who have had symptoms of the disease(s). If both biological parents are schizophrenic, the risk of offspring showing symptomatology is 50 percent. If one parent or a sibling is schizophrenic, the risk of the illness is about 15 percent.[74] However, possible genetic predisposition to the disease is believed to interact with environmental factors in exacerbating or waylaying symptoms.[75]

Biological hypotheses about the causes of schizophrenia(s) include metabolic abnormalities, some toxic factors circulating in the blood, endocrine dysfunctions, idiosyncratic responses to drugs or stress, circulating antibrain antibodies, and a chemical imbalance in the brain affecting the transmission of messages over the synaptic clefts between nerve endings. Despite long years of study, cause(s) have not yet been successfully explained. Schizophrenia is occasionally believed not to be a disease. For example, Ronald Laing states that perhaps the schizophrenic's insanity is more sane than our sanity.[76] Thomas Szasz believes we have invented a myth of schizophrenia and calls for an abolition of the whole concept.[77]

Treatment of schizophrenia(s) may include drug therapy, psychotherapy, and occasionally hospitalization. There are many antipsychotic drugs available today. Thorazine, first introduced in the early 1950s, is still one of the most frequently used. The antipsychotic drugs are not simply tranquilizers that sedate or reduce anxiety; they have unique properties that effectively interrupt acute psychotic behaviors. Experimentation with massive doses of vitamins (especially C and some of the B complex) to treat schizophrenia has not been scientifically successful.[78]

Psychotherapy can be beneficial to both a schizophrenic and his or her family. While such intervention may not be a remedy, it does help those involved to learn to live with a condition characterized by phases of quiescent and active symptomatology. It may also contribute to more long-lasting remissions of symptoms.

Hospitalization may be necessary for schizophrenia when psychotic behaviors threaten to disrupt or cause injury to the lives of patients or others. However, physical restraints and locked doors are now less necessary due to the effectiveness of antipsychotic drugs.

Depression is the most frequently treated psychiatric disorder. It contributes heavily to problems of alcoholism, drug abuse, family break-ups, and suicides. The usual features of depression are sadness, loss of appetite, insomnia, lack of concentration, indecision, and a waning interest in one's usual pursuits. However, some depressed persons show opposite symptoms. They compulsively overeat or sleep practically around the clock.

There are many types of depression. Depression that occurs as a consequence of the death of a loved person, loss of property, change in lifestyle, separation from a friend, or loss of job or status is called reactive depression and is a normal response. A depressive neurosis is an excessive reaction of depression employed by some persons to cope with stress or anxiety. In depressive neurotics there is typically a pattern of self-criticism, low self-esteem, brooding, guilt, and feelings of helplessness. The cyclothymic personality disorder is characterized by recurring periods of depression and elation not easily explained by a person's circumstances. While the cause is unknown, it is hypothesized that this reaction may be related to deprivation or severe emotional trauma in childhood.[79]

Some forms of depression can be very serious and long-lasting. Involutional depression (also called involutional melancholia) is one of them. It occurs following the menopause in some women or following life-situation changes for both older men and women. Symptoms generally begin with difficulty in concentrating, lack of attention, indecision, increased suspicions of others' good intentions, insomnia, pessimism, and spells of weeping. Later, affected persons become anxious, agitated, and hypochondriacal, lose weight, and are deeply depressed. They may have delusions of great sins and unworthiness and frequently discuss death. They may whine, pace, abuse themselves with scratching or head banging, and be verbally hostile and abusive to others. Suicide and physical deterioration from lack of food and rest loom large enough as threats in some persons that they are given protective hospitalization. In some cases electric shock therapy brings marked improvement in the condition of persons with involutional depression.[80]

Manic-depressive psychosis is another well-known form of very serious depression treated by psychiatrists. In this condition a patient has alterations of excitement and depression that may each extend for months. In the manic, agitated state a person may show increased energy and actually accomplish great works. However, mania may also bring in its wake undesirable behaviors such as irrepressible, uninhibited, unconventional, assertive, or mischievous speech and actions that hurt others. In the depressed state the individual may be suicidal or show symptoms similar to the person with involutional depression. If the psychotic state is not improved with psychotherapy or drugs, hospitalization and sometimes electric shock therapy may be added to the treatment regime.[81]

Summary

Persons in their forties devote much of their time to home and/or job. They often reassess their aspirations and accomplishments, their status and their life satisfactions. After this midlife survey some make changes. Others work harder at whatever it is they are doing.

The decade of the forties may be a period of excellent health and physical fitness or a time when activities become limited by chronic conditions such as joint diseases or digestive disturbances. Grey hairs and wrinkles are more evident.

The end of the female reproductive cycle is marked by menopause. Menopausal symptoms vary from woman to woman and range from negligible to psychologically and physically traumatizing. The end of the male reproductive cycle is gradual and less obviously concluded.

Socially, the forties are often charged with restlessness. It is hard for many persons in this age span to realize that young people view them as old. Marital relationships are often troublesome. Spouses may be anxious about loss of youthfulness and about their reproductive slowdowns. Spouses' midlife reassessments may take them in different directions, creating problems of readjustment. Often parents have to deal with teenagers' identity crises as well as their own psychological changes. Research indicates that these are years when married couples are least satisfied with each other.

Aging parents often turn to their fortyish children for support—financial, emotional, and physical—as they reach their retirement years. Assisting aging parents causes many forty-year-olds emotional turmoil. It is hard to realize that the persons on whom one depended for many years are now dependent instead.

Contributions to civic and community causes often peak in the forties. Persons may become more strongly identified with their political party, their religion, their social clubs. They may run for, or be appointed to, positions of leadership. An interest in social activities climbs, but the nature of the activities engaged in changes from the more active pursuits of youth to less rigorous sports—golfing, bowling, games—or social or family gatherings.

Health problems that may appear in the forties include vascular diseases (arteriosclerosis, varicose veins), heart disease (ischemic heart disease, hypertension), cancer, and mental illness. Many health problems are related to inability to handle the stresses of everyday living (alcoholism, depression) or to dietary factors (arteriosclerosis, obesity) or to both. As in other decades of life, health maintenance is enhanced by attention to diet, exercise, rest and relaxation, safety precautions, and prompt treatment of any symptoms of illness.

Questions for review

1. Treatment of menopausal symptoms with estrogen replacement therapy has recently caused a great deal of controversy. List some of the pros and cons of using this form of therapy.
2. Some women experience feelings of worthlessness and lack of sexual appeal after the menopause. Why do you think this is so?
3. As people age, we tend to think of them as less sexual and less able. List some of the myths and facts you know about the biological process of aging.
4. Describe a midlife transition you have witnessed occurring in a friend or a relative. If possible, illustrate your example with conversations you have had with this person about or during this transition.
5. Much literature has focused recently on middle age as a time of crisis and transition. Assuming this is true, do you believe it is possible for individuals to prepare for this transition? Explain.

6. American society seems to be one in which it is especially difficult to face and cope with one's own aging. Do you agree or disagree with this statement? Discuss.
7. Describe some of the ways husbands and wives can avoid using each other as scapegoats for their failures and insecurities as they go through their lives together, especially during this fourth decade of unrest.
8. Many individuals in their forties going through a midlife crisis are also dealing with teenagers and aging parents. How would you counsel a woman who feels overwhelmed by her own needs and those of her children and aging parents?
9. Describe some of the ways you think environment contributes to the high incidence of heart disease and cancer in this country. Consider in your answer the social, emotional, and physical components of environment.
10. Individuals who seek help from psychiatrists often receive various kinds of labels for their condition. They might be called manic-depressive, schizophrenic, mild depressive, or neurotic. Describe the pros and cons of the use of such labels. In your answer consider especially the effects on the individual.

References

[1]E. Bierman and W. Hazzard, "Adulthood, Especially the Middle Years," *The Biologic Ages of Man*, D. Smith and E. Bierman, eds. (Philadelphia: W. B. Saunders Co., 1973).

[2]J. Crough, *Human Anatomy and Physiology*, 2nd ed. (New York: John Wiley, 1976).

[3]P. Timiras, *Developmental Physiology and Aging* (New York: Macmillan, 1972).

[4]L. Wharton, *The Ovarian Hormones* (Springfield, Ill.: Charles C. Thomas, 1967).

[5]F. Appel, *Understanding Your Body* (London: Aldus Books, 1972).

[6]B. Neugarten, V. Wood, R. Kraines, and B. Loomis, "Women's Attitude Toward the Menopause," *Vita Humana*, 6 (1963).

[7]Ibid.

[8]G. Sheehy, *Passages: Predictable Crises of Adult Life* (New York: E. P. Dutton & Co., Inc., 1976).

[9]M. Gray, *The Changing Years* (Garden City, N.Y.: Doubleday & Co., Inc., 1967).

[10]J. Birren, "The Experience of Aging," *Aging: Prospects and Issues*, R. Davis and M. Neiswender, eds. (Los Angeles: Andrus Gerontology Center, 1973).

[11]J. Kangas and K. Bradway, "Intelligence at Middle-Age: A Thirty-Eight Year Follow-Up," *Developmental Psychology*, 5 (1971).

[12]L. Sontag, C. Baker, and V. Nelson, *Mental Growth and Personality Development: A Longitudinal Study.* Monograph of the Society for Research in Child Development, 23(2), Serial No. 68 (1958).

[13]M. Horner, "Toward an Understanding of Achievement-Related Conflicts in Women," *Journal of Social Issues,* 28(2) (1972).

[14]R. Havighurst, *Developmental Tasks and Education,* 3rd ed. (New York: McKay, 1972).

[15]D. Levinson, "The Psychological Development of Men in Early Adulthood and the Mid-Life Transition," *Life History Research in Psychopathology: III,* D. Ricks, A. Thomas, and M. Roff, eds. (Minneapolis: University of Minnesota Press, 1974).

[16]R. Gould, "The Phases of Adult Life: A Study in Developmental Psychology," *American Journal of Psychiatry*, 129(5) (1972).

[17]J. Hillman, "Archetypal Theory: C. G. Jung," *Operational Theories of Personality,* A. Burton, ed. (New York: Brunner/Mazel, 1974).

[18]E. Erikson, *Childhood and Society*, 2nd ed. (New York: W. W. Norton, 1963).

[19]B. Neugarten, "The Awareness of Middle Age," *Middle Age and Aging,* B. Neugarten, ed. (Chicago: The University of Chicago Press, 1968).

[20]Ibid.

[21]B. Neugarten and J. Moore, "The Changing Age-Status System," *Middle Age and Aging*, B. Neugarten, ed. (Chicago: The University of Chicago Press, 1968).

[22]B. Neugarten, "Adult Personality: Toward a Psychology of the Life Cycle," *Middle Age and Aging*, B. Neugarten, ed. (Chicago: The University of Chicago Press, 1968).

[23]D. Levinson, "The Psychological Development of Men in Early Adulthood and the Mid-Life Transition."

[24]Ibid.

[25]R. Gould, "The Phases of Adult Life."

[26]Ibid.

[27]B. Neugarten, "The Awareness of Middle Age."

[28]D. Woodruff and J. Birren, "Age Changes and Cohort Differences in Personality," *Developmental Psychology*, 6 (1972).

[29]E. Kelly, "Consistency of the Adult Personality," *American Psychologist*, 10 (1955).

[30]A. Kinsey, *Sexual Behavior in the Human Male* (New York: W. B. Saunders Co., 1948).

[31]M. Scarf, "Husbands in Crisis," *Annual Editions: Readings in Human Development*, P. Rosenthal, ed. (Guilford, Conn.: The Dushkin Publishing Group, Inc., 1974).

[32]B. Rollins and H. Feldman, "Marital Satisfaction Over the Family Life Cycle," *Journal of Marriage and the Family*, 32 (1970).

[33]J. Bernard, *The Future of Marriage* (New York: Bantam Books, 1973).

[34]B. Rollins and H. Feldman, "Marital Satisfaction Over the Family Life Cycle."

[35]I. Deutscher, "The Quality of Post-Parental Life," *Journal of Marriage and the Family*, 26 (1964).

[36]Ibid.

[37]E. Duvall, *Family Development*, 4th ed. (Philadelphia: Lippincott, 1971).

[38]P. Bart, "Depression in Middle-Aged Women," *Women in Sexist Society*, V. Gornick and B. Moran, eds. (New York: Basic Books, 1971).

[39]B. Neugarten, "The Awareness of Middle Age."

[40]R. Gould, "The Phases of Adult Life."

[41]M. Scarf, "Husbands in Crisis."

[42]B. Neugarten and J. Moore, "The Changing Age-Status System."

[43]Ibid.

[44]N. Seligman, "Working Mobility for Women," *Quality of Life: The Middle Years* (Acton, Mass.: Publishing Sciences Group, Inc., 1974).

[45]Ibid.

[46]P. Swerdloff, *Men and Women* (New York: Time Inc., 1975).

[47]Ibid.

[48]R. Gould, "The Phases of Adult Life."

[49]American Public Health Association, *Vital and Health Statistics Monographs: Mortality and Morbidity in the United States*, C. Erhardt and J. Berlin, eds. (Cambridge, Mass.: Harvard University Press, 1974).

[50]Ibid.

[51]Ibid.

[52]S. Kety, "From Rationalization to Reason," *The American Journal of Psychiatry*, 131(9) (September 1974).

[53]D. Fredrickson, "Atherosclerosis and Other Forms of Arteriosclerosis," *Harrison's Principles of Internal Medicine*, M. Wintrobe et al., eds. (New York: McGraw-Hill, 1974).

[54]Ibid.

[55]D. Strandness, "Vascular Diseases of the Extremities," *Harrison's Principles of Internal Medicine*, M. Wintrobe et al., eds. (New York: McGraw-Hill, 1974).

[56]J. Stamler, "Epidemiology of Coronary Heart Disease," *Medical Clinics of North America: Symposium on Coronary Heart Disease*, L. Resnekov, ed. (Philadelphia: W. B. Saunders Co., 1973).

[57]Ibid.

[58]S. Robbins, *Pathologic Basis of Disease* (Philadelphia: W. B. Saunders Co., 1974).

[59]B. Sobel and E. Braunwald, "Sudden Cardiovascular Collapse and Death," *Harrison's Principles of Internal Medicine*, 7th ed. M. Wintrobe et al., eds. (New York: McGraw-Hill, 1974).

[60]S. Robbins, *Pathologic Basis of Disease.*

[61]P. Jagger and E. Braunwald, "Hypertensive Vascular Disease," *Harrison's Principles of Internal Medicine*, M. Wintrobe et al., eds. (New York: McGraw-Hill, 1974).

[62]S. Robbins, *Pathologic Basis of Disease.*

[63]E. Silverberg, "Cancer Statistics, 1977," *CA-A Cancer Journal for Clinicians*, 27 (1) January 1977.

[64]Ibid.

[65]C. Zippin and N. Petrakis, "Identification of High Risk Groups in Breast Cancer," *Cancer*, 28 (1971).

[66]E. Silverberg, "Cancer Statistics, 1977."

[67]S. Robbins, *Pathologic Basis of Disease.*

[68]Ibid.

[69]Ibid.

[70]M. Kramer, C. Taube, and R. Redick, "Patterns of Use of Psychiatric Facilities by the Aged: Past, Present, and Future," *The Psychology of Adult Development and Aging*, C. Eisdorfer and M. Lawton, eds. (Washington: American Psychological Association, 1973).

[71]Ibid.

[72]M. Victor and R. Adams, "Alcohol," *Harrison's Principles of Internal Medicine*, M. Wintrobe et al., eds. (New York: McGraw-Hill, 1974).

[73]R. Baldessarini, "Schizophrenia," *The New England Journal of Medicine*, 297 (18) (Nov. 3, 1977).

[74]I. Gottesman and J. Shields, "A Critical Review of Recent Adoption, Twin, and Family Studies of Schizophrenia: Behavioral Genetics Perspectives," *Schizophrenia Bulletin*, 2 (1976).

[75]Ibid.

[76]R. Laing, *Self and Others* (London: Tavistock Publications, 1969).

[77]T. Szasz, *Schizophrenia: The Sacred Symbol of Psychiatry* (New York: Basic Books Inc., 1976).

[78]R. Baldessarini, "Schizophrenia."

[79]T. Hackett and R. Adams, "Grief, Reactive Depression, Manic-Depressive Psychosis, Involutional Melancholia, and Hypochondriasis," *Harrison's Principles of Internal Medicine*, M. Wintrobe et al., eds. (New York: McGraw-Hill, 1974).

[80]Ibid.

[81]Ibid.

10

Contents

Elizabeth Hamlin/Stock, Boston

The Fifties and Early Sixties

At some point in the decade of the fifties, most people think of themselves as middle-aged. Those in poor health may consider themselves old. Those in excellent health may consider themselves young. However, such hallmarks as children leaving home and grandchildren being born serve to remind people where they are chronologically, regardless of how they feel physically and emotionally.

The fifties and early sixties are often years of peak status and power. Past accomplishments may be recognized and rewarded with a measure of respect. Financial earnings are probably greater than they have been in the past, while expenses may be lowered due to the departure of children from the home. Persons in their fifties and early sixties are often regarded as reservoirs of wisdom and good judgment. A vast number of them really are in the prime of their lives due to an emphasis on diet, exercise, and physical fitness and to new and better ways of curing or alleviating problems of ill health.

Physical development

The physical changes that normally occur in the fifties were once difficult to ascertain because of the high incidence of debilitating diseases that masked normal development. Now, however, because of improved medical techniques and an increased concern for protection from disease and

Figure 10–1. *The fifties are often years of peak earnings and great productivity. Men and women in this decade may experience a sense of achievement at work and pleasure and pride in their family and community relationships.*
Leslie Davis

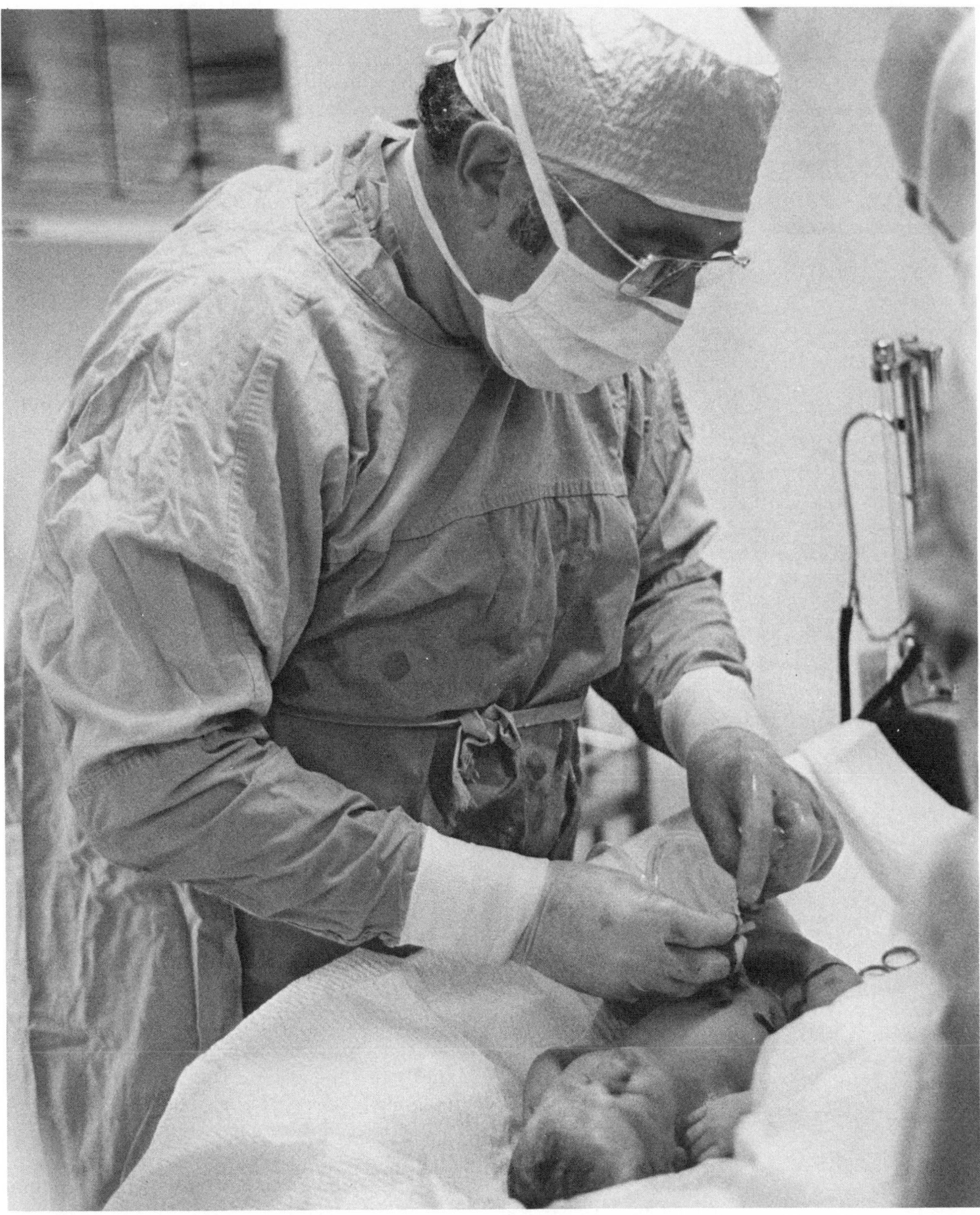

environmental hazards (including unhealthy diets and lack of exercise), a larger number of normal people survive. The changes that occur with age are becoming more obvious.

While neurons stopped dividing in the prenatal days, other cells (like those of the liver, pancreas, bowel, and skin) continue to actively divide for a much longer time. There are conflicting theories about why some body cells eventually die without replacing themselves and why some lose their ability to function properly over time. There are probably several different causes for cell deterioration and cell malfunctions. Most biologists agree that the aging of cells, including structure and function, must be programmed in the cells' genetic material. Changes seen in the aging of cells include more frequent mutations of DNA (deoxyribonucleic acid), more frequent errors in the synthesis of RNA (ribonucleic acid), changes in the rate of protein synthesis and breakdown, changes in endocrine organ functions, and faulty internal control of the cells by regulator substances such as cyclic AMP (adenosine monophosphate).

The changes of aging are gradual and continue in the same directions described for the thirties and forties, except to a greater and greater extent. Muscles have diminished strength, size, and reflex speed; bones lose mass and density, break more easily, and heal more slowly; skin become less elastic, drier, and more wrinkled; hair thins out and greys; vision and hearing become less keen; digestive disturbances occur more frequently; fat accumulation is a threat unless eating habits are curbed; there are changes in the patterns and amounts of production of many hormones; energy is diminished, and with each passing year it takes slightly longer to catch one's breath after exertion.[1]

Considerable retarding of physical decline can be accomplished through regular exercise to increase cardiovascular efficiency, elimination of excess calories from the diet, diminished cholesterol and saturated fat intake, adequate calcium and protein intake, cessation of cigarette smoking, a curbed use of alcohol and drugs, and avoidance, whenever possible, of environmental pollutants such as external radiation, emissions from internal combustion engines, exhaust fumes, smoke, and contaminated waters.

As reported in Chapter 9, sexual interests and performance need not cease with the decrease in fertility following female menopause and the male climacteric. Both men and women can remain sexually active through their fifties and sixties when their libido is kept alive by an interested and stimulating partner and when no physical disabilities interfere with performance.

Many women experience a renewed interest in sex (and in making their physical appearance more attractive to men) after the menopause. Masters and Johnson described this unleashed sexual drive as a "second honeymoon" phenomenon and attributed it in part to women's newly found freedom from fears of pregnancy.[2] Social factors such as no children in the home, fewer tiring household tasks, and a desire for more companionship may also contribute to this new burst of sexuality.

Men generally experience a gradual waning of sexual interests with age, uninterrupted by dramatic changes in their levels of sexual libido. This waning of interest varies greatly from man to man and reflects, in part, sexual stimulation received and past history of sexual responsiveness. Masters and Johnson reported that men in their studies with the most evidence of maintained sexuality in their later years were those who had had more sexual activity in their early years. The men with problems of sexual inadequacy and impotence usually had one or more of the following six problems: (1) monotony of a repetitious sexual relationship (usually translated into boredom with his partner); (2) preoccupation with career or economic pursuits; (3) mental or physical fatigue; (4) overindulgence in food or drink; (5) physical and mental infirmities of either the man or his spouse; (6) fear of performance associated with or resulting from any of the former categories.[3] Masters and Johnson reported a high cure rate for impotence in men over age fifty. Therapy successes indicate that a willingness to return to active sexual practice and an interested partner are more important than any hormonal, medicinal, or other physiological routines in restoring potency.

Intellectually, people in their fifties continue to add words to their vocabularies and organize and process new information they take in from the external environment. However, Baltes and Schaie have reported that a reduction in motor skills may begin to interfere with certain aspects of intellectual functioning.[4] Eye-hand coordination, for example, is not as acute as it was in earlier years, and reaction time slows due to a decline in the velocity of nerve impulses. Botwinick reported that a person's intellectual functions in middle age are still more dependent on motivation, education, experience, intellectual activity, and intellectual stimulation than on age.[5]

Social development

People in their fifties typically have fewer family responsibilities than in earlier decades and more time for leisure and social activities. They seldom have personality shifts towards a more extroverted party-going, party-throwing lifestyle. Rather they are apt to become more introverted and satisfied with a few, narrow, well-defined life goals and interests. They also tend to view themselves more favorably than they have done in the past. They begin to reap the rewards of their lifetime of stresses and joys, pains and pleasures. Just as there is a feeling among youth that people over thirty cannot be trusted, there is a feeling among adults that many people over fifty have accumulated the wisdom of the ages through their experiences. Many people are glad to have arrived at fifty and have no desire to relive their thirties and forties.

Family interactions

Evelyn Duvall conceptualized the family life cycle as having six major divisions: (1) marriage, (2) birth of the first child, (3) family with school-age children, (4) family with adolescents, (5) launching/empty nest, and (6) the retired family.[6] While fifty-year-olds may fit into any of these divisions, they are more apt to fall into the classification of the family launching its children and adjusting to an empty nest. Family interactions decrease in the home, but family dynamics are active as new in-laws and grandchildren join the extended family.

Launching/empty nest. The time when the first child (usually the oldest) leaves home is a momentous occasion in most families. For some parents (especially the mother) the child's going away may be comparable to a death in the family. For years the parents have hovered over and protected the child. To then release the child into the world and to cut off the daily ministrations brings an acute sense of loss. Launching the first child is usually the hardest.[7] However, families may feel acute pain as each offspring moves out of the family home. The beginning of the empty nest usually coincides with the marriage of the last child or a comparable declaration of independence from the family of origin by the remaining offspring. While circumstances in every individual household make the timing and paths of entry into the empty nest slightly different, many married couples or single parents approach this phase of their lives during middle age. In general, women are more affected by this change in the family than are men. Whether they work outside the home or not, women usually assume the primary role as nurturant, social, emotional caregivers for their families. These nurturing tasks take up a considerable amount of time, both in contemplation and in actual deeds of sustenance and support. When children leave the home, the woman's twenty to thirty years' practice suddenly has few outlets for employment. Many mothers find surrogate children to nurture (e.g., their husbands, infirm friends, their aging parents, pets). Some try to hold on to their own children and may meet with varying degrees of success. More often than not, mothers who refuse to let go and accept the empty nest phase are considered meddlesome and intrusive by their newly independent children. Fathers may be equally reluctant to accept the empty nest, although most men are less involved with the social and emotional aspects of parenting and more heavily involved in their careers. Consequently, they are less upset by the absence of their offspring in the home. The empty nest phenomenon may be felt most acutely by men as a proof of acquired middle age.

Son- and daughter-in-law relations. The family both contracts and expands with the empty nest phase. While the number of persons living in the family home dwindles, the extended family may grow through marriage to include the new spouses and their offspring. Some parents are pleased with their children's choices of mates. They welcome them into the family with open arms. They may also seek to establish closer ties and frequent contacts with the parents of their children's new spouses. Not infrequently, however, parents have a degree of difficulty in accepting the persons their children choose as mates. This is more common when the chosen mate is from a different social class, ethnic group, religion, or region of the country, or demonstrates beliefs, values, or lifestyles that are distasteful to the parents. As reported in Chapter 8, there are often special problems that arise between mother and daughter-in-law and father and son-in-law. A mother may resent her son's preference for his new bride's attention over her own. A father may be especially bitter toward the groom who has taken away his "little girl." All interactions may be problematic. A mother and father may resent the fact that their daughter now seeks her husband's over her parents' advice. Or they may want their son to take social and economic favors and advice from them, not from his wife or his wife's family. Designing good in-law relations takes a great deal of tact and skill. Parents must remember that their children need to be independent to be mature human beings. It is difficult, however, not to be intrusive or overgenerous with advice or financial or social assistance after years of practice. On the other hand, parents who sever all ties with their offspring at the empty nest phase may be contributing to their own future conflicts and stresses with their sons- and daughters-in-law and alienation from their possible grandchildren. Some interactions and interdependencies are conducive to the establishment of good relationships that remain workable over time.

Leslie reported that parents are more apt to intrude in their offsprings' lives if children marry while still quite young rather than waiting until they have finished their education and begun a career.[8] Mothers are more apt to intrude in their offsprings' lives than are fathers, probably due to their greater investment in the nurturing role.[9] This is in keeping with the previously reported idea that mothers feel the empty nest more acutely than fathers.

It is not always the parents who intrude into or sever ties with their offsprings' mates. Many empty nest problems relate to the fact that the departed child and spouse cut off ties with the parents. Many mothers and fathers would dearly love to give housekeeping or child care aid, gifts, and the like to their children but find their offers of assistance rejected. This causes some parents to suffer great pangs of confusion and disappointment. Invariably they question their own performance as parents.[10] Many initial problems of parent-in-law and children-in-law discord are worked out in time with honest communication and a bit of pride swallowing on both sides. However, some problems may persist.

Interiority of personality. Carl Jung, one of Freud's most famous student dissenters, was the father of life-span studies of personality development. He rejected the idea that the personality remains stable once adulthood is reached. He described the early years of adulthood as years in which expansion into the outer world is the prevailing manner of operating or working. He felt that middle age brings noticeable personality changes. The maturing adult's manner of dealing with the outer world becomes more constricted or contracted. Older individuals begin to integrate outer reality with inner fantasy and move toward more self-realization, which Jung called individuation.[11]

Bernice Neugarten, after her extensive interviews with middle-aged and aging persons in the 1950s and 1960s, came to a similar conclusion. She described the move inward toward more preoccupation with satisfying personal needs as an increased "interiority of the personality."[12] This movement generally occurs around the fifth decade. "It is in this period of the life line that introspection seems to increase noticeably and contemplation and reflection and self-evaluation become characteristic forms of mental life."[13] Neugarten held that the reflections of the middle years of life differ from the reminiscences of old age. Middle-aged adults restructure their personalities after their reflecting. They develop new concepts of self, time, and death with a consideration for how they will spend the rest of their lives. Very often they emerge with a feeling of being more fully in charge of their destinies than ever before. This satisfaction does not lend itself to many desires to relive their thirties and forties. As one person interviewed by Neugarten put it: "There is a difference between wanting to *feel* young and wanting to *be* young. Of course it would be pleasant to maintain the vigor and appearance of youth, but I would not trade those things for the authority or the autonomy I feel—no, nor the ease of interpersonal relationships nor the self-confidence that comes from experience."[14]

Roger Gould's recent descriptions of the principal characteristics of personality over the life span support the conclusions of Jung and Neugarten that persons in their fifties begin to turn inward. He stated that these patterns of reflection and contemplation seem to give people much more self-acceptance and self-approval in their fifties. They "look within themselves at their own feelings and emotions, although not with the critical 'time pressure' eye of the late thirties or with the infinite omnipotentiality of the early thirties but with a more self-accepting attitude of continued learning from a position of general stability."[15]

David Gutmann found that the increased interiority of personality that occurs during the middle years of life has important repercussions on men's social behaviors.[16] In early adulthood men tend to be bold and active in their dealings with the external environment. They tend to act on their impulses and maintain a position of control over their own lives to the greatest extent possible. However, after midlife men become less bold. They begin to see the external world as more complex and dangerous. They conform and accommodate to it more. Gutmann studied men in a preliterate Mexican farming culture, Navajo Indians, and urban American men and determined that this personality shift occurs with age in all three cultures, regardless of the male sex-role expectations.[17] While the degree of shift varies from male to male and men without any obvious personality changes can be found, men generally become less self-assertive and more conforming with age. Gutmann describes this as a shift from alloplastic (active) mastery to autoplastic (passive) and omniplastic (magical) mastery of the outer world.[18]

Figure 10–2. *Spouses must make adaptions in their marital relationships in middle age as children leave home. Some marriages grow in interdependency, support, and affection. Other partnerships may be dissolved at this time.*
Esaias Baitel from Rapho/Photo Researchers, Inc.

Neugarten, in conjunction with Gutmann, found that a personality shift also frequently occurs in women.[19] They, like men, become more constricted and more detached from active mastery of their environments. However, they also tend to have less inhibitions about expressing their aggressive feelings. This finding has led some people to conclude that women become more "masculine" after the menopause. Perhaps with society's current movement for less emphasis on sex-role stereotyped behaviors in younger adults, this perception of postmenopausal women will transcend the age barrier and be applied at earlier and earlier ages. Or perhaps society's concepts of "masculine" and "feminine" behaviors will alter sufficiently to make obsolete the attributions of aggression, nurturance, and other such behaviors as more appropriate for one sex than for the other.

Marriage and divorce. Many social scientists have reported an upsurge in marital happiness after the nest empties. Rollins and Feldman found that the number of wives who were very satisfied with their marriages more than doubled from the launching period to the postparental period, while the number of husbands who became very satisfied postparentally nearly tripled.[20] Couples often find a new pleasure in marriage and a new intensity in their personal relationships once the children leave.[21] Roger Gould's clinical work revealed that this increased marital happiness and contentment is often associated with a change in attitude toward the spouse.[22] The postparental individual, according to Gould, is more apt to look to his or her spouse for approval and companionship and less likely to view the spouse as a parent or source of supplies.

The postparental period is often a time to harvest the rewards of the hard work of earlier adulthood. The family income is usually at a higher level than before, but the financial burdens are lighter. Bills for education, food, clothing, shelter, and leisure activities for the children diminish. By the fifties adults have also usually carved a niche for themselves in their society. Their abilities, merits, and contributions are recognized by their associates, and they are granted a certain degree of honor and esteem. They no longer have to work so hard to prove themselves from day to day.

While marital happiness increases for some postparental couples, others seek divorce soon after the children leave home. In many cases the spouses involved have lost touch with each other long before the empty nest. They have only been biding their time, waiting for the children to depart before separating and divorcing. In other cases the empty nest proves distressing. Both husband and wife may experience new identity crises. The husband may have stayed at work more in the preceding years to meet the expenses accrued by college educations or weddings. Suddenly he has more time on his hands and no interests to fill the empty hours and days. Hobbies that just occupy time do not relieve boredom and restless feelings. Or the husband may be afraid to quit working so hard for fear of demotion, early retirement, or loss of job. These frustrations may be displaced from their real cause and blamed on the wife.

Identity crises after the empty nest also may occur in women. As mentioned earlier in this chapter, a woman whose predominant role has been mothering is left unemployed when children depart. She may find it difficult to redirect her childrearing time into new efforts and to find new outlets for her nurturing skills. She may begin to make more and more demands on her husband. She may try to recapture her youth through extramarital affairs. While many women find new interests in jobs, school, politics, or religion after the children leave, others wait for their husbands to solve the crises for them and may divorce him if he fails.

Sex is often a problem in postparental marriage conflicts. As every man ages, he may experience some delayed erection time and reduced ejaculatory volume, pressure, and demand.[23] Women may experience slowed production or reduced volume of vaginal lubrication, thinning and loss of elasticity of vaginal walls, and a shortened orgasmic experience.[24] These sexual problems may be alleviated or cured when both partners are willing and interested in discussing them and finding new ways to stimulate sexual activity. However, many couples either do not know where they can get professional help for their problems or do not trust the sexual dysfunction experts in their community to be effective or to maintain confidentiality. Society's new openness about sex may help some individuals feel more comfortable in seeking professional attention for these problems.

Grandparenting. In spite of an American vision of grandparents as old, heavy-set, rosy-cheeked, wrinkled, benevolent persons enjoying rocking chairs and home-baked foods, most grandparents are quite different from this stereotype. Today's grandparents are more apt to be actively working, involved, middle-aged persons. Great-grandparents (and there are many of them alive today) are much more apt to approach the popular notion of how a grandparent should appear.

Approaching grandparenthood speeds on the realization of aging for many people. It also may contribute to the process of personality restructuring that leads to a more conforming, accommodating, passive mastery of the external world. Grandparents are seldom asked to assume the primary, active, assertive task of shaping their grandchildren's behaviors. Rather, they are expected to conform to, supplement, and support the decisions and rules about their grandchildren handed down to them by their children. The former pattern of active mastery and control is usurped by the younger generation. In a study of contemporary middle-class American grandparents, Neugarten and Weinstein found that about 60 percent of the persons they interviewed felt comfortable in the role of grandparenthood.[25] About 30 percent of them were uncomfortable, however. They had difficulty viewing themselves as grandparents, or they had conflicts with the parents about the rearing of the grandchildren, or they

Figure 10–3. *The majority of today's grandparents enjoy their roles with grandchildren. They can often spend more pleasant, relaxed moments with them than they could with their own children.*
Anna Kaufman Moon/Stock, Boston

found that their grandparenting responsibilities were void of positive rewards and full of disappointments.

Neugarten and Weinstein identified five major classifications into which grandparents fall in terms of style of interacting with grandchildren: (1) formal, (2) fun seeking, (3) parent surrogate, (4) reservoir of family wisdom, and (5) distant figure.[26] Formal grandparents do no childrearing beyond occasional baby-sitting. They maintain a clearly demarcated line between parents' responsibilities and grandparents' roles. Fun-seeking grandparents see their role primarily as playmates. Authority lines are irrelevant. The principal goal is that all parties involved should enjoy the interaction. Parent surrogates take on all the caregiving responsibilities for the grandchildren and are more parents than grandparents. The reservoir of family wisdom is a grandparent who is really an authority figure for parents as well as grandchildren. He, she, or they use interaction time to pass on special skills or resources. The distant figure stays remote from grandchildren except possibly to observe rituals such as birthdays or religious observances. The fun seekers and the distant figures are now the most common styles adopted by grandparents in their fifties. Older grandparents and great-grandparents are more apt to be formal.

Relations with aging parents. Bernice Neugarten and Roger Gould both report that during the fifties people tend to mellow and develop warmer, more sympathetic feelings toward their own parents. One of Neugarten's interviewees said, "I sympathize with old people, now, in a way that is new. I watch my parents, for instance, and I wonder if I will age in the same way."[27] Gould reported that middle-aged adults less frequently see their parents as the source of their problems. They begin to call them "Mom" and "Dad" with more warmth and affection.[28]

While feelings mellow, responsibilities for aging parents often grow. The older generation may gradually require more assistance in managing their own lives and households. Housekeeping chores, shopping trips, transportation, financial arrangements, holiday preparations, and the like may be more and more troublesome for aging parents. They are more likely to turn to their children for help than to strangers and are more likely to request assistance from their daughters than from their sons.[29]

Many aging parents, particularly widows, move in with their daughters or sons. The tensions of trying to share a household are usually not as great as they are among younger adults with live-in parents. The middle-aged adult tends to be more sympathetic toward the older adult. Many over-fifty persons also tend to be more conforming and accommodating toward each other. If the nest is empty, the frictions commonly associated with differences of opinion about childrearing do not exist. The older parent can often be a help with light housework and may even be able to contribute some financial assistance for equipping and maintaining the household. In addition, aging parents can be a source of companionship to the postparental middle-aged adults with whom they live.

Community interactions

Middle-aged adults in the postparental phase of their family life cycle often have much more time, freedom, and financial resources for pursuing leisure and social activities. However, their restructured personalities tend to make them proceed along tried and tested paths of entertainment rather than striking out at new and different pastimes. Careers still occupy many of their waking hours. Women in the empty nest phase may be reentering the labor force or renewing or increasing their efforts at work in politics, religion, or education to fulfill their needs for active participation in the outside world. Community participation is generally still at a high point.

Careers. Men and women who have worked throughout their adult lives generally reach the zenith of their careers in their fifties. Not only are their salaries as high as they will probably go, but their prestige and power are at their peak. Persons at all other stages of life—children, adolescents, young adults, older adults—look to middle-aged experts for advice and direction and expect middle-aged adults to help them solve their problems and make appreciable changes in the society. Middle-aged persons are expected to be stable. They seldom make the radical shifts or impulsive moves that may have characterized their younger years. They are expected to remain in their present jobs until retirement. By this time the threat of being fired or laid off is usually low due to seniority status. For many people the years of work between approximately age fifty and sixty-five are the most comfortable, satisfying years of their careers. They are doing what they know how to do best with fewer threats of moves or job changes. For a few people, however, this lack of upward mobility after approximately age fifty may be a frustration. They may become bored with their work and simply mark time until they can retire. Some people are now opting to retire early, at fifty, or fifty-five, or whenever they have enough money to live at a level they deem comfortable. Work for them is so boring that they give it up gladly to do what they prefer to do for the rest of their lives.[30]

For women who have been predominantly homemakers until the empty nest, a first retirement occurs in their forties or fifties. Many women then choose to embark on a second career. For this group, jobs are approached with expectations of upward mobility during their fifties. They do not view themselves as winding down their lives but rather as renewing themselves—starting all over again. Some go back to school before embarking on a job. Career boredom is less apt to occur in women who begin their out-of-the-home jobs later in life.

Leisure and social activities. Neugarten noted an interesting facet of our changing American society. "A hundred years ago, the higher one's education and income, the more leisure one had. Now . . . the best educated and the most skilled professionals . . . put in sixty- and eighty-hour weeks. As you go down the occupational scale, people are working fewer hours. . . . It is the blue-collar worker who has gained leisure over the past 100 years."[31]

The postparental phase often brings in its wake increased pocket money and greater opportunities to get up and go out for many adults. While some couples may strike out anew and attempt to go places and do things foreign to their previous lifestyles, it is more common for leisure pursuits to follow tried and trusted paths of the past: watching

Figure 10–4. *Each person decides how he or she will spend free time. Most people have plenty of work to do at home or at social- or job-related obligations that take up many of their leisure hours.*
Leslie Davis

television, eating out, socializing with friends, attending cultural or sports events, or participating in activities centered around religion, politics, or involving their extended families.

The second honeymoon phenomenon, described by Masters and Johnson as an unleashing of sexual drive in fiftyish women, spills over into social activities.[32] Wives, freed of child care responsibilities, may devote more time to seeking out their husbands' affection and companionship. They may develop an interest in the sports, games, television programs, clubs, hobbies, or projects of their husbands in order to be included in more of their leisure time activities. Husbands, in turn, may develop an interest in the sports, games, television programs, clubs, hobbies, or projects of their wives for the same reasons.

Many people in their fifties have a very limited amount of actual time for pursuing enjoyable leisure activities. The professional workers may be tied up with eighty-hour-plus work weeks. They may spend considerable amounts of their free time getting to and from work or doing work-related reading, entertaining, or preparations. Blue-collar workers, who supposedly have the most leisure time, often take on a second job to supplement the income from the first job. Most people have work to do at home (e.g., do-it-yourself projects, home repairs, meals, housework) that also cuts into their planning of leisure and social activities. Kelly proposed that people's use of their nonworking time can be classified according to whether they chose an activity for the free time or had it determined for them, and whether the free time activity is independent of their career or dependent on it.[33] A great deal of a person's nonworking time is actually used in career-related activities. Kelly labeled the work-related activities that are freely chosen by individuals "coordinated leisure." Examples include reading in one's professional field or improving one's technical skills at home. Work-related activities that are determined by others are called "preparation and recuperation" by Kelly. Examples may include entertaining clients or preparing teaching aids at home. Free time that is not used in career-related activities is classified by Kelly as either "complementary leisure" or "unconditional leisure." Complementary leisure is determined directly or indirectly by others. It includes those activities that a person pursues because he or she is expected to do so (e.g., religious activities, voluntary services, community activities). Unconditional leisure includes the things freely chosen because one enjoys doing them. Many people have little free time left over in their lives for unconditional leisure. When one does have this ideal leisure, he or she often chooses to do enjoyable work (e.g., hobbies, handicrafts).

Erikson's concept of ego integrity. Erik Erikson saw the nuclear conflict of the later adult years as that of achieving ego integrity versus despair (see Table 10–1).[34] In Erikson's view, ego integrity involves an acceptance of the fact that one's life and work and leisure have been one's own responsibility. Attaining a sense of ego integrity necessitates a great deal of self-acceptance as well as acceptance of other family and community members. While aspects of this last stage of Erickson's "eight ages of man" theory are suggestive of the midlife transition described in the last chapter, this final Eriksonian stage goes far beyond the self-assessment of a midlife transition. An individual in the process of achieving ego integrity looks back over his or her own life experiences with a degree of acceptance. Mistakes, faults, failures, and disappointments are not denied or overlooked. Accomplishments, assets, successes, and satisfactions are ap-

Table 10–1. *Erikson's eighth nuclear conflict: ego integrity versus despair.*

Sense	*Eriksonian descriptions*	*Fostering behaviors*
Ego integrity	– ego's accrued assurance of its proclivity for order and meaning	– associates recognition of ego's lifestyle as meaningful
	– love of the human ego	– demonstrations of human integrity and human dignity by others
	– acceptance of one's one and only life cycle as something that had to be and that permitted no substitutions	– recognition of style of integrity of culture and civilization
vs.		
Despair	– fear of death	– lack of ego integration
	– nonacceptance of one's life cycle	– feedback from others that own resources have not been sufficient during life cycle

Source: Based on material from "Eight Ages of Man" from *Childhood and Society,* 2nd Edition, Revised, by Erik H. Erikson, with the permission of W. W. Norton & Company, Inc. Copyright 1950, © 1963 by W. W. Norton & Company, Inc.

preciated. The individual feels content with the outcome of his or her life. Family and community members are accepted in a new way. The individual no longer wishes that others had been different but accepts responsibility for the course of many life experiences based on the way he or she acted and reacted to the deeds of others. When a person can look back on life with the satisfaction of ego integrity, death becomes much more acceptable. The whole process of achieving ego integrity may take many years. Some middle-aged adults have the nuclear conflict of generativity versus stagnation still very much at the forefront of their lives during their fifties. Others are more concerned with developing ego integrity.

The opposite of ego integrity in Erikson's theory is despair. If an individual cannot accept what his or her life has been by the later adult years, a feeling of hopelessness develops. Despair, in Erikson's view, involves low self-esteem, feelings of incompetence, speculation on what things one would like to change about one's past, a lack of acceptance of one's age and status and lifestyle, and a fear of death. Failures are emphasized more than assets, accomplishments, and successes. Despairing persons would like to start life again but realize that it is too late and consequently become discouraged, frustrated, and resentful rather than accepting. Just as different people work at the eight nuclear conflicts of life at varying chronological ages, different persons resolve their conflicts in contrasting ways. It is possible for a person to go through a period of despair before achieving a sense of ego integrity.[35]

Health considerations

As reported in Chapter 9, the five leading causes of death between the years of forty-five and sixty-four are heart disease, cancer, vascular lesions, accidents, and liver cirrhosis.[36] During the last few years the general health of Americans has improved a great deal. The number of deaths from heart disease declined 15 percent between 1965 and 1975, but the number of cancer deaths rose 4 percent.[37] There has also been a significant rise in the number of deaths from respiratory diseases, kidney, and liver ailments. In spite of these increases, life expectancy continues to climb slowly. Many Americans are health wise. They have discovered that such things as a healthful diet (e.g., with more lean proteins, green, leafy vegetables, and less saturated fats), plenty of exercise, and a cutback on smoking and drinking can help them avoid costly medical bills. For other Americans the excessive use of alcohol and tobacco, nutritiously unsound diets, and a lack of exercise still constitute the major causes of disease and disability.

The discussion in Chapter 9 of the causes and ways to avoid heart disease will not be repeated here. However, it is reemphasized that exercise, dietary discretion, and avoidance of smoking are foremost as preventive measures. More information will be presented about the forms of cancer that typically have their onset in the fifties and early sixties. The increased occurrence of dental problems in middle age, diabetes mellitus, and the onset of visual disorders will also be presented.

Cancer

Lung cancer is the most frequent form of cancer in American men (22 percent of all cancers), followed by prostate cancer (17 percent) and colon cancer (14 percent).[38] As mentioned in Chapter 9, breast (26 percent) and uterine (14 percent) cancers are the most common for women. Women are also frequent victims of colon cancer (15 percent), leukemia or lymphomas (7 percent), and lung cancer (6 percent). Urinary tract carcinomas account for 9 percent of cancers in men and 2 percent of cancers in women, while oral tumors account for 5 percent of cancer in men and 2 percent of cancer in women.[39] Lung, prostate, colon, urinary tract, and oral cancers plus leukemia and lymphomas will be discussed in this section.

Lung cancer. There has been a rapid increase in lung cancer in recent years. It is the leading cause of cancer deaths in men, accounting for one in four deaths. It takes a heavy toll from the female population as well. The ratio of male to female lung cancer is about five to one.

Lung cancer is one of the most treacherous, rapidly spreading, and dangerous cancers. Early symptoms—a persistent cough, coughing up blood, difficult breathing—may be mistaken for other problems. Early diagnosis of lung cancer may be difficult, even with annual or semiannual chest x-rays. In view of the significant numbers of lung cancer deaths and the difficulty of early diagnosis by x-ray, researchers have sought new means of early detection. Experienced pathologists can detect early cases by examining the sputum of smokers for malignant cells. Late signs and symptoms of lung cancer include weight loss, hoarseness, and chest pain. Often a malignancy is diagnosed after a metastatic lesion (caused by the shifting of disease from one organ of the body to another) from it is discovered elsewhere.

The most widely publicized cause of lung cancer is cigarette smoking. The risks increase with the number of cigarettes smoked per day, inhalation, and duration of the habit. However, we all swim in a sea of carcinogens. Atmospheric pollutants are believed to irritate the lungs and possibly contribute to our rising rate of lung cancer. There are also numerous known hazards associated with certain occupations such as working with asbestos, beryllium, and ionizing radiation.

Lung cancers are sometimes resected through a lobectomy (removal of one of the lobes of the lung). Inoperable pulmonary cancers are treated with radiotherapy and chemotherapy to alleviate the symptoms. The earlier the tumors are detected and treated, the better. However, the overall five-year survival rate for lung cancer is very low, only 7 percent.[40]

Prostate cancer. Prostatic cancer exists in two forms: small tumors with slow growth that may persist unchanged for many years and aggressive, quickly metastasizing tumors that often prove fatal.[41] This cancer is rarely manifest in early adulthood but becomes increasingly common from the forties onward. An early symptom may be some difficulty associated with urination caused by pressure on the urethra from the growing tumor. However, back pain due to metastasis to the vertebral column may also be the first symptom noticed. Surgical removal of the prostate gland is used to treat cancers that are small or still confined within the prostatic capsule. With demonstrated bone or extrapelvic involvement, radiation or chemotherapy may be used in addition to or instead of surgery. The cure rate is best if the cancer is detected and removed early. Hormone therapy is an important mode of treatment in this disease. These cancers depend on androgens (testosterone from the testes and other androgens from the adrenal gland) for their growth. Treatment, therefore, may consist of removal of the testicle (orchidectomy) and/or the use of estrogens, the female steroid hormones.[42]

Cancer of the colon. Cancer of the large intestine is one of the most common causes of cancer deaths in the United States.[43] Symptoms usually occur a considerable time after the cancer develops. They include changes in bowel habits, constipation, or blood in the stool. They are frequently ignored or considered normal bowel function disturbances. Many persons do not seek medical advice until they also experience weakness, weight loss, or obstruction of the bowel. If the tumor can be removed before it spreads to the regional lymph nodes or lungs, the five-year survival rate is high (97.7 percent).[44] However, all too frequently the tumors are not discovered until metastasis has occurred. Cancer of the colon shows a markedly high intrafamilial occurrence rate, suggesting some genetic factors affecting susceptibility. With a known family history of colonic carcinoma, adults should request periodic sigmoidoscopic examinations from middle age onward.[45]

Resection of colonic cancers often entails a colostomy. This surgery usually involves removing the end of the colon (rectum), closing the anal opening, and establishing an artificial opening (stoma) for the colon through the lower abdominal wall. A person with a colostomy must wear a small bag attached to this opening to collect fecal materials that may be discharged at any time. Colostomy patients regularly irrigate their colons to evacuate the feces. Many establish once-a-day elimination patterns that make any appreciable amount of discharge into their bags a rare occurrence. Some colostomies can be reversed; bowel functions can then be returned to the anus after a period of time. However, after cancer of the colon permanent colostomies are more common. Ostomy societies have sprung up all over the country to enable persons who have had artificial openings made into their gastrointestinal canals (colostomy, ileostomy) to share problems, solutions, and self-care techniques with each other. The comradeship of these groups often helps to alleviate the problems of withdrawal and depression that may plague a person after an ostomy operation. If others can accept that an ostomy is not calamitous or even too unusual, the patient can usually return to his or her normal activities and lifestyle quite successfully.

Urinary tract cancer. Cancer of the bladder or kidneys seldom occurs prior to middle age. It is much more common in men than in women,

Figure 10–5. Persons who have had an ostomy operation often find that others like themselves provide the most help and encouragement in readjusting to the normal activities of daily living.

Oneonta Star

and its occurrence has been linked especially to exposure to certain industrial chemicals and dyes and to chronic irritation from bladder parasites.[46] There are suggestions that heavy cigarette smoking may also contribute to an increased incidence of bladder cancer due to irritation from tobacco tars that may be excreted in the urine. Symptoms of bladder cancer may include blood in the urine, frequent urination, or painful urination. As with other cancers, the cure rate depends on the rapidity of the treatment after detection and the extent of any metastasis. Treatment may be radiation, fulguration (destruction of tissue by means of heat from an electric current), or surgical resection of the tumor. Many bladder cancers have a tendency to recur following excision, making the prognosis for a cure somewhat guarded.[47]

Leukemias and lymphomas. Leukemias are cancerous growths of the blood cells originating in any of the blood-forming organs (bone marrow, liver, spleen, lymph nodes, thymus). Any of the different types of blood cells may be involved in the cancerous process, but the disease is characterized by an abnormally large number of a specific type of white blood cell found in the circulating blood and elsewhere without a demonstrable cause.[48]

The causes of leukemia are unknown, although researchers have recognized several probable contributing factors. Viruses, ionizing radiation, chemical agents (especially benzine derivatives), and genetic factors are all suspect and subject to ongoing investigation.

Leukemias are usually classified as acute or chronic and subclassified according to the predominant, abnormally growing cells. In the acute form symptoms develop rapidly; in the chronic form their onset is very gradual and may go unrecognized. Prior to currently available therapy, the categorizations into acute and chronic forms had some value in terms of predicting life expectancy. Now, some patients with acute leukemias may have their diseases brought into remission; they may live longer than some patients with chronic forms of leukemia.

As a consequence of the large growth of cancerous blood cells, there is an increase in the number of cells in the bone marrow and very often enlargement of the liver, spleen, and lymph glands. The crowding out of normal cells by the cancerous cells produces a loss of red blood cell production leading to anemia and its attendant fatigue. A loss of the normal white cell response causes increased susceptibility to infection, and a loss of the platelet-producing cells leads to easy bruising and abnormal bleeding.[49]

The treatment of acute leukemia usually reduces many of the attendant symptoms and complications of the disease and prolongs life.

Whether it prolongs life in chronic leukemia is not always clear. The different subclassifications of leukemia require different drug therapy programs, all aimed at reducing the number and controlling the rate of growth of leukemic cells. Adjunctive therapy including antibiotics, blood transfusions, and radiation therapy are aimed at controlling the complications of leukemia.

Lymphomas are malignancies arising in the lymph cell-producing areas (lymph nodes, spleen, liver, and areas in the intestine). The lymphomas include the lymphosarcomas and Hodgkin's disease. In lymphosarcoma, complaints and physical findings vary with the location of the tumors, which usually appear as large, firm lymph nodes matted together. Hodgkin's disease can take on several forms. It is a chronic, progressive illness with the same organs involved as in lymphosarcomas but with a different course. Pruritus (itching), fevers, anemia, and weight loss are all typical features. Treatment of both lymphosarcomas and Hodgkin's disease includes chemotherapy, radiation therapy, and sometimes surgical excision of isolated growths. The inherent nature of the tumor itself seems to be the most important factor in determining the course of these disorders. Some cases run chronic courses. Others run rapid, downhill courses despite treatment. In general, cases of localized disease with no fever or weight loss seem to have the best chance for long survival. Cases of cure, especially in Hodgkin's disease, are not unusual.[50]

Oral cancer. About 4 percent of all human cancers occur in the mouth.[51] Most oral cancers involve the lower lip. Many of the intraoral cancers involve the tongue. Environmental factors are important in these cancers. The major causative factor in lip cancer appears to be exposure to a lot of the sun's radiation. Intraoral cancers seem to be related to pipe and cigar smoking, use of chewing tobacco, and excessive consumption of alcohol. Oral cancers may at first be mistaken for canker sores or other mouth or lip irritations. They are frequently painless. Eventually they interfere with speech and/or chewing as they enlarge. Surgery is indicated as soon as the diagnosis is confirmed, before metastasis to lymph nodes, sinuses, bones, or lungs occurs.[52]

Dental considerations

During the first forty years of life, the main cause of tooth loss is dental caries, the bacteria-induced decay of the tooth's outer enamel. During early adulthood the worst problems most people have with their dentists are paying for the bills on their children's teeth or submitting to cleaning jobs, fillings, repairs on broken teeth, or replacement of lost fillings. After the fourth decade, however, gum diseases may become problematic. A new type of dental caries, the caries of maturity, occurs. It attacks the cervix (neck) of the teeth near the gumline. It is caused by a type of oral pathogen, the *Odontalmyces viscosis*, which is not prevalent in the mouths of younger adults.[53] An enzyme, collagenase, produced by bacteria that accumulate in plaques on the surface of the teeth, breaks down the attachments of the teeth to the surrounding bone.[54] As a result, middle-aged people may begin to develop pyorrhea (loose teeth and sometimes even emanation of pus from the gingiva around the teeth). Treatment is largely preventive and is aimed at removing the plaques with frequent, careful brushing. While proper tooth and mouth cleansing and avoidance of excess sugars can eliminate the need for extractions of teeth in the later years, many Americans fail to pay attention to their teeth until it is too late. Consequently, it is common for people to begin wearing partial or complete dental plates by middle age.

Improperly fitted false teeth can cause chronic mouth irritations and possibly contribute to the development of malnutrition in some people. Denture plates may need periodic adjustments to assure continued good fit with advancing age because the bony structure of the mouth often changes as bone mass and amount of mineralized tissues decrease. In spite of preparations that are advertised to hold dentures firmly in place "no matter what one eats," people with false teeth may find it impossible or extremely difficult to chew some foods like charcoal-broiled steaks and corn on the cob.

Diabetes mellitus

Diabetes mellitus, or simply diabetes, is a disorder with metabolic and vascular (small blood vessel disease) components. It is one of the most common diseases of metabolism, affecting millions of Americans. Diabetes increases in frequency with every decade of life. The United States Public Health Service estimates that there are thirty-three diabetics out of every 1000 Americans between forty-five and fifty-four years old, fifty-six diabetics out of every 1000 Americans between fifty-five and sixty-four years old, and sixty-nine diabetics out of every 1000 Americans between sixty-five and seventy-four years old.[55]

The main feature of diabetes is a high blood glucose level (hyperglycemia) often associated with glucose in the urine. This hyperglycemia results from underutilization of glucose by the tissues and overproduction of glucose by conversion from other substances (mainly from amino acid subunits of protein and from liver glycogen). The central hormones associated with diabetes are insulin and glucagon, both products of the pancreas. Insulin has many actions, but its essential role is in promoting entry, storage, and utilization of glucose, amino acids, and fats in tissues. In its absence, or in the excessive presence of its antagonist, glucagon, glucose, amino acids, and fats cannot enter tissues. On the contrary, the muscle and fat tissues break down and release amino acids and fats into the blood. Many of these products then spill into the urine in large amounts to the detriment of the body. The condition is really one of starvation of the body's cells.

In Chapter 5 juvenile diabetes was briefly discussed. It should be pointed out now, for clarification, that in the juvenile form of diabetes there is a total or almost total lack of insulin production. In order to survive, the diabetic must have insulin administered. Thus, juvenile diabetics are better termed insulin-dependent diabetics. There is further confusion in that persons in their twenties and thirties sometimes develop the "juvenile," insulin-dependent type of diabetes. Typical symptoms of this form of the disease are loss of weight, weakness, excessive hunger and thirst, and frequent urination.

Maturity-onset diabetes has a less stormy beginning. It is very often completely asymptomatic. It may be discovered in routine diabetes screening, which consists of measuring blood glucose in the fasting state or during the two-hour period after a glucose loading. It is often looked for when other disorders are observed that are known to be related to diabetes. In maturity-onset diabetes insulin is present. In fact, in obese diabetics it is often found in even higher levels than it is in slender, healthy persons. Maturity-onset diabetics most often do not require insulin. They can, therefore, be referred to as non-insulin-dependent diabetics. It has become recognized that tissues become less sensitive to insulin with aging. In order for normal blood sugar levels to be maintained, more insulin must be secreted. Obesity at all ages produces insulin resistance in tissues. This phenomenon is not well understood to date. The tendency to being overweight with increased age is surely related to the increased prevalence of diabetes with every decade. In addition to the factors of aging and obesity, there is clearly a genetic predisposition to maturity-onset diabetes.[56]

The relative lack of insulin causes the hyperglycemia that is thought to lead to the complications of diabetes. Recently, attention has also been given to the production of a substance called sorbitol from glucose present in high amounts in the blood. Sorbitol has also been implicated in the complications of diabetes. It accumulates in some tissues, causing swelling and dysfunction. It is currently accepted as the biochemical explanation for the high prevalence of cataracts and peripheral neuropathies in diabetics.[57] Peripheral neuropathies are manifested by feelings of tingling, numbness, or burning, generally of the feet. Diabetics with peripheral neuropathies often develop painless breakdown of the skin of their feet, leading to infected ulcers or gangrenous toes. Elevated blood glucose levels also lead to abnormalities in the walls of blood vessels, resulting in renal (kidney) and retinal (eye) disease.[58]

Often the adult with mild diabetes (mildly elevated blood sugar, no complications) can reduce blood sugar by weight loss, by decreased intake of refined sugars in the diet, and by exercise to promote glucose utilization. Drug treatment of maturity-onset diabetes includes agents that promote the release of insulin from the pancreas. Insulin must also be administered to some maturity-onset diabetics. When drugs or insulin are used, caution must be taken to recognize symptoms of low blood sugar and to respond appropriately.

Adult diabetes should be carefully controlled by a combination of actions that may include drug or insulin administration, weight reduction, limited use of refined sugars, and exercise. Close attention to the above, in addition to extra attention given at times of infection or injury, gives diabetics the best chance for longer lives free of complications.

Visual disorders

The causes of impairment of vision may vary with age. By the fifties and early sixties cataracts, glaucoma, and disorders of the retina such as retinal hemmorrhage are the most frequent causes of impaired vision. This is in contrast to the first four decades when the most frequent problems were refractive errors that could be corrected easily with glasses.

Glaucoma, characterized by increased pressure within the globe of the eye, is a common problem occurring in 2 percent of all persons over the age of forty.[59] Most of the time the cause is unknown. It may be asymptomatic and progress slowly in producing loss of vision. Glaucoma can and should be easily recognized by physicians and is easily treated with medication. Because it so often is not detected early in its course, it is a major cause of visual loss in the later adult years.

A cataract is a density of the lens of the eye, most often due to degenerative changes in the lens. It also may follow trauma to the eye or lens and is often associated with diabetes. A cataract first occurs as a progressive, painless loss of vision. The amount of visual loss depends on the location and the degree of density in the lens. Surgical removal of the lens is indicated when there is significant density producing loss of vision.[60]

Summary

The fifties and early sixties can be years of peak status and power: in the family, in the community, in the world of work. Health may continue to be excellent or begin to decline. Physical strength and stamina are diminished, and signs of aging are evident. Yet, vast numbers of persons in this age span still feel in the prime of their lives.

Family responsibilities can be problematic—launching children (to jobs, to marriage, to higher education), adjusting to the empty nest, reworking marital relationships, helping aging parents. Typically, however, family responsibilities will decrease, and time for work, leisure, and social activities will increase during these years.

Women are generally more affected by the empty nest syndrome than men. Many seek new postparental roles in paid jobs or as volunteers. This embarkation on a second career may be seen as a revving up rather than as a winding down of one's life.

Women and men who have been pursuing careers for many years often find that in their fifties and early sixties they are regarded as experts by their coworkers. Many become mentors (loyal advisors and friends) to younger adults who are just starting careers.

Marriages, when they survive, tend to become more stable and satisfying after the traumas of launching offspring. Spouses may look to each other more for approval and companionship.

Specific circumstances and points of view may make the experiences of designing son- and daughter-in-law relationships problematic, gratifying, or both for persons in their fifties and early sixties. Likewise, grandparenting and caring for one's own aging parents can be hard work, rewarding, or a little of each.

Introspection, a looking into one's own mind, feelings, and reactions, is a common tendency in the fifties. Individuals often restructure their concepts of self and time and plan for the rest of their lives. Most tend to be more self-accepting and less self-assertive than in previous decades.

Erik Erikson saw the conflicts associated with these years as leading either to a state of ego integrity or one of despair. When adults can acknowledge that their work and leisure are their own responsibility and accept the accomplishments and failures, satisfactions, and disappointments of their lives, they move toward ego integrity. Despair results if they overemphasize their frustrations, blame others for them, and refuse to accept their life cycle as something that had to be.

Health maintenance requires attention to diet, exercise, safety precautions, rest and relaxation, and prompt treatment of disease symptoms. The most common health problems of this age span are heart disease, cancer, vascular lesions, accidents, and cirrhosis. Dental problems, visual disorders, and maturity-onset diabetes also increasingly occur during these years.

Questions for review

1. What sorts of things might mothers do to prepare themselves for coping with the "empty nest" situation? What might fathers do?
2. Recent articles indicate a revitalized interest in physical activity and exercise. What do you think are some of the causes of this renewed interest, especially in older persons?
3. Why do you think it is true that parents tend to intrude more in their children's married lives when their children marry young?
4. Divorce rates tend to be high within the first five years of marriage. They are also substantial after children are grown and leave home. Discuss what sorts of adjustments or stresses occur in these periods that might lead to high rates of divorce.
5. It has been said that women's lives involve constant shifts into new roles. From the chapters you have read thus far, give examples of these various forms of role shifts.
6. Recent literature suggests the work ethic is changing, saying that Americans no longer feel so compelled to work hard. Do you agree or disagree with this? Discuss.
7. Erikson describes ego integrity as self-acceptance and labels the opposite as a sense of despair. How do you think family and friends affect the achievement of ego integrity? Discuss.
8. Individuals who have cancer often speak of rejection, avoidance by others, and inability to discuss their feelings with others. Why do you think these reactions prevail? What sorts of information would help others react more openly to the cancer patient?
9. Differentiate between juvenile diabetes and maturity-onset diabetes. What are the variations in treatment for these two diseases?

References

[1]E. Bierman and W. Hazzard, "Old Age," *The Biologic Ages of Man from Conception Through Old Age*, D. Smith and E. Bierman, eds. (Philadelphia: W. B. Saunders Co., 1973).

[2]W. Masters and V. Johnson, *Human Sexual Response* (Boston: Little, Brown and Co., 1966).

[3]Ibid.

[4]P. Baltes and K. Schaie, "Aging and IQ: The Myth of the Twilight Years," *Psychology Today*, 7 (1974).

[5]J. Botwinick, *Cognitive Processes in Maturity and Old Age* (New York: Springer, 1967).

[6]E. Duvall, *Family Development*, 4th ed. (Philadelphia: Lippincott, 1971).

[7]Ibid.

[8]G. Leslie, *The Family in Social Context* (New York: Oxford University Press, 1967).

[9]D. Kieren, J. Henton, and R. Marotz, *His and Hers: A Problem-Solving Approach to Marriage* (Hinsdale, Ill.: The Dryden Press, 1975).

[10]Ibid.

[11]J. Hillman, "Archetypal Theory: C. G. Jung," *Operational Theories of Personality*, A. Burton, ed. (New York: Brunner/Mazel, 1974).

[12]B. Neugarten, "Adult Personality: Toward a Psychology of the Life Cycle," *Middle Age and Aging*, B. Neugarten, ed. (Chicago: University of Chicago Press, 1968).

[13]Ibid.

[14]B. Neugarten, "The Awareness of Middle Age," *Middle Age and Aging*, B. Neugarten, ed. (Chicago: University of Chicago Press, 1968).

[15]R. Gould, "The Phases of Adult Life: A Study in Developmental Psychology," *American Journal of Psychiatry*, 129(5) (1972).

[16]D. Gutmann, "Aging Among the Highland Maya: A Comparative Study," *Journal of Personality and Social Psychology*, 7(1) (1967).

[17]A. Krohn and D. Gutmann, "Changes in Mastery Styles with Age: A Study of Navajo Dreams," *Psychiatry*, 34(3) (1971).

[18]Ibid.

[19]B. Neugarten and D. Gutmann, "Age-Sex Roles and Personality in Middle Age: A Thermatic Apperception Study," *Middle Age and Aging*, B. Neugarten, ed. (Chicago: University of Chicago Press, 1968).

[20]B. Rollins and H. Feldman, "Marital Satisfaction Over the Family Life Cycle," *Journal of Marriage and the Family*, 32(1) (1970).

[21]D. Kieren, J. Henton, and R. Marotz, *His and Hers: A Problem-Solving Approach to Marriage.*

[22]R. Gould, "The Phases of Adult Life."

[23]W. Masters and V. Johnson, "Emotional Poverty: A Marriage Crisis of the Middle Years," *Quality of Life: The Middle Years* (Acton, Mass.: Publishing Sciences Group, Inc., 1974).

[24]Ibid.

[25]B. Neugarten and K. Weinstein, "The Changing American Grandparent," *Middle Age and Aging*, B. Neugarten, ed. (Chicago: University of Chicago Press, 1968).

[26]Ibid.

[27]B. Neugarten, "The Awareness of Middle Age."

[28]R. Gould, "The Phases of Adult Life."

[29]E. Shanas and G. Streib, *Social Structure and the Family: Generational Relations* (Englewood Cliffs, N.J.: Prentice-Hall, 1965).

[30]L. Epstein and J. Murray, "Employment and Retirement," *Middle Age and Aging*, B. Neugarten, ed. (Chicago: University of Chicago Press, 1968).

[31]B. Neugarten, "The Roles We Play," *Quality of Life: The Middle Years* (Acton, Mass.: Publishing Sciences Group, Inc., 1974).

[32]W. Masters and V. Johnson, *Human Sexual Response.*

[33]J. Kelly, "Work and Leisure: A Simplified Paradigm," *Journal of Leisure Research*, 4(1) (1972).

[34]E. Erikson, *Childhood and Society*, 2nd ed. (New York: W. W. Norton & Co., Inc., 1963).

[35]Ibid.

[36]American Public Health Association, *Vital and Health Statistics Monographs: Mortality and Morbidity in the United States*, C. Erhardt and J. Berlin, eds. (Cambridge, Mass.: Harvard University Press, 1974).

[37]United States Department of Health, Education and Welfare, *Health: United States, 1975*, T. Cooper, ed. (Washington: U.S. Government Printing Office, 1976).

[38]E. Silverberg, "Cancer Statistics, 1977," *CA-A Cancer Journal for Clinicians*, 27(1).

[39]Ibid.

[40]S. Robbins, *Pathologic Basis of Disease* (Philadelphia: W. B. Saunders Co., 1974).

[41]R. Flocks, "Carcinoma of the Prostate," *Journal of Urology*, 101 (1969).

[42]B. Lytton and F. Epstein, "Tumors of the Urinary Tract," *Harrison's Principles of Internal Medicine*, 7th ed. M. Wintrobe et al., eds. (New York: McGraw-Hill, 1974).

[43]S. Robbins, *Pathologic Basis of Disease.*

[44]Ibid.

[45]Ibid.

[46]Ibid.

[47]Ibid.

[48]D. Boggs and M. Wintrobe, "The Leukemias," *Harrison's Principles of Internal Medicine*, 7th ed. M. Wintrobe et al., eds. (New York: McGraw-Hill, 1974).

[49]Ibid.

[50]M. Wintrobe and D. Boggs, "Hodgkin's Disease and other Lymphomas," *Harrison's Principles of Internal Medicine,* 7th ed. M. Wintrobe et al., eds. (New York: McGraw-Hill, 1974).

[51]E. Silverberg, "Cancer Statistics, 1977."

[52]S. Robbins, *Pathologic Basis of Disease.*

[53]M. Massler, "Dental Considerations in the Later Years," *Quality of Life: The Later Years,* E. Brown and E. Ellis, eds. (Acton, Mass.: Publishing Sciences Group, Inc., 1975).

[54]Ibid.

[55]J. Steinke and G. Thorn, "Diabetes Mellitus," *Harrison's Principles of Internal Medicine,* 7th ed. M. Wintrobe et al., eds. (New York: McGraw-Hill, 1974).

[56]Ibid.

[57]D. Villee, *Human Endocrinology: A Developmental Approach* (Philadelphia: W. B. Saunders, Co., 1975).

[58]J. Steinke and G. Thorn, "Diabetes Mellitus."

[59]M. Victor and R. Adams, "Common Disturbances of Vision, Ocular Movement, and Hearing," *Harrison's Principles of Internal Medicine,* 7th ed. M. Wintrobe et al., eds. (New York: McGraw-Hill, 1974).

[60]Ibid.

Contents

Dennis Stock/Magnum Photos, Inc.

The Later Years

The voters of the United States during the 1976 presidential campaign did very little to suggest that they felt the sixties were retirement years. Gerald Ford and Ronald Reagan were sixty-three and sixty-five respectively. Nowhere was it suggested that their ages were responsible for their defeats. Consider the meaning of old age in persons like George Burns, who won an Oscar as a septuagenarian (seventy-nine), or Arthur Rubenstein, who gave demanding and brilliantly performed piano concerts as an octogenarian, or nonagenarian Pablo Picasso, who painted masterpieces until his death at ninety-two, or centenarian Grandma Moses, who painted popular landscapes until age 101. (Grandma Moses did not start painting until age seventy-four.) Many individuals maintain their vim, zest, vitality, and a real *joie de vivre* (keen enjoyment of the pleasures of life) well beyond their sixty-fifth year.

Old age is a difficult topic for many to discuss. Our youth-loving culture generally fears growing old. Sometimes this translates into a fear of older persons. Society creates euphemisms for them: senior citizens, retirees, golden-agers, the sunshine crowd. Some older individuals are healthy, some are ill. Some are crippled, some rich, some poor. Some are venerable and revered, some feisty, some mellow, some ageless. In every imaginable category they account for about 10 percent of the population of the United States or 23 million persons.[1] Older adults will be discussed just as persons in all other decades of the life span—in terms of physical changes, cognitive abilities, social interactions (especially as they involve the family and the community), and in terms of health.

Physical changes

The physical appearances of individuals over sixty-five vary as much as those of individuals of earlier decades. Call forth mental images of two or more persons you know who are beyond sixty-five. Consider various aspects of these persons: hair color, skin tone, posture, mobility, voice, eating behavior. These persons may have few if any similarities. Despite the fact that you may have chosen persons at the far extremes of a thirty-or-so year age range, the external appearances of old people are not identical. The physical changes that accompany aging appear at different times and in different ways in all individuals. Persons who have escaped chronic or debilitating diseases into their later years and who exercise regularly and watch their diets carefully stand a much better chance of retaining a vigorous appearance than persons who have experienced debilitating illness, chronic disease, obesity, or muscular atrophy.

Chronological age cannot be used as a predictor of physical decline. In some cultures (e.g., Hunza, Pakistan; Georgia, Russia; Vilcabamba, Equador) and even in some American families, longevity is the rule, not the exception. One elderly Russian who died in 1966 claimed to be 160 years old and to have fathered 130 children.[2] While his story has been recorded as within the realm of possibility, it is not considered fact (nor are Methuselah's 969 years, Genesis 6:27), because of the imprecise methods of recording age in past centuries. The reasons for physical decline, or the lack of it, are poorly understood. Some hypothetical reasons for the failure of cells to reproduce themselves in old age were discussed in Chapter 10 and will be continued here. More of the changes that accompany advanced old age will also be described.

Senescence

The term *senescence* refers to the process of growing old, with the accompanying decrease in functional abilities. It is sometimes confused with senility. Senility refers to some degenerative condition of the brain with problems of confusion and disorientation. It does not occur in all old persons, as senescence does. We will discuss senility further in the health section of this chapter (see pp. 450–451).

Explanations of why senescence occurs differ among the biologists studying the phenomenon. Some feel that hormones act on cells to inhibit their reproductive ability. Others feel that every individual has a genetically preprogrammed "clock of aging" within their cells that dictates how and when the cells will slow down and eventually die.

Research by W. Donner Denckla suggests that aging occurs partially because the pituitary gland controlled by the hypothalamus of the brain stimulates the production of less thyroid hormones by the thyroid gland.[3] The active form of thyroid hormone is triiodothyronine. The thyroid gland secretes some triiodothyronine, but most of what is found in the blood is derived from the other thyroid hormone, thyroxine. Although thyroxine levels do not decrease with aging, triiodothyronine levels do. The thyroid gland does not secrete more thyroxine to compensate for this. Denckla's research also points to the possibility that the pituitary gland secretes another hormone, called DECO (decreased consumption of oxygen). It may have a blocking effect on cells, preventing them from using the thyroxine normally circulating in the blood.

Research studies by other scientists, notably Leonard Hayflick, suggest that the DNA molecules in genes may have coded instructions for the cell to slow down, stop dividing, and ultimately die after a certain period of time.[4] Cells that Hayflick raised in culture mediums typically divided a certain number of times (depending on the life span of the species from which they were taken), then stopped. If cells were frozen before they reached the end of their life span, they seemed to remember how far they had come once they were thawed and continued to divide the number of times typical for their species before dying.

During the gradual onset of senescence, the body undergoes degenerative structural and functional changes. Lean body mass decreases slightly because of a gradual decrease of bone, muscle, cartilage, and connective tissue mass.

The loss of bone density and mass causes a compression of the bones, especially in the vertebral area, creating a slight decrease in height. The loss of mass in the mandible (jawbone) produces a change in the physical appearance of the chin. All bones break more easily and recuperate more slowly. A loss of cartilage makes painful joint complaints more common and contributes to a decreased range of movement and mobility. A curved posture becomes increasingly more common with age: the head down, the back and knees bent, and a forward pitch with small, shuffling steps when walking.[5] Older persons usually do most tasks slowly. James McCracken offered this remembrance of how his elderly father got out of a chair. "He'd sit in his chair just thinking about getting up. He'd run his hands up the arms of the chair a little way, brace, and push. And he'd stand up. Well, he was up. He'd stand for a moment, put his hands on the back of his hips. He'd still be bent over a little bit. But then he'd straighten up and be off about his business."[6]

Vision deteriorates steadily beyond the sixties, and problems of cataracts, glaucoma, retinal disease, and presbyopia continue. Anderson and Palmore reported finding a best corrected vision of 20/50 in approximately 8 percent of persons in their sixties, 14 percent of persons in their seventies, and 36 percent of persons over eighty.[7] Changes in the eye also decrease the rapidity with which older persons can accommodate to variations between dark and light. Vision may be adequate when the darkness or light is constant, but sudden changes to more or less light may cause temporary blindness. Night driving is more hazardous for older persons for this reason. Color perception and depth perception also become less accurate.[8]

Hearing losses are so common among old people that persons who have lived or worked among the aged for any length of time habitually raise their voices to all older persons. Higher tones are more difficult to hear than low ones.[9] Many old people, either unaware of their hearing losses or hesitant to admit such a loss, may pretend to understand messages that they actually did not hear completely. Or they may try to piece together what they did hear and fill in the blanks. As a result, they may receive the wrong message. Noise pollution (background noises) may further distort or mask messages for hard-of-hearing persons.

A loss of vestibular function in the inner ears may give old people difficulty with balance. They may sway slightly when standing or experience dizziness when rising, when viewing heights, or when trying to climb hills. They may lose their balance and fall quite frequently.

Because of the loss of lean body mass, there is a relative increase in the body's fat content. While many old persons have problems with obesity, appetites usually are less keen. Stamina and strength are greatly diminished regardless of caloric intake. The basal metabolic rate (BMR), a measure of the body's uptake of oxygen for metabolism, decreases.

Eating is often problematic. Many aged people are poorly nourished, whatever their weight. A decreased number of taste buds makes food less interesting. A reduced amount of saliva and digestive juices of the stomach makes indigestion more common. Reduced absorption from the intestines, sluggish peristaltic movements, and decreased secretions of the intestinal mucosa add to constipation problems, as do diets low in bulk and fiber. A loss of teeth may make chewing many foods difficult. Diets are often unbalanced for reasons of economics (protein foods are expensive) and preparation procedures (cooking may be difficult due to arthritis and visual disturbances).[10]

Hair may turn white in old age due to loss of pigmentation at the roots. Pigment deposits in skin cells may produce "age spots" on the hands, face, and other body surfaces. The skin gradually loses its elasticity and may develop folds or jowls. If an old person loses weight, skin is apt to hang loosely for a long time in areas once filled by deposits of fat. Skin surfaces that are allowed to dry out may take on a withered look. Decubitus ulcers (bedsores, pressure sores) may develop in places where circulation is impaired by prolonged sitting or lying.

All of the above descriptions may make growing old seem painful or cruel. Remember that the types and degrees of change occur gradually over a long period of time and vary greatly from individual to individual. A great many of the twenty million people beyond age sixty-five in the United States enjoy their lives. They would not all agree that being old is intolerable. They might argue, quite persuasively, that being sixteen, or twenty-six, or thirty-six is more difficult.

Cognitive abilities

Just as not all people become senile, not all people experience cognitive disabilities in old age. The questions of whether intelligence declines, how much it declines, and why are not yet adequately answered by research.

The idea that intellectual abilities do fall off with age has been suggested and demonstrated in numerous cross-sectional research studies. For example, using the Wechsler Adult Intelligence Scale (WAIS) to ap-

Figure 11–1. A great many healthy, aged persons resemble healthy, young persons in their physical, cognitive, social, and emotional needs and behaviors. When old people feel accepted as loved and useful members of their families and society, their lives continue to have meaning and value.

Leslie Davis

praise the IQs of large numbers of aging persons, Wechsler in 1958, Eisdorfer and Cohen in 1961, and Botwinick in 1970 all reported that the oldest people scored less well than the younger subjects.[11, 12, 13] However, the latter two research reports expressed concern about interpreting the results as conclusive of an age-related IQ decline. In cross-sectional research the subjects cannot be matched for their initial level of intelligence, since they are only tested once. Even if chance allowed for an equal distribution of persons of initially high, average, and low IQ to be tested in each age group, other factors make the results inconclusive. The WAIS questions are geared to predict adult success in learning various academic subjects. They are not particularly relevant to the concerns of old people. Consequently, the elderly may become bored, tired, or lack the motivation to do well on the examinations. Younger adults are apt to be both better educated and more test-wise than their elders. Test wisdom refers to one's knowledge of how to choose right answers on an examination. Some students may know less of the material covered in a course than others but score better on tests because of this test wisdom.

Cross-sectional researchers have also used nonverbal and less culture bound tests of intelligence with old people. For example, Heron and Chown used the Raven Progressive Matrices Test and Schaie used Thurstone's Primary Mental Abilities Test.[14, 15] These studies also reported results indicating that older subjects perform below the level of younger adults.

Longitudinal studies are felt to be more accurate indicators of intellectual changes since they test and retest the same persons over a period of years. Schaie and Strother's seven-year longitudinal study and Eisdorfer and Wilkie's ten-year study are representative of this kind of research.[16, 17] They found some IQ decline with age, but results were very individualistic. While some persons showed a decline, others demonstrated quite stable ability levels over time. Wilkie and Eisdorfer, Riegel and Riegel, and others have suggested that there probably exists a "terminal decline" in intelligence.[18, 19] A significant drop in IQ test scores often precedes death. Researchers have repeatedly observed that old persons who score poorly have died before the next year's retest period. This intellectual loss may reflect other pathological processes in the body that cause death. For example, blood vessels that are narrowed by atherosclerosis can cause diminished blood supply to the brain as well as cause coronary heart disease with its associated sequelae. Malignancies may metastasize to the brain as well as to other body parts. Biological processes may account for many of the intellectual difficulties noted in some older persons. Cardiovascular disease, emphysema, acute infections, poor nutrition, lack of exercise, injuries, or surgery may all temporarily or permanently diminish, to some degree, the blood supply of oxygen to the brain. Hearing or visual losses may interfere with comprehension of incoming information. Senescent changes in the electrical and chemical functioning of the brain cells may diminish their ability to code and store new memories. Even the decreased speed of transmission of information along the neurons may slow down learning. While biological processes may set limits on the intellectual functioning of many elderly persons, learning and problem solving are still possible, especially if the pace is slow and information is imparted loudly and clearly.[20] Remember that some individuals show little or no cognitive disabilities in spite of advanced old age.

Environmental events, alone or in conjunction with biological processes, may also interfere with cognition. A loss of self-esteem or self-confidence, a loss of interest in external events, a loss of motivation to do well, and feelings of rejection or depression may cause an apparent or real decline in abilities to perceive, remember, and reason.

Social interactions

The preceding adulthood chapters have highlighted the social theories and research findings of Carl Jung, Erik Erikson, Bernice Neugarten, Robert Havighurst, Daniel Levinson, Roger Gould, and George Vaillant. Charlotte Bühler, who collected data on Europeans in the 1920s and 1930s, also wrote especially rich descriptions of adult personality changes. She defined the retirement phase as beginning at approximately age sixty-four.[21] While her findings are old, they have been, in large part, supported by more recent research. This chapter will briefly review Havighurst's and Bühler's work and then present the ways in which Neugarten and Maas and Kuypers describe personality orientations of contemporary elderly Americans.

Robert Havighurst called old age "later maturity." He saw the following as developmental tasks to be accomplished:

> Adjusting to decreasing physical strength and health.
>
> Adjusting to retirement and reduced income.
>
> Adjusting to death of spouse.
>
> Establishing an explicit affiliation with one's age group.
>
> Adjusting and adapting social roles in a flexible way.
>
> Establishing satisfactory physical living arrangements.[22]

Interfamilial relationships and the relations that elderly persons may have with others in their communities will be described in this section.

Family interactions

In some societies, and in a few American families, the old reside with the young and are an integral, honored part of the household, whether they help with the work load, add to it, or do a little of both. However, more often in our culture (in about 75 percent of all cases) the old live apart from the young.[23] Families differ in the ways they regard their elders: as beloved grand- or great-grandparents, as dons or dowagers to be courted with favors in hopes of an inheritance, as burdens, as persons already three-quarters dead. Just as younger adults vary in the ways they regard their elders (sentimentally, solicitously, disdainfully, neglectfully), old persons vary in the ways in which they treat the younger generations (lovingly, angrily, disparagingly). Research has not shown that any particular racial, religious, or cultural group categorically experiences a better old age. Factors such as health, wealth, longevity, past experiences, surviving kin, and intrafamilial communication patterns make the personalities and lifestyles of persons in America over sixty-five very diversified.

Personality orientations. Charlotte Bühler found that most of the older European people she studied in the 1920s and 1930s could be classified into one of four personality types: (1) those who were satisfied with their past lives and were content to relax; (2) those who would not sit back but felt they must strive to the end; (3) those who were dissatisfied with their past lives and sat back with an unhappy air of resignation; and (4) those who were dissatisfied with their lives and continued to experience regrets, frustrations, and feelings of guilt until the end.[24]

Neugarten, Havighurst, and Tobin more recently described four similar personality patterns of older Americans: (1) integrated personalities, (2) armored-defended personalities, (3) passive-dependent personalities, and (4) unintegrated personalities.[25] While integrated persons all faced up to their emotions and experienced rich inner lives, their outward behaviors varied from those who reorganized their activities, substituting new ones for old ones, to those who focused on one or two activities, to those who just chose a rocking-chair approach to old age. Armored-defended personalities held their impulses and emotions in tight harness and were satisfied to restrain their creativity. Passive-dependent personalities were less satisfied with life. While some remained apathetic, others gleaned a measure of contentment from leaning on and receiving succor from other persons. Unintegrated personalities were characterized by dissatisfactions, disorganization, and low activity levels.[26]

Maas and Kuypers described seven personality patterns of

Figure 11–2. *Persons over sixty-five do not fit into any one stereotype. They are just as different as the persons included in any other age bracket. They vary in abilities, in person orientations, in activities, in health, and in life satisfaction.*
Burk Uzzle/Magnum Photos, Inc.

elderly, middle-class, white subjects studied in California over a forty-year time span, ending in the 1970s.[27] Four of the patterns pictured women and three detailed men. The 142 subjects ranged in age from sixty to eighty-two, with the average woman's age being sixty-nine and the men's seventy-one. All of the persons studied had been married and had had children.

Women were grouped as (1) person-oriented mothers, (2) fearful-ordering mothers, (3) autonomous mothers, and (4) anxious-asserting mothers.[28] Person-oriented women were giving, sympathetic, warm, and well liked. Fearful-ordering women were withdrawn, reassurance-seeking, anxious individuals who found little personal meaning to their worlds. Autonomous mothers were involved more with formal organizations than with their families. They kept others at a distance and were independent, productive, and self-defensive. Anxious-asserting women were histrionic and self-dramatizing and were apt to be moody and hostile as well as talkative.

The Maas and Kuypers data argued against the stereotype of

all old people being negative, depressed, and disabled. Everyone was very individual, even down to his or her physical manifestations of age. Men were grouped as (1) person-oriented fathers, (2) active-competent fathers, and (3) conservative-ordering fathers.[29] The person-oriented men were warm, sympathetic, and giving. They sought more reassurance and were less socially poised than the person-oriented women but were still popular. Active-competent men were power conscious, aloof, verbally fluent, charming persons who were also rebellious and nonconforming to social expectations. Conservative-ordering men were similar to the fearful-ordering women. However, they were not as anxious and afraid. They were self-satisfied but also overcontrolled, repressive, and conventional.

Maas and Kuypers reported that personality changes very definitely occurred over the forty-year time span. Not all person-oriented older men were gregarious young men, for example, nor were all fearful-ordering women anxious in early adulthood.

Lifestyles. Maas and Kuypers identified ten different lifestyles into which the elderly could be clustered. While the lifestyles were not matched to the personality types in any meaningful way, certain personality types were noted to be more likely to pursue various components of a particular lifestyle. The lifestyles into which women could be clustered were (1) husband-centered wives, (2) uncentered mothers, (3) visiting mothers, (4) work-centered mothers, (5) disabled-disengaging mothers, and (6) group-centered mothers.[30] Husband-centered women were more interested in their spouses than in their children, grandchildren, and siblings. Uncentered women were most apt to live alone, be in poor health, and have meager financial resources. Visiting mothers had frequent social interactions in churches, clubs, and their own or others' homes. Work-centered women were more apt to be widows or divorcees, to live alone, to be in good health, and to enjoy full- or part-time jobs. The disabled-disengaging mothers were frequently in poor health but lived with others from whom they would withdraw. The group-centered mothers differed from the visiting mothers in that they preferred formal social functions. They were usually from well-to-do families and had high education levels.

The lifestyles of the men developed independently from those of the women. A husband-centered wife was not, for example, necessarily married to a family-centered man. The four groupings into which the elderly men fit were (1) family-centered fathers, (2) hobbyists, (3) remotely sociable fathers, and (4) unwell-disengaged fathers.[31] The family-centered men had children living nearby whom they visited often. The hobbyists lived farther from their children. The core of their lives was their leisure-time interests and activities. Remotely sociable fathers were more involved in formal activities (politics, social organizations) than in interpersonal relationships. Unwell-disengaged fathers were most apt to be in poor health and have few friends.

The lifestyles of the men showed more continuity over the forty-year span into old age than did the living modes of women. This may be due to the fact that women are more affected by loss of children, loss or gain of outside employment, and changing marital and family situations than men. They make more adaptations in their lifestyles to cope with these altered circumstances.

Maas and Kuypers saw disengagement (withdrawal and detachment from obligations, occupations, relationships) as a phenomenon mainly affecting people in ill health. Cumming and Henry theorized that disengagement is a natural part of aging and that old people and society mutually separate from each other.[32] Kuhlen, after looking at the data on disengagement, felt that the separation is due more to the attitudes of society; old people withdraw because they feel unloved and unwanted, and they often resent being neglected.[33] Havighurst, Neugarten, and Tobin found that feelings in older people of satisfaction with life were correlated more with participation than with disengagement.[34]Robert Butler, who was appointed the first director of our National Institute on Aging in 1975, stated in his Pulitzer Prize-winning book, *Why Survive: Being Old in America,* that disengagement of all old people from society is a myth. It is merely one of many patterns of reaction to old age.[35]

Spouse relationships. Another myth attacked by Butler, but still prevalent in our society, is a belief that emotions become dulled as people age. The myth of serenity portrays the elderly as peaceful, carefree, relaxed persons, beyond the storms and stresses of their earlier years. In fact, emotional reactions of the elderly remain powerful enough to trigger divorces, marriages, outbursts of rage, psychosomatic illnesses, deep depressions, or any of the other manifestations of tumultuous emotions that affect younger adults. Some aging individuals perceive that they have lost their power to accomplish change by giving vent to their emotions. Consequently, they may practice silence. However, this reaction does not indicate that they are immune to insults, injustices, rejections, feelings of despair, and the like.

Many people also believe sexual desire is dulled with age. However, as reported in Chapters 9 and 10, sexual interests and performance need not cease after menopause or after a male experiences slowed erection time and diminished ejaculatory volume. When partners are interested and willing to help each other find ways to stimulate libido, sexual activity can often be maintained throughout the life span.

Butler described a sentiment in our society similar to racism and sexism, but aimed at old persons, that he termed ageism.[36] It is a process of systematic stereotyping of old people in which they are seen as old-fashioned in morality, rigid in thought and manner, and senile. Ageism allows younger adults to see the elderly as something very different from themselves and consequently permits them to stop identifying with old people. Ageism takes a cruel turn where sexuality is concerned. Old people often become the butt of sexual jokes; they are portrayed as exhibitionists, dirty old men (or women), or as never-say-quit impotents who will try every quack nostrum or gadget offered them to improve libido. In fact, young adults buy more of the sexual gadgets and potions. And the average age of a "dirty old man" is reported to be twenty-seven.[37]

Marital happiness is probably as varied in degree among the aged as in any other group. Some elderly persons turn increasingly to each other for approval and companionship. Some become increasingly bored by or hostile toward each other as they spend more and more of their waking hours together under the same roof. Some file for divorce. Some separate. Extramarital affairs are not unknown among the elderly. Nor are late-life marriages. Butler found that a poignant sense of tenderness—a feeling that each encounter is precious because it may be the last—often exists and characterizes the relationships between persons who have met and married late in life.[38]

Widows and widowers. There are many more widows than widowers in our country.[39] This is because life expectancy for women exceeds that of men by about eight years. Life expectancy for white women is about seventy-seven years compared to sixty-nine years for white men. Nonwhites' average life span is about seventy-one years for women and sixty-three years for men.[40] Since the custom for women to marry men older than themselves is prevalent in the United States, many women outlive their husbands for a decade or more. There are many widows and widowers under, as well as over, age sixty-five. Our discussion, however, will be concerned with older persons who have lost their spouses.

The last chapter of this book will focus on death and bereavement and examine the ways in which people handle their emotions at the time of death. The death of a beloved person, especially one with whom another has had an amiable, daily relationship over a number of years, leaves the survivor feeling lost, threatened, and as if some part of the self had died also. A numbness and disbelief follow immediately after death. The more difficult period of bereavement occurs a month or more after the loss.[41]

A person's reactions to losing a spouse vary according to how companionable the marriage was, how much warning the person had of the approaching death, how independent the survivor is, how supportive family and friends are, and how many financial burdens (or lack of them) are left to the widow or widower. In general, women have a less difficult time adjusting to the death of a spouse than men.[42] A widow is more apt to have observed the reactions of other women to their husbands' deaths. She usually knows other widows to whom she can talk confidentially, pouring out her grief, fears, loneliness, or bitterness. Women are more apt to have harmonious ties to many persons, both within and outside the family from whom they can seek sympathy, nurturance, and support.

The widower is more apt to suffer acute loneliness after the death of his wife. Often she was his only true confidant. A man may feel that he has to be courageous and unemotional in his bereavement. He may refuse to discuss death with others, hiding his intense emotions rather than defusing them through conversation. Widowers are also apt to be less independent in terms of living alone than are widows. While they may have been fiercely independent in their work-a-day worlds, many know little about cooking, laundry, and the like. About twice as many widowers remarry as widows.[43] True, they have a greater number of widows from whom to choose a new mate, but they also have more desire for marriage. Many women, once they adjust to widowhood, enjoy their new sense of freedom. On the other hand, there are a few widows and widowers who cannot adjust to being alone. The suicide rate among widowed persons is considerably higher than that of married persons.[44]

Becoming single after years of marriage requires several lifestyle changes. Some persons choose to move in with other family members or move into a smaller house (or trailer, or apartment, or home for the aged). Some try to find a companion to move in with them. Many acquire pets, plants, or new time-absorbing hobbies. Having adequate financial resources makes adjustment to widowhood much easier. Greater difficulties arise for men and women who are saddled with debts from their previous marriage or from the funeral or who must cope with diminished income because of the spouse's death.

Communications with children. The fact that about three-quarters of the 23 million old people in the nation today live apart from their families is not entirely a matter of ageism or the young rejecting the old. In research by Marvin Sussman, several hundred American families were interviewed to determine their attitudes about the aged. A majority (60 percent) of them indicated they would be willing to let their elderly parents move in with them.[45] Many old people prefer to live alone, maintaining their privacy and their sense of competence and self-determination for as long as possible. They do not want to impose on their children or become burdens to them. It is difficult for parents to move in and become dependent on children, a reversal from the years and years of having their children dependent on them.

A preference for self-help as long as possible generally does not mean that old people prefer to be disengaged from their families and friends (see the myth discussed on page 438). Parents still appreciate phone calls, letters, and visits from children, grandchildren, and great-grandchildren if the reasons for the communications are friendly, not demanding or hostile.

A majority of elderly people live within a half hour's driving time of at least one of their family.[46] Families differ greatly in the amount and quality of time spent with their old people. In general, while contacts with children may be frequent, contacts with grandchildren decrease as the second generation move into their teens, become young adults, or have children of their own.[47]

Elderly persons frequently prefer to have family members come to visit them rather than making trips to see family due to some of their physical disabilities. Here are three typical comments about children and grandchildren made by people in the Maas and Kuypers study: (1) "The children always want me to come more than I can. . . ." (2) "I kind of wish they did live closer. . . . When you get older, you miss them." (3) "It's a pleasure for a little while [to be with grandchildren]. I wouldn't say that I could be with them all day long."[48]

Community interactions

Just as families differ in the way they regard their elders, and elders differ in the way they regard the younger generations, so too do various community officials, agencies, and citizens differ in their regard for old people, and vice versa. Some older people prefer a slower pace to their activities (e.g., "I'm not like I used to be. I'm calming down. I was ambitious and eager and did so much . . . I've driven everywhere and anywhere . . . ").[49] Others resent being retired and having their activities limited. Some seek out new friends (e.g., ". . . They're more important. We depend on [friends] for companionship").[50] Some accept the loss of friends passively (e.g., "People that we used to see from time to time are gone now and they simply have not been replaced"), and some withdraw from their friends (e.g., "The strain of being with people makes me terribly nervous").[51]

Community interactions will be examined in terms of three of Havighurst's developmental tasks of later maturity: adjusting to retirement, establishing an affiliation with one's age group, and establishing satisfactory living arrangements.

Retirement. The move from an agrarian society to a predominantly industrialized society brought in its wake the phenomenon of retirement. Not too long ago people worked until they became physically incapacitated or until they died. They worked less as they got older or did more advising and less manual labor, but they still felt a part of the job. When Congress established the Social Security Act in 1935, it arbitrarily set sixty-five as the age when men could first collect government retirement benefits (sixty-two for women). Many industries in turn set sixty-five as a mandatory retirement age for men (sixty-two for women). Some corporations with their own pension plans ask employees to retire even earlier, while others allow them to work beyond age sixty-five. However, about 86 percent of Americans retire or are already retired when they first become eligible for social security benefits.[52]

There is a prevalent belief in our society that the transition from working to retirement brings in its wake a shock syndrome, a decline into illness, depression, loneliness, anxiety, self-doubt, feelings of uselessness, or financial worries. While it is true that the transition requires substantial changes in one's lifestyle, it is not true that shock and decline are necessary results. For some people retirement is a welcomed relief from the toils of daily labor. For others it means a change from a disliked job to a more enjoyable, self-directed form of employment. For still others it does generate feelings of uselessness and impending death. There are a great many differences in how retirees view their changed status, just as there are a wide variety of ways in which people handle every other developmental milestone throughout life.

Simpson, Back, and McKinney reported that feelings of job deprivation and lack of a role are often related to the kind of work performed prior to retirement.[53] Upper status workers (executives and professionals) objected more to forced retirement and often feared the consequences of being unemployed. They enjoyed the wages, recognition, and power of their jobs. However, once retired, they were more often able to organize and plan for their leisure hours in such a way as to minimize some of their feelings of job deprivation. Unskilled workers had less to lose with retirement. They had low autonomy, low pay, and often little or no satisfaction in their jobs. However, they were often less able to adapt to loss of work roles. Simpson and her associates suggested that two factors helped many retirees make better unemployment adjustments: a prior orderliness of work habits with experience in planning for time and an involvement with other activities. Streib and Schneider found that persons who retire early tend to adjust better than employees who continue at their jobs beyond the expected age of retirement. They also found that persons who are compelled to retire fare less well than persons who retire voluntarily.[54]

Retirement is a financial blow for many persons. On the average, social security benefits and other pension plans total less than 50 percent of preretirement income.[55] It is often easier for persons with low preretirement wages to learn to live on their social security checks than it is for persons who were once more affluent. Shanas and her associates asked nearly 700 retirees what they missed most in their retirement. They found that almost one-half (45 percent) missed money most, as compared to 18 percent who missed the work itself, 16 percent who missed the people at work, 8 percent who missed feeling useful, 4 percent who had miscellaneous reasons, and 9 percent who missed nothing.[56] Many elderly Americans (approximately 4.5 million of them) live at subpoverty levels after their retirement.[57]

Health frequently improves after retirement. While health decrements are to be expected with age, the end of job-related stress and strain leaves many persons feeling better. Ryser and Sheldon asked 500 retirees about their postemployment health and found that 25 percent felt better, as opposed to 10 percent who felt worse.[58]

A less mentioned problem of retirement is the adverse effect it has on some marriages. After years of one or both partners hurrying to dress, eat breakfast, and depart for a job, the change to both persons staying home can be stupefying. Conversation may be difficult. Partners may get in each other's way. Disputes often arise about how to do even the most trivial of household tasks. One woman in the Maas and Kuypers study summarized her feelings this way: "I think it's harder on a wife when her husband retires. I mean, he was around underfoot all the time—and it meant three meals a day—you know—to get and prepare and clean up after and so on."[59]

Leisure activities. Humans are social beings. Retirement often means the loss of contact with friends at work. With each passing year older people are also apt to experience through death the loss of other relatives, friends, and/or acquaintances. The diminution of social contacts can mean low morale, low self-esteem, and depression for many persons.

While there is doubt about the theory that disengagement is a phenomenon that characterizes aging, it is true that disengagement characterizes some old people. However, many gerontologists (people who study aging and the personalities of the aged) now believe that old people who remain active usually have a higher level of satisfaction with their lives. To argue whether activity itself brings greater enjoyment to life in old age is debatable. Neugarten pointed out that her own research as well as studies by others concerned with activity versus disengagement show that personality type is the pivotal factor in predicting whether high or low activity will contribute to a more successful aging.[60] One must remember that factors such as family relationships, health, and finances also play an important role in life satisfaction or dissatisfaction in old age. They also influence how much activity a given old person can have. Some dissatisfied elderly persons resent the fact that their health, their caretakers, and/or their lack of finances prevent them from getting about and socializing more. Some satisfied elderly persons accept their limitations and their diminished social contacts and are still satisfied.

The leisure activities available to retired persons who want them and are able to enjoy them vary from community to community and from state to state. Because of the great numbers of retirees who move to warmer regions of the country, areas such as southern California, southern Arizona, and Florida have a considerable selection of recreations planned, produced, and maintained for older adults. Northern cities and larger towns are also becoming increasingly aware of the large numbers of retired persons who comprise their population and are planning, building, and supporting centers for senior citizens. At-home activities pursued by many elderly include household tasks, repairs, cooking, laundering, hobby or handicraft projects, reading, card playing, entertaining, and television viewing. Out-of-the-home activities are less rigorous sports (e.g., bowling, shuffleboard, golfing, hiking, cycling, touring, visiting, shopping, and church or club-sponsored events).

Figure 11–3. *Elderly persons, as is true of all persons, have a need to reminisce. This contributes to a sense of continuity of past with present and greater self-awareness. The ability to accept events and experiences of the past as something that had to be and allowed for no substitutions contributes to ego integrity and greater life satisfaction in old age.*
Leslie Davis

Some retired persons become active as volunteers in hospitals, churches, and other community facilities. One of the more popular volunteer projects for old people today is the Foster Grandparents Program, in which old people become involved in teaching, supporting, and helping children with special needs.[61] Eisdorfer recalls having lunch with a group of Foster Grandparents working at a home for profoundly retarded children.[62] He found them a lively, aggressive, involved group of human beings. A child psychiatrist then told him that when the elderly first arrived for in-service training sessions, they were a pitiful, depressed group of old people. They even refused to talk. However, after giving love and affection to the children, they changed as much, if not more, than the children. While some volunteer projects provide a tremendous feeling of self-worth to the elderly, others are frought with difficulties. Carp warns that volunteer work does not necessarily enhance well-being.[63] The work must be meaningful and must be rewarded with honest praise and genuine appreciation if the worker is to feel good about it.

Living facilities. As has been mentioned, three-quarters of the elderly live apart from their families. The large majority of them still live in homes of their own. Many live in rented facilities. Only about 5 percent (approximately one million) live in hospitals or homes for the aged.[64]

The old people living in their own homes will be discussed first. For many persons who still enjoy relatively good health, few physical disabilities, and adequate income, and a spouse, relation, or companion(s) to share the house, this situation may bring great happiness. However, it may be difficult to keep up a home if one is chronically ill or crippled. Without an adequate income, household repairs and upkeep costs can be staggering. Plumbing, electrical wiring, furnaces, pipes, or drains may require attention. Termites or rodents may create problems; heavy winds or rains can do considerable damage, and one must face continual bills for utilities, heating, and taxes. About two-thirds of the elderly home owners live in rural areas.[65] One-third of them own substandard dwellings.[66] This means that they exist without inside flush toilets, or hot water showers or baths, and that they may have minimal heat in winter and general conditions of deterioration. Many of the six million impoverished elderly homeowners are trapped in their poverty. They cannot find buyers for their homes or afford to move elsewhere.

Some elderly people rent dwellings for their later years. Satisfaction or dissatisfaction is very much dependent on what one can afford to rent and the services provided by the landlord or landlady. While all repairs and services should be the responsibility of the owner of the rental property, rentals are often neglected. Tenants may be afraid of being evicted if they complain. Most retirees have a fixed income. Regular rent increases are a hardship to them. Some rental properties available to the elderly are in poor condition (i.e., walk-up flats, dingy rooms in hotels or boarding houses, poorly heated trailers), and they reflect the meager amount spent to maintain them. The government has tried to alleviate some of the problems of inadequate housing for the aged by making public housing units available to them. Tenants generally are not required to pay more than 25 percent of their income to rent such federally supported dwellings. However, annual income eligibility requirements generally are fixed at about $4500 to $9800.[67] This range excludes many elderly who are either too poor or slightly too rich for public housing.

Retirement communities are popular places for people to move in their later years if they can sell their own home, have sufficient income to move, and are well enough to adjust to a new place. Carp studied many old persons who volunteered to move from their own housing to a federally financed community for the elderly. He reported that after one year 99 percent of them rated the project as a very good place to live. More importantly, after eight years 90 percent of them still rated the place as very good, with another 9 percent rating it as okay.[68] They were able to adjust to the modern setting and make new friends in the adjacent Senior Center. He suggested that morale is generally good in planned societies where the inhabitants are of a comparable age range and activities are designed to be of interest and within the ability levels of the participants. However, many inhabitants also miss their old friends, families, and their former lifestyles.

Living alone can be a devastating experience for an old person who is accustomed to having a spouse and/or neighbors and friends around. Many elderly persons volunteer to move into a housing project or even into a nursing home to escape the loneliness and isolation that follows widowhood or death of friends. Those who opt to live alone can often escape their feelings of solitude by doing volunteer work or visiting geriatric activity centers. Some programs such as meals-on-wheels, dial-a-bus, and homemaker services bring help to people who are too disabled or ill to get about easily by themselves when living alone.

Nursing homes are generally regarded as a last resort as a living facility for the aged. They have pros and cons. The pros generally concern problems of family, economics, and health. Butler found that 50 percent of all older persons in nursing homes have no significant family.[69] They may have a distant cousin, niece, or nephew somewhere but no relation who could reasonably be expected to take care of them. The poverty that affects about one-third of the elderly also makes nursing homes desirable. Widows, in particular, often cannot cope financially due to inequities in the social security system. Finally, over 75 percent of the elderly have at least one chronic health problem.[70] There are four major areas of problems: (1) degenerative diseases of the heart and arteries (coronary occlusion, stroke), chronic brain syndrome; (2) cancer; (3) degenerative processes of the bones and joints; and (4) mental defects. These leave many persons in need of around-the-clock medical supervision beyond that which can be provided by family members or nurses in private homes. Thus, for many persons nursing homes or extended-care hospital settings are the best living facilities available for the later years.

Other positive aspects of nursing homes relate to the reasons the persons are there. If a man or woman has no living family, or is ignored and neglected by relatives, he or she may find friends among the residents of the home. If a person is destitute, Medicaid will pay the costs of care in a nursing home. Medicaid rules vary from state to state. In some states a person must be rid of all financial assets (home, stocks and bonds, savings for a funeral) before he or she is eligible. In others they may hold on to a few possessions and valuables and still receive Medicaid. Both Medicaid and social security checks go right to the nursing home once a person resides there. However, the law provides that each resident of a nursing home should receive an allowance of thirty dollars a month for his or her own personal use. While medical attention varies from home to home, nursing homes are theoretically better equipped to handle medical emergencies than most private residences could be.

Nursing homes are becoming big business in America. In the 1950s and early 1960s they were small and relatively personal. Now they are growing larger and larger. Most have over one hundred beds.[71] Many are chain-operated—run by the same owner as several other nursing homes in the region. Chains large enough to be listed on either the New York or the American Stock Exchange control about 10 percent of all the old age homes in the country.[72] With such far-reaching interests, it is difficult for the adminstrators of the homes to be concerned about the problems of individual patients. In the best homes the staff members show concern for each person, using respectful titles (e.g., Mr. Hine) rather than nicknames (e.g., "Pops," "Gramps") or diagnoses (e.g., the coronary in room 402). However, personnel in many homes are poorly trained, disrespectful, or even cruel to the patients. In the best homes the residents are helped to get out of bed, dress, and participate in exercises (walks, physical therapy) and social activities (outings, games, parties, recreational therapy). However, in many homes the highlights of the day are meals and bed changes. Some patients are never dressed and taken out of bed. Others are taken out and placed in chairs, where they sit all day, sleeping or staring at the walls, other patients, or television until they are moved back to bed. Some homes provide nutritionally balanced diets planned to meet each patient's particular needs. Others serve inexpensive foods, quickly prepared and uninteresting, or occasionally serve unsanitary or even spoiled foods.[73] There are questions individuals can ask and observations to make in assessing a potential nursing home for a friend or relative. Do a number of patients have bedsores? Are most patients up and dressed? What's the rapport with the staff? Do patients receive regular baths? Are their teeth well cared for? Do doctors make regular visits? Is there enough staff? Is the place clean and well-maintained? These are only some of the questions. Often, local social service agencies or offices for the aging can provide information about nearby facilities.

Health considerations

Old age is different for every person who experiences it. Remember that many elderly persons maintain their vim, zest, and vitality throughout their seventies, eighties, and nineties. Various centenarians interviewed in our country and abroad have attributed their longevity to hard work, diet, religion, or heredity. American scientists are trying to unlock the secrets of cell biology and discover what causes aging. For example, is it caused by hormones or something coded on the DNA molecules? Meanwhile, the best advice for extending one's life still rests in the elimination or avoidance of known hazards: stress, smoking, excessive use of alcohol, abuse of drugs, obesity, contagious diseases, pollutants. Experts also advise an increased concern for exercise and proper diet (adequate fluid intake, adequate vitamins and minerals, fewer excess calories, less cholesterol, and less saturated fats). Finally, prompt, suitable, and sufficient treatment of diseases can often further extend one's life span.

As more and more people become aware of how they can protect their health, and as medical science finds ways to elimate and cure more diseases, our aged population increases. Average life expectancy is now hovering about the late sixties and early seventies and is continuing to climb.[74]

General health

The statistic that over 75 percent of the elderly have at least one chronic health problem was mentioned earlier in this chapter. As more and more people reach their seventh or eighth decade, frequently occurring or prolonged conditions become more obvious. Many of the problems that are chronic in the elderly had their origins in childhood or earlier adulthood. Most of these long-term or recurrent disease conditions have been discussed in preceding chapters. The following are common problems of the elderly. The chapter in which they were discussed is indicated in parentheses: obesity (6); general malnutrition (6); anemia (6); digestive disturbances (8); diabetes (5 and 10); gallbladder disease (8); cirrhosis (6); urinary tract disorders (8); psychosomatic illnesses (5 and 7); excessive self-medication or drug abuse (7); depression (9); mental disorders (9); arthritis (8); lung and respiratory diseases (8); cancers (9 and 10); hypertension (9); heart diseases (9); and arteriosclerosis and other vascular diseases (9). The most common chronic health problems of the elderly are all the heart and vascular conditions (cardiovascular diseases), cancer, degenerative diseases of bones and joints, and mental defects. While the number of deaths from heart disease declined in the early 1970s (due both to improved medical care and greater individual concern for disease prevention measures), the incidence of cancer, arthritis, respiratory diseases, cirrhosis, and diabetes climbed.[75]

This chapter will examine problems not previously discussed: cerebrovascular accidents (strokes); chronic brain syndrome (senility); osteoporosis, and osteoarthrosis. The special acciddent hazards that old people face and some safety precautions will also be discussed.

Cerebrovascular accidents (strokes)

The term stroke, along with the abbreviation CVA, is often used to describe a cerebrovascular accident, a sudden, crippling, sometimes fatal occurrence. While young people, and even children, occasionally suffer strokes, they most typically affect older people. When a stroke occurs, the blood flow through blood vessel(s) of the brain is disrupted, either by obstruction or by rupture of the vessel(s). There are several different factors that may cause the disruption of flow. Whatever the cause, confusion or loss of consciousness and/or some degree of physical impairment follow. The impaired blood flow can occur in any part of the brain and can be brief, prolonged, or recurrent. The symptoms and degree of disability from a stroke depend on where in the brain the disruption occurs, how long it lasts, and how extensive an area of tissue is damaged. While over 1,800,000 Americans suffer some form of stroke each year, only about 11 percent die from it.[76] Approximately 1.5 million survivors are left with some form of disability. In many patients stroke sequelae demand lifelong extensive care.

The majority of strokes, especially in the elderly, are caused by cerebral embolism, hemorrhage, or cerebral thrombosis.[77] A description of the mechanisms behind these most common types of strokes follows.

A stroke may result from an embolus, which may be a dislodged blood clot, a plaque from the atherosclerotic deposits of cholesterol and platelets in the arteries of the neck leading to the brain, or some other foreign material (e.g., air, fat). Embolic strokes are usually abrupt in onset, like a bolt out of the blue. They are often associated with a recent heart attack, a diseased or recently surgically replaced heart valve, or the abnormal heart rhythm called atrial fibrillation.[78]

Hemorrhagic strokes may result when a cerebral blood vessel

ruptures and hemorrhages into an area of the brain. Such ruptures are frequently the consequence of microaneurysms (outpouchings of an artery) produced in the cerebral blood vessels in severe and prolonged hypertension. The onset of hemorrhagic strokes may be rapid or gradual, depending on the speed of the bleeding. Disabilities will vary according to the area and extent of the damage.[79]

Cerebral thrombotic strokes occur because a blood clot forms in one of the blood vessels of the brain. Thrombotic strokes may have either a rapid or a gradual onset but more generally are slow to develop, over a few hours. They may be referred to as thrombosis-in-evolution or stroke-in-evolution. Warning signs may precede the actual stroke (e.g., weakness, numbness, difficulty with speech, trouble understanding speech, dizziness, or diminished vision).[80]

Treatment of strokes may be aimed at the primary cause, at preventing complications and recurrences, and at restoring as much function as possible. Surgery is rarely used, as in the case of hemorrhage due to large aneurysms. Anticoagulant and/or antihypertensive drugs may occasionally be prescribed. It has recently been learned that aspirin prevents the clumping of platelets seen in clotting.[81] This clumping is an important part of the sudden narrowing of vessels in an area of atherosclerosis. Platelet clot particles can become dislodged and embolize and thereby obstruct vessels in the brain. Asprin, consequently, may be useful in preventing strokes in persons with atherosclerotic heart disease and atherosclerotic plaques in the large neck arteries leading to the brain.

Restoration of function after a stroke depends on the extent of the physical impairment, the part(s) of the body affected, the kinds of therapy given the patient (including encouragement from and determination of the therapists), and the victim's own will to recover.

Chronic brain syndromes

Chronic brain syndromes describe various conditions of persons who have permanent, diffuse areas of brain tissue damage and/or atrophy, as opposed to focal areas of damage that occur with strokes. The permanency of chronic brain syndromes differentiates them from various acute brain syndromes that are reversible. All brain syndromes have similar symptoms: confusion, memory loss, disorientation, and disordered thinking. Acute brain syndromes can be caused by such things as blows to the head, high fevers, overuse of tranquilizers, malnutrition, anemia, alcohol, some viral infections, exhausting illnesses, and untreated congestive heart failure. The causes of irreversible syndromes with brain tissue changes and possible atrophy are not well understood.[82] When the same condition occurs in younger adults, it is called Alzheimer's disease or presenile dementia.[83]

The term *senility* is from the Latin root *senilis*, meaning old. It is used most often to describe old persons with chronic brain syndromes. It is not, however, a true diagnosis of any specific disease condition. Unfortunately, senility is often used as a label or diagnosis for older persons who have acute, reversible problems that cause them to become temporarily restless, forgetful, irritable, or disoriented. It may also be used to describe old persons who are depressed or anxious. Medical personnel are sometimes guilty of gross neglect for diagnosing old people as senile without searching for reversible disease conditions and providing them with proper and adequate medical care.

Some of the suggested possible causes of chronic brain syndromes include severe atherosclerosis, chronic alcoholism, uncontrolled high blood pressure, or a long history of severe or poorly controlled diabetes, epilepsy, or emphysema. It is suspected that other, as yet unknown, factors also play a part in causing atrophy of brain tissue in some old people.

Persons with chronic brain syndromes show a progressive loss of intellectual abilities and increasingly abnormal behaviors over time. They may have swings from relatively good days with near normal functioning to bad days marked by memory loss and antisocial behaviors before the brain dysfunction becomes extensive. In the later stages of chronic brain syndromes, patients may become incontinent (lose the ability to prevent discharge of urine or feces), incoherent, and often fail to recognize even their closest friends and relatives. They may exist in a vegetative state, requiring total custodial care.

Degenerative bone and joint diseases

The skeletal system is particularly vulnerable to degenerative changes in old age. Bones and the cartilage and synovial membranes of the joints between bones can lose cells and become both more susceptible to injury and disease and less able to heal rapidly. The most common disease conditions affecting the musculoskeletal system of the elderly are osteoporosis, osteoarthrosis, and rheumatism.

Osteoporosis. Osteoporosis is a metabolic disorder of bones characterized by a decreased amount of the protein and mineral components of bone. It occurs in older people, both men and women. The lack of estrogen after menopause may account for the high prevalence of the disease in elderly females, since a lack of estrogen is known to accelerate bone protein loss and, with it, mineral loss. Other factors that are believed to play a role in causing increased bone resorption in some people include inadequate calcium and phosphorus in the diet and lack of muscle use in active exercising. Symptoms of the disease include pain in the bones and a bending of the back. Some of the vertebrae in the lumbar and thoracic spine may undergo compression fractures. Bones may fracture quite readily during falls or bumps. Bierman and Hazzard have suggested that osteoporosis severe enough to predispose an individual to fractures occurs in as many as 30 percent of persons over sixty-five.[84] The progress of osteoporosis can be slowed somewhat in older women with estrogen replacement therapy and dietary supplements of calcium, but it is not halted. Many osteoporotic persons wear special corsets or back braces to help support their curving spines.

Osteoarthrosis. It has been estimated that 80 percent of persons over age sixty have some osteoarthrosis.[85] This condition, also called osteoarthritis, degenerative arthritis, or degenerative joint disease, is characterized by degeneration and loss of the cartilage at the ends of the bones and by sharp "spur" formations. Pain is confined to the joints, especially on motion and weight bearing. It most typically affects the large joints, particularly the hips and knees, but can also affect the vertebrae, ankles, and fingers. Obesity, or the bearing of too much weight on weakened joints, is thought to contribute to osteoarthrosis, as do the normal jolts of everyday living. Treatment is usually aimed at relieving pain and preventing further joint trauma. Medication used for pain consists of aspirin or other analgesic drugs. Dietary regimes for weight loss may be prescribed for the obese person. Regular range-of-movement exercises for the affected joints may also be recommended. Surgical replacement of a painful, crippled joint with a prosthesis is occasionally used for persons with a great deal of pain and joint destruction. Many persons with osteoarthrosis use walking aids to help them get around.

Accidents

The fifth leading cause of death in the elderly is some form of accident.[86] Traffic fatalities and in-house mishaps are most common in these statistics.

About 12 percent of the drivers on our roads are over age sixty.[87] Most of them drive cautiously. They fear revocation of their licenses if they are arrested for some traffic violation. Driving for them signifies freedom, independence, and a relatively safe, accessible, inexpensive form of transportation. Most elderly people prefer back roads to super highways and often avoid night driving. Many are also duly cautious not to drive when tired or while under the influence of alcohol. Nevertheless, the traffic accident rate per miles driven is approximately the same for old people as it is for teenagers.[88] While teenagers generally err in the direction of high speed, elderly drivers have more mishaps while failing to yield, signaling incorrectly, changing lanes, making turns, missing stop signs and stop lights, or parking.[89]

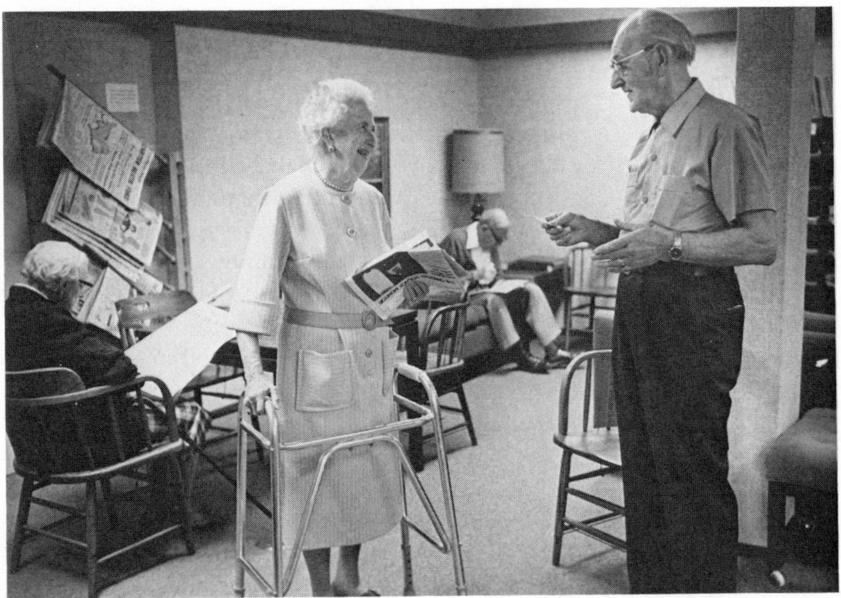

Figure 11–4. *Physical disabilities can restrict movement in all age brackets but are more common in aged populations. Age-related changes in bone and joint structure contribute to diseases such as osteoarthrosis and rheumatism. Many persons continue to get around in their communities by using canes or walkers.*
© Liane Enkelis/Jeroboam, Inc.

In-house accidents commonly affecting the elderly include burns, scalds, explosions, poisonings, and especially falls. Waxed floors, loose carpets, slippery bathtubs, high beds, misplaced furniture, and stairs cause many old people to trip and fall. About one-third of all home accidents of the elderly occur on stairs.[90] Living quarters of the elderly should have elevators or well-lighted, well-railed, wide, nonslippery steps or be on one level to help avoid some of these stairway disasters.

Summary

The later years may be spent in active pursuit of goals or at a leisurely pace, by healthy individuals or by those debilitated by disease. The ecological settings of persons over sixty-five are as varied as those of other adults.

Senescence, the process of growing old, is marked by body changes in structure and function (e.g., loss of bone density and mass, loss of some visual and auditory acuity, loss of pigmentation in skin and hair). The changes are gradual and often begin quite early in adulthood.

Research has not sufficiently demonstrated that cognitive disabilities occur in all older persons. Many persons demonstrate stable cognitive abilities until very late in life. However, intellectual abilities do seem to show a terminal decline just preceding death.

Personality orientations and lifestyles in the later years are diverse. Personalities may range from integrated to armored-defended, to passive-dependent, to unintegrated, with many variations of personalities in each category. Lifestyles may range from spouse-centered to family-centered, to visiting-centered, to work-centered, to group-centered, to uncentered, to hobby-centered, to remotely sociable, to disabled, unwell, and disengaged. Men's lifestyles show more continuity over the adulthood years than do women's situations. Women, in general, cope with and adapt to more changes in their lifestyles as they age.

Life expectancy for women exceeds that of men by about eight years, making many more widows than widowers in our country. About twice as many widowers remarry as widows. Becoming single after years of marriage alters one's lifestyle in many ways, most of which require difficult readjustments.

About three-quarters of the nation's older people live apart from their children, but a majority live close enough to visit or be visited by one or more children or grandchildren at frequent intervals. Most older persons maintain their own homes or apartments for as long as possible. Only about 5 percent live in hospitals or homes for the aged.

Mandatory retirement at age sixty-five can be a blow to the finances, social life, and self-esteem of men and women after years of steady, paid employment outside the home. Conversely, it may also be welcomed. Some workers opt to retire even before age sixty-five. Retirees, when asked what they missed most after retirement, mentioned money, the work itself, the people at work, and the feeling of usefulness. However, 9 percent of them missed nothing at all. Many retired persons become active as volunteers in hospitals, churches, and community projects. Many also pursue leisure activities planned for older adults in their communities.

Over 15 percent of the elderly have at least one chronic health problem. The most common include cardiovascular disease, cancer, and degenerative diseases of bones and joints. Exercise, proper diet (adequate fluid and nutrients, fewer excess calories, less cholesterol and saturated fats), and prompt treatment of disease symptoms can often further extend one's life span.

Questions for review

1. Describe the various physical changes that occur during senescence.
2. Various studies have concluded that intelligence declines over time. Critique these studies. Are they valid? In your critique use the information in Chapter 1 on evaluating research.
3. Communities and housing projects have been established for older persons. Some people feel that these living situations tend to isolate older individuals, while others feel they are beneficial. What is your opinion? Discuss.
4. Describe life experiences that might lead to the four personality patterns outlined by Neugarten, Havighurst, and Tobin.
5. Men's lifestyles tend to have more continuity than women's. What sorts of changes could be made in women's lives to give them more continuity?
6. Describe some examples of ageism that exist in the mass media—in newspapers, magazines, and television.
7. Why do you think it is true that widowers tend to remarry at a much greater rate than widows?
8. Mandatory retirement has recently come under attack. Do you believe people should be forced to retire at a specific age? Discuss the pros and cons of mandatory retirement.
9. Disengagement mainly affects people of ill health. Why do you think this is so?
10. Would you feel guilty about putting one of your parents in a nursing home? Explain your answer.
11. Describe the various causes of strokes and the various forms of treatment.

References

[1]U.S. Department of Health, Education, and Welfare, *Health: United States, 1975* (Washington, D.C.: U.S. Government Printing Office, 1976).

[2]N. McWhirter and R. McWhirter, *Guinness Book of World Records,* 1977 edition (New York: Sterling Publishing Co., 1976).

[3]W. D. Denckla, "Pituitary Inhibitor of Thyroxine," *Federation Proceedings: Federation of American Societies for Experimental Biology,* 34(1), 1975.

[4]L. Hayflick, "Current Theories of Biological Aging," *Federation Proceedings: Federation of American Societies for Experimental Biology,* 34(1), 1975.

[5]E. Bierman and W. Hazzard, "Old Age," *The Biologic Ages of Man From Conception Through Old Age,* D. Smith and E. Bierman, eds. (Philadelphia: W. B. Saunders Co., 1973).

[6]J. McCracken, "The Company Tells Me I'm Old," *Saturday Review,* August 7, 1976.

[7]B. Anderson and E. Palmore, "Longitudinal Evaluation of Ocular Function," *Normal Aging II: Reports from the Duke Longitudinal Studies, 1970-1973,* E. Palmore, ed. (Durham, N.C.: Duke University Press, 1974).

[8]B. Anderson, "The Aging Eye," *Postgraduate Medicine,* 50(3) (1971).

[9]M. Riley and A. Foner, *Aging and Society: Volume 1, An Inventory of Research Findings* (New York: Russell Sage, 1968).

[10]P. White, J. Pelcovits, R. Shank, "Nutritional Considerations: A Panel Discussion," *Quality of Life: The Later Years,* L. Brown and E. Ellis, eds. (Acton, Mass.: Publishing Sciences Group, Inc., 1975).

[11]D. Wechsler, *The Measurement and Appraisal of Adult Intelligence,* 4th ed. (Baltimore: Williams and Wilkins Co., 1958).

[12]C. Eisdorfer and L. Cohen, "The Generality of the WAIS Standardization for the Aged: A Regional Comparison," *Journal of Abnormal and Social Psychology,* 62 (1961).

[13]J. Botwinick, "Geropsychology," *Annual Review of Psychology,* 21 (1970).

[14]A. Heron and S. Chown, *Age and Function* (Boston: Little, Brown, 1967).

[15]K. Schaie, "Rigidity-Flexibility and Intelligence: A Cross-Sectional Study of the Adult Life Span from Twenty to Seventy," *Psychological Monographs,* 72(9) (1958).

[16]K. Schaie and C. Strother, "The Effects of Time and Cohort Differences on the Interpretation of Age Changes in Cognitive Behavior," *Multivariate Behavior Research,* 3 (1968).

[17]C. Eisdorfer and F. Wilkie, "Intellectual Changes," *Intellectual Functioning in Adults,* L. Jarvik, C. Eisdorfer, and J. Blum, eds. (New York: Springer Publishing Co., 1973).

[18]F. Wilkie and C. Eisdorfer, "Terminal Changes in Intelligence," *Normal Aging II: Reports from the Duke Longitudinal Studies, 1970-1973,* E. Palmore, ed. (Durham, N.C.: Duke University Press, 1974).

[19]K. Riegel and R. Riegel, "Development, Drop, and Death," *Developmental Psychology,* 6, 1972.

[20]J. Birren, "Age Changes in Speed of Behavior: Its Central Nature and Physiological Correlates," *Behavior, Aging, and the Nervous System,* A. Welford and J. Birren, eds. (Springfield, Ill.: Charles C. Thomas, 1965).

[21]C.Bühler, "The Developmental Structure of Goal Setting in Group and Individual Studies," *The Course of Human Life*, C. Bühler and F. Massarik, eds. (New York: Springer, 1968).

[22]R. Havighurst, *Developmental Tasks and Education*, 3rd ed. (New York: McKay, 1972).

[23]R. Wernick, *The Family* (New York: Time, Inc., 1974).

[24]C. Bühler, "The Developmental Structure of Goal Setting in Group and Individual Studies."

[25]B. Neugarten, R. Havighurst, and S. Tobin, "Personality and Patterns of Aging," *Middle Age and Aging*, B. Neugarten, ed. (Chicago: The University of Chicago Press, 1968).

[26]Ibid.

[27]H. Maas and J. Kuypers, *From Thirty to Seventy* (San Francisco: Jossey-Bass Publishers,1974).

[28]Ibid.

[29]Ibid.

[30]Ibid.

[31]Ibid.

[32]E. Cumming and W. Henry, *Growing Old: The Process of Disengagement* (New York: Basic Books, 1961).

[33]R. Kuhlen, "Developmental Changes in Motivation During the Adult Years," *Relations of Development and Aging*, J. Birren, ed. (Springfield, Ill.: Charles C. Thomas, Publisher, 1964).

[34]R. Havighurst, B. Neugarten, and S. Tobin, "Disengagement and Patterns of Aging," *Middle Age and Aging*, B. Neugarten, ed. (Chicago: The University of Chicago Press, 1968).

[35]R. Butler, *Why Survive? Being Old in America* (New York: Harper and Row, 1975).

[36]R. Butler and M. Lewis, *Aging and Mental Health: Positive Psychosocial Approaches* (St. Louis: C. V. Mosby, 1973).

[37]P. Gebhard, W. Pomeroy, C. Christenson, and J. Gagnon, *Sex Offenders: An Analysis of Types* (New York: Harper and Row, 1965).

[38]R. Butler, "Sex After Sixty-Five," *Quality of Life: The Later Years*, L. Brown and E. Ellis, eds. (Acton, Mass.: Publishing Sciences Group, Inc., 1975).

[39]U.S. Department of Health, Education, and Welfare, *Health: United States*, 1975.

[40]Ibid.

[41]S. Morris, *Grief and How to Live with It* (New York: Grosset and Dunlap, 1972).

[42]G. Gorer, *Death, Grief and Mourning* (Garden City, N.J.: Doubleday and Co., 1965).

[43]R. Butler and M. Lewis, *Aging and Mental Health: Positive Psychosocial Approaches.*

[44]F. Bernardo, "Widowhood Status in the United States: Perspective on a Neglected Aspect of the Family Life-Cycle," *Love, Marriage, Family: A Developmental Approach,* M. Lasswell and T. Lasswell, eds. (Glenville, Ill.: Scott, Foresman, 1973).

[45]J. Jones, "Aging Parley Plugs Research and Action," *American Psychological Association Monitor,* 7(12) (1976).

[46]E. Shanas et al., eds., *Old People in Three Industrial Societies* (New York: Atherton Press, 1968).

[47]Ibid.

[48]H. Maas and J. Kuypers, *From Thirty to Seventy.*

[49]Ibid.

[50]Ibid.

[51]Ibid.

[52]U.S. Bureau of the Census, "Some Demographic Aspects of Aging in the United States," *Current Population Reports,* Series P-43(43) (Washington: U.S. Government Printing Office, 1973).

[53]I. Simpson, K. Back, and J. McKinney, "Work and Retirement," *Social Aspects of Aging,* I. Simpson and J. McKinney, eds. (Durham, N.C.: Duke University Press, 1966).

[54]G. Streib and C. Schneider, *Retirement in American Society: Impact and Process* (Ithaca, N.Y.: Cornell University Press, 1971).

[55]Ibid.

[56]E. Shanas et al., *Old People in Three Industrial Societies.*

[57]J. Schulz, "The Economics of Old Age," *Quality of Life: The Later Years,* L. Brown and E. Ellis, eds. (Acton, Mass.: Publishing Sciences Group, Inc., 1975).

[58]C. Ryser and A. Sheldon, "Retirement and Health," *Journal of the American Geriatrics Society,* 17(2) (1969).

[59]H. Maas and J. Kuypers, *From Thirty to Seventy.*

[60]B. Neugarten, "Personality Change in Later Life: A Developmental Perspective," *The Psychology of Adult Development and Aging,* C. Eisdorfer and M. P. Lawton, eds. (Washington, D.C.: American Psychological Association, 1973).

[61]C. Eisdorfer, "Making Life Worth Living," *Quality of Life: The Later Years*, L. Brown and E. Ellis, eds. (Acton, Mass.: Publishing Sciences Group, Inc., 1975).

[62]Ibid.

[63]F. Carp, "Differences Among Older Workers, Volunteers, and Persons Who Are Neither," *Journal of Gerontology*, 23 (1968).

[64]E. Shanas, "Family Relationships," *Quality of Life: The Later Years*, L. Brown and E. Ellis, eds. (Acton, Mass.: Publishing Sciences Group, Inc., 1975).

[65]R. Butler, *Why Survive? Being Old in America* (New York: Harper and Row, 1975).

[66]Ibid.

[67]Ibid.

[68]F. Carp, "Housing and Living Arrangements," *Quality of Life: The Later Years*, L. Brown and E. Ellis, eds. (Acton, Mass.: Publishing Sciences Group, Inc., 1975).

[69]R. Butler, "Aging's Best Advocate: An Interview with Robert Butler," *APA Monitor*, March 1976.

[70]R. Butler, "A Life Cycle Perspective: Public Policies for Later Life," *Retirement*, F. Carp, ed. (New York: Behavioral Publications, 1972).

[71]S. Jacoby, "Waiting for the End: On Nursing Homes," *The New York Times Magazine*, March 31, 1974.

[72]Ibid.

[73]Ibid.

[74]U.S. Department of Health, Education, and Welfare, *Health: United States, 1975.*

[75]Ibid.

[76]American Heart Association, *Heart Facts* (Washington: American Heart Association, Inc., 1976).

[77]C. Fisher, J. Mohr, and R. Adams, "Cerebrovascular Diseases," *Harrison's Principles of Internal Medicine*, 7th ed., M. Wintrobe et al., eds. (New York: McGraw-Hill, 1974).

[78]Ibid.

[79]Ibid.

[80]Ibid.

[81]W. Folger and J. Whisnant, "Acute Ischemic Cerebrovascular Disease" *Current Therapy 1977*, H. Conn, ed. (Philadelphia: W. B. Saunders Co., 1977).

[82]J. Brocklehurst, *Textbook of Geriatric Medicine and Gerontology* (London: Churchill Livingstone, 1973).

[83]Ibid.

[84]E. Bierman and W. Hazzard, "Old Age."

[85]J. Brocklehurst, *Textbook of Geriatric Medicine and Gerontology.*

[86]American Public Health Association, *Vital and Health Statistics Monographs: Mortality and Morbidity in the United States,* C. Erhardt and J. Berlin, eds. (Cambridge, Mass.: Harvard University Press, 1974).

[87]D. Gianturco, D. Ramm, and C. Erwin, "The Elderly Driver and Ex-Driver," *Normal Aging II: Reports from the Duke Longitudinal Studies, 1970-1973,* E. Palmore, ed. (Durham, N.C.: Duke University Press, 1974).

[88]T. Planek, "The Aging Driver in Today's Traffic," *North Carolina Symposium on Highway Safety* (Chapel Hill, N.C.: University of North Carolina Press, 1972).

[89]Ibid.

[90]E. Bierman and W. Hazzard, "Old Age."

Contents

Joseph Flack Weiler/Stock, Boston

Death and Bereavement Throughout the Life Span

Thanatology, the study of death, is growing as a field of scientific inquiry. Mortality and immortality have always been concerns of theologians and philosophers. Meanwhile, most humans remain afraid of death. According to Shakespeare, Julius Caesar reasoned thus with his wife:

Cowards die many times before their deaths;
The valiant never taste of death but once.
Of all the wonders that I yet have heard,
It seems to me most strange that men should fear;
Seeing that death, a necessary end,
Will come when it will come.[1]

Calphurnia and the servants still feared. John Dryden, an English poet, stated:

Death in itself is nothing; but we fear
To be we know not what, we know not where.[2]

Today social scientists probing death and dying are attempting to break down the taboos against discussing the end of life. By discussing death they hope to help us all learn to live more comfortably with a knowledge of our finite state.

Perspectives on death

The emotions a loved one's death evokes are disquieting: fear, anger, anxiety, jealousy, recriminations, weeping, and anguish. And yet, recent researchers tell us that a proximity to death can be an enriching, growth-promoting experience.[3] If a dying person honestly can express a host of negative and confusing feelings, he or she can move to a final stage of peaceful acceptance of death. If a mourner can express a host of chaotic, anguished feelings, he or she can move to a stage of rebuilding a rewarding new life. And if doctors, nurses, social workers, religious, and other counselors can learn to accept their own fears and concerns about death, they can be enormously helpful to dying patients. They can help terminally ill persons grow and find harmony. In addition, they can be inspired rather than depressed by such experiences.

In this chapter death will be examined first from the point of view of the dying individual: child, young adult, and older adult. Then the ways in which death affects bereaved persons will be discussed. Finally, death will be viewed as a catalyst to enjoying life more fully. The text will end by exploring some perspectives on living.

Approaches of children to death

Children are minimally aware of death when very young. In fact, the finality of death may not be fully realized until children approach the end of their elementary school years. Each child's understanding is very much dependent on his or her own experiences with death, teachings about death, and cognitive maturity.

In general, preschool children view death as changed circumstances.[4] They do not recognize that it is a final process. Rather, they seem to believe that the deceased will someday return from a visit or come to life again. For many preschool children death is experienced first through the loss of a pet. The fact that pets are often rather quickly replaced with new pets may help perpetuate a young child's belief that death is temporary or causes only a slight change in ongoing situations.

When preschool children are hospitalized with terminal illnesses, their reactions of fright are more often related to separation anxiety than to any awareness or fear of death. Preschoolers are still very much dependent on their caregivers for physical help with their activities and for emotional support and nurturance. When caregivers are replaced by strangers, as often occurs in hospital settings, the preschooler may become very anxious. Not only are caregivers absent, but all of the other familiar sights and sounds (home, siblings, pets, friends) that add to a feeling of security are lost. The terminal illness itself is seldom a threat beyond the fact that the child may experience pain and discomfort from it.

School-age children develop a greater understanding of death with each passing year, with each new experience of learning about death of another animal or person, and with each new lesson about death taught to them by caregivers, teachers, religious leaders, or friends. Very often school-age children personify death. They see it as some invisible force that carries people off. Many still believe that death does not have to be permanent. They believe that a dead person may come back to life for a while to finish some tasks or see loved ones and then die again. The personification of death is often individualistic and ranges from invisible animal, to monster, to some deceased person, to angel, to God. The following quote from a school-aged child exemplifies the personification of death as God. "You know, God is going to come down from Heaven and take me back with Him."[5] Death is generally believed to occur at night, in the dark, when nobody can see. Many nightmares and night terrors of children may stem from their anxieties about the link between death and night. Morrison found that school-age children who are hospitalized with terminal illnesses often have more anxiety about medical procedures (e.g., intravenous feedings, blood transfusions, x-rays, bone marrow aspirations, blood tests, or injections) than about approaching death.[6]

If a school-age child still views death as a temporary phenomenon, he or she will have hopes of everything eventually returning to normal, despite death. In some children, especially younger ones, parents and medical personnel may have tried to shield the patient from knowledge of the seriousness of the illness. Even when a prognosis has not been given, the child often perceives the seriousness of the situation. The grief of the parents becomes obvious to the child. Eventually the child may ask, "Am I going to die?" Opinions differ as to how to answer. Many professionals believe that honesty is best. For example, an answer may be worded carefully, "Yes, but we are not certain when this will be."[7] If parents or professionals hedge on such questions, the child may become extremely anxious. The fear of death is worse when one cannot discuss it. It is especially traumatic for a child to be left alone when family members are feeling that the future is too terrible to mention.

In some cases children may realize that they are dying and try to shield their parents from the fact.[8] This lack of open, honest communication can prevent acceptance of death and the growth that accompanies acceptance in both the dying child and the parent(s). The dying child is still alive. He or she needs comforting, loving, and help to overcome some of the overwhelming terrors being experienced. If parents and professionals listen, children will usually give an indication of how much they know or suspect and what particular concerns they wish to discuss. Once a child is aware of impending death, one of three patterns of reaction are common: (1) anxiety expressed symbolically and physiologically, (2) anger with acting-out behaviors, or (3) depression with withdrawal.[9] The reactions may be sequential or may even occur almost simultaneously. There is a danger that the dying child who misbehaves and makes demands on the parents may be overindulged. Such overindulgence can be more upsetting than helpful. Children feel more secure when they know their limits. When limits are stripped away, the child may make preposterous requests to test the parents. Parents will invariably come to resent this. The dying child usually senses this resentment and may accuse them of not being loving any longer. If demands are then met to prove love, a vicious cycle is begun. The child will make more and more requests. The parents will become more and more frustrated and resentful. The child will sense the hostility and, ultimately, the child may die feeling unloved and/or rejected. The parents may feel relieved of their demanding child as well as grieved. The guilt feelings for feelings relieved can be enormous.[10]

Approaches of younger adults to death

Adults with fatal illnesses usually know or guess their prognosis quite soon after physicians and family members learn the facts of the disease. The physician is responsible for imparting the information to the patient. However, this is often frought with difficulties. Many adults resist having the prognosis spoken aloud. They may not be ready to deal with this information about their own death. In addition, many physicians have great personal conflicts and anxieties about death. They may avoid dying patients, rationalizing that their time would be better spent with the living. Such neglect from health professionals (nurses may also avoid communications with their dying patients) makes it especially difficult for an adult to approach the knowledge that he or she has but a short time left to live.

Kübler-Ross identified five stages through which persons pass when they realize death is imminent. (Teenagers and cognitively mature children may also progress through the same stages in trying to accept their deaths.) The stages are (1) denial, (2) anger, (3) bargaining, (4) depression, and (5) acceptance.[11] Some persons may move back and forth across these stages or experience two of them simultaneously. On occasion they occur out of the sequence presented. Some persons may never reach the acceptance stage. However, there is general agreement among professionals who have worked with dying individuals that these behaviors are typical.

In the first stage, that of denial, the patient may vigorously oppose the notion that the end is near. As Thomas Bell wrote:

> *This can't be happening to me. Not to me. Me with a malignant tumor? Me with only a few months to live? Nonsense.... Such things happen, should happen, only to other people.... People who are strangers... born solely to fill such quotas.*[12]

The patient may hop from doctor to doctor, or from clinic to health spa to faith healer to miracle worker seeking a different diagnosis or a cure for the illness. He or she may become isolated, insulated from friends or acquaintances who know the truth. A reaction of shock, in which the person seems dazed, temporarily helpless, and confused, may ensue. Eventually, when the patient can no longer say, "This can't be happening to me," he or she will move to the second stage, that of anger. The question becomes, "Why me?"

At the second stage the patient may strike out especially hard at loved ones. The terminal illness may be blamed on the spouse, best friend, parent(s), doctor, employer, or God. Frequently, a vehement jealousy arises against people in good health. It is not unusual at this time for the patient to behave in agonized ways: cursing, accusing, condemning, screaming, being aggressive, being destructive, demonstrating hate and bitterness. The venting of such strong emotions may help a patient pass through this stage more readily than trying to choke back the mental and physical anguish being experienced.

The next stage, that of bargaining, usually begins when the anger is somewhat dissipated. The patient may agree to alter his or her behavior, become devoted to a religion, give away goods, buy some special treatments, or purchase wares for doctors or persons responsible for his or her health; in short, he or she may attempt to strike almost any kind of bargain in exchange for a longer life. Bargaining with God through prayers or exchanges with a religious representative are common. Variations of the Faust legend, in which people try to sell their souls to the devil to prolong their lives, have also been written, based on the tumultuous experiences of this stage.

Eventually, when the patient gives up hope that bargaining will effect a cure, he or she usually becomes depressed. The patient may refuse visitors, show little interest in external events, may be silent even with loved family members and friends, and may simply cry softly or stare into space. It is as if the patient is preparing for the time when he or she will no longer be able to see or hear others. This mourning need not be the final stage before death.

Kübler-Ross identified a fifth stage that many persons reach—acceptance. The patient leaves depression behind and goes about saying and doing all the unfinished business of his or her life. Rather than acting defeated or bitter, the patient seems to accept impending death with a peaceful, quiet sense of expectation. Often the acceptance is expressed by a desire to have just one or two close friends near, to hold hands, to listen to reading or quiet music, or simply to share silence. The patient seems to have reached the ego integrity described by Erikson: "acceptance of one's one and only life cycle as something that had to be and . . . permitted of no substitutions."[13] The fear of death is removed.

Kübler-Ross not only described the stages through which dying persons pass, but also identified what others can do to be of most help to terminally ill patients. She taught many physicians, nurses, social workers, religious counselors, and others at seminars at the University of Chicago to overcome their own anxieties about death. In so doing, they became better able to communicate with persons with fatal diseases. She shared this information through articles and books. In *Death: The Final Stage of Growth,* she presented five rules that summed up one minister's notes from a seminar:

> 1) . . . I must try to be myself. If the dying patient repulses me, for whatever reason, I must face up to that repulsion. I also must let the other person be himself. . . .
>
> 2) . . . when we talk to each other about ourselves, we will find something in common.
>
> 3) . . . let the patient "tell him" (the counselor) how he feels. . . . "let the patient be." This simple rule does not imply granting all of the patient's demands and jumping whenever the patient wants the counselor to jump. . . . The belief that "I know what's best for the patient" is not true. The patient knows best.
>
> 4) I must continually ask myself "What kind of a promise am I making to this patient and to myself?". . . . [Is it to] save this person's life or to make him happy in an unendurable situation,(?) . . . stop trying to attempt both. If I can learn to understand my own feelings of frustration, rage, and disappointment, then I believe I have the capacity to handle these feelings in a constructive manner.
>
> 5) My fifth and last rule . . . is expressed in the Alcoholics Anonymous prayer: "God grant me the serenity to accept the things I cannot change, the courage to change the things I can, and the wisdom to know the difference."[14]

The persons who are most helpful to a dying person are those who allow communication to proceed honestly and those who have come to terms with their own frustrations and anxieties about death. However, family members may find it extremely difficult to talk about death or to understand and control their own emotions. Family members may go through stages similar to those of the patient—denial, anger, bargaining, and depression—before they can accept the prognosis. Their own grief sometimes leaves them as much in need of support as the patient approaching death. Occasionally, the patient may try to help family members or may simply prefer not to see them.

Approaches of old people to death

Old people are generally less afraid of death than young adults who have not yet had a chance to pursue careers or raise families. However, the approaches of individual old people to death vary tremendously. While some welcome death, others try to postpone it in every way possible. Some will discuss it; to others it is a taboo topic. The variety of views old people have about death were expressed in interviews conducted by Maas and Kuypers:

> Person A: I think death would be wonderful. . . . There's a time for everybody and when it comes, it comes. . . . Death to me is a way out of this troubled world that we're in. And I think sometimes that death is going to be peaceful.
>
> Person B: Talk about death? No, we never have thought to talk about it. We're always too busy doing something.
>
> Person C: Life and death go together—that's the natural way. . . . I don't like to—just—think about death. . . .We're ready to die before we're ready to know how to live.[15]

Old persons have all had experience witnessing the deaths of others around them. This practice in mourning and coming to terms with grief and anxieties concerning the death of others gives them some degree of preparation for facing their own finiteness. Robert Butler pointed out that many older persons show a perseveration in reminiscing about their lives.[16] Did they make sense? Were they worthwhile? By so doing, they seek to find some way to assure themselves that their lives were meaningful and thus prepare themselves to face death more peacefully.

When an elderly person is terminally ill, he or she is still apt to go through the stages described by Kübler-Ross: denial, anger, bargaining, depression, and finally acceptance. Physicians or family members may try to shelter the elderly from knowledge that his or her illness will be fatal. However, dying persons usually know their status, whether or not the prognosis is put in words. They may have financial or personal matters that they want to put in order. Older persons should be allowed to take care of such matters when they desire. The terminal decline in intelligence that precedes death (see pp. 433–434) may render some individuals incapable of accomplishing logical, ordered thinking when death is near. Some persons sign what is called a "living will" before a terminal illness becomes advanced. This legal document, which must be witnessed and notarized, states that the individual does not desire to be kept alive by artificial means but rather would like to be allowed to die with dignity (see Figure 12–1). A standardized "living will" is available from euthanasia

To my family, my physician, my lawyer, my clergyman,
To any medical facility in whose care I happen to be,
To any individual who may become responsible for my health, welfare or affairs:

Death is as much a reality as birth, growth, maturity and old age—it is the one certainty of life. If the time comes when I, ____________, can no longer take part in decisions for my own future, let this statement stand as an expression of my wishes while I am still of sound mind.

If the situation should arise in which there is no reasonable expectation of my recovery, I request that I be allowed to die and not be kept alive by artificial means or "heroic measures." I do not fear death itself as much as the indignities of deterioration, dependence and hopeless pain. I therefore ask that medication be mercifully administered to me to alleviate suffering even though this may hasten the moment of death.

This request is made after careful consideration. I hope you who care for me will feel morally bound to follow its mandate. I recognize that this appears to place a heavy responsibility upon you, but it is with the intention of relieving you of such responsibility and of placing it upon myself in accordance with my strong convictions that this statement is made.

Signed ____________________ Date ____________________
Witness ____________________ Witness ____________________

Copies of this request have been given to: ____________

Figure 12–1. *The living will.*

societies throughout the United States. The concept of euthanasia (literally meaning happy death) has become a controversial one, generally associated with mercy killing. Various religions and philosophical groups differ in their opinions of where one draws a line between not making heroic efforts to sustain life and actually allowing or even hastening death by withholding life-supporting equipment or medicines.

Bereavement and grief

Thus far this chapter has focused on the reactions of persons to their own approaching deaths. The reactions of others to the death of a loved one are also painful. It does not matter that death may relieve the suffering of the loved person, or, depending on religious convictions, that the departed is believed to have passed into a better afterlife. Surviving individuals will still miss a loved person who dies and will need to work through an assortment of disturbing emotions concerning the meaning of that death to their lives.

Reactions to the death of a child

There is no one way parents react when one of their offspring dies. Some parents go into a state of shock. They may be confused and unable to act or react. Some parents may refuse to believe that the death has occurred. They behave as if the child will return soon. Some parents have emotional breakdowns. Some become agitated and acutely anxious about trivia and innumerable smaller events. Some parents are overcome with unreasonable fears. Others may become deeply depressed. Some parents show their grief in emotional outpourings. Others give no visible signs of their feelings. In other words, the sorrow parents feel manifests itself in different ways for different people.

The death of a child generally leaves everyone feeling that a great injustice has been done. The child had no chance to live out his or her life. A sense of bitterness compounds the grief. The work of mourning is to come to terms with the fact of death and to work out some of the bitterness, sense of loss, hurt, disappointment, and frustrations that accompany it. Parents who can express their feelings and allow others to comfort them are able to emerge more rapidly from their bereavement than parents who refuse to discuss their pain or who refuse the sympathy, compassion, and support of others. Grief that is hidden may burst forth later in psychosomatic illnesses or even mental illnesses.[17] Eventually, it must be expressed and worked out for the parent to return to normal. It is not always possible to enable a person to express his or her feelings, but it is helpful to reassure a parent that another person will be available to listen at any time he or she wishes to talk.

Siblings and close playmates of a dead child also experience a number of painful emotions associated with death. Often their sense of loss is accompanied by an overwhelming sense of fear. "If it could happen to ______________, it can happen to me." In addition, due to their limited understanding of death, they may see themselves as being, in some way, responsible for it. Children need to be given a chance to express all of their emotions after experiencing the death of a sibling or friend. They will cue adults on what they most want to know: Will it happen to me? Was I responsible? Will I ever see ______________ again? Bereaved children need extra emotional support and a sense of security in their environments. A sudden change in rules, discipline, or schedules can be especially upsetting to them when they are trying to cope with their anxieties and fears about death.[18]

Reactions to the death of a young adult

In general, the death of a young adult is met with feelings of injustice in much the same way as is the death of a child. It is especially hard to understand or accept the death if the adult had many persons dependent on him or her (e.g., children, employees), or if he or she were doing some great humanitarian work.

The death of young adults not only brings grief to loved ones but also causes a sense of discomfort in most associates. An untimely death makes us all remember how unpredictable are our own futures, how finite we all are. However, the process of grieving, while painful, can be a growth-promoting experience. If people can come to terms with their concerns and fears of death, they can begin to live each day in a more meaningful way.

The ways in which individuals express their grief vary from tight control of emotions to hysterical outpourings of anguish. However, a certain underlying sequence of events is typical.[19] Initially, bereaved persons are disbelieving. When the realization of death finally sets in, protests (silent or otherwise) are common. Confusion follows. Bereaved persons feel hopeless, without direction, desperate. They may move slowly, think slowly, and detach themselves from others and from the course of everyday living. Finally, the work of mourning must occur. Bereaved persons must break their emotional ties to the past and rid themselves of the hopes and dreams they shared with the dead person. This is extremely painful. It can take weeks and months to accomplish. Sometimes bereaved persons fear they are losing their minds. They find it difficult to be aware of the things that are happening around them or to react to events in their customary fashion. Their personalities may change (e.g., short tempers replacing patience or reserve replacing gregariousness). During a period of grieving, persons may be unusually sensitive to criticism. One of the more difficult aspects of grief is a feeling of regret at things left undone or unsaid to the departed. Guilt feelings are a common ingredient in mourning and must be resolved.

Fear is still another emotion common to grieving. On occasion real reasons for fear exist (e.g., economic instability, deprivation of primary social-emotional support). On other occasions the fear is nameless and often more frightening because its cause cannot be ascertained.

Another very difficult aspect of grieving may be coping with the attitudes of some friends and neighbors. Some persons do not recognize the beneficial, necessary work of mourning. They feel it would be better if the bereaved would forget, quit talking about the dead, and stop crying. In a study of attitudes about grieving in persons in England and the United States, Gorer found that mourning is most often viewed as a form of self-indulgence.[20] On the other hand, having supportive family and friends helps a grieving person to work through his or her emotions, to reach the stage of accepting the death.

When a child loses a parent, grief and bereavement are especially agonizing, especially if the child does not understand the permanency of death.[21] Some children react with loud protesting and increased aggressiveness. Others withdraw and become detached. Recurrent attacks of anxiety are common whenever some reminder of the dead parent appears. Guilt may also be a part of a child's grief. The child may believe that he or she was in some way responsible for the parent's disappearance. Children must be told the truth about the parent's death. They also must be encouraged to work out all their feelings of anger, hurt, loneliness, guilt, fear, and anxiety.

Reactions to the death of an older adult

Mourning for an aged person who dies is generally less painful than mourning the death of a child or young adult. One senses that the death is more a part of a natural process. The aged person can be viewed as having lived a long and full life. Death in the elderly is also generally anticipated, consciously or unconsciously, for a period of time before it occurs. Family and friends have a chance to anticipate what life will be like when the older person dies. Grief is most severe in the persons who may still have been dependent on the departed (e.g., widow, widower, children). The sequence of feelings in accepting the death of an elderly person is the same as the sequence following the death of a younger person: disbelief, possibly anger, confusion, and finally the painful process of disassociating oneself from the departed. Survivors must go through the work of mourning. They also must find a meaning and purpose to their own lives that no longer center around or include the dead person in order to overcome their grief and return to normal functioning.

Perspectives on living

An understanding and acceptance of the totality of the human life span, including death, can make all feel more kin to each other, whatever one's age or life stage.

Experiencing death can be a catalyst to living more fully. Most people have good intentions. Most people would like to live lives that benefit others, but, when one lives as if life will go on forever, it is too easy to postpone until tomorrow all those things that ought to be done today. Eventually one looks back and sees life as being self-absorbed, selfish, and not very beneficial to others. This is embarrassing and unpleasant. Such negative feedback from the internal valuing system prevents one from becoming all one is capable of being. It is difficult, if not impossible, to like others if one does not first like oneself. One of the secrets of building up a positive self-image and of learning to like oneself is to spend a portion of each day reaching out to some other human being(s). This must be done lovingly, unselfishly, not because one wants something in return, but simply because it is in us to care for someone else. When concern and affection is given another, the reward is not only the appreciation of the one served, but, more importantly, a feeling of self-satisfaction, self-esteem, and personal growth. By repeated giving, one is able to learn to like and understand other human beings more fully. There will still be times when one experiences frustrations, exploitations, insults, and inhumanity. However, loving, caring relationships will also develop. One can come to trust others by reaching out to them, more than one ever can by remaining isolated. The concept of death, the idea that our future is uncertain, is one of the major keys to continued personal growth and giving. As Kübler-Ross put it, "When you fully understand that each day you awaken could be the last you have, you take the time, that day, to grow, to become more of who you really are, to reach out to other human beings."[22]

Take a moment to consider who you really are. How and where do you fit into the fellowship of humankind? Consider the wise command spoken by the sage Chilon (but generally attributed to Socrates), "Know thyself."

Homo sapiens (humans) have existed on earth for about 100,000 years.[23] Most of this time they have been hunters and gatherers. Farming in a primitive form only started about 10,000 years ago.[24] The industrial revolution occurred only 200 years ago. Now every single generation sees fantastic changes in the way society lives. Society must take risks to survive. The future is uncharted, unpredictable. There are difficult problems in trying to adapt and cope with the ever-changing world around us. Life exists with conditions of stress and fear. Alvin Toffler calls this "future shock" and suggests that our fear may at times nearly paralyze us.[25] It can prevent us from behaving rationally with respect to future planning. How does one plan for a world that may in a short time include such things as test-tube babies, computerized robots capable of holding important societal offices or positions, a cancer cure, a prevention of aging, an accidental nuclear explosion, the spread of anarchism over large parts of the world, a diminution of fresh air and fresh water?

Try to view living in the world today and tomorrow from a more positive perspective. In 1972 a meeting of experts considered our quality of life and determined that several special kinds of environments should be reasonably available to all people to help shape a more peaceful, humane world.[26] The first is an environment of health. All members of society should be able to breathe clean air, drink clean water, eat uncontaminated, nutritious food, and afford medical attention to prevent and treat disease processes. A vital part of this environment of health is physically fit parents of our future generations. Our world should make it possible for parents, especially the mother, to confer optimum health benefits to offspring. The mother should not have to conceive at too young an age or in a malnourished, drug-addicted, or chronically diseased state, all of which could adversely affect the baby-to-be.

A second environment that all people should reasonably be expected to enjoy is a quality home life. One cannot become all one is capable of being without love and freedom from physical dangers at home. People also need family environments that are free from racial discrimination and abject poverty.

A third specialized kind of environment that should be available to all humans is that of quality education. One of our priorities must be to provide educational opportunities flexible enough to allow all people to learn to read and reason about the various areas of human knowledge.

A fourth environment needed by everyone for a better world is that of constructive outlets for aggression (which many persons believe is an instinctual behavior in the human species[27]). Society needs to provide opportunities for persons to direct their aggressive urges at righting environmental obstacles to a quality life, or at improving their health and physical fitness through such outlets as sports, or at enriching the lives of others through outlets such as the arts or scientific inquiry, or at defusing the tense emotions triggering aggressive urges through laughter.

Another environment generally recognized as both a necessary and reasonable right is that of employment.

Still another environment that should be available to all persons is equal treatment under the law. We must not have a double standard of justice, one divided between the rich and/or powerful and the poor and/or powerless of the world. Every human being deserves a feeling of her or his own dignity as part of the fellowship of humankind.

Where do you see yourself in the scheme of the total fellowship of humankind? What will you give to the population of the world in

Figure 12–2. *We all should consider our responsibilities for providing the next generation with a quality of life that matches (or surpasses) our own: clear air and water, nutritious food, energy, freedom, love, quality education, outlets for aggression, employment, and equal treatment under the law.*
Leslie Davis

order to assure a better quality of life and a peaceful, humane future for all peoples?

Conclusion

This text has discussed development throughout the life span, considering physical, cognitive, social, and health components. The notion of development throughout adulthood is rather a recent one. For years developmental texts focused primarily on growth during childhood, ending with adolescence. Adulthood was generally viewed as encompassing years of gradual decline rather than of change and progress. The trend now is to view development as occurring throughout life.

Along with this change is a trend that encourages persons to discuss and consider the end of the life span—death—something that for years was considered morbid or at least to be avoided. This healthy opening up of discussions about death, in part brought about through the work of Kübler-Ross, has enabled individuals to consider their own mortality, their own finiteness. Rather than being gruesome, such awareness can be liberating. An awareness of one's finiteness can help a person to look at each day as one filled with opportunity and potential for accomplishment. Rather than living one's life in the future, this awareness can help people to focus on what can be achieved here and now.

While development occurs as a process throughout life, it is generally divided into definable stages. Development through infancy and childhood proceeds from sensory and motor responses to verbal communication, thinking, conceptualizing, and relating to others (modeling, responding, asserting the self). These basics normally continue with the individual throughout her or his life.

In adolescence the individual begins to test out an independent life. Values are questioned and identity is engraved. Behavior is fluctuating and often unpredictable.

Early adulthood establishes the individual as a separate person. Employment, further education, the beginning of one's own family are all aspects of setting up a distinct life, with both its own characteristics and the characteristics and customs of previous generations.

During middle and late adulthood persons have new situations to face, new transitions with which to cope. Children grow up and leave home. Aging becomes apparent. Relationships change, sometimes becoming stronger, sometimes ending. Roles shift. New abilities are found, and opportunities are sought.

Finally, during late adulthood, people assess what they've accomplished. Some are pleased. Some feel they could have done more or lived differently. In the best of instances, individuals accept who they are and are comfortable with themselves.

The human developmental process, therefore, is always changing. It is exciting and scary, joyful and disappointing. In each person's developmental process, he or she brings unique characteristics and contributions to the surrounding ecological settings. The environment that is established and continues for future generations hinges upon what each person contributes and values. Step by step, the process continues—with potential for a quality of life for everyone.

Questions for review

1. Some research says that proximity to death can be a growth-producing experience. Do you agree or disagree with this? Explain your answer.
2. Describe some ways in which parents, other relatives, friends, and health professionals can help alleviate the fears of a seven-year-old who is terminally ill and is hospitalized.
3. Kübler-Ross defined five stages that terminally ill persons experience in facing their own deaths. Describe the characteristics of each of these stages.
4. Are you in favor of "living wills" or do you believe it is best left up to a person's loved ones to determine whether or not to maintain life-sustaining equipment? Explain your answer.
5. American society tends to be more critical of men who cry and show emotion than some other societies. What sorts of implications does this have for a man who has recently lost someone he loved?
6. Describe the special kinds of environments that should be reasonably available to all people for a more peaceful, humane, and healthy life span.

References

[1]W. Shakespeare, *The Tragedy of Julius Caesar* (New York: The Airmont Publishing Co., Inc., 1965).

[2]J. Dryden, *A Collection of Critical Essays*, B. Schilling, ed. (Englewood Cliffs, N.J.: Prentice-Hall, 1963).

[3]E. Kübler-Ross, *Death: The Final Stage of Growth* (Englewood Cliffs, N.J.: Prentice-Hall, 1975).

[4]M. Nagy, "The Child's View of Death," *The Meaning of Death*, H. Feifel, ed. (New York: McGraw Hill, 1959).

[5]J. Morrissey, "Death Anxiety in Children with a Fatal Illness," *Crisis Intervention*, H. Parad, ed. (New York: Family Service Association of America, 1965).

[6]Ibid.

[7]D. Marlow, *Pediatric Nursing*, 4th ed. (Philadelphia: W. B. Saunders Co., 1973).

[8]C. Binger, C. Mikkelsen, and E. Waechter, "Terminal Illness-Implications for Patient, Family and Staff," *The Hospitalized Child, His Family, and His Community*, H. Thorpe, ed. (San Francisco: American Association for Child Care in Hospitals, 1970).

[9]J. Morrissey, "Death Anxiety in Children with a Fatal Illness."

[10]D. Marlow, *Pediatric Nursing.*

[11]E. Kübler-Ross, *On Death and Dying* (New York: Macmillan Co., 1969).

[12]T. Bell, *In the Midst of Life* (New York: Atheneum, 1961).

[13]E. Erikson, *Childhood and Society*, 2nd ed. (New York: W. W. Norton Co., 1963).

[14]E. Kübler-Ross, *Death: The Final Stage of Growth.*

[15]H. Maas and J. Kuypers, *From Thirty to Seventy* (San Francisco: Jossey-Bass, Inc., 1974).

[16]R. Butler, *Why Survive? Being Old in America* (New York: Harper and Row, 1975).

[17]S. Morris, *Grief and How to Live with It* (New York: Grosset and Dunlap, 1972).

[18]D. Marlow, *Pediatric Nursing.*

[19]S. Morris, *Grief and How to Live with It.*

[20]G. Gorer, *Death, Grief and Mourning* (Garden City, N.J.: Doubleday and Co., 1965).

[21]D. Marlow, *Pediatric Nursing.*

[22]E. Kübler-Ross, L. Braga, and J. Braga, "Omega," *Death: The Final Stage of Growth* (Englewood Cliffs, N.J.: Prentice-Hall, 1975).

[23]E. Lanning, "Human Evolution," *The Columbia History of the World*, J. Garraty and P. Gay, eds. (New York: Harper and Row, 1972).

[24]Ibid.

[25]A. Toffler, *Future Shock* (New York: Random House, 1970).

[26]H. Downs, "Prologue," *Quality of Life: The Early Years* (Acton, Mass.: Publishing Sciences Group, Inc., 1974).

[27]K. Lorenz, *On Aggression*, M. Wilson, trans. (New York: Harcourt, Brace and World, Inc., 1966).

Index